# REASSESSMENT IN PSYCHOLOGY

## The Interbehavioral Alternative

Edited by

# Noel W. Smith
# Paul T. Mountjoy
# Douglas H. Ruben

UNIVERSITY
PRESS OF
AMERICA

Copyright © 1983 by

**University Press of America, Inc.**

P.O. Box 19101, Washington, D.C. 20036

ISBN (Perfect): 0-8191-3082-6
ISBN   (Cloth): 0-8191-3081-8

To

## J. R.  KANTOR

In His Ninety-fifth Year


Whose stalwart insistence on a psychology whose constructs
are continuous with observation,

Whose untiring devotion to the explication of the fundamental
assumptions of science in general and psychology in particular,

Whose interbehavioral field psychology provides a revolutionary
program for moving from recurring problems to scientific
advancement.


We Dedicate This Book With Gratitude and Affection

## CONTRIBUTORS

Bickel, Warren K.  University of Kansas

Bijou, Sidney W.  University of Illinois

Blewitt, Edward.  University of Cardiff

Cone, Donna M.  Director of the Division of Program Standards, Planning and Evaluation, Department of Mental Health, Retardation, and Hospitals, State of Rhode Island

Delprato, Dennis J.  Eastern Michigan University

Herrick, J.W.  SUNY College of Technology

Higgins, Stephen T.  University of Kansas

Lichtenstein, Parker E.  Denison University

MacRoberts, M.H.  Shreveport, Louisiana

MacRoberts, B.R.  Shreveport, Louisiana

Morris, Edward K.  University of Kansas

**Mountjoy, Paul T.**  Western Michigan University

Parrott, Linda J.  West Virginia University

Pronko, Nicholas H.  University of Wichita.

Ray, Roger.  Rollins  University

Ribes, Emilio.  Universidad Nacional Autonoma de Mexico

**Ruben, Douglas H.**  Western Michigan University

Shaffer, Lawrence C.  State University of New York at Plattsburgh

**Smith, Noel W.**  State University of New York at Plattsburgh

Verplanck, William.  The University of Tennessee, Knoxville

vi

# CONTENTS

vii

x

# PREFACE

William S. Verplanck

In 1938 I took a course, "Systems of Psychology," with Frank Geldard at the University of Virginia. We covered everything in Frank's typical dispassionate, systematic and thorough style. Our primary text was Boring's **Physical Dimensions of Consciousness.** The course provided a more or less general background reflecting Nafe, rather than Hunter, in Frank's Clark education. That introduced me to positivistic thinking. The course was thorough, so we covered behaviorism, too, in a not entirely sympathetic, but thorough manner. This was my first introduction to the name, **J.R. Kantor.** I learned that Kantor and Weiss were extreme behaviorists of the 1920's period. Needless to say, Geldard in his moderate way gave a good deal more attention to Watson, Lashley, Hunter, and Dunlap. Somehow I formed the impression that Kantor was dead--and his thinking deader.

The next year at Virginia was my first year of graduate work, and Ken Spence's first year of teaching graduate students, which he did there at the University of Virginia. Our little band of graduate students that year took two full-year courses with him and were thoroughly trained (perhaps I should say "indoctrinated") in Pavlovian research, Hullian practice and theory, with special emphasis on Spence's own theory of discrimination learning, and on the Spence-Krechevsky confrontation. The blackboards were covered with **N** (drops of saliva), **S**'s and **R**'s in both upper and lower cases, and arrows.

An exciting year, indeed. It was a year in which Machian-Pearsonian positivism was superseded by logical positivism, a year of indoctrination in one view of scientific logic and method.

With Master's done, I went on to Brown to work with Clarence Graham in the department headed by Walter S. Hunter. Walter Hunter, "the old Doctor," was surely the most prominent behaviorist of the time, and the department bore his stamp. More important for me, and perhaps for many others, it was also a fuller introduction into psychology of exciting ideas on science, new in the early 1920's. Here, with the leadership of Clarence Graham and using source material, not advanced texts, we learned how to **Do Science.**

xi

From Hunter, we learned that one could not be a properly scientific psychologist unless one was accepted as a scientist by other **hard** scientists, that is, by chemists, physicists, mathematicians, probably even astrophysicists, and (more marginally) biologists. So, at Brown, built-in reductionism was omnipresent, and exemplified by careful experimental research in the laboratory.

When finished, we knew as scientific psychologists (experimental psychologists)--rigorous behaviorists--what we should do and why we should do it. Hunter himself, had somehow forgotten his proposal years before that the skin is the boundary that separates Psychology from Physiology. We took courses in neuroanatomy and were excited by theories of synaptic transmission. On the one hand, we thrived on elegant mathematical models exemplified by Selig Hecht's work, and, on the other hand, we physiologized. Some were ardent Hullians; among these, I could be counted. After all, who could resist the combination of hypothetical-deduction method, with strict behaviorism, and physiologizing? Not I. Still I was not immune to what appeared to be another kind of positivistic thinking in psychology--Fred Skinner's--whose views entered the department through the research and personal friendship of Clarence Graham, who, indeed, undertook to translate Fred's views into a mathematical model (!)

**The Behavior of Organisms** had just come out, and the graduate students at Brown accounted for a goodly percentage of its first year's sales.

Yes, we read, we learned more about behaviorism. Again, both Kantor and Weiss would occasionally be mentioned, then to be ignored. So far as we knew, they had done nothing since 1925, and my conviction that Kantor was dead was unimpaired. Kantor's continuing contributions never came to the attention of us parochial Northeasterners.

Then came four years of World War II, during which I learned that you could find something outside the laboratory and in real life.

Nineteen forty-six was job-hunting time, and I had the good fortune of being recommended to Fred Skinner, who was just starting at Indiana University. There I went for an interview. To my astonishment, Fred introduced me, first of all, to J.R. Kantor. Wasn't he dead? No, he was very much alive and kicking, in his understated way. He thrived in a large office lined with full bookshelves and filled with tables stacked with journals and open books. I was a little awestruck by what seemed a resurrection. Only years later did I realize how awestruck I should have been.

It wasn't hard to decide to take the job, which split my time down the middle. Half-time I taught and did such research as I chose (it was in vision, on behavioral psychophysics). The other half I was administrative assistant to Fred, and took over almost all the ordinary housekeeping duties of running a department, particularly those of routine bookkeeping matters in dealing with course-offerings and of the much more critical and interesting problems of admissions and the care and feeding of both undergraduate and graduate students. I was expected to know just about everything, and just about anything about everybody. I was geographically split, too. One office was for teaching and research, and the other, in a partitioned office space of the main office, filled with departmental matters. This was where I shuffled all of the papers that needed to be shuffled. It was an exposed position, accessible to all.

The department was a lively one, to put it mildly. There were the Skinnerians, led by Fred, who included the Minnesotans--Bill Estes, Norm Guttman, and George Collier, plus Sam Campbell and many others. There were the Kantorians--Parker Lichtenstein, Irv Wolf, Harris Hill, Bod Neu, Bob Lundin among them. There were the Hullians and near Hullians, a leaderless and small group that included Doug Ellson, Bill Jenkins (who had been converted to Hullian thinking by Neal Miller at Yale; he'd been super-Skinnerian at Brown), and myself. Winthrop Kellogg's conditioning group was made up of students, not followers, and Roland Davis whose pioneering psychophysiological studies and cool objectivity required lots of electronic knowhow as well as a degree of detachment stood on the sidelines.

Intellectual rivalry and argument were everywhere. The battle lines were drawn. Kantorians vs. Skinnerians. But also, the hometeam vs. the visitors--or interlopers, from Minnesota. What do you believe? Tell me, whose student are you?

In the intellectual melee, the Hullian behaviorists, Ellson, Jenkins, and I did not get far; we attracted no students to Hullianism. After all, when you choose up sides, you choose between **two** sides, not three. (In the late forties, we were joined by two fresh Iowa-Spence Ph.D.'s, Sid Bijou and Clete Burke. Both missed the first days of heated debate, but both profited by it; Sid's contribution elsewhere in this book will speak for itself.)

It was an ideological battlefield and certainly a very exciting place to be, what with the fortified positions and the various patrol parties, with snipers behind every tree. I managed to stake out my own little hill-top position from which I was able to fire in various directions at will. I taught a course called "Scientific Method and Theory and

Construction," which most of the graduate students took. You might say it was logical positivism for the multitude, with emphasis on measurement, and psychological theory (hypothetics-deductive), preferably in mathematical form, but formal logic was acceptable. This was a revision and extension of the course I had taken (plus some further thoughts about operationism) from Clarence Graham. Most of the material in that course emerged everywhere else as well as over the next years, and it now appears as absolute doctrine, revealed truth, in most textbooks on experimental method. (I was one of the first to climb on this bandwagon, and took many students with me. I am now happy to have been among the first to get off it. But, it is still much too crowded. What can one do, when ideas get pickled in textbooks, which in turn provide the multiple-choice questions and hackneyed finals that define the subject-matter of scientific psychology?) As the reader will have noted, that course was indeed an excellent vantage point from which a Hullian hypothetico-deductive, mathematical-model could make its presence felt in the ongoing strife.

Yes, it was a sort of war there at Indiana in 1946-1947, and 1947-1948. The ongoing confrontation between Kantorian and Skinnerian students wouldn't cease. There shouldn't have been any such confrontation. Robert had brought Fred to Indiana in the first place, and is said to have more than once commented that Aristotle was the first Interbehaviorist, himself the second, and Skinner the third. Here, as usual, he was quite correct, as I failed to understand for some years. I couldn't understand Kantor at all; my reductionistic-behavioristic-theoretical "sophistication" was an unfailing blindfold. Skinner, I **thought** I understood, but only as an alternative "learning theory" to which I much preferred Hull's.

In his autobiography, Fred puts it this way: "I was never able to come very close to Robert Kantor's way of thinking about behavior, although our differences were trivial compared to our similarities....we held doggedly to our own positions." To the onlooker or perhaps overhearer, both then and now, what each person stuck to so doggedly was his **language,** his terminologies, and neither budged an inch.

Their greatest difference was perhaps the one least discussed by Kantor and Skinner themselves, but was subject of loudest and longest argument and greatest passion among students. Fred did **experimental** research. Robert's disregard for laboratory experimentation contrasted with Fred's fascination with pigeons, boxes, apparatus and circuitry. The outcome, thirty-five years later? Kantor's contributions and systems remain intact, but without great manifest influence; Skinner's vocabulary and acceptance of the holy status of the laboratory have led both him and his followers to victory over competing behavioral systems--to writing "finis" to Hull-Spence--and also to loss of all that was fundamental to and most valuable in the Skinnerianism of the thirties and forties.

What was indeed Skinner's interbehaviorism regressed to becoming the super-successful but still garden variety of early Watsonian behaviorism. This feat was accomplished by the Skinnerians' continuing neglect of the characteristics and activities of environments, except as a source or way of talking about the gadgets they put in these apparatus and the contrived set-piece actions of the behavior-therapist and by equivocal use of the word "stimulus."

But, that is getting ahead of the story.

Primarily, then, two vocabularies and styles in using them confronted one another when Kantor and Skinner led their weekly well-attended seminars. Almost all faculty and students, plus a few from other departments attended regularly. Perhaps Fred's "need" to be original, to be unique, and to be a leader made these open discussions more brittle and less productive than they might have been. Skinner then, as now, was unwilling to take second place to anyone, much less third. Aristotle-Kantor-Skinner? Never! Nor was Robert likely to yield. He was, one might say, much more committed in papers which Fred had clearly not read.

So these weekly seminars went, with Kantor and Skinner taking their turns expounding their points of view, with Robert emphasizing the similarities between Skinner's position and his own, and Fred turning the deaf ear. Each would discuss what the other had said. Then, general discussion: Communication was not facilitated by vociferous and heated "student participation"--sometimes illuminating but more often misleading.

At these meetings, Bill Jenkins, my fellow Hullian (or close-to) and I would sit on the sidelines, largely silent, except for our whispers back and forth, mostly amused, but occasionally upset by these people who were so far from what **we** believed, and who, not one of them, stated postulates, derived theorems, or developed quantitative theories.

One discussion that I remember well concerned turkeys. The question--if you have two turkeys, both roasted for Thanksgiving dinner and then sit down and gorge to satiation on one of them, is the surviving turkey the **same** turkey (but colder and drying out) after dinner as it was before dinner? For the Kantorians, No! For the Skinnerians, Yes! The question of the relevance of physical specification to a degree permitting replication to psychology somehow did not come up. Skinnerians and Hullians agreed; they demonstrated their basic view of behavior as taking place in a **physical** world, in contrast to the far more sophisticated ideas of interbehaviorism by Kantor, which are not all that dissimilar to views espoused by some phenomenological thinkers, who use still another language. On this and other occasions when the discussion heated, Kantor remained calm, but clearly was uncomfortable with the intensity shown by the group.

Throughout my association with Kantor at Indiana, both in these seminars and as administrative assistant to him when he was Acting Head during Fred's absence, he was invariably a gentle man, a kind man, and a persistent man. But, he was also a man whose viewpoint seemed hopelessly misguided to me, the reductionistic, logical positivist, who was persuaded that all truth could be wrested only by conforming with reconstructions of scientific methodology done by philosophers in their efforts to figure out what scientists do and have done.

In sum, I liked and admired Robert Kantor very much indeed, but I thought that interbehaviorism was an unintelligible, scientifically worthless if not downright destructive literary enterprise.

Not that the Kantorians weren't interesting and articulate. In my exposed position in the little glass cubicle near the main office where I worked long and late I was vulnerable not only to interruption and insult but also to reason.

Reason was personified by Parker Lichtenstein who, as a graduate student, spent a good deal of evenings around the office. He seemed to have taken on the mission of getting me into endless didactic discussions about Kantor and interbehavioral psychology.

I'd been a bit miffed that Parker had not (and would not) take my methodology course but was agreeable to using these opportunities to try to convert him. (From the vantage point of the present, his judgment in refraining from taking the course was better than mine in offering it.)

That they were discussions rather than arguments is a tribute to Parker's manner and social skills. We did discuss; he was impervious to my Hullian reductionism, just as I was then impervious to understanding J.R. Kantor. But, I did listen a lot, I heard, even though I was unable to think except in terms of my "sophisticated" and superscientific training.

One of the many outcomes of the intellectual and experimental ferment among the Skinnerians and their fellow-travelers was the conference at Dartmouth in 1950 which led to the book **Modern**

**Learning Theory.** This conference aimed at scrutinizing and evaluating each of the then current learning theories. Each member chose the learning theory which he would most like to dissect. (Each of us was well aware that dissection would usually require antecedent trial and éxecution.) Kantor's writings, of course, did not enter into consideration. The writer was still a faithful Hullian, but also a Skinnerian fellow-traveler. My faith in the correctness of the Hullian enterprise had been only a little shaken by his attempt to measure "E-bar-dot," or momentary effective excitatory potential. (You will remember that he succeeded but only by making something like 35 consecutive assumptions, many of them far short of the reasonable.)

I chose to "do" Skinner. I was sure that hard-core review and evaluation of Fred's work in terms of "scientific methodology" would produce the correct, well-stated criticisms which might lead him and his students to reform, and behave more like Hull, complete with axioms, postulates, and "experimental hypotheses." After the summer's work of reading and of discussion, followed by a couple of years of thinking, I completed the job; I hope carefully. I put together the exposition and evaluation of the writings and research of "Burrhus F. Skinner" for **Modern Learning Theory.** Choice of this name, I think, was my way of reminding the readers of Burris, **Walden Two**, while I wrote about Frazier. The outcome of my exploring Skinner's "flaws" as a scientific theorists was a new understanding, as a Skinnerian, of Skinner's behaviorism (as of 1952). His was not a theory, but a descriptive system that provides the framework for an ongoing functional taxonomy of behavior. At the same time I understood and also grasped that interbehaviorism is **also** not a theory, but as Parker had told me over and over, a systematic view, a different way of looking at all matters behavioral.

For the first time, the Aristotle-Kantor-Skinner progression made sense; Robert Kantor recognized early where Skinner's research would lead him if he continued thinking and working the way he had done as a graduate student at Harvard and then at Minnesota. For me, writing that paper shifted me into a path very different from the one I had followed until then.

In 1953, a sabbatical with Niko Tingergen and his students at Oxford, with visits to other ethologists, led to a glossary which assembled the vocabularies of ethology and "learning theory" in psychology. It followed strict operational-interbehavioral principles, requiring careful analysis in writing each definition. Twenty-five years later, they're still good.

This application of operational thinking forced more detailed examination of measurement for psychology, and led me to the position which I have held now for 15 years. Despite the differences in terminology I believe it is indeed interbehavioral. This view turns its back on everything in which I had been indoctrinated through my own schooling, and which I had passed on to others. It is, for me, the inevitable outcome of persistence in pursuing the conceptual framework of Skinner (up to 1953) and which Kantor had recognized as a fragment of his own.

What then, are the views to which events in this history have guided me, for which I believe we are indebted to J.R. Kantor? I would identify four major characteristics of a Kantorian position. Here, I will necessarily state them in my own terms, and in my own way; Kantor is not responsible for any misunderstandings, distortions or misstatements of his writings that the reader may identify.

1. Naturalism
2. Scientific Pluralism
3. Interbehavior as Subject-Matter
4. Rejection of Causal-Deterministic "Explanation"

These must be recognized as probable obstacles to the adoption of interbehavioral thought by the great majority of living psychologists. Each represents a departure if not a negation of the eternal verities of "the science of psychology" learned and accepted by most who work in the discipline.

### Naturalism

Scientific advance in psychology must depend upon the full adoption of naturalism, the viewpoint that all explanations, all accounts we give of the antecedents prior to what we observe must be given in terms of other observables of the same sort--of other natural, uncontrived, uninvented events, and **not** by appeal to transcendent entities or forces--to the supernatural.

The gods we invent, whether gentle and loving, cruel and vindictive, whether lascivious or chaste, are modeled after people we know, and love, or fear, or both. The plans, the pleasures, the habits, the whims of these supernatural entities are then used to "explain," "give reasons for" the events in the world we live in. The rise of modern science, foreshadowed by Aristotle and other Greeks, was made possible by the adoption of the naturalistic viewpoint--as "supernaturalism," or explanation in terms of our inventions, was rejected.

The success of the naturalistic viewpoint has been accompanied by the development of new families of human inventions, scientific constructions, and these function appropriately in explanation in the sciences within which they were developed, and to whose observable concepts they bear direct and immediate relationship.

When, however, a psychologist appeals to such constructions (adding, of course, additional and convenient traits) as theoretical explanation for the behaviors we observe, that psychologist is appealing to unobservable causes for observable events, and is doing no differently than our pre-scientific forbears. In psychology, "brain centers in the hypothalamus" account for feeding no more and no less than Zeus accounts for lightning or Jehovah for creation. Brain centers are "spooks," as Kantor would say. They are explanatory fictions. They are, for psychology, **supernatural,** appealing to events external to the behaviors they purport to explain.

Between these two extremes of the supernatural--between a god or gods and "hypothetical constructs"--fall most of psychologists' supernatural concepts--its spooks. "Minds," "personalities," "libido," "drive," "motives," "attitudes," "traits,"... the list is nearly inexhaustible.

Kantor's naturalism is extreme. When William James, in the first years of this century, rejected the very explanatory fictions (including "consciousness") that he had so fully expounded in **The Principles of Psychology,** he used the term "radical empiricism." Kantor, who shares so much with the late James, could well term his position "radical naturalism." Having identified his subject-matter interbehavior, he has refused to accept any description or explanation of a behavioral event that is not itself observable **and** statable in terms of **other** behavioral events. Skinner, in "Are Theories of Learning Necessary," adopts this same viewpoint. He seems to have heard more of what Robert Kantor was saying in those seminars than he had thought.

### Scientific Pluralism

There is and can be no "one science." Methods and concepts will necessarily differ with the differing subject matters and the differing education and training of scientific investigators, who will intervene differently, and with differing consequences for what they study.

The methods of investigation and the conceptual system that are appropriate for and which have worked effectively in the science of physics apply only to the physical sciences--the sciences that deal with the environment as energy, and that attempt to exclude the observers from consideration, and attempt to minimize their role, although even here, as the Heisinberg Principles show, the observer intrudes. Concepts applicable to living individuals, much less to behaving ones, are singularly inappropriate. A second set of methods, concepts, and vocabulary distinguish the biological sciences, which treat the organisms and their functions generically. A third set of methods, concepts and language will define psychology, given the subject matter of psychology as the science of behavior--of the interaction of the individual and his environment. Its methods of investigation and concepts will necessarily differ from those of the physical and biological sciences. Other sciences with unique or overlapping subject matters should be expected to develop their own framework of methods, concepts and conceptual systems.

There is no limit to the number of sciences, to the new scientific languages that may be developed, which may include some of the concepts of other sciences. Among the psychologies, psychophysics deals with those limited sets of physical and behavioral phenomena that come into immediate relationship with one another. It is neither physics nor psychology, but shares some of both. It weds some of the concepts of physics, e.g., electromagnetic radiant energy with a limited set of activities of the individual ("yes, I see it."). At present, Psychophysics may seem to be an all but complete science; its triumphs in producing acceptable replicas of environments have given us the "Tonight Show," technicolor, and Stravinsky on the HiFi. Other such interstitial sciences that stand separately but borrow from its neighbors are ecology and physiological psychology.

These views anticipate much of the later writings of Wittgenstein, who emphasized the limitations on scientific and all other knowledge set by the various languages developed in linguistic communities: People sharing common interests. "Universal truths" have not been found within any science or within any culture; each investigation is limited by the context within which it is developed, and the language in which it is cast and reported.

Finally, given this pluralistic conceptual framework, the pursuit of "explanation" through reductionistic thought is not merely futile but misleading and necessarily destructive of the development of further knowledge in any one field.

### Interbehavior as Subject Matter

Psychology is the science of **behavior.** Behavior is the interaction of parts of the activities of the individual ("responses"), with parts of the activities of the environment--the events surrounding that part. No event in Psychology can be specified without equal reference to both the individual and to the individual's environment. Psychological events--interactions--lie in between. Activities of the individual that can occur and be described without reference to the environment fall outside the interests of the psychologists, however much they may concern the biologist.

Society is now coming to recognize this as did Aristotle 2,500 years ago: The biologically intact individual who is completely unresponsive to the environment and shows no interaction with it is judged legally dead and his still sound, biologically living tissues are available for transplant.

The interaction is bi-directional: The individual changes his environment, whether physically or functionally, and the environment changes the individual in turn. Each "controls" the other; each interacts with the other. When the environment ceases to respond to the individual, the individual ceases to respond to the environment. From this it follows that psychological events all have duration in time; the "instantaneous" concept of causality implicit in the physical sciences and in the calculus as the tool for the physical science theory does not apply.

## Rejection of Causal-Deterministic Explanation
## "The Field"

From an interbehavioral point of view, both causal and deterministic thinking must be rejected. We can discuss at most only the prediction of an event, B, from our antecedent knowledge of event, A, of the context("field") in which event A occurs and of the reactional biography of the individual in question. Exact, precise predictions are not to be expected except in trivial matters, nor is trans-situational prediction or control possible except **a posteriori.** We can only to a limited degree make our predictions "come true" by physical or psychological intervention. When we can make a prediction, we need not be disturbed by the duration of time intervening between the occurrence of event A and the later occurrence of event B; an individual may interact with an environmental event only some years after the event. Physical-theoretical limitations to interactions across physical time or space do not apply to psychological events. In psychology, such limitations are empirically established.

In sum, physical causality, as it has been conceptualized by Hume, and applied in physics and elsewhere, whether overtly or tacitly, with its requirements of immediate contiguity in infinitely divisible time and space, is rejected, whether in its implication of perfect predictability , or in its use as "explanation."

If any view of "causality" as necessary antecedents to an event were acceptable, it might be the Aristotelian analysis, with omission of "final causes," although it is tempting to remind the reader of what we call a "self-fulfilling prophecy."

From the foregoing it follows that attempts to develop a science of psychology using the experimental methods that have proven fruitful in the physical sciences and that aim to identify "causes" will be necessarily futile, since they neglect individual reactional biographies, context ("setting factors"), and the activities of the intervening experimenter. The most that can be expected from laboratory research are statements about what happened in specific laboratories at particular times using specific methodologies with particular kinds of subjects. These are data incapable of supporting applicable generalizations.

In short, Psychology must expect to be and to remain a descriptive and a classificatory science, whose findings will enable us to live more comfortably in the world and to relate more readily to other people.

As a descriptive and classificatory science, psychology must be concerned with developing a language, a method of talking about and writing about behavior that will bring to a maximum our ability to predict what we will do and what others will do under what circumstances, and to make those predictions and descriptions in the world outside the laboratory.

Perhaps this last is the greatest point of possible coincidence, or possibly distortion of the interbehavioral viewpoint by my own. For thirty years I have been concerned with the vocabulary of psychology and both the semantics and syntax of language we use in speaking and writing to one another as well as with our students of behavior, such as ethologists. Pursuit of that goal led me to what I hope is a fuller understanding of Kantor's interbehaviorism, and of its relevance to what all psychologists do. The attempt to provide operational--empirical--definitions for the terms we use required close examination of the operations carried out, both in the laboratory and outside. The operations, the sequence of events linking individual and environment prove indispensible for those predictions of behavior we can make, as well as for clearly communicating what happened. Given a specification of the operations that define our various terms, then arranging the terms in order of their appearance in subsequent definitions brings us to the set of such empirical generalizations as can now be made. The process is both descriptive and classificatory, and not one of "theory-construction."

Very close examination of the operations carried out by psychologists in specific experiments in laboratory research led to two further conclusions. The definitions tell us what we know. First, the operations are developed out of simplistic views of causality and by the demands of one or another elegant theory based on some "scientific model"; and second, the operations are of a complexity that renders unlikely the generation of any results of interest or significance in any other context than that of the laboratory and the theory in terms of which they were developed.

It is no accident that Robert Kantor has not done experimental research. It is no accident that those who understand the viewpoint and apply it successfully both in doing research and in communicating with one another (if not to the classical hard core pseudo-physicists of the experimental psychologists) keep their methodology simple, and carry out their work elsewhere than the lab.

In sum, the experimental literature does not reward **close study**. The most productive experimental research has been that using the simplest of operations, most free of theory, and most close to the straightforward interactions of individuals in natural (uncontrived) environments.

This set of views may be a gross misrepresentation of Robert Kantor's thinking. I hope not. It is unwelcome to experimental psychologists who prize the experimental method and who seemed baffled when they discovered that 10 or 12 years of intensive experimental research, say on "Mathematical Learning Theories" wind up with a net product of zero. Careers are made, and honors won; libraries fill up. But there is little by way of "cumulative knowledge."

Those who read and absorb interbehavioral views will thereafter think and act differently; they alter their ways. But, at what explicit point in a paper by one so affected can he refer to him? In 1947 Kantor published **Problems in Physiological Psychology.** Since this critical analysis, many physiological psychologists no longer are subject to the criticisms he first made. Did they read Kantor's book? Did they accept his criticisms? How does one measure the influence this book has had on the thinking of the physiological psychologists of the time, and in turn on the thinking of their students?

A specific case. In the early fifties, in conversation on psychological matters, Fred Skinner said something like this to me: "Yes, Bill, Robert was right--drive is a spook." To my own knowledge, Skinner has not made reference to Kantor on this point except for in the preface to the seventh edition of **The Behavior of Organisms,** nor does my probably unreliable remembering recall a paper explicitly rejecting the concept "drive." But, it is no trick to observe that the Indiana years mark a change in Skinner's treatment of this concept, and of the experimental procedures(and their outcomes) that had entered into it. Kantor drove this spook out.

Where, in a paper, can or should one write, "This statement is made because I've read Kantor?" And if one wants to make such acknowledgment, who could cite what specific line or page, in which specific book, as an editor would demand?

When, one might ask, should a fish refer to the sea?

In short, Kantor's influence has surely been greater than is at first apparent, however difficult (if not impossible) it may be to document. But, still, the question: Why has Kantor's work not reached for greater recognition and acceptance? There has probably been one great barrier, one which has led this preface to take the form it has. Kantorian views on what psychologists should do, and how they should do it, run precisely opposite to all the concepts of "psychology as a science" developed by the masterful and effective efforts of psychologists in the first part of the century to join the respected "scientific" community. Ensconced in the departments of the Ivy League, these successful men stamped out a pattern for what is, and what is not, "scientific." The efforts of these scientists have pervaded and impeded the progress of psychology by adopting an inappropriate model, the activity of "hard-core" scientists, of physical scientists as they were at the turn of this century. "Research" is "experimental" research, carried out in the laboratory. "Scientific method" is that specified by philosophers of science. The Ph.D. requires original **experimental** research as the measure of professional success, and the **sine qua non** of promotion and raises in the academic community.

As William James foresaw in **The Ph.D. Octopus,** before the century began, our society has placed a premium on "research," and in psychology, on "experimental research" which has in turn given plausibility and force to any and all procedures, statistical devices, epistemologies, and techniques, that make it easy to do "good research"--to perform "experiments." Results and the doctorate are guaranteed irrespective of importance. The "quality" of this research is measured by the degree to which it conforms with the rules set down by the "philosophy of science."

Little wonder that Kantor, the outsider way out in Indiana, who expounded a very different view of psychology and of what psychologists should do, could be thought dead or at least missing, as early as 1938.

To this date, interbehavioral views remain unwelcome--unwelcome by the great majority of psychologists, to the point of refusal to consider, much less to examine and study the works of Kantor. This would require them to question all the techniques, all the eternal verities, that the academic world still requires for professional achievement and success, both in reputation and salary.

A contributing factor, not to be neglected, is the difficulty of Kantor's prose, both in sentence structure and vocabulary, and in his frequent stylistic use of allusion rather than direct statement in developing his arguments. He places demands on his reader, that the reader too often cannot meet.

"There are no such phenomena as monochromatic light." Reading that, as a researcher in vision, with no small investment in "monochromatic filters," and who had peered at many spectra, I was appalled. Twenty or so years later, encountering it again--"Of course, who could have thought otherwise?"

Through his career, Robert Kantor has been patient with this lack of earned recognition. But, patient he can be; he knows, and has written to the effect, that so long as investigators continue to interact with their subject matter, they will move forward to fuller understanding and scientific knowledge in psychology. Passing trends and fads of equipment, or "sophisticated" methodology, of systematic viewpoint, and of theories may accelerate or slow this movement, but they will not stop it. Time, in which research (however misguided) continues, will inevitably lead us all to interbehaviorism, if not necessarily to its vocabulary.

This personal history may prove the paradigm--where time after time, when I thought I had reached a new position, I'd stop myself short...."Hey, wait a minute, Kantor wrote that"--or "that's what Kantor would say." He's always been there first.

This is the way it will happen for others, over coming years.

Then, this great psychologist will reach the recognition he has earned.

But, for now, this is preface to contributions prepared for you in honor of J.R. Kantor, by others who share the systematic viewpoint for a science of psychology that Robert Kantor has so fully developed.

Knoxville, Tennessee
November, 1982

# INTRODUCTION

Is psychology an authentic science? This question has been asked repeatedly for more than a century. Such a question is kept alive by the fact that even today psychology's speciality fields include those that are dedicated to studying an "inner" or "subjective" world or the operations of alleged processing in the person, often by use of questionable analogies such as computers and holographs. This approach has delayed the achievement of a unified scientific orientation in psychology. What, then, would constitute an authentic science of psychology? We submit that psychology must become a discipline which examines **natural events**, not reified constructs. If psychology were removed from the harness of its ancient mentalism and transformed into a study a humankind concerned with the situations that comprise behaviors, it would be on its way toward such a goal. It would also move closer to providing solutions to human problems. In this book we have tried to take that direction and to treat physiological, clinical, developmental, and other branches of psychology in the context of such naturalism.

The role of objective analysis in science has been carefully articulated by J.R. Kantor in his formulation of interbehavioral psychology. The authors of this volume champion the interbehavioral alternative because it represents a clear departure from the traditions of dualism and simple reductionism: It identifies with natural science. J.R. Kantor's contributions to an event-based psychology have been in the direction of discarding final principles, mechanisms, and imaginary constructs. In short, the paradigmatic assumptions which most versions of psychology have accepted are replaced with a system that is fully naturalistic. With this volume we present a challenge to the conventionalism of contemporary psychology by encouraging a different outlook on human behavior. While operant psychology has been content to espouse environmental relations between antecedents, behaviors, and consequences, and mentalism has relegated behavior to an unseen inner process or to a homunculean brain, the interbehavioral alternative instead begins with the observed events of an integrated field involving an organism in reciprocal or ecological relation with other factors in the field.

Psychology seems to be ready for a change in direction that we propose. This is attested to by the following. In recent years several movements have appeared in psychology that seek a replacement for mechanism, mentalism, and reductionsim. One, contextualism, has stressed the necessity of dealing with setting or context in which the individual is situated and the interactions between them. Other competing psychologies include dialectic psychology, and the more recent versions of European phenomenological psychology. In general, these approaches seek a field type of formulation; but they retain elements of mentalism and organocentrism. They have not achieved a fully integrated field approach to psychology or even a fully event-based orientation. A second development is that many students of behavior analysis have sought a broader framework for their operant work and have turned to interbehaviorism for it. At the same time, laboratory and clinical applications of behavior modification have been in transition, shifting from a purely overt response orientation to one that is more sympathetic to cognitivism. Interbehaviorists have always considered cognitive behavior (as opposed to cognition **and** behavior) as a genuine form of interbehavior and have analyzed it as such. A third development is that numerous students of Kantor, and now their students, have taken positions in colleges and universities and have integrated interbehaviorism into their work. Together, these developments provide both an impetus for reassessment and an event-based alternative to the traditional construct-based psychologies. Toward that end we have prepared this volume.

This book is divided into three sections: Part I is devoted to an analysis of the contemporary historical states of psychology vis a vis the interbehavioral alternative. In Chapter 1 Lichtenstein provides general orientation for the reader by succinctly describing the interbehavioral approach to theory. This is followed by Smith's discussion of the implications contained in interbehavioral theory for viable alternatives to contemporary mentalistic and behavioristic failures to adequately deal with manifold and recurrent empirical and theoretical problems. Finally, Morris, Higgins, and Bickel summarize empirical data which validates the relevance of interbehavioral psychology as a potent inluence within radical behaviorism.

Part II contains examples of successful research applications. Cone, in Chapter 4, describes the origins of scientific psychology in antiquity, the exclusion of psychology from the group of natural sciences on purely metaphysical grounds, and the consequent struggle by many psychologists to regain for psychology a place among the company of natural sciences. Pronko then expounds upon one blind alley of the attempt to restore psychology to its rightful niche among the natural sciences: Physiological psychology. The actual role of physiological psychology as a setting factor is presented, and this alternative thus provides an alternative to the conventional wisdom that connecting the mind to physiological events establishes psychology as a natural science. In Chapter 6 Delprato disposes of the convenient and conventional notion that the new term for mental mechanisms ("cognitions") solve the problem of the inner world by exposing "cognition" as a type of behavior to be investigated within the interbehavioral framework. Smith combines the basic core of the preceeding chapters to elucidate the interbehavioral interpretation of perception of behaviors, which constitute one of the oldest technical problems in psychology.

Three chapters are devoted to language behavior. Bijou elucidates the earliest stage of language acquistion and the continuity with non-language behavior. Chapter 9 presents Ribes's careful analytic critique of the operant treatment of verbal behavior. Parrott continues this critical analysis in her presentation of an interbehavioral description of implicit interbehaviors. In the last chapter of this section Herrick describes the failure of contemporary psychologists to adequately appreciate the scientific value of the aging process. "Ageism," as it reflects individual biological systems, is presented through a paradigm that refutes traditional constructions of behavioral disorders resulting from organic deterioration.

In Part III on interbehavioral implications for other disciplines the authors describe how certain principles of ecological systems apply to sibling fields. MacRoberts and MacRoberts explore dimensions in social psychology consonent with Kantor's reformulations. Shaffer discusses common reductionistic assumptions in animal behavior and demonstrates how these assumptions have subverted the understanding of the genuine role of behavior in evolution by natural selection. Cone's account of "interbehavioral ethology" continues this elucidative theme by challenging contemporary comparative psychology's emphasis upon subjective inferences. Ray, Blewitt and Mountjoy consider the influence of today's technology through an interbehavioral perspective. Blewitt raises the antinomy of memory as either interbehavioral or information processing as he probes into the collective realms of science and computer technology for a resolution. Ray's chapter continues this investigation into technically adaptive methods for interbehavioral study by encouraging a temporal analysis of natural events related to physiological dispositions. Mountjoy, also intrigued by aspects of technology, follows the course of its evolutionary progress in psychology from Prehellenic days forward to current day technology, isolating at each stage the cultural changes that contributed to this volution. Finally, interbehavioral psychology is not to remain unaccredited by clinicians. Ruben's formulations for clinical therapy are twofold. First he attempts a reconciliation between a "response repertoire" and "reactional biography" and then, secondly, to incorporate this improved concept into an application he designs a model for clinical diagnosis and treatment.

Lastly, we owe a debt of appreciation to persons directly involved in all preparation phases of this book. Assistance from Dr. David Lyon and secretaries in the Department of Psychology at Western Michigan University made it possible to begin editing manuscripts fairly quickly. Assistance from the contributing authors was especially valuable in the many contacts we had during these past two years. And finally, special recognition is given to Marilyn J. Ruben, wife of the third editor, for her cooperation in proof-reading the entire book and offering constructive comments on layout design.


N.W.S.
P.T.M.
D.H.R.

Kalamazoo, Michigan, 1982

Part 1

HISTORICAL CONTEMPORARY ANALYSES

# THE INTERBEHAVIORAL APPROACH TO PSYCHOLOGICAL THEORY

Parker E. Lichtenstein

Interbehavioral psychology has been evolving since the early 1920's. The early definitive statement of the interbehavioral position was Kantor's (1924, 1926) two volume work which still stands as the most comprehensive and ambitious to date. Certain basic constructs have, however, undergone modification and these changes have been detailed in two fairly recent books; Kantor and Smith (1975) and Pronko (1980).

In his reexamination of the foundations of psychology Kantor urged that the discipline abandon completely the traditional dualistic approach together with ancient epistemology and metaphysics. He contended that if this were done, no barrier would remain to the erection of a sound naturalistic psychology or an authentic behaviorism. All of the sciences arise from a single, vast matrix of events and all are alike natural. There is no sound basis for the doctrine which regards men as in part natural and in part transcendental.

The subject matter of psychology is defined as the interactions of organisms with objects and events. Psychology is not the study of mere biological responses to extra-psychological energies or physically defined stimuli. An illustration of Kantor's approach can be seen in his handling of perception. Traditionally, perceptual theory has postulated light rays or colorless energies impinging on the retina, initiating nerve conduction, and culminating in a sensation of color in the mind. J.B. Watson did not depart in any radical way from this construction in spite of his condemnation of mentalism.

Kantor asked that we start over with the observation of a person or animal discriminating a color or colored object. When we do so we do not see light rays, retinal response, or nerve conduction; we see an object being reacted to appropriately or inappropriately as the case may be. How the person responds to the colored object is dependent upon a variety of factors which can be further investigated. These might be illumination, contrast effects, bodily conditions, past conditioning, etc. At no point in the observation of another person or oneself do we see a sensation. Sensation becomes a dualistic fiction.

If there are no sensations, no more is there experience, the supposed matrix from which all science is derived. Experience, which was seen as inner and private, gives way to interaction or interbehavior. Interbehaviors range from the overt to the very subtle. Perception, imagery, thinking, and feelings may be difficult to observe in another but they are not out of the range of investigation; they are not private. Furthermore, one has access to aspects of his own behavior not readily observed by another. We may speak of the relative accessibility of the field of interaction recognizing that each of us has a unique perspective from which to view his own behavior. Self-observation can be a significant source of information particularly with respect to the more subtle behaviors. At the same time we should note that a trained outside observer can frequently observe the operation of factors of which the behaver himself is quite unaware.

According to Kantor, part of Watson's error lay in treating behavior or response as simple biological action. Kantor sought functional descriptions of both stimulus and response, recognizing that a single stimulus object may operate in different ways depending upon the total immediate situation and the history of contact of the organism with the object and similar or related objects. In a similar manner, a response such as raising the head may be a bid for attention, a salute, a greeting, or an attempt to keep the sun out of one's eyes. The constructs of stimulus function and response function identify the coordinate poles of the psychological interaction. These constructs are at least somewhat similar to the stimulus and response classes of Skinner, and the stimulus function bears a resemblance to Lewin's valence.

To continue with our perception illustration we may consider the child's response to an orange. Through progressive contacts it becomes a ball to be rolled or tossed, food to be peeled and eaten, etc. Early responses are called out by the color of the orange, its sweetness, etc. By the time the child is five or six the orange means many things. Thus an orange on the table is perceived as something sweet for breakfast even though the child is responding to the sight of the orange and not directly to its taste. Perceptual responses, then, have the character of being partially implicit, that is, the response is made to an aspect of the object not immediately present to the senses.

Perception, of course, involves sense organs, peripheral nerves, and the brain. Like all other psychological activities, however, it should be seen as involving the organism-as-a-whole. The organism does not act part by part. It is particularly important that we not look upon the brain as a unique psychological organ. Psychological actions are not brain functions even though they probably always require brain

participation.   To seek      explanations    of behavior           in
brain terms or even in terms of total biological response is to place
undue emphasis upon what can only be a part of a complex field of
interaction.

The interactional perspective can be applied in analyzing any
psychological activity as, for example, thinking, imaging, imagining,
remembering, planning, intelligence, instinct, feelings, emotion, and
willing.   As might be expected, the interbehavioral psychologist's
analyses of human and animal behavior differ radically from
conventional descriptions which usually have an organocentric or
internal principle emphasis.  The organocentric attitude leads readily
to mentalism once it is observed that biological action is insufficient
to provide an adquate description of psychological    data.

Kantor has been particularly interested in such complex behaviors
as language, reasoning, and dreaming.  With respect to such events
Kantor (1968) says,

> As long as we cleave to the fundamental pri-
> ciple that psychology is the study of the inter-
> actions between response functions and stimulus
> finctions there is no type of behavior that eludes
> observation. In dealing with the most refined and
> difficult behavior we need  only exclude the influence
> of venerable traditions.  Imagery, for example, can
> be readily described in terms of incipient and ves-
> tigial action based upon prior contacts with partic-
> ular objects and surrounding circumstances (p. 165).

### Philosophical Foundations of Psychology

As psychology became an experimental science in the late
nineteenth century, it seemed natural to assert its independence of
philosophy.   With behaviorism came an even bolder attempt to rid
psychology of ancient metaphysics.  It is a bit ironic that about the
same time physics, one of the oldest of the sciences, was being forced
by scientific developments in its own field  to a renewed interest in
philosophical issues.

The situation in psychology was not, however, a simple one. To a
great extent psychologists who wished to avoid philosophical questions
allowed assumptions drawn from traditional epistemology and
metaphysics to dominate their thinking. Because these  assumptions,
such as mind-body dualism, private experience, and sensation were
accepted uncritically, they tended to have insidious effects. The anti-
position was defended on the grounds that some assumptions are
inevitable and since they are  not capable of empirical validation ,

one should simply get on with collecting data. What was overlooked was that facts, once observed or interpreted, are theory-laden.

Kantor (1963, 1969) seeing the extent to which psychology has been dominated by ancient philosophical and theological beliefs, concluded that all such traditional assumptions could be extruded. The assumptions of scientific psychology would be such as to place psychology on a comparable footing with the other natural sciences. Kantor, almost alone among psychologists, has made his postulates and assumptions explicit in order that they might be identified and criticized. It is only when one understands fully the implications of Kantor's postulates that one begins to realize how radically he has departed from traditional psychology. If Kantor has devoted a great deal of attention to the influence of mind-body dualism on psychological thinking, it is because he believes that this influence has been and continues to be an extremely pernicious one.

**The Logic of Science**

Interbehavioral psychology claims the merit of deriving its descriptions and interpretations directly from interbehaviors of the psychological type. It sees its task as identifying and describing psychological events and the conditions under which they will occur as fully as possible. Such a psychology is strictly a scientific enterprise. The broad appraisal of this or any other scientific system falls within the logic of science. The logic of science summarizes and organizes the work and products of the various sciences. Inevitably it must include positions regarding the data of science, approaches to investigation, and the construction of general propositions or laws. A sound scientific psychology requires a satisfactory logic of science which in turn demands the extrusion of traditional metaphysics. Kantor and Smith (1975) have formulated two basic rules for the sciences:

1. To be aware of and to avoid as much as possible the cultural institutions unfavorable to the prosecution of scientific work.
2. To persist in interacting exclusively with confrontable events whether directly or by reliable inference (p. 409).

Depending upon the cultural conditions prevailing at a particular time and place science may flourish, decline, or even be proscribed. Western civilization has for nearly two thousand years supported transcendental beliefs which have made the evolution of scientific pscyhology difficult indeed. While interbehavioral psychology rests on postulates which find increasing acceptance, it must be admitted that such postulates run counter to widely accepted beliefs.

6

The level of philosophy establishes the philosophy of science regulating scientific systems. Kantor refers to assumptions about the nature of science as protopostulates. Most philosophies of science have included supernatural elements which an interbehavioral philosophy of science emphatically excludes. Interbehavioral protopostulates emphasize that science is interbehaving with specific things and events, that science is not concerned with existences which transcend the scientific enterprise, that scientific constructions (theories, laws) must be derived from interbehavior and not imposed from cultural sources, that science is evolutional, cumulative, and corrigible, and that it can be relatively autonomous within a cultural complex (Kantor, 1959).

Each particular science may have postulates specific to it and which constitute the foundation of a scientific system. These may be called metapostulates and are said to constitute a metasystem (Kantor and Smith, 1975). The psychological metasystem according to Kantor and Smith (1975) involves seven metapostulates.

Metapostulate 1. "Psychology is homogenous with all other sciences" (p. 413). Psychology isolates an aspect of the complex manifold of events for study. Psychology is no more and no less naturalistic than the other sciences.

Metapostulate 2. "Psychology is a relatively independent science though in constant interdisciplinary contact with other relevant sciences" (p. 414). Psychology has its own subject matter, methods, and accumulation of facts. Constructs and models borrowed from other sciences are generally to be avoided.

Metapostulate 3. "Psychology must be freed from all traditional philosophies" (p. 414). Events must be described as they occur and not as seen through the distorting lenses of traditional epistemology and metaphysics. Unfortunately rationalistic and experiential metaphysics are deeply embedded in the fabric of our culture and their influence is pervasive.

Metapostulate 4. "An adequate psychological system should take account of events, operations, and theory construction" (p. 414). There is no need to limit psychological investigation to a restricted range of data as, for example, animal learning. All types of animal and human interbehavior can and should be studied and interpreted. Complex human behavior requires careful observation and description and cannot be understood simply by extrapolation from simpler animal behavior.

Metapostulate 5. "Psychological systems must be oriented" (p. 414). The psychologist must pay attention to the system building enterprise in order to correlate such factors of the system as postulates, descriptions, definitions, hypotheses and laws.

Metapostulate 6. "Psychological systems are irreducible" (p. 414). It is widely postulated that physics is the basic science and that psychology can be reduced to physiology and eventually to physics and chemistry. While cooperation among the sciences is essential, each science should aim at full description at the level of the observed events themselves.

Metapostulate 7. "All scientific systems are subject to changes in circumstances" (p. 415). Events may change requiring modifications in procedure and new hypotheses.

All psychological systems rest upon postulates whether these are openly stated or not. Interbehavioral psychology makes its postulates explicit, readily available for inspection and criticism.

The system postulates of interbehavioral psychology are given by Kantor and Smith (1975) as eight in number.

Postulate 1. "Psychology studies interbehavioral fields. The specific events which psychology investigates consist of the interactions of organisms with other organisms, objects, and events" (p. 415). Interbehaviors include everything from simple overt acts to the most subtle reflections or imaginings. The mental events postulated by traditional psychology, such as thinking, feeling, and willing, are seen as interbehaviors. And bodily movement, often taken as a basic datum by behaviorists, is viewed as a factor in a more complex field event but not as a fundamental datum for the psychologist. It is the total field of activity which is basic.

Postulate 2. "Psychological events are evolved from bioecological interbehaviors" (p. 415). Just as complex organisms have in the course of evolution developed from simpler types, so has there been continuity in the development of complex interbehaviors from simpler biological behaviors such as the reflex. The simple conditioned reflex in an animal has its basis in the bioecological evolution of a particular species. As evolution has proceeded interbehavioral capacities have become extremely complicated but in all cases they retain their biological roots.

Postulate 3. "Psychological fields are multiplex" (p. 415). Psychological fields embrace many factors in addition to organisms and the objects with which they interact. There are media of stimulation such as light for vision and air waves for hearing. Surrounding circumstances, called setting factors, include the biological state of the organism and the presence or absence of objects which may facilitate or inhibit certain action.

Postulate 4. "Psychological events are interrelated with societal events as well as with events studied by physicists, chemists, and biologists" (p. 416). At the level of human behavior it is quite apparent that objects may take on cultural properties. A watch does not normally elicit time-telling behavior apart from an individual life history evolved within a particular kind of culture. A psychology which limits itself to physical and chemical properties of objects gains precision only at the price of understanding.

Postulate 5. "Psychological interbehavior involves the performance of entire organisms not special organs or tissues" (p. 416). The field concept rules out the belief that psychological action resides in the organism alone. Behavior is not simply the operation of muscles or glands, nor is there any organ, not even the brain, which performs psychological actions. Important as it undoubtedly is, the brain is a biological organ with biological functions. There is no evidence that the brain is a "thinking machine" in spite of the growing appeal of computer or information processing analogies.

Postulate 6. "Psychological events are ontogenetic" (p. 416). Psychological events evolve during the lifetime of particular individuals. In contrast with biological actions such as the reflex, they have an inevitable historical dimension. How an organism will interbehave with an object will depend upon previous interactions with the object or with similar or associated objects.

Postulate 7. "Psychological events occur without any internal or external determiners" (p. 416). Behavior has often been explained as due to mental states, instincts, drives, faculties, or innate capacities. In contrast interbehavioral psychology holds that an adequate description of a psychological event requires only a naturalistic description of the media of stimulation, setting factors, and historical circumstances in addition to the interacting organism and objects.

Postulate 8. "Psychological constructions are continuous with crude data events" (p. 417). Scientific constructions should be based upon direct confrontations of events by the scientist. Interbehavioral constructs, whether descriptions or theories, must be derived from direct observation. Too often speculative constructs and theories have had their sources in tradition, including religion, mythology, and folklore.

# Basic Interbehavioral Constructs

## Interbehavioral Field

As defined by Pronko (1980) the interbehavioral field is "that complex or totality of interdependent factors that constitute or participate in a psychological event" (p. 5). The psychological field is dynamic and continuously evolving and is specific to a particular person. The field at a given time is a function of previous fields and of other factors participating at that moment.

## Behavior Segment

William James spoke of consciousness as a continuous flowing stream. Interbehavioral psychology rejects consciousness in favor of interbehavior but finds the analogy an apt one. Think of the behavior life of a person as a stretched-out string. In order to have a convenient unit we can isolate for scientific study we might cut out a small segment. This unit is called the behavior segment. Behavior segments vary by type and complexity. When the segment has a clear beginning and end we may speak of an "operation" behavior segment. Less determinate situations may involve relatively complex processes rather than simple acts and are called "process" behavior segments.

Some behavior segments are completed quickly while others like problem-solving require considerable time. We may then distinguish between "momentary" and "protracted" behavior segments.

An important distinction may be made between "witting" and "unwitting" behavior segments. Commonly we speak of unwitting behavior as absent-mindedness and think of it as maladaptive. In the case of well-established habit, however, close attention to the sequence of acts may be disruptive while habitual attention suffices for efficient action and frees the person to some extent for other activity. Unwitting behavior provides the factual basis for the constructs of the subconscious and the unconscious. Through reification a process becomes an entity and a basis is found for the elaborate constructions of Freudian psychology.

## Response Function

Interbehavioral psychology is sometimes viewed as a stimulus-response psychology and while there is some truth in this idea, the interbehavioral conceptions of stimulus and response stand in sharp contrast to more biologically oriented positions. The reflex is a biological response. Such responses as blushing or wincing, while they may be evoked by biological stimulation, are usually coordinated in adults with complex stimulus conditions; they have been conditioned to various stimuli such as verbal barbs, laughter, etc. Interbehavioral psychology, while taking the biological response into account, is primarily ·interested in the response function which is directly correlated with a stimulus function. The blushing response, for example, may be correlated with a friend's verbal reference to an embarassing episode. Laughter is a response with many functions; it may express great pleasure, cover up embarassment, subject another to ridicule, etc. We commonly distinguish between laughing at another and laughing with another. The difference is accounted for by different interbehavioral fields with their appropriate stimulus functions and settings.

It should be clear that the same biological response may have different functions depending upon the situation. Raising the arm, for example, may protect one from a blow, shield the eyes from the sun, provide a signal or a greeting, stretch a sore muscle, etc. Different biological responses may have the same function; the rat in a Skinner box may depress the lever with one or both forepaws, with his head, by sitting on it, etc. The boxer may avoid a punch by blocking, ducking, or slipping it. Language behavior reflects many subtleties. The same spoken words may have different functions depending upon whether they are spoken with a smile or in anger. The child's request for a new toy may be answered with a blunt, "No," or with a lengthy explanation which adds up to the same thing from the child's point of view.

## Stimulus Function

Any object becomes a stimulus object when it enters into a psychological event. The specific role played by the stimulus object in the psychological event may be termed the "stimulus function." Stimulus function and response function are coordinate and evolve in the course of the life history. One can watch the young boy learning to bat a ball. At first uncoordinated movements result in a poor swing and a wide miss. Eventually a smoothly coordinated swing is accurately timed according to the speed of the pitch. The appropriate response does not occur, however, except as there has developed a corresponding stimulus function. Thousands of interactions may undergird the stimulus-response functions of the expert's behavior. The elaboration of stimulus functions and correlated response functions in a subtle form is seen in wine testing. The inexperienced taster may simply find white wine different from red and prefer white. Subtleties of aroma and taste are for him quite meaningless. By sampling and tasting many wines he finds characteristics he had not previously thought existed. Even without specific instruction he begins to be a bit of a connoisseur. The process of developing more stimulus functions and response functions may proceed without one's knowing exactly how it takes place. While some stimulus functions are clearly based upon physical properties of the stimulus object, others are dependent upon cultural influences. Just how one will react to the hammer and sickle is a function primarily of the culture in which one has been reared. Again, snails may be eaten as a delicacy or avoided as inedible, if not disgusting.

Stimulus functions are extremely varied and it is instructive to classify them as to type. However, a few brief examples must suffice. The telephone rings, I pick it up and answer. Here the stimulus function is "direct." Quite a different situation arises when the radio announcer reports the continuation of dry weather and I respond by going out and turning on the sprinkler. In this case the speaker's words constitute a "substitute" stimulus function since they lead me to respond to another object, in this case the sprinkler.

Stimulus functions may be "endogenous" or "exogenous." Muscular strain which leads me to shift my position in my chair harbors an "endogenous" function. The father's command to his son to sit up straight is "exogenous."

In much of our behavior the object in which the stimulus function inheres is quite "apparent." There are puzzling cases, however, where this is not the case. I may find myself thinking of an acquaintance from long ago with no awareness of the stimulus. The stimulus function is quite "inapparent."

**Interactional Setting**

It is a commonplace observation that the behavior of children may change markedly if the teacher leaves the room. The presence or absence of other people may inhibit or facilitate certain behaviors depending upon who those other people are. Exactly which stimulus and response functions will operate at a given time depends upon such setting factors as the place (church, boxing arena, roller skating rink), certain people (minister, policeman, close friend), and conditions of the organism (headache, fatigue, well-being).

**Media of Contact**

Obviously light rays play a role in vision and sound waves in hearing. It is at this point, however, that interbehavioral psychology makes a sharp departure from traditional psychology. The long established position is that light rays are the stimuli for vision setting off a chain reaction from the retina to the optic nerve and thence to the visual cortex of the brain. Color quality comes into existence as a result of the cortical response or it is the cortical response.

For the interbehaviorist color is an object quality which one can respond to only in the presence of light which operates as the medium of contact. Each of the special senses has, of course, its proper medium. Failure to grasp the difference in approach outlined here has made it difficult for many psychologists to understand the interbehavioral position.

## Interbehavioral History

The interbehavioral history is "the complete behavior experience of an individual" (Kantor and Smith, 1975, p. 59). When one considers that psychological events are frequently phenomena occurring in milliseconds, he quickly realizes the complexity of the interbehavioral history. Behavior is evolutional; it is an outgrowth of past behavior. While biological differences between persons may account in part for individual differences of a psychological kind we must look to differences in the interbehavioral histories for a full understanding of their nature. The biological factor always enters into the interbehavioral history but it is important to keep biological development and psychological development distinct.

Psychological events involve stimulating objects and reacting organisms and we may describe their corresponding evolutions as the stimulus evolution on the side of the object and reactional biography on the side of the organism.

Biological and cultural factors provide both possibilities and limitations for psychological development. Yet those who see behavior as the unfolding of biological potential and those who can see only the stamp of culture on the individual are alike wide of the mark. It is the total field which is changing as a function of previous fields. Both biological and cultural factors are extremely important but overemphasis upon either leads to such theoretical distortions as sociobiology or extreme environmentalism. If we are to develop an adequate understanding of personality, genius, psychopathology, or almost any important psychological topic, it is to the intimate details of the interbehavioral history that we must look.

### Interbehavioral Positions on Controversial Issues

## Description vs. Explanation

A frequent criticism of interbehavioral psychology is that it is simply a descriptive approach and not explanatory. Yet in what sense can a scientific psychology do more than provide a relatively complete description of behavior and its conditions? A typical answer to this question is that behavior is explained by reference to conscious or unconscious mental events. Such an answer has generally satisfied the

13

layman and the psychoanalyst and, today, the cognitive psychologist. It is argued that mind is a perfectly good psychological construct as an inference from behavior if not an actual datum. Unfortunately, mind has been postulated to be non-spatio-temporal and thus, it seems, forever unobservable. It was once argued that although no one had ever seen a mind, neither had anyone seen a gene. Of course, with improved techniques it has been possible to photograph genes. Clearly, then, mind and gene belong in quite separate categories.

A somewhat different answer to our question is that what we call mind is actually the brain and therefore we should look to the brain for the explanation of behavior. A general term for this approach is reductionism, or explaining psychological events in terms of events at a lower (physiological) level. Reductionistic thinking is anathema to interbehaviorists since it is an attempt to explain what the interbehaviorist postulates as a complex field event in terms of a single field component. The basic postulates of interbehaviorists and reductionists could scarcely be at greater variance.

In brief, psychology does not require constructs other than those derived directly from its own behavioral data. There is no virtue in explanations which have recourse to metaphysical assumptions (mentalism) or to a brain surrogate for the ancient mind (reductionism).

**The Definition of Behavior**

Behavior is a term to which psychologists have assigned several meanings, with resulting confusion. Sometimes behavior has meant a muscular or glandular response while again it has referred to the response of the organism-as-a-whole. Generally speaking, psychologists have identified behavior with movement and thus have eliminated mental (intracerebral?) events from the behavioral realm. Here is the foundation for the view that psychology studies both behavior and experience.

Kantor (1922) objected to the position that behaviors or psychological data are actions of muscles , nerves, and glands. He recognized that at a pre-analytic level we can see that an animal or person may "do the same thing" in different ways, i.e., with different movements. He then postulated that the basic psychological datum is the interaction of organism and object, with movement playing an important but not defining role. Once we accept Kantor's definition of behavior it becomes relatively easy to embrace thinking, feeling, perceiving, etc. within a    behavioral framework.

**Private vs. Public—the Data of Psychology**

Traditionally psychology has been the science of the mental life, experience, or consciousness. Mental events were almost universally regarded as subjective and private, known only through the method of introspection. Such psychology differed radically from the natural sciences which dealt with objective subject matters. As some saw it psychology studied private experience itself while the natural sciences studied objective events revealed through private experience. In general, it was believed that all of the sciences rest upon private experience.

With the coming of behaviorism psychology appeared to make an "about face." Psychology was to be the science of observable human and animal behavior, as objective as any of the natural sciences. Private experience, while the ground and guarantor of all science, would no longer be the subject matter of any science. Psychology was to be known as the science of behavior. But because behavior was usually defined as neuro-muscular-glandular responses, behavioristic psychology failed to provide adequate analyses of perceiving, thinking, reasoning, memory, and so on. For this reason, and perhaps others, subjective psychology lived on and several textbooks defined psychology as the science of behavior and experience. Recently Kendler (1981) has defended the distinction between private experience and public behavior. He then finds that the psychololgist has options; he can view psychology as the science of experience, or as the science of behavior, or as some combination of the two. Under such circumstances it is little wonder that psychology is "a science in conflict" with little unity or even the hope of it.

It should be noted that behaviorists who, like Tolman, Boring, Stevens, and Spence accepted private experience as the starting point of science could only escape a dualism of subject matter by fiat or by ruling out experience as a proper subject of scientific investigation. They were in the difficult position of stating that perceiving events, for example, could only be handled by cumbersome indirect methods and theoretically through the brain, which was held to be the physical seat of the mind.

Subjective psychology has been undergirded by doctrines which many accept as readily as fact. These doctrines include Locke's distinction between primary and secondary qualities, Muller's doctrine of specific nerve energies, and the causal theory of perception. Together these add up to the position that the world does not exist independently but only as a construct of the human mind. Interbehavioral psychology dismisses such an analysis and asks for a new beginning. It cuts through the accumulation of metaphysical and theological notions from the past with one bold assumption, i.e., that all psychological behaviors , whether of the so-called mental type or overt actions, are interactions of organisms with stimulus objects. But, the reader may ask, "What about privacy?" "How can private events be handled in a natural science?" "Isn't the pain of my toothache fundamentally different from turning my head away from a bright light?" The answer is that of course interbehaviors vary by type but they are alike natural and observable. While all aspects of the interbehavioral field may not be readily accessible to an outside observer, the field is objective and capable of study. In some cases the subject's own observation of his behavior may be particularly helpful. Privacy means uniqueness of occurrence; there is nothing mysterious about the fact that B cannot have A's toothache. Both B and A can study A's toothache  and describe its conditions. In spite of detailed differences in the interbehavioral fields A's toothache  is no more private than A's reading of a thermometer.

Interbehavioral psychology achieves a unity of subject matter for psychology by eliminating mind, consciousness, and private experience and by defining behavior in terms which embrace the traditional mental event as well as overt acts.

### Heredity vs. Environment

No question in psychology has proved to be more troublesome than that regarding the relative infulence of heredity and environment upon behavior. It is a common misconception that interbehaviorism represents an extreme environmentalism and almost total denial of any role to heredity. Such misunderstanding rests upon a failure to grasp the distinction between biological behavior and psychological behavior. Biological behavior is essentially a matter of structure, and in lower animals there are striking examples of complex behaviors performed immediately after birth. Such apparently inborn behaviors may be remarkably well adapted to particular environments and may be regarded as evolutionary adaptations.

Psychological behavior builds upon biological behavior and always involves it as a participating factor. Simple biological action can be described in terms of structure-function, ecological behavior in terms of the fit of structure-function and environment, but psychological behavior only in terms of a sequence of organism- object interactions. The ability to speak French, for example, is not simply accounted for in physiological terms but requires elaborate and continued contact with a French-speaking culture.

The phenomena of heredity are biological, and while genes may be thought of as the carriers of heredity, they operate through interaction with their environment and not in a foreordained way. In any case the genes act upon the development of bodily structure and to the extent that they operate upon psychological behavior they do so through structural characteristics. From the standpoint of psychology, then, heredity plays a remote role in behavioral development since, as we have pointed out, psychological behavior is not the simple functioning of bodily structures.

If interbehavioral psychology finds only a limited role for heredity, it makes practically no use of environment taken in the usual sense. Recall that the stimulus object harbors stimulus functions developed through the interbehavioral history, and it is the reciprocal stimulus-function,response-function interaction which is the particular concern of the psychologist. A field interpretation of behavior, while embracing any relevant facts regarding biological heredity and the physical environment, radically reconstructs the situation so as to render the traditional heredity-environment controversy quite meaningless.

## The Brain and Behavior

There is in our culture a deep-seated belief that the brain is the organ of thinking, the seat of learning and of personality. Laymen and scientists alike generally accept the idea that if A should receive a brain transplant from B he would no longer be A but would become B. A brain with such functions would truly be a homunculus, a little man inside who knows, feels, decides, and controls. The study of brain function might then be regarded as the road to a scientific explanation of man while behavioral science could provide only simple description.

What must appear puzzling about the view which makes the brain a surrogate for the mind is the fact that no other bodily organ has anything but biological functions. The brain, too, has its biological functions of conduction and integration but in addition is endowed with psychological functions. The basis for this position seems to rest upon the observed intimate connection between brain activity and behavior. No one denies the importance of the brain in the biological economy or its role as a participant in psychological events. But to regard thinking, a complex field event involving many participating factors, as an activity within the skull is to commit the fallacy of "nothing but" with a vengeance. One of the most serious defects of the brain view is that its acceptance can easily lead to the failure to investigate other factors involved in the full description of behavior.

The brain view, or dogma, has its source in the mind-body tradition. An immaterial mind seemed to require a bodily seat through which it might operate and there were many reasons for choosing the brain as the most likely candidate. While Descartes' interactionist solution to the mind-body problem has few advocates today, there are many philosophers , psychologists, and physiologists who find identism, the position which makes mind and brain one and the same, quite attractive. Yet, if we have no need for postulating the immaterial mind, we have no need for its substitute. the brain as homunculus.

## Operant Behaviorism and Interbehaviorism

Skinner's operant behaviorism has been in a process of continuous development for over forty years. It has a great many adherents today carrying on research, writing, and practical applications in such diverse areas as programmed instruction, behavior modification (including token economies, care of infants and the retarded and behavior therapy), psychopharmacology, and language.

Skinner has been primarily interested in the prediction and control of the motor and verbal behavior of human beings and animals. These activities are observed, recorded, and measured without preconceptions from self-observation or other contaminating sources. Starting with studies of rat and pigeon behavior Skinner moved on by extrapolation to human verbal behavior,work with  psychotics, and to problem behaviors such as obesity.

From his lever-pressing experiments emerged the analysis of behavior in terms of (I) the stimulus which sets the occasion for the occurrence of the response, (2) the response or response- class (e.g., any response which results in depression of the bar), and (3) a reinforcing stimulus defined as a stimulus the presentation of which strengthens a response or increases its probability of occurrence. One of the attractions of the Skinnerian system is that widely diverse data can be embraced within this simple analytic scheme.

Behavior, which is Skinner's basic datum, is defined in terms of observable movement, but emphasis is placed upon the consequences of a particular act.  While Skinner appears to lean toward the exactness of physical definitions of stimulus and response, in practice his approach is clearly a functional one.

Long ago Verplanck (1954) observed that there is a resemblance between operant behaviorism and interbehaviorism.  He said, "Skinner's approach, then, bears no more than a terminological resemblance to Hull's or to Pavlov's , but it is at least first  cousin to Kantor's system, which explicitly rather implicitly  accepts a metaphysical position, naive realism , and rejects even the logical possibility of reductionism" (p. 308). Verplanck stressed the point that Skinner (like Kantor) asked that psychology make a new beginning and base its constructs on data rather than the bias of tradition. Since Verplanck's paper, many others have noticed the close resemblance of operant behaviorism to interbehaviorism, and it has even been suggested that operant behaviorism may be viewed as a subsystem within the broader interbehavioral framework. An analysis of the similarities between the two systems provides support for this position but differences exist and these are striking enough to lead Kantor and Skinner to rule out such an amalgamation.

A few of the similarities of the operant and interbehavioral systems are worth mentioning. Both advocate a descriptive, behavioral psychology; both are anti-mentalistic; both place great emphasis upon the behavioral-environmental history; both desire to keep constructs close to crude data; both oppose reductionism; and both avoid meditational states in the form of hypothetical constructs or intervening variables.

On the other hand, differences are found which cannot be easily removed. Skinner advocates a functional analysis stressing the reinforcement principle; Kantor prefers a field analysis. Skinner's psychology is deterministic while Kantor dismisses both determinism and indeterminism as metaphysical. Skinner and Kantor disagree over the definition of behavior. Skinner extrapolates freely from animal to human behavior while Kantor emphasizes direct contact with complex human data. While Kantor's psychology is a special version of stimulus-response psychology, Skinner's is better characterized as a response psychology. While Skinner emphasizes controlled experimentation, Kantor relies heavily upon field observation. Thus, while reconciliation is not out of the question, it will not readily be achieved. As the situation stands a growing number of psychologists have been encouraged to work within both operant behaviorism and interbehaviorism, seeing them as broadly compatible and allied in their opposition to all forms of non-naturalistic psychology.

## Footnotes

1. Kantor prefers to see his position as asserting an uncommitted view of the nature of objects rather than as a metaphysical realism.

## References

Kantor, J. R. 1922. Can the psychophysical experiment reconcile introspectionists and objectivists. **American Journal of Psychology** , 32, 481-510.

Kantor, J.R. 1924. **Principles of Psychology.** (Vol. 1). New York: Knopf.

Kantor, J.R. 1926. **Principles of Psychology.** (Vol.2). New York: Knopf.

Kantor, J.R. 1959. **Interbehavioral Psychology**. Chicago: Principia Press.

Kantor, J.R. 1963. **The Scientific Evolution of Psychology** (Vol. 1) . Chicago: Principia Press.

Kantor, J.R. 1969. **The Scientific Evolution of Psychology** (Vol. 2). Chicago: Principia Press.

Kantor, J.R. 1968. Behaviorism in the history of psychology. **Psychological Record,** 18, 151-166.

Kantor, J.R. and Smith, N.W. 1975. **The Science of Psychology: An Interbehavioral Survey.** Chicago: Principia Press.

Kendler, H.H. 1981. **Psychology: A Science in Conflict.** New York: Oxford Univeristy Press.

Pronko, N.H. 1980. **Psychology from the Standpoint of an Interbehaviorist.** Monterey, California: Brooks/Cole Publishing Company.

Verplanck, W.S. 1954. Burrhus F. Skinner. In W.K. Estes, S. Koch, K. MacCorquodale, P. Meehl, C.G. Mueller, W.N. Schoenfeld, and W.S. Verplanck (Eds.) **Modern Learning Theory.** New York: Appleton-Century-Crofts.

# THE IMPERATIVE FOR REVOLUTIONARY ALTERNATIVES TO RECURRING PROBLEMS IN PSYCHOLOGY

Noel W. Smith

## Some Recurring Problems

A characteristic feature of the various fields of psychology is the occurrence and recurrence year after year, decade after decade of the same unresolved problems, those of fundamental assumptions about the basic character of psychological events. These intractable problems stand in the way of the advancement of knowledge and of the realization of a science of psychology. They can be traced throughout the discipline's modern period, the last 100 years, although they have their roots in a turbulent and insecure social milieu of 2000 years ago when investigation of nature was replaced with deference to theological constructs. A sample of these problems is posed by such traditional questions as these:

1. Is behavior caused by internal processes or external forces: Is the locus of motivation inside the organism or in the enviornment?

2. What are the biological bases of psychology? What is their causal role?

3. To what extent is behavior determined by heredity and to what extent by environment?

4. Is intelligence innately determined or is it acquired or how much does each source contribute?

5. How do neurological events give rise to subjective experience? How are neurons able to store memories and perform thoughts?

6. Does "will" or determinism reign supreme or is there some mixture?

7. Is the organism only a behaving body or is there a mind (or cognitive processing) in the body?

8. How are percepts related to the real world?

9. Since physical input and response output are often not isomorphic how does the mind work in transforming the input into the output form?

10. How does the mind or cognition mediate between words and the things that words represent? How are ideas transmitted from one mind to another?

11. Are private events knowable?

One could go on with this list, but suffice it to say that problems such as these have absorbed enormous amounts of effort both empirical and theoretical and remain as intractable as ever. They will continue to be intractable and the efforts toward solving them counter-productive--they divert efforts away from scientific enterprises--until the assumptions on which they rest are replaced. These assumptions provide for an existence of constructs that derive from verbal creations. The situation calls for nothing less than a revolution. That revolution will demand that any claims to knowledge be self-correcting. To allow for correction the postulates must be based on events. This is a prerequisite for a science. A postulate system that is explicit and meets these requirements is provided by interbehaviorism (Kantor, 1959; Kantor and Smith, 1975). It offers a revolutionary and viable alternative to tradition and its recurring problems. In brief, the postulates state that psychological events (1) are continuous with all other events of the universe and equally objective and naturalistic, (2) consist of occurrences that follow their own principles of organization and are therefore relatively independent of and irreducible to those of any other domain of events such as culture, biology, or chemistry although these fully participate, (3) require the bioecological evolution of species as a preceding condition for their level of organization, (4) must be dealt with as concrete occurrences from which constructs such as relationships and laws are derived and not have traditional constructs such as mind-body diremptions or a homunculean brain imposed on them, (5) consist of multiplex fields of interactions involving stimulating objects with evolved stimulus functions, responding organisms with corresponding response functions, setting factors, history of past interactions, and media of contact between the organism and the stimulating objects, (6) and have their causality not in internal or external factors but in the total interbehavioral field.

A postulate that specifies continuity of psychology with other events obviates mind-body, physical-nonphysical, behavior-cognition constructs. There is no ghost in a machine. There is not even a machine but rather a field of interactions of which the organism is but one part. A postulate that requires contact with events rules out self, ego, drives, instincts, engrams, and information processing. These have no basis in observation, yet the worker who starts with these assumed entities and powers interprets the results of observations in such terms. Much of psychology began with constructs derived from historical nonscientific sources and then interpreted its observations in terms of those same constructs. To that extent it has been less than scientific. Science begins with observation and develops its constructs from them. Even good inference must be anchored in observable events that provide means of validation. The interbehaviorist has a cardinal rule that all interpretations must be consistent with observation.

The characteristics of interbehaviorism are such that it is not so much a theory as a systematic program. As an indication of that program and its operation the following brief account of how it would generally deal with the eleven stated questions is suggestive.

### 1. Is Behavior Caused by internal Processes or External Forces : Is the locus of Motivation Inside the Organism or in the Environment?

Why is Mary looking out the window? Why is she not motivated to listen to the teacher? The traditional approach is that either (a) Mary is lacking in self-motivation or (b) the teacher is providing insufficient external or environmental motivation. What Mary needs is heightened "arousal" or an "energizer." But who has ever observed a motive, whether internal or external, or arousers and energizers? What we do observe is Mary with a particular past history of interactions, interacting in the presence classroom situation with objects outside the window. The interbehaviorist insists that it is these observed events rather than proposed invisible forces that we must work with. Stemming from the postulates, especially the last one listed above, psychological events can be best handled as a field of observable events involving (1) the orgnism with a history of past interactions or interbehaviors, (2) the object or situation with which the organism is presently interacting and which has meanings or functions constituted by past interactions, (3) an immediate setting, and (4) a medium of contact such as light or sound between the organism and the object which permits it to see or hear the object. In the case of Mary, the concrete question is not, "Why is she not motivated?," but rather "Why does she not behave in the manner that is preferred by the educator?" Or more importantly, "What conditions will improve the probability that she will behave in a manner the educator prefers?" We can then begin to examine her interactional history in connection with stimulus objects to learn what things she will attend to, these then serving as a basis of programmatic learning. Such setting factors as the classroom decor and the teacher's mode of expression may be also important. Even the medium of contact may be relevant; Mary may attend better to visual than to auditory presentations or better to the two together. In this approach internal and external forces are obviated. "Causality" used concretely can only mean that an event occurs and it is

23

interrelated with other occurring events, all of which comprise the entire interbehavioral field. No "arouser" or "energizer" is needed, for the organism is not passive but an active component of an active field. Interbehaviorism objects to the all-too-common procedure of starting with such constructs as energizers, motives, or other forces and interpreting observations in terms of those constructs. To use motivation as a description presents no problems. But when such a descriptive construct is used to explain the same behavior it describes, circularity occurs. We can describe or define Mary's looking out the window as non-motivated and her attending to the teacher as motivated. We cannot also use that definition as an explanation. If a highly motivated student is one who works hard we cannot also say that he works hard because he is motivated. For the explanation we must go to the observed relationships of the field. The only admissable constructs for science whether in the form of verbal statements, numerical formulae, or diagrams are those derived from these observed relationships. Even inferential constructs must have concrete referents and be subject to verification (see Kantor, 1942; Kinnie, 1978).

## 2. What are the Biological Bases of Psychology? What is Their Causal Role?

It is often contended that psychology springs from biology and that biology is therefore more basic. The argument continues that if we could examine biological structure and processes more minutely and completely they would be found to contain the basis of all that we call psyhological behavior. More particularly, the brain would be the seat of behavior for it controls behavior, contains awareness, interprets what the senses bring to it, produces intelligence, processes information and stores and retrieves it, etc. This particular contention fails to recognize that the psychological event is a field of factors. A field event is not reducible to any of its components, for the field consists of a different level of organization thn any of the components. Various levels of organization, each with their own principles of interaction, occur throughout nature. For instance, the two gases , hydrogen and oxygen, behave quite differently as gases than when they are combined into a molecule of water. At the level of biology are cells which behave in an organized fashion qualitatively different form the molecules that compose them although knowledge of the biochemistry of those molecules may help understand how cells are able to function as they do? Even though chemical reactions provide some of the means by which the cells carry out their functions cellular behavior is not reducible to them. And certainly cells do not behave in the fashion of their constituent atoms; what the physicist discovers about atomic particles with a high volatage accelerator is quite different from what the biologist discovers about cellular metabolism.

The psychologist is dealing with a still larger organization of events than cells or even multicellular organisms. This organization is one that involves organisms in interaction with stimulus objects in a context. Biological conditions provide the organismic structure with which the interactions develop but are causative only as limiting or facilitating conditions. They participate in the psychological field with numerous other factors such as those of a social nature. As for the latter, it may be important to study the cultural meaning of a particular gesture in order to understand the reactions to it of those in that culture. Similarly, it may be important to study the nervous, muscular, and skeletal systems in order to know how actions are coordinated. It may also be important to study the setting--classroom, tribal ceremony,factory assembly line--where the interaction occurs. These all participate in the total field and only in that respect are caustive. The field is not reducible to any one of them. Nor is any one of them a basis or a cause of the field. Thus the brain--to return to the contentions listed above--is no more the seat of behavior for the situation involving the gesture than is the gesture itself or the light medium by which it is seen. As for control, the brain has no more autonomous power than does the gesture or the light. Indeed, there is no controlling force but rather contributions of various factors as they interact in the field. Neither is there any awareness or intelligence except as these are descriptions of concrete interbehaviors. And there is no information processing and retrieval but rather complex interactions of field factors involving such adaptive acts as perceiving, thinking, and learning. The seat or basis of behavior, if one is needed, is the interactional field in which biology is only one of the contributing factors (see Delprato, 1979; Kantor, 1947; Observer, 1969a; Kantor and Smith, 1975; Kuo, 1967; McKearney, 1976).

## 3. To What Extent is Behavior Determined by Heredity and to what Extent by Environment?

Heredity and environment are not causative factors but merely labels or logical categories abstracted from a field of interdependent conditions. Heredity is not the transmission of a "unit character" but the interaction of germ cells with various molecular, chemical, and cellular conditions in a sequence of events that make for biological similarities with the parent organisms. These interactions are inseparable from the environments of which they are a part. Similarly, environment has no independent identity. On the biological level it consists of conditions with which cells interact. On the psychological level such biological factors as morphological structure and function, health, fatigue, and hunger are part of the environment as are such diverse factors as lighting conditions, immediate setting, culture, stimulating object or situation, and history of interactions with that object. Rather than setting heredity against the environment as reified forces it is necessary to examine the way in which particular

25

morphological structures with their potentialities for action (such as dextrous hands or bipedal posture) interact with specific objects and under what conditions. Both a passive organism shaped by its environment and a hidden genetic force producing behaviors are replaced by interactional development (see Bijou, 1963; Mountjoy, 1957; Pronko, 1957; Smith, 1976).

## 4. Is Intelligence Innately Determined or is it Acquired or how much does each Source Contribute?

Various forms of this question or the declaratory forms of it have linked intelligence with nationality, race, sex, and socio- economic status. Pronouncements abound that women are inferior to men in mathematics, but superior in language; Blacks are less intelligent than Whites; the level of intelligence decreases as the proportion of Indian blood increases; children's IQ's are closer to those of biological as opposed to adoptive parents. These may be true as descriptions are based on the assumption that intelligence exists and that it is a regulatory power located somewhere within the organism, albeit in an unknown form, and that from the very moment of conception in some degree it dictates the level of intelligence. Some psychologists have tried to control this power by asserting that a stimulating environment enriches intelligence and a deprived one detracts from it. Other proponents state that no force or forces can push a person over the innate upper limit. Both factions are dreamers because palpable, tangible, intelligence has never been seen, felt, heard, or in any way sensed. It has always been a hypothetical construct and one whose reality base is confined merely to human belief.

The interbehavioral approach is to search for all the variables from all sources which contribute to competency and incompetency rather than dealing with mythical constructs. On a realistic basis intelligence is not a thing, but can be an adjective. Performance that society honors is called superior, talented, skilled, or genius, and that which is disparaged is termed inferior, incompetent, dull, or stupid. When intelligence is used as an explanation of the behavior it describes, circularity is invoked. The construct becomes a mythical causal power for described characteristics. After the myth is cast out, there is no mandate to observe the same level of proficiency in all aspects of a single repertoire. A surgeon can be accepted as commendably superior in his surgery, grossly inefficient in interpreting hieroglyphics, skilled in skiing, incometent in art. He will not be incorrectly defined as intelligent in everything he does. Likewise, a successful mother can be perceived as unskilled in skiing, incompetent in surgery, and proficient as a decorator. The correct questions are not what are the sources of intelligence--nature or nurture--but rather they lay in the generators of efficiency and inefficiency: Varieties of experience, developmental contexts, reinforcement schedules, activity levels, feelings of efficiency and competency, etc. The scientist does

26

not ask whether women are inferior to men in intelligence. Rather, he asks what sex aligned variables promote competence in mathematics, problem solving, verbal skills, and others of interest (see Bowles and Pronko, 1969; Kantor, 1920; Observer, 1970).

## 5. How do Neurological events give rise to Subjective Experience? How are Neurons able to Store Memories and Perform Thoughts?

The interbehaviorist regards the brain as a biological not a psychological organ. Its major role is one of coordination of the actions of the whole organism. It must be seen as an integral part of the organism in which its actions are as much affected by other components of the organism as it affects them. It is not a master organ biologically. Neither is it a master organ psychologically; it is not a man inside a man. It is a necessary participant in psychological activity but not a locus or determiner of them. All empirical work points to its participant role; but the weight of tradition imposes the constructs of a determiner, interpreter, image and thought producer and manufacturer of ideas and consciousness. There is no evidence that neurons store memories or perform thoughts, nor is such an assumption needed. Nor is the construct "subjective experience" needed; the psychological event as an interbehavioral field obviates it as a separate ontological category.

## 6. Does Will or Determinism Reign Supreme or is there some Mixture?

An individual browses in a library, looks at several books of possible interest, and finally selects one to read. Is this individual exercising free will or is the decision a product of a series of antecedent causal events that determine the selection? The determinist would argue that the individual actually had no choice in the matter but selected the book on the basis of lawful cause and effect sequences. Each act was cause of the next and so on **ad infinitum** with any "choice" being also determined. The free will proponent would contend that humans can rise above physical cause and event relations and make free choices by exercising will power. Still others integrate various mixtures of freedom and determinism. Some make a distinction between determinism and causality; causality is a motivating force; in a choice situation an individual uses will power to reject all motives but one, thus rendering the decision as one that is caused but not strictly determined.

The argument advanced by the interbehaviorist is that the debate is a pointless one for it invokes metaphysical forces, namely, will and determinism (and sometimes motives), and imposes them on the events. What are will power or determinism but empty abstractions? Where are these constructs tied to actual events? Such verbal creations should not be confused with events. What the observer actually observes are fields of interrelating objects and events. In the example of

27

selecting a book, an event-approach would require examining the individual's interests, his or her momentary pressing problems that the book might have been considered to help solve, length of time available for reading as compared with the book's length, recommendations by a friend, or other relevant factors. After fully describing the essential factors including the deliberating and choosing, there is no need to add a special force of any kind. The interacting and interdependent factors that comprise a field of psychological events are themselves the causal conditions. This is a "descriptive" rather than a "prescriptive" approach. Each event occurrence can be correlated with particular sets of conditions—examining a book, considering its desirability or appropriateness in terms of interests, needs, reading time .Change in a field of events comprises a new arrangement of field factors-- deliberating on another book, rejecting the previous book. As new properties and conditions are present the organization must be a different one, a different correlation or co-presence. Finding the book that is most suitable, in which case it is chosen, is the final field of events for that series. Noting the time and walking to a check-out desk would be further ongoing fields or events. No invisible or impelling force is necessary (see Kantor, 1950; Pronko, 1972; Smith and Shaw, 1979).

## 7. Is the Organism only a Behaving Body or is there a Mind (or cognitive processing) in the body?

The organism as a mindless body or a mind in a body are both construct-based approaches. So is social learning theory which posits a triadic interaction of behavior, mind (person), and environment. Such perennial and intractable problems of how body and mind affect each other or how body operates without a mind are pointless exercises in verbal puzzles and must be discarded. The field approach as event-based obviates these puzzles: The psychological event is not localized in the organism, nor is it a mere organismic act. Thus it is not reducible to structure or function. The psychological event is not just action of the organism but **inter**-action of objects and organisms; it is not just behavior but **inter**-behavior. It is mutual and reciprocal activities, activities in a field. If mind or consciousness has any concrete meaning at all it is not an invisible entity or process but rather interbehaviors as relationship.

## 8. How are Percepts related to the Real World?

The traditional notion of percepts assumes that light waves are stimuli whose energy causes receptors in the eye to send neural messages to the brain where the messages become "sensations." Sensations are then compounded to form "percepts." These percepts as creations of the brain (mind) are our experiences of the outer world.

Thus the light reflected from a tree or the sound from a bell, the argument continues, are meaningless forms of energy until they are internally processed into an experience. It is further contended that this experience or percept may or may not be true to the tree or the bell, the true nature of the "real world" is forever unknowable. In a sense, we live in a double world, one inside of us and one outside.

If we reject an abstract power such as a percept and turn to the events that can be observed we discover that we are concerned with an act--the act of perceiving. This act involves (a) an organism which has the organs for sensing, (b) the object which has properties that can be sensed, and (c) a medium that facilitates the contact. Eyes, a tree, and a medium of sound waves are required to hear the bell. The medium requires no mysterious transformation into a percept which represents the object and bears an unknown degree of correspondence with it. The medium, instead, is the vehicle of the interbehavior of organism and object. The joint activity of the eyes and tree or ears and bell through their respective media of contact is the sensing act itself (or perceiving act, there being no objective distinction). Perceiving is not contained in the organism or in the object but in their relationship. It is an organism-object interaction. A history of action comprises the meanings that things have for us: Friends and enemies, familiar places, objects that have particular uses or meanings to us, social sanctions and prohibitions, etc. These meanings are not mysterious internal processes that reflect the external world but are inteactions that develop as part of and are comprised by interbehavioral fields. Internal-external dichotomies are artificial; the question of real versus an unreal or illusory world has no concrete referent (see Kantor, 1924; Kantor and Smith, 1975; Lichtenstein, 1959, 1971; Observer, 1969a, 1969c, 1974; Pronko, 1961; Pronko, Ebert and Greenberg, 1966).

## 9. Since Physical Input and Response Output are Often not Isomorphic, how does the Mind Work in Transforming the Input Into the Output Form?

With a field approach the fact of imperfect correlation between the measured characteristic of a stimulus condition and that of a response presents no problem and requires no invisible mental processing to bring about a transformation. If red looks redder against green than against grey, if racial prejudice influences a person to perceive according to his prejudices, if a violent explosion is merely reflected upon, if a slight smile stimulates great joy, these are the conditions of the different fields. Thus perceiving, feeling, believing, and other interbehaviors often do not and need not correspond closely to the magnitude or character of the stimulus object. (That they do not, indicates also that a psychological response is interbehavior and not just biological functioning of structures.) It is only by postulating a mechanistic assumption of inputs and outputs which call for equal exchanges of energy that an unseen power must be postulated to account for the presumed discrepancy. This model and all intervening variables must be discarded and replaced with the actual interrelationships that comprise the event. The individual's past interactions and the ambient conditions as well as the nature of the stimulus object are all factors in any psychological event. The stimulus object itself is not energy but something which has meaning as derived from previous interbehaviors. That meaning may change from interaction to interaction and from setting to setting. For the lion tamer, for example, chairs come to mean something to ward off lions as well as something to sit on. The tamer will perceive the chair and act upon it as either of these functions depending on whether he is in a setting of facing a lion or one where sitting down is appropriate. A book on a desk means clutter when we are searching for something but a source of information when its contents are needed. Inputs and outputs are relevant to the kickback from firing a gun, the rebound of a ball on a pool table, or to principles of conservation but totally inapplicable to psychological events. We do not find and should not expect to find one-to-one correspondence of intensity, size, form, or other dimension. Psychology consists of a level of organization that requires attention to its own events rather than analogies transferred from other sciences.

## 10. How does the Mind or Cognition Mediate Between Words and the things Words are supposed to Represent?

Words, phonemes, grammatical forms, sentences, and other abstracted components of speech acts are derived from acts by a process of analysis. They are not psychological data. The implicit postulate that speech consists of sounds which form strings of words must be replaced with the explicit postulate that speaking is a field of events involving speakers, listeners, and things referred to. It then becomes clear that living language involves a speaker interacting simultaneously both with a listener and the object that is being referred to while the listener is simultaneously interacting both with the speaker and the object of reference. Thus language is bistimulational interaction for both speaker and listener. In short, language is speaking about something to someone. As for ideas, they are constructs derived from thinking, anticipating, and knowing acts. Speech is the overt reference to those things thought about, anticipated, or known and the means by which the listener refers to the same things. There is transmission only in
the sense of simultaneous reference to the same thing by speech, gesture, or other language interbehavior (see Kantor, 1929, 1977; Kantor and Smith, 1975; MacRoberts and MacRoberts, 1979-80, 1980; Observer, 1971a, 1971b; Pronko, 1946; Ratliff, 1962; Rosenberg and Cogen, 1966).

## 11. Are Private Events Knowable?

This question involves two major circumstances: Individuality of a psychological event and the accessibility of the various components of the interactional field that comprise that event. In a sense all psychological events are private; that is, they are individualistic and unique. But such covert events as joy or a toothache or seeing a color are no different in principle from more overt activities such as speaking or walking, both overt and covert events being equally individualistic and equally concrete. The only difference is in the degree of accessibility to other observers. The astronaut on the moon who is reporting crater formations is having a private experience in that others are not in a position to engage in the same interbehaviors. Although in any interaction any component of the field may vary in accessibility to others, one or another component of the field is usually accessible. In many cases the stimulus is easier to observe than the response.

For example, any number of persons may interact with a television commercial as a stimulus object but their responses may be less accessible and quite individualistic; for one person the commercial is informative and for another irritating, and we might not know this response without asking the person, but a knowledge of that person's past history might lead us to infer the response. In other cases the response is accessible or readily observed by others while the stimulus conditions may be unknown. For example, we may know that a person has committed a crime but be uncertain about the "motive." Similarly, if we observe someone suddenly smile for no observable reason (which in fact was due to the recollection of an amusing incident) the stimulation is not known to us even though the response is. In still another situation, such as a toothache, both the stimulus object and the response are primarily accessible only to the person engaged in the interaction. This is to say that it is a unique event as all other events are unique. The same stone does not fall in exactly the same way twice; one does not say the word "tree" in precisely the same way twice. The toothache is not only one of a universe of unique events but is not entirely inaccessible. Some phase of the field of events which comprise it remains accessible, even if only by inference, just as some aspects of a distant star are inferred by an astronomer. The inflammation of the tooth may be observable by the dentist who would expect it to be painful. The verbal reference may also be indicative of the interaction, and the dentist makes use of it in his identification of the problem; similarly, we often rely on a technician's report of a dial reading that is no longer available to others. When the object of stimulation or the response to it or the entire interaction are largely covert, accessible to only one person, we often rely on self-reports. We do this regularly in psychological studies and often successfully; subjects' reports to questionnaires predict the outcome of elections and their reports of phi phenomena give us reliable information for rate of presentations of still pictures that are perceived as motion pictures. Psychology is in the fortunate position of dealing with human subjects who can give these self-reports; this contrasts markedly with the inert rocks of geology or the mute potshards of prehistory. In respect psychology has an advantage in its efforts to acquire knowledge, not a disadvantage in relying on self-reports as some have maintained. This is not to overlook the fact that not all self-reports are valid or even informative. The person with anxiety reactions may not know the source of the reactions. Consequently, self-reports may be treated as (1) the equivalent of the investigator's own observation of the stimulus object or the response or both concerning the topic on which the subject is reporting or (2) as data to be interpreted--for example, as errors, lies, distortions, judgments, etc. Observation of other components of the field might suggest whether the first or second category is likely to obtain for any given situation or subject; do we have a reliable or unreliable witness, a trained or untrained observer? Do we have a situation given to accurate or inaccurate observation?

The contrast between private and non-private events may be useful for indicating what components of the interaction are more or less accessible to more than one person at any given time but as a distinction between internal-external, knowable-unknowable, mental-physical it is artificial and should be discarded. In sum, private and non-private or covert and overt responses are continuous with each other and are both made of the same stuff--fields of interacting factors. As with all sciences there are various conditions under which knowledge may be obtained and various means and degrees of difficulty of obtaining it. All components of psychological events, wherever they may lie on the overt-covert continuum, are, on the whole, as amenable to being known as those of any other science [1] (see Kantor, 1922, 1963; Lichtenstein, 1971; Observer, 1973, 1981; Pronko, 1976; Ratliff, 1962; Stevenson, 1953, 1961; Schoenfeld and Cumming, 1963; Taylor, 1962; Woodbridge, 1913; Zuriff, 1979).

Perhaps the interbehavioral approach to these recurring problems will illustrate that it is a system that provides a perspective on a number of topics and that this perspective is nothing less than a revolutionary approach. It calls for reformulating basic postualtes so that old questions with their recycled presuppositions and unanswerable puzzles and paradoxes fall away. It calls for moving beyond the stalemated problem of body-with-a-mind or body-with-out-a-mind that has entrenched our thinking for so many years. It calls for discarding questions about brain and consciousness, electronic or mechanical models, biological bases, and internal and external determiners. By starting with new and explicitly formulated postualtes based on the observation of nature, it provides a genuine alternative. The postulates, in sum, propose a universe of interacting objects from which may be abstracted the interactions of organisms and objects. The focus, then, is on a field of interrelationships which constitute thinking, imagining, choosing, deciding, learning, and all other interbehaviors. Field approaches are those toward which some sciences have moved as they developed from "substance-property" to "statistical-correlation" to "integrated-field" stage (Kantor, 1969). Psychology's mainstream of assumptions based on culture doctrines has kept it firmly in the first two. It can complete its evolution toward full scientific stature involving fruitful research, acquisition of knowledge, and service to society only by replacing those assumptions.

## Two Divergent Trends: A Critique

### The Mentalistic Trend

A recent posthumous and uncompleted book by MacLeod (1975), **The Persistent Problems of Psychology,** also examines recurring problems. The similarity between that work and this one ends there, however, for MacLeod apparently accepts as legitimate questions those which the writers of the present volume would consider to be illegitimate; they are based on implicit and probably unrecognized assumptions that stand on a vacuous foundation.

> The Psychologist asks: What are the concrete, observable ways in which mental and physical processes are related to one another? What is the precise chain of causation that leads from a physical event (like a stimulus) to a mental response (like a thought or an act), or from a mental event (like a choice) to a consequent change in the physical situation? Questions such as these require detailed studies of the properties of physical stimuli, the behavior of receptors and effectors, the nature of the coordinating mechanisms of the brain and the relation of all these to the observed facts of experience and behavior...(p. 33).

The mental-physical distinction originated in metaphysical constructs from a doctrinaire past; non-physical agents and processes were developed by the Church Fathers in the Greco-Roman period and became an intrinsic part of Western thought down to the present day. While MacLeod invokes concreteness and observability he links these to metaphysical constructs. Elsewhere MacLeod (1969) argues for a private world of the inner consciousness and the unknowability of it; it is pointless, he maintains, for the psychologist to attempt to gain information about it.

This view is in line with the current swing of psychology from a dominance of behaviorism to cognitive and phenomenological (American as distinct from European versions) approaches. For example Boneau (1974) contends that information from the environment is internalized and "structured into an internal model of the environment" (p. 299). McKeachie (1976) notes the turn toward an "information-process in memory, problem-solving, and decision making" which "brings these areas into a single framework" (p. 827). He observes the adoption of cognitive approaches to motivation and emotion as well and holds that the change has made psychology "human rather than mechanical, ratlike, or even computerlike" (p. 831). Since "cognitions influence, and are influenced by, behavior" (p. 831) he seems to be saying that they must be something other than behavior but does not specify what. He also fails to recognize that these cognitive approaches that often rely on information processing schemes are more mechanistic than the systems they criticize and propose to replace. Under a subtitle of "Progress During the Last Quarter Century" Atkinson (1977) similarly stresses the importance of what he calls "the information-processing viewpoint" (p. 205). He accepts without question the assumption of the validity of the construct of memory as an existing thing (neglecting that we never observe memory or a storage bank but only organisms reperforming or reenacting a previous action) and the constructs that serve it: "How information is stored, how it is retrieved from that memory store" (p. 205). Also as a part of "progress" is his uncritical acceptance, along with other brain doctrines, of "Sperry's dramatic demonstration that the two hemispheres of the human brain carry out quite different psychological functions" (p. 205). He likewise accepts as real "the psychology of consciousness" (p. 288) though disapproving of other unobserved constructs such as "psychic forces" and those involved in such practices as "astrology, voodoo, [and] witchcraft" (p. 208).

In an attempt to deal with the mind-body problem Sperry (1977) rejects psychophysical identicalism, parallelism, epiphenomenalism, and reductionism and replaces them with "consciousness as an emergent property of brain activity" (p. 289). He asserts that "mind can rule matter in the brain and exert causal influence in the guidance and control of behavior" (p. 239). In a reply to Sperry, Wile (1977) notes the logical contradictions "in contending that the events from one realm of discourse (the mental and subjective realm) can stand in direct causal relationship with events from a very separate realm (the physical or behavioral-neurological realm)" (p. 988). Despite his recognition of the contradictions Wile asserts that interaction of mind and body is nevertheless a necessity because of the "obvious fact that subjective decisions do have behavioral outcomes" (p. 988). Neither Sperry nor Wile is able to recognize that one need not make the assumption on which this dilemma is based: Wile is unaware that his "fact" rests on a dichotomy that nature does not provide, that this dichotomy exists only in the form of words. He declares that "the mind-body problem has always been, and continues to be, the central unrecognized issue in psychology" (p. 988). If he extended his reading of history back to the Classical Greeks or earlier he would discover that such a presumed dichotomy has not "always" existed (Smith, 1974, 1981) .

34

But he is correct in his appraisal if "always" is limited to the past 2000 years of Western history. Also he correctly identifies psychophysical dualism as lying at the heart of the interactable problems in psychology.

Psychology has gone from mind-and-body to body-without-mind and back again to mind-and-body. It would seem that psychology has been chasing its tail over the past half century. Today's psychophysical dualism is directly expressed in current references to behavior and consciousness, behavior and experience, and behavior and cognition or when such constructs as motivation or personality or emotion are said to cause behavior or when behavior causes one of these.

This dualism also appears in such forms as the eleven problems treated briefly in the preceding section. Brain forces, causation by inner and outer powers (motivation), cognitive processing, unconscious process, and other ascriptions--as opposed to what is actually observed--all represent attempts to convert non-physical entities into scientific constructs. The verbal contradiction represented by psychophysical dualism, positing utterly disparate realms of non-physical and physical nature cannot, however, be resolved: One cannot conjoin matter and non-matter, the spatial and the non-spatial. The conversion to other intangibles such as motives, unconscious forces, brain animism , and the like, does not overcome the problem. It merely puts the unobservables into scientific guise with the result that investigators observe organisms interbehaving with their surroundings and infer these intangibles. Inferences of this kind are metaphysical constructs rather than scientific constructs.

But there is no need to resolve psychophysical dualism. It is an assumption out of our theological past that need no longer be made. It is as irrelevant and fatuous as the number of angels that can dance on the head of a pin. It must be replaced with a postulate system that is tied to concrete referents such as that of interbehaviorism which postulates confrontable events of nature in general and psychology in particular and insists that investigation and interpretation of events must be consistent with the postulation.

Some observers have been optimistic about psychology's recent progress (McKeachie, 1976; McKinney, 1976) but others view the continuation of dualism as a stifler or progress and are less optimistic. They note unscientific constructs such as (a) those involving adoption of common usage terms such as sensation, will, emotion, and ego which cause confusion because they are borrowed from historical notions of "bipartite and tripartite systems of mental states" (Observer, 1977, p. 353); (b) those that are based on fashion (Observer, 1976) such as information-processing, consciousness raising, and right-left mind/brain contentions; and (c) those that occur in the age-old practice of ascribing characteristics to events that are not those observed

35

such as motives, percepts, etc.

A further example of the last is that of offering unobserved neurological accounts in experiments rather than the response observed. The work of Pavlov involved observing responses to sequentially paired stimuli but was interpreted in terms of unobserved neruological activities. Similarly, Pribram (1970) has contended "that psychology must concern itself with the problems of mind" (p. 46) and this is to be accomplished by brain-environment relationships "tease[d] out" by behavior.² In other instances the investigator speaks of such non-observed events as how long it takes the brain to make a discrimination when what he actually observes is how long it takes the individual. Attribution to an organ,which is a participating factor among other factors, the full power of determination of the event is to confuse necessary with sufficient conditions and to overlook the contributions of the other factors and their respective roles. Biological organs--whether neural, glandular, muscular, etc.--have never been observed to be other than participants in interbehaviors and never independent of numerous other factors with which they interact. Any of these factors may have limiting or facilitating roles but no single one has been observed to independently control or determine the others. The relationships always involve complex interactions. Interbehaviorism allots biological factors their full biological role just as it allots other factors their appropriate roles. Consequently, it repudiates the "empty organism" conception just as it does the conversion of biological organs into psychological powers. Descriptions must fit observations.

The problem of circularity also enters, for in most cases of attempted mind-brain explanations mind-brain is inferred from the same behavior which it is used to explain. For example, mind-brain powers are inferred from thinking behavior and then used to explain the thinking. Likewise, information processing, usually also a brain power, is inferred from behavior and used to explain that behavior. Ebel (1974) notes that in psychology when hypothetical constructs are used rather than descriptive constructs the result is inevitably circularity. In those sciences where such hypothetical constructs as atoms or genes have been salutory the "expected functional relations between then and observable variables are specified exactly so they can be tested experimentally" (Ebel, 1974, p. 487). In psychology hypothetical constructs have been drawn from metaphysical sources, computer analogies.,³ brain powers, and other non-events. The interbehaviorist rejects these and insists on confining scientific work to descriptions of observed relationships. In such a field description no hypothetical brain determiners or processors of information appear, for they are not part of the observation described. Two rules are important here (Observer, 1969b): (1) "...the rule of specificity; no thing or event is something else, so each must be described as a field of its own specific factors"; (2) "...the rule of natural limits;

no confrontable event can be described in transcending the limits of observation..." (p. 146).

All constructs must have an observable referent at least in principle. Such constructs as processing centers, motives, consciousness, and sensations in the brain have no existential status and are not even potentially observable. Constructs must be continuous with events. This holds for inferential constructs as well as those of description, calculation, or other forms.

No doubt the shortcomings of the mechanistic approach of some of the S--> R positions (stimulus input and response output) led to the reversion to cognition as the new mentalism. As the mechanistic approach was seen wanting--that is, the organism is not passively shaped by environmental forces--the critics and sometimes former S-->R supporters rushed in with consciousness, will power (or "freedom"), genetic determiners, and other intangibles conjured up from the metaphysical past. Consequently, the ghostly middle term was reintroduced or given renewed emphasis. Woodworth's old S-O-R and its many variations seemed to be the necessary corrective. Thus the new mechanism of S-->CP-->R (stimulus input, cognitive processing, and response output) came on the scene.

The perpetuation of intervening variables or hypothetical constructs (the two are distinguishable only by laborious verbal abstraction; see Marx, 1963) such as cognitive processing is due to the failure to recognize that they violate a basic criterion of science: Corrigibility. Inasmuch as they are not observable they are never corrected. Thus we may account for their occurrence and longevity, not by their scientific validity but by (1) their origins in historical metaphysical propositions, (2) their inseparability from mentalistic systems and their roles as props for simplistic ones, and (3) their incorrigibility.[4] Interbehaviorism in contrast, (1) steps outside historical tradition, (2) proposes a field of events, and (3) is subject to correction because of its observational base and explicit postulate system.

Atkinson (1977), who supports the intervening variable of information- processing, advocates the need for a science of psychology that will contribute to solving national problems. This is a psychology, he avers, that must be dedicated to "understanding thenature of the human mind" (p. 210). Mischel (1976) argues that mentalism is necessary because of powers that biology has given the organism even if these powers are not yet explained. These, he believes, do not invoke homunculi or other occult powers and do not reduce psychology's scientific character. However, they are a necessary corrective to biological reductionism and to account for intentionality ("agency, self-direction, choice, purpose, and meaning," pp. 195-196) and the lack of input-output isomorphism in perception. What Mischel overlooks is the field of interrelationships that render notions of isomorphism irrelevant and analogical models, whether applied to mind-in-a-body or body-without-a-mind, as unnecessary and even misleading.

But to return to mentalism is not entirely satisfactory even to one such as Neisser (1967) who, among others, led the way back to it. Neisser (1976) turns largely from internal states or information-processing modes to seeking mind in the stimulus array; environment rather than mind becomes central, but mental schemata receive the environmental information. The struggle to break away from mentalism and mechanism is ongoing but the failure to recognize the basic postulate on which these are based, to distinguish constructs from events, obscures the alternatives. Psychology is still being pursued by many as a **Geisteswissenschaft** even while it is aspired to as a **Naturwissenschaft** . The alternative to mechanism or to mentalism goes unrecognized. Thus there is no informed choice.

The focus on the organism rather than organism-environment relationship of both mechanism and mentalism is a continuation of the 2000 year tradition of the internal spirit-psyche-mind. The cognitivist peers into the organism for psychological events or their causes, cannot see them there, and invents analyzers, retrievers, feedback loops, and attenuators as analogical substitutes for what he does not observe. The response outputs. He also calls the inputs "independent variables" or "antecedent conditions" under the assumption that an object can be stimulating independently of and prior to any response on the part of the organism. The response then is a "consequent" for it is assumed to follow after the stimulating event. It is also a "dependent variable" for it is a product of the stimulus. The mechanist, like the cognitivist, confuses what he observes with what he assumes.

The psychologist must widen his vision if he is ever to break the impasse between mentalism and mechanism. The interbehaviorist looks beyond both of those forms of organ-ocentrism to the full field of interactions. He notes the continual interbeahvior between the organism and its stimulating objects and conditions, that each interbehavior is different from the previous one, and that this interbehavioral history continually builds and adapts as both the organism and conditions change. With this response equipment, overt and covert, new contingencies are met, new interactions developed. There is here no passive receiving of information, no input-output. Neither is there room or need for some unobservable processing mechanism centered in the organism. And yet interbehaviorism gives full treatment to such activities as thinking, believing, judging, recollecting, perceiving, knowing, dreaming, imaging (see Kantor, 1924, 1926, 1971)--those that may be called cognitive interbehaviors. Rather than treating them in one or another framework or psychophysical dualism--brain powers, conscious states, machine

38

processes, etc.--they are observed, analyzed, and described as concrete interbehaviors. Interbehaviorism provides a clear alternative to both mechanism and mentalism. The choice only needs recognition.

## The Contextual Trend

A trend that interbehaviorists would hold to be more salutoy recognizes that the entire focus cannot be on the organisms or even on the organism plus the object of stimulation. This trend seems to be gaining the appellation of "contextualism." Interbehaviorism has long insisted on the importance of setting factors (Kantor, 1924, 1926) but recently social learning theorists have been giving increased attention to it as a factor in accounting for changes in responses when successive stimuli are the same. Several writers in the 60's (Barker, 1963, 1969; Bevan, 1968; Kuo, 1967; Sells, 1963; Sommer, 1968) have stressed the conceptual and programmatic importance of it. During the 70's Jenkins (1974), Cronbach (1975), Rennert (1975) and Bronfenbrenner (1977) called for the recognition of context . Bijou (1976) has used it extensively as has Sarbin (Sarbin, 1976 ; Sarbin and Coe, 1972; Sarbin and Mancuso, 1980). Even a mental-processing framework (Mischel, 1977) has emphasized it. A symposium called "Contextual Interactionists" (Smith, 1973) dealt with the figures who have most prominently contributed to this viewpoint from antiquity to the present yet were never before brought together or given a title. They included Aristotle, George Herbert Mead, John Dewey, Arthur Bentley, J.R. Kantor, and B.F. Skinner.[5] Lichtenstein (1980) has also described a trend in psychology toward contextual and ecological approaches that have some of the essential characteristics of interbehaviorism; these, he suggests, could be well served by its explicit postulate system.

The radical behaviorism of Skinner has long offered important points of correspondence with interbehaviorism. Skinner (1975) states: "We can analyze a given instance of behavior in its relation to the current setting and to antecedent events in the history of the species and of the individual" (p. 42). As the operant movement has broadened its scope into complex human activities a number of its supporters have felt the need for a broader framework for their work. The framework that has been most appealing has been the interbehaviorism of J.R. Kantor. Yet, how to put these two approaches together has not been altogether clear (Lichtenstein, 1973), although Morris (1978, 1979) has made a careful analysis and has attempted strides in that direction. In 1969 Kantor addressed the APA Division of Experimental Analysis of Behavior on an analysis of the operant analysis of behavior (Kantor, 1970) and in 1974 was Honorary Chairman at the first Mexican Congress on Behavior Analysis. This was held at Xalpa, Veracruz, Mexico. His address was "How is Interbehavioral Psychology Related to the Experimental Analysis of Behavior?" Bijou (e.g., B ijou and Baer, 1961, 1965; Bijou, 1976) has been a proponent of an integration, especially in the area of child development, and Lundin (1969) in personality studies. Natalicio and Kidd (1971) suggested means of integration and Ray and Brown (1975), Ray and Ray (1976), and Ray and Upson (1977) gave further explication by way of a systems approach, this having also been suggested by Fuller (1973). In 1975 the **Mexican Journal of Behavior Analysis** began publishing papers by Kantor and others on interbehaviorism and on interbehavioral analyses of various topics. In one of these Mountjoy (1976) explored the operant behavior issue. Further interest from the operant quarter is indicated by the category of "interbehaviorism" listed as a topic for papers by the Association for Behavior Analysis.

Kvale and Grenness' (1967) paper indicates that current European phenomenology finds a close kinship with radical behaviorism; there may be an even closer one with interbehaviorism (Kvale, 1977). "Being-in-the-world" can be handled as interbehavior, but in a critique Bucklew (1955) argues that " a phenomenological revision of science will introduce a neo-mentalism into psychology and a neo-vitalism into biology" (p. 299). American phenomenological psychology as represented by MacLeod, Maslow, Allport, Rogers, and others has its roots in the phenomenological tradition of Gestalt psychology and the philosophy of Kant. It is clearly mentalistic. The current European versions as interpreted by Kvale seem to be on a more objective track. The resemblance to interbehaviorism may be superficial or actual. The trends will bear watching.

Direct empirical attacks on setting factors have also begun to appear. (They have long been the sole concern of Barker's (1963, 1969) research.) Bloom (1974) notes their important but neglected role in S-R relationships and experimentally examines them as does Redd (1974). Gewirtz (1972) replaces drive with studies of settings as he recognized that settings can account for variation in response to a given stimulus while an abstract force cannot. Ray (1973) observes that "compared to conditioning, what we know about setting factors is almost nothing" (p. 3). He continues, "setting conditions, situation factors, species differences, and specificity of response measures will almost likely be found to have profound influence on conditioning than current research would lead one to suspect" (p. 7). In a series of papers Ray and others (Ray, 1976; Ray and Brener, 1973; Ray and Brown, 1975; Ray and Ray, 1976; Ray and Upson, 1977) have reported several experimental and field studies of animal and human behavior that show the close relationships between subtle and often ignored setting factors and behavioral measures. Similarly, McKearney (e.g., 1976, 1977) has given considerable emphasis to multiple factors in his research into drug effects on behavior. For example:

> Knowing the physiological concomitants of a behavior
> could be very useful information and yet not be an
> explanation. Since behavior is a complex product of

many interacting factors, it is erroneous to attribute primary causal status to any one of these acting in isolation... (1977, p. 111-112).

At the Fourth Annual Summer Community of Scholars held June 16-20, 1969 at Miner Institute in Chazy, New York the topic was "The Emerging Role of Interbehavioral Psychology." But the trends seen in 1969 are even more apparent now. After 100 years of postulating intangibles and vainfully searching for them psychology seems ready to consider new directions that have been available but largely ignored for over half a century. A brief analysis of eleven problems and an interbehavioral alternative to the dilemmas they pose has been presented in this chapter. The authors of the chapters that follow set forth some additional problems that have beset psychology and offer some new directions for the future. They also provide a further explication of the interbehavioral system.

### Acknowledgment

The author is grateful to the following persons for their helpful suggestions on this introductory chapter: Donna Cone, Philip DeVita, Parker Lichtenstein, Marion McPherson, Paul Mountjoy, N.H. Pronko, and Nancy Shaw.

### Footnotes

1. Overtness and covertness do constitute a continuum rather than a dichotomy. A person who is sitting quietly thinking about an argument is behaving covertly. But as he continues to develop the arguments he begins to murmur audibly and to gesture slightly. As he becomes more involved in the argument with the absent opponent he eventually speaks aloud, paces the floor, and gestures fully. There is no definitive point that separates covert from overt and the continuity rules out any mental-physical distinction. At all times in this example the event is one of an integral organism interacting with a substitute stimulus, the interaction varying in degree of observability to others.

2. Although Pribram insists that we must study mind, the real subject of psychology, he gives two different meanings for it. At times he implies, but not very clearly, that it is brain-environment relationships of which behavior is its effect. At others he equates it with awareness which "accompanies... states of the neural apparatus" or, in the same vein of psychophysical parallelism, defines it as "contents and processes which become subjectively experienced" (p. 46). In the first case it is biology and in the second a non-physical abstraction. The researcher can infer ("gain access" to) mind, he claims,

by observing verbal and instrumental behaviors. He further claims that intention, volition, affect, and other "mental" acts cannot be studied by behavior but only by measuring such brain events as electrical responses to stimulation. He often posits such unobservables as "unconscious determinants," coding, and "subjective experience," these being supposedly known by their effects. There is here much confusing of constructs with events and the imposing of them on the events. Further, biological participating factors are confused with determiners. Behavior he views mechanistically: It is produced by brain in conjunction with environment and hence follows from the first meaning of mind. Mind produces behavior. Presumably, if activity is covert it is mental and thus either brain-environment relationship or some abstraction parallel to brain. If overt, it is behavior and produced by brain-environment. This conception again is in marked contrast to observation. There is no evidence that nature cleaves the organism into disparate functions along the lines of covertness and overtness, the former being mind functions and the latter body functions produced by mind. Pribram's statements point to the fact that direct brain studies, when guided by traditional assumptions, result in the same practice of imposing neurological and metaphysical powers that are not observed at it does when using those assumptions in conjunction with conditional responses or other behavioral studies whether overt or covert. Johnson (1932) gives an example of the behavioral type. In a task of card sorting in which the response rate increases with performance he notes that it would be fashionable to explain this as reduced resistance in conduction paths of certain synapses. "By 1933, we may think it queer that we ever burdened such meager facts of observation with so much unnecessary assumption" (p. 301).

3. If a computer model or information processing model is said to be merely an analog of behavior then it is proposed as something which behavior is not.

4. A device for attempting to give them legitimacy has been to define them operationally. The result of this has been both to give apparent reality to transcendentals and to rob events of their objectivity (e.g., Bridgman, 1936; Kendler and Spence, 1971; Stevens, 1936). To use operationism to amalgamate scientific operations with properties of things, to assimilate the known into the knower, to doubt the existence of the world, to transform nature into sensations, and to convert abstractions into events and vice-versa is to build verbal mountains. Operational procedures, however, as contituting the actions taken by the investigator with respect to the objects and their properties under investigation are an intrinsic part of science.

5. Another new trend that has developed is interactionism. It seems to be confined for the most part to personality studies (see Endler and Magnusson, 1976). In its efforts to move away from emphasis on either the environment of the "situationist" or the person of the

psychoanalyst the new interactionists accept many of the fictitious constructs of tradition and assume that those are what the data show to be interacting. One of the new interactionists (Ekehammer, 1974) has even confused interbehaviorism with presumed mental or phenomemal interaction. He attributes to Kantor the importance of distinguishing "between the physical and the psychological world." The necessary correction to this is perforce at arm's reach (Kantor, 1975; Kuo, 1967; Smith, 1973).

## References

Atkinson, R.C. 1977. Reflection on psychology's past and concerns about its future. **American Psychologist**, 32, 205-210.

Barker, R.G. 1963. On the nature of the environment. **Journal of Social Issues**, 19, 17-38.

Barker, R.G. 1969. Wanted: An eco-behavioral science. In E.P. Willems and H.L. Raush (Eds.) **Naturalistic Viewpoints in Psychological Research.** New York: Holt, Rinehart and Winston.

Bevan, W. 1968. The contextual basis of behavior. **American Psychologist**, 23, 701-714.

Bijou, S.W. 1963. Theory and research in mental (developmental) retardation. **Psychological Record**, 13, 95-110.

Bijou, S.W. 1976. **Child Development: The Basic Stage of Early Childhood.** Englewood Cliffs, New Jersey: Prentice-Hall.

Bijou, S.W. and Baer, D.M. 1961. **Child Development** (Vol. 1). **A Systematic Theory.** New York: Appleton-Century Crofts.

Bijou, S.W. asnd Baer,D.M. **Child Development** (Vol. 2). **Universal Stages of Infancy.** New York: Appleton-Century-Crofts.

Bloom, K. 1974. Eye contact as a setting event for infant learning. **Journal of Experimental Child Psychology**, 17, 250-263.

Boneau, C.A. 1974. Paradim regained? Cognitive behavior restated. **American Psychologist**, 29, 297-309.

Bowles, J.W. and Pronko, N.H. 1960. A new scheme for the inheritance of intelligence. **Psychological Record**, 10, 55-57.

Bridgman, P.W. 1936. **The Nature of Physical Theory.** New Jersey: Princeton University Press.

Bronfenbrenner, U. 1977. Toward an experimental ecology of human development. **American Psychologist, 32,** 513-531.

Bucklew, J. 1955. The subjective tradition in phenomenological psychology. **Philosophy of Science,** 22, 289-299.

Cronbach, L.J. 1979. Beyond the two disciplines of scientific psychology. **American Psychologist,** 30, 116-127.

Delprato, D.J. 1979. The interbehavioral alternative to brain-dogma. **Psychological Record,** 29, 409-418.

Ebel, R.L. 1974. And still the dryads linger. **American Psychologist,** 29, 485-492.

Ekehammer, B. 1974. Interactionism in personality from a historical perspective. **Psychological Bulletin,** 81, 1026-1028.

Endler, N.S. and Magnusson, D. 1976. Toward an interactional psychology of personality. **Psychological Bulletin,** 83, 956-974.

Fuller, P.R. 1973. Professors Kantor and Skinner--the "Grand alliance" of the 40's." In N.W. Smith, Contextual interactionists: A symposium. **Psychological Record,** 23, 318-324.

Gewirtz, J.L. 1972. Some contextual determinants of stimulus potency. In R. D. Parke (Ed.) **Recent Trends in Social Learning Theory.** New York: Academic Press.

Jenkins, J.J. 1974. Remember that old theory of memory? Well, forget it. **American Psychologist,** 29, 785-789.

Johnson, H.M. 1932. Some follies of "emancipated" psychology. **Psychological Review,** 39, 293-323.

Kantor, J.R. 1920. Intelligence and mental tests. **Journal of Philosophy,** 7, 260-268.

Kantor, J.R. 1922. Can the psychophysical experiment reconcile introspectionists and objectivists? **American Journal of Psychology,** 32, 481-510.

Kantor, J.R. 1924. **Principles of Psychology.** (Vol. 1). New York: Knopf.

Kantor, J.R. 1926. **Principles of Psychology.** (Vol. 2). New York: Knopf.

Kantor, J.R. 1929. Language as behavior and as symbolism. **Journal of Philosophy**, 26, 150-159.

Kantor, J.R. 1942. Toward a scientific analysis of motivation. **Psychological Record**, 5, 225-275.

Kantor, J.R. 1947. **Problems of Physiological Psychology.** Bloomington, Indiana: Principia Press.

Kantor, J.R. 1950. **Psychology of Logic.** (Vol. 2). Chicago: Principia Press.

Kantor, J.R. 1959. **Interbehavioral Psychology: A Sample of Scientific System Construction.** Bloomington, Indiana: Principia Press.

Kantor, J.R. 1963. **Scientific Evolution of Psychology. (Vol. 1).** Chicago: Principia Press.

Kantor, J.R. 1969 **Scientific Evolution of Psychology.** (Vol 2.). Chicago: Principia Press.

Kantor, J.R. 1970. An analysis of the experimental analysis of behavior (TEAB). **Journal of The Experimental Analysis of Behavior,** 13, 101-108.

Kantor, J.R. 1971. **The Aim and Progress of Psychology and other Sciences: A Selection of Papers by J.R. Kantor.** Chicago: Principia Press.

Kantor, J.R. 1975. A commentary. **Interbehavioral Quarterly,** 6, 3-4.

Kantor, J.R. 1977. **Psychological Linguistics.** Chicago: Principia Press.

Kantor, J.R. and Smith, N.W. 1975. **The Science of Psychology: An Interbehavioral Survey.** Chicago: Principia Press.

Kendler, H.H. and Spence, J.T. 1971. Tenets of neo-behaviorism. In H.H. Kendler and J.T. Spence (Eds.) **Essays in Neo-Behaviorism: A Memorial to Kenneth W. Spence.** New York: Appleton-Century Crofts.

Kinnie, J.F. 1978. The interbehavioral approach and motivation. **The Interbehaviorist,** 8, 6-10.

Kuo, Z.Y. 1967. **The Dynamics of Behavioral Development: An Epigenetic View.** New York: Random House.

Kvale, S. 1977. Personal Communication, September 28.

Kvale, S. and Grenness, C.E. 1967. Skinner and Sartre: Toward a radical phenomenology of behavior? **Review of Existential Psychology and Psychiatry,** 7, 128-150.

Lichtenstein, P.E. 1959. Perception and the psychological metasystem. **Psychological Record,** 9, 37-44.

Lichtenstein, P.E. 1973. A behavioral approach to "phenomenological data." **Psychological Record,** 21, 1-6.

Lichtenstein, P.E. 1973. Discussion: "Contextual interactionists." In N.W. Smith, Contextual Interactionists: A Symposium. **Psychological Record,** 30, 447-458.

Lundin, R.W. 1969. **Personality: A Behavioral Analysis.** Toronto: MacMillan.

MacLeod, R.B. 1969. Interdisciplinary relationships and cross-cultural research. In M. Sherif and C. W.Sherif (Eds.) **Interdisciplinary Relationships in the Social Sciences.** Chicago: Aldine.

MacLeod, R.B. 1975. **The Persistent Problems of Psychology.** Pittsburgh, Duquesne University Press.

MacRoberts, M.H. and MacRoberts, B.R. 1979-1980. Interbehaviorism and animal communication theory. **The Interbehaviorist,** 9, 4-11.

MacRoberts, M.H. and MacRoberts, B.R. 1980. Toward a minimal definition of animal communication. **Psychological Record,** 30, 387-396.

Marx, M.H. 1963. The general nature of theory communication. In M.H. Marx (Ed.) **Theories of Contemporary Psychology.** New York: Macmillan.

McKeachie, W.J. 1976. Psychology in America's bicentennial year. **American Psychologist,** 31, 819-832.

McKearney, J.W. 1976. Drug effects and the environmental control of behavior. **Pharmacological Reviews,** 27, 3.

McKearney, J.W. 1977. Asking questions about behavior. **Perspective in Biology and Medicine,** 21, 109-119.

McKearney, J.W. and Barrett, J.E. 1975. Punished behavior: Increases in responding after d-amphetamine. **Psychopharmacologia,** 41, 23-26.

McKinney, R. 1976. Fifty years of psychology. **American Psychologist,** 31, 834-842.

Mischel, T. 1976. Psychological explanations and their vicissitudes. In J.K. Cole and W.J. Arnold (Eds.) **Nebraska Symposium on Motivation,** 1975. Lincoln: University of Nebraska Press.

Morris, E.K. 1978-1979. Some relationships between the psychologies of Kantor and Skinner. **The Interbehaviorist,** 8, 3-12.

Mountjoy, P.T. 1957. Differential behavior in monozygotic twins. **Psychological Record,** 7, 65-69.

Mountjoy, P.T. 1976. Science in psychology: J.R. Kantor's field theory. **Mexican Journal of Behavior Analysis,** 2, 3-21.

Natalicio, L. and Kidd, R.V. 1971. A conceptual shift: An operant approach to human interaction. **Psychological Record,** 21, 521-526.

Neisser, V. 1967. **Cognitive Psychology.** New York: Appleton-Century-Crofts.

Neisser,V. 1976. **Cognition and Reality: Principles and Implications of Cognitive Psychology.** San Francisco: Freeman.

Observer, 1969a. The basis fallacy in psychology. **Psychological Record,** 19, 645-648.

Observer, 1969b. The condioned reflex and scientific psychology. **Psychological Record,** 19, 143-146.

Observer, 1969c. On the reduction of psychology to physics. **Psychological Record,** 19, 515-518.

Observer, 1970. Innate intelligence: Another genetic avitar. **Psychological Record,** 20, 123-130.

Observer, 1971a. Wanted: A better direction for linguistic psychology. **Psychological Record,** 21, 269-273.

Observer, 1971b. Words, words, words. **Psychological Record,** 21, 269-272.

Observer, 1973. Private data, raw feels, inner experience, and all that. **Psychological Record, 23,** 563-565.

Observer, 1974. On the role of chemistry in the domain of psychology. **Psychological Record, 24,** 267-296.

Observer, 1976. The science of psychology 1976: What progress? **Psychological Record, 26,** 289-296.

Observer, 1977. Concerning cognitive reversionism in psychology. **Psychological Record, 27,** 351-354.

Observer, 1981. Concerning the principle of psychological privacy. **Psychological Record, 31,** 101-106.

Pronko, N.H. 1946. Language and psychological linguistics: A review. **Psychological Bulletin, 43,** 189-236.

Pronko, N.H. 1957. "Heredity" and "environment" in biology and psychology. **Psychological Record, 11,** 311-314.

Pronko, N.H. 1961. Some reflections on perception. **Psychological Record, 11,** 311-314.

Pronko, N.H. Notes for a freshman: On the free will versus determinism controversy. **Interbehavioral Psychology Newsletter, 3,** 3-4.

Pronko, N.H. 1976. Personal Communication, July 8.

Pronko, N.H. , Ebert, R. and Greenberg, G. 1966. A critical review of theories of perception. In A.L. Kidd and J.L. Rivoire (Eds.) **Perceptual Development in Children.** New York: International Universities.

Ratliff, F. 1962. Some interrelations among physics, physiology, and psychology in the study of vision. In S. Koch (Ed.) **P sychology: A Study of a Science** (Vol. 4). **Biologically Oriented Fields.** New York: McGraw-Hill.

Ray, R.D. 1973. Conditions conditioning conditioning. Paper presented at the Southeastern Psychological Association Meeting, New Orleans, Louisiana, April 6-8.

Ray, R.D. 1976. Oscillating behavioral dynamics in temporally paced environmental settings. Unpublished manuscript.

Ray, R.D. and Brener, J. 1973. Classical heart-rate conditioning in the rat: The influence of curare and various setting operations. **Conditional Reflex, 8,** 224-235.

Ray, R.D. and Brown, D.A. 1976. The behavioral specificity of stimulation: A systems approach to procedural distinctions of classical and instrumental conditioning. **Pavlovian Journal of Biological Sciences,** 11, 3-23.

Ray, R.D., and Ray, M.R. 1976. A systems approach to behavior II: The ecological description and analysis of human behavior dynamics. **Psychological Record,** 26, 127-180.

Ray, R.D. and Upson, J.D. 1977. A systems approach to behavior III: Organismic pace and complexity in time-space fields. **Psychological Record,** 27, 649-682.

Redd, W.H. 1974. Social control by adult preference in operant conditioning with children. **Journal of Experimental Child Psychology,** 17, 61-78.

Rennert, M. 1975. Der Einflus der Versuchssituation bei Imitationsexperimenten. **Archiv fur Psychologie,** 127, 70-77.

Rosenberg, S. and Cohen, B.D. 1966. Referential processes of speakers and listeners. **Psychological Review,** 73, 208-231.

Sarbin, T. 1977. Contextualism: A world view for modern psychology. **Nebraska Symposium on Motivation,** 1976. Lincoln: University of Nebraska Press.

Sarbin, T.R. and Mancuso, J.C. 1980. **Schizophrenia: Medical Diagnosis or Moral Verdict?** New York: Pergamon Press.

Sarbin, T.R. and Coe, W. 1972. **Hypnosis: The Social Psychology of Influence Communication.** New York: Holt, Rinehart and Winston.

Schoenfeld, W.N. and Cumming, N.W. 1963. Behavior and perception. In S. Koch (Ed.) **Psychology: A Study of a Science** (Vol. 5) **The Process Area, the Person, and Some Applied Fields.** New York: McGraw-Hill.

Sells, S.B. 1963. An interactionist looks at the environment. **American Psychologist,** 18, 696-702.

Skinner, B.F. 1975. The steep and thorny way to a science of behavior. **American Psychologist,** 30, 42-49.

Smith, N.W. 1973. Interbehavioral psychology: Roots and branches. **Psychological Record,** 23, 153-167.

Smith, N.W. 1973. Contextual interactionists: A symposium. **Psychological Record**, 23, 281-282.

Smith, N.W. 1974. The ancient background to greek psychology and some implications for today. **Psychological Record**, 24, 309-324.

Smith, N.W. 1976. Twin studies and heredity. **Human Development**, 19, 65-68.

Smith, N.W. and Shaw, N.E. 1979. An analysis of commonplace behaviors: Volitional acts. **Psychological Record**, 29, 179-186.

Sommer, R. 1968. Hawthorne dogma. **Psychological Bulletin**, 70, 592-595.

Sperry, R.W. 1977. Bridging science and value: A unifying view of mind and brain. **American Psychologist**, 32, 237-245.

Stephenson, W.S. 1953. **The Study of Behavior: Q-Technique and its Methodology.** Illinois: University of Chicago Press.

Stephenson, W.S. 1961. Consciousness out--subjectivity in. **Psychological Record**, 18, 449-501.

Stevens, S.S. 1936. Psychology, the propaedeutic science. **Philosophy of Science**, 3, 90-103.

Taylor, J. 1962. **The Behavioral Basis of Perception.** New Haven: Yale Unviersity Press.

Wile, D.B. 1977. Questioning Sperry's bridge from brain to mind to value. **American Psychologist**, 32, 987-989.

Woodbridge, F.J.E. 1913. The belief in sensations. **Journal of Philosophy, Psychology, and Scientific Method**, 10, 599-608.

Zuriff, G.E. 1979. Covert events: The logical status of first-person reports. **Psychological Record**, 29, 125-133.

# CONTRIBUTIONS OF J.R. KANTOR
# TO CONTEMPORARY BEHAVIORISM

Edward K. Morris
Stephen T. Higgins
Warren K. Bickel

Contemporary behaviorism has many varied roots, some of which can be attributed to broad philosophical movements (e.g., naturalism, objectivism, functionalism), and others of which can be attributed more specifically to particular individuals (e.g., Darwin, James, Pavlov, Watson, Thorndike, Mach). B.F. Skinner and his radical behaviorism, of course, are pre-eminent forces in this movement. Numerous conceptual and technical advances in the study of behavior stem directly from his empirical research and theoretical formulations (cf. Ferster and Skinner, 1957; Skinner, 1938; 1953, 1957, 1969, 1972, 1974). Overlooked in the development of contemporary behaviorism, however, have been the contributions of J.R. Kantor and his system of interbehavioral psychology.

It may appear that Kantor's contributions to the field have been modest; however, a careful search of the literature suggests a much broader influence--one that is subtle and often difficult to ascertain. To date, the most obvious form of Kantor's influence can be seen in the interest behaviorists have had in the relationships between radical behaviorism and interbehavioral psychology. This interest apparently began in the 1940's (cf. Fuller, 1973; Lichtenstein, 1973), and continues today. During the past ten years, in particular, papers have been published on the compatibility of the two systems (e.g., Handy, 1973; Mountjoy, 1976); on the common stance each takes towards various philosophical aspects of the two systems (e.g., Bijou and Baer, 1978; Morris, 1981). Moreover, within the past five years, numerous presentations have been made at national conferences on these and similar topics. Most of the presentations have been delivered at the Association for Behavior Analysis (ABA) (Bijou, 1981a; Cone, 1981; Delprato, 1980; McKearney, 1981; Morris, 1979, 1980a; Morris, Higgins and Bickel, 1981; Mountjoy,1980a; Parrott, 1980a, 1980b, 1982) but papers also have been delivered at least twice at the annual meetings of the American Psychological Assocaition (Delprato and Holmes, 1980; Morris, 1980b; Morris and Hursh, 1979; Mountjoy, 1980b).

The concerns of those interested in the relationships between radical behaviorism and interbehavioral psychology have been for the improvement of one or the other of the two systems or for an integration of the two approaches that will promote the effective evolution of contemporary behaviorism in general. Despite this interest, however, little attention has actually been paid to the contributions Kantor has made to the field. The interest evinced thusfar warrants such an investigation. At the very least, the historical record should be formally examined. That is the purpose of this chapter.

In examining Kantor's contributions to contemporary behaviorism we (a) assess his influence on indvidual behaviorists and their scientific formulations, (b) describe the increased recognition of interbehavioral psychology has been receiving within the field, and (c) evduate how the future directions of behaviorism can and may be influenced by Kantor. This investigation is based on two sources of information. First, we document the extent and depth of Kantor's contributions on the basis of the published historical record. And second, we present the results of a questionnaire on this topic sent to all present and past editorial board members of the **Journal of the Experimental Analysis of Behavior (JEAB)**, the **Journal of Applied Behavior Analysis (JABA)**, and **Behaviorism.** Upon concluding our investigation, we evaluate Kantor's influence on contemporary behaviorism with respect to the past, present, and future of the field.

Before commencing, however, two brief comments are in order. First, some of our statements about contemporary behaviorism and interbehavioral psychology cannot be supported by empirical evidence or literature citations. These comments represent the scientific and social perspectives we have acquired through our professional development, and should be viewed in this light. Second, this chapter is not designed to present a comprehensive description of interbehavioral psychology or of its conceptual relatitonship with radical behaviorism. These analyses are available elsewhere in this book and from other sources (cf. Kantor, 1959, 1970; Morris, 1981; Mountjoy, 1976; Pronko, 1980). We turn now instead to the first section in which we present the historical record documenting Kantor's contributions to contemporary behaviorism.

### The Historical Record

Jacob Robert Kantor, born in 1888, received his Ph.D. in 1917 under James Rowland Angell from the Department of Philosophy at the University of Chicago. It is of interest to note that Angell was also the co-advisor of J.B. Watson (with H.H. Donaldson) and that Kantor , while at Chicago, took a course from Watson who returned from John Hopkins University for the summer of 1914. Later, in the

1920's, Kantor was once a guest lecturer in a course Watson taught at the New School for Social Research in New York. Kantor was influenced by the functionalists at Chicago (e.g., Dewey, Angell, Carr), as well as by the early objectivist trend in psychology. The influence of functionalism can be seen in Kantor's emphasis on the inseparable interactive relationships between stimulus and response functions, as opposed to the separable and formal properties of environment and behavior. The influence of objectivism is seen in the naturalism of his approach, and in the early stances he took against mentalism (Kantor, 1920a) and the instinct doctrine (Kantor, 1920b). Kantor was, however, at variance with aspects of both the functionalist and objectivist movements. He castigated the former for its acceptance of "mental fictions," and the latter for its inherent mechanism which left stimuli and responses devoid of any substantial psychological meaning. Kantor has continued to be a vociferous critic on these points throughout his long career (cf.Kantor, 1971).

As these criticisms apply to behavior analysis, even Skinner has acknowledged Kantor's influence on his thinking. With respect to mentalism, Skinner (1967) has stated: "Another behaviorist whose friendship I have valued is J.R.Kantor. In many discussions with him...I profited from his extraordinary scholarship. He convinced me that I had not wholly exorcised all the 'spooks' from my thinking" (p. 411). As an example of Kantor's influence in this regard, in the preface to the seventh printing of **The Behavior of Organisms** (Skinner, 1938), Skinner (1966, p. x) credits Kantor with convincing him of the dangers inherent in the concept of drive--a concept Skinner used regularly in his earlier work (LaShier, 1974). Skinner has again acknowledged Kantor's contribution with respect to Kantor's ability to avoid mechanisms with the concepts of stimulus and response function and with the adoption of a behavioral field system. As a footnote in **The Behavior of Organisms,** Skinner (1938) cited Kantor (1933), noting that "The impossibility of defining a functional stimulus without reference to a functional response, and vice versa, has been especially emphasized by Kantor" (p. 35). Fuller (1973, p. 319) has made this same point and gone even further stating that "The rereading of the whole of the first chapter of **The Behavior of Organisms** reveals many passages which could pass as Kantorian" . Skinner (1979) has also acknowledged the usefulness of a field or systems perspective, commenting that he found it "helpful in thinking about the behavior of an organism as a whole" (p. 101). Expanding on this, Skinner (1953) has commented elsewhere:

> ...any **unit** of operant behavior is to a certain extent
> artificial. Behavior is the coherent, continuous ac-
> tivity of an integral organism. Although it may be
> analyzed into parts for theoretical or practical pur-
> purposes, we need to recognize its continuous nature
> in order to solve certain common problems (p. 116).

Thus, as Krechevsky (1933) pointed out,

> ...Skinner reflex is **not** a "molecular" unit, as understood
> and criticized by the Gestalt psychologists...We find
> Skinner following the best traditions of Tolman, Lewin,
> Koffka, et al., for he stops with his process of analysis
> at the point beyond which no **psychological** sense can
> result, he is not differing from the Gestaltist's concept
> of what is proper analysis (p. 406-407).

Verplanck (1954) has commented on why Skinner may be misunderstood
on this point

> In his choice of terminology, Skinner has assured that
> his works and those of his fellows will be read easily
> by the followers of Hull and Guthrie and only with
> emotion, if not with difficulty, by those who have
> selected the organismic-field-Gestalt-force family
> of words to work with. Skinner's conditioned respon-
> ses seem to many readers just as **mere** as those of
> Pavlov or Hull,with the extraordinary result that he
> has been classed with Guthrie rather than with Lewin,
> in his general position (p. 307).

Kantor spent his academic career in the Department of Psychology
at Indiana University from 1920 to 1959. For much of his tenure
there, that department was, as it continues to be, one of the leading
centers for behavioral science in this country (Capshew and Hearst,
1980; Goodall, 1972). Aside from Kantor's prolific publishing career
(cf. Smith, 1976), the most obvious contribution he made to
behaviorism at Indiana University was his founding of **The Psychological Record (The Record)** in 1937. Throughout the late 1930's,
Skinner published a number of single and co-authored papers in that
journal (Cook and Skinner, 1939; Heron and Skinner, 1937, 1939, 1940;
Skinner, 1937, 1939; Skinner and Heron, 1937), and during the mid 1940's
served as one of its associate editors. Although Skinner no longer
contributes to **The Record,** many behavior analysts have found this
journal supportive of their views, both before and after the
development of speciality behavioral journals for basic research (e.g.,
Verhave and Owen, 1958), applied research (e.g., Ferster, 1967; Ferster
and Simmons, 1966; Rice and McDaniel, 1966) and theory (Burgess and
Akers, 1966; Homme, 1966). To this day, **The Record** continues to
serve as an important outlet for work in these areas (e.g., Kileen,
Wald and Cheney,1980; Moore, 1980; Picker, Poling, and Parker, 1979;
Vukelich and Hake, 1980).

In addition to founding **The Record,** Kantor was also responsible
for bringing Skinner to Indiana from Minnesota in 1945. During
Skinner's stay there, he and Kantor jointly taught a seminar entitled

"Theory Construction in Psychology," and were especially influential for their thoroughgoing functionalism and criticisms of conventional operationism (Fuller, 1973, p. 319, 321). It should be noted, though, that despite their relationship at Indiana, Kantor and Skinner did not interact professionally to a great degree then, nor have they since. Thus, in contrast to comments cited earlier, Skinner (1979) has noted, "I was never able to come very close to Robert Kantor's way of thinking about behavior, although differences were trivial compared to our similarities" (p. 325).

Both Kantor and Skinner had their followings at Indiana, and the differing approaches of the two men was apparently the basis for much intellectual discussion among the students there (Fuller, 1973; Lichtenstein , 1973). Fuller (1973, p. 321) and Lichtenstein (1973, p. 332), for instance, both observed that during this time it was Kantor, not Skinner, who was the more adamant about extending behavioral psychology to human activities (cf. Carter, 1937), whereas most radical behaviorsts tended to pursue basic animal research in search of the basic principles of behavior, before extending those principles to the complex content and substance of human activity. Of those particularly affected by Kantor in this regard were Greenspoon, Kanfer, and Fuller, himself. Indeed, Fuller's 1949 report of his research with a vegetative human is often cited as the first behavior modification study conducted in the operant tradition (e.g., Ulrich, Stachnik and Mabry, 1966, p. 65). Moreover, Fuller (1973) commented: "Without the influence of Kantor, operant studies might have stayed exclusively in the animal laboratories for a long, long time" (p. 324). The accuracy of this comment is difficult to assess , and may be slightly overstated, because by this time Skinner had worked out some of his preliminary analysis for **Verbal Behavior** (1957) (Skinner, 1979) and was nearing completion of **Walden Two** (1948). Soon to follow would be Keller and Schoenfeld's **Principles of Psychology** (1950) and Skinner's **Science and Human Behavior** (1953). In any event, between the two of them, Kantor and Skinner influenced a whole generation of students, staff, and summer conference participants (Dinsmoor, 1980) at Indiana, many of whom went on to become well-known, or better known behavior analysts. Among them were Bernal, Bijou, Dinsmoor, Ferster, Homme, Kanfer, MacCorquodale, Malott, Mountjoy, Schoenfeld, and Ulrich (Lichtenstein, 1973).

Skinner left Indiana in 1947 to return to Harvard, and no substantial interaction between him and Kantor seems to have occurred since. Starting in the 1950's, however, some of the relationships between the two systems began to be noted in the psychological literature. Stephenson (1953), for instance, commented on the similar approaches Kantor and Skinner took towards investigating psychological activity. In 1954, Verplanck published "the finest critical assessment of **The Behavior of Organisms** [Skinner, 1938] that has been made to date" (Day, 1980, p. 242) and in it described briefly the relationship between Skinner's and Kantor's systems:

> Skinner's approach...bears no more than a terminolo-
> gical resemblance to Hull's or Pavlov's, but it is at
> least first cousin to Kantor's system [Kantor, 1924]
> which explicitly rather than implicitly accepts a meta-
> physical position, naive realism, and rejects even the
> logical possibility of reductionism (p. 308).

In the 1960's, the implications of Kantor's system became even better recognized and appreciated which has been increasingly evident ever since. Bijou and Baer(1961) published the first volume of their series on child development in which they formally established the behavior analysis approach to child development. In developing this position, they integrated several aspects of Kantor's system with Skinner's, notably the concept of setting events (p. 17) and the descriptive stage sequences of the universal (or functional), basic, and societal periods (p. 24). In Bijou and Baer's second volume (1965), these features were retained and two others added-- Kantor's concept of ecological behavior (pp. 5-7)and his distinction between the domains of biology and psychology (pp. 10-12). Gewirtz (1969, p. 89; 1972, p. 9), we should note, also used the concept of setting events in the analysis of child development, especially social development. Finally, in the March, 1969 issue of **JEAB**, Schoenfeld published an intelligent and sensitive retrospective review of Kantor's books on grammar and logic (e.g., 1935, 1945, 1950), in which he noted similarities to Skinner's system, especially in regard to the functional elements of verbal episodes (p. 331, 333), the nature of meaning (p. 332),and cause-and-effect (p. 339). Skinner, himself (1979, p. 213), has mentioned that he thought Kantor was "on the right track" in his analysis of language.

The 1970's have seen a further expansion of these interrelationships. Bijou (1976) published his description and analysis of the basic stage of child development in which he maintained his interbehavioral stance and his intention of integrating it with radical behaviorism. Evidence of this can be seen clearly in the preface of that volume:

> The analysis presented here...is theoretical in
> interpreting behavior in terms of the empirical
> concepts and functional laws that have been generat-
> ed by laboratory and field experimental research in
> the last fifty years and organized into a system
> founded on the assumptions embodied in the philo-
> sophy of modern behaviorism presented by B.F. Skinner
> and J.R. Kantor (p. xi).

In 1977, Bijou again mentioned the usefulness of combining Skinner's experimental theory and methodology with Kantor's philosophy of science (Krasner, 1977, p. 590), and again emphasized the importance of both the field approach and the concepts of stimulus and response functions to a behavior analysis of child development (Krasner, 1977, pp. 598-599). Shortly thereafter, Bijou and Baer (1978) revised their first volume, this time presenting an even more forceful integration of the two systems, especially in the functional analysis of stimulus and response relationships, and by adding Kantor's view on emotional activity that distinguishes between feelings and emotions (cf. Kantor, 1966). Brady (1975) also published a chapter in 1975 in which he adopted this interbehavioral distinction between feelings and emotions; moreover, Brady (e.g., Brady and Emurian, 1979) has continued to use the language of Kantor's system, for instance "interbehavioral" analysis (p. 82) and "behavior segments" (p. 85). In a paper published in **Behaviorism** , Jay Moore (1975) cited the similar positions Skinner and Kantor have taken in the interpretation of operationism, especially as it relates to the development of scientific knowledge. In another paper published in **Behaviorism,** Powell and Still (1979) examined the contributions of several early behaviorists to the psychology of language. In doing so, they devoted a section to Kantor (1922, 1936), describing his theses that language is behavior (rather than a "thing") and that the meaning of language can only be understood in terms of its social contact (pp. 83-85). Paul Mountjoy (1976) published a paper in the **Mexican Journal of Behavior Analysis** **(MJBA)** in which he described Kantor's theoretical system and pointed out that it could be usefully combined with Skinner's experimental program, to the benefit of both approaches and psychology in general. The benefit for psychology, Mountjoy said, would be in the clarification of persistent problems such as the relationship of biology to psychology (pp. 16-17), the hereditary doctrine of intelligence (pp. 17-18), and the uniqueness of humans in their thought and language (pp. 18-19). It is of interest to note that Mountjoy's was but one of eight articles citing Kantor published in **MJBA** between its founding in 1975 and the middle of 1980; this suggests that Kantor's influence is stronger in Mexico and other Latin countries than in the United States. Finally, in the realm of applied behavior analysis, both Kanfer (Kanfer and Phillips, 1970, p. viii) and Krasner (1979, p. 2) have mentioned the important but often overlooked influence Kantor has had on the conceptual development of the field. More specifically, Grossberg (1972) in discussing brainwave feedback experiments, cited Kantor in arguing against physiological reductionism. Also , Wickramasekera (1972) commented that the relaxation instructions provided during systematic desensitization may be regarded as Kantorian setting events that sensitize subject to subsequent treatment procedures.

Compared to the attention behavior analysts have given interbehavioral psychology, Kantor has very infrequently commented in turn, except for his eight publications in the **MJBA**. He has in the past cited Skinner (1938) positively in making arguments against physiological reductionism and for psychology as an independent natural science (Kantor, 1947). In addition, he has served as an editorial board member of **Behaviorism** since its inception. Kantor's most substantive comments were those delivered at a 1969 invited address to the APA Division on the Experimental Analysis of Behavior (Division 25) in which he presented his own analysis of the experimental analysis of behavior, which he referred to as TEAB. In that presentation, and subsequent 1970 **JEAB** article, Kantor (1970) was both supportive and critical. On the one hand, he called the audience friendly, proclaimed his high regard for its anti-mentalism, complimented its naturalism and objectivism, and praised TEAB for being "one of the first adequate scientific formulations of experimental psychology" (p. 102). On the other hand, he criticized TEAB of the late 1960's for being a constrained and specialized science of the simple, arbitrary, and laboratory- generated behavior of non-human species, especially that behavior influenced simply by "reward conditions" (p. 102). He stressed that TEAB must be conducted from a "wide-open perspective" (p. 106) and that it not restrict itself to specialized patterns of research. As in the past, he called for the behavior analysis of everyday, complex human behavior in its natural setting. Among those behaviors that Kantor said we must analyze are those referred to as feeling and emotion, as well as remembering, perceiving, thinking, inventing, and problem-solving. He felt that the lack of attention to these behaviors left them to what he called the "untender mercies" of the cognitivists (p. 105).

We have been able to find only one published reaction to this paper--one by Winokur (1971), in his **JEAB** review of Skinner's **Contingencies of Reinforcement** (1969). Winokur called Kantor's paper "perspicacious" (p. 253), but felt that Kantor was perhaps unnecessarily harsh in his criticisms, due in part to an unsympathetic and incomplete reading of the behavior analysis literature. Nonetheless, the TEAB paper has been cited since by those seeking to make points similar to Kantor's. Salzinger (1973), for instance, cited the paper in arguing that TEAB should begin to address problems behavior analysts have left to cognitive psychology. Malone (1975, p. 149) described Kantor's position as one that offers an alternative to current experimental practices, especially those that focus solely on the effects of reinforcement, because even simple cases of animal learning, such as "behavioral contract," have proven troublesome for traditional operant analyses (Malone, 1975; Malone and Staddon, 1973). Finally, Shimp (1976) cited Kantor's paper as he argued that TEAB has made little progress in developing and experimentally analyzing a useful or relevant concept of memory. We should note, though, that Shimp's suggestions, and more recently those of Wasserman (1981), which argue that TEAB should adopt cognitive language and concepts, are deemed mentalistic by many behavior analysts and interbehavioral psychologists (e.g., Branch, 1977; Morris, Higgins and Bickel, 1982). As will be later emphasized, interbehavioral psychology offers an important alternative to the limitations of mechanistic behaviorism so that a return to mentalism through cognitive psychology is not necessary.

This ends the review of the historical record. Our evaluation of it will be presented later in the chapter so that we can integrate it with our findings from the next section--the results of our questionnaire study.

## The Questionnaire Study

A six-page questionnaire was developed to ascertain further the influence Kantor and his interbehavioral psychology have had on contemporary behaviorism. We took as our sample all present (1980) and past editorial board members of **JEAB, JABA,** and **Behaviorism** in order to obtain opinions form the primary divisions within behavior analysis--basic research, applied research, and theory. Of the 346 board members, we were able to locate the correct addresses and send the questionnaire to 318 (91.9%), 143 (45%) of whom returned it. Comments were neither solicited from the first author of this chapter, nor from Skinner or Kantor; the latter two, however, were sent copies of the questionnaire and a letter explaining its purpose.

We asked the board members about their familiarity with the approach, and its relevance to teaching, research, and theory. In addition, we asked questions about the strengths and weaknesses of interbehavioral psychology, its past and future influence on behavior analysis, and the compatibility of the approach with behavior analysis. A consent form was included so that the comments of the assenting respondents can be cited and reproduced here. Passages from already published material are also cited in this section where they illuminate the comments of our respondents.

## Familiarity with Interbehavioral Psychology

Fifty-eight of the respondents have had some contact with Kantor and interbehavioral psychology, primarily through professional reading (18.2%) and coursework as students (17.5%); as for the former, some respondents said they wished they had read more of Kantor. Ten percent (10.5%) had contact through peers and colleagues, 7.7% had contact as students through faculty members other than their instructors, 2.1% had contact by other means , and 6.3% could not recall the nature of their first contact.

Of those who have had contact, 32.9% have read from at least one of Kantor's 16 published books. Of this group, 44.7% have read from one book, 29.8% from two, 10.6% from three (among them Shull, Zeiler, and Zuriff), and 14.9% from more than four (among them Bijou, Brady, Catania, Moore, and Sarbin). The most influential of Kantor's books for these respondents has been the outline of his system, entitled **Interbehavioral Psychology** (Kantor, 1959); this book was also the most frequently cited of Kantor's texts in the **Social Sciences Citations Index** (SSCI) (1969-1980). Also mentioned prominently, though, were his books on grammar (Kantor, 1935), problems in physiological psychology (Kantor, 1947), and the history of psychology (Kantor, 1963, 1969). The last was the second most frequently cited set of Kantor's books in the **SSCI** ; close behind these were his tests on the **Principles of Psychology** (Kantor, 1924, 1926).

Thirty-seven percent (37.1%) of the sample have read at least one of Kantor's numerous published articles (cf. Smith, 1976). Seven percent have read one article, 16.1% have read two to three, 4.9% have read four to five, 2.1% have read six to ten articles (among them Shull and Zeiler), and 7% have read more than ten articles (among them Bijou, Blackman, Brady, McKearney, Moore, Sarbin and Zuriff). The most influential of Kantor's articles were his 1966 **The Record** feeling and emotions as scientific events, and his 1970 **JEAB** paper; the latter was clearly the most frequently cited reference in the **SSCI**.

### Relevance to Teaching, Research and Theory

**Teaching.** Seventeen percent (17.5%) of our sample reported that they thought it was important to teach students explicitly about Kantor's interbehavioral psychology; they favored this instruction for graduate students over undergraduate students by about three-to-one. more than half (56%) of this group said that they refer to interbehavioral psychology in their teaching, though typically as lecture material (63.2%) rather than as course readings (36.8%). Eleven respondents (7.7%) reported that they teach courses having an interbehavioral orientation; among these instructors were Bijou, Brady, Falk, Sarbin, Schnelle, Pennypacker, and Wahler. The content of these courses include abnormal psychology, applied behavior analysis, child development, environmental design, the experimental analysis of behavior for medical students, and social psychology.

When asked whether students should be taught about Kantor's interbehavioral psychology, 81.4% said "yes," while 18.6% said "no." The predominant reason given for not teaching interbehavioral psychology was the greater necessity for teaching radical behaviorism. Radical behaviorism was described as more current, well-known, and recognizable; as similar to Kantor's system, it does not lend itself readily to immediate use in basic and applied research. Radical behaviorism, however, does lend itself to these particular matters, and hence is viewed as easier and more relevant to teach. In this regard, Shull added that other psychologists make the same points as Kantor, but make them in relationship to specific content areas in which reference is not made to Kantor. Finally, two respondents said that it was more important to teach the approach then to be concerned about to whom or to which "school" it should be attributed.

As for why interbehavioral psychology should be taught, several themes may be discerned from the respondents' answers. The most frequent comment centered on the historical value of the approach. Pennypacker and other respondents viewed Kantor as having played an important role in the development of modern behaviorism, hence exposure to his ideas increases students' understanding of psychology in general. Several respondents said that more students should know about Kantor, and that they should be encouraged to conceptualize and broaden their perspectives with what Eckerman called Kantor's "careful and thoughtful general system" and with what Shull called Kantor's "useful framework." Several respondents said that, at the very least, students should become acquainted with Kantor in a history and systems course.

On a more substantive level, it was mentioned that one specific value of teaching Kantor was to provide students with an understanding of a behavioral field theory that avoids the reductionism that detracts from so many other forms of behaviorism. McKearney mentioned this in particular and, in a related comment, Gelfand noted that she specifically instructs her students about setting events. Wahler was the most adamant about this issue, especially as it relates to research and application in the natural environment: Interbehavioral psychology is "crucial knowledge for anyone concerned with social ecology and change procedures applied therein."

Finally, we had several strong statements on the general value of teaching Kantor's system. Sarbin thought it important to teach students about interbehavioral psychology because it gives "them an option other than mentalism and mechanism." Bijou added: "It is a way to acquaint them with the nature of a scientific analysis of behavior...it orients them to basic assumptions, theory, and methodology...it sensitizes the student to the many guises of mentalism." Brady provided the most compelling argument, at least in its forcefulness: "It's the propaedeutic science--the basis for understanding all other sciences and forms of human knowledge!!" To summarize the findings from this section of the questionnaire, let us quote Schoenfeld (1969) who provides an eloquent statement on the value of teaching interbehavioral psychology:

...a teacher, no matter what his personal views, can
do no better for his students than to make them at
least for a time students of Kantor,knowing they will
find it an enriching interlude, one that will contribute
to their growth as psychologists (p. 346).

**Research.** Ten percent (9.8%) of our sample reported that
interbehavioral psychology has influenced their research practices or
formulations, among these individuals were Bijou, Brady, Eckerman,
Sarbin, Schnelle, and D.R. Williams. More than half of this group
(58.3%) reported citing Kantor in their references. Another subgroup,
comprising 4.2% of our sample, reported that they had conducted
research that was specifically influenced by interbehavioral
formulations; among these individuals were Brady, Patterson, Sarbin,
and Wahler.

The influence Kantor has had on the research of these respondents
is in some cases broad and profound, while in others more specific. As
for the former, Bijou commented that "It helped me to discriminate
between meaningful and meaningless problems" and "to see the
weakness of problems, studies, and interpretation in the literature." In
noting the influence Kantor has had on the research practices of
students at Indiana, Hopkins said

He taught us to stay close to our facts (data) when
making inferences. He taught us to be explicit
about what we did in our research. He showed us
many examples of how people got into scientific
trouble when they failed to do these things.

In this regard, Hopkins said that "these lessons seemed much more
fundamental than interbehavioral psychology." Along these same lines,
Williams added: "The clarity of the approach is agreeable and
contributes to the clarity of germane formulations." McKearney said
that while none of his research had been stimulated by interbehavioral
formulations, it is concordant with them. The value of the approach
for him, then, is that it plays "a part in the way I think about my
work and the ways in which it may fit into a bigger picture."

As for more specific interbehavioral contributions to the research
of behavior analysts, Eckerman said he valued the thoroughgoing
functionalism of the approach. Schnelle was stimulated by the
emphasis Kantor places on the multiple determination of behavior,
while another respondent said that Kantor made him appreciate the
importance of measuring both subject behavior and environmental
stimuli simultaneously. One respondent was made more sensitive to
radical behavioral concepts such as sensory reinforcement, while
others found value in the concept of setting events as an independent
variable and in Kantor's explication of the role of the history of the

organism in the analysis of lengthy behavior-environment interactions.

A final set of comments should be noted. Several respondents felt that Kantor had had an influence on their research formulations, but not one they could cite explicitly. The source of this influence, they suggested, was in Kantor's influence on the historical development of behaviorism or on the professional development of their teachers.

**Theory.** Fifteen percent (14.7%) of our sample reported that interbehavioral psychology has influenced their theoretical or conceptual formulations; among these individuals were Baer, Bijou, Blackman, Brady, Gelfand, Hopkins, Newsom, Pennypacker, Sarbin, Schnelle, and Spradin. Forty-three percent of this group reported citing Kantor in their theoretical publications. Another subgroup, comprising 4.2% of our sample, reported that they had written articles that dealt with interbehavioral psychology or positions similar to it; among these individuals were Bijou, Brady, Moore, Patterson, and Wahler.

The influence of Kantor's system on the theoretical and conceptual formulations of our respondents can be graded from general to specific. On the general level, Moore said that Kantor's influence was

> more corrective and prescriptive. [He] asks for
> clarification of theoretical assumptions to be sure
> they aren't dualistic. [He is] more a comment on
> the factors that exert stimulus control over the
> verbal behavior of scientists than a way to do
> research.

Sarbin credited Kantor with giving him the conceptual tools for taking "a critical stance toward modern psychology." Along the same lines, Hopkins said, "Kantor taught me to be an empiricist (modern definition) and he taught me to operationalize." Finally, another respondent said that interbehavioral psychology stimulated him to view psychology as a natural science.

As for the influence of Kantor's work on the theoretical and conceptual formulations related to radical behaviorism, two respondents mentioned that Kantor had positively affected their conceptualization of language and private events. More generally, Newsom pointed out that interbehavioral psychology "added conceptual breadth and depth to Skinner's system." Blackman responded more specifically. He said that interbehavioral psychology made him more aware of "the essentially interactive approach of Skinner and the science of contemporary behaviorism." With respect to behavioral concepts, Blackman added that Kantor's system made him more aware of the importance of discriminative stimuli (as opposed to reinforcers)

63

in the analysis of behavior. Another respondent commented that the concept of the setting event ( a likely source of Blackman's views on discriminative stimuli) was a useful supplement to the concept of stimulus control. Gelfand, again, commented on the usefulness of the setting event concept. As the last point in this regard, Schnelle said that is is to Kantor that he attributes his ecological orientation.

As in the section on research practices and formulations, a number of respondents felt that Kantor had influenced their theoretical and conceptual perspectives, but that they could not specify the nature or extent of this influence, nor the mechanism by which it was transmitted.

## The Strengths and Weaknesses

**Strengths.** One of the major strengths of interbehavioral psychology was seen to be its comprehensiveness as a behavioral system. As Baer said, "It is a very comprehensive, truly behavioral approach to the understanding of behavior and environment." Zuriff noted that "it has a clearly defined philosophical and historical context," to which we may add Brady's comment that it is the "most logical and consistent conceptualization of behavioral interactions--easily operationalized." The approach was additionally praised for being creative, clear-headed, and unremitting.

Several other respondents noted that another strength of the system is that it sensitizes us to what Bijou called "the many disguises of mentalism" or, in Catania's and Hopkin's use of Kantor's term, it calls attention to the "spooks" in our thinking. In this regard, our respondents said taht Kantor was seen as being one of the leaders in criticizing mentalistic psychology. The elegance of the interbehavioral system on this point is perhaps the basis for Brady's comment that it "requires [the] fewest assumptions about observed and unobservable phenomena." As for the future, Sarbin was bold in stating that Kantor's "attacks on mentalism ought to be renewed by the current generation of interbehaviorists, lest 'cognition' become the new ghost-in-the-machine."

Several points were raised specifically about the strengths of Kantor's approach for basic and applied research, and for theory. With respect to basic research, Bijou's comments were the most compelling: "It encourages psychologists to believe that the legitimate approach to understanding behavior must be through the long and arduous methods of the natural sciences" and that it "helps in formulating problems and interpreting results," to which he added: "It makes psychologists face some of the difficult problems facing the field," for example, in such areas as implicit behavior and the effects of early influences on development. Sarbin concurred, noting that "the approach makes us take into account specific contexts." In regard to applied research, Wahler argued that Kantor's "system compels us as researchers to deal with all parts of environment-behavior systems, regardless of our a priori assumptions about how the systems operate." Sarbin made a similar point, noting that "the approach makes us take into account specific contexts." The reason for doing so is best gleaned from McKearney's comment: "The obvious strong point [of interbehavioral psychology] is its explicit attention to the fact that behavior is multiply determined." Breiling was more specific about this:

> [Interbehavioral psychology is] another reminder of
> the number of variables and complex interactions
> among them that probably need to be taken into
> account in behavioral and social science theory, research,
> and technological planning and implementations. As
> I see it, the implications of the number of and nature
> of variables to be taken into account, and the complex-
> ity of their interactions, are such as to put into serious
> doubt the value of much behavioral/social research,
> to require much more sophisticated designs and analyses
> than are usually done, and very probably also to point
> up why behavioral/social planning, analyses, and inter-
> ventions may account for only a small portion of the
> variance with most dependent variables.

As for the strengths of interbehavioral psychology for theory, Sarbin pointed out that

> Kantor's system is less a system than a metaphysical
> orientation, a set of guidelines for penetrating human
> problems...a set of rules for doing intellectual or em-
> pirical work on human problems. The metaphysic is
> most closely related to contextualism. Kantor's work
> is most congenial with the pragmatism of Dewey,
> Meade, and Pierce.

Bijou, Eckerman, and Sarbin, each in his own way, made note of the emphasis that the system places on thorough functional analyses in which the interaction of stimulus and response functions are emphasized, as opposed to the search for stimuli and responses possessing some inherent psychological property. Additional strengths were seen by Bijou to be the system's clarification of the relationship among the sciences, and the distinctions among stimuli, setting events, and media. Blackman was impressed by its naturalism. Finally, one respondent noted the potential usefulness of the classification system Kantor set up in his **Principles of Psychology** (1924, 1926) for organizing the field of behavioral science.

**Weaknesses.** Despite the strengths of Kantor's interbehavioral psychology noted by behavior analysts, several weaknesses were also described. The most consistently negative comments centered on Kantor's writing style (cf. Stevens and Stove, 1947). His work was said to be difficult to read and understand because his old school germanic writing style is too complex, abstract, and obtuse. It was noted that, despite the importance of what Kantor had to say, his work has been made somewhat inaccessible and less interesting because of this problem; Kantor should have had an editor, and been more quotable. Several other respondents added that they had turned to Skinner because his writing was more understandable to them than Kantor's.

In addition to this formal quality of Kantor's writing, his style was also viewed as being excessively critical, negative, and combative towards cognitive psychology and psychological theories not in keeping with his own. One respondent noted that he thought Kantor missed some of the significant aspects of behavior in favor of making logical points. Moreover, Kantor was criticized for using a language of logical and psychological constructs that appeared to be remote from data or operations on data. This is a style, then, that some said make his theoretical work appear unclear and even mentalistic to a radical behaviorist. Kantor (1970), however, defended his position on this point in his TEAB paper, stating that he believed

> TEAB should repudiate the mistaken view that it is
> a virtue to liquidate the traditional categories of
> psychology as though names were things instead of
> social constructs. Undeniably, it is reasonable to
> advocate the abandonment of the conventional names
> of psychology in the hope of avoiding their mentalistic
> connotations, but it appears a futile gesture as long
> as we are enlisted under the banner of psychology
> or psychonomics (p. 103).

Despite Kantor's plea, many behavior analysts would argue that the retention of a mentalistic language has a deleterious influence on the logic and theory thereby constructed with it (cf. Branch, 1977; Branch and Malagodi, 1980). With respect to all the points raised above, and othes similar to them, Schoenfeld sought to explain the relative lack of influence Kantor has had with his books on grammar and logic (Kantor, 1935, 1945, 1950).

The second primary weakness seen in Kantor's approach was clearly its lack of a research tradition, or even relevance to research, either basic or applied. These points contradict those reported in the earlier section on the relationship of interbehavioral psychology to research, and represent a divergence of opinion among behavior analysts. Despite the previous comments, however, the balance seems to be on the negative side. Interbehavioral psychology was viewed as being too strongly philosophical to offer substantial implications or guidance for the conduct of science. To this point, McKearney commented that "...the approach badly needs people who actually go out and do things, whether this is basic research or application." We concur with McKearney's comments and agree that if interbehavioral psychologists followed his advice then they could make an important contribution to the influence of the approach within psychology. Nonetheless, the field of psychology has room for contributors on many levels, some of which lead to greater recognition than others. Schoenfeld (1969) has spoken on this point in defending Kantor, and his comments seem appropriate here:

> The contribution a scholar makes to the general fund
> of society's knowledge can take various forms. In
> science, the accolade is usually bestowed on a man
> who offers his colleagues the means for extending
> his line of work, who describes or designs a set of
> practical tools or procedures, who suggests a method
> for concrete application. Such a man will, everything
> else aside, stand out in the scientific community, while
> one who leaves others to their own inventive resources
> will reap neither the fame nor the followers that are
> the rewards of science-in-the-market-place. Kantor's
> position in psychology is to be seen in this light...
> (p. 329-330).

These are strong words. That they come from a pre-eminent behavior analyst ought to be cause for reflection by others in the field.

Two other points were brought up in this section. First, McKearney noted that interbehavioral psychology is weak because its "proponents have to a great extent been talking only among themselves...The practical influence will be nil so long as interbehaviorists remain in the closet." We concur! The second point was that "interbehavioral" is an unattractive term. One respondent said that the term has become associated with Kantor's combative style, and hence many readers may be dissuaded from delving into the system to any appreciable degree. (The "radical" in radical behaviorism, we should note, also makes for similar difficulties.) A term that had more obvious connotations for the theory it labels was thought to be more valuable. Baer, for instance, suggested "comprehensive," "ecological," or "interactive" behaviorism. Within the field of psychology, perspectives have been developing that are increasingly consonant with Kantor's approach, but interbehavioral is a term that is rarely used. These perspectives oftne go by such labels as "interactional" (Cairns, 1979; Patterson, 1979), "transactional" (Handy, 1973), or "dialectical" (Riegel, 1978). If interbehavioral psychologists desire to make Kantor's work more influential, they will have to point out the relationships between their approach and those that go by other labels, or they will have to begin working under a different title.

## The Influence of Interbehavioral Psychology

Of the respondents who commented on this item, a fair number said that Kantor and his interbehavioral psychology have had little influence on psychology or behavior analysis during the past sixty years; this point was especially emphasized in regard to empirical research. Kantor's approach was viewed as intriguing and interesting, and its advocates as erudite, but as having little observable impact. As evidence for this, Bijou pointed out that Gibson (1979) apparently had to "rediscover" the field-ecological approach to perception even though Kantor had outlined it years ago (Kantor, 1920a; Observer, 1981). Patterson, in turn, noted that the influence of an interactional behavioral psychology has been gaining, but not in the manner expressed by Kantor or attributed to him. Finally, Pennypacker said that the influence of the system should be stronger than it is.

Several reasons were offered in explanation of Kantor's relative lack of influence. Baer argued that a large part of the problem lay in Kantor's inaccessibility, due in part to his writing style. Along this same line, another respondent said that Kantor was in some ways actually ahead of Skinner in championing a truly behavioral psychology, but that Skinner has received most of the credit because he could communicate better. It was also suggested that not all behavior analysts are trained enough in philosophy and theory to appreciate Kantor's arguments. Mountjoy (1976) also referred to this as a possiblity. He said that the most reasonable interpretation for Kantor's lack of influence is the "tendency of the majority of psychologists to ignore the theoretical aspect of psychological science and to exalt exuberantly the amassing of data" (p. 19). These latter comments on theory have some merit, we think. However, they may have been more descriptive of the field a few years ago than now. The founding of the journal **Behaviorism** in 1972 stands as clear evidence for a growing interest in theory. Other, more recent publications also underscore this point (Day, 1980; Harzem and Miles, 1978). As Day (1980, p. 257) has pointed out, there appears to be a growing interest among younger behavior analysts in examining conceptual issues. With these changes may also come a growing appreciation of Kantor's work.

Another set of respondents offered some comments of an historical nature. Rozeboom, for instance, agrees with Kantor's orientation and his efforts, but argues that Kantor has had little impact. He said that Kantor's work, which was in the style of late 19th century philosophy, would have been valuable to psychology in the first two decades of this century, but that by the 1940's and 1950's behavioral psychology and technical philosophy of science had passed him by.      Sarbin mentioned that the time of Kantor's early writings, the 1920's, was also a factor in his lack of influence:

> Psychology was entering a mechanistic (S-R) phase.
> Interbehaviorism was better adapted to narrative
> explanations, therefore Kantor's influence was not
> widespread...By the time psychology became interested
> in social (i.e., human) problems, Kantor's work was
> dated.

On a more social note, one respondent said that the influence of interbehavioral psychology was profound and diffuse at the time when behaviorism had some flexibility in it.    Blackman    made a similar point and tied it in with a comment on the relevance of Kantor's approach for contemporary psychology.

Many respondents, however, were much more positive in their estimations of Kantor's influence.    One said that all modern behaviorism, especially behavior analysis, has been influenced by Kantor in ways that were uncited and untraced.  The mechanisms for this influence were attributed to several sources.  For instance, one respondent said that Kantor had had a positive influence on Skinner, which we illustrated earlier in the chapter . Two more commented that his influence was widely disseminated through Bijou and Baer's books.   Both Catania and Patterson mentioned that Kantor had been an influential teacher, which seems to be another likely means by which his views have become known. Finally, Erikson and one other respondent asserted that an important reason for Kantor's apparent lack of influence was that he was ahead of his time, that what he offered psychology was too early and too soon to be appreciated.  In this regard, Schoenfeld (1969) suggested that

> Sometimes the work of a man of scholarhsip and
> intellectual daring plunges ahead of the learned
> community he is addressing, it does not immediately
> receive the honor it deserves.  Instead, it blends
> unmarked into the scholarly landscape, it becomes
> somehow taken for granted.  Something like this
> has happened to the writings of J.R. Kantor (p. 329).

Of those respondents who commented on the future influence Kantor and his system   are likely to have, almost all were very positive.  Bijou, for instance, said that he was very enthusiastic about the potential of Kantor's system.  Eckerman noted that contemporary psychology is now "...in a structuralist phase.   Hopefully, the next antithesis will read Kantor to aid in bringing a functional theme back."  Brady made similar comments and was a little more specific about what Kantor's influence would be. With respect to basic research, he felt that the clearest impact would be in "areas involving interdisciplinary activities like physiological psychology and the currently fashionable 'neuroscience' craze." Another respondent mentioned that the new emphasis on "contextual" determinants of behavior, conditioning, and memory will make Kantor's work worth restudy and application. With respect to applied work, Wahler and Schnelle both commented on the importance Kantor's ecological orientation has for the future. Wahler, in particular, was adamant:

> His work will ultimately be recognized as an important set of guidelines in applied behavior analysis. Once proponents of applied behavior analysis discover the crucial importance of the complete ecosystem, Kantor's contributions will attain greater value than they have now.

Another respondent mentioned that applied behavior analysts who work in institutions and other circumscribed settings have been able thus far to ignore historical variables and the ecological context of behavior, but that as they attempt to analyze more complex problems, Kantor's position on the role of the organism's behavioral history and on behavioral fields may prove increasingly useful. Finally, Bijou, McKearney, and Patterson mentioned that although the evolution of psychology may move towards Kantor's system, these changes will not necessarily be attributed to him, but to other approaches, most notably interactional psychology systems theory, ecological psychology, contextualism, transactionism, and parts of radical behaviorism.

## Compatibility and Incompatibility

Comments from our respondents on the compatibility or incompatibility of interbehavioral psychology and behavior analysis were clearly in favor of their compatibility--by about three-to-one. And, of the comments on their incompatibility, most of them seemed more a matter of emphasis than necessarily true. A sympathetic reading of the behavior analysis literature, especially of Skinner's writings, by interbehavioral psychologists, and a sympathetic reading of the interbehavioral literature by behavior analysts would likely dispel some of these apparent incompatibilities. In this regard, Baer commented, quite accurately we think, that the incompatibilities reflect not so much differences in principle as unnecessary "tribal hostilities."

**Incompatibility.** A number of apparent incompatibilities were mentioned by our respondents, though in each case the radical behavioral literature makes it clear that the incompatibilities are probably misunderstandings or stem from a failure to distinguish between radical behaviorism as the philosophy of science of behavior (Skinner, 1974) and what some radical behaviorists do or do not do. Some respondents described possible differences between the two systems in the admissability of private events into the science of behavior. Moore (1975, 1980, 1981), however, illustrates the compatibility of the two approaches on this point. Others mentioned that radical behaviorism tended to be mechanistic, while interbehavioral psychology was historical and contextualistic (cf. Pepper, 1942; Sarbin, 1977). Skinner (1938, pp. 433, 436-437; 1974, p. 222 ), however, has often argued against the usefulness of mechanistic models of human activity. Finally, another respondent said that radical behaviorists were closed to new principles of behavior, whereas interbehavioral psychologists remained open to new principles and relationships. Skinner (1938, p. 438), however, clearly states that it would be an anomaly in science if more than one variable were not found as a scientific system was developed. Indeed, radical behaviorists have prided themselves on advocating the inductive development of an open system (cf. Skinner, 1950, 1956).

Several other differences were also noted that are more a matter of emphasis than of principle. For instance, one respondent mentioned that the logic of scientific development for radical behaviorists was to attack simple problems and relationships before proceeding to complex cases, whereas interbehavioral psychologists preferred to go directly to complex problems in their natural context. Another difference of this same type was the linear functional relationship described by radical behaviorists in comparison to the field system of the interbehavioral psychologists (cf. Mountjoy, 1976, pp. 14-15). It was also mentioned that the practitioners of the two systems tended to ask questions of a different sort, and not that one set of questions was better than the other.

More difficult to reconcile, however, were a number of additional points. Brady mentioned that he felt that radical behaviorists sometimes "appear to persist in the conceptual error of regarding their subject matter (i.e., behavior) as a property of the organism rather than as a unique product of the interaction between organism and environment." Another important issue which was raised was that of the status of reinforcement and operant behavior in the analysis of behavior. To the interbehaviorist, reinforcement and operant behavior are just another facet of conditioning (cf. Kantor and Smith, 1975), and conditioning is only a minor part of the development of stimulus and response functions. For radical behaviorsts, however, reinforcement and operant behavior tend to be central to the principles of behavioral development. Parrott (1982) and Kantor, himself (1970) have commented cogently on this apparent incompatibility.

**Compatibility.** Despite these potential problems, most of the respondents pointed to the very strong compatibility of the two approaches. Among the respondents who said the systems are compatible in one way or another were Baer, Baum, Bijou, Blackman, Brady, Breiling, Catania, Eckerman, Holland, McKearney, Moore, Patterson, Pennypacker, Sarbin, and Shull.

The dimensions of this compatibility range from their fundamental philosophy to the details by which they attacked specific problems in psychology. Among their compatibilities in fundamental philosophy were their naturalism, functionalism, interactionism, holism, anti-mentalism, non-reductionism, operationism, and parsimony. With respect to any possible differences here, Moore wrote:

> Interbehavioral psychology is in many ways a more
> abstract summation and integration of many of the
> assumptions expressed more technically and partic-
> uarly in radical behaviorism. I do not mean, however,
> that either is superior theoretically...Interbehavioral
> psychology is simply on a more abstract level.

In a similar comment, Erickson said that her impression was that "interbehavioral psychology is more elegant in its conceptualization of the history and current stimulus environment of the organism." McKearney, however, provided a useful perspective on these points: "Interbehavioral psychology is more comprehensive in its field orientation, but this may be a broadness that is possible only for an approach that relies more on the armchair than the laboratory."

In a comment that is relevant to why interbehavioral psychology has apparently not been influential, Baer said that "...the research and application that embodies it embodies radical behaviorism a la Skinner just as well, and far more economically." In similar comments, two other respondents said that the positions fit together so well that a slight revision of radical behaviorism ends up incorporating most of the value of Kantor's position. With this, these respondents could maintain one position (radical behaviorism) to do the work of both.

In addition to the compatibilities of this philosophical level were those relating to more detailed analyses of a broad range of psychological behavior. Of those specifically mentioned were their compatibility in the areas of perception, feeling, thinking, language, and, as Breiling put it, "the power and complexity of 'behaving' that is done within the body and for which there often do not appear to be clear, immediate, and distinctive behavioral manifestations." In summary, the compatibility of the two approaches was clearly evident in the answers of our respondents, and is consistent with the conclusions of the present authors (cf. Morris, 1981).

72

## Evaluation of Kantor's Influence

Having examined the historical record and presented the results of our questionnaire study, we now offer an evaluation of the influence Kantor has had on contemporary behaviorism, and on the contributions he and his thinking may have for the future.

### The Historical Record

First, we may say of the results of our literature search and the questionnaire that Kantor has had a profound influence on some behavior analysts, but that their number is limited. We think, however, that this limitation is more apparent than real. Several respondents to the questionnaire were clear in pointing out that Kantor's influence has been substantial, but unrecognized. Moreover, other respondents qualified their comments by stating that they could not explicitly ascertain the influence Kantor had on them. They said that because Kantor's influence was so much a part of the academic milieu in which they were educated and in which they continue to work that his views and theirs were often indistinguishable. The most common mechanism for transmitting this influence was Kantor's students who tended to be dedicated teachers, rather than well-known research scientists.

### Contemporary Behaviorism

As pointed out by Schoenfeld (1969) and by many of our respondents, contemporary behaviorism has moved in the directions Kantor has been advocating, even if Kantor's contribution has gone unnoticed or even if he has contributed nothing to these changes. But what about the current and future practice of behaviorism? Let us examine the influence of Kantor's ideas in this regard, or at least the changes that might be consonant with this approach. In doing this, we will comment on each of the three primary divisions within the field--basic research, applied research, and theory.

**Basic Research.** In the area of basic research, Nevin (1980) published a **JEAB** editorial that made points similar to those raised in Kantor's TEAB paper. In assuming the role as editor of **JEAB** Nevin wrote,

> I believe that it is essential that we attract work
> on topics that have received little attention in this
> journal, such as taste aversion learning, and in areas
> that are just now developing in verbal behavior and
> other complex processes that have tempted some into
> a cognitive orientation (p. ii).

In line with Kantor's and Nevin's positions, we have seen a growth in behavior analysis in this direction in the past ten years.

First, on a conceptual level, we should cite the **JEAB** publication of Michael's (1982) article in which he argues for a new term--"establishing operation"--to refer to operations on the organism, such as deprivation, that have effects different from those of discriminative stimuli: It "alters the effectiveness of some object or event as reinforcement and simultaneously alters the momentary frequency of the behavior that has been followed by that reinforcement " (pp. 150-151). In making this distinction, Michael added in a footnote that "Students of J.R. Kantor may see some similarity here to his term 'setting factor,' but I believe that his term includes operations that have a broader or less specific effect on behavior than the establishing operation..." Despite this qualification, which we believe to be an accurate one, the publication of this paper suggests that TEAB is displaying an increasing appreciation for distinguishing among sources of multiple determination and has begun to focus more on the broader contextual determinants of behavior. Both of these changes are consonant with Kantor's approach.

At an empirical level, we can also see the development of research in areas Kantor has been emphasizing as being in need. For instance, behavior analysts have conducted research with humans and infrahumans in areas traditionally left to cognitive psychologists, such as concept formation (e.g., Dixon, 1977; Sidman, Cresson and Willson-Morris, 1974; Sidman, 1979), memory (Jans and Catania, 1980; Kendrick, Rilling and Stonebraker, 1981), problem-solving(e.g., Parsons, Taylor, and Joyce, 1981), self-awareness (e.g., Epstein, Lanza, and Skinner, 1981), self-control (e.g., Grosch and Neuringer, 1981), language (e.g., Lee, 1981), emotion (e.g., Brady and Emurian, 1979) and on behavioral hierarchies and broader segments of human beahvior (e.g., Bernstein, 1978; Bernstein and Ebbesen, 1978; Emurian, Emurian , Bigelow and Brady, 1976). Even within the more traditional topics of operant research, such as drug effects on behavior, investigators are emphasizing the need to adopt a systems perspective in order to give greater consideration to multiple control and historical causation (cf. McKearney and Barrett, 1977). Along similar lines, more   recognition is being given to the previously unrecognized relationships  operating in human schedule performance (cf. Lowe, 1979).   Progress is also being made in the analysis of complex human social interactions such as trust (Hake and Schmid, 1981) and cooperation (e.g., Hake and Olvera, 1978). Consonant with Kantor's (1970) call for examining more than "rewards," we see the emergence of research on the multiple effects of reinforcing stimuli and their patterns of delivery. Of interest here is the research on adjunctive behavior (Falk, 1971; Hamm, Porter and Kaempf, 1981), autoshaping (e.g., Brown and Jenkins, 1969; Prem ck and Klipec, 1981), shock-maintained behavior (e.g., Gardner and Malagodi, 1981; Kelleher and Morse, 1968; Malagodi,

Gardner, Ward and Magyar, 1981), and superstition (e.g., Sizemore, and Lattal, 1977; Staddon and Simmelhag, 1971).

Overall, this growth in the experimental analysis of behavior reflects, perhaps, the pressure Day (1980) sees within radical behaviorism "...to develop new and innovative research strategies capable of assessing variables controlling behavior in nonlaboratory situations" (p. 222). Whatever the source of this pressure, these developments are clearly in line changes called for by Kantor (1970) in his TEAB paper.

**Applied Research.** In applied behavior analysis, research and conceptual analysis are also progressing in directions consonant with interbehavioral psychology. With respect to conceptual issues, Grossberg (1981) has recently cited Kantor extensively in arguing for an interactive perspective towards behavior therapy, as opposed to simple-minded cognitive or mechanistic approaches. Kanfer and Karoly (1972) had commented on this issue before:

> Almost 50 years ago, Kantor (1924) argued eloquently
> against the use of psychology of metaphysical abstrac-
> tions, which find extreme representations in the
> "bodyless mind" of the psychists and the "mindless
> body" of the mechanists. His analysis retains its
> timeliness (p. 399).

Generating greater interest in the field, however, has been the recent emphasis on behavioral ecology (e.g., Harshbarger and Maley, 1976; Rogers-Warren and Warren, 1977; Williams, 1974). This concern with the ecological setting centers on these points: (a) The complex nature of the activities occurring within organism-environment interactions must be more fully taken into account, (b) change in one domain may have multiple effects on others, and (c) both positive and negative side-effects may be produced. Handy (1973, p. 322) mentioned the need for applied behavior analysts to adopt this perspective in 1973. The most recent statement of concern over these matters comes from Wahler and Fox's recent **JABA** article (1981) in which the authors make a case for including Kantor's concept of setting factors within applied behavior analysis. This conceptual expansion, they argue, encourages a more complete analysis of the complex conditions of the behavioral ecology, which will be necessary as behavioral psychologists begin to broaden their units of measurement and analysis across behaviors, settings, and time. Also important, Wahler and Fox said there is a need to know more about how temporally distant events affect current and future organism-environment interactions (cf. Fowler and Baer, 1980) and about how these events affect initial behavior change (Krantz and Risley, 1977). response generalization (cf. Peterson, Merwin, Mayer and

75

Whitehurst, 1971; Steinman, 1970; Rincover and Koegel, 1975), and response maintenance (cf. Wahler, 1980). The authors conclude by stating that the inclusion of the setting factor concept within the functional analysis of behavior will serve an important heuristic function--better questions will be asked and more fruitful hypotheses generated (e.g., Patterson, 1978).

In addition to these conceptual considerations, applied behavior analysts are also moving with increasing sophistication into complex problems of application, such as in behavioral medicine (e.g., Katz and Zlutnick, 1975), language training (MacDonald, in press), community psychology (e.g., Glenwick and Jason, 1980; Neitzel, Winett, McDonald, and Davidson, 1977), program evaluation (e.g., Davidson, Koch and Lewis, 1981), and social validity (e.g., Kazdin, 1977; Wolf, 1978). Again, these changes are clearly in line with the emphasis of an interbehavioral orientation.

**Theory.** In recent years, behavior analysts have begun to focus more attention on the history, theory, and philosophy of behaviorism, a trend that is clearly consonant with Kantor's interests. For many years, Kantor has argued that it is essential to scrutinize one's theoretical assumptions in order to clarify how cultural variables affect the hypotheses, experimental methodology, and data interpretation of beahvioral scientists (Kantor, 1963, 1969). Among these issues of special interest to interbehavioral psychologists being discussed in journals such as **Behaviorism** are the need to distinguish between the different varieties of behaviorism (e.g., Kitchner, 1977); the unrecognized mentalistic assumptions of methodological behaviorism (e.g., Moore, 1975, 1981); scientific practice and epistemology (e.g., Zuriff, 1980); causation (e.g., Staddon, 1973); and language (Powell and Still, 1979; Tweney, 1979). Over and above this, the theoretical foundations of contemporary behaviorism and psychology are evolving into more of an interactional, contextual, or transactional model--a model that is clearly Kantorian.

## Conclusion

The interests and perspectives of contemporary behaviorists are clearly evolving, as are those of psychologists in general--both of them in directions compatible with those urged by Kantor. Examples of the former have been described throughout this chapter. Examples of the latter can be seen in the adoption of field ecological perspectives in psychology, especially in the areas of perception, development, and in the adoption of interactive approaches within social learning theory and personality theory.

Despite the positive evaluation we have made of Kantor's past, present, and future contributions to contemporary behaviorism, we feel that it is proper to conclude this chapter with a more conservative evaluation. Some of the intellectual foundations behind the changes, and prospects for future change, which we have described, clearly come from Kantor, either directly or indirectly. We suspect, however, that this is not true for most of the changes the field has seen and is likely to see in the future. Rather, many of the trends we have described reflect changes in the field of behavioral sciences necessitated by the complex nature of the subject matter. Nonetheless, if contemporary behaviorism and the rest of psychology are evolving in these directions, then although Kantor may exert little influence over these trends, he does offer a rich and appropriate literature for how they might promote further change consonant with their basic metatheoretical assumptions. Moreover, if Kantor was once ahead of his time, as some of our questionnaire respondents noted, then perhaps he still is. If so, then behavior analysts may look to him and his interbehavioral psychology for future directions in the field, especially as they attempt to promote a comprehensive and logical system of behavioral science.

## Acknowledgments

An abbreviated version of this chapter was presented as the introduction to an invited symposium at the 1981 meeting of the Association for Behavior Analysis held in Milwaukee. The symposium, entitled, "The Relevance of Interbehavioral Psychology for Behavioral Research," was chaired by Edward K. Morris. The other papers presented on that symposium were by J.W. McKearney, S.W. Bijou, and D.M. Cone; P.T. Mountjoy served as discussant. We would like to thank Donald M. Baer and Nancy J. Wert for their assistance in developing the questionnaire described herein, as well as those who completed and returned the questionnaire to us.

## References

Bernstein, D.J. 1982. (Ed.) **Response Structure and Organization: Nebraska Symposium on Motivation.** Lincoln: University Of Nebraska Press.

Bernstein,D.J. and Ebbesen, E. B. 1978. Reinforcement and substitution in humans: A multiple-response analysis. **Journal of the Experimental Analysis of Behavior,** 30, 243-253.

Bijou, S. W. 1976. **Child Development: The Basic Stage of Early Childhood.** Englewood Cliffs, N.J.: Prentice-Hall.

Bijou, S.W. 1981a. Child development and interbehavioral psychology. Presented at the meeting of the Association for Behavior Analysis, Milwaukee, May.

Bijou, S.W. 1981b. Interbehavior analysis of developmental retardation. **Psychological Record**, 31, 305-329.

Bijou, S.W. and Baer, D.M. 1961. **Child Development I: A Systematic and Empirical Theory**. Englewood Cliffs, N.J.: Prentice-Hall.

Bijou, S.W. and Baer, D.M. 1965. **Child De velopment II: Univesal State of Infancy**. Englewood Cliffs, N.J.: Prentice-Hall.

Bijou, S.W. and Baer, D.M. 1978. **Behavior Analysis of Child Development**. Englewood Cliffs, N.J.: Prentice-Hall.

Brady, J.V. 1975. Toward a behavioral theory of emotion. In L. Levi (Ed.) **Emotions: Their Parameters and Measurements.** New York: Raven Press.

Brady, J.V. and Emurian, H.H. 1979. Behavior analysis of motivational interactions in a programmed environment. In R.A. Dienstbier (Ed.) **NebraskaSymposium on Motivation** (Vol. 26). Lincoln: University of Nebraska Press.

Branch, M.N. 1977. On the role of "memory" in the analysis of behavior. **Journal of the Experimental Analysis of Behavior,** 28, 171-179.

Branch, M.N. and Malagodi, E.F. 1980. Where have all the behaviorists gone? **The Behavior Analyst,** 3, 31-38.

Brown, P.L. and Jenkins, H.M. 1968. Auto-shaping of the pigeon's key-peck. **Journal of the Experimental Analysis of Behavior,** 11, 1-8.

Burgess, R.L. and Akers, R.L. 1966. Are operant procedures tautological? **The Psychological Record,** 16, 305-312.

Cairns, B.B. 1979. **Social Development: The Origins and Plasticity of Interchanges.** San Francisco: W. H. Freeman.

Capshew, J.H. and Hearst, E. 1980. Psychology at Indiana University: From Bryan to Skinner· **Psychological Record,** 30, 319-342.

Carter, J.A. 1937. A case of reactional dissociation (hysterical paralysis). **American Journal of Orthopsychiatry,** 7, 219-224.

Cone, D. 1981. Behavioral applications: Complexity of the true state of affairs. Presented at the meeting of the Association for Behavior Analysis, Milwaukee, May.

Cook, S.W. and Skinner, B.F. 1939. Some factors influencing the distribution of associated words. **Psychological Record,** 3, 178-184.

Davidson, W.S., Koch, J.R., Lewis, R.G. and Wrensinski, M.D. 1981. **Evaluation Strategies in Criminal Justice.** New York: Pergamon.

Day, W.F. 1980. The historical antecedents of contemporary behaviorism. In R.W. Rieber and K. Salzinger (Eds.) **Psychology: Theoretical-Historical Perspectives.** New York: Academic Press.

Delprato, D.J. 1980. Interbehavioral psychology as a palliative to the excess of cognitionism. Presented at the meeting of the Association for Behavior Analysis, Dearborn, May.

Delprato, D.J. and Holmes, P.A. 1980. Interbehaviorism: A non-reductionistic alternative to the heredity-environment question. Presented at the meeting of the American Psychological Association, Montreal, September.

Dinsmoor, J.A. 1980. 1947-1950: The first CEAB's. Presented at the meeting of the Association for Behavior Analysis, Dearborn, Michigan, May.

Dixon, L.S. 1977. The nature of control by spoken words over visual stimulus selection. **Journal of the Experimental Analysis of Behavior,** 27, 433-442.

Emurian, H.H., Emurian, C.S., Bigelow, G.E. and Brady, J.V. 1976. The effects of a cooperation contingency on behavior in a continuous three-person environment. **Journal of the Experimental Analysis of Behavior,** 25, 293-302.

Epstein, R., Lanza, R.P. and Skinner,B.F. 1981. "Self-awareness" in the pigeon. **Science,** 212, 695-696.

Falk, J.L. 1971. The nature and determinants of adjunctive behavior. **Physiology and Behavior,** 6, 577-588.

Ferster, C.B. 1967. Arbitrary and natural reinforcement. **Psychological Record,** 17, 341-347.

Ferster, C.B. and Simmons, J. 1966. Behavior therapy with children. **Psychological Record,** 16, 65-72.

Ferster, C.B. and Skinner, B.F. 1957. **Schedules of Reinforcement.** Englewood Cliffs, N.J.: Prentice-Hall

Fowler, S.A. and Baer, D.M. 1981. "Do I have to be good all day?" The timing of delayed reinforcement as a factor in generalization. **Journal of Applied Behavior Analysis,** 14, 13-24.

Fuller, P.R. 1949. Operant conditionign of a vegetative human organism. **American Journal of Psychology,** 62, 587-590.

Fuller, P.R. 1973. Professors Kantor and Skinner--the "grand alliance" of the 40's. **Psychological Record,** 23, 318-324.

Gardner, M.L. and Malgodi, E.F. 1981. Responding under sequence schedules of electric shock presentation. **Journal of the Experimental Analysis of Behavior,** 35, 323-334.

Gewirtz, J.L. 1969. Mechanisms of social learning: Some roles of stimulation and behavior in early human development. In D.A. Goslin (Ed.) **Handbook of Socialization Theory and Research.** Chicago: Rand McNally.

Gewirtz, J.L. 1972. Some contextual determinants of stimulus potency. In R.D. Parke (Ed.) **Recent Trends in Social Learning Theory.** New York: Academic Press.

Gibson, J.J. 1979. **The Ecological Approach to Visual Perception.** Boston: Houghton-Mifflin.

Glenwick, D. and Jason, L. (Eds.) 1980. **Behavioral Community Psychology: Progress and Prospects.** New York: Praeger.

Goodall, K. 1972. Shapers at work. **Psychology Today,** 6, 53-62, 132-138.

Grosch, J. and Neuringer, A. 1981. Self-control in pigeons under the Mischel paradigm. **Journal of the Experimental Analysis of Behavior,** 35, 3-21.

Grossberg, J.M. 1981. Comments about cognitive therapy and behavior therapy. **Journal of Behavior Therapy and Experimental Psychiatry,** 7, 25-33.

Hake, D.F. and Olvera, D. 1978. Cooperation, competition, and related social phenomena. In A.C. Catania and T.A. Brigham (Eds.) **Handbook of Applied Behavior Analysis: Social and Instructional Processes.** New York: Irvington.

Hake, D.F. and Schmid, T.L. 1981. Acquisition and maintenance of trusting behavior. **Journal of the Experimental Analysis of Behavior,** 35, 109-124.

Hamm, R.J., Porter, J.H. and Kaempf, G.L. 1981. Stimulus generalization of schedule-induced polydipsia. **Journal of the Experimental
Analysis of Behavior,** 36, 93-99.

Handy, R. 1973. The Dewey-Bentley transactional procedures of
inquiry. **Psychological Record,** 23, 305-317.

Harshbarger, D. and Maley, R.F. (Eds.) 1974. **Behavior Analysis
and Systems Analysis: An Integrative Approach to Mental
Health Programs.** Kalamazoo: Behaviordelia.

Harzem, P. and Miles, T.R. 1978. **Conceptual Issues in Operant
Behavior.** New York: Wiley.

Heron, W.T. and Skinner, B.F. 1937. Changes in hunger during
starvation. **Psychological Record** , 3, 166-176.

Heron, W.T. and Skinner, B.F. 1939. An apparatus for the experimental
study of animal behavior. **Psychological Record,** 3, 166-176.

Heron, W.T. and Skinner, B.F. 1940. The rate of extinction in
maze-bright and maze-dull rats. **Psychological Record,** 4,
11-18.

Homme, L.E. 1965. Perspectives in psychology XXIV. Control
of coverants, the operants of the mind. **Psychological Record,**
15, 501-511.

Jans, J.E. and Catania, A.C. 1980. Short-term remembering of
discriminative stimuli in pigeons. **Journal of the Experimental
Analysis of Behavior,** 34, 177-183.

Kanfer, F.H. and Karoly, P. 1972. Self-control: A behavioristic
excursion into the lion's den. **Behavior Therapy,** 3, 398-416.

Kanfer, F.H. and Phillips, J.S. 1970. **Learning Foundations of
Behavior Therapy.** New York: John Wiley.

Kantor, J.R. 1920a. Suggestions toward a scientific interpretation
of perception. **Psychological Review,** 27, 191-216.

Kantor, J.R. 1920b. A functional interpretation of human instincts.
**Psychological Review,** 27, 50-72.

Kantor, J.R. 1922. An analysis of psychological language data.
**Psychological Review,** 29, 267-309.

Kantor, J.R. 1924. **Principles of Psychology** (Vol. I). Granville,
Ohio: Principia Press.

Kantor, J.R. 1926. **Principles of Psychology.**(Vol. II). Granville, Ohio: Principia Press.

Kantor, J.R. 1933. In defense of stimulus-response psychology. **Psychological Review,** 40, 324-336.

Kantor, J.R. 1936. **Objective Psychology of Grammar.** Bloomington, Indiana: Principia Press.

Kantor, J.R. 1945. **Psychology and Logic** (Vol. I). Bloomington, Indiana: Principia Press.

Kantor, J.R. 1947. **Problems in Physiological Psychology.** Bloomington, Indiana: Principia Press.

Kantor, J.R. 1950. **Psychology and Logic** (Vol. II). Bloomington, Indiana: Principia Press.

Kantor, J.R. 1959. **Interbehavioral Psychology.** Granville, Ohio: Principia Press.

Kantor, J.R. 1963. **The Scientific Evolution of Psychology** (Vol. I). Granville, Ohio: Principia Press.

Kantor, J.R. 1969. **The Scientific Evolution of Psychology** (Vol. II). Granville, Ohio: Principia Press.

Kantor, J.R. 1970. An analysis of the experimental analysis of behavior (TEAB). **Journal of the Experimental Analysis of Behavior,** 13, 101-108.

Kantor, J.R. 1971. **The Aim and Progress of Psychology and Other Sciences.** Chicago, Ill.: Principia Press.

Katz, R.C. and Zlutnick, S. 1975. **Behavior Therapy and Health Care: Principles and Application.** New York: Pergamon Press.

Kazdin, A.E. 1977. Assessing the clinical or applied importance of behavior change through social validation. **Behavior Modification,** 1, 427-452.

Kelleher, R.T. and Morse, W.H. 1968. Schedules using noxious stimuli, III: Responding maintained with response produced electric shocks. **Journal of the Experimental Analysis of Behavior,** 11, 819-838.

Keller, F.S. and Schoenfeld,W.S. 1950. **Principles of Psychology.**
Englewood Cliffs, N.J.: Prentice-Hall.

Killeen, P., Wald, B. and Cheney, C.D. 1980. Observing behavior
and information. **Psychological Record,** 30, 131-190.

Kitchener, R.F. 1977. Behavior and behaviorism. **Behaviorism,**
5, 11-17.

Krantz, P.J. and Risley, T.R. 1977. Behavioral ecology in the
classroom. In S.G. O'Leary and K.D. O'Leary (Eds.) **Classroom
Management: The Successful Use of Behavior Modification.**
New York: Pergamon Press.

Krasner, L. 1977. An interview with Sidney W. Bijou. In B.C.
Etzel, J.M. LeBlanc and D.M. Baer (Eds.) **New Developments
in Behavioral Research: Theory, Methods, and Application.**
Hillsdale, N.J.: Lawrence Erlbaum Associates.

Krasner, L. 1979. History of a revolutionary paradigm? Review
of A. E. Kazdin's **History of Behavior Modification.**
**Contemporary Psychology,** 24, 1-2.

Krechevesky, I. 1939. Review of Skinner's **The Behavior of Organisms.**
**Journal of Abnormal and Social Psychology,** 34, 404-407.

LaShier, C.J. 1974. B.F. Skinner on motivation: A critique.
**The Interbehaviorist,** 5, 4-9.

Lee, V.L. 1981. Prepositional phrases spoken and heard. **Journal
of the Experimental Analysis of Behavior,** 35, 227-242.

Lichtenstein, P.E. 1973. Discussion: "Contextual interactionists."
**Psychological Record,** 23, 325-333.

Lowe, C.F. 1979. Determinants of human operant behavior.
In M.D. Zeiler and P. Harzem (Eds.) **Reinforcement and the
Organization of Behavior.** New York: John Wiley.

MacDonald, J.D. in press. Language through conversation: A
communication model for language intervention. In S.F.
Warren and A. Rogers-Warren (Eds.) **Teaching Functional
Language.** Baltimore: University Park Press.

Malone, J.C. 1975. Stimulus-specific contrast effects during operant
discrimination learning. **Journal of the Experimental Analysis
of Behavior,** 24, 281-289.

Malone, J.C. and Staddon, J.E.R. 1973. Contrast effects in maintained generalization gradients. **Journal of the Experimental Analysis of Behavior,**19, 167-179.

McKearney, J.W. and Barrett, J.E. 1978. Schedule-controlled behavior and the effects of drugs. In D. E. Blackman and J.D. Danger (Eds.) **Contemporary Research in Behavioral Pharmacology.** New York: Plenum.

McKearney, J.W. 1981. Organism-environment relations in the analysis of behavior. Presented at the meeting of the Association of Behavior Analysis, Milwaukee, May.

Michael, J. 1982. Distinguishing between discriminative and motivational functions of stimuli. **Journal of the Experimental Analysis of Behavior,** 57, 149-155.

Moore, J. 1975. On the principle of operationsim in a science of behavior. **Behaivorism,** 3, 120-138.

Moore, J. 1980. On behaviorism and private events. **Psychological Record,** 30, 459-475.

Moore, J. 1981. On mentalism, methodological behaviorism, and radical behaviorism. **Behaviorism,** 9, 55-77.

Morris, E. K. 1979. Some relationships between the psychologies of Kantor and Skinner. Presented at the meeting of the Association for Behavior Analysis, Dearborn, June.

Morris, E.K. 1980a. The evolution of interbehavioral psychology and radical behaviorism. Presented at the meeting of the Association for Behavior Analysis, Dearborn, May.

Morris, E.K. 1980b. Historical and philosophical evolution of interbehaviorism and radical behaviorism. Presented at the meeting of the American Psychological Association, Montreal, September.

Morris, E.K., Higgins, S.T. and Bickel, W.K. 1981. The influence of Kantor's interbehavioral psychology on behavior analysis. Presented at the meeting of the Association for Behavior Analysis, Milwaukee, May (and in press in **The Behavior Analyst**).

Morris, E.K., Higgins, S.T. and Bickel, W.K. 1982. Cogniphilia and cogniphobia in behavioral science. Presented at the meeting of the Association for Behavior Analysis, Milwaukee, May.

Morris, E.K. and Hursh, D.E. 1979. Some basic considerations and concepts. Presented at the meeting of the American Psychological Association, New York, September.

Mountjoy, P.T. 1976. Science in psychology: J.R. Kantor's field theory. **Mexican Journal of Behavior Analysis,** 2, 3-21.

Mountjoy, P.T. 1980a. The interrelationships between interbehavioral psychology and radical behaviorism. Presented at the meeting of the Association for Behavior Analysis, Dearborn, May.

Mountjoy, P.T. 1980b. Conceptual relationships between inter-behaviorism and radical behaviorism. Presented at the meeting of the American Psychological Association, Montreal, September.

Neitzel, M.T., Winett, R.A., McDonald, M.L. and Davidson, W.S. 1977. **Behavioral Approaches to Community Psychology.** New York: Pergamon Press.

Nevin, J.A. 1980. Editorial. **Journal of The Experimental Analysis of Behavior,** 33, i-ii.

Observer. 1981. Priority and the pace of scientific progress. **Psychological Record,** 31, 285-292.

Parrott, L.J. 1980a. Radical- and inter-behavioral perspectives on knowing. Presented at the meeting of the Association for Behavior Analysis, Dearborn, May.

Parrott, L.J. 1980b. Beyond radical behaviorism: The interbehavioral alternative. Presented at the meeting of the Association for Behavior Analysis, Dearborn, May.

Parrott, LJ. 1982. Psychology as an interdisciplinary science. Presented at the meeting of the Association for Behavior Analysis, Milwaukee, May.

Parsons, J.A. , Taylor, D. C. and Joyce, T.M. 1981. Precurrent self-prompting operants in children: "Remembering." **Journal of the Experimental Analysis of Behavior,** 36, 253-266.

Patterson, G.R. 1978. A performance theory for coercive family interactions. In R.B. Cairns (Ed.) **The Analysis of Social Interactions: Methods, Analysis and Illustrations.** Chicago: University of Chicago Press.

Pepper, S.C. 1942. **World Hypotheses.** Berkeley, CA.: University of California Press.

Peterson, R.F., Merwin, M.R., Mayer, T.J. and Whitehurst, G.J. 1971. Generalized imitation: The effects of experimenter absence, differential reinforcement, and stimulus complexity. **Journal of Experimental Child Psychology**, 12, 114-128.

Picker, R.P., Poling, A. and Parker, A. 1979. A review of children's self-injurious behavior. **Psychological Record, 29,** 435-452.

Powell, R.P. and Still, A.W. 1979. Behaviorism and the psychology of language: An Historical reassessment. **Behaviorism, 7,** 71-89.

Premock, M. and Klipec, W.D. 1981. The effects of modifying consummatory behavior on the topography of the autoshaped pecking response in pigeons. **Journal of the Experimental Analysis of Behavior,** 36, 277-284.

Pronko, N.H. 1980. **Psychology from the Standpoint of an Interbehaviort.** Monterey, CA.: Brooks/Cole.

Rice, H.K. and McDaniel, M.W. 1966. Operant behavior in vegetative patients. **Psychological Record,** 16, 279-281.

Riegel, K. 1978. **Psychology, Mon Amour: A Countertext.** Boston: Houghton-Mifflin.

Rogers-Warren, A. and Warren, S.F. (Eds.) 1977. **Ecological Perspectives in Behavior Analysis.** Baltimore: University Park Press.

Salzinger, K. 1973. Inside the black box, with apologies to Pandora. A review of Ulric Neisser's **Cognitive Psychology. Journal of the Experimental Analysis of Behavior** , 19, 369-378.

Sarbin, T.R. 1977. Contextualism: A world view for modern psychology. In A.W. Landfield (Ed.) **Nebraska Symposium On Motivation** (Vol. 24). Lincoln: University of Nebraska Press.

Schoenfeld, W.N. 1969. J.R. Kantor's **Objective Psychology of Grammar** and **Psychology and Logic:** A retrospective appreciation. **Journal of the Experimental Analysis of Behavior,** 12, 329-347.

Shimp, C.P. 1976. Organization in memory and behavior. **Journal of the Experimental Analysis of Behavior,** 26, 113-130.

Sizemore, O.J. and Lattal, K.A. 1977. Dependency, temporal contiguity, and response-independent reinforcement. **Journal of the Experimental Analysis of Behavior,** 27, 119-125.

Sidman, M. 1979. Remarks. **Behaviorism,** 7, 123-126.

Sidman, M., Cresson, O., and Willson-Morris, M. 1974. Acquisition of matching to sample via mediated transfer. **Journal of the Experimental Analysis of Behavior,** 22, 251-273.

Skinner, B.F. 1937. The distribution of associated words. **Psychological Record,** 1, 71-76.

Skinner, B.F. 1938. **The Behavior of Organisms.** New York: Appleton-Century-Crofts.

Skinner, B.F. 1939. The alliteration in Shakespeare's sonnets: A study in literary behavior. **Psychological Record,** 3, 186-192.

Skinner, B.F. 1948. **Walden Two.** New York: MacMillan.

Skinner,B.F. 1950. Are theories of learning necessary? **Psychological Review,** 57, 193-216.

Skinner, B.F. 1953. **Science and Human Behavior.** New York: MacMillan.

Skinner,B.F. 1956. A case history in scientific method. **American Psychologist,** 11, 221-233.

Skinner, B.F. 1957. **Verbal Behavior.** Englewood Cliffs, N.J.: Prentice-Hall.

Skinner, B.F. 1967. B.F. Skinner. In E.G. Boring and G. Lindzey (Eds.) **A History of Psychology in Autobiography.** New York: Appleton-Century-Crofts.

Skinner, B.F. 1969. **Contingencies of Reinforcement.** Englewood Cliffs, N.J.: Prentice-Hall.

Skinner, B.F. 1972. **Cumulative Record.** Englewood Cliffs, N.J.: Prentice-Hall.

Skinner, B.F. 1974. **About Behaviorism.** New York: A.A. Knopf.

Skinner, B.F. 1979. **The Shaping of a Behaviorist.** New York: A.A. Knopf.

Skinner, B.F. and Heron, W.T. 1937. The effects of caffeine and benzedrine upon conditioning and extinction. **Psychological Record,** 1, 340-346.

Smith, N.W. 1976. The works of J.R. Kantor: Pioneer in scientific psychology. **Mexican Journal of Behavior Analysis**, 2, 137-148.

Staddon, J.E.R. 1973. On the notion of cause, with applications to behaviorism. **Behaviorism**, 1, 25-63.

Staddon, J.E.R. and Simmelhag, V.L. 1971. The "superstition" experiment: A reexamination of its implications for the principles of adaptive behavior. **Psychological Review**, 78, 3-43.

Stephenson, W. 1953. Postulates of behaviorism. **Philosophy of Science**, 20, 110-120.

Stevens, S.S. and Stove, G. 1947. Psychological writing, easy and hard. **American Psychologist**, 2, 230-245.

Tweney,R.D. 1979. Reflections on the history of behavioral theories of language. **Behaviorism**, 7, 91-103.

Ulrich,R., Stachnik, T. and Mabry, J. ( Eds.) 1966. **Control of Human Behavior.** Glenview, Ill.: Scott, Foresman and Co.

Verhave, T. and Own, J.E. 1958. The effects of Bulbo capine administration on avoidance behavior. **Psychological Record**, 8, 49-52.

Verplanck, W.S. 1954. Burrhus F. Skinner. In W.K. Estes, S. Koch, K. MacCorquodale, P.E. Meehl, C.G. Mueller, W.N. Schoenfeld and W.S. Verplanck (Eds.) **Modern Learning Theory: A Critical Analysis of Five Examples.** New York: Appleton-Century-Crofts.

Vukelich, R. and Hake, D.F. 1980. Basic research in a natural setting: Auditing or social comparison behavior as a function of class rank. **Psychological Record**, 30, 17-24.

Wahler, R.G. 1980. The insular mother: Her problems in parent-child treatment. **Journal of Applied Behavior Analysis**, 14, 327-338.

Wahler, R.G. and Fox, J.J. 1981. Setting events in applied behavior analysis: Toward a conceptual and methodological expansion. **Journal of Applied Behavior Analysis**, 14, 327-338.

Wasserman, E.A. 1981. Comparative psychology returns: A review of Hulse, Fowler and Henig's **Cognitive Processes in Animal Behavior.** Journal  **of the Experimental Analysis of Behavior,** 35, 243-257.

Wickramasekera, I. 1972. Instructions and EMG feedback in systematic desensitization: A case report. **Behavior Therapy,** 3, 460-465.

Williams, E.P. 1974. Behavioral technology and behavior ecology. **Journal of Applied Behavior Analysis,** 7, 151-165.

Winokur, S. 1971. Skinner's theory of behavior. An examination of B.F. Skinner's **Contingencies of Reinforcement: A Theoretical Analysis. Journal of the Experimental Analysis of Behavior,** 15, 253-259.

Wolf, M.M. 1978. Social validity: The case for subjective measurement. **Journal of Applied Behavior Analysis,** 11, 203-214.

Zuriff, G.E. 1980. Radical behaviorist epistemology. **Psychological Bulletin,** 87, 337-350.

# Part 2

# RESEARCH APPLICATIONS

# THE HISTORICAL DEVELOPMENT
# OF SCIENTIFIC PSYCHOLOGY

Donna M. Cone

Beginning students of psychology receive little, if any, exposure to the history of the subject as science. Those texts which contain a chapter on history generally list the names of several famous men, display a few dark portraits and proclaim that psychology became a science when it broke with philosophy and began conducting psychological experiments. A few lucky students may hear anecdotes about the famous men described in the text and fewer still may learn from their professors that history is not best understood as a genealogical exercise. For the most part, however, the beginning student is exposed to a superficial prologue.

The present paper will show that it is possible to introduce the beginning student to that complex set of interrelated intellectual movements and technological advances which comprise the history of scientific psychology. To do this, one need only follow the lead given by J.R. Kantor in his two volume work, **The Scientific Evolution of Psychology**(1963, 1969).

The chronological point at which one begins to study the history of any science depends greatly on one's definition of that science's subject matter. In their simplest form, the philosophical assumptions underlying science are naturalistic. This means that the subject matter of all sciences must be restricted to events which are confrontable, i.e., events which occur in time and space.

Psychology has had more difficulty than the other sciences in defining its subject matter. Even today, people in general do not regard psychology as a science in the sense that biology, chemistry, and physics are sciences. This failure to give psychology its proper place in the scheme of sciences is due to the continual influence of nonscientific cultural institutions. As a result of these influences, many people naively assume that psychology is the study of unique and private mental events. By their very definition, such events are not confrontable and therefore violate the philosophical assumptions which separate the sciences from the nonsciences.

The present paper sketches the historical development of authentic naturalistic psychology from its origin in Hellenic Greece (4th century BC) to the present. This general orientation to the history of psychology is based on the work of J.R.Kantor (1963, 1969).

## The Six Stages of the Development of Scientific Psychology

The development of scientific psychology can be divided into six stages or periods beginning approximately five hundred years before the birth of Christ.

## Stage 1: The Hellenic Period (4th Century BC)

During this period the naturalistic study of the behavior of living organisms was developed by the Greeks, especially Aristotle (384-322 BC). In a society which not only accepted naturalistic assumptions about the universe but which also provided stability and leisure for its scholars, great progress emerged in the objective analysis of both human and nonhuman behavior. Aristotle's psychology, contained in several treatises including **De Anima,** has a remarkably modern tone. While his work in psychology is clearly naive and not adequately differentiated from biology, it is clearly naturalistic since it does not appeal to unobservable forces for explanations of psychological events. Aristotle not only held objective attitudes about the nature of the universe but he also identified and classified a number of behaviors which constitute the nucleus of what is still regarded as the subject matter of scientific psychology. Among these are discrimination, memory and cognition, along with many others. He also inquired into the relationship among various classes of behavior and studied the origins and development of behaviors both within and between species.

Aristotle, of course, acknowledged his debt to his predecessors, for example, Socrates (469-399 BC), who set up a model for science. This model is derived from his more general use of the syllogism and consists of two aspects, the universal definition and the inductive procedure. Greek thinkers who viewed their universe as limited and bounded sought all-inclusive, or universal principles and conclusions. For psychology, such an emphasis on universal definitions serves to direct investigations toward behavioral essentials and aids in the analysis and description of these events. The inductive procedure indicates that the general propositions (or universal definitions) which psychology and the other sciences make arise from the study of particular natural events or samples of events.

92

## Stage 2:  The Hellenistic Period (ca. 300 BC-200 AD)

The transition from a naturalistic, scientifically-oriented culture to a supernaturalistic, religiously-oriented culture occurred gradually during the period of the Roman Empire.  The emphasis on observable events was replaced by increasing attention to, and reliance on, verbal substitutes for things.   Allegories and myths replaced scientific treatises.  Appeal to the authority of  earlier workers by citing their writings replaced the collection of new scientific data.   While the applied aspects of the physical and biological sciences (e.g., engineering and medicine) thrived, basic research, in which knowledge is sought for its own sake, declined.

The Roman intellectuals of the early Hellenistic period continued to use naturalistic models, but their subject matter shifted from the basic behavioral events to applied social matters.  The Cynics, Stoics, Skeptics, and Epicureans all sought to remove man from an increasingly chaotic and stressful world.  Thus, the way was paved for an acceptance of spiritual concepts, many of which originated in the Orient and were brought westward by traders and migrants.  The rise of a different social life centered around the nonscientific institution of religion, described by many writers. Murray's comments, quoted by Kantor (1963) are among the most colorful and often cited.   In part, he said:

> There is a change in the whole relation of the writer
> to the world about him...It is an atmosphere in which
> the aim of the good man is not so much to live justly,
> to help the society to which he belongs, and enjoy the
> esteem of his fellow creatures; but rather, by means
> of a burning faith, by contempt for the world and its
> standards, by ecstasy, suffering, and martyrdom, to be
> granted pardon for his unspeakable unworthiness, his
> immeasurable sin.  There is an intensifying of certain
> spiritual emotions; an increase in sensitiveness, a failure
> of nerve (pp. 230-231).

## Stage 3:  The Dark Ages (200-1200)

For our purposes, the central event of this millenium is the institution of the doctrine of dualism.   This doctrine assumes there are two worlds, the physical and the psychical.  The beginnings of this philosophical model are apparent in the writings of such early Christian Apologists as Tertullian (160-240 ?).  By the 4th century, the Syrian Nemesius had as his first proposition: "Man is composed of an understanding soul and body" (Kantor, 1963, p. 250).   The dualistic model was believed by writers of this period to represent the assumptions of Plato (427-347 BC) because of misinterpretations of Plato's works by the Roman, Plotinus (204-270). A century later, St.

Augustine (354-430), following the lead of Plotinus, completed the reinterpretation of Plato's works. For Augustine, the Soul (the psychical side of the dualistic model) was totally personal. It represented a microcosm of the universe, so that all experience became internal. Certainly the activities of such a Soul could not be studied scientifically! Hence arose the persistent belief that psychical events are private and unique.

St. Augustine represents the high watermark of anti-scientific attitudes among established philosophers and, at the same time, the low watermark in the historical development of scientific psychological.

### Stage 4: The Renaissance (13th-17 Century)

The word Renaissance means "rebirth." In general terms, the classical (or Hellenic) Greek values and interests were reawakened. In terms specific to the history of our science, an interest in the natural world was revived.

A key transitional figure during the early Renaissance was St. Thomas Aquinas (1225-1274). While fully dedicated to his role as a Catholic Theologian, St. Thomas contributed significantly to the slow return to an intellectual climate in which naturalistic sciences could flourish. Like other intellectuals of his time, St. Thomas had access to Arabic translations of Aristotle's **De Anima** . Despite the fact that St. Thomas retransformed the ideas of Aristotle to serve the needs of the Church, his promotion of this classical work assured that psychology would be given a chance to develop along with the other modern sciences.

Prior to St. Thomas' era, medieval society had begun to expand. The aspects of this growth which are of direct importance for the rebirth of science include: The founding of universities, which served as centers for intellectual activities; and the development of lenses, which made possible the invention of such scientific tools as telescopes and microscopes. Other more general aspects of the expansion which characterized late medieval and early Renaissance times, such as the growth of towns, the discovery of new lands, and the challenges to Church authority offered by leaders of the Protestant Reformation, helped to lessen the hold which the clergy and the nobility had on the lives of most individuals. As Kantor (1963, p. 329) expresses it: "Theology's monopoly of the realm of thought is broken to the extent, at least, that nature was accepted as a parallel to grace."

The first sciences to develop in this new intellectual atmosphere were astronomy, physics, and chemistry. This was the era of such eminent men as Copernicus (1473-1543), Galileo (1564-1642), Kepler

(1571-1630), Newton (1642-1727), van Helmont (1580-1644), and Boyle (1627-1691). The Copernican Revolution led to a rejection of Earth as the center of the universe and thereby stimulated interest in other planets and stars. Newton's laws contributed greatly to making physics the "Queen of the Sciences." In chemistry, the study of gases predominated.

Biology, and especially its applied branch, medicine, also advanced rapdily. Taxonomists gathered the data which would allow Linnaeus (1707-1778) to devise his famous classification system. The study of human anatomy thrived as da Vinci (1452-1519) and Vesalius (1514-1564) used data from dissections to challenge the authority of Galen (130-200). Harvey (1578-1657) also challenged Galenic authority on the nature of the circulation of the blood and helped to dispel culturally transmitted superstitions about the spontaneous generation of animals with his research in embryology. Leeuwenhoek (1632-1723) developed the microscope and first viewed human sperm. And, in toto, moden physiology was born with the scientific study of respiration.

The great philosophers of the 17th century laid the groundwork for psychology's acceptance as a member of the sciences. Now that people were relatively freed from political and religious domination, questions arose concerning their ability to govern themselves. The physical aspect of the dualistic universe was slowly changed from Soul to Mind, an evolution which Kantor calls the "naturalization of the soul."

This transmutation took various forms in the writings of Hobbes (1588-1679), Descartes (1596-1650), Leibniz (1646-1716), and Spinoza (1632-1677). The dualism of Descartes, called **Cartesian Dualism,** appears to be the most persistent form of this modernized dichotomization of the universe. Descartes was sensitive to the technological and scientific advances around him. He responded with the radical concept of man as a machine, but allowed psychical components to maintain control of the body via an area in the brain called the pineal gland. Descartes is often cited as the first physiological psychologist, primarily because he discussed reflex action and instincts. As far as scientific psychology is concerned, the major effect of his writings has been to perpetuate dualism.

Our discussion of 17th century philosophy would not be complete without reference to the private physician, John Locke (1632-1704). He refined the definition of the psychical aspect of humans so that it became more personal, a "cognitive soul" as it were. This shift in emphasis stimulated discussion of the nature and activities in this aspect of people and began a tradition which led more or less directly to the widely held definition of psychology as the study of the operations of the mind.

## Stage 5: The Rise of the New Mental Science (18th and 19th Centuries)

Final preparation for the rise of the new mental "science" were made by Locke's intellectual heirs, Berkeley (1685-1753) and Hume (1711-1776). Kantor (1969, p. 94) characterizes the effects of their thought as follows: "Soul in a sense was reduced to a function, a primarily cognitive one...the function of the soul became empirical and localized in human experience." The cosmological soul of St. Augustine was being brought down to Earth.

Credit for systematizing the new "science" goes to Christian Wolff (1679-1754) and Thomas Reid (1710-1796). They organized their own ideas and the writings of others into the first modern textbooks of psychology. Although this new discipline was to perpetuate traditional dualism, its formalization at least insured that the swing back toward a naturalistic intellectual atmosphere would continue.

The 18th century has been called the "Age of Enlightenment," in reference to the culmination of man's struggle to free himself from the total authority of medieval cultural institutions. One characteristic of the era of political revolutions and social reform was an increased emphasis on individual human rights and needs. The humane treatment of the insane by Phillippe Pinel (1745-1826) and others reflects this emerging attitude. The psychical component of humans was now viewed as having the function of feeling as well as the functions of willing and thinking attributed to it earlier by medieval and Renaissance thinkers.

French Materialism flourished during the 18th century. This viewpoint, which represents yet another variant of traditional dualism, generally conceptualized the mind as dependent on the body. In line with the new concept for people as social and political creatures, and in keeping with increasing information about their biological composition, scholars became interested in studying humans as an integral part of nature.

Before describing the areas of research which developed during the scientifically-oriented century, attention must be given to the great philosopher Immanuel Kant (1742-1804). His philosophy is synthetic in that he sought to reconcile Newtonian science with such traditional concepts as those of "God," "Immortality," and "Freedom." In his system, the psychical side is the victor. The "Things in Themselves" which were organized by the innate "Principles" and "Categories" of the mind were really creations of the mind. Despite the fact that Kant himself believed that psychology could not be a science, physiologists of his time and subsequent physiological psychologists have sought a biological basis for his model of the mind. Individuals working within this tradition seek to understand how the brain (as the residence of the mind with its innately-organized principles and categories) converts incoming sensations (Things in Themselves) into a perception, or knowledge about something in the outside world.

## Psychology Emulates the Established Sciences

In its struggle for recognition as a science, psychology began more and more to imitate its successful sister sciences. Kantor (1969) summarizes this development in terms of four means by which scholars interested in promoting the new mental "science" attempted to naturalize the soul: ' (1) Psychobiology; (2) quantization; (3) experimentation; and (4) evolution.

### (1) Psychobiology

This approach has already been alluded to in our treatment of the evolution of the dualistic model. The disproportionate emphasis on Soul which characterized the Dark Ages and the early Renaissance was superseded by the Materialistic view of the 18th century, in which Soul and Body were seen as essentially equal. By the 20th century, the emphasis had shifted so that the Body was viewed as much more important than the Soul. With increased understanding of brain activities, the psychical component of the organism was redefined as merely "the 'integration' of subtle processes in the cortical parts of the brain" (Kantor, 1969, p 362). By thus attributing nonnaturalistic functions to the brain, the objective study of this biological system has been impaired.

### (2) Quantization

The tradition of mathematics has two aspects, a mystical one, seen in the assertions of St. Augustine and St. Thomas of the mystical absoluteness of numbers, and a practical one, seen in the success which the Renaissance physicists and astronomers had in dealing with the quantitative aspects of their subject matter. Leibniz (1646-1716) and Herbart (1776-1841) conceptualized mind as composed of units similar to the atoms of Newton which could be subjected to mathematical manipulations. Combining the mystical and practical traditions, Gustav Fechner (1801-1887) launched the study of psychophysics, an area of psychology whose name belies its dualistic bias. The famous psychiatrist, Sigmund Freud (1856-1939), drew on the Leibniz-Herbart tradition for his concepts of the "conscious" and the "unconscious" aspect of the mind.

### (3) Experimentation

Like psychology, physiology was relatively younger than the other modern sciences. During the 19th century, such men as Johannes Muller (1801-1894) guided both fledging sciences toward more intimate confrontation with events. The work of Helmholtz is particularly noteworthy. He dispelled the traditional notion that nervous impulses are instantaneous by actually measuring the speed of conduction in a frog's sciatic nerve. He formulated theories of vision and audition which still shape the study of these sensory systems. And he invented a number of instruments still used by physicians, physiologists, and psychologists to measure physiological activities.

The extent to which people assume that experimentation is the aspect of psychology which makes it a science can be gauged by examining most modern introductory psychology textbooks. They follow the tradition delineated by E.G. Boring (1886-1968) when, in 1924, he published a book which has been regarded as the first comprehensive history of experimental psychology. This tradition holds that psychology became a science when Wilhelm Wundt (1832-1920) established a laboratory of psychology at Leipzig University in 1879.

### (4) Evolution

The fourth attempt to naturalize the soul involved adopting certain aspects of Charles Darwin's (1809-1882) theory of the origin of the species. Evolutionary theory established the continuity of humans with other animals and thereby made possible a modern rebirth of the Aristotelian comparisons of behaviors across species. Of more importance is that evolution, unlike the other three attempts to naturalize the soul, provided an authentic and objective scientific model for psychology. Later we shall see how Kantor has developed this model.

### Stage 6: Psychology's Recent Century (Late 1800's to the present)

Before describing the contemporary theoretical positions or systems which have developed in psychology, some attention is due to the general state of the science. In a real sense, the four attempts to naturalize the soul and thereby render psychology scientific succeeded. As Kantor (1969, p. 320) expressed it, by the late 1800's workers in psychology believed that"...nothing was left to be done but gather data and induce laws."

The first data were gathered with instruments borrowed from the physicists and physiologists. As the data accumulated and the science expanded, instruments were devised by psychologists for their own use.

98

Among the most uniquely psychological instruments are mazes and operant chambers for testing learning in nonhuman animals.

## The Specialized Areas of Modern Psychology

A number of specialities developed within psychology. Conditioning (a subclass of learning) and physiological psychology (including perception) form the core of what is today called "experimental psychology." Basic research is conducted in a number of other subject matter areas, many of which are related to applied areas. Among these areas which have both research and applied aspects are abnormal (or clinical) psychology, social psychology, developmental psychology, and industrial psychology. Professional categories in applied psychology have multiplied during the past forty years, a growth correlated with the steadily increasing population of clients produced by our relatively affluent industrialized society.

Early American psychology was continuous with European psychology. The four attempts to naturalize the soul survived the journey to the New World and appeared in several variant forms. These forms are often referred to as "Schools of American Psychology" are associated with the names of famous men and universities. A careful analysis of the activities and writings of these early schools reveals that all of them assumed a form of mind-body parallelism.

## Varying Attempts to Naturalize the Soul of American Psychology

(1) **Structuralism.** Quantization and experimentation characterized the transplanted German psychology which thrived at Cornell University under E.B. Titchener (1867-1927), a student of Wundt. While the attempt to study "pure experience" via introspection and thus determine the number of basic mental units is now of historical interest only, structuralism is credited with winning academic recognition for psychology as an independent science.

(2) **Gestalt Psychology.** The clearest example of psychobiology in American Psychology is found in the concept of isomorphism held by the three German scientists, Max Wertheimer (1880-1943), Wolfgang Kohler (1887-1967), and Kurt Koffka (1886-1941). This concept, which was invoked to explain many of their observations of complex perceptual phenomena and "insight" learning, referred to a hypothetical one-to-one relationship between brain activity and mental activity. The general Gestalt system is often referred to as a "field theory." Field postulation is a desirable point of view in that it encourages an appreciation of the complexity of psychological events. Unfortunately, the Gestaltists replaced the observable event field with a nonobservable psychical field when they moved from collecting data to writing explanatory principles.

(3) **Associationism.** Following the tradition of mental associationism, several early American psychologists developed a movement widely regarded as experimental learning in memory and school attainment. The German Ebbinghaus (1850-1909), who studied the memorization of nonsense syllables by humans, was the immediate European predecessor of this American group. The effect of the work of the associationists was to establish in America a tradition of correlating various observations, some of which were believed to be totally under the observer's control (independent variables), while others were seen as performed or emitted by the subject (dependent variables). This arbitrary division of the psychological event field is evident in the studies of animal behavior and in the work of the functionalists to be considered next.

(4) **Animal Behavior Studies.** Evolutionary theory entered into the work of a number of men who studied the so-called psychical activities of nonhuman animals. The latter approach, which provided the foundation for modern conditioning , included the work of Pavlov (1849-1936) and Bechterev (1857-1927) on respondent conditioning, the work of Thorndike (1874-1949), whose Law of Effect is the classic statement of reinforcement, the work of Guthrie (1886-1959) who equated learning with simple associations of stimuli and responses, and the work of Estes (1919-   ), who has expressed Guthrie's contiguity principle in mathematical (statistical) terms. These men share a common belief that the association of variable is the primary task of all sciences. As Kantor (1959, p. 14) notes, this statistical-correlation stage is the second stage in the evolution of science, being more advanced than the earlier substance-property stage in which traditional sense qualities cause changes in mental powers, but less sophisticated than an integrated field approach.

(5) **Functionalism.** Evolution was also the principal attempt to naturalize the soul used by the most widespread and most charactersitic of American schools of psychology. As the name **functionalism** implies, emphasis ·was placed on the funciton of an organism's behavior as it adapts to its environment. While such studies often dealt with several variables, the general approach was still statistical-correlational. Three major areas of study were undertaken by functionalists. The first was animal behavior. Its pioneers included Guthrie and Thorndike, who were mentioned earlier under animal behavior studies, as well as the great comparative psychologist Yerkes (1876-1956) and the inventor of the rat maze, Small (1870-1943). By invoking Darwin's assumption of mental continuity between animals and man, these pioneers made the study of animal behavior an integral part of American psychology.

A second area of psychology dominated by the functionalists involved mental testing and the development of statistics for the evaluation fo individual differences. Inspired by the work of Chales Darwin's cousin, Francis Galton (1822-1911), several American psychologsits devised and administered various tests and then developed statistical procedures for dealing with their data. Prominent among the Americans in the testing movement was the active editor, founder and publisher of psychological journals, James McKeen Cattell (1860-1944). Other notable men who worked in the area of individual differences were America's first Ph.D. in psychology, G. Stanley Hall (1844-1924), a leading author of textbooks, R.S. Woodworth (1869-1962), and the famous philosopher and innovator of educational methodology ,John Dewey (1859-1952).

Several famous Americans contributed to the third area in which evolutionary theory was applied in a broad manner. William James (1842-1910), the renowned Harvard Philosopher and psychologist, did much to promote the science of psychology in the eyes of the general public as well as with academicians. He wrote books suitable for the general reading public,and on several occasions he sympathized with the investigation of such alleged phenomena as psychics contacting the dead through mediums. Two psychology professors, James Angell (1869-1949) and Harvey Carr (1873-1954), were instrumental in making the University of Chicago the center for functionalism. Their influence on the American Psychological Association insured that this organization would be largely applied in its orientation to the science.

(6)  **Behaviorism.**  The first American movement to break deliberately with the traditional ways of attempting to naturalize the soul was behaviorism.  Of the various systems formalized in 20th century America, this one most nearly approximates a truly naturalistic science of psychology.  Popularized by John B. Watson (1878-1958) and stated as a formal system by Paul Albert Weiss (1879-1931), behaviorism is the most influential and most controversial of the schools.  Watson conducted many animal studies, but is most famous for his work on the conditioning of emotional responses in young children.  His greatest contribution was his vociferious insistence that psychology use objective methods and terminology.

Edward C. Tolman (1886-1961) and Clark L. Hull (1884-1952) are among the prominent learning theorists who are considered as behaviorists.  Tolman's assertion that organisms consult "cognitive maps" during remembering helped to break down the distinctions between rodent and human behavior.  Working primarily with complex mazes, Tolman called attention to various factors in the test situation which combine to produce a given response pattern. He provided psychology with a number of puzzling phenomena, including "latent learning." Hull, who favored rats in runways, attempted to formulate a comprehensive mathematical model of mammalian learning and remembering. Physiological factors, particularly drive states associated with varying hours of deprivation, figured prominently in his writing.

One of Watson's students, Karl Lashley (1890-1958), is referred to as a neuropsychologist for his classic studies of the effects of various brain ablations on rat behavior. It is important to note that Lashley moved toward a field theory of nervous system function when he failed to find experimental evidence for memory storage in the rodent brain. Another prominent behaviorist whose research led him to a field-type theory was Z.Y. Kuo (1898-1970), who is best known for his work on the behavioral development of chick embryos.

A man who is currently the most famous of all living psychologists, B.F. Skinner (1904- ), belongs to the behavioristic tradition. Skinner made the operant a basic unit of behavior and pioneered work on schedules of reinforcement, using the apparatus which bears his name. He is also known for his discussions of verbal behavior (Skinner, 1957) and for two books which have received public attention: The Utopian novel, **Walden Two** (1948) and **Beyond Freedom and Dignity** (1971), both of which advocate wide application of the principles of conditioning to human social and political activities.

The behavioristic tradition has done much to shape contemporary American psychology. Watson sought to solve the problem of mind-body dualism by denying the existence of mind and emphasizing the body, a "solution" which tacitly accepts the original division of the world into two aspects. As Kantor (1969, p. 366 ff) notes, however, this "solution" not only failed to free psychology of the dualistic tradition but also produced the significant problems of specialism, organocentrism, reductionism, and analogism. Since these problems are still evident in much of American psychology, they will be briefly discussed.

While denying the psychical self of the dualistic mind-body model, behaviorists embraced the physical half. This led them to regard the organism as a mindless body filled with such nonobservables as "drives" and "needs." Once this viewpoint was accepted, specialism developed in a choice of behaviors to be studied: Simple conditioning tasks were favored, while pscyhological events traditionally regarded as functions of the mind (e.g., thinking), were neglected. Organocentrism is related to reductionism and refers to the belief that psychological data are concentrated in the organism,i.e., that organisms **emit** behaviors. By reductionism is meant the belief that these behaviors can only be understood in terms of physiological activities; a belief which, when carried to its logical conclusions, would reduce all the sciences to physics! The problem of analogism refers to the tendency of behaviorists to view all or part of the organism as a glorified machine (e.g., "the brain is like a computer") and represents an extreme effect of the attempt to devise concrete and objective descriptions of psychological events. Kantor (1969, p. 368) ends his critique of behaviorism by stating that "...what is lacking in its naturalistic description of psychological events is their field character. In addition to eliminating all transcendentalism, it is necessary to take account of the complete situations which comprise psychological events."

Kantor's interbehavioral psychology possess this field character. Unlike earlier schools, Kantor's approach is a general logic of science applicable to all areas of psychology. In general, the essence of a field construction is that all events are regarded as complex interactions of many factors in specified situations. A study of 20th century physics, chemistry, and biology reveals that these sciences, too, have incorporated field constructions. For psychology, the field refers to the sum total of things and conditions, including the organism which contributes to a psychological event. Thus, psychology has as its subject matter not simply the behavior of an organism, but the mutual interbehavior of an organism and its stimulus object through time.

Kantor (1959) suggests this formula for a psychological event (PE):

$$PE = C(\ k,\ sf,\ rf,\ hi,\ st,\ md\ )$$

**C** indicates that the field consists of the entire system of factors in the interaction; **k** symbolizes the uniqueness of interbehavioral fields. The behavior segment (or Unit PE) centers around a **response function (rf)** and a **stimulus function (sf)**; the first is identified with an action of the organism, the second with an action of the stimulus object. The **historical interbehavior** process **(hi)** refers to the series of contacts of organisms and objects which has occurred prior to the present PE. The **setting factors (st)** consist of the immediate circumstances influencing which particular sf-rf will occur. The **medium of contact (md)** refers to the medium of interbeahvior such as air, light, or water. Organisms respond, objects stimulate. Both organisms and objects increase the number of response and stimulus functions through repeated interbehavioral contacts in different settings.

As indicated earlier Darwin's evolutionary theory provides an authentic model for the sciences. Kantor uses this model in dealing with the factors which contribute to the behavior of mature organisms. He delineates four evolutions (Kantor, 1959, pp. 44 ff):

Planetary, phylogenetic, ontogenetic, and interbehavioral history. The study of natural history focuses on planetary evolution, during which the habitat of living organisms developed. The study of phylogenetic evolution points to man's behavior as a member of species, Homo Sapiens. The process of species development constitutes phylogenetic evolution. For man, we can point to the possibilities for the development of psychological interbehaviors which result from the evolution of the hand, an erect posture, and a general agility. (Note that these phylogenetic characteristics are to be viewed merely as "possibilities" for the development of psychological interbehaviors, not as "predeterminers" of what will develop.) The third evolution, the ontogenetic biological evolution, begins with the union of individual gametes. At this point a complex set of interactions of the new individual with intrauterine environmental conditions begins. During the embryonic and fetal periods, numerous physical, chemical, and biological interactions occur. If abnormal conditions exist during this time, a malformed organism may be produced instead of the average biological product. That is, psychological interbehavior which depends upon specific biological characteristics cannot occur if they are absent, e.g., a person born without legs cannot walk though he may transport himself by other means. When ontogenetic evolution reaches a certain point, psychological development begins. At first, psychological interactions are scarcely different than biological interactions. They consist of fetal adjustments to such factors as varying pressure and temperature. When the organism is born, and thus comes into direct contact with a complex world of stimulus objects, psychological development proceeds rapidly. Early postnatal psychological development continues to parallel biological development, e.g., before an infant can turn his head toward his mother in response to her call, he must develop the necessary neuromuscular coordination. The most characteristically psychological activities are to a greater extent independent of biological development, being composed of interactions with stimulus objects on the basis of the organism's prior contacts with those objects.

At this point, we can properly speak of the importance of an individual's interbehavioral history. This fourth evolution continues throughout the life of the individual. Man's psychological interbehaviors are involved with what are called social factors, those essentially human features of one's surroundings. Consequently, individuals build up specific ways of speaking and feeling, of appreciating thenature and uses of objects. A characteristic human development involves learning to name things in the environment. A given object stimulates different people in different ways; e.g., a statue is reacted to as a fertility god by one person and as an art object by another. An appreciation of the natural development of the organism through four evolutions renders unnecessary any appeal to traditional nonobservables such as "drives" and "needs."

With a discussion of interbehaviorism, our sketching of the historical development of scientific psychology comes to a close. While many areas of psychology (particularly physiological psychology) still suffer from reductionism and analogism, other areas are moving more rapidly toward field type theories. Two examples illustrate this trend.

In the study of animal behavior, the "innate vs. acquired" simplistic explanation is essentially a dead issue; partially as a result of increased contact with ethologists, animal behaviorists are attempting to study more of the factors which comprise the event field. In clinical psychology, attempts are underway to insure that the therapies which work in the clinical setting continue to work when the factors in the event field change (i.e., when the client returns to his home and job). As the simplistic solutions fail, more and more psychologists are turning to the complex field-type approach. Only time can tell if this progress toward an objective, naturalistic science of psychology will continue.

## Value of an Interbehavioral Approach to the History of Psychology

At the outset it was noted that the history of psychology is best viewed as a complex set of interrelated intellectual movements and technological advances . Kantor (1963, p. 54) refers to this criterion as one of "continuity" and "corrigibility." The history of all the sciences is continuous in that elementary causal factors are replaced with more complex propositional systems as scientists become more familiar with the natural events included in their specialty. It is corrigible in that both specific constructs and the total system are constantly being corrected and improved.

This interbehavioral approach applies objectve, scientific methods to the study of historical events. Over time, more and more sophisticated techniques becomes available (e.g., carbon dating of fossils) which allow for a more direct confrontation with historical data. More data become available as diaries, scrolls, and other primary records of past events are discovered. The specific constructs of history are corrected and improved in line with new data. In recent years, women's studies have forced a reexamination of history as the story of military and political events. Quilts and diaries should be viewed as authentic artistic creations and the contributions of wives and mistresses should be acknowledged. Furthermore, during the Renaissance when men were freed from medieval shackles, women lost much of the protection offered by their status in a feudal society. And while world wars are regarded as devastating for the male population, they provide unique opportunities for career advancements for many women.

The cultural background and biases of the historian are viewed as an integral part of his work. To appreciate this, one might contrast the history of the Inquisition as written by a Catholic clergyman with that written by a Russian novelist or the history of obstetrics written by a female physician.

The scientific approach to the history of psychology serves as an object lesson for the beginning students. He learns to seek accurate and direct contact with events and to beware of his own biases. He realizes that the historical evolution of all the sciences are interrelated and that progress has not been steady and linear. The naive objectivity of the Hellenic Greeks was soon lost in a world preoccupied with personal salvation. Attempts to revise this early naturalism met with powerful opposition from the medieval church. The past seven centuries have witnessed various attempts to free science from traditional dualism. Field approaches now characterize all the sciences. An appreciation of the historical struggles which led to this evolution will help insure that non-scientific institutions do not again dominate and weaken the sciences.

## References

Kantor, J.R. 1959. **Interbehavioral Psychology.** Gransville, Ohio: Principia Press.

Kantor, J.R. 1963. **The Scientific Evolution of Psychology** (Vol. 1) Chicago: Principia Press.

Kantor, J.R. 1969. **The Scientific Evolution of Psychology** (Vol. 2) Chicago: Principia Press.

Skinner, B.F. 1948. **Walden Two.** New York: Macmillan.

Skinner, B.F. 1957. **Verbal Behavior.** Englewood Cliffs, New Jersey: Prentice-Hall, Inc.

Skinner, B.F. 1971. **Beyond Freedom and Dignity.** New York: Alfred Knopf.

# WHITHER PHYSIOLOGICAL PSYCHOLOGY?

N.H. Pronko

A representative article in an issue of **American Psychologist** helps to set the stage for a consideration of the current status of physiological psychology. "Human vision: Some objective explanations," an article by Riggs (1976), constitutes his address on the occasion of a Distinguished Scientific Contribution Award bestowed upon him at the 1974 meeting of the American Psychological Association. Because Riggs' publication explicitly states the theoretical framework within which his laboratory work is embedded, it is especially suitable as a model for our analysis. Even a casual scanning of psychological journals that publish experiments reveal an apparent endemic allergy to a statement of the theoretical orientation of the experimenter. Riggs deserves praise for the unambiguous statement of his theoretical stance, which we shall now consider.

## Riggs' Dualistic Approach

Essentially, Riggs makes the point that while subjectivity has played an important part in the early history of every intellectual field, it is the sciences that have made the greatest advances by adopting objective methods. To make things clear, Riggs defines his terms. For him, "subjective" means "existing in the mind" or "introspective." "Objective" is also defined in the dictionary sense as "belonging to the object of thought rather than to the thinking subject" or "intent upon dealing with things external to the mind rather than thoughts or feelings." Beyond this point, Riggs traces out the trend in physics and in biology from subjectivity toward objectivity. Using Descartes as an example, he points out Descartes' attempt toward a mechanical interpretation of man's walking, breathing and other automatic responses. But how about man's will, memories, emotions and such? The best that Descartes could do at that time was to assume a semi-automatic soul residing in the pineal gland and directing somehow the flow of animal spirits.

Riggs does not stop with Descartes. He sketches out the continued trend toward "objectivity" in the biological sciences, a trend that culminated in the recent, rich development of molecular biology. Riggs makes an emphatic point about "objectivity" as he sees it by quoting extensively from the Nobel lecture of Albert Claude (1975). In his lecture, Claude expounds on the wonders of the cell "mechanisms" (sic) "which reveal...an unparalleled knowledge of the laws of physics and chemistry..." (p. 434). Claude continues his praises of the cell for its memory of its past and foreknowledge of the future (e.g., as an egg). The cell "plans," with great specificity, the patterning and growth of the organism. According to Claude, as accomplished as man may become, he may easily forget

> Whether awake or asleep, that he is a colony of cells
> in action, and that it is the cells which achieve, through
> him, what he has the illusion of accomplishing himself.
> It is the cells which create and maintain in us, during
> the span of our lives, our will to live and survive, to
> search and experiment, and to struggle (p. 434).

Riggs commends Claude's hosannahs in behalf of the marvels of the cell and sees the latter's words "as a beautiful statement of materialistic objectivity" (p. 128).

According to Riggs, the above remarks attest to biology's successful development toward "objectivity" with a place for the cell but not for the organism. But how about psychology? On this point, Riggs thinks that our sciences has been, for too long, plagued with a preoccupation with "subjectivity." It struggled through Structuralism and Functionalism and with the objectivity of Behaviorism had finally achieved a scientific respectability which permits psychologists to work by the side of engineers, physiologists and such. But, Riggs concludes on a cautionary note: We should be careful to avoid slipping back into subjectivity which would isolate us from other scientists once more. In working out the basic laws of behavior, "let us not forget Dr. Claude's admonition to give due credit to the cells of the body" (p. 129). Such fascinating studies as hypnosis, biofeedback, TM, and other altered states of consciousness should challenge us to "continue to search for the physical and chemical bases for such phenomena..." (Riggs, 1976, p. 129).

Let us appraise Riggs' interpretation of his data, granting that his laboratory work is technically correct, even fastidious. However, of greater interest to us is the way he thinks about psychological matters "before" and "after" he leaves his laboratory. In other words, what, for Riggs, basically and fundamentally, are psychological "things?" The answer is obvious. Riggs has adopted a dualistic approach for his work. According to his lights, the human organism consists of a body and a mind; the body is physical, material, and objective while the mind is spiritual, a derivative of the soul and immaterial and subjective. For further elucidation of the two opposed terms, objective and subjective, we turn to Warren's **Dictionary of Psychology** (1934). According to Warren, the term **objective** is used as a : (1) Synonym for physical; (2) admitting of record by physical instrument;

108

(3) not open to verification by other investigators; (4) localized in psychological space within the observer's body, et. cetera. The above definitions are elaborations of the ones offered by Riggs (p. 125). The reader should really examine Riggs' paper carefully so as to convince himself that none of the above is "being read into" his statements.

Before turning to other matters, I want to emphasize that Riggs is not some obscure, rare and randomly selected psychologist. In a sense, his Distinguished Scientific Contribution Award honors him above others. Indeed, he becomes a kind of model for other psychologists. If so, then the dualistic theoretical structure that guides his laboratory work must also be acceptance to his colleagues who chose to recognize him with a special award in a special ceremony. In fact, as we shall wee, his theoretical approach is the established doctrine in contemporary psychology. The outstanding feature of Riggs' formulation is his frank and open espousal of the mind-body approach. Riggs seems to admit that the traditional split of the organism into body and mind causes him trouble. But, because the mind is too evanescent and difficult to apprehend, he opts for the physical or bodily alternative. And, now, having examined Riggs' underlying theoretical stance, we are ready to have a brief look at his laboratory work.

## Riggs' Objective Vision Research

Starting with microelectrode recording in the visual cells of the brain, Riggs began a series of experiments in an attempt to get at some of the facts of pattern vision. By means of ingenious devices, he measured human and animal cortical potential responses aroused by visual stimulus patterns. Forced choice or matching tasks were demanded of subjects and EEG electrodes on the scalp recorded the correlated cortical potentials. With this set-up it was possible for Riggs to compare experimentally-induced visual deprivation in animals with such clincial conditions in human subjects as high astigmatism or early cataract.

In another study of visual acuity, Riggs found that the electroretinogram and visually evoked cortical potential waves dropped off in amplitude as vision was distorted by means of positive or negative eye lenses. These measures corresponded to lower scores o'n standard chart tests of visual acuity administered to his subjects.

In other experiments during which the subject reported disappearance of the visual stimulus, the recorded cortical potentials showed a surprising stability. The same results occurred in the supression of vision obtained by means of binocular rivalry. How does Riggs reconcile these seemingly incompatible results? For him, the unmistakable conclusion is that the suppression of vision obtained at the moment of the subject's introspective report "must have taken place at some higher level in the brain than the one generating the visually evoked cortical, potentials" (Riggs, 1976, p. 131). In fact, these findings suggested still other experiments to Riggs, extensions of which "may help us solve the riddle of what parts of the brain may be resopnsible for sensory awareness...(Riggs, 1976, p. 131).

Riggs reports still other studies in color vision similarly approaches via microelectrodes and computer, but those discussed above are an adequate sample for our purposes.

A bit of reflection about Riggs' laboratory procedure reveals a certain interesting pattern. He certainly sets up genuine psychological problems for research: There is no doubt about that. For example, he confronts a human organism with a checkerboard stimulus pattern, a few-weeks-old baby with successive flashes of light, and so forth. Now, when we ask how he works at his visual research, we find him resorting to the use of physiological measures. As the organism interacts with the various visual stimuli, his scalp and eye are wired up to certain devices. Riggs records the visually evoked cortical potentials from the subject's scalp and the electroretinogram from the eye. His procedure yields response amplitudes which he then computer-averages for differential analysis. Suppose a neurologist by training should ask to join Riggs' enterprise, should we ask what function would be indicated for him? The answer is simple: The same as for the psychologist. Obviously we have caught Riggs in an attempt to "reduce" his data to a physiological form. he is, thus, a reductionist. As to Riggs' motive for his reductionistic act and the consequences thereof, we shall leave this for a later examination following a short excursion into reductionism.

### Reductionism

Reductionism:  **A Philosophical stance adopted by various sciences which holds that in the hierarchy of sciences the phenomena at one level are to be explained and understood by reducing them to the data or principles of a science at a lower level.**

As rampantly as reductionism appears in psychological literature, one rarely finds it discussed or indexed in text books. The explanation may lie in its "unwitting" adoption and usage. Awareness of reductionistic modes of thinking may be as difficult for psychologists to detect as is the realization by fish that they live, and move, and have their being in a watery medium.

It may be of advantage to approach reductionism indirectly by considering how it works in some field other than psychology. As a

110

convenient target, let us take biology which is presently undergoing a civil war between "molecular biologists" and "classical biologists." The work of Paul Weiss will furnish us with a suitable source of instruction.

In his book, **Dynamics of Development,** Weiss (1968) has gathered together scattered papers that he had published over a period of half a century. His focus throughout his creative years was upon understanding the morphogenesis or the "dynamic order" of living systems via rigorous experimental analysis. The theme that runs through the whole series of papers is that "a whole contains and conveys more information than does the sum of its unassembled parts" (p. ix). Before proceeding with this exposition, I should point out that Weiss, simultaneously with another biologist, coined the term "molecular biology." He intended for it to take its order at the bottom of a hierarchical arrangement, according to functional principles which, in ascending order, would include cellular, genetic, developmental, regulatory, group, and environmental biology. According to his conception, no level was to be dominant over any other level; each was to make its contribution to add to the totality and the molecular was simply the lowest on a scale of orders of magnitude of study.

Trouble arose when molecular biologists acted as if the principles of biological development might be solved by reducing organismic, organ or tissue events to the molecular level. Weiss' work throughout his half century of experimental investigation denies the validity of the reductionists' claim to a monopolistic status. Here is the way he puts it:

> ...there is no phenomenon in a living system that is
> **not** molecular, but there is none that is **only** molec-
> ular, either. It is one thing not to see the forest for
> the trees, but then to go on to deny the reality of the
> forest, is a more serious matter; for it is not just a
> case of myopia, but one of self-inflicted blindness
> (1969a, p. 368).

In other words, a tissue, organ, system, or organism has properties, attributes or characteristics beyond thsoe found in its component cells. Order, system, pattern or relationship appear at levels of organization above the cell that simply are not to be found in the ultimate conceptual biochemical unit, i.e., the molecule.

Let us hear from another biologist, one who is alarmed at the molecular rebellion in his field. Here is how Commoner (1966) views the radical approach.

111

Anyone who learned biology by dissecting a frog must
find the reports of present-day biological research strange
and unsettling:  molecules that reproduce themselves;
a molecular 'code' that tells an egg whether it should
turn into a turtle or a tiger; efforts to create life in
a test tube of chemicals...(p. 31).

Such notions seem to go against the grain for many biologists. For, if
a molecule can duplicate itself, then biologists must relinquish the cell
theory, according to which life characterizes the whole cell and not
some fine unit in the cell.  If life can really be created in the test
tube, then the traditional notion of "all life from life" must be
relinquished.  And if all the characters of the adult  are contained in
the molecular "code," then we will have to regress to the ancient
doctrine of "preformation,"according to which the features of the
adult are fully formed in the germ cell and need only to increase in
size.

According to Commoner, classical biologists such as he argue that
the accumulated observations of organisms, organs, and cells have
demonstrated that one must have the cell at minimum in order to
demonstrate life attributes.    But the molecular biologists, as
reductionists, talk about a "living molecule," which with proper
analysis, they think, will reveal chemical secrets that will throw light
upon life.

Sociology    and    other    disciplines    that    study    groups    (e.g.,
anthropology, ethnology, culturology) are no more immune from
involvement in reductionism than biology, as we discussed above. As
our prime exhibit of group-study, let us inspect White's (1949) work.
He starts from the premise that the terms "physical," "biological," and
"cultural " identify "three qualitatively different and scientifically
significant classes of forms of reality" (p. 15).   The designation
"qualitatively different" immediately tells us that White is not a
reductionist.  He distinguishes among the levels, not on the basis of a
difference in the composition of their substance, but on the basis of
the form or pattern into which their component parts are organized.
The physical level consists of the non-living; the biological, of the
living;  and  the  cultural  pointing  to  the  "extra-somatic"  or
"supra-biological" category.  The last include such phases of culture as
languages, beliefs, tools, utensils, customs, and institutions.

Having defined his discipline in relation to the other two, White
argues cogently for the right to study it independently of the
techniques of any other science.   The following quotation states his
position clearly.

With the advance of science...came a recognition of
culture as a distinct class of events, as a distinct order
of phenomena...In short, it was discovered that culture

112

may be considered, from the standpoint of scientific
analysis and interpretation, as a thing **sui generis,** as
a class of events and processes that behaves in terms
of its own principles and laws and which consequently
can be explained only in terms of its own elements
and processes. Culture may thus be considered as
a self-contained, self-determined process; one that can
be explained only in terms of itself (p. xviii).

White is highly critical of those of his colleagues who would
explain culture in a psychological way or, as formerly, by way of
biological principles. The former would study culture by becoming
psychiatrists and using Rorschach tests. To those who would attempt
to explain culture psychologically, White would respond that it is the
other way around. Differences in the behavior of people of diverse
populations is to be understood in terms of their cultures. Their
behaviors are expressions of their culture and not vice versa.

As for biological determinants of culture, White states that "all
evidence points to an utter insignificance of biological factors as
compared with culture in any consideration of behavior variations"
(speaking **en masse,** not of individual organisms) (p. 124). Whether one
speaks of the American Indians or of African Blacks, "it cannot be
shown that any variation of human behavior is due to variation of a
biological nature" (p. 124). In sum White seems to be saying that
cultures have a dimension and a framework of their own and must be
studied as cultures, rather than psychologically or biologically. To
transform them to terms of the latter two disciplines is to do an
injustice to them.

Webster (1973), an investigator of a closely related field, sociology,
has also expressed himself in a straightforward fashion on the question
of reductionism. He points to a certain reluctance on the part of
sociologists to embrace reductionism. Taken in its extreme form, it
would make sociology obsolete. Even a cursory acceptance of
reductionism would tend to belittle the status of sociological
phenomena by suggesting that "they are simply special cases of
something; more 'fundamental'" (p. 258). Without going into Webster's
elaborate rationale for his argument, suffice it to say that, in his
opinion, psychological explanations for social phenomena are just not
available. But that proposition hardly settles the question. The
debate goes on. The foregoing discussion of reductionism thus makes
two critical points.

## (1) Psychology is not the only Discipline Plagued with this Problem

The "two-part system" runs across the sciences so that one can be
a reductionist or a non-reductionist, whether one is a sociologist,

113

psychologist, biologist, or so forth.  To carry the political analogy further, it seems a bit far-fetched that scientists join one party or the other through (a) a dramatic and self-aware conversion or (b) through a subtle indoctrination by way of the cultural atmosphere. The latter hypothesis seems more attractive when one considers that every psychologist has been the child of his culture long before he becomes a psychologist[1].

## (2)  A Reductionistic View Perpetrates the "Nothing but" Fallacy

In the study of groups in the sociological realm, groups are converted, as in methodological individualism, into a collection of individuals and lose their identity as groups.  In biology, likewise, to revert to Weiss' complaint, an attempt to explain all biological happenings in molecular terms is to provide only a "worm's eye view" (Weiss, 1968, p. 96).  And, it needs to be emphasized that molecular analysis is perfectly acceptable to Weiss if it is intended as a partial contribution to an understanding of the total picture under observation.   But when it tries to gain monopolistic control in the explanation of biological events, Weiss pushes for a "bird's eye view of the cell in its integrity," (p. 96), i.e., an approach from the standpoint of cellular biology--both approaches united in a joint enterprise. Weiss' objection to an exclusively molecular view is that it gives a distorted picture of the phenomena under inquiry.   Apparently, the view is widespread among biologists according to which, a cell is a body of protoplasm,   a complicated mixture of organic and inorganic substances, or a seat of various processes. An analysis in terms of molecular biology loses sight of  the attributes provided by the bird's eye view that has characterized Weiss' life-long work.   These living features of the cell vanish and what remains is a pale aggregate of molecules.

## Back To Riggs

Having seen what consequences different views have in sociology and biology, let us return to Riggs' study and its reductionistic interpretation.   It was earlier work on the visual cells of the brains of anesthetized monkeys and cats that really stimulated Riggs to set up his own program.  He was apparently impressed with his predecessors' use of microelectrodes that could be inserted into the individual cells of the visual cortex.  More impressive, yet, was the revelation of the manner in which "brain cells are organized for detection of lines, color, distance, and other features of the visual world" (p. 129).  His own work proceeded with the same orientation and, in his study, he reports a number of findings in terms essentially of patterns of cortical potentials and retinograms.

114

Let us note the facts before us. Both Riggs and his predecessors must begin with animal or human subjects. They confront them with visual stimulus objects. We hve before us an obvious psychological situation, i.e., an organism and stimulus object. However, at this point Riggs' theoretical position intrudes upon both his laboratory operations and the way he talks about his doings. Essentially, Riggs admits that the traditional split of the organism into body and mind causes him trouble. Since the mind is too evanescent and spooky to apprehend, he opts for the physical or bodily to deal with. As indicated above, Riggs is a reductionist.

What are the consequences of Riggs' reductionism? We have already noted that violence to the facts occurs in sociology and biology when events on one level are transformed into the units of a simpler level. Why shouldn't we expect to find similar consequences here? Consider how Riggs' organism and stimulus object disappear entirely in deference to "cortical potentials." The latter now become the center of attention similar to the manner in which "molecules" upstaged the cell as Weiss so strikingly demonstrated.

There is another consequence to this procedure, one that is frequently overlooked. Let us go about the matter this way. Suppose the proverbial man-from-Mars should step into Riggs' laboratory shortly after the departure of Riggs' subjects for the day. He interrogates Riggs who exhibits his records in the form of cortical potentials and retinograms as proof of his objective research in visual patterns. Exactly how much understanding of visual perception would the man-from-Mars gain from looking at Riggs' experimental protocols? The answer is obvious. Now, it would be a different matter if the subjects and stimulus patterns could be seen in interaction **while** the action potentials are being recorded. In other words, the so-called "objective data" have no meaning of their own without support from the psychological situation from which they were derived. They are really by-products of the experiment proper. As long as one has **both** available for inspection simultaneously, one can make sense of the data. Without them, they are as meaningless as the molecular biologist's molecules in isolation from the cell of which they are components. The main point is that, however objective the data are, they will not stand on "their own feet" but rather will derive meaning only from the **psychological context** which is either implicitly or explicitly overlooked and not stated.

Riggs' problems are not yet over and his desertion of the mental for the bodily alternative causes as much trouble as the Structuralist option for the mental. For, the body will now have to do what the mental used to do. Flesh will have to carry out executive and other functions for Riggs that mind used to perform for the Structuralists. It will be able to do so only by Riggs' verbal attribution and not factually as by experimental demonstration.

Let us turn once more to Riggs' discussion of Descartes and the views of Claude's regarding the cell that had an impression on Riggs. Recall that excpet for the reflexes, Descartes' mechanical model would not work in explaining human choices, memories, will, and passions. For the non-reflex states and for inhibition of the reflex actions, Descartes postulated the soul. The soul was the governor, so to speak, and had power over the body, a **deus ex machine.** Today, no psychologist would admit to a study of the soul. Even mind, soul's successor, is abhorrent because it is no longer scientifically respectable. One alternative, as Riggs has suggested, is to "renounce the soul in favor of governance by the billions of brain cells that we now have observed " (Riggs, 1976, p. 127). The powers of the soul have been transferred to the nerve cells. Claude (1975) assigns similar powers to the cell--knowledge, resourcefulness, efficiency. Man has only the illusion of accomplishment.

Both Riggs and Claude have declared an equivalence of function for the traditional opposition, soul (or mind) and body, thus yielding the formula: Flesh=soul (or mind). The spiritual or immaterial has been transformed or reduced to the material, but at the price of making "the material " carry a burden which it cannot sustain. And this proposition requires a clarification of self-action, to which we turn next.

### Self-action, Interaction, Transaction

### Self-action[2]

Once upon a time, people were not unduly exercised about the origin of life because it was a commonplace observation that life arose "spontaneously." For example, maggots just somehow made their appearance out of rotting meat. Lice came from sweat, fireflies from fire, mice from the mud of the Nile, and water bugs from the water puddles left behind by a Spring rain. And some societies are said to have no notion yet of where babies come from. Even our myths about babies being found under a bush or delivered by a stork do not answer the question as to where babies really come from; only where they are left after they come from wherever it is that they come from. The preceding parade of bits of folklore is easily recognized today as naive if not downright superstitious. The notions displayed reveal a thing as being the cause of itself or, viewed otherwise, as an effect without a cause. Another illustration comes from the befuddled student who says, "O.K. I'm all by myself and, right out of the blue, an idea 'popped into my head.'" Where did it come from and how? The belief is that the "idea" originated by itself, from inside somewhere, unconnected with any other variable. In other

116

words, the mind is believed to be self-actional. So was the soul. And so were other 'free agents" such as the unconscious, preconscious, conscious, id, ego, superego, libido, death instincts, "I.Q." and will-power, since each is alleged to be the very fountainhead of forces that can produce certain effects.

## Interaction

Hula-balls is the clearest possible example of interaction. If one raises the outermost ball and lets go of it, he will observe a demonstration of Newton's third law which states that action and reaction are equal. In more obsolete terms, the situation can be observed as cause-effect or, in more up-to-date terms, as a correlational case, in which the two outermost hula balls are seen "in causal interconnection" (Dewey and Bentley, 1949, p. 108). They operate upon each other in a balanced way. Their inter-action is reciprocal or mutual and they may be viewed as if separate when not inter-acting. Other examples are provided by eliciting the knee jerk, the "separates" being the patellar tendon and reflex hammer. The muscle-nerve and heart-lung preparation will suffice, too. For example, do something to the lungs and note what happens to the heart.

## Transaction

The terms "occurrence," "situation," "field," "process," or "event," approximate Dewey and Bentley's definition of their favorite term "transaction." Consider such an event as a hurricane. There is no way in which it can be treated the way that hula balls in interaction can be described. For one thing, the hurricane is more complex in that it will not permit reduction to two simple things in interaction as will the hula balls. Secondly, it is constantly changing from moment to moment and over a considerable period of time by comparison with the hula ball situation. Therefore, the hurricane is more properly treated as a transaction while the hula balls will permit an interactional treatment. Another example from astronomy , namely, a galaxy with a diameter of 100,000 light years would never permit viewing it from either a self-actional or interactional stance. To attempt, verbally or otherwise, to isolate the component starts, planets, and asteroids in their myriad relationships out of the total system would be futile and senseless. Under transactional auspices, interpretations must not violate the totoality of the field observed, although aspects of it may be analyzed mor specifically, but never without awareness of the context from which they are abstracted. A transactional view emphasizes the dynamic, ongoing event and avoids imputing "phases of action to independent self-actors, or to independently interacting elements or relations" (Dewey and Bentley, 1949, p. 121).

117

If we may, at this point, reexamine our foregoing discussion of reductionism, we may find further help in achieving a clearer understanding of self-action, interaction and transaction. Weiss' cellular view is readily subsumed under a transactional approach. His stress on organization order ( or system) as attributes of the cell shows a transactional orientation by contrast with the reductionistic view of the molecular biologists, who do their work with an interactionist procedure in which a cell is considered a plastic bag of component elements in interaction with each other. But "when a molecular 'code' tells an egg whether it should turn into a turtle or a tiger" (Commoner, 1966, p. 31), we observe the workings of a self-actional approach. "The gene" and DNA as "the secret of life" are likewise self-actional. Let us recall, too, White's insistence on viewing culture as a distinct stream of events in its own right, with its determinants to be found at the same level without a forced reduction to some lower level. Webster's refusal to reduce the sociological to the psychological should also be noted. In sum, then, as with reductionsim, we observe that the three positions discussed in this section not only cut across various disciplines but all three points of view may be found in any one discipline.

### Exhibit A: How Does Endocrinology Fit In?

In an outstanding paper, "Sex Hormones and Executive Ability," Ramey (1973) displays a keen awareness of the levels of integration which the manifold scientific data fall into. As an endocrinologist, she discusses the role of endocrinological factors in various behaviors. As such, one would expect her to plug the role of hormones as behavior determinants. One soon discovers that, according to Ramey, in general, hormones merely serve as organismic setting factors for behavior rather than as causes, and the following discussion of her paper will attempt to show it.

In tune with the women's liberation movement, Ramey considers whether behavioral differences between men and women can be explained in terms of hormonal differences. She chides Freud and others for their attempted promulgation of the "anatomy-is-destiny" theory. She complains that, even today, " a bastardized endocrinology is being invoked to keep her (i.e., women) in her place" (p. 237), as when some physicians assert that women cannot be placed in jobs of top responsibility because of their monthly "hormonal imbalances." Even as an endocrinologist, Ramey is forced to reject the physiological control of sexuality. Why? Because of the tremendous diversity of the human sexual response. She is impressed by such facts as exclusive homosexuality, bisexuality, pedophilia, zoophilia, fetishism, the complete reversal of sex roles, and the total repression or sublimation of the sexual response. Since glands don't "produce" the variety of such behaviors, the implication is clear that the factors involved lie in the variety of conditions confronting the human organism. Ramey says as much when she asserts that in place of Freud's innate psychologic bisexuality, "we must substitute a concept of psychologic sexual neutrality in humans at birth" (p. 238-239).

Ramey catalogues other lines of evidence against a strict hormonal interpretation of human sexual behavior. For example, profound gonadal abnormalities (such as hermaphroditism or anatomical sexual ambiguities or contradictions) show no correlation with that individual's sex gender role. However, whatever sex assignment is made in such cases cannot be changed after the first year of life. As to homosexuality, acceptance of it in such societies as ancient Greece and Nazi Germany does not argue for an abnormal hormonal balance. Also pertinent is the discovery that injection of male hormones to either male or female homosexuals may provide a boost to the libido but without change of direction of the sex drive. Furthermore, the male sex hormone, testosterone, is supposed to be "take charge" or "mucho macho" hormone. For that reason, it has figured in studies of aggression in animals. but, in primate studies, testosterone levels were correlated with pecking order only under certain conditions. Since stress may also lower testosterone levels, how about our captains of industry? Should one select them on the basis of "low" secretion of the "manly hormone?" And how about aggressive women leaders such as Joan of Arc or the Viet Cong and Israeli women in battle, or the women guerrilas in the IRA or the underground Nazi fighters? Are they to be explained in terms of a higher level of testosterone in their blood stream? Do varying hormonal factors cause the behavioral variations that are so striking? Here is Ramey's answer:

> Men are different biologically from females. They
> are also different sociologically. Men become United
> States Presidents and women do not. But then women
> do become Premiers of Israel and India and Ceylon.
> Endocrinologists have nothing to contribute to the
> explanation of these national differences (p. 244).

What a beautiful recognition of levels of integration! Endocrines are endocrines and behavior is behavior and no amount of the former can attain the behavioral level. This is what Ramey appears to be saying. In fact, if anything, behavioral factors can influence the physiological ones. In some of her statements, she approaches a transactional behavioral position. But, what's the final upshot of her report? We find that, at bottom, she is caught up in a self-actional framework of traditional psychology. Here is the incriminating evidence in the form of direct quotation:

...the experiential component plays a dominant role
in shaping human sexual behavior. The primary importance of individual experience is in turn due to reduced
reliance upon gonadal hormones and increased intervention of the cerebral cortex (p. 244).

When it is a matter of endrocrinology, Ramey obviously
acknowledges the properiety of levels of integration. Accordingly, she
dethrones the glands of internal secretion, which she thinks play a
minor role (as in human sexuality). but she elevates the flesh known
as the cerebral cortex by attributing to it the storing of experience
and intervening in certain life situations. In other words, the brain,
but not the endocrine glands, is said to possess special powers.
Previously, we noted self-actional, interactional, and transactional
viewpoints within a given discipline. Here, we see a switch from
transactional to a self-actional view in the case of a single individual.
Ramey has obviously adopted the conventional view of the brain as a
special agent.

### Exhibit B: Pribram's Work

Pribram's (1971) labors in neuropsychology are brought together in
**Language of the Brain: Experimental Paradoxes and Principles in
Neuropsychology.** Because of Pribram's conspicuous position as a
leader in his field, his book deserves extra attention as representative
of current theory and experimentation in physiological psychology.
However, its tremendous range in coverage demands selectivity as
well in what we shall focus upon.

First, some general comments. Part I of Pribram's treatise deals
with basic brain function and the logic of neural wetware which
enables codes to be found within the brain; Part II concerns the role
played by such psychological processes as perception, motivation, and
emotion; Part III "focuses on the neural control and modification of
behavior"; and Part IV is "devoted to the structure of communication
between brains in terms of signs and symbols, and of the affairs of
man (p. xi).

The subtitle, "experimental paradoxes and principles in neuropsychology," points to the recurrent theme of Pribram's record
of theoretical evolution. According to the author, " The manuscript,
while primarily a theoretical statement, consists of formulations
arising from paradoxes and puzzles which emerged from experimental
results..." (p. ix). Did Pribram, then, reexamine his theories and their
underlying assumptions? No, he retained the same approach, an
approach which is essentially dualistic, reductionistic, and
self-actional. Pribram's avowed aim is to solve " the relation of the
brain to behavior and to subjective experience" (p. ix). That statement

presages the author's inevitable pursuit of the "brain mechanisms" of "subjective experience," an orientation which demands the duality, body and mind, and sets the stage for Pribram's extensive and thorough experimental program.

Not all of Pribram's views are in accord with conventional psychoneurology. For example, while he accepts the neuron doctrine of Sherrington which relied on the synapse to make it work, he notes the substitutability of receptor cells, spontaneous motor reorganization, and the fact tht "extremely large holes can be made in the brain with very little effect on just that highly complex behavior which one would expect to be especially sensitive to disruption if integration depended entirely on the presence of permanent associative connections" (p. 10). Therefore, he reasons, there must also be neuroelectric states in the brain, a fact which requires amendation of the neuron doctrine. The result is a two-process model of brain function: "Nerve impulse unit discharges on the one hand, and graded slow potential changes on the other" (p. 15). The former are propagated; the latter wax and wane and respond to a variety of non-neuronal influences such as chemical factors. A simple, ikonic isomorphism cannot explain the facts of percpetual constancy or pattern perception in cases of scotomata. Pribram reports that loss of 80% of the visual cortex ( and visual field) produces "little difficulty...in making discriminations" (p. 124). Such facts force Pribram to hypothesize the lasting phenomena with such a severely disturbed brain "must"[3] take place..."in the microstructure composed of junctional slow potentials" (p. 47). The hypothetical "mechanism" required to do the job is readily available in an optical process devised by mathematicians and engineers known as "holography."

Thus a theory evolved by a physicist working in the field of optics is imposed upon (forced to do service in) biological and behavioral data. To this reviewer, all of the foregoing theoretical borrowings from physics and their uninhibited ascription to biological tissues is too far-fetched. The Central Nervous System has been truly transformed into a highly Conceptual Nervous System. Is this not necessarily so when, as one limited aspect of an organism, the nervous system must carry the entire theoretical burden of what others structure as organism-stimulus object transition or field events?

One more point concerns a frequently missed defect of traditional brain dogma. The neuropsychologist agrees to tell his explanatory story about behavioral events strictly in neurological terms. But he does not do it without occasionally leaning upon the crude datum at hand or without revealing the slip that Pribram shows in the following example. He is making a point about behaviors that involve awareness or absence thereof, a point that does not need to be disputed here. Only the following concens us:

Thus, even the production of speech is unconscious
at the moment the words are spoken. My hypothesis
therefore is an old-fashioned one: we experience
in awareness some of the events going on in the brain,
but not all of them (p. 105).

How did "we" get into the act? If brains are involved in
awareness, unawareness, perception, memory, etc., with what other
brain are the brain's goings-on perceived? Or is it that when
psychological data are reduced to or transformed into mere
anatomical and physiological functioning, as they are here, they leave
out part of the data that we started with and we are, thus, forced to
drag in the whole organism, the "we" that we begin with[5].

**Languages of the Brain** provides a record of a dedicated worker in
the area of neuropsychology, one with an enviable mastery of its facts
and theories. It also serves as a model of the way in which
scientists study their data and how they construct their theories.
There is much more to the book than we have touched upon here, but
the preceding permits setting down certain propositions.

**(1).** Pribram starts with certain assumptions, namely, that the
human organism consists of a viable portion, the body, and an invisible
entity, the mind. Another assumption concerns the relationship
between the two. Pribram admits that, since he rejected strict
behaviorism, he has come to terms with Ryle's (1949) "Ghosts in the
Machine." He declares "images and feelings are ghosts that inhabit
my own and my patients' subjective worlds. ...They reside 'in' that
machine called the brain, yet they cannot be pointed at...I am
interested in the ghosts, the psychological functions--not just the
machine/brain nor just its regulation of overt behavior" (pp. 100-101).

**(2).** When Pribram comes upon explanatory paradoxes in his
experimentation, he resorts to amending his theories with supplementary principles that require further assumptions. Should one not heed
Goldstein's (1939) advice on patching up old theories, stated so
eloquently in the following statement? "The real crisis arises when
even in the face of new findings, the investigator cannot free himself
from the former theory; rather he attempts to preserve it... (p. 377).

**(3).** Pribram's brain constructs are entirely hypothetical and there
they remain unless and until they are substantiated. Only then can
they be used as explanatory principles. As presented, they do no
service in prediction or control.

**(4).** Pribram's theories are reductionistic and self-actional. The
brain is assigned "power-in-a-spot" which has a pseudo-location since

the ghosts residing in it  cannot be pointed at.

(5). The brain cannot do its explanatory work alone without silent support from the whole organism and stimulus object. Woodger's (1929) comment on biology of his era somehow seems relevant here: "Nothing is more striking in this science than the contrast between the brilliant skill, ingenuity, and care bestowed upon observation and experimentation, and the almost complete neglect of caution in regard to the definition and use of the concepts in terms of which its results are expressed" (p. 3).

Isn't it shocking how casually, and without explanation, Pribram made the radical switch from a Behavioristic to a Mentalistic position? A "Body Minus Mind " formula which had guided his work up to a certain point in his career is all-of-a-sudden traded for a "Body Plus Mind" formula. How would one go about explaining such a sudden conversion to the proverbial Man-from Mars?

### Exhibit C:  Retreat to James?

The American Psychological Association's Seventy-fifth Anniversary convention in 1967 coincided (almost) with the golden jubilee celebration of the publication of Willam James' **Principles of Psychology.** A small group organized a series of lectures and discussions to honor William James. The separate contributions have been published in a little book, **William James:  Unfinished Business** under the editorship of R.B. McLeod (1969).

In his contribution to the series, Krech (1969) aims to discuss the "mind-body" problem in praise of James. He sees the mind-body problem today as being essentially unchanged from the manner in which James formulated it as an interactionist, for as Krech admits, "we have advanced little beyond his ken of the matter" (p. 2). The reason is that we have neglected for too long the mind-body problem and William James' stricture to view brain events and behavior events in interrelation rather than as independent variables. As a result of our refusal to follow in William James' footsteps, we have lost much ground in solving the mind-body problem. In hsi sad state, Krech laments: "I cry for so many lost years of work by so many good and true and bright minds" (p. 6). Had we continued as James directed us to do, Krech is of the opinion that we would long ago have parted company with the learning theorists who are in hot pursuit of general descriptions and laws of learning that have profited us not at all. As a consequence, "we have just begun to work on the program he bequeathed us so many years ago" (p. 10).

Mandler (1969) discusses Krech's chapter. He questions the need to retreat 70 years to William James' psychology and, as for a general physiological theory for psychology, asks how would one know what is relevant and appropriate? Shouldn't one's theory really stand on its own? In fact, it is as difficult for a psychologist to choose among the various physiological conceptions as it is for physiologists to pick from among the variety of psychological theories. The more we learn about the increasing complexity of the neuron, the more difficult it becomes to know how to restrict neurological models for psychological purposes.

Even William James realized the dangers of a Conceptual Nervous System[5], or so James' advised, "Let us...relegate the subject of the **intimate** workings of the brain to the physiology of the future" (James, 1890,p. 81). Mandler agrees with James in pushing our problems to the future for solution. The pertinent question is: How long must we wait? And is it scientifically justifiable to hand over our problem to **another science** to solve at sometime in the future? Isn't it our responsibility to solve our own problems and **now** instead of taking refuge in evasion by "letting George do it?"

Mandler is not certain as to whether or not behavior needs a brain, but since the theoretical structure underlying behavior is in terms of "the mind" (p. 15), then a theory of the brain is needed. However, since it is difficult or impossible to prescribe or proscribe, let's see what the future will bring. He appears to wind up with a suggestion which might be paraphrased: "For no good reason, let us maintain the status quo. Let's wait and see."

"Does behavior really need a brain?" (p. 17) begins Millner's (1969) discussion of Krech's paper. He answers it by referring to plants, which perform many integrated responses without anything remotely resembling a nervous system. But, when it comes to organisms making choices, then much analysis of the behavior in question is called for "to reduce it to questions that can be entrusted to other disciplines" (p. 188). What Milner is apprehensive about is that if psychologists turn into physiologists with all sorts of fancy gadgetry, they will not return to the thorny problems of psychology. Besides, stress on neurophysiological and biochemical factors is likely to restrict research to a narrow set of problems that gadgetry can handle readily.

Because **William James: Unfinished Business** is a recent publication by leaders in the field who attempt to assess the current status of physiological psychology, it is noteworthy and must not be glossed over. What is the state of the art 75 years after the publication of James' great **Principles of Psychology**? Mandler (1969) speaks eloquently to that point in the following statement: "We must still leave the intimate or detailed workings of the brain to the future some 80 years after...In the meantime, psychology as well as physiology is working toward that future. It has not arrived yet" (p. 15). Compare the final pronouncement of Pribram's (1971) epic treatise with Mandler's assertion. In assessing the role of the brain in the mind-brain problem, Pribram declares: "The power of this peculiar biological organ, the brain, especially in man, is only beginning to be fathomed" (p. 385). Unfinished business? Will we hear the same refrain in the sesquicentennial celebration of William James' **Principles of Psychology**?

## Exhibit D: Drowning in Data?

I was intrigued with Krech's lamentations over "the lost years" for the research-deprived field of physiological psychology. Is it true, as Krech alleges, that little or no research has been carried out in this area over the years? Superficial inspection seemed to indicate a considerable literature, enough to warrrant an actual analysis of publications.

Let us consider the year-by-year output of papers published in the area of physiological psychology for the last 12 years. From a low of 800 papers per year in 1964, there is a steady increase to 2800 in 1970, with the annual figure hovering up around there for the last five years. In two different years, the figure rises to just over 3100 each. The sum of the 13 years' output yields a grand total of nearly 25,000 separate pieces of work! It seems that such lavish productivity should count toward a massive onslaught upon the mind-body or behavior-brain problem. One sees no reason why Krech should deplore the situation when we have such an extravaganza of work. But there is only one way to really appreciate this tremendous GNP which averages out (for the 12 years considered) about 10% of all the publications in **Psychological Abstracts.** One needs to scan experiment after experiment appearing in page after page of the successive volumes of **Psychological Abstracts.** Again, it does not seem impertinent to ask: "When will the breakthrough come? If not after 25,000 jobs, then after 50,000? And, is the resolution of the problem of the interaction of brain and behavior likely to manifest itself after some **one** single, just-right experiment or somehow by a summation of a certain number of them? Will they somehow fit into the jigsaw puzzle to create a meaningful design? How? Are there overall plans for achieving such a goal or are the individual experiments conducted piecemeal and helter-skelter, and if the latter, are the results likely to get us anywhere?

It is possible to take a contrary view, and suggest that we are already drowning in data. Kendig (1973) reports that this is true of all the sciences, a situation that has evoked the suggestion that, perhaps, a ten-year moratorium on scientific publications should be declared. Kendig places the blame largely on universities, whose "publish or perish" policy stimulates the accumulation of publications for the purpose of gaining advancement by their faculty publishers.

Isn't there a certain similarity in the titles? No matter where one looks, one has a **deja vu** experience. Have I seen this before? Let the reader do as I did: Have someone put before you the 1950 and the 1975 volumes of the **Journal of Physiological and Comparative Psychology** both opened at the Table of Contents but with volume number and dates of publications masked out. Can you tell which one was published 25 years earlier? I doubt it (unless one of the factors mentioned above cues you in). Apparently, since William James, psychologists have been delving into a myriad of widely scattered mini-problems. Paul Weiss (1969b) comments on this diversification in an article assessing the progress, or better, the lack of progress of biology in the past half-century. Comparing modern science to a giant industry, he notes certain benefits and drawbacks. "One of the drawbacks is that, by its sheer momentum,a mass of single-tracked workers tends to amplify any trend once that trend has started rolling" (p. 19). Is it possible that traditions of working in physiological psychology can spread and build up in the same way as traditions do in other areas of life? The generally rising number of publications would support such a notion.

As if the analysis of the literature in physiological psychology described above is not overwhelming enough, consider the possibilities for the future. The basic plan for experimentation appears to be to correlate some physiological measure with some psychological variable. When one ponders the billions of neurons, tissues, organs, plus the whole organism in infinite detail, the number of publications in physiological psychology could reach epidemic proportions!

## Toward an Authentic Physiological Psychology[6]

Let us revisit Riggs' laboratory. It is obvious that we have an organism-stimulus object relationship , but, for Riggs, the retinograms and brain waves are "the thing." Actually, what do the records say? How do they fit into the total picture? Do they signify anything more than the following: That when an organism views a visual pattern, certain neurological events occur in its eyes and brain? Is it not also true that when an organism views a visual pattern, there are simultaneously certain "goings-on" in its circulatory or endocrinological systems? Or, possibly, still other organs or systems?

### An Alternative to the Conventional Approach

Consider a psychological situation involving an organism and a visual stimulus object, set in a laboratory, and under specific conditions of illumination, temperature, and instructions from the experimenter. The stage is now set for our entrance upon the scene. How shall we play our role as scientists?

How about starting with the stricture that Pavlov enjoined upon his laboratory staff but abandoned himself in his theoretical construction: Observation, and then more observation. If one approaches the situation without any pre-observational prejudices, silent assumptions, or expectations about what he will see, or ought to see, all that he can see is an organism and a visual stimulus in confrontation. Of course, we must note that respiration, circulation, digestion and assimilation and, naturally, neurological action are all going on at the same time, but we leave these to the specialized interest of the physiologist.

Our specialized interest lies on a different level in a different dimension. As Bentley (1954) puts it: "The great task of psychologists, as of all other scientists, is to observe. Precision of observation is their goal. Without it their science stumbles" (p. 176). Bentley has criticized psychologists for making "direct, literal, observations of their own primary phenomena in the sense in which other sciences observe" (p. 182). If one thinks about it, one must admit that physicists do make direct literal observation of gravitating bodies, light, heat and chemical interactions. Why then do not psychologists report the situation as they see it ?

The localization of the psychological event in a field is the position Kantor assumes in interbehaviorism. In a recent paper in which Kantor (1973) considers what kind of system structure is essential for a scientific psychology, he first dissociates himself from certain preceding systems. Ancient mentalistic systems adhered to the formula **Psychology=Body plus Mind.** More recent behavioristic approaches rejected the mind part of this formula and were left with **Psychology=Body minus Mind,** which amounted to a coverup for the mind. Under that slogan, Body had to do the same job alone that Mind used to do under the old dispensation.

What is the alternative, according to Kantor? A fresh start altogether. In his approach, Kantor begins with observables. His raw data are field events as in all the sciences and these interbehavioral fields include an observer or investigator. Among his basic postulates are the following. The investigator must derive his constructs solely from observables rather than from pre-observational cultural impositions (such as mind, consciousness, et cetera) because, as a child of his culture, one is loaded with certain traditional ways of thinking about psychological events. Taken in order, the most fundamental starting point is the view that events consist of multifactorial fields. Some act by an organism in reciprocal relationship with another organism or thing, under certain setting conditions, media of contact,

127

such as light, et cetera, all constitute the field. Note that there is no glorification of the organism over the stimulus object, any more than a physicist would "favor" one of two gravitating objects. Each is equally important because each is indispensable to the event. Also, there is no postulation about governing or controlling "centers" in the organism simply because observation doesn't warrant such a claim and all preobservational preconceptions have been purged as rigorously as possible. This step, in itself, is an innovation with Kantor, a step which is obviously ignored in wholesale fashion in contemporary psychology. It need hardly be pointed out that Kantor's system is a far cry from a self-actional orientation. The organismic variable obviously cannot carry the burden alone. And if one applies the term "interactional" to the traditional model of a stimulus triggering a response as in the occipital lobe of the subject (i.e., a piece of the organism), then, it doesn't do full justice to Kantor's interbehavioral field conception which covers much more territory. Hence, the term transactional seems justified. The important point is to not identify the piecemeal interactional in the illustration above with Kantor's event or field orientation[7].

Viewed overall, Kantor's system is simplicity in itself when compared with the theories we have encountered in the area of physiological psychology. The latter are so complex that they can make no attempt to explain how "the bodily" produces or yields "the mental" or "discriminations," whichever is correlated with the bodily. Felix Deutsch (1959) helps to make this point in his book, **On the Mysterious Leap from the Mind to the Body,** in which he quotes a passage from Freud's autobiography. In that passage, Freud expresses his disappointment in physiology's failure to localize mental processes in the brain, even though he believed that they must be there somewhere His reaction is revealed in the following passage: "Many tried, and much research has been carried on in this direction, but to this very day we are still far from closing the 'mysterious leap' from the psychic to the physiologic" (p. 5). Should a more recent statement be sought, here is the last word from Penfield (1972), that "the ancient riddle of how brain and mind do interact is still unsolved" (p. 309). If one subscribes to the law of parsimony or the principle of economy, according to which the simplest available explanation is to be preferred, then the outcome of a comparison of the self- actional with the transactional or field view is qui te obvious.

My review of the recent literature persuades me to believe that an opposite view holds sway. Reductionistic theories that are obscure prevail over economical ones. Perhaps, another silent assumption governs the work of physiological psychologists, namely, that to be truly scientific is to be obscure.

The foregoing outline of Kantor's systematic approach to psychology may nevertheless be sufficient to enable us to examine how the data and theory of conventional physiological psychology fit into that approach. Kantor's fullest treatment of this area is to be found in his **Problems of Physiological Psychology** (1947), a work which may, in some future period, rank as a classic. Kantor first traces out the philosophical and scientific backgrounds of physiological psychology and the role of the brain in the history of science. The biology and psychology of the nervous system is treated next, with full attention to the dogma connected with the nervous system. An exhaustive survey of the data and theory of physiological psychology follows with a final consideration of ways of amending conventional physiological psychology, the intent being to formulate it as an authentic discipline. The last consideration is of special interest to us.

According to Kantor, the transformation of conventional physiological psychology to an authentic arm of general psychology requires the ejection of its underlying dualistic philosophy. And, if we grant the validity of deriving all constructs from observation, then certain criticisms are in order. (1) Physiological psychology as a theory of general psychology must be rejected simply because we know more about biological factors than we did 100 years ago and we can build constructions from observation. (2) Physiological psychology as a philosophy of parallelism or identity is not needed. In its place, we can derive a useful, scientifically-derived philosophy to guide our scientific work. (3) Physiological psychology as an investigative method (so prominent today) must be disowned because it forces physiological factors into the role of causes or counterparts of alleged intangibles in the psychological process; in other words, the anatomy or physiology becomes solely an anchorage for the ethereal "mental."

### The Role of a Genuine Physiological Psychology

If one were to deny biological factors any share whatsoever in psychological events, one woudl wind up with a disembodied spirit. Interbehavioral psychology, therefore, must acknowledge the organism's participation **qua** living "thing" in interbehavioral events. But, as Kantor (1947, p. 342) indicates, such participation varies tremendously. For example, in explaining a person's speaking German or Chinese or English what would be gained by including the action of diaphragm, vocal chords, tongue, etc.? However, any biological defectiveness such as absence of arms, legs, eyes or brain calls for different treatment. Even more general conditions such as glandular, fatigue and drug conditions can influence the interbehavioral outcome.

A comparison of conventional physiological psychology's handling of such factors is called for at this point. The classic case which the discipline leans upon is one in which speech disappears after a certain brain injury. The usual simplistic explanation has been that "the speech center" has been disrupted. Skinner's (1938) reply to such an explanation is that

> It is not difficult to point to a mere damage to verbal behavior and a corresponding damage to the nervous system, but almost no progress has been made toward describing neurological mechanisms responsible for the positive properties of verbal behavior (p. 424).

For illustrative purposes, let us again take the case of speech disruption with an interbehavioral treatment of same. A brain-injured organism is in one field and the uninjured organism in another. We now compare the two fields and find they are not by any means equal even when the "same(?)" organism is involved in both. Obviously, one factor can change the entire field. As a comparison, let us consider a person seeing a painting (a) with the lights out in total darkness and (b) with the lights turned on. One factor can change the entire field whether found in the medium of contact, in the biological conditions of the organism or in absence of the stimulus object. Note again, that the above condition (absence of light) can be equated (in its behavioral consequences) with an organism going suddenly blind. An authentic physiological psychology is free to derive such equivalences without ascribing a special status to the biological factors because all are neutral until assigned their proper role as determined by observation. In sum and essence, the biological organism provides a nucleus of setting factors as an aspect of the total event.

Another important platform in a transactional view of physiological psychology calls for an organismic biology. An organism viewed as an aggregate of so many cells, tissues, organs, and systems, each functioning in pieces and allegedly separately as a "governing" brain or a "speech-center," "pleasure center," et cetera is not very serviceable. Such disjointed entities are not in harmony with an evert or field orientation.

## A Sampling of Contradictions and Dissident Voices

From our categorizing of physiological psychologists as conventional, one should not infer that they are a 100% solid block that speaks with one voice. There are, here and there, departures from the orthodox viewpoint either (a) as outcome of the particular investigation engaged in or (b) as statement of differing viewpoint. We indicate some specimens of both briefly.

130

We are accustomed to read or hear that the brain effects behavior but can behavior affect brain? Psychologist know that Krech (1964) and his colleagues have demonstrated that "an enriched environment increases the depth of the cortex in the rat brain" (p. 118). They, therefore, recommend a Head Start Program for rats and for people. The whole point of this citation is that although Krech and associates find behavior influences upon brain development, that finding has no effect on their theoretical behavior. They hold to a reductionistic framework anyhow, despite a tremendously important finding in which the usual "cause" (i.e., the brain) and "effect" (behavioral response) are reversed. A convenient theoretical blind spot prevents them from detecting any threat to their narrow self-actional viewpoint, the threat of a need for a wider observation base than the one they are using. Perhaps, an accumulation of such findings can force a reconsideration of conventional theory.

Sidman (1960) discusses the various ways in which variability is treated. The psychologist may be ever so ready to attribute the variability of his data to physiological factors which may be beyond his competence to analyze physiologically. In turn, the biochemist may blame his lack of uniformity of the data he works with upon a certain whimsey in the subject's biochemistry. The biochemist blames the gene while the genetecist reverses the charges and tries to get the biochemist involved. Sidman cautions psychologists to make certain that they determine whether the variability of their data really stem from variables that lie outside their field of competence or from adequate experimental control. Until the psychologist has succeeded in eliminating all his sources of variability, there will be little advantage in joining forces with the genetecist or physiologist. Then, he reminds us (p. 183) of Skinner's argument for an independent science of behavior.

**Biofeedback**

All publication explosions are not to be decried, since those in the area of biofeedback have opened up a new area of raw data that we never knew existed. It seems that practically every nook or cranny of the organism which bears a muscle can be brought under operant control. When we inquire as to the significance of this type of investigation, note what Bernard Engel (1972) has to say:

> There is...[a] question which has never been made ex-
> plicit, but which I think should be raised. The question
> is, "of what importance is it to the science of psychology
> that autonomic responses can be operantly conditioned?"
> And my answer is, "probably none whatsoever." Whether
> or not autonomic responses can be operantly conditioned

is an empirical question which adds nothing conceptually
to our knowledge about the principles of learning. In
my opinion the great importance of operant conditioning
of autonomic responses comes from what it tells us
about the autonomic nervous system. It is physiology,
not psychology, which is going to have to revise some
of its principles...(p. 205).[8]

What a dismal judgment . on the standard dogma of conventional physiological psychology, with its reliance on the nervous system as an anchorage or, to change the metaphor, as a rock of ages! The following statement Skinner made many years ago is again articulate in this regard:

Not only are laws of behavior independent of neurological
support; they actually impose certain limiting conditions
upon any science which undertakes to study the internal
economy of the organism. The contribution that a science
of behavior makes to neurology is a rigorous and quantitative statement of the program before it (1938, p.432).

Kantor (1922) has been making similar criticisms against the psychologists' reliance on fictitious neurology for over half a century and preceded Skinner with the formulation of an independent science of behavior. The question is: Will the recent observations result in producing changes in the interpretation of physiology, or will they go as unheeded as the earlier criticisms? We as interbehaviorists would hope the message is received.

### Acknowledgments

I wish to thank my colleague, Grant Kenyon, for his critical reading of this paper and for his helpful suggestions.

### Footnotes

1. Kantor (1938) has long and assiduously urged psychologists to check the influence upon them of their cultural tradition.

2. Self-action, interaction, and transaction are discussed by Handy (1964) .

3. "There is no 'must' at all in natural science; 'must' belongs to for-mal logic" (Woodger, 1929). Is not the **must** here a function of the assumption that Pribram started with?

132

4. Many of the preceding statements are excerpts from my review of Pribram's book (Pronko, 1972).

5. Although Skinner (1957) has not outright rejected a neurological correlate of behavior, he has for long inveighed against "a conceptual nervous system" for psychology.

6. This term was lifted "bodily" from Kantor's **Problems of Physiological Psychology** (1947, p. 331).

7. In his earlier work, Kantor used the term "interaction" for which he has more recently substituted the term "interbehavioral."

8. This gem was called to my attention by my colleague, Grant Kenyon.

## References

Bannister, D. 1968. The myth of physiological psychology. **Bulletin of the British Psychological Society**, 21, 229-231.

Bentley, A.F. 1954. **Inquiry into Inquries.** Boston: The Beacon Press.

Chargaff, E. 1971. Preface to a grammar of biology. **Science,** 172, 637-642.

Claude, A. 1975. The coming of age of the cell. **Science,** 189, 433-435.

Commoner, B. 1966. **Science and Survival.** New York: The Viking Press.

Deutsch, F. 1959. **On the Mysterious Leap from the Mind to the Body.** New York: International Universities Press, Inc.

Dewey, J. and Bentley, A.F. 1949. **Knowing and the Known.** Boston: The Beacon Press.

Diamond, M.C., Krech, D. and Rosenzweig, M.R. 1964. The effects of an enriched environment on the histology of the rat cortex. **Journal of Comparative Psychology,** 123, 111-119.

Goldstein, K. 1939. **The Organism.** New York: American Book Company.

Handy, R. 1964. **Methodology of the Behavioral Sciences.** Springfield, Ill.: Charles C. Thomas Publisher.

Hanson, N.R. 1958. **Patterns of Discovery.** Cambridg e: Cambridge University Press.

James, W. 1890. **Principles of Psychology.** New York: Holt (2 volumes).

James, W. 1909. **The Meaning of Truth: A Sequel to Pragmatism.** New York: Longmans, Green.

James, W. 1912. **Essays in Radical Empiricism.** New York: Longmans, Green.

Kantor, J.R. 1922. The nervous system: Psychological fact or fiction. **Journal of Philosophy,** 19, 38-49.

Kantor, J.R. 1938. The nature of psychology as a natural science. **Acta Psychologia,** 4, 1-61.

Kantor, J.R. 1947. **Problems of Physiological Psychology.** Bloomington, Indiana: Principia Press.

Kantor, J.R. 1973. System structure and scientific psychology. **Psychological Record,** 23, 451-458.

Kendig, F. 1973. Downing in data: Editorial. **Saturday Review,** April, p. 26.

Laver, A.B. 1972. Precursors of psychology in ancient Egypt. **Journal of the History of the Behavioral Sciences,** 8, 181-195.

Lynch, G. 1975. Aftermaths of brain lesions (a review). **Science,** 187, 736.

Mandler, G. 1969. Acceptance of things past and present: A look at the mind and the brain. In R.B. McLeod (Ed.) **William James: Unfinished Business.** Washington: American Psychological Association.

Milner, P. 1969. Do behaviorists really need a brain drain? In R.B. McLeod (Ed.) **William James: Unfinished Business.** Washington: American Psychological Association.

Penfield, W. 1972. The electrode, the brain and the mind. **Zeitschrift fur Neurologie,** 201, 297-309.

Pribram, K.H. 1971. **Languages of the Brain: Experimental Paradoxes and Principles in Neuropsychology.** Englewood Cliffs, New Jersey: Prentice-Hall.

134

Pronko, N.H. 1972. Pribram, Karl H. **Languages of the Brain** (a review). **Psychological Record,** 22, 280.

Ramey, E.R. 1973. Sex hormones and executive ability. **Annals of the New York Academy of Sciences,** 208, 237-245.

Riggs, L.A. 1976. Human visions: Some objective explorations. **American Psychologist,** 31, 125-134.

Ryle, G. 1949. **The Concept of Mind.** New York: Barnes and Noble.

Sidman, M. 1960. **Tactics of Scientific Research.** New York: Basic Books.

Skinner, B.F. 1938. **The Behavior or Organisms.** New York: Appleton-Century Company.

Skinner, B.F. 1957. **Verbal Behavior.** New Jersey: Prentice-Hall.

Warren, H.C. 1934. **Dictionary of Psychology.** New York: Houghton Mifflin Company.

Webster, M. 1973. Psychological reductionism, methodological individualism and large-scale problems. **American Sociological Review,** 38, 258-273.

Weiss, A. 1968. **Dynamics of Development: Experiments and Inferences.** New York: Academic Press.

Weiss, A. 1969a. The living system: Determinism stratifield. **Studium Generale,** 22, 361-400.

Weiss, A. 1969b. Living nature and the knowledge gap. **Saturday Review,** November 29, 19-56.

White, L.A. 1949. **The Science of Man.** New York: Groves Press.

Woodger, J.H. 1929. **Biological Principles: A Critical Study.** London: Kegan, Paul, Trench, Trubner and Company Ltd.

136

# AN INTERBEHAVIORAL ALTERNATIVE TO COGNITIVE-BEHAVIORISM

Dennis J. Delprato

Cognitionism is by no means a new force on the psychological scene. Observer (1978) drew a humorous parallel between what has been pretentiously proclaimed as the "cognitive revolution" (Dember, 1974; Mahoney, 1977; Marzillier, 1980; Segal and Lachman, 1972) and another feature of our times. He stated that:

> Recycling has recently become a distinct institution
> in the economics of modern living. Old paper, glass
> metals, are hoarded and recycled as new materials.
> The basis of this collecting and reprocessing is a
> presumed need to replenish declining stockpiles of use-
> ful materials, or to ameliorate the need to efface
> environmental amenities. Psychology has not escaped
> the recycling fashion, but in a reverse manner. It was
> not the scarcity of basic materials that has induced
> the refurbishing process and procedure. On the contrary.
> Recycling in psychology consists of the reintegration
> of sensations and other mental processes that should
> long have been disposed of forever (p. 28).

## Renovations of Cognition in Behavior Theory

The view that has been referred to as cognitive-behavior theory (e.g., Barber, Spanos and Chaves, 1974; Kendall and Hollon, 1979) or the cognitive-learning perspective (e.g., Mahoney, 1977) is the major point of focus for this chapter. The most important reason for this is that advocates of cognitive-behaviorism have promised us a view of human behavior that integrates the best of cognitive and behavioral approaches that is free of the pitfalls of internalism, intrapsychism, or mentalism. And there is no question that cognitive-behavioral theory is a positive step toward a naturalistic rather than a transcendental approach to behavior. Unfortunately, transcendentalism nevertheless contaminates the cognitive-behavioral solution.

Numerous interrelated circumstances contributed to renovations of cognition in behavioral theory. Some of these are overviewed below.

## (1). Dualism

The notion that transcendental powers propel human activities follow from the distinction between spirit and matter and between mind and body that is fundamental in our Western cultural tradition. Because of this, the dualistic character of the cognitive (or mind)-behavioral (or body) language is completely consistent with the years of cultural training psychologists receive.    The dualistic hypothesis is unequivocally evident in numerous statements made by advocates of cognitive-behaviorism.    Note the inherent assumption that the organism is separated into two components, mental and physical (behavioral), in the following quotations that examplify central features of contemporary cognitive-behavioral theorizing:

>    ...cognition has causal influence on behavior...(Bandura, 1977b, p. 10).

>    Ideas are rarely transformed into correct actions without error on first attempt...(Bandura, 1977b, p. 28).

>    Knowledge [cognition] of results...enhances performance [behavior]...(Bandura, 1977b, p. 163).

>    ...internal personal factors and behavior...operate as reciprocal determinants of each other...(Bandura, 1977b, p. 195).

>    ...cognitive representations are said to causally influence ...feelings, actions, and so on (Mahoney, 1977, p. 8).

>    ...beliefs or expectancies [are] better predictors of human behavior than external variables...(Mahoney, 1977, p. 8)

>    From the cognitive-behavioral viewpoint, **subjects carry out so-called 'hypnotic' behavior when they have positive attitudes, motivations, and expectancies toward the test situation**...(Barber et al., 1974, p. 5).

## (2) Mechanistic View of Conditioning and the Involuntary-Voluntary Dichotomy

In the turbulent transformation of the subject matter of psychology from transcendental soul to that of organisms in contact with their surroundings, materialism and mechanism played prominent and, probably necessary, roles (Kantor, 1969).    One outcome of psychology's affiliation with nineteenth-century science in an attempt to free itself of psychiatric formulations was the mechanistic conditioning conception. The Pavlovian conditioning paradigm stemmed from the physiological concept of the reflex and, thus, at the time appeared to provide a properly "scientific" model to those attempting to bring psychology into the realm of naturalistic science. Thus, the mechanistic S->R model of reflexology became the interpretative framework of early behaviorists such as Watson, Smith and Guthrie, and Weiss. The result was that behavioral outcomes of respondent procedures were interpreted in terms of the reflexological model.

The mechanistic view of reflex action is closely related to the traditional distinction between involuntary and voluntary action. If all psychological behavior is a matter of the conditioning of automatic, mechanical reflexes, no room is left for voluntary acts. Furthermore, since voluntary behavior is, according to tradition, always conscious, consciousness has no place in the mechanistic interpretation of conditioning. This thinking is so entrenched that many psychologists today define respondent conditioning as repeated pairings of a CS and UCS that produce involuntary, automatic, unconsciousness reactions to the CS. Typifying such a view is the title of a chapter appearing in the 1970's--"There is no convincing evidence for operant or classical conditioning in adult humans" (Brewer, 1974). Is the author implying that respondent (and operant) procedures or interactions are ineffectual in modifying behavior? No, he insists to have marshalled evidence that conditioning effects are always the result of "conscious hypotheses and expectations" (Brewer, 1974, p. 2). Empirically, of course, this author identified phenomena not well-accounted for by mechanical principles. Theoretically, too, these phenomena (instances of which are discussed below) are related to the voluntary, cognitive side of the traditional voluntary-involuntary and cognitive-noncognitive dichotomies that are implied by the mechanical hypothesis.

### (3). Respondent Conditioning as Representative of all Non-Innate Behavior

Early behaviorists' acceptance of the traditional innate-learned distinction combined with a dearth of systematic formulations concerning behavioral development led to the equation of learning with development and of conditioning with learning (Hilgard and Marquis, 1940). Thus, traditional behaviorism often appeared to attempt to explain virtually all human behavior with the concepts of reflex, conditioning, and learning. As Observer (1978) notes, "mentalists assumed that psychologists on the whole were too deeply bitten by Pavlov's dogs" (p. 158). Especially troublesome was the S->R model borrowed from biology. The reliance on overt stimuli and responses led many to get something in between the S and R--this something, as mentioned above was part of our cultural heritage--the mind or cognitive structures and processes.

139

## (4). Effects of Instructional and Informational Variables

The results of numerous investigations reveal shortcomings with the mechanistic theory. An implication of the reflexological view is that CS-UCS pairings result in the CS serving as a substitute for the UCS and thus the UCS-evoked reflex UCR is transferred to the CS such that the CR is a replica of the UCR. Zener's (1937) experiment, among others, showing several differences between the CR and UCR with food and acid UCSs pointed out the inaptness of such a view. It is a common observation in aversive conditioning with rats that the UCR to a footshock UCS consists of vellicative foot movements but that the response developing to the CS is often immobility. As Zener observed with his dogs, the rat appears to "expect" the UCS and the CR, therefore, seems to function as a preparatory response (see Tolman, 1932).

Of notable importance for cognitive theories of behavior is the large number of studies of human electrodermal conditioning implicating instructional and informational factors, especially but not restricted to, language variables (Bandura, 1969, Brewer, 1974; Grings, 1965, 1973; Grings and Dawson, 1973). Experiments such as that of Cook and Harris (1937) represent one way in which researchers have studied the role of instructional variables in conditioning situations. That is, subjects are supplied with verbal descriptions of CS-UCS relationships, e.g., "the CS will be followed by shock." Other strategies for investigating informational variables (cognitive mediation) have involved the use of subjects' verbal reports concerning their identification of CS-UCS relationships and masking tasks to minimize identification of the CS-UCS relationship.

The theoretical issue in this work is whether or not responding to CSs varies as a function of cognitive mediation or "awareness" (of the CS-UCS relationship). Empirically, awareness is related to the experimenter's procedures, e.g., informing the subject of the CS-UCS relationship, or to the subject's behavior, e.g., verbal report of the CS-UCS relationship. Positive correlations between awareness so defined and responding to the CS have been interpreted as support for the role of cognitive mediation in respondent conditioning as against the original mechanical, noncognitive hypothesis. Since behavioral effects of CS-UCS pairings are not always related to the cognitive variables (experimenter supplied information, subjects' reports of CS-UCS relationships), some have suggested that a distinction be made between "true" conditioning and perceptual or mediated behavioral change (Grings, 1965; Mowrer, 1938; Razran, 1955). This distinction amounts to a preservation of the mechanistic hypothesis ("true" conditioning) and the addition of a "new" principle (cognitive mediation) to handle cases in which the S->R translation is inadequate.

### (5). Problems with the Generality of CS-UCS Pairings in Nonhuman Research

The mechanistic, reflexological foundations of conditioning have contributed to the view that temporal contiguity between the CS and UCS is the critical ingredient of the conditioning procedure. However, several discoveries in animal conditioning laboratories suggest that temporal contiguity between the CS and UCS is not sufficient for conditioning effects (see review by Rescorla, 1972). Representative of this research is Rescorla's (1968) experiment using response suppression to a CS as the measure of fear behavior. Rescorla found that suppression was not accounted for by the number of CS-UCS pairings; rather, the amount of suppression (a) increased with increases in the probability of the shock UCS during a CS and (b) decreased with increases in the probability of the UCS in the absence of the CS. Regardless of the number of CS-UCS pairings, when the UCS was equally likely in the presence and absence of the CS, little or no conditioning occurred. Findings such as these suggest that fear behavior develops to a CS not when the CS is paired with shock but when the CS predicts shock. Rescorla has offered the hypothesis that the correlation between the CS and UCS (involving mediating expectancy relationship), not their contiguous pairing (leading to an automatic connection of stimulus and response) is the critical factor in respondent conditioning (cf. Bolles, 1979).

### Advantages and Deficiencies of Cognitive-Behaviorism

Despite interbehaviorism's pessimistic view of cognitive solutions to the problem of behavior, several key features of interbehaviorism are in complete agreement with certain basic assumptions of cognitionism, especially the influential cognitive-behavioral movement (see also Grossberg, 1981). For example, interbehaviorism is an interactional or even transactional system. This means that the one-way stimulus-response model is rejected in favor of a recognition of the reciprocal relationship between the organism and its environment or between response and stimulus. Second, and related to this, is the conceptualization of the organism as actively, rather than passively, involved with its surroundings. Thus, while original behaviorism borrowed the reflexive stimulus-response formula, which signifies that some condition puts an otherwise inert organism into action, interbehaviorism and cognitive-behaviorism emphasize the active nature of psychological activity. Third, cognitive-behaviorists argue, as have cognitionists in general, that traditional behaviorism's insistence that we concentrate only on overt behavior is restrictive and incomplete. Kantor always agreed with this as indicated by his analyses of non-overt acts such as perceiving, knowing, feeling, emotional behavior, thinking, and imagining. A fourth point of agreement between cognitionism and interbehaviorism is the recognition

141

that learning, conditioning, and reinforcement are but part of the story.

Given these points of agreement with cognitive-behaviorism, what then, does interbehaviorism find deficient with the view? In many ways, the overall major porblem with cognitive theorizing is that it is a throwback to traditional transcendentalistic dualism. Cognition and behavior are substituted for spirit and matter or mind and body. Observer (1977) forcefully addressed the alleged "broadening" of behavior theory via the "cognitive revolution" as follows:

> The dichotomization of psychological activities is obviously
> not based on any observation, whether informal or exper-
> imental . Now this disjunction is not merely the careless
> use of language. No. The style of the rhetoric harks
> back to venerable mind-body assumptions which are
> only masked by linguistic drapery....The entire reversionary
> movement is symbolized by the term cognitive, which
> historically was employed to differentiate between
> different structures and functions of the spiritistic entites
> called consciousness. The unfortunate result is that
> psychistic ways of description are imposed upon the
> occurring behavior of organisms (pp. 351-352).

The classic problem of how a nonspatial, occult, entity can lead to spatial movements of tongues and arms, how a physical change in the auditory nerve can give rise to auditory sensations, and how a decision inside a person's head can activate movement of his muscles never has been resolved and it is safe to say it never will be. I refer to this state of affairs as the "somehow problem." How do images produce action? Somehow. How do thoughts give rise to writing? Somehow. How does the expectation of success contribute to success? Instead of relying on cognitive mediators to "somehow" produce behavior, interbehaviorism offers an alternative to the traditional conceptualization of cognitive mediators. Note that classical S->R theory also confronts us with the somehow problem--stimuli somehow (automatically) produce responses; thus, S->R theory is not a very satisfying alternative to cognitionism.

Another problem with cognitionism is that it locates psychological events inside the organism. Kantor refers to this as organocentrism. This organocentrism, in combination with the desirability of anchoring cognitions in the nervous system to "keep them from floating off into diaphanous realms represented only by words" (Kantor, 1947, p. 137), leads to brain dogma. Brain dogma is the assumption that psychological behavior is a causal product of the brain (Delprato, 1979; Kantor, 1947). Brain dogma, in turn, contributes to neglect, sometimes subtle, of the fact that human behavior is very much a matter of social conditions. The result is that we look inside the person's brain or presumed mental apparatus for solutions to what are actually social problems. The individual who commits socially undesirable acts is said to have a problem with his mind (e.g., distorted cognitions) or brain.

Several features of interbehaviorism enable us to avoid the pitfalls of cognitionism. Let us now turn to them.

## Holistic Nature of Organismic Activity

The very basic assumption of cognitive-behaviorists that in order to adequately deal with the human condition we must work with both behaviors and cognitions(seen in the dualistic statement that cognitions influence behavior) is put in a different light if we consider interbehaviorism's suggestion that we need not artificially devide up the organism into bits and pieces. I am referring to the interbehaviorist's emphasis on a total, integrated organism. In other words, "interbehavioral psychology assumes that only the activities of the total organism participate in psychological events" (Kantor, 1942, p. 181). While mentalistic and behavioristic approaches have led to attempts to correlate psychological phenomena with particular organs, parts of organs, or mental structures or functions, interbehaviorism focuses on the whole organism. Of course, holism thus makes unnecessary the reductionsitic sorts of analyses that seek to reduce psychological activity to biological or mental bases. The holistic perpsective offers an alternative to the separation of cognitions and behavior. Instead of a dichotomy of cognitions and behavior that amounts to the culturally transmitted notion that humans are made up of mind and body, the interbehaviorist recognizes the unitary, integrated nature of organismic activity.

## The Interbehavioral Field and the Causation Problem

Holism is closely related to another feature of interbehaviorism that confronts head on a basic assumption of cognitive theories. This is the issue of causation. Cognitionists insist that cognitive concepts are indispensable in behavior theory because cognitions are critical causes of behavior. There appears to be something of a circularity or self-fulfilling prophecy problem here. First, the nineteenth-century view of science is taken that behavior is produced by specific causal agents. Then, after behavior occurs, a causal agent, often in the form of a cognition, is contrived. Antagonists on both sides of the dispute argue over whether the S->R or cognitive model is necessary to account for behavior have not disagreed with the causal assumption. Indeed, they have each argued for their own favorite class of causes--external stimuli or internal cognitions.

143

Interbehaviorism takes a different tack from that of the S->R versus cognitive disputants by substituting for cause the view of participating field factors. Kantor maintains that the traditional causal construct has been an important contributor to what is referred to above as the somehow problem. As he stated in **Psychology and Logic** (1950):

> The widely held view that when thinkers adopted the
> causal notion to account for things they discarded mystic
> processes and became exclusively occupied with events
> as caused by other events is, however, scarcely true.
> The evolution of thecausality construct did not once
> and for all establish a mode of thinking concerned
> only with laws derived from observed things and events.
> Actually, the interest in cause in no sense excluded
> the mystical from the explanations ofnatural happenings.
> Worse, from time to time cause itself was made into
> a mystical process, for under this rubric were placed
> innumerable magical forces which were presumed to
> bring things about in some unknown, and sometimes
> impossible manner (p. 148).

The interbehaviorist recognizes that attempts to account for organismic activities by seeking causes for them in stimuli, the brain, or cognitions represents acceptance of the nineteenth-century view that the purpose of science is to identify cause-effect sequences. Instead of directing the psychologist to identify internal or external causes of behavior, interbehaviorism adopts the view of twentieth-century science that psychological events are components of event fields (Mountjoy, 1976). Psychological phenomena are defined in fields according to their space-time boundaries, the factors that comprise the field, and the interrelationship among the factors. The factors contained in psychological fields include (a) the organism, (b) those objects, events, and other organisms with which the organism interacts, (c) the medium of contact through which the organism interacts with the other events of the field, e.g., light which permits the organism to see an object, and (d) the setting or context of the organism- environment interactions. The field-theoretical conception rules out the traditional creative-agent view of cause with its intimations of ultimacy and absoluteness because "causation basically amounts to the copresence of a given number of components [in a field]" (Kantor, 1950, p. 159; also see Smith, 1973, p. 157).

Kantor (1947) and Staddon (1973) have shown how the view of cause as the copresence of the factors of a field enables psychologists to avoid causal-chain determinism that provides the rationale for viewing behavior in terms of either stimulus-response sequences or as the effects of postulated internal, mediating processes such as neural events and cognitions. Causal forces such as stimuli and cognitions are constructed in attempts to bridge temporal and spatial gaps between developmental and hereditary factors that participate in psychological activities. As Staddon argues, these attempts are simply versions of the hook-and-eye systems of early physics in which clockwork-like streams of hooks and eyes were used to account for action at a distance phenomena. As physicists studied their events more carefully they abandoned the simple cause-effect, hook-and-eye theories in favor of field-theoretical views. Perhaps psychology's version of hood-and-eye theory--cognitionism--will undergo a similar fate as psychologists become more intimately involved with the events of behavior.

## Developmental-Interactionism

Another feature of interbehaviorism that goes far toward placing cognitions in a different light is its developmental-interactional orientation. When we ignore the developmental history of an organism, it is very easy to load it with all sorts of internal forces and agencies in an attempt to account for its current behavior. Interbehaviorism's view that all psychological interactions are historical, which is to say that they originate in the organism's concrete interactions with its surroundings, suggests that we must become intimately involved with the history of organisms if we are to detect the development of psychological fields and abandon attempts to construct internal mediators of behavior. It is perhaps unfortuante that careful study of the actual developmental (or interactional) history of organisms is so difficult. The difficulty of observing an organism's actual interbehavioral history in combination with the failure to recognize its necessity, however, has often led to the type of situation where we thrust two individuals into an "intelligence testing" situation, observe different criterion behaviors, then proceed to claim differences in the cognitive capacity. Had we observed the interbehavioral histories of the two individuals, we would have discovered developmental factors accounting for their different performances in the testing situation, thereby making any cognitive and genetic constructions superfluous. The main point of developmental interactionism is that the individual's present behavior is an outcome of the entire history of interactions with its surroundings. The interactions are actual happenings, although they are "minute interactions with objects that occur through milliseconds of time" (Kantor, 1971, p. 139). It is "during these interactions [that] the organism takes on or builds up its response configurations--some of which we call traits--while the objects take on reciprocally stimulational functions" (Kantor, 1971, p. 139). In relation to the previous discussion of cause, note that there is little use in attempting to locate "cause" at any particular location in the devlepmental stream. At best, "it" is all of the factors of the current field. Thus, cognitions as causes of current behavior are not needed for a complete account.

## Cognition as Interbehavior

Having ruled out thoughts, images, perception, desires, knowledge, memory, learning, etc., as mentalistic states or processes, what does interbehaviorism do with these concepts. It does much the same thing that radical behaviorism (Skinner, 1953, 1963) later came to do. That is, interbehaviorism views cognitions as organismic acts or as interbehaviors. Specifically, the referents to the term "cognition" are identified as subtle or implicit responses that, as Kantor stated in 1924, are "morphologically and functionally          continuous with our overt responses" (p. 298).    Thus, instead of the dualistic claim that thoughts affect actions, which involves the bifurcation of the individual into two parts, the interbehavioral view is that thoughts are actions.

The suggestion that "mental" can only refer to action is a central feature that distinguishes interbehavioral psychology and radical behaviorism from traditional or methodological behaviorism. The latter basically admits mental or cognitive as separate from behavior (dualism); presentations of cognitive-behaviorism have not shed this aspect of methodological behaviorism. It is noteworthy, however, that certain points raised by cognitive theorists emphasize the unity of psychological activity of psychological activity and the corollary that cognitions are actions rather than mental  phantasms. As an example of this, consider the following:

> ...None of the four fundamental life operations--sensing,
> moving, emoting, and thinking--is experienced in isolation.
> If an individual senses something (e.g., sees a stick),
> he also tends at the very same time, to do something
> about it (pick it up, kick it, or throw it away), to have
> some feeling about it (like it or dislike it), and to think
> about it (remember seeing it previously or imagine
> what he can do with it).   Similarly, if he acts, emotes,
> or thinks, he **also** consciously or unconsciously involves
> himself in the other behavior processes....As in the
> case of thinking and the sensori-motor processes, we
> may define emotion as a complex mode of behavior
> which is integrally related to the other sensing response
> processes (Ellis, 1962, p. 39).

This statement is made by Albert Ellis in his **Reason and Emotion in Psychotherapy**. Several years later, the cognitive theorist, Ellis (1977), warned against the arbitrary separation of perceptual- cognitive from "other" behavior. Writers in addition to Kantor, Skinner, and Ellis, opposed to the dualism of mind-body, inner-outer, and cognition-behavior, have emphasized the centrality of action, conduct, or behavior in psychology; hence, they have taken steps that resolve the "somehow problem" that results from the separation of cognition and behavior revealed in the cognitionists' claim that thoughts affect actions. Some of these writers include Dewey and Bentley (1949). Wittgenstein (1958), Ryle (1949), and Schafer (1976, 1978). Lang and his associates (Lang, 1977, 1979; Lang, Kozak, Miller, Levin and McLean, 1980) have recently taken steps toward an interbehavioral view of the cognition problem in their theoretical and empirical work in the area of emotional imagery: "We firmly reject the dualism implied by phenomenological analysis; the image is **not** a stimulus in the head to which we respond; it is itself an active response process" (Lang, 1979, p. 500). Additional considerations pertaining to "cognition" will be presented below in the course of a consideration of some specific events.

## Interbehavioral Interpretations of Selected "Cognitively Induced" Behaviors

For the final section of this chapter, I have selected for inter-behavioral analysis three phenomena that are noteworthy for the apparent support they provide to cognitive theory. While it would be misleading to suggest that the accounts of these phenomena offered below are complete, they nonetheless demonstrate some of the specific ways in which the interbehavioral perspective approaches behaviors that have traditionally stimuluated cognitive renditions.

### Magnetized Finger Instructions

Let us present instructions to subjects that their index fingers are magnetized:

> With your elbows resting against your body, firmly interlace
> your hands together with your fingers interlocking.
> Next, separate your index fingers so they are pointing
> outward parallel to each other. Do this. Now, imagine
> that your index fingers are two magnets that are being
> attracted to one another. See them going together.
> Feel them going together.

Next, suppose the subjects are instructed to imagine that an iron bar is placed between their index fingers as follows:

> With your hands and index fingers in the same position,
> that is, your index fingers are again pointing outward
> parallel to each other, imagine an iron bar between
> the fingers keeping them apart. The fingers are resting
> on the bar and remain rigidly pointing outward because
> of the iron bar.

A highly reproduceable consequence of the magnetized fingers instructions is that subjects' fingers move together and they verbally report no deliberate attempt to move the fingers (e.g., Delprato and Holmes, 1978; Sparks, 1975). Furthermore, the fingers are considerably less likely to move together to the "iron bar" instructions than to the former ones. This latter finding rules out a purely muscular interpretation (e.g., fatigue) of the response to the magnetic fingers instructions. Thus, the cognitionist might argue that central, rather than peripheral, factors account for the fingers "involuntarily" moving together and that the image of the fingers moving is the cause of the motor behavior. Additionally, the subject's expectations that the fingers would go together in combination with a positive attitude and motivation to succeed might be invoked (see Barbar et al., 1976). Individual differences in the behavior--some people exhibit no movement, for example--would be accounted for by differences in cognitive states and processes. Some subjects have a better power of imagination than others, some "wanted" to foil the experimenter, etc. Some people (e.g., the "retarded") simply are not "gifted" with much in the way of cognitive ability.

From an interbehavioral perspective, however, we recognize that the particular instructions for the fingers to move together are tantamount to requesting the subject to move them together. (Likewise, the iron bar instructions specify the behavior of keeping the fingers apart.) The interbehavioral history of many subjects is sufficiently similar such that they are prepared to interact with the instructions in a particular predictable way. Of course, the key variables in the magnetic fingers instructions were several words and phrases, such as "imagine," "two magnets attached to one another," and "fingers moving together." But the total context in which the words were embedded (setting factors) is also importantly related to the magnitude of occurrence of the target behavior. The total context includes the numerous circumstances of the current environment as well as behavioral tendencies to respond in certain ways to various stimuli which in turn are not separable from environmental factors. For example, if the instructions are administered to a group and immediately prior to their presentation, someone stands up and loudly states, "This is absurd and unscientific," the histories of some individuals will preclude finger movement in the context of this particular setting factor.

Because of these considerations, the interbehaviorist holds that if the subject follows the instructions in their entirety, the fingers must go together. Those subjects whose fingers do not go together are not following instructions--they are not doing what the instructions specify. But note that following or not following instructions is not a matter of decisions, attitudes, or expectations; rather it is a matter of the unique history of the subject and the contemporary setting. The individual does not decide to follow instructions, then do so. He or she does not create an image which then produces the action, but interacts with the described meanings as developed from past history.

## Chevreul's Movement

The magnetized finger demonstration is representative of a class of phenomena that mentalistic psychologists interpreted in terms of an early version of cognitive-mediational theory, viz., the construct of ideomotor action. This is the dualistic notion that "the bare idea of a movement's sensible effects is its sufficient mental cue" (James, 1890, p. 522). An even more striking phenomenon of the same class was reported in an 1808 book entitled "Le Pendule Explorateur," which hailed the inauguration of a "new" chapter in physics (Jastrow, 1937). This work was based on numerous experiments with an apparatus consisting of a hand held pendulum. The experimenters observed that the direction in which the pendulum oscillated varied as a function of its physical composition and of materials placed beneath it. For example, when an iron bob was held over copper and silver , it moved from right to left. When the same bob was held over zinc or water, it swung from left to right. Such differential movements of the pendulum were alleged to provide evidence of a supernatural force not addressed by naturalistic science (see also Rawcliff, 1959).

Jastrow (1937) reported that, with his experiments in 1812, the distinguished scientist and founder of organic chemistry, M.E. Chevreul, demonstrated that the "exploring pendulum" was better accounted for in terms of psychological constructs than with supernaturalistic notions. (Lemay and Oesper, 1948, provide further information on the career of this outstanding pioneer of naturalism.) Chevreul concluded that pendulum movement was the result of minute, involuntary muscular movements that occurred in response to the subject's expectations regarding how it should move. In recognition of Chevreul's analysis, the hand-held pendulum is now referred to as Chevreul's Pendulum, and its movement is called Chevreul's Movent. Chevreul's Movement is empirically defined as movement of the bobo in a direction consistent with the subject's thinking or "expectations" as inferred from independent manipulations and observations. For example, the subject is told that the bob will move in a particular direction, or the subject reports the direction to which he or she was covertly responding (thinking of). An additional defining characteristic of Chevreul's Movement is that the subject reports no deliberate attempt to move the bob (Delprato, 1977a).

The interbehaviorist finds Chevreul's Movement especially noteworthy because the history of its interpretation so conspicuously parallels views of human behavior in general. In other words, the pendulum movement

149

initially was viewed as a manifestation of occult forces. With the advent of naturalistic science, some (such as Chevreul) offered interpretations that were less obviously occultistic than were the earlier views. That is, human behavior was interpreted in terms of the causal effect of psychological factors or mind. Contemporary cognitive-behavioral theory substitutes for mind cognition, information processing, memory stores, encoding and decoding, retrieval operations, executive routines, and other constructs that are designed to appear far removed from earlier mentalistic concepts and even further removed from supernaturalism. The interbehavioral perpsective shows how we can go even further toward eradicating the last vestiges of spiritualism in the science of behavior.

**Contemporary cognitive-behavioral analysis of Chevreul's Movement.** Perhaps the obvious identification of Chevreul's Movement with occultism (Rawcliffe, 1959) has contributed to the lack of interest it has received in the science of psychology. Nonetheless, it appears that Chevreul's analysis continues to predominate. Indeed, one twentieth-century writer appears to resort to views that clearly antedate those of Chevreul: "Now fix your eyes on the bob and **will** it to move...This question of willing has never been properly described anywhere and...it is likely that it will not be for some time to come" (Weitzenhoffer, 1957, p. 86). (Willing is not a construct advanced by sophisticated cognitive-behavioral theorists.)

Chevreul's Movement is ideally suited for analysis in terms of contemporary cognitive-behavioral theory. Consider Bandura's (1977b) claim that ideas are transformed into actions and Mahoney's (1977) related assertion cognitive representations cause actions. According to these views, ideas or images of pendulum movement (somehow) become transformed into muscular movements of the hand which are amplified by the pendulum. (It should be clear that the pendulum unquestionably functions as an amplifier of bodily movement, e.g., Easton and Shor, 1976.) Such an interpretation amounts to a resurrection of the ideomotor construct. In fact, Easton and Shor (1975, 1976, 1977) conducted a series of careful, well-designed experiments on Chevreul's Movement and concluded that the dualistic notion of ideomotor action is a viable interpretation. Furthermore, the cognitive-behavioral theorist might suggest that pendulum movement is facilitated by positive attitudes, motivations, and expectancies in the test situation (e.g., Barbar et al., 1974).

**Interbehavioral analysis of Chevreul's Movement.** The interbehavioral analysis of Chevreul's Movement basically follows that outlined for the magnetized fingers experiment. However, since Chevreul's Pendulum has been used with a wider variety of instructional conditions that has been the case with the less complex magnetized fingers phenomena, additional considerations are raised. One common circumstance used to demonstrate Chevreul's Movement involves having subjects hold the bob over a target line while they follow instructions to imagine the bobo swinging back-and-forth along the line (e.g., Delprato, 1977a; 1977b). In this case, we are especially exploiting the subject's history of interactions wit the verbal stimulus "imagine." Specifically, "imagine" has typically been applied to describe implicit action to substitute stimulus objects; like all behavior, such implicit (covert) actions have their origination in the individual's interbehavioral history of direct contacts with stimuli (Kantor, 1924; Kantor and Smith, 1975). As Kantor (1924) noted, imagining (like thinking and remembering) refers to implicit behaviors, and the fundamental principle of these actions is that "they operate when the original stimulus responsible for their development and operation is not present... [T]he implicit reaction can only be morphologically in some cases a partial or diminished form of response..." (p. 298). In effect, the instruction to the subject to "imagine pendulum movement" amounts to instructing him or her to partially move it, i.e., engage in a sufficient degree of bodily movement to move the pendulum in the direction specified. The subject who is instructed to imagine pendulum movement in a particular direction and who shows no movement in the opposite direction is not (a)being hostile, (b) lacking cognitive ability, (c) displaying a poor attitude, or (d) manifesting a decision to foil the experimenter. Instead, such cases indicate a subject whose interbehavioral history prepares him or her to react in this particular way in the particular test setting.

One class of developmental interaction that appears to contribute to the preparation of subjects to respond in the way specified by Chevreul's Movement instructions is the Pavlovian (respondent) interaction. Delprato (1977b), with Chevreul's Movement, and Holmes and Delprato (1978), with a similar behavior--"involuntary" arm movement, demonstrated that these actions transferred to previously ineffective stimuli after these stimuli were presented in conjunction with effective stimuli a number of times. For example, Delprato (1977b) instructed subjects to repeatedly verbalize a consonant-vowel trigram (ineffective stimulus) while they followed instructions to imagine pendulum movement (effective stimulus) for either 10 or 20 trials. When subjects were subsequently tested for Chevreul's Movement to the trigram alone, probability of movement to the trigram increased in comparison with control conditions; movement was greater following the larger number of training trials.

The use of Chevreul's Pendulum as a "mind-reading" or "thought-reading" instrument (Delprato, 1977a; Hull, 1933) points out additional aspects of the interbehavioral analysis of this phenomenon. Suppose we place the name of three presidential candidates in different spatial positions in front of a subject--call them X, Y , and Z. Next, we ask the subject to hold the pendulum while he simply thinks of the candidates of his choice. Observation of the bob will reveal that it will quitely reliably move in the direction of the subject's preferred candidate and we can impress him by using this to "read his thoughts." Certainly, mystical forces are not emanating from the preferred candidate's name to attract the bob. Neither are the subject's thoughts, expectancies, etc., activating muscles that are amplified by the pendulum. The interbehavioral perspective recognizes that thinking is an interbehavior of the whole organism with an actual or implied stimulus object. If the subject is thinking of X, he is interacting more with X than with Y or Z. He is making implicit approach responses toward X and, since he is holding the pendulum, these movements are amplified. As Kantor indicated in 1924, " By very diligently observing a person under various stimulating conditions we can understand and predict what kind of implicit reactions he is performing" (p. 312). The pendulum is an economical aid to our observation of the subject. Furthermore, if we observe carefully while the subject holds the pendulum and follows the instructions to imagine its movement along a line or to think of X, we often can detect movement of the entire body in the instructed direction (Easton and Shor, 1976; Hull, 1933); this further reflects the holistic nature of interbehavioral activity as well as the fact that implicit or covert actions are the same as explicit or overt behaviors but reduced in degree.

## The Self-Efficacy Construct

Bandura (1977a, 1977b) has proposed a general theory of behavioral change based on the notion of self-efficacy . This author's most comprehensive presentations of his views have been in the context of human defensive behavior (fear, anxiety, inhibitory behavior, withdrawal, avoidance). The basic model has been the "phobic" who does not approach a phobic object or situation. Efficacy expectations refer to the individual's conviction that he can success-fully perform behavior that produces certain outcomes. Thus, while an individual may have the performance-outcome expectation that giving speeches will eventuate in a passing grade in a speech class and a college degree (as when speech is a required class), the person may not perform the requisite behavior because of a belief that he is unable to effectively give a speech. Efficacy expectations regarding the performance of a particular behavior in a specific situation or general range of situations are assumed to develop especially as a result of the individual's history of successful performances (personal mastery experiences). Vicarious experiences (seeing others perform successfully ) and verbal -informational processes may also contribute to the development, or lack thereof, of efficacy expectations. Furthermore, situationally-evoked fear can interfere with (lower) perceptions of efficacy because of the individual's history of generally unsuccessful performance when anxious. In sum, deficiencies in efficacy expectations can contribute to the withdrawal from or avoidance of situations and, according to Bandura (1977a, 1977b) are necessary for a complete account of defensive behavior. It is clear that self-efficacy fits the classic dualistic, cognitive-mediational framework. That is, a mentalistic process inside of the person and separate from action is a presumed cause of behavior . Significantly, Bandura and others , e.g., Rosenthal, 1978; Wilson, 1978; Wilson and O'Leary, 1980) offer the self-efficacy construct as representative of the "state of the art" in behavioral theory.

Bandura (1977a) proposed a specific methodology for measuring self-efficacy and for testing his theory. Let us examine his methods, results, and reasoning from an interbehavioral perspective. Efficacy judgments were obtained from subjects in the context of behavioral avoidance tests on which experimenters observed subjects' degree of approach to a phobic stimulus , e.g., snake (Bandura and Adams, 1977; Bandura , Adams, and Beyer, 1977; Bandura, Adams, Hardy and Howells, 1980). After pretreatment avoidance testing and before posttreatment testing, subjects were provided with stepwise descriptions of the approach hierarchy and requested to designate those steps they could perform as of that moment. High positive correlations between the self-report (efficacy expectations) and subsequent performance measures are interpreted as support for the theory that self-efficacy is a critical determinant of approach to the phobic stimulus. This assumes that efficacy judgments are "signs" of an underlying cognitive expectancy that is separate from the observed samples of approach behavior. An alternative to this dualistic viewpoint is that efficacy judgments, rather than providing access to privileged internal determinants of action, represent personal descriptions of behavioral dispositions. Subjects in Bandura's experiments are making statements similar to that of an individual who states, "I expect to play golf tomorrow." This individual means, "I have arranged my schedule to play," "John and I will be playing," "I will play even if my wife objects," and the like. Correspondence between verbal reports of expectancies to play golf and performance does not require the assumption that the individual's expectation is an inner determinant or cause of golf-playing. Neither does correspondence between self-reports of approach and actual approach to phobic objects require a similar assumption.

Bandura et al. (1980) place great weight on data sugesting that efficacy judgments are more reliable than past performance (during treatment) in predicting posttreatment performance on a behavioral avoidance test. The implication is that an internal experience of mastery is reflected by the efficacy measure and this causal factor accounts for approach behavior. Again, these data are compatible with the view of efficacy judgments as reports of behavioral dispositions. The usefulness of self-observation in predicting performance is upsetting to a form of behavioral psychology that rules out self-observation in favor of overt behavior. On the other hand, Kantor (1924) finds self-observation indispensable in a complete psychology. Individuals often are in positions to observe aspects of their biosocial lives that pose difficulties for other observers. If, for example, several individuals were contacted in a gymnasium in the morning and asked to designate "how long they expected to play handball" on the particular morning, it would not be surprising to find a substantial relationship between the "expectancy" reports and overt performance In light of the numberous factors that are involved in the moment to moment lives of individuals, expectancy judgments may be better predictors of performance on a given day than are the most precise measurements of past performance duartions. Observations of past performance would not reveal A's typical Saturday luncheon meeting scheduled to take advantage of a fortuitious business opportunity, D's dental appointment to replace a filling lost yesterday, G's agreement to return early for his son's birthday, etc. The hypothetical handball players are reporting their disposition to play and are taking into account factors that participate in setting time limits as to how long they play. It is not necessary to assume their self-reports of expectancy are manifestations of inner determinants.

## Summary and Conclusions

This paper addressed contemporary renovations of cognition, especially as advocated by cognitive-behavior theorists. The central feature of this allegedly revolutionary view is that organismic actions are caused by antecedent cognitive events that mediate organisms' intercourse with their surroundings. Deficiencies in the mechanistic, stimulus-response model advocated by many early versions of behaviorism have especially stimulated cognitionism, which places mentalistic states, structures, and processes in between stimulus and response. The notion that mind-like factors underlie psychological action is entirely compatible with the dualistic theme of Western culture; consequently, cognitive- behaviorism is consistent with the interbehavioral histories of many psychologists in our culture. In short, cognitionism violates one basic datum of scientific behavior, viz., constructs are to be derived from events not cultural tradition. Students of interbehaviorism begin with events and take the revolutionary view that cognition can only refer to action. Some of the features of the interbehavioral perspective that buttress its alternative to traditional accounts of "cognitively mediated" behavior include (a) recognition of the integrated nature of organismic activity, (b) the field-theoretical conception as an alternative to the creative -agent view of causality, and (c) developmental interactionism.

In the final section of this chapter three phenomena varying in complexity were analyzed from an interbehavioral point of view. Interbehaviorism proposes no simple solution to the interpretation of apparently mediated behavior. It does offer a cohesive, naturalistic account that brings the analyst into contact with actual biosocial lives of individuals.

## Acknowledgments

I gratefully acknowledge the valuable comments made on an earlier version of this chapter by Peter Holmes and Noel W. Smith. F. Dudley McGlynn assisted with the presentation of efficacy theory and Barbara Delprato made important contributions to preparation of the manuscript. Finally, the unequivocatingly empirical approach to behavior consistently taken by Donald E. Jackson contributed greatly to the author's search for an alternative to cognitionism.

## References

Bandura, A. 1969. **Principles of Behavior Modification.** New York: Holt, Rinehart and Winston.

Bandura, A. 1977a. Self-efficacy: Toward a unifying theory of behavioral change. **Psychological Review,** 84, 191-215.

Bandura, A. 1977b. **Social Learning Theory.** Englewood Cliffs, New Jersey: Prentice-Hall .

Bandura, A. and Adams, N.E. 1977. Analysis of self-efficacy theory of behavioral change. **Cognitive Therapy and Research,** 1, 287-310.

Bandura, A., Adams, N.E. and Beyer, J. 1977. Cognitive processes mediating behavioral change. **Journal of Personality and Social Psychology,** 35, 125-139.

Bandura, A., Adams, N.E., Hardy, A.B. and Howells, G.N. 1980. **Cognitive Therapy and Research,** 4, 39-66.

Barber, T.X., Spanos, N.P. and Chaves, J.F. 1974. **Hyponosis, Imagination, and Human Potentialities.** New York: Pergamon Press.

Bolles, R.C. 1979. **Learning Theory** (2nd ed.). New York: Holt, Rinehart and Winston.

Brewer, W.F. 1974. There is no convincing evidence for operant or classical conditioning in adult humans. In W.B. Weimer and D.S. Palermo (Eds.) **Cognition and the Symbolic Processes.** Hillsdale, New Jersey: Lawrence Erlbaum Associates.

Cook, S. W. and Harris, R.E. 1937. The verbal conditioning of the galvanic skin reflex. **Journal of Experimental Psychology,** 21, 202-210.

Delprato, D.J. 1977a. Observing covert behavior ("mind-reading" with Chevreul's Pendulum. **Psychological Record,** 27, 473-478.

Delprato, D.J. 1977b. Pavlovian conditioning of Chevreul's Movement. **American Journal of Clinical Hypnosis,** 20, 124-130.

Delprato, D.J. 1979. The interbehavioral alternative to brain-dogma. **Psychological Record,** 29, 409-418.

Delprato, D.J. and Holmes, P.A. 1978. Facilitation of arm levitation by response to previous suggestions of a different type. **International Journal of Clinical and Experimental Hypnosis,** 26, 167-177.

Dember, W.N. 1974. Motivation and the cognitive revolution. **American Psychologist,** 29, 161-168.

Dewey, J. and Bentley, A.F. 1949. **Knowing and the Known.** Boston: Beacon Press.

Easton, R.D. and Shor, R.E. 1975. Information processing analysis of the Chevreul Pendulum illusion. **Journal of Experimental Psychology: Human Perception and Performance,** 1, 231-236.

Easton, R.D. and Shor, R.E. 1976. An experimental analysis of the Chevreul Pendulum illusion. **Journal of General Psychology,** 95, 111-125.

Easton, R.D. and Shor, R.E. 1977. Augmented and delayed feedback in the Chevreul Pendulum illusion. **Journal of General Psychology,** 97, 167-177.

Ellis, A. 1962. **Reason and Emotion in Psychotherapy.** New York: Lyle Stuart.

Ellis, A. 1977. Can we change thoughts by reinforcement? A reply to Howard Rachlin. **Behavior Therapy,** 8, 666-672.

Grings, W.W. 1965. Verbal-perceptual factors in the conditioning of autonomic responses. In W.F. Prokasy (Ed.) **Classical Conditioning: A Symposium.** New York: Appleton-Century-Crofts.

Grings, W.W. 1973. The role of consciousness and cognition in autonomic behavior change. In F.J. McGuigan and R. Schoonover (Eds.) **The Psychophysiology of Thinking.** New York: Academic Press.

Grings, W.W. and Dawson, M.E. 1973. Complex variables in conditioning. In W.F. Prokasy and D.C. Raskin (Eds.) **Electrodermal Activity in Psychological Research.** New York: Academic Press.

Grossberg, J.M. 1981. Comments about cognitive therapy and behavior therapy. **Journal of Behavior Therapy and Experimental Psychiatry,** 12, 25-33.

Hilgard, E.R. and Marquis, D.G. 1940. **Conditioning and Learning.** New York: Appleton-Century-Crofts.

Holmes, P.A. and Delprato, D.J. 1978. Classical conditioning of "hypnotic" arm movement. **Psychological Record,** 28, 305-313.

Hull, C.L. 1933. **Hypnosis and Suggestibility.** New York: Appleton-Century-Crofts.

James, W. 1890. **The Principles of Psychology** (Vol. 2). New York: Holt.

Jastrow, J. 1937. Chevreul as psychologist. **The Scientific Monthly,** 44, 487-496.

Kantor, J.R. 1924. **Principles of Psychology** (Vol. 1). Granville, Ohio: Principia Press.

Kantor, J.R. 1942. Preface to interbehavioral psychology. **Psychological Record,** 5, 173-193.

Kantor, J.R. 1947. **Problems of Physiological Psychology.** Granville, Ohio: Principia Press.

Kantor, J.R. 1950. **Psychology and Logic** (Vol. 2). Bloomington, In.: Principia Press.

Kantor, J.R. 1969. **The Scientific Evolution of Psychology** (Vol. 2). Chicago: Principia Press.

Kantor, J.R. 1971. **The Aim and Progress of Psychology and Other Sciences.** Chicago: Principia Press.

Kantor, J.R. and Smith, N.W. 1975. **The Science of Psychology: An Interbehavioral Survey.** Chicago: Principia Press.

Kendall, P.C. and Hollon, S.D. 1979. Cognitive-behavioral interventions: Overview and current status. In P.C. Kendall and S.D. Hollon (Eds.) **Cognitive-Behavioral Interventions.** New York: Academic Press.

Lang, P.J. 1977. Imagery in therapy: An information processing analysis of fear. **Behavior Therapy,** 8, 862-886.

Lang, P.J. 1979. A bio-informational theory of emotional imagery. **Psychophysiology,** 16, 495-512.

Lang, P.J. , Kozak, M.J., Miller, G.A., Levin, D.N. and McLean, A. 1980. Emotional imagery: Conceptual structure and pattern of somato-visceral response. **Psychophysiology,** 17, 179-192.

Lemay, P. and Oesper, R.E. 1948. Michel Eugene Chevreul (1786-1889). **Journal of Chemical Education,** 25, 62-70.

Mahoney, M.J. 1977. Reflections on the cognitive-learning trend in psychotherapy. **American Psychologist,** 32, 5-13.

Marzillier, J.S. 1980. Cognitive therapy and behavioural practice. **Behaviour Research and Therapy,** 18, 249-258.

Mountjoy, P.T. 1976. Science in psychology: J.R. Kantor's field theory. **Mexican Journal of Behavior Analysis,** 2, 3-21.

Mowrer, O.H. 1938. Preparatory set (expectancy)--a determinant in motivation and learning. **Psychological Review,** 45, 62-91.

Observer, 1977. Concerning cognitive reversionism in psychology. **Psychological Record,** 27, 351-354.

Observer, 1978. The recycling of cognition in psychology. **Psychological Record,** 28, 157-160.

Rawcliffe, D.H. 1959. **Occult and Supernatural Phenomena.** New York: Dover.

Razran, G. 1955. Conditioning and perception. **Psychological Review,** 62, 83-95.

Rescorla, R.A. 1968. Probability of shock in the presence and absence of CS in fear conditioning. **Journal of Comparative and Physiological Psychology,** 66, 1-5.

Rescorla, R.A. 1972. Information variables in Pavlovian conditioning. In G.H.Bower (Ed.) **The Psychology of Learning and Motivation** (Vol. 6). New York: Academic Press.

Rosenthal, T.L. 1978. Bandura's self-efficacy theory: Thought is father to deed. **Advances in Behaviour Research and Therapy,** 1, 203-209.

Ryle, G. 1949. **The Concept of Mind.** London: Hutchinson and Company.

Schafer, R. 1976. **A new Language for Psychoanalysis.** New Haven: Yale University Press.

Schafer, R. 1978. **Language and Insight.** New Haven: Yale University Press.

Segal, E.M. and Lachman, R. 1972. Complex behavior or higher mental process: Is there a paradigm shift? **American Psychologist,** 27, 46-55.

Skinner, B.F. 1953. **Science and Human Behavior.** New York: Macmillan.

Skinner, B.F. 1963. Behaviorism at fifty. **Science,** 140, 951-958.

Smith, N.W. 1973. Interbehavioral psychology: Roots and branches. **Psychological Record,** 23, 153-167.

Sparks, L. 1975. **Self-Hypnosis: A conditioned Response Technique.** North Hollywood, Ca.: Wilshire.

Staddon, J.E.R. 1973. On the notion of cause, with applications to behaviorism. **Behaviorism,** 1, 25-63.

Tolman, E.C. 1932. **Purposive Behavior in Animals and Men.** New York: Appleton-Century.

Weitzenhoffer, A.M. 1957. **General Techniques of Hypnotism.** New York: Grune and Stratton.

Wilson, G.T. 1978. The importance of being theoretical: A commentary on Bandura's "Self-efficacy: Towards a unifying theory of behavioral change." **Advances in Behaviour Research and Therapy,** 1, 217-230.

Wittgenstein, L. 1958. **Philosophical Investigations.** New York: Macmillan.

Zener, K. 1937. The significance of behavior accompanying conditioned salivary secretion for theories of the conditioned response. **American Journal of Psychology**, 50, 384-403.

# SENSING IS PERCEIVING: AN ALTERNATIVE TO THE DOCTRINE OF THE DOUBLE WORLD

Noel W. Smith

Perceiving is one of the most fundamental psychological activities in which we engage. Each act, such as stepping on a stone to cross a brook, calling out to a friend in a crowd, finding a gasoline station when our fuel supply is low, placing a piece in a jigsaw puzzle, or entering a bakery that exudes a savory aroma is preceded by an act of perceiving. As Aristotle indicated, even our covert acts such as dreaming, reasoning, and imagining can occur only in terms of what we have previously perceived. Perceiving has been a topic of interest from the time of ancient Greece, and perhaps earlier, right through this millenia. The volume of literature dealing with it has become enormous and greatly diversified as writers have treated perceiving in relation to social behavior, cognitive behavior, personality, and other complex issues as well as elementary discrimination acts and reaction times. Yet confusion abounds, puzzles recur, constructs get imposed on events, and assumptions prevail that come straight out of medieval theology though dressed up in a terminological guise that appears scientific.

In the days of Aristotle and before Western psychophysical dualism evolved, the approach to perception was direct and naturalistic (Kantor, 1963; Smith, 1974). But in the ensuing period the whole mode of thinking and its assumptive base shifted so that the perplexities and unscientific doctrines have been recurring in never ending fashion ever since. A topic of such fundamental importance to psychology cries out for reexamination and reform. This reform will not occur by merely collecting more data or making more precise measurements. A century of such empirical work has resulted in no change in basic assumptions. Only a reexamination a of these assumptions and a recognition of alternative assumptions that are consistent with naturalistic science can provide the basis for such a reform.

## Development of the Recurring Problem: The Dualistic Heritage

In all but a few treatments of perceiving in the literature of psychology there is an assumption regarding an outer world and an inner world, the inner being a mere reflection and perhaps a distorted one at that of the outer. Kvale and Grenness (1967) refer to this as "the illusion of the double world." We do not see a tree but merely have a mental image. We do not here a bell but have a sensation resulting from processing of neural impulses. This view has its origin in the Graeco-Roman period when conditions of life were so tumultuous that intellectual leaders developed philosophies based on self-satisfaction, asceticism, contemplation, inner peace, and similar matters that turned away from the world of nature and actual events. At the same time large numbers of people turned to salvationist cults that offered a better life in the hereafter. From these trends emerged the verbally constructed soul as the basic essence of life and the source of eternity. This inner abstraction, regarded as the vital or life source of the individual, became the entity that performed thinking, sensing, willing, and other psychological activities, and directed or caused the actions of the material body.

Acting on the assumption that an inner creational entity operates within us, Galileo was one of the first modern writers to relegate tastes, odors, colors, heat, tickling, and other events to the soul while figure, number and motion he held to be externally real. Similarly, Newton designated the "sensorium" as the place where colors were converted from light waves. John Locke used the term "secondary qualities" to distinguish those non-physical sounds, colors, etc. from "primary qualities" which, as Galileo had indicated, were physical or real. George Berkeley, a bishop of the Church of England, carried the matter to its final extreme and made all things non-physical and resident in the non-physical mind. Thomas Reid, the Scottish philosopher and theologian, first distinguished between sensations and perceptions. In sensation the mind passively receives a feeling; the odor of a rose is felt. Perception is an act of mind giving a belief in the quality of the object. The odor of the rose is the quality of the object perceived by way of the sensation and this is perception. The object is directly intuited.

Drawing primarily from Locke, Kant held that unknown sources produced the qualities of things. Where Berkeley had transformed thses unknown sources into mental creations Kant rendered them as unknowable: The thing-in-itself. From the Thing-in-itself came sensations. These are synthesized into phenomenal products. The unified transcendental mind finally produces the phenomenal mind and its contents. The Thing-in-itself such as a tree or a bell remains unknowable. We know only the mental representations.

In the nineteenth century the development of physiology led to the transformation of this spiritualistic view into a biological one. When Charles Bell (and almost simultaneously Francois Magendie) discovered the difference between sensory and motor nerves he suggested that a variety of mental functions might be based on a variety of distinct neural elements: Each sensory nerve conveys one kind of quality or experience. Visual nerves convey only visual impressions, auditory only auditory impressions. Johannes Mueller extended this to mean that various qualities of experience come only through specific qualities or energies of particular nerves. Each particular nerve trait has a specific-energy--it is correlated with specific kinds of sensation regardless of the type of stimulus[1]. The influence of Kant with his near disregard of the stimulus object is apparent here. Few clearly recognized then or now that Mueller's concept was a continuation of the old mentalism with a mere change of words from metaphysical to biological and no change in basic assumption.

Herman von Helmholtz, who was a student of Mueller, accepted the Galileo-Newton-Locke-Kant model of perceiving as elaborated upon Mueller's doctrine of specific nerve energies. He proposed that special kinds of impulses determined special sensations. End organs were analyzers. It was a minor step for others to move the analyzers to the brain as the culminating effort to naturalize the soul. Much of this conceptual development was promoted by the fact that a subject that claims to be dealing with intangibles and unobservables cannot be a science. Consequently, there was "much groping about for some concrete material with which to work. Finally, psychologists seized upon the nervous system as a tangible basis for the intangible consciousness" (Kantor, 1920, p. 212).

## The Consequences

Through this line of descent, especially as given form by Kant and physiological status by Mueller and Helmholtz, comes the assumption that has largely dominated psychology: That the world is unknowable for we can only know our sensory impressions or percepts of it as given to us by our brain. This view is clearly explicated by Attneave (1974) writing in the **American Psychologist**[2]:

> Naively, it seems to us that the outside world, the
> world around us, is a given; it is just there...We all
> feel as if our experiencing of the world around us were
> quite direct. However, the apparent immediacy of
> this experience **has** to be more or less illusory because
> we know that every bit of our information about external
> things is coming in through our sense organs, or has
> come in through our sense organs at some time in the
> past. All of it, to the best of our knowledge, is mediated
> by receptor activity and is relayed to the brain in the
> form of Morse code signals, as it were, so that what
> we experience as the "real world", and locate outside
> ourselves, cannot possibly be anything better than a
> **representation** of the external world (p. 493).

163

Perhaps one of the most unfortunate things about this statement is the conviction that there is no alternative: "This experience **has** to be...illusory." Writing also in the **American Psychologist** Mason (1976) seeks "representational processes" or "constructions of reality" in the great apes that he assumes to be characteristic of humans. He offers almost an echo of Attneave:

> The question is not whether representational processes
> exist but whether we must treat them as a serious object
> of study. All behavior that is guided by sensory informa-
> tion, that is, most of the behavior that interests us,
> implies some type of schema or functional"image" of
> the environment. Behavior is the endpoint of an infor-
> mation processing sequence (p. 284).

The descent of our mode of thinking from the Graeco-Roman period through medieval theology is so pervasive that the underlying assumptions from this theology often go unrecognized, with the result that current psychology is dominated by it and alternatives appear as impossible.

Here we have, passing for science, the assertion that we must deal with an unknowable organism that merely represents it. This direct us to start our investigations not with events whch must perforce remain forever illusory but with verbal constructs: A "conceptual nervous system," to use Skinner's term, which converts the sensations into representations. And what is then to view the representations? At one time a homunculus was proposed. And another to sense what that one sensed and so on **ad infinitum.** The absurdity of this has led us to ignore the problem these constructs pose, but no diminuation in the use of the constructs results.

It must follow from this assumption, although it seems to go largely unrecognized, that all studies of perceiving, whether empirical or conceptual, and the results of these studies are equally illusory. These illusory results are then interpreted in terms of the false original assumptions. The entire procedure is antithetical to science. When we begin with constructs such as an interpretive nervous system or sensations and percepts we impose these on whatever results we may find. A scientific study of perceiving, in contrast, must formulate hypotheses in terms of events, not constructs, and interpret results in terms of these same events. For example, when we observe that responses to sound frequency do not correspond precisely with that frequency, a scientific approach hypothesizes a consideration of biological limitations or other concrete factors that enter into a field of events comprising sound discrimination. Traditional influences, on the other hand, will impose a mental sensation or neural transformation produced by a physical stimulus; a rectangular table

164

that is seen from an oblique angle and reported as rectangular will be interpreted as demonstrating unconscious inference; colors will be assumed to be unreal and attributed to the brain which must excrete them.

Skinner (1974) points out that the "copy theory" is often used for vision but less often for hearing. It is difficult to assume that orchestral sounds are internally created. It is even more difficult, he notes, to assume this for taste and odor and almost impossible for touch. We hear almost no arguments that the texture of paper is only an inner representation.

## The Sensation and Perception Coupling Reexamined

The distinction between sensation and perception has been defined in various ways since the time of its first differentiation by Reid. It usually involves the assumption that when the sense organs are stimulated the resulting sensation must be analyzed by some inner power to result in perception. A sensation is unanalyzed and uninterpreted " 'mental stuff', a correlate of the nervous system," and is exemplified by such conditions or qualities as pressure , color, warmth, sound, odor (English and English, 1958, p. 490 ) . Perception, on the other hand, "enables the organism to receive and process information on the state of, and alterations in, the environment" (**Encyclopedia of Psychology,** 1972, p. 377). Perception, then, is commonly regarded as the inner interpretation of sensory data form the outer world. Hebb(1966) regards perception as mediating between sensation and behavior. Helmholtz proposed that separate sensations were combined by "unconscious inference," and Oatley (1978) has built a brain theory of perception around this construct that challenges mechanistic brain assumptions but replaces them with equally dualistic, emergent mentalisms based on computer analogies of the brain. Segall, Campbell, and Herskovits (1966) assert that the ordinary individual "does not recognize that his visual perception is **mediated** by indirect inference systems" (p. 5). Others who make similar assumptions are legion. Allport (1955) asks who is there to make the inference. "Can a neuron or a group of synapses in the brain make an inference " (p. 83)? The homonculus or animistic power is as unsatisfactory as it is pervasive.

Considerable effort has gone into the study of the anatomy and physiology of the sense organs[3]. Much of the attention, however, has followed the traditional doctrine of the primacy of the nervous system and has concentrated on the role of this one system to the neglect of others. That which is designated perception has been broadened to consider the effects of motivation, personality, past experience, and other factors. While these are encouraging developments the basic assumptions of psychophysical dualism and the constructs that follow from it will almost invariably bias the data.

The sensation-perception dichotomy has long been a subject of analysis by philosophers and seldom questioned as a basic doctrine. Many philosophers have argued, especially those such as Bertrand Russell, C. D. Broad[4], H.H. Price, and G.E. Moore who follow in the tradition of British empiricism, that the world is illusory and we perceive "sense-data" rather than physical objects. The few philosophers who have seen the fallacies may offer something instructive to psychology.

## Skeptical Philosophers

W.H.F. Barnes (1944-45/1965) observes that if this illusoriness be true there is no distinction between seeing a table and having an illusion, the latter often being offered as proof of the unreliability of our senses and the uncertainty about the physical world. He argues a common-sense approach and notes that in daily life we observe that appearances change and that things are not always what they seem. it is only because we are sometimes successful in seeing things as they are that we can distinguish between how things actually are and how they sometimes appear. "...The only naivete about naive realism is that philosophers should have thought the ordinary man believed it " (p. 166). Similarly, F.J.E. Woodbridge (1913b) points out that "the relativity of sensations witnesses to the relativity of thing " (p. 410), not relativity to a mind. The stick that appears bent in the water is no illusion. Under conditions of differential refraction of air and water it should appear bent. If it appeared straight, that would be an illusion. He takes up Locke's claim that when water is warm to one hand and cool to the other the sensation is in us and not the water, that we sense only the effects in us produced by the water. As a counter, he offers that "the relativity cited is evidence only of the fact that the water is warmer than one hand and colder than the other" (p. 409)[5]. John Dewey (1961) argues similarly for a field of interactions for the situation of the bent stick and even for all events in the universe, of which sensing is no exception.

N.R. Hanson (1961) considers the matter of what we see when we look at an object. If the two astronomers Tycho Brahe and Johannes Kepler were to both observe a sunrise would they see the same thing? Tycho who believed in a fixed Earth and a revolving sun would see the sun moving upward against a fixed horizon while Kepler who had established the motion of the planets around the would see the horizon dropping below the sun. (This ignores the figure-ground effect in which the smaller object is seen moving against the larger as when the moon appears to move against stationary clouds regardless of what we know about them.) The two would be seeing the same objects and would draw the same picture of them yet they would mean different

166

things to each man.

It is not that they have sensations which are alike and then they perceive or interpret them differently but that their seeing is different. They do not see similarly then interpret differently. They do not see the same thing at all, for their experiences with regard to the event are different. This in spite of the fact that their optical and neurological reactions may be identical.

> Seeing is an experience. A retinal reaction is only a
> physical state--a photochemical excitation...People,
> not their eyes, see. Cameras and eyeballs are blind.
> Attempts to locate within the organs of sight (or within
> the neurological reticulum behind the eyes) some nameable
> called 'seeing' may be dismissed....There is more to
> seeing than meets the eyeball (Hanson, 1961, p. 7).

Other examples can be offered in profusion. Ambiguous figures may be seen differently by different people and yet the configuration of lines is the same for all. A physicist looking at an X-ray tube would see an instrument of specific function. A layman who looks at the same object sees a combination of glass, wires, and odd shaped constituents within the glass. The layman could see it as an X-ray tube and the component elements for their specific role in producing X-rays only after undergoing some of the same education as the physicist. Again, we do not sense and then interpret but perceive according to our learning history and the conditions of the moment.

If perceiving consisted of registration of an image on a retina we would continuously perceive the entire visual field of about 180°. But we perceive only those objects that we attend to. As an optical instrument the eye has numerous defects (Evans, 1974) but with visual scanning, observation under a variety of conditions, the use of other senses, and the build up of meanings seeing becomes acute for what is significant to us. There is, indeed, much "more to seeing than meets the eyeball."

In another work Hanson (1969) takes up the problem more extensively and considers the notion that the interpretation occurs unconsciously:

> ...there is something logically askew about the accounts
> of seeing that make it all sound as if we soak up light
> radiation like blotters and then clamp our interpretations
> on our visual impulses, **click-clack**--but oh so very quickly.
> This is not anything like what I **mean** when I say I see
> a bicycle, or a duck, or a bear, or an X-ray tube. If
> there were something corresponding to our good old

word "interpretation" going on in me while I see, then
I ought to be able to consider such an act by myself
as I can when I interpret history, art, or an ambiguous
remark. I should not have to invent such an act just
in order to set into motion my philosophical theories
about seeing...But then notice the comprehensive difference
between conscious act of interpretation--from which
the world draws most of its force--and **unconscious**
**interpretation**, a curiously timeless, colorless, ineffable,
intangible, invisible, unlocatable, indiscoverable entity.
Talk about ghosts in machines! (p. 130-131).

Ryle, too, who popularized the term "ghost in the machine" and attempted to excise it (1949), points out (1965) that inference and thinking are not involved in perceptual recognition but that perceiving involves previously acquired knowledge. Soltis (1966) expresses the mutual relationship of knowing and perceiving as one in which we come to see and know the world as consisting of the meanings that we develop from our daily encounters with it. Shaw and Bransford (1977) arrive at similar conclusions about knowing and perceiving. They reject the assumption that perceiving is inferring. Pitcher (1971) argues that to see is just to come to know by use of the eyes. No assumption of sensation or sense data is necessary.

## An Alternative to Tradition

### The Scientific Beginnings

If we go back in time more than two millenia to the time when Hel-
enic culture was in flower we find a mode of thinking that contrast
sharply with traditional doctrine, one that did not find itself in quandries and contradictions. The Greeks took nature exactly as they found it and tried to understand it in a straight-forward manner. There was no assumption of an illusory world nor of an inner spirit interpreting an outer world.

The interactional approach to perception which is seen in Protagoras has its culmination and fullest analysis with Aristotle, who begins with the viewpoint of a biologist. He observes that organisms have the potential for sensing by means of their biologically specialized sense organs, and correspondingly objects (called "sensible objects") and their qualities have the potential to be sensed. The joint action of the potentials produce the actualization of the sensing act. This sensing is not in the sense organ nor is it in the object but is an **interaction** of the two. We do not see in our eye or hear in our ear but see and hear with these organs. When we see we see an object, when we smell we smell an object, when we feel we feel an object. Sensing is a joint product, an organism-object continuity

168

(Aristotle, 418a-424b).

Aristotle does not distinguish between sensing and perceiving but does differentiate sensing a quality from sensing an object. (Sensing and perceiving are used for this distinction in translation but do not appear in the Greek. The single Greek word is **aisthesis**.)

Seeing, Aristotle says, occurs by means of light as a medium of contact. (Actually he designates the "transparent" as the medium which is actualized by light.) It is not the light that is the stimulus but rather the object. The light merely provides the means for interaction with the object. In contrast, current notions suggest that forms of energy such as light waves register on the sensory organ and must then be transformed by the brain into an interpretation of the object. Some versions continue with the brain interpretations being projected back out onto the object so that it appears outside us rather than in our eye or in our head. Objects are thus reduced to sensations. If we look at a tree it is said to form an inverted image on the retina, then, second, transmitted by neural coding to the brain, and, lastly, "somehow" interpreted as a tree outside the skull. Unstated is (1) how a neuronal action or neuronal pattern can look like a tree, (2) what does the looking at the neuronal pattern, and (3) how it looks to be outside. In this connection Pronko (1961) asks "With what mind's eye could the 'image' be seen and what is really being seen--the three out there, the picture in the eye, the one on the visual cortex?" (p. 314).

With Aristotle there is no transformation of light to object and object to neural pattern--no such mysterious transformations are necessary--and consequently no questions arise about what is reality; for there is no "inner" interpreting an "outer" or "sensation" as opposed to "reality." Sensing is constituted by the interaction and consists of this quite physical activity. No "mental" or "spiritual" or "intervening variable" notion is invoked, for such had not been invented. To Aristotle sensing consists of the sensible organism and sensible object in interaction in conjunction with a medium of contact, such as light or sound. It is, then, not a matter of internal creations but of ongoing events whose occurrences can be objectively studied and thereby offer the beginning of scientific elucidation (Smith, 1974). On this basis Aristotle was able to work out a rather detailed analysis of perceiving6 that is completely naturalistic (Smith, 1971). Because of the subsequent eclipse of scientific thinking this approach was not understood or redevleoped until the 20th century. Although the philosopher of science Hanson was able to see the difficulties of the current dualism and offer a corrective, Woodbridge (1909/1965) before him had not only seen the difficulties but offered in a sketchy fashion an interactional replacement.

169

Seeing would thus appear to be, not a process set up
exclusively in the organism itself, but an interaction
or relation between the organism and its surroundings
effected by means of the eye. It is not a reaction solely
but an interaction as well (p. 368).

He observes that this eliminates the mysteries including the Lockian
contention of intervening existences "between a supposed mind and a
supposed world" (p. 368), as well as the mysterious projection of these
intervening sensations to an outer world that they only appear to
constitute. Sensing as interactions are objective events of the world
and have the same status as any other natural event. They may be
studied as objectively as all other events and their "antecedents and
consequents" (p. 369) discovered. The variety of the sense organs
provide for a variety of organism-environment intractions that account
for our many sensory experiences of the world and that obviate the
need for postulations of an additional power of awareness.

Woodbridge deals with Lockian secondary qualities in a manner
that seems to be like Aristotle's potentialities of the sense organs:
The organs "make the secondary qualities effective according to their
specific characters" (p. 370) but do not make the existence subjective.
Qualities such as color and sound operate when "the appropriate means
for making such operation effective" (p. 370) are present.

The role of the nervous system, in Woodbridge's view, is to
connect and coordinate the organism as a whole to any stimulated organ. The sense organs are specific to specific stimulus
conditions but the nervous system is constructed for coordianted acts.
It prevents isolated and discontinuous reactions. The nervous system
cannot see or hear, for neural impulses are much alike whether from
eye or ears. The differentiation is by means of the sense organs
with their varied structures for sensitivities to varied environmental
conditions. These biological capabilities enable the organism to be
coordinated and unified and thereby make adjustments to expectations.
An organism that can interact differentially with the differences in
its surroundings and still remain unified and coordinated is
demonstrating consciousness. Consciousness is "a relational system
integrating and unifying its differentiated interaction with its
surroundings" (p. 351). Consciousness, if it means anything at all, is
constituted by concrete interactions.

Both Woodbridge and Hanson, spanning a half-century between
them, seem to be so involved with refuting and correcting the major
tenets of the pervasive doctrine of 2000 years that little attention is
given to the developing of a full account of a naturalistic approach
to perceiving. But perhaps this would not be a task to interest philosophers.

170

## Interbehaviorism

It remained for J.R. Kantor to offer this formulation. His first statement on perception (1920) set forth the non-traditional view that perceiving consists of the individual "in direct contact with objects develop[ing] reaction patterns enabling him to differentiate and distinguish the various objects affecting him" (p. 192). Subsequent to the initial contact the perceptual interactions can be considered **knowing interactions** as well. What we have perceived is part of what we know. Kantor emphasized, apparently independently, the medium of contact which Aristotle had used so effectively. Significantly, both derived their formulations from a straight-forward examination of events and arrived at the same position. This we would expect from two observers who do not depart from their observations.

By means of light rays we contact objects visually, by air waves auditorily, by pressure tactually. More proximate media are chemical solutions for taste and tissue pressure or laceration for pain (Kantor, 1924). Similar media are involved in kinesthetic, vestibular, and other sensory interactions. When we react to a sound or a light the object and medium coincide. The importance of media are frequently encountered in our technological society where we become accustomed to a variety of effects from colored lights. The media are not to be confused with the object but well examplify their role in the object-organism act of perceiving. As with Aristotle, this approach obviates the mentalistic interpretive assumption of tradition.

Among the few other writers who have also observed this role of the medium are Cox (1966), Taylor (1962), and Ratliff (1962). Cox, an optical physicist, notes:

> The link betwen our eyes and the objects we see is
> **light.** This defines what we mean by light without,
> at the moment, saying anything about its nature.
> Light is primarily defined as the link between the
> viewing eye and the object that is viewed (p. 15).

Taylor describes more fully its role in perception:

> All visual perception is mediated by light, but when
> a bird flies overhead we do not say that the flux of
> of light is interrupted in a particular manner, and with
> certain rhythical fluctuations; we say that a bird is
> flying overhead. Surely nobody in his senses would
> claim that this knowledge is misleading on the ground
> that it is knowledge not about light, the medium through
> which it is conveyed, but about a bird (p. 344).

Ratliff observes that "we do not see light as a distinct entity; we see objects of various colors and brightnesses" (p. 419).

The traditional assumption that we see     light but not the object has led to endless metaphysical problems about an illusory world. The writers referred to here have provided a naturalistic alternative that begins with Aristotle but did not appear again until the  twentieth century.

## Attending and Perceiving as Preparatory Acts

Perceiving further finds its place in an interaction event as the preparatory act for some final act with respect to the stimulus (Kantor, 1924; Smith, 1973; Smith and Shaw, 1979). When we are in the process of finding a name in a telephone directory we must attend to any number of names, perceive their alphabetical relation to the one we seek, and proceed further accordingly. Finally we attend to and perceive the name we seek, attend to and perceive the number which follows it, then overtly begin dialing that number. Thus attending and perceiving prepare us for a final action that has been stimulated by some need to make the phone call. Nuttin and Greenwald (1968) find the separation of performance into a preparatory phase followed by an executive phase, the latter being overt, an important distinction in their studies of learning. They observe that the preparatory stage is seen even in animals as they anticipate alternative responses and their consequences and    this becomes an essential consideration in human behavior. Similarly, Garner's studies lead him to note that the individual "select[s] the structure to which he will attend and react" (p. 11). Green (1958) finds that the observed behavior in the experimental setting shows the three reaction systems of  a behavior segment depicted by Kantor.

There are a myriad of possible stimuli we can respond to at any given time. Those which we do respond to constitute the stimulus aspect of the attending act. It may be influenced by changes in the medium, immediately preceding interactions, salient features of the stimulus object such as size of loudness, biological conditions of the organism such as illness or invigorating effects of exercise, and surrounding conditions constituting the context of setting in which the interactions occur.

The mentalistic assumption which is the typical framework for attention is illustrated by Berlyne's (1974) definition of it as "processes or conditions within the organism that determine how effective a particular stimulus will be" (p. 124). Similarly, Egeth and Bevan (1973) refer to attending as "any mode of information processing that permits a subject to respond on the basis of a limited portion of the available stimulus information" (p. 396).

172

How do we attend to something prior to perceiving it? Broadbent (1958) proposes a brain filter that selects one message or another on the basis of its bias and then forwards it to neural analyzing systems. Studies in which each ear listens to a different speaker show the location of this filter to be very elusive. Deutsch and Deutsch (1967) propose a modified neurological mechanism and Norman (1967) offers one that excites representation in a storage system which chooses which message to perceive. Following similar lines are the mechanisms proposed by Moray (1969) and Kahneman (1973).

The alternative offered here is seldom considered. It consists, first, of observing the beginning of a behavioral event comprising a field of factors that involve ambient conditions, such as characteristics of the object, and total factors of the organism including immediate interests. Second, the manner in which these factors enter into that beginning to constitute the actualization of some object as a stimulus is observed (Kantor and Smith, 1975, Chapter 10). The question concerning how we select something prior to perceiving is handled within this field framework. For example, the "cocktail party phenomenon" in which one sometimes listens to one conversation then to another and even to a voice from a group of which one is not immediately a part requires no mysterious filter or animistic neurological center. It requires instead an observation of whether the conversation with which one is confronted is of slight or greater interest, whether the voice from an adjacent group is shrill or loud or otherwise distinctive, whether a smoker in the immediate group is rendering discomfort so that attention is shifted to that and then to the adjacent voice. In shifting attention from on object to another a perceiving act occurs in each instance. Re-attending and perceiving may continue in this manner until one recognizes (perceives) a word or phrase of significance and continues to follow the utterances. As for the contention that perceiving may precede attending, we may ask how an object could be perceived that is not yet actualized as a stimulus.

### Perceiving as Meaning: The Stimulus Function

After initial contact involving perceiving, an object has meaning. Renewed contact may bring new meanings. On this basis a stimulus object can be distinguished from a stimulus function. A chair as an object has the functional meaning of something to sit on for a student entering a classroom, something to stand on for someone needing to change a light in the ceiling, or something to prop open a door when a draft is closing it. These are meanings developed as part of the interactional history consisting of successive interactions with the chair. Any given stimulus function may be actualized depending on the conditions as in the case for the chair.

Stimulus objects, then, are not mere physico-chemical structures but have meanings that are conditioned by past interactions and in turn condition those that follow. This is basic to problem solving. Those problems requiring for their solution functional meanings out of the ordinary are difficult to solve. Those who have had the opportunity to develop a wide variety of perceptual functions for objects are usually good problem solvers while those who have not more often exhibit "functional fixedness."

In the problem consisting of two strings hanging from the ceiling eight feet apart, a pair of pliers lying on a table, and the task of grasping both strings simultaneously, the solution consists of using the pliers as a pendulum bob so that one string may swing toward the other. Such a stimulus function for pliers is almost never previously developed and requires **generalizing** from other interactions in the individuals' repertoire. Setting factors also influence the ease of developing new stimulus functions for problems. When a ping pong ball is down a rusty pipe just large enough to receive it, it is easier to perceive that a dented pitcher containing muddy water may be used to bring it to the top for retrieval than if the pitcher is shiny and full of clean water. A student who will not ask questions of the instructor in class may do so when the class is over. In all of these cases the perceiving of the stimulus object as having a stimulus function is preparatory so some act. As with Hanson, interbehaviorism objects to the notion that the object is sensed and mentally interpreted. Rather, the perceiving is a unitary act based on an interactional history with the object. It is not a matter of perception transformed into meaning. Nor of interpreting "cues." Rather, the perceptual interaction constitutes that meaning. Moreover, when the individual's past interactions with the object have been sufficient to develop more than one meaning or stimulus function, the perceiving then involves anticipation of alternative acts with regard to it. The child who has had experience with snow looks out the window and perceives a new layer of snow in which he can lie down to impress his form, use to make and throw snowballls, or pack into a fort. Further contacts modify or add new stimulus functions: Something that makes mittens wet and hands cold or the basis for a game of fox and geese. The school youth who skies perceives more complex consequences. It offers good skiing today but if he skips school that will have consequences and if he waits until the weekend it may be icy or swept down to bare ground by the skis of previous skiers. Greenwald's (1968) observation that "this stage, in which the organism [rat] presumably anticipates the consequences of alternative response possibilities, must be regarded as especially important when one considers behavior at the human level" (p. 127) is significant here.

## Perceptual Development

Perceiving develops in both an integrative and a differential manner. Each contact with an object is integrated with the next contact. In this way we make finer discriminations and differentiations of these objects. We perceive not isolated qualities, such as greenness unless we attend directly to that quality, but a green object such as a green automobile. And we perceive the object as a unit. The green automobile is not unrelated doors, wheels, body, etc., although we may differentiate these. Further, we perceive it integrally with its setting, its relational character. If it is moving down the street toward us it is an object to be dodged. If it is a taxicab and we need to get to another location it is perceived as a conveyance. If it is our own it may be perceived as an object of pride or as an expensive piece of machinery constantly requiring payments, maintenance, and repairs.

This integral charcater of perceiving is well illustrated when a picture is inadvertently shown upside down from a slide projector. Some members of the audience will be seen to tilt their heads in an effort to approximate the usual relationship. Similarly, if we look at the negative of a photograph it is difficult to perceive the full detail and relationships of the positive print. In those situations the usual integral meanings are put out of harmony and no longer integral. That readaptation is possible is shown by the printer who is quite adapted to reading print backward because of his constant interactions with this form and by the astronomer who studies photographic negatives rather than positive prints of celestial objects.

Frequently we encounter situations that require a novel or partially novel response. Problems are of this type: They are problems by virtue of the fact that we do not have a ready-at-hand solution. We react with partial reproductions of past actions and much covert or overt trial and error until a new and satisfactory stimulus function (actually, as in all interactions, an independent stimulus function-response function) is found.

By continually building up and differentiating response functions from birth onward in integration with thinking, judging, and other activities we are able to solve problems more and more readily. The child cannot be left alone in a large city nor given college level class assignments but as an adult he will manage these. This development is different for every individual. It is this uniqueness of each individual's interactional history that constitutes personality.

## Perceiving Without Dualism

The mentalist claims that fragrances, melodies, the view from an airplane, the woods in autumn, someone's suffering, or a toothache are experiential or cognitive and must be added to behavioral approaches (Zener and Gaffron, 1962). Thus these are different events--an inner versus an outer[7]. Interbehaviorism is able to handle--in fact, demands--a full analysis of such activities that make up our daily lives (see Smith and Shaw, 1979). At the same time it obviates internal versus external or experience and behavior notions. It also obviates the dilemma that Ames (Ittelson, 1968, p. 13) finds, the solipsism of a subjective mind and the mechanism of materialism. The rich meaning or experience of the world that the mentalist points to is exactly what human interactions comprise, neither metaphysical internal processes nor mechanisms of the cognitivist, nor external mechanisms of the behaviorist, but objective fields of events that are continuous with the events that other sciences study.

In Allport's (1955) monumental review of theories of perception, there is no mention of the interbehavioral approach and yet all those reviewed show the same tangle with medieval assumptions. In addition to Kantor himself, Pronko (1961), Lichtenstein (1959, 1971), and Pronko, Ebert and Greenberg (1966) have offered the interbehavioral formulation.

Gregory (1974) poses ten questions about known facts of perception and judges how well they are answered by viewpoints of reflexes and tropisms, Gestalt and brain fields, phase sequences of Hebb, the ambient array of Gibson, unconscious inference, and brain analyzers. he gives them all a poor score. Most the questions involve lack of correspondence or consistency between one thing and another. For example, "how do we see a table as hard?" (p. 267). The questions cry out for a field approach where stimulus functions constituting meaningfulness to the organism, biological conditions (such as in after-images), attending acts (such as in impossible figures and shifting figures like the Necker cube), and others might be brought to bear. With the interbehavioral field "all the variables share the burden and the organism is freed from its crushing and perplexing job of doing a theoretical solo. The job becomes one of determining how, what, when,and where (i.e., in **terrestrial** space) percpetual interactions arise and change" (Pronko, Ebert and Greenberg, 1966, p. 77).

### Some Topics and Issues

Based on the fact that the lens of the eye inverts rays, Descartes proposed in the seventeenth century that everything would appear upside down if the image did not reinvert before reaching the pineal

176

gland, the seat of the soul and of perception. Others, too, have proposed theories based on an internal interpreter, often with physiological assumptions that are in some cases erroneous and in others unobservable. It is an error to assert that there is any retinal image although the literature is replete with the assertion that there is. The retina actually consists of ten layers that are transparent. Only in death do they become translucent and support an image that is sometimes shown in photographs (Bentley, 1954a; Gibson, 1950). The belief that the optic nerve transmits a picture or even that it encodes a picture involves an unobservable. What is observed are neural impulses like the impulses from any other nerve. How those electro-chemical impulses could constitute an image is a great mystery. Nor is it observable that there is any image on the occipital lobe of the brain quite apart from any righting of the image. Again, a great mystery.

When the eye structure and its interrelated neural, vascular, metabolic, and other systems are considered biological rather than psychological organs, they can be examined for their role along with the object and medium of contact in enabling visual perceiving to occur.

It is quite unnecessary to assume any righting of any image when we examine the individual's interactional history with visual objects. As the child contacts objects they acquire meanings and relationships to other objects and then involve motor as well as visual activities. Thus vision becomes coordinated with movements (and directions of sounds, the tug of gravity on the vestibular organs, etc.) and in this way he knows the world. There is no meaning to right-side-up or upside-down apart from an accustomed orientation. The world as adapted to is normal. There is nothing by which to contrast it[8].

This has been demonstrated by experiments with subjects, human and nonhuman, wearing inverting lenses (Ewert, 1949; Foley, 1940; Snyder and Pronko, 1952; Stratton, 1897). After considerable confusion and disorientation for a few days, perceiving becomes newly adapted and the subjects are able to function in a normal manner. In Gibson's (1969) terms it "requires discovery of new invariants" (p. 213). In some of the studies subjects reported that they knew how things looked before but the inversion had come to seem normal. When the lenses are taken off there is again some temporary disorganization. Never is there any inverting or re-inverting but rather object-organism adaptation. In a follow-up of the Synder-Pronko study two years later (Snyder and Synder, 1957) the subject readapted to the inversion almost immediately. The body is seen in correct orientation with other visual objects whether inverting lenses are worn or not.

This gradual development of a meaningful world is further illustrated by studies of the congenitally blind who have had their sight restored (London, 1960; Senden, 1932). The process of developing meaningfulness for what is visual to what is already meaningful by touch is very slow and visual generalization must be gradually built up. Riesen's (1947) study of chimpanzees reared in the dark offers similar conclusions.

## Constancies

Constanies, too, have been traditionally analyzed as "retinal images" that change but are interpreted by the brain as remaining constant. The traditional assumption is that a door locked at from an oblique angle and forming a trapezoidal pattern on the retina, as we would have to draw it for an illustration, gets transformed into a rectangle. For as the door moves back and forth on its hinges we do not perceive it as a changing shape but continue to perceive it as a rectangle. Alternatively, we may observe that by varied interactions with doors, tables, chairs, rooms, and other objects we know that they do not change shape as we move with respect to them. Their meaning to us is rectangularity or other known shape and is stable. We perceive them according to what they mean--that meaning being constituted of previous interactions. We do not need to assume that our nervous system translates sensory "images" or "messages" into stability or constancy. And without this assumption the corollary that we perceive and then interpret is obviated.

Similarly for size constancy. By knowing the size of familiar objects, we judge them as of constant size whether close or far. A man two blocks away is perceived to be of equal size to one standing beside us. And as he approaches he does not grow in size but is perceived nearer. The notion of changing retinal size and reinterpretation again is seen as fiction. It is by throwing known sizes out of their usual context that movie makers can use scaled down models that appear full size. Objects that are of uncertain size such as some airplanes cannot be judged as to size with distance unknown nor of distance with size unknown and thus remain entirely ambiguous. But most objects are sufficiently familiar to us so that they are perceived in size according to known distance and distance according to known size.

The well known rotating trapezoidal window (Ames, 1951; Ittelson, 1968) is a case where both shape and size constancy is put in a context contrary to our adaptations. Since we have almost no experience of windows being trapezoidal but constantly encounter them as rectangular, the smaller end of the window is perceived as farther away. As the small end approaches us we perceive it in terms of its meaning to us. Windows are rectangular and therefore a smaller end is such only because it is farther away. It is not a matter of perceiving as smaller and then interpreting as further away, but rather, an immediate and singular perception of the small end as more distant. Consequently, the smaller end is perceived as oscillating back away from us rather than continuing in a complete rotation. The motion picture film of Ames' demonstration of this is so compelling that some students insist it is trick photography. In this case the illusion is enhanced by the fact that the image on the screen is strictly two-dimensional. Further, the Zulus resist this illusion because they live in round structures and seldom see anything rectangular (Allport and Pettigrew, 1957). Another finding is the minimal illusions non-Western people perceive in the Ponzo and Mueller-Lyer drawings, since their environments include few parallel lines, square corners, or other usages of perspective to simulate depth (Segall, Campbell and Herskovits, 1962). For our own culture it is significant that as the number of millions is increased and shadows painted in so that it becomes a better representation of a window the illusion increases, for then the small end must be perceived as more distant.

The many other illusions of Ames such as distorted rooms, size brightness, bouncing balls, parallax, and others are ingenuous arrangements for altering the usual meaningful relationships and characteristics of objects that vividly demonstrate this basic character of perceiving. The interpretations of Ames and his followers, however, largely miss this essential character and resort to dualism by postulating "unconscious assumptions" and "interpretations."

The "Honi phenomenon" (Wittreich, 1952) demonstrates extraordinarily well the role of meaningfulness. In some of the distorted rooms a human figure appears to be larger or smaller depending on where he is standing in the room. In this case size constancy of the human figure is in conflict with distance, constancy, as it appears in the distorted room when viewed monocularly or in two-dimensional photographs. A figure at a far rear corner will look smaller than one at a near rear corner because both corners appear equidistant. That is, the far figure, in harmony with the room, is perceived as equidistant to the near figure and can thereby only appear as smaller. When they change places, the figure that was previously far appears to grow larger and the figure previously near to shrink because they appear to stay equidistant from the viewer. However, when the person is marital partner the distortion is less than for a stranger, and the room takes on distortion instead. Kilpatrick (1961, pp. 201-202) advances an explanation based on "stress" or "insecurity": Size distortion of one's spouse is "threatening and tension arousing" because of the ever present possibility of loss of that partner. In contrast to this questionable assumption it would be more in keeping with the events to start with the observation that successive interactions with an object build up meaning and that one would therefore expect a marital partner's size to have greater meaningfulness--size constancy--than a stranger's. This could be tested out with well known objects compared to those less well known, and objects too impersonal to be linked with such "stress" as proposed for spouses could be included.

Wittreich's (1961) limited data show a negative correlation between length of marriage and constancy of spouse but the original observation on which the eponym "Honi phenomenon" is based constitutes a major exception. It is possible that other characteristics of meaningfulness besides knowledge of size are involved, such as value. The effect of value on perceived size has been demonstrated by Bruner and Goodman (1947), and Bruner and Rodrigues (1953), and reviewed by Tajfel (1957). Value of spouse for some may decline with time--witness divorce--but not for others. We could then hypothesize that objects of high value to an individual would be perceived as maintaining more constancy than objects of lesser value when in conflict with size-shape constancy of a room.

Returning to the meaning of perspective, another facet of it can be found in children's drawinings. A child will draw both ends of a house along with the side--and occasionally both sides. He is not making a "mistake" in showing both ends which cannot be seen simultaneously but is indicating what a house **means** to him. He draws it as he knows it to be--having two ends. Some of the drawings of Picasso are like this. They show various sides of a human figure that are in violation of perspective. But representation of perspective is one meaning and representation of knowledge of an object is another and both can have their constancies. Similarly, African tribesmen interpret distance in a drawing according to actual distance on the paper, not distance as it is represented by relative size of objects and perspective. Perceiving is interacting in accordance with previously developed meanings and these vary with age, culture, and even artistic interest.

## Color

Newton (1782) in 1666 experimented with sunlight and a prism, and handed us the legacy that the world is entirely colorless. Colorless light waves enter the "sensorium" where color is created and imposed on a colorless world, a world that is only an assemblage of associated sensations anyway. Among other shortcomings Newton confused (1) the spectral colors with the full range of colors, many of which are not spectral, and (2) the production of colored light from interaction of solor or white light with a prism with the belief that the prism separated white light into components of which it was a mixture (Kantor, 1950, 1953). Goethe (1810) argued for the objectivity of colors and demanded to know how white light could be compounded out of colors all of which are darker than it. Apparently no one has yet answered Goethe. Ehrenstein (1943) points to four of Goethe's observations that have held up and Evans (1974, pp. 5-7) emphasizes two others including the importance of white. Yet the Newtonian creationist constructs continue to preponderate in both physics and psychology today. Kaufman (1974) has been unusually frank about the traditional dilemma:

> In the older psychology the nineteenth century the colors were sensations--mental events existing in a mental domain, they were simply parallel to neural events; and for that reason many thinkers were explicitly psychophysical parallelists. Today we are still parallelists, although we rarely admit it (p. 205).

In line with Newton and parallelism Guttman (1963) holds that color is not in the object as naive realism believes. He argues (1973) that redness or greenness depends on the excitation of one subsystem of the central nervous system and yellow or blue to another, and that to refer to "sensitivity to redness" (1974) is a mistake, for these qualities of "sensory experience" must be separated from the object and placed in the nervous system. He seems unaware of the alternative and more naturalistic approach that these different subsystems of the central nervous system are factors in the facilitation of seeing particular colors. Rather, he starts with the presupposition that colors are unreal and imposes this on the data.

It is ironical that something held to be so ghostly as color could be so tangible and reliable in modern chemistry, pigment research, photography, and the like as well as in human conduct for which its occurrence is codified into laws such as those involving traffic lights. It is often observed that psychology engenders suspicion among physicists and other scientists by presuming to deal with unreal things. Yet, as pointed out in this paper, physicists have been equally guilty from the time of Galileo to the present. Some of them have even been mystical with respect to both physics and psychology.

Kantor (1950) has observed that it would be impossible to correlate wave length with color unless the workers were in contact with both phases of the color event. Despite the correlatibility-- much as we can correlate tables with rectangularity even when viewed from an oblique angle--there are innumerable factors that influence color perception. We view human skin as about the same color whether in sunlight or incandescent light. Yet a color photograph will show the latter as quite orange if taken with film balanced for sulight. Skin color is so familiar to us that it has a meaning that remains constant unless grossly changed by colored lights.

A variety of effects are obtained by contrasting colors or shades and these have enjoyed considerable research. Similarly, instructions, prior experience, length of exposure, and many other conditions affect color perception. Land's (1959 a 1959b, 1967, 1977) experiments in producing perceiving of colors by specially contrived monochromes are extremes of this. As with all other perceiving the entire field must be considered and in some instances may be very complex. Extensive programs of research will undoubtedly be required to explore it9. What could more clearly indicate the necessity of turning to this full interbehavioral field than the fact that there is often less than perfect correspodnence between loudness and sound level, pitch and frequency, brightness and illumination, color and wave length, etc., and all of these with physiological dimensions? And is not a field of interactions of concrete things more in keeping with a scientific approach than postualting unobservables such as "phenomenal percepts?" Such a field framework does not require a 1:1 relationship among any of the factors. Nor does it require the burden of causality to be carried by any one. It does require all the factors that participate to be physical and it seeks causality in the total interrelationship of all the factors.

In a departure from the Newtonian doctrine of colorless light waves that are transmuted by the organism into color, Taylor (1962, pp.334-345) argues that light rays are the media for color. It is an "erroneous assumption" that seeing in color is a reaction to a wave length. He goes onto note that we react to the colored object, not the light ray. Mixtures of colors tell us about properties of objects which reflect the mixture of lights but not about the light itself. Accurate information about light can be obtained only when it is unmixed. Only when we study physics do we react to wave lengths as objects. This does not deny the effect that light of varying wave lengths has on the optic system. And as we react to the changing character of a bird in flight through the medium of light , colors are also reacted to and so color is no more illusory than the bird. He notes that Newton who rejected color as real used it to gain knowledge about the spectrum and physicists today continue to use it for attaining knowledge even while rejecting its objectivity.

Aristotle's analysis is also instructive (418b-419a). He starts with the transparent as something which is visible but not from its own power; it obtains its visibility from the color of something else. Light is the color of what is transparent. It causes it to become visible as it is also its color. Color is the power to set in movement the actualized transparent--the light. Without light the color is only a potential and remains invisible.

Once the transparent as a medium has been actualized the object has the power or potentiality to exhibit color but cannot actually do so until there is an eye for it to be exhibited to--a viewer of the color as well as a color to be viewed. When all of the requisite potentialities are present the exhibiting of color (there is no verb form for color but we might use "colorizing") and seeing of color are actualized as one. Thus object and organism interact by means of a medium and although they are interdependent they are not fused. Aristotle's naturalistic culture enabled him to grasp this full continuity of organism, object, and medium as ongoing events of nature while our dualistic culture has continued to stumble over its constructs of intenal and external determiners.

Although Aristotle did not know about color-blindness his analysis would lead us to say that the color-blind person lacks the potentiality for seeing color even though the object has the potentiality for exhibiting color, and so there is no seeing of color. This does not make color a creationist act on the part of others who can see it. Rather, they have the requisite biological structures which together with the requisite condition of the object result in the joint activity of seeing color.

Kaufman (1974) points out that all of the theories of color vision are actually of color mixing, and Armington (1973) observes that the "methods of color addition and colorimetry...are often more descriptive of the stimulus than of the visual system" (p. 336). And yet there is constant recourse to the central nervous system as an explanation or source of creation (often called "correlation") of the quality despite the fact that neural activity "that I, as an experimenter, can experience, is not the redness or greenness that you as a subject can experience" (Kaufman, 1974, p. 205). This might be less of a puzzle if we observe that the experimenter is interacting with neurons while the subject is interacting with a colored object.

## Binocular Stereopsis

Binocular disparity is the special means by which we see in three dimensional space (Zajac, 1964). As disparity becomes minimal at about 25 feet, perception of depth becomes dependent upon monocular factors. Most of the theories of three dimensional perceiving utilize some form of fusion theory in which disparate "images" or "signals" are fused in the brain to "somehow" look like three dimensions "out there." This theory has the same conceptual shortcomings as other brain centered theories of perception and Kaufman (1975) has reviewed the empirical difficulties.

Gibson (1950) has shown that the gradient of disparity changes with the point of fixation and with distance of the object from the eye in an algebraic fashion. These complex conditions he holds can best be

handled as stimulus gradients while "some graded process in     the
brain of the observer reacts to the disparity of his binocular images"
(p. 104).     He explores other stimulus conditions in addition to
gradients and indicates that in most cases they operate  concurrently.
He concludes that "Depth...is not built up out of sensations but is
simply one of the dimensions of visual experience" (p. 108).

While recognizing that the brain is intimately involved in biological
coordination of the eyes as well as motor functions and other
structure-function relationships of the organism, might it not be more
fruitful and more in line with observation to approach the problem as
one in which the complex relationships of objects with the two eyes
are adapted to as in the individual develops? There is gradual
improvement in accuracy in reaching for things and moving toward
things as the musculature, eyes, and other biological components
mature and as practice takes place and objects acquire the meanings
of their discovered spatial relationships. Could these maturing
visual-motor interactions involving relationships of the eyes and
objects provide what we call stereoscopic vision? Could these
developed interactions in themselves be the stereopsis? Individual
differences, effects of practice, and other variables seem to require a
field of interactions.  This is well illustrated by the finding that a
different photograph to each eye in a stereoscope will provide a
combination that is more aesthetic than either alone (Ross, 1976).

In the case of stereopsis produced by stereoscope and by polarized
pictures on a flat screen viewed through polarized lenses the same
gradient relationships hold but in simulation.  It is as unnecessary as
undesirable to assume "mental rays" that converge in  front and
behind the flat screen.  Gibson's work provides a useful  empirical
basis for a field framework with which to handle binocular stereopsis.

## Phi Phenomenon

From his studies of the illusion of movement from one position
to another as the timing  and spacing was right, Wertheimer (1912)
coined the term **phi phenomenon** and argued that there was more
involved in perception than  stimulus elements.  There     was    a
whole configuration, the Gestalt.  From this contention Wertheimer
founded Gestalt psychology and its research that largely centered
around perception.  The Gestalt psychologist came close to a field
approach but they, too, fell victim to the cultural belief in an internal
determiner.

That setting factors influence phi is shown in the Benussi (1916)
study in which movement will appear to curve  around         an
obstacle placed between two lights. If the duration of time between

the two lights is too short they will appear to go on and off simultaneously. As space is increased the time must also be increased if phi is to be obtained. If the second light is brighter than the first an apparent reversal of direction may occur (Korte, 1915; Sgro, 1963).

Subjects who have had little experience with successively flashing lights report that the lights flash simultaneously or in succession. With practice they give more and more consistent reports of motion. direct instructions to see motion also facilitates such perceptions (Neuhaus, 1930).

There is no satisfactory explanation of phi phenomenon. Every explanation that has been proposed has met with some contradictory evidence (Hochberg, 1971). Part of this difficulty is that the explanations invariably invoke the age-old dualisms. Here it is important to examine the biological potentialities and limitations as an important condition of the perceptual interaction, for there seems to be such a limit on the rate at which the human organism can visually perceive successive forms clearly. (The dualist will say something about rate of processing information.) The maximum is at the rate of about 300 milliseconds. Within this limit visual forms interact: The receiving of one light affects the perceiving of the next and this seems to be involved in the illusion of movement (Kolers, 1964). As we have seen, setting factors, instructions, and the interactional history play a role as well as the operational characteristics of the biological development. Here is a clear example of the interdependence of all field factors although the specific roles and interrelationships remain to be further explored.

## Privacy

Are not perceptions along with desires, feelings, and many other covert activities private? And does this not indicate that they are internal and inaccessible? Can we ever really know what another person sees, hears, smells, tastes? Is our toothache private?

Kantor answers by observing that,

> The famous and perennial argument that only the possessor of the aching tooth could have direct experience or knowledge of the toothache is simply the product of the evolution of psychic doctrine. Those who accept the doctrine have always been influenced by the dogma of mind to overlook the fact that all events are unique. What A is digesting is not digested by B. The fall of A is not the fall of B. Nor does the fact that neither A nor B can see what the other is digesting nor observe the fall of the other, unless

both happen to be in a favorable situation, indicate that psychic stuff or principle is involved (p. 292).

Pronko (1976) points out that the chemist cannot be the reaction he studies or the entymologist the insect he observes; yet this does not make the events any less knowable. The psychologist may, in fact, have an advantage over other scientists in that he has a commonality with other people's perceptions and feelings as expressed in the phrase "I feel for you" or, similarly, " I know how you feel."

When privacy is analyzed into concrete events it appears to have two major referents: (1) The accessibility of the stimulus object or the response to more than one person and (2) the meaning of the stimulus object to the individual--that is, the individuality or uniqueness of the interaction.

(1). The availability of the stimulus object to one or more than one person often depends on whether it resides within the individual organism or outside of it. Ratliff (1962) makes a similar point--a visual stimulus, though different for each observer, has the same source for all and is highly correlated among them while a pain stimulus rarely has a common source and therefore has a low correlation.

(2). In all cases each individual may react differently from any other. To you the sighting of a rare bird may be something to enter into your record book. To a deer hunter it is just a distraction. To a small boy it is something to throw a rock at. That is, the same stimulus object has different stimulus functions for different persons depending on each person's prior reactions and the circumstances of the moment. As for the present circumstances or setting, the hunter might be more interested if he is not looking for deer; the boy might not throw a rock in the presence of an adult; and the bird watcher will be less than enthusiastic if he is lost in the woods. Privacy merely refers to the fact that no two people interact in the same way with the same stimulus object even when that same object can stimulate more than one person.

However, there is no need to assume that a mental state or phenomenal field resides inside each person constituting his or her own private reality. Rather, the different interactions are themselves objective events comprising a part of the reality or ongoing events of the universe.

Lichtenstein (1971) notes that under the influence of Locke and Mueller we have traditionally placed seeing red in the organism and this in turn leads us "very easily to a subjective psychology in which the world does not exist independently but only as a construct of the human

186

mind."

Lichtenstein further points out that covert behaviors may be more difficult to deal with than overt ones but do not differ in principle regardless of the difficulty of the technical problems. Even so, other sciences also have their difficulty of observation of some of the phenomena of which they are concerned: The nuclear reactions of the center of the sun, the basic particles of the atom, the causes of cancer, social organization of prehistoric people, the origin of the solar system. Difficulty of observation makes them no less objective. Ratliff (1962) emphasizes that all sciences have "equal objectivity in observation" (p. 477). Homme's (1965) success in applying operant procedures to "coverants" is indication that the problem is far from unsurmountable. In fact psychologists regularly study covert interactions by asking subjects to fill out questionnaires about their attitudes, interests, and desires and by such procedures as asking what they see projected on a screen. Jacob and Sachs (1971) have edited a book on "private events" and note that the evidence contained therein "support[s] the proposition that covert events operate as if they are amenable to some of the same learning processes and manipulations as other classes of responses" (p. 2-3). Watson and Raynor (1926) were offering the same kind of demonstration in conditioning a child to fear a white rat. Lichtenstein observes that the question about whether seeing red or the verbal statement "I see red" is the "actual datum" for the psychologist is well handled by Schoenfeld and Cumming (1963) who take the seeing red as the verbal response for exactly what it is --a report. Thus there is a perceptual response and a verbal response as reference to it. One cannot be reduced to the other nor should there be any confusion about them, but dualistic assumptions inevitably produce such confusion (e.g., Alston, 1973).

Greenspoon (1961) offers two resolutions to the privacy "problem." One is to recognize that experience is behavior and thus thee really is no problem. The other solution, a methodological refinement of the first, is to consider objectivity to be high reliability of either intra- or inter-observer reports and subjectivity to be low reliability. Stephenson (e.g., 1953, 1968, 1980) has developed an entire methodology, Q-sort, that is totally objective out of a recognition of the objectivity of subjectivity as illustrated by the title of one paper: "Consciousnes Out--Subjectivity In" (1961).

The perennial problem of how do I know that the red I see is the same red that you see involves both the assumption of privacy and creationism. The privacy and the color matters have been dealt with, but the question can still be a meaningful one with regard to possible color blindness and to different viewing arrangements. These problems are easy to resolve: Color blindness can be checked with appropriate tests and viewing arrangements can be standardized. This results in high inter-observer reliability. We can then say with a high degree of confidence that the red I see is the same as the red you see. (This assumes a simple discrimination or identification and disregards any differences in meaning--e.g., the red is harsh to you but attractive to me.) As for the retort that we may have learned the same word while seeing different things, this same claim might be made for the names we give to anything in our surroundings. The objects I call by the names "house" and "dog" are the same for all those who share the same language reference system. The color red can in no way differ from this unless we assume that the organism creates that color and that different organisms may create different colors. And that takes us back to the original assumption of creationism.

There is abundant evidence that the notion of "privacy" as distinct from objective events of the universe is a factitious and confusing impediment to psychology as a science. It should be summarily dismissed.

## Individual Differences and Illusions

Individuality has already been referred to with respect to perceiving. if we do not all see, hear, taste, and smell the same, does this not indicate the unknowability of the "real" world? It indicates only that interactions differ from person to person and even change with the same individual as successive contacts are made with objects. Individuality is true for other characteristics of the world as well. Snowflakes, ocean waves, elm trees, and other things come in infinite varieties and so do their interactions with still other objects. All of nature consists of constantly changing events and relationships and so the sciences must deal with these changes whether they occur in stars, physiological processes, or human behavior. As the investigator explores changing behavior, his own behavior changes as he engages in successive interactions. These behavioral changes constitute development of knowing of the changes themselves.

But if the perceiving involves knowing and it keeps changing for a given individual and is different or different individuals, how can we ever know with certainty? Probably there is much that we never can. But as we continue to engage in such interactions as perceiving, thinking, judging, and reasoning, we improve our knowledge. We make errors and correct them. We also develop instrumentation and refined methods of observation that improve our knowing. And, where appropriate, we can develop methodologies that mitigate these factors of individual differences in observation (e.g., interjudgmental reliiability). The contention here is that the world is quite knowable even if imperfectly. Once again we can fall back on Aristotle: The joint activity of a knowing organism and a knowable world is the actualization of knowing.

Another consideration in the problem of changeability is that it is not thorough. Most of the things we deal with on a day to day basis develop relatively constant meanings for individuals. That is to say that even though events are technically never identical, for practical purposes they are similar enough that we can react as if they were. This is so whether these meanings are natural properties of things such as size and shape or whether they are social attributes. And such meanings are shared by others to an extent that we maintain a stable social order. Inasmuch as the problem in any appreciable degree of continuous change is not always present it simplifies knowing.

If the world were illusory and unkowable there would be no point to science. It would be a mere compounding of illusions. With our eyes we perceive a tree. With a microscope we perceive its cellular structure. Neither is illusory. From my position I perceive the tree as pointed at the top and from yours you perceive it as rounded. Again, neither is illusory, but merely incomplete. The story of the blindmen feeling the elephant illustrates this well. The rattle-snake perceives its victim because of its sensitivity to infrared produced by the warm blooded rodent. My world is not distorted or erroneous or illusory because I am insensitive to infrared as a medium; it is merely incomplete. And illusions do exist. Psychologists are fond of experimenting with a variety of them. But they are not misperceptions so much as perceptions under unusual or misleading conditions. Along with Barnes' observation previously referred to we may note that the person on the street recognizes many illusions and "errors" of perceiving, such as a mistaken shape in dim light or at a distance, and he or she also recognizes the corrections upon further contacts that allow errors and illusions to be recognized as such and differentiated from what is actual. The world is ineed knowable, illusions notwithstanding.

Segall, Campbell and Herskovits (1966) find that illusory effects are greater within cultures than between cultures. The very fact that illusions are not the same for everyone and that the experimenters themselves can determine what is illusory and what is not is antithetical to their own initial thesis that the world is illusory. Perhaps they are assuming that there are illusions within an illusory world that are more illusory than the rest of the illusory world--whatever that would mean.

## Psychophysics

Psychophysics has long confused events with constructs. The very term refers to a duality of physical and nonphysical. Fechner's law written as $S=C \log R$ considers S to be a mental sensation, C the constant for the ratio, and log R the logarithm of **Reitz** (stimulus). He regarded the relations as one of subjectivity or mental sensation to physical quantity. Despite Fechner's assumption about sensations, he was dealing with events, not constructs. All that anyone can deal with are events--natural events. As a science of events psychophysics may be considered the study of the relationships of the intensity of stimulation (often media and stimulu objects coincide in these studies) to intensity of response. Accordingly, Fechner's law may be rewritten as $R=C \log S$, where R is the response, C the constant ratio for each particular type of interaction, and log S the logarithm of the stimulus function. In this formula stimulus intensity increases in geometric progression while response intensity increases arithmetically. Steven's power law may be rewritten as $R=C (S-S_o)^n$ where R is the percpetual response, C the constant for the unit of measurement, S the stimulus, So the threshold value or "effective threshold" of the stimulus, and n a power function. Since S is usually very small the formula can become $R=CS^n 10$. In this formula equal stimulus ratios produce equal response ratios. Helson's adaptation level can also be written in interbehavioral terms: $R=C \log (S/A)$ where R is a response, C a constant, and A the adaptation level-- an empirically given constant (Kantor and Smith, 1975, pp. 188-190). It might be charged that such rewriting is of no consequence since the values remain the same and only the terms change. Yet such rewriting reflects an interpretation that recognizes the empirical basis of these formulae and interprets them consistently with that empirical basis. That is, it gives them an orientation toward an interrelationship of events rather than toward mythical constructs.

That the psychphysical formulas have perhaps a greater degree of accuracy than any others in psychology is a reflection of the fact that they are primarily based on biological capabilities. Yet it is well known that threshold values vary from time to time and situation to situation even using the same method of measurement. They depend on setting factors and interactional history as well as on biological sensitivity. Sensitivity is not an absolute condition but is what exists under specific conditions including instructions, attentiveness, nature of the task, and many others. Whenever there are organism-object relationships the field factors may not be safely ignored even when biological conditions are paramount.

Helson's (1959) adaptation level goes the furthest toward such a re-cognition. It considers past stimulation and present complx of stimula-tion as well as contextual and relational factors. The very title "adaptation" is significant. Of special interest is its handling of visual illusions (Avant and Helson, 1973).

## Biological Factors Versus a Biological Basis

Although the role of biological factors has been indicated in some of the preceding sections it needs more direct consideration. The interbehavioral approach neither minimizes them nor gives them any greater emphasis than any of the other factors comprising the interbehavioral field of events. A field approach does, however, rule out any acceptance of the belief that biological organs are also psychological organs and that they can be the container and producer of the event. It also rules out placing a psychological event in the organism as a totality. Such organocentrism is contrary to the nature of events comprising a field. Perceiving, as has been argued here, is inseparable from the stimulus object, setting, media of contact, interactional history, and the biology of the organism. Its locus is not in the object, the organism, the medium, or any other factor but is constituted by the interrelations of all of them.

The interbehavioral position gives due allowance to the role of the organism in the field of events of which it is a part. The role that particular biological components may provide in enabling such acts as seeing red or tasting sweetness is important, especially since these acts are closely tied to simple discrimination which are of necessity delimited or facilitated by the biological equipment. The emphasis on biological research in these areas is therefore of far greater importance than in acts where the nature of the stimulus is more distinctly that of an evolved meaning for the individual through his history of past contacts. For example: Recognizing a friend in a crowd or adjusting the sail on a boat as the wind shifts. But even in the simple sensory tasks where biology looms large we must ask whether biology is the whole event. Is not the object reacted to as important as the organism that reacts to it? Does not seeing red require a red object to be seen? Does not tasting sweetness require a sweet object? To the extent that we eliminate the stimulus object in our experiments and artificially stimulate biological tissue we may learn something about the reaction of the tissue under such conditions, but have we learned anything about perceiving the qualities or characteristics of objects? In what way does the stimulation of a single cell or system of cells in the retina relate to looking at a red flower? We may learn that certain biological structures and processes are required for seeing red--and this may be worth knowing--but does redness lie therein? How do neurological events comprise redness? The interbehaviorist holds that experimental hypotheses must come out of events rather than presuppositions and that results of the experiments be interpreted in terms of the events. The researcher should

191

by all means pursue his investigations and find the answers to his questions. But those answers will only be as close to the actual domain of nature as are the questions he asks.

The need for a field approach can be seen in Pfaffmann's (1959, 1962) work. He has shown that in gustation the Mueller-Helmholtz sense organ or afferent-fiber-specificity does not hold. Single neural fibers respond to all classes of stimulation. Unable to use this doctrine, he resorts to a patterning hypothesis to account for the creation of taste rather than questioning the basic doctrine itself of which the Mueller-Helmholtz notion is one form. A hypothesis in keeping with events would offer patterning and other physiological events as factors on the organism side of object-organism relationships, without giving it causal efficacy for the entire event. For example, is the existence of sourness in fiber A plus fiber C as Pfaffmann holds? He does not observe it there. How could the action of neural fibers possibly be sourness? Is it then in the object? How can an object be sour apart from an organism engaged in tasting it? Is it not, after all, as Aristotle says, a potentiality of the organism (which might very well include joint actions of fibers A and C) to taste sourness and a potentiality of certain objects to taste sour and a mutual action or interaction of both to actualize sourness? Isn't sourness constituted by this interaction? If so, the physiological research will help us understand the organismic conditions for potentially discriminating sourness, just as chemical research will help us understand conditions of potentiality of sourness of the object. However, physiological research will never reveal sourness in the organism nor chemistry reveal it in the object. It will be found only as an interaction.

Held (1965) shows the indispensable role the muscles and efferent components of the nervous system play in sensing. The interbehaviorist would insist that the entire integrated-organism must be considered, while allowing for what Kuo (1967) calls behavior gradients (the relatively greater role played by some organic parts or processes than others in any given activity), but that the analysis must go further than the organism. It must involve the entire field of interdependent events. Neisser (1968) delineates the errors in assuming that seeing is a result of the retina representing an outer world but he then makes the usual retreat to the nervous system for "conscious experience." Pfaffmann will not find a sour taste or Neisser a "conscious experience" in the brain, but organic factors in continuity with the nature of the object occurring in a particular context and often with individually evolved meanings of the object must be the "locus" if one is needed, for all of these are involved. Yet it is perhaps better to seek the factors that constitute the act of perceiving than to search for a thing or its locus.

That such a search in the brain has been less than successful can be illustrated by a number of experiments. To test the assumption that an electrical brain field is basic to supposed brain integration in perception, Sperry (1957) worked with cats in a series of experiments. He placed metallic inserts in their brains to short circuit the fields, placed insulators to block it, sliced up the visual cortex, and excised the corpus callosum--all without appreciable change in the cat's visual discrimination. He notes that these findings are embarrassing to the usual concepts of brain organization, especially when severance of the largest neural tract, the corpus callosum, produces no clear changes in humans. Even when large areas of cortex are destroyed previously learned responses are unchanged and new discriminations can be learned almost as well as before. He also observes the failure to find memory traces or engrams. Other investigators come to similar conclusions; for example, "today we know of no cellular or biochemical changes which correspond to, are produced by, or underlie learning" (Diamond and Chow, 1962).

Sperry (1964) has also split the brain of a monkey so that all neural fibers passing from one side to the other are severed. Since the brain is bilaterally symmetrical, each half still retains a full complement of components, but no cross connections. Almost no change in learning ability, coordination, cooperation, or other behavior occurs or can be distinguished from that of a normal monkey. However, when a split-brain monkey learned to discriminate a square from a circle for a food reward with the right eye it could not also make the discrimination with the left eye. A split-brain cat that was taught a task with one paw could not do it with the other paw, but had to learn anew with that paw. The animal has, in some respects, become two biological entities. Where the animal is not confined to such artificialities as one-eyed or one-pawed arrangements, there is little effect. It is hardly surprising that an animal with its vital coordinating organ split and one-half of itself treated in isolation from the other would show some of the characteristics of two separate organisms. The integrity it maintains when allowed to function in its entirety is more to the point. A man who had his corpus callosum cut to arrest epilepsy showed normal behavior in his daily activities. Under special tests some bilateral discontinuity was found--especially with the left side. Sperry speaks of commands to the left hemisphere (said to control the right side) that are not executed by the right, but the events are simply that the man cannot execute commands with his left side. He speaks of preoccupation of the left hemisphere with a task and the right hemisphere being oblivious, but the events consist of the man's attending to tasks on the right and not on the left. Where the monkey has been taught one response with the left eye and an opposite response with both eyes, and then the conflict presented to both, he speaks of one hemisphere taking command, but what he observes is that the monkey chooses. He speaks of engrams in one hemisphere and not in the other, but his words have no concrete referent: The engram exists only as a word. If the psychological event consists of the organism in interaction with its surroundings (rather than a locus in the brain) but with the brain participating as a feature of the organism, then the continued integrity of the split-brain organism (with some bilateral disruption) is what should be expected. The fact that a nineteen year-old with congenitally absent corpus callosum showed no impairment indicates that disruption occurs only when the interactional history includes that component of the organism. In contrast to the event-based approach offered here, Sperry concludes by stating that split-brain studies provide a new way "for investigating the mysteries of the mind" (p. 52). In another work (1970) he observes that "mental phenomena are seen to transcend the phenomena of physiology and biochemistry" (p. 136).

Similar studies and interpretations have been applied to humans (e.g., Gazzaniga and Freedman, 1973; Gazzaniga and Le Doux, 1978; Sperry, 1968. Gazzaniga (1970) avers that "it is not that the researcher lacks the will or even the know-how. Rather, it is clearly a problem of not knowing what are the proper and most important questions to ask... " (p. vii). The proper questions derive from a more fundamental level of postulation that Gazzaniga considers. A postulate system that starts with events rather than mind-brain constructs is required. In another passage Gazzaniga (1970) avers that his tack is purely descriptive and that it avoids the construct of consciousness. Consciousness is assumed to have a real existence; in subsequent statements it is imposed on the observed behaviors. However, his entire work fails to recognize that the observations made are not actually those of what the hemispheres do but what the organism does under contrived conditions. There is also a failure to distinguish between necessary and sufficient conditions--the distinction between whether one or the other or both hemispheres are necessary for certain coordiantions and whether they are sufficient for them. It is the latter that is assumed when only the former has been demonstrated. The approach is not descriptive but entirely ascriptive. It results in a thoroughgoing homunculean approach that permeates Gazzaniga's and Sperry's works.

Similar errors obtain in abscribing language, logic, writing, and mathematics to the left hemisphere and perception, creativity, and revery to the right. Is perception a **thing** that is contained in one hemisphere? Or is there an **observed act** of perceiving that requires that hemisphere among other factors for action? At most, all that is shown is a necessary and intimate participation of the respective hemispheres in these activities. More recent work casts doubt on even that specificity and seems to repeat the history of retreat, as noted below, of earlier localization assertions. Even so the animistic accounts and **non sequiturs** continues (e.g., Day, 1977).

Repeated attempts to localize psychological functions in particular portions of the brain have met with little success. A site for "character" has been sought but not found. Musical ability was for a time thought to be contained in the gyrus of Heschl, but the evidence was insubstantial. Broca's area in the left frontal lobe and Wenicke's area in the left temporal lobe were once held to be involved in speech, but this is now seriously doubted. Aphasia can occur from lesions in almost any part of the cortex, while Broca's area can sometimes be removed without producing it (Von Bonin, 1962).

Livingston (1962) reports that dysfunction of a sensory performance such as seeing or hearing are specific to the particular seeing or listening task rather than to seeing as such or hearing as such. He recognizes the futility of searching for a localization in the brain where the function of that part is necessary for all discriminations of a sensory system.

The whole difficulty with brain localization efforts has been one of seeking to find brain anatomy that correlates with **fictitious mental states.** More fruitful results would be obtained by investigating the manner in which biological defects in brain, gland, or other tissue or a dysfunction in metabolism or other physiological processes affects the functioning of the organism in its concrete interactions with particular objects and conditions and in what types of situations.

Leeper (1963) finds it unfortuante that Kantor's interbehavioral approach to perception has been ignored, but feels that a severe and unnecessary handicap of the system is in the rejection of internal determiners for some of the principal properties of the interactions. It is true that determiners are rejected as in a biological basis of behavior, but it is perhaps not fully recognized that biological conditions as components are considered essential factors in the field. They are necessary conditions for perceiving but are not sufficient. Seeing occurs **with** the eye and the brain, not in them. The anatomy and physiology of the sense organs are legitimate and important fields of investigation and may assist us in more fully understanding perceiving with respect to the biological facilitating factors, ranges, and limitations. Such an understanding is in no way consistent with assertions that such biological factors contain or determine or create the event. Now that a few others are arriving at similar conclusions, interbehaviorism may be seen to have a distinct advantage rather than a severe handicap.

## Some Approaches to Perceiving as Interbehaving

The works of several persons who have departed from traditional perception concepts and moved toward a systematic naturalistic orientation have been reviewed in conjunction with other topics. Aristotle has been given considerable emphasis, although he came prior to the advent of the pernicious doctrine. Kantor's interbehaviorism has served as the model for a scientific framework that treats psychological acts as homogenous with all other events in the universe. Taylor's work also deserves mention among recent writers, as does a report of studies by Garner (1966) who shows that perceiving is knowing and that what is perceived depends on the context or "sets" of which the stimulus is a part. In this section two additional formulations will be considered.

A view known as **transactionalism** was developed by Arthur Bentley and John Dewey (e.g., Bentley, 1935, 1954b; Dewey and Bentley, 1949). This proposed that self-actional theories that assumed a "mind," "will," "consciousness," or other internal prime Actor were unsatisfactory. Transactionalism, in contrast, insists that inquiry must consider the organism-in-the-environment. Organism and environment are so interdependent that they are separate entities only in abstraction and are said to be parts of a transaction rather than an interaction. Knowing is inseparable from the field of which it is a part and from the one who investigates the transaction. While there are some important philosophical differences between transactionalism and interbehaviorism (Handy, 1973; Lichtenstein, 1973), especially the former's roots in Hegelian objective idealism (Mitsorg, 1970; Observer, 1975), it offered a corrective to internal Actors and stressed the full field of factors, even if there resulted too much fusion of these factors.

Unfortunately the best features have been transmogrified by Ames, Kilpatrick, Cantril, and Ittelson into "transactional psychology" which imposes internal "assumptions," "registration," and "unconscious weighting process" (Ittelson, 1962) as over against an "external world." In common with the phenomenalists they hold that "our 'assumptive world'" is "the only world we know" (Kilpatrick, 1952, p. 89); perception involves the "externalization" of some aspects of the experientially created world and the "internalization" of other aspects, thereby providing recognition of one's own subjective experience. These constructs are added to the weakest parts of the Dewey-Bentley thesis of "an indissoluble whole" (Kilpatrick, 1961, p. 3) where stimuli are inseparable from the organism[11]. Nevertheless, the transactionalists have provided some of the most remarkable of demonstrations and research in perception and these offer clear alternative interpretations of the type advocated in this paper.

A second important viewpoint and one that offers in its later stages a promising naturalistic system is that of Gibson. Perceiving, he holds, is a function of stimulation, a matter of physical energies which affect the sense organs and "specify the world" (Gibson, 1959). Organisms do not reflect or interpret or construct the world but detect it from the flux of energy which maps itself onto the functional groupings of receptor systems and motor organs. The systems extract from the infinite stimulus array invariant features that inform the individual about stable characteristics of the environment. The brain "resonates" to these invariant features of the environment in comparable fashion to a radio receiver (Gibson, 1966). There is no transformation of stimuli into percepts through associations, no ghostly intervening variables in learning. Instead, the perceiving act is one of becoming more focalized and more specific with practice. Perceptual learning involves extracting increasing amounts of information from the array of stimulation from the environment in an ever increasingly differentiated manner.

There is a mixture of orthodoxy and heterodoxy in the writings covering these ten years. From orthodoxy we find a phenomenal world corresponding to stimuli, a consciousness construct added to a behavioral event, organocentrism, brain doctrine, a mechanistic analogy, biological stimulation confused with psychological, stimulus regarded as energy, and some continuing distinction between sensation and perception. But of greater interest are the departures from orthodoxy. Gibson treats the world as directly knowable. Perceiving is not interpretation but selection. Attention is treated as orienting rather than an invisible filtering. "Cues" are discredited. The retinal "image" is discounted, and the notion of seeing movement by successive single cell stimulation is rejected. The interrelationship of perceptual systems and these in turn with both motor systems and conditions of the environment is stressed. Slightly later (1973) he notes that belief in the senses as channels of sensation or of sensory and motor distinctions is mentalistic. The assumption of a "mind that can copy, store, compare, match, decide, and issue commands" requires "a man in the brain" (pp. 396-397). He repudiates "sensory signals and motor commands" and the brain as "the seat of the mind" (p. 397). Gibson's final book (1979) argues that we cannot see light, only its effects on the environment. Hence there are no sensations of light to be converted to mental perceptions. We do not perceive stimuli but conditions of the environment. Instead, perception is an **ecological** event, one involving the interrelationship of the individual and surrounding objects and conditions.

The major thrust of Gibson's work is interbehavioral, although it differs in many details. Most importantly, like interbehaviorism, it holds that perception is an activity in which the individual gets acquainted with the world. A recognition of Kantor's analysis more than half a century earlier could have saved Gibson the long independent struggle toward a similar position. Observer (1981) points out that failure to recognize this alternative has caused psychology to spend that half century in struggling with metaphysic postulates rather than pursuing naturalistic ones. There is still very limited signs of change. Scientific psychology could make a quantum leap foreward if ecological-interbehavioral psychology could gain recognition. At the very least, psychologists would have available the basis for a more informed choice.

## Summary and Conclusions

This paper has dwelt primarily on the fundamental considerations of the nature of perceiving. The large and very important body of literature on the role of personality, attitude, interests, knowledge, values, expectations, affect, and needs in perceiving has been hardly mentioned but they do illustrate the importance of meaning in perceiving whether derived from interactional histories, the structure of the stimulus situation, or the context. Often, however, any such categorization is somewhat arbitrary because of the interdependence of these factors and merely indicate a direction of emphasis. Learning studies have also been ignored here though they too are of considerable importance12.

What has been emphasized is that perception need not be the mysterious process fraught with puzzles that history has handed us. Its concrete character was clearly seen by the Helenics, especially Aristotle, and in more recent times by a number of philosophers and psychologists who have cast aside some or all of the dualistic heritage and recounted the same objective events that Aristotle described. The earliest and fullest such account has been that of J.R. Kantor starting in the 1920's. This view insists that perceiving consists in the development of interactions of stimulus object and responding organism in which new stimulus functions and their correlated response functions accumulate over succesive contacts. Perceiving is thus an **activity between organism and object.** This differs radically from the traditional view which comes in two forms, each being a mere variation of the other. In the first a mind or nervous system actively interprets an outside world; that world is known only by means of the organization of subjective qualities. Most of the traditional views considered here are of this type. They range from notions of unconscious inference to information-processing. The second stems from John Locke and other British empiricists: The mind-brain passively records an active environment which is known as the subjectively recorded qualities. The term "receptor" belongs to this assumption.

As a distinct alternative an attempt was made to indicate how interbehaviorism would apply to a number of issues in contrast to traditional approaches and their dilemmas. It is contended here that interbehaviorism offers not only a vastly more scientific and more succesful program to deal with these issues than psychophysical dualism, but that its insistence on dealing solely with concrete events and their interrelationships is so fundamental to science that it cannot be ignored if psychology is ever to overcome its malaise.

### Footnotes

1. Pfaffman (1962) further modifies the doctrine to eliminate the rigid specificity for each sensory organ and allow for sensations based on patterns of neural activity. See section "Biological factors versus biological bases."

2. The prestige of this journal which carried the statement is indicated by the fact that it was rated highest for important materials by members of the American Psychological Association (Koulack and Keselman, 1975). White and White (1977) found it ranked second in mean citations per article including self-citations and first when self-citations were excluded.

3. Graham and Ratoosh (1962) shows that data on duration threshold indicate that there is no meaningful distinction between sensing and perceiving.

4. Lean (1953) offers an extensive critique of Broad's position and argues that the entire distinction of physical objects and subjective perception of them or "external reality" and "private mental events" is a fallacy based on artificial verbal distinctions. Similarly, five philosophers (Warnock, 1967) have reexamined the issues and assumptions of this doctrine and found it wanting. Unfortunately, most psychologists have not given the same critical appraisal to this matter.

5. See also Woodbridge, 1913a.

6. Sensing and perceiving are used here as synonomous terms, not two separate things. It might be noted that the reference here is to a verb form of these two words rather than to noun form in order to emphasize an action rather than a mysterious thing or state or process.

7. It is noteworthy that Zener and Gaffron speak of "an ongoing interaction between organism and environment" but seem unable to escape the assumption that an internal psychic component must be added. Another point of their incipient interbehavioral approach is

in their observation that it is more correct to speak of perceiving an "illuminated object" than light.

8. Rock (1966) offers a similar anlaysis but heavily laden with such constructs as retinal image, phenomenal objects, phenomenal directions, phenomenal self, etc., and those in turn further laded with constructs of brain traces. There have been several revisions of this subject. For a recent one see Welch (1978).

9. Land (1977) had demonstrated that colors are accurately discriminated throughout a wide variety of lighting arrangements but that certain triplets of wave lengths are particularly involved. He postulates creationist factors in either the retina or the cortex ("retinex"). But the factors may well be considered as conditions of lighting media which permit the seeing of colors, especially since reflectance is correlated with discrimination, while flux is independent. As a follow-up on Land's assumptions about color as a product of the cortex, Zeki (1980) claims to have found color-coded cells in the cortex of the rhesus monkey that correspond to sensations of color. However, he observed no excreted colors, only neural discharges.

10. Nihm's (1976) recent polynomial law uses the form $R = a(0-0)^k + b$, but R is interpreted not as responses but as sensation.

11. Professor Rollo Handy (1976) believes that while Bentley (1954c) objected to fragmenting the organism-environment relationship and arued for observation of their joint operations he did not intend that they should be undifferentiated. Perhaps so, but Bentley (1941) refers to "the fusion of organic and environmental participations in behaviors" (p. 10) and in a "Postcript" to the reprinting of the 1941 paper (1954b) similarly refers to "the full subjective -objective fusion (except as linguistically dissected with careful semantic anethetic and antiseptic)" (p. 211). Handy also feels that Dewey and Bentley left behind Dewey's earlier Hegalian influence and supported no idealism. He points out that in the Dewey-Bentley correspondence (1964, pp. 619-620, 626) they voiced objections to Ames' group's misusing and misunderstanding transactionalism.

12. See Epstein (1967) for a review of the research and critique of the theories concerning the role of learning in perception.

### References

Allport, F.H. 1955. **Theories of Perception and the Concept of Structure: A Review and Critical Analysis with an Introduction to a Dynamic-structural Theory of Behavior.** New York: Wiley.

Allport, G.W. and Pettigrew, T.F. 1957. Cultural influence on the perception of movement: The trapezoidal illusion among Zulus. **Journal of Abnormal and Social Psychology,** 55, 104-113.

Allston, W.P. 1972. Can psychology do without private data? **Behaviorism,** 1, 71-102.

Ames, A.A. 1951. Visual perception and the rotating trapezoidal window. **Psychological Monographs,** 65, 324.

Aristotle. 1908. De Anima. In W.D. Ross (Ed.) **The Works of Aristotle Translated into English.** Oxford, 1952.

Armington, J.C. 1973. Color vision. In B.B. Wolman (Ed.) **Handbook of General Psychology.** Englewood Cliffs, New Jersey: Prentice-Hall.

Attneave, F. 1974. How do you know? **American Psychologist,** 29, 493-511.

Avant, L.L. and Helson, H. 1973. In B.B. Wolman (Ed.) **Handbook of General Psychology.** Englewood Cliffs, New Jersey: Prentice-Hall.

Barnes, W.H.F. 1944-45. The myth of sense-data. **Proceedings of the Aristotelian Society,** 45, A.A. Karsman (Ed.) (reprinted in R.S. Swartz (Ed.) **Perceiving, Sensing and Knowing.** New York: Doubleday, 1965.)

Bentley, A.F. 1935. **Behavior, Knowledge, Fact.** Bloomington, Indiana: Principia.

Bentley, A.F. 1941. The human skin: Philosophy's last line of defense. **Philosophy of Science,** 8, 1-19.

Bentley, A.F. 1954a. The fiction of the retinal image. In A.F. Bentley (Ed.) **Inquiry into Inquiries.** Boston: Beacon.

Bentley, A.F. 1954b. **Inquiry into Inquiries.** Boston: Beacon.

Bentley, A.F. 1954c. Kennetic inquiry. In A.F. Bentley (Ed.) **Inquiry into Inquiries.** Boston: Beacon.

Benussi, V. 1916. Versuche zur analyse taktil erwickter scheinbewegungun. **Archiv fur die Gesamte Psychologie,** 36, 59-135.

Berlyne, D.E.1974. Attention. In E.C. Carterette and M.P. Friedman (Eds.) **Handbook of Perception** (Vol. 1) **Historical and Philosophical Roots of Perception.** New York: Academic Press.

Broadbent, D.E. 1955. **Perception and Communication.** London: Pergamon.

Bruner, J.S. and Goodman, C.C. 1947. Value and need as organizing factors in perception. **Jounral of Abnormal and Social Psychology, 42, 33-44.**

Bruner, J.S. and Rodrigues, J. 1953. Some determinants of apparent size. **Journal of Abnormal and Social Psychology,** 48, 17-24.

Chaplin, J.C. 1968. **Dictionary of Psychology.** New York: Dell.

Cox, A. 1966.Photographic Optics: **A Modern Approach to the Technique of Definition.** (13th edition). New York: Focal Press.

Day, J. 1977. Right-hemisphere language processing in normal right-handers. **Journal of Experimental Psychology.** Human **Perception and Performance,** 3, 518-528.

Deutsch, D.A. and Deutsch, D. 1963. Attention: Some theoretical considerations. **Psychological Review,** 70, 80-90.

Dewey, J. 1925. The naturalistic theory of perception by the senses. **Journal of Philosophy,** 22, 596-605.

Dewey, J. and Bentley, A.F. 1964. **John Dewey and Arthur F. Bentley: A Philosophical Correspondence, 1932-1951.** In S. Ratner, J. Altman and J.E. Wheeler (Eds.). New Jersey: Rutgers University.

Dewey, J. and Bentley, A.F. 1949. **Knowing and the Known .** Boston: Beacon.

Diamond, I.T. and Chow, K.L. 1962. Biological psychology. In S. Koch (Ed.) **Psychology: A Study of a Science,** Vol. 4, **Biologically Oriented Fields.** New York: McGraw-Hill.

Egeth, H. and Bevan, W. 1973. Attention. In B.B. Wolman (Ed.) **Handbook of General Psychology.** Englewood Cliffs, New Jersey: Prentice-Hall.

Ehrenstein, W. 1943. Theoretisch fruchtbare gedanken in Goethes Farvenlehre. **Archiv fur die gesamte Psychologie,** 12, 196-206.

**Encyclopedia of Psychology.** 1972. New York: Herder and Herder.

English, H.B. and English, A.C. 1958. A **Comprehensive Dictionary of Psychological and Psychoanalytic Terms: A** Guide to Usage. New York: Longmans, Green.

Epstein, W. 1967. **Varieties of Perceptual Learning.** New York: McGraw-Hill.

Evans, R.M. 1974. **The Perception of Color.** New York: Wiley.

Foley, J.P. 1940. An experimental investigation of the effect of prolonged inversion of the visual field in the rhesus monkey **(Mucaca Mulatta).** Journal of Genetic Psychology, 56, 21-51.

Freeman, K. 1965. **The Pre-Socratic Philosophers: A Companion to Diels, Fragmente der Vorsokratiker,** (2nd edition). Oxford: Blackwell.

Garner, W.R. 1966. To perceive is to know. **American Psychologist, 21, 11-19.**

Gazzaniga, M.S. 1970. **The Bisected Brain.** New York: Appleton-Century-Crofts.

Gazzaniga, M.S. and Freedman, H. 1973. Observations on visual processes after posterior callosal section. **Neurology, 23, 1126-1130.**

Gazzaniga, M.S. and LeDoux, M. 1978. **The Integrated Mind.** New York: Plenum.

Gibson, E.J. 1969. **Principles of Perceptual Learning and Devleopment.** New York: Appleton-Century-Crofts.

Gibson, J.J. 1950. **The Perception of the Visual World.** Boston: Houghton Mifflin.

Gibson, J.J. 1959. Perception as a function of stimulation. In S. Koch (Ed.) **Psychology: A Study of a Science,** Vol. 1, **Sensory, Perceptual, and Physiological Formulations.** New York: McGraw-Hill.

Gibson, J.J. 1966. **The Senses Considered as Perceptual Systems.** Boston: Houghton Mifflin.

Gibson, J.J. 1973. Direct visual perception: A reply to Gyr. **Psychological Bulletin, 79, 396-397.**

Gibson, J.J. 1979. **The Ecological Approach to Visual Perception.** Boston: Houghton Mifflin.

Goethe, J.W. von. 1810. **Zur Farbenlehre** (2 vols.). Tubingen: Cotta.

Graham, C.H. and Ratoosh, P. 1962. Notes on some interrelations of sensory psychology, perception, and behavior. In S. Koch (Ed.) **Psychology: A Study of a Science** (Vol. 4), **Biologically Oriented Fields.** New York: McGraw-Hill.

Green, E.J. 1958. A simplified model for stimulus discrimination. **Psychological Review,** 65, 56-60.

Greenspoon, J. 1961. Private experience revisted. **Psychological Record,** 11, 373-381.

Gregory, R.L. 1974. Choosing a paradigm for perception. In E. C. Carterette and M.P. Friedman (Eds.) **Handbook of Perception** (Vol. 1) **Historical and Philosophical Roots of Perception.** New York: Academic Press.

Guttmann, N. 1963. Laws of behavior and facts of perception. In S. Koch (Ed.) **Psychology: A Study of a Science** (Vol.5 ). New York: McGraw-Hill.

Guttman, N. 1973. Guttman's reply. **Contemporary Psychology,** 18, 570.

Guttman, N. 1974. Rejoinder to Noel Smith. **Contemporary Psychology,** 19, 72.

Handy, R. 1973. The Dewey-Bentley transactional procedure of inquiry. In N.W. Smith "Contextual Interactionists: A Symposium." **Psychological Record,** 23, 281-334.

Handy, R. 1976. Personal Correspondence., July 1.

Hanson, N.R. 1961. **Patterns of Discovery: An Inquiry Into the Conceptual Foundations of Science.** Cambridge: University Press.

Hanson, N.R. 1969. **Perception and Discovery: An Introduction to Scientific Inquiry.** San Francisco: Freeman, Cooper.

Hebb, D. 1966. **A Textbook of Psychology** (2nd edition). Philadelphia: Saunders.

Held, R. 1965. Plasticity in sensory-motor systems. **Scientific American,** November, 213, 93-84.

Helson, H. 1959. Adaptation level theory. In S. Koch (Ed.) **Psychology: A Study of a Science** (Vol. 1) **Sensory, Perceptual, and Physiological Formulations.** New York: McGraw-Hill.

Hochberg, J. 1971. Perception II. Space and movement. In J.W. Kling and L. A. Riggs (Eds.) **Woodworth and Schlosberg's Experimental Psychology** (3rd edition). New York: Holt, Rinehart and Winston.

Homme, L.E. 1965. Control of coverants, the operants of the mind. **Psychological Record,** 15, 501-511.

Ittelson, W.H. 1962. Perception and transactional psychology. In S.Koch (Ed.) **Psychology: A Study of a Science** (Vol. 4) **Biologically Oriented Fields.** New York : McGraw-Hill.

Ittelson, W.H. 1968. **The Ames Demonstrations in Perception with an Interpretive Manual by Ames.** New York: Hafner.

Jacobs, A. and Sachs, L.B. 1971. Private events. In A. Jacobs and L.B. Sachs (Eds.) **The Psychology of Private Events: Perspectives on Covert Response Systems.** New York: Academic Press.

Kahneman, D. 1973. **Attention and Effort.** Englewood Cliffs, New Jersey: Prentice-Hall.

Kantor, J.R. 1920. Suggestions toward a scientific interpretation of perception. **Psychological Review,** 27, 191-216.

Kantor, J.R. 1922. Can the psychophysical experiment reconcile introspectionists and objectivists? **American Journal of Psychology,** 32, 481-510.

Kantor, J.R. 1924. **Principles of Psychology** (Vol. 1). New York: Knopf.

Kantor, J.R. 1950. Goethe's place in modern science. In **Goethe Bicentennial Studies,** Indiana University, Humanities Series.

Kantor, J.R. 1963. **The Scientific Evolution of Psychology** (Vol. 1). Chicago: Principia.

Kantor, J.R. and Smith, N.W. 1975. **The Science of Psychology: An Interbehavioral Survey.** Chicago: Principia.

Kaufman, L. 1974. **Sight and Mind: An Introduction to Visual Perception.** New York: Oxford University.

Kilpatrick, F.P. 1952. Statement of theory. In F.P. Kilpatrick (Ed.) **Human Behavior from the Transactional Point of View.** Hanover, New Hampshire: Institute for Associated Research.

Kilpatrick, F.P. 1961 (Ed.) **Explorations in Transactional Psychology.** New York: New York University.

Koler, P.A. 1964. The illusion of movement. **Scientific American,** October, 211, 98-106.

Korte, A. 1915. Kinematoskopische untersuchungen. **Zeitschrift fur Psychologie,** 72, 193-296.

Koulack, D. and Keselman, H.J. 1975. Ratings of psychology journals by members of the American Psychological Association. **American Psychologist,** 30, 1049-1053.

Kuo, Z. Y. 1967. **The Dynamics of Behavior Development:** An **Epigenetic View.** New York: Random House.

Kvale, S. and Grenness, C.E. 1967. Skinner and Sartre: Toward a radical phenomenology of behavior. **Review of Existential Psychology and Psychiatry,** 7, 128-150.

Land, E.H. 1959a. Experiments in color vision. **Scientific American,** May, Freeman Reprint.

Land, E.H. 1959b. Color vision and the natural image. Part II. **Proceedings of the National Academy of Sciences,** 45, 636-644.

Land, E.H. 1967. Retinex theory of color vision. **Journal of the Optical Society of America,** 57, 1428.

Lean, M. 1953. **Sense-Perception and Matter: A Critical Analysis of C.D. Broad's Theory of Perception.** New York: Humanities Press.

Leeper, R.W. 1963. Learning and the fields of perception, motivation, and personality. In S.Koch (Ed.) **Psychology: A Study of a Science,** (Vol. 5). New York: McGraw-Hill.

Lichtenstein, P.E. 1959. Perception and the psychological metasystem. **Psychological Record,** 9, 37-44.

Lichtenstein, P.E. 1971. A behavioral Approach to "phenomenological data." **Psychological Record**, 21, 1-16.

Lichtenstein, P.E. 1973. Discussion: "Contextual interactionism." In N.W. Smith, "Contextual interactionists: A symposium. **Psychological Record**, 23, 281-334.

Livingston, R.B. 1962. How man looks at his own brain: An adventure shared by psychology and neurology. In S.Koch (Ed.) **Psychology: A Study of a Science** (Vol. 4) **Biologically Oriented Fields.** New York: McGraw-Hill.

London, I.D. 1960. A Russian report on the postoperative newly seeing. **American Journal of Psychology**, 73, 478-482.

Mason, W.A. 1976. Environmental models and mental modes: Representational processes in the great apes. **American Psychologist**, 31, 284-294.

Mitsorg, A. 1970. Interaction: Transaction: Which? **Interbehavioral Psychology Newsletter**, 1, 4-5.

Moray, N. 1969. **Attention: Selective Processes in Vision and Hearing.** London: Hutchinson.

Neisser, U. 1968. The processes of vision. **Scientific American**, September, 219, 204-214.

Neuhaus, W. 1930. Experimentalle untersuchung der scheinbewegung. **Archiv fur gesamte Psychologie**, 75, 315-458.

Newton, I. 1782. **Isaaci Newtoni Quae Exstant Omnia** (Vol. 4). Horsley (Ed.), London: Nichols.

Nihm, S.D. 1976. Polynomial law of sensation. **American Psychologist**, 11, 808-809.

Horman, D.A. 1969. **Memory and Attention: An Introduction to Human Information Processing.** New York: Wiley.

Nuttin, J. and Greenwald, A.G. 1968. **Reward and Punishment in Human Learning: Elements of a Behavior Theory.** New York: Academic Press.

Oatley, K. 1978. **preceptions and Representations: The Theoretical Basis of Brain Research and Psychology.** New York: Free Press.

Observer. 1973. Private data, raw feelings, inner experience, and all that. **Psychological Record**, 23, 563-565.

Observer. 1975. On reviewing psychological classics. **Psychological Record**, 25, 293-298.

Observer. 1981. Priority and the pace of scientific progress. **Psychological Record**, 31, 285-292.

Pitcher, G. 1971. **A Theory of Perception.** Princeton, New Jersey: Princeton University Press.

Pfaffmann, C. 1959. The afferent code for sensory quality. **American Psychologist**, 14, 226-232.

Pfaffmann, C. 1962. Sensory processes and their relation to behavior: Studies on the sense of taste as a model S-R system. In S. Koch (Ed.) **Psychology: A Study of a Science** (Vol. 4), **Biologically Oriented Fields.** New York: McGraw-Hill.

Pronko, N.H. 1961. Some reflections on perception. **Psychological Record**, 11, 311-314.

Pronko, N.H. 1976. Personal Communication, July 8.

Pronko, N.H. , Ebert, R. and Greenberg, G. 1966. A critical review of theories of perception. In A.L. Kidd and J.L. Rivoire (Eds.) **Perceptual Development in Children.** New York: Internaltional Unviersities Press.

Ratliff, F. 1962. Some interrelation among physics, physiology, and psychology in the study of vision. In S. Koch (Ed.) **Psychology : A Study of a Science.** (Vol. 4). **Biologically Oriented Fields.** New York: McGraw-Hill.

Riesen, A.H. 1947. The development of visual perception in man and chimpanzee. **Science**, 106, 107-108.

Rock, I. 1966. **The Nature of Perceptual Adaptation.** New York: Basic Books.

Ross, J. 1976. The resources of binocular perception. **Scientific American**, March 234, 80-86.

Ryle, G. 1949. **The Concept of Mind.** New York: Barnes and Noble.

Ryle, G. 1965. Sensations. In R.J. Swartz (Ed.) **Perceving, Sensing and Knowing: A Book of Readings from Twentieth-Century Sources in the Philosophy of Perception.** Garden City, New York: Anchor Books, Doubleday.

Schoenfeld, W.N. and Cummings, W.W. 1963. Behavior and perception. In S. Koch (Ed.) **Psychology: A Study of Science** (Vol. 5) **The Process Areas, the Person, and some Applied Fields.** New York: McGraw-Hill.

Segall, M.H. ,.Campbell, D.T. and Herskovits, M.J. 1966. **The Influence of Culture on Visual Perception.** Indianapolis: Bobbs-Merrill.

Senden, M.V. 1932. **Raum and Gestaltauffasung bei operierten Blindegeboren vor und nach Operation.** Leipzig: Barth.

Sgro, F.J. 1963. Beta motion thresholds. **Journal of Experimental Psychology,** 66, 281-285.

Shaw, R. and Bransford, J. 1977. Introduction: Psychological approaches to the problem of knowing. In R. Shaw and J. Bransford (Eds.) **Perceiving, Acting, and Knowing: Toward a n Ecological Psychology.** Hillsdale, New Jersey: Erlbaum Associates.

Shute, C. 1964. **The Psychology of Aristotle: An Analysis of of the Living Being.** New York: Russell and Russell.

Skinner, B.F. 1974. **About Behaviorism.** New York: Knopf.

Smith, N.W. 1971. Aristotle's dynamic approach to sensing and some current implications. **Jouranl of the History of the Behavioral Sciences,** 7, 375-377.

Smith, N.W. 1974. The ancient background to Greek psychology and some implications for today. **Psychological Record,** 24, 309-324.

Snyder, F.W. and Pronko, N.H. 1952. **Vision with Spatial Inversion.** Wichita: University of Wichita.

Snyder, F.W. and Snyder, C.W. 1957. Vision with spatial inversion: A follow-up study. **Psychological Record,** 7, 20-30.

Soltis, J.F. 1966. **Seeing, Knowing, and Believing: A Study of the Language of Visual Perception.** Reading, Mass.: Addison-Wesley.

Sperry, R.W 1957. Brain mechanisms in behavior. **Engineering Science Monthly,** May.

Sperry, R.W. 1964. The great cerebral commissure. **Scientific American,** 210, 42-52.

Sperry, R.W. 1965. Hemisphere deconnection and unity in conscious awareness. **American Psychologist,** 23, 723-733.

Sperry, R.W. 1970. Perception in the absence of the neocortical commissures. **Perception and its Disorders.** Research Publications, 48, The association for Research in Nervous and Mental Diseases. Baltimore, Maryland: Williams and Wilkins.

Stephenson, W. S. 1953. **The Study of Behavior : Q-Technique and its Methodology.** Chicago: University of Chicago.

Stephenson, W.S. 1961. Consciounsess out--subjectivity in. **Psychological Record,** 18, 499-501.

Stephenson, W.S. 1980. Newton's fifth rule and Q methodology: Application to educational psychology. **American Psychologist,** 35, 882-889.

Stratton, G.M. 1897. Vision without inversion of the retinal image. **Psychological Review,** 4, 341-360, 463-481.

Tajfel, H. 1957. Value and the perceptual judgment of magnitude. **Psychological Review,** 64, 192-204.

Taylor, J. 1962. **The Behavioral Basis of Perception.** New Haven: Yale University Press.

Von Bonin, G. 1962. Brain and mind. In S. Koch (Ed.) **Psychology: A Study of a Science** (Vol. 4) **Biologically Oriented Fields.** New York: McGraw-Hill.

Warnock, G.J. (Ed.) 1967. **The Philosophy of Perception.** London: Oxford University.

Watson, J.B. and Rayner, N. 1920. Conditioning emotional reactions. **Journal of Experimental Psychology,** 3, 1-14.

Welch, R.B. 1978. **Perceptual Modification: Adapting to Altered Sensory Environments.** New York: Academic Press.

Wertheimer, M. 1912. Experimentalle studien uber das sehen von bewegung. **Zeitschrift fur Psychologie,** 61, 161-265.

White, M.J. and White, K.G. 1977. Citation analysis of psychology journals. **American Psychologist**, 32, 301-305.

Wittreich, W.J. 1961. The Honi phenomenon: A case of selective distortions. In F.P. Kilpatrick (Ed.) **Explorations in Transactional Psychology.** New York: New York University.

Woodbridge, F.J. 1909. Consciousness, the sense organs, and the nervous system. **Journal of Philosophy, Psychology, and Scientific Method,** 7, 449-455.

Woodbridge, F.J. 1913a. The deception of the senses. **Journal of Philosophy, Psychology, and Scientific Method,** 10, 5-15.

Woodbridge, F.J. 1913b. The belief in sensations. **Journal of Philosophy, Psychology, and Scientific Method,** 10, 599-608.

Zajac, J.L. 1964. Is binocular correspondence and disparity still a dominant factor in depth perception? **Psychological Bulletin,** 62, 56-66.

Zecki, S. 1980. The representation of colours in the cerebral cortex. **Nature,** 284, 412-418.

Zener, K. and Gaffron, M. 1962. Perceptual experience: An analysis of its relations to the external world through internal processing. In S. Koch (Ed.) **Psychology: A Study of a Science** (Vol. 4) **Biologically Oriented Fields.** New York: McGraw-Hill.

# THE INITIAL DEVELOPMENT OF
# LINGUISTIC BEHAVIOR

Sidney W. Bijou

## Introduction

Current general behavior theories must be revised substantially if they are to be serviceable for analyzing all of the complexities of human behavior (Kantor, 1970; Kazdin, 1979; Ribes, 1977). As they stand, they consist of concepts and principles derived primarily from non-verbal, infra-human data. Consequently, complex human interactions are analyzed in terms of conceptual analogies rather than in terms of conceptualizations based on actual relationships. The treatment of the initial development of linguistic behavior presented here is an attempt to contribute a needed revision.

Current behaivor theories of initial language development (e.g., Lewis, 1959; Mowrer, 1954; Risely, 1977; Skinner, 1957) suffer from inadequacies similar to those of the general theories which we alluded to above. Specifically, the tend to deal with only a single aspect of initial language development--the transition from random vocalizations to the utterance of conventional speech. Furthermore, they view the developing language capacities of an infant according to the learning paradigm, i.e., as successive adaptations to the dialectic sounds and sentences of the group into which he or she is born (Kantor, 1977).

This paper is organized into five parts. Part One describes the systematic orientation of the analysis; Part Two presents a brief outline of the initial interactional equipment of a human organism; Part Three, the pre-verbovocal stage of linguistic development; Part Four, the primary stage of conventional verbovocal behavior; and Part Five, the complex stage of conventional verbovocal behavior.

## Systematic Orientation

Before developing our main thesis we shall briefly outline the major areas of study that pertain to language development to show the scope of the field and to indicate how the various specializations differ from the functional analysis presented here.

1. **Phonology** concerns the relationship between the biological structure and functioning of the speech apparatus and speech sounds. It also deals with changes in sounds as a function of biological maturation, sounds used in children's words, and sounds used in corresponding adult words, and includes both developmental and experimental phonetics.

2. **Lexis** deals with the development of words and vocabularies as a function of age and the meaning of words. It is the domain of normative language development and the semantics of words.

3. Grammar encompasses the beginnings of word combinations and the development of syntax (the major components of sentences and inflectional morphology).

The functional analysis of the initial development of linguistic behavior presented here is based on the natural science or interbehavioral approach which"...regards psychological events as definite organized fields in which organisms and stimulus objects interbehave; and that what happens in detail is based upon previous confrontations of the organisms and stimulus objects under specified conditions prevailing at the time" (Kantor and Smith, 1975, p. xiv).

Language, from this point of view, is an aspect of the psychological behavior of an individual and is studied in terms of observable interactions with stimulus objects that include, of course, the behavior of others and the products of social interactions (customs, conventions, artifacts, etc.). Therefore, language development is analyzed in the same way as other forms of behavior, such as manual dexterity, locomotion, and self-care. This statement succinctly expresses our basic hypothesis.

Note that this approach does not include the concept of language faculty, innate disposition to language, built-in language acquisition devices, mental faculty, innate processing ability, nor the linear analogical analysis of learning and behavior theories.

### Definition of Linguistic Behavior

Kantor (1977) briefly states the essence of psychological linguistics:

> Psychological linguistics focuses upon the psychological acts or adjustments of organisms as they adapt themselves to their congeners, along with the things which they encounter, either directly by means of vocal utterances and gestures, or indirectly by means of writing and symbolizing behavior (Kantor, p. xiii).

Linguistic behavior, then consists of three components: (1) referential verbovocal language, (2) gestural language, or communication by body movements, postures, facial expressions, etc., and (3) symbolic behavior, or acts of relating signs or marks in a surrogate association with other signs or things.

An analysis of the initial development of linguistic behavior must take into account the evolutionary order of verbovocal communication, gestures, and symbolic behavior, and the interrelationship among them. Considering that research on these topics is extremely limited, and that the data available are derived from studies designed for purposes other than those prescribed by a functional analysis approach, behavior theorists are confronted by an enormous task. Nevertheless it will be helpful to proceed with this analysis for at least to reasons: First, to get some conception of what we do know about the subject, and second, to point up the kinds of studies that will advance the study of linguistic development. We begin by inventorying a newborn's interactional equipment for linguistic development, and progress to descriptions of the circumstances development and changes in linguistic behavior at three stages of development.

The concept of stage is used here as analytical tool to identify the appearance and status of responses that constitute an individual's linguistic behavior. Stages have no properties of their own, neither hypothetical, as in the Piagetian system, nor physiological in the form of analogues to embryological structures and functions, as in the Gesellian approach. Progressions in linguistic behavior are related here to changes in the circumstances of development, conceptualized as stimulus and response functions, setting factors, media of interaction, and reactional systems (Kantor and Smith, 1975).

## Initial Linguistic Interactional Equipment

Our defintiion of linguistic behavior, as refential speech, gestures, and symbolic behavior, requires us to describe not only the vocalizing equipment of a neonate but also his or her motor status. To do so , we shall follow the lead of the typcial child development textbook which reviews the neonate's psychological endowment in terms of random movements, reflexes, vocalizations, and conditionability.

## Random Movements

Random movements describe the activities of an infant when awake and free from aversive stimulation or deprivation of appetitive substances; they are the unorganized, uncoordinated, and diffused movements of the arms, legs, and head, as well as the squirms and shifts that are difficult to relate to observable conditions or events.

Viewed as transitional responses--transitional between biological and psychological activities--their functioning depends on structural differentiation and biological maturation on the one hand, and on the raw material for the development of complex psychological behavior, on the other. Through interactions first with the ecological environment, then with the combination of ecological and social environments, and finally with only the social environment, behaviors develop that are categorized in various ways but mostly as self-care, motor skills, socialization, language, and cognitive behaviors.

Our interest in random movements naturally centers on the gestural aspect of linguistic behavior.

## Vocalizations

An infant is capable of two types of vocal behavior. One is crying, which isrelated to specific antecedent stimulation, such as blows, pricks, restraint, or internal pain (e.g., colic), and to setting events, such as deprivation of appetitive stimuli, like food and water. Although crying serves a most essential survival function, it appears to be of little importance in the initial development of speech. The other type of vocal behavior--the so-called "comfort sounds"--consists of undifferentiated soft noises that are most likely to occur in the absence of conditions that produce crying or restlessness.

Osgood (1953) has characterized the vocal sounds produced during the first few months of life, stating that the vocal apparatus "is a muscular system, and activity here partakes of the gross, mass activity of the total organism. Just as arms and legs are randomly exercised, and whne air happens to be pushed through the oral cavity, varying patterns of sound are produced" (p. 684). He goes on to say that the vocal productions are composed of an infinite variety of sounds: "...within the data from the first two months of life may be found all of the speech sounds that the human vocal system can produce, including French vowel and trills, German unlaut and guttural sounds and many that are only describable in phonetic symbols" (p. 684).

Osgood's conclusion that the infant can make all the speech sounds that the human system can produce is contrary to the traditional position that an infant gradually "becomes more capable" of making various sounds. The discrepancy between these views is probably due to the relatively primitive speech recording devices available earlier. More modern tape recording systems, even those in use in the 1950's, make possible detailed and repeated study of an infant's vocalizations, and enabled Osgood to observe "that the comparative frequencies of various speech sounds change as development proceeds: Owing to a number of anatomical factors, there is variation in the **probability** of given combination of jaw, lip and tongue positions being assumed" (and

216

hence the probability of various sounds being produced) (pp. 684-685).

If Osgood's contention is correct that an infant can make all speech sounds (phonemes) in any language, it follows that the transition from primitive utterances to verbal behavior in the language structure of an infant's particular culture comes about through interactions with the people and events that comprise his or her history. This view is compatible with our interbehavioral formulation.

## Reflexes

The large array of reflexes displayed by the neonate and young infant may conveniently be divided into biologial and psychological behaviors. Biological reflexes, such as the patellar tendon, abdominal, and achilles, are rather precise reactions to specific stimuli and are related to the health status of an individual's nervous system. Because they are not conditionable they have only a small role in the development of psychological behavior.

Psychological reflexes, on the other hand, are diffuse forms of behavior coordinated with antecedent stimulation, as in respondent (classical) conditioning, or with consequent stimulation, as in operant conditioning. Infants show unconditioned reactions to light, chemicals on the tongue, odors, temperature, pin pricks, electro-tactual stimuli, and changes in body orientation and movement. To sounds--important stimuli for the development of language--newborns respond to differences in pitch, loudness, and the duration of sounds. Pitches within normal speech range tend to produce quieter, more attentive behavior; those outside the normal range tend to produce startle behavior.

## Conditionability

Early in the history of child development, psychologists were intent on determining whether the neonate was conditionable ("conditionable" at that time meant making conditioned responses to conditioned stimuli in accordance with the Pavlovian paradigm) because they believed it was important to establish how soon after birth the human organism is capable of learning.

But not until the early 1960's, when sensitive measuring and controlling techniques became available, was it possible to demonstrate that the neonate was indeed capable of respondent (classical) conditioning. In 1964 Lipsitt and Kaye provided the clearest evidence that non-nutritive sucking could be conditioned to a tone.

In 1961, Papousek opened the way to study operant conditioning by his discovery that head-turning was a sufficiently stable response in an infant's limited repertoire to assess the functional properties of contingent stimuli. Following this lead, Siqueland and Lipsitt (1966) showed that head-turning, stimulated by a touch on the cheek, could be conditioned in the newborn on the basis of consequent stimuli. Later, Siqueland (1968) demonstrated that head-turning in the newborn could be conditioned in accordance with the operant model, and that intermittent reinforcement led to greater resistance to extinction than continuous reinforcement, a fact well documented in infrahuman organisms.

## Stage One: Pre-Verbovocal
## Linguistic Development

In Stage One of initial linguistic development, which begins at birth and ends sometimes between 9 and 12 months, depending upon the specific developmental circumstances, vocalizations (babbling) evolve into first-approximation language utterances, and initial comprehension and gestural repertoires develop progressively.

### Transformations in the Topography of Vocalizations

The beginnings of vocalizations are contingent upon a certain level of biological maturation which, using age as an indicator, is at about three months for a normal infant. One indication that an infant will soon begin to babble is his or her control of the articulatory apparatus in which the airstream from the lungs is interrupted by an articulation between the tongue and the roof of the mouth.

Ensuing changes in vocalizations, which are orderly, are correlated with certain biological physical, and social setting factors, and with opportunities (a) to explore the vocal apparatus (ecological behavior) and (b) to interact with people.

**Role of exploratory (ecological) interactions.** Another harbinger of babbling is said to be an infant's discovery that sounds are "fun" (Cruttenden, 1979), a criterion that may have been inferred from the observation that normal infants in a state of contentment engage in babbling with oru without prompting. Initial babbling, and preconventional idiosyncratic utterances ("expressions"), like random motor behaviors, are ecological activity which results in skills and knowledge with respect to the immediate physical environment (Bijou, 1980; Kantor and Smith, 1975). The mechanism is as follows: When a 3-month or older normal infant is under setting factors usually described as "feeling good," or is in a state of biological equilibrium (e.g., not deprived of appetitive substances, not exposed to aversive stimulation, and not tired or sleepy) he or she will probably engage in babbling. This activity produces vibrating and auditory stimulus consequences that influence both the form, frequence, and content of the vocalizations as well as their relationships with currently acting stimuli. We might say that a normal infant with healthy biological equipment and a responsive social environment babbles for the sake of babbling.

**Functional properties of social stimuli.** On the assumption that conditioning (including imitation) is a critical process in the modification of babbling, a key question arises: Are an infant's vocalizations sensitive to consequent social stimuli, as in operant conditioning, or to antecedent social stimuli, as in respondent conditioning, or to both? This becomes an issue of significance in light of Skinner's hypothesis (1957) that vocalization as the forerunner of conventional speech is operant behavior and therefore sensitive to consequent stimulation. A series of interrelated experiments shed considerable light on the importance of temporal relationships between social stimulation and infant vocalizations. Because Rheingold, Gewirtz and Ross (1959) set a pattern for studies on this subject, their procedures are described in some detail. in their first investigation they evaluated the role of contingent social stimuli (response-dependent) on the vocalizations of 3-month-old infants. During the first two days of the study, the baseline period, an investigator stood by the infant's bed, looking down at him or her with "an expressionless face" while an observer recoreded the infant's vocalizations. On the third and fourth days, at each vocalization by the infant, the investigator immediately smiled (visual stimulus), said, "tsk, tsk, tsk" (auditory stimulus) and lightly touched the infant's abdomen (tactile stimulus). The fifth and sixth days constituted the extinction period during which the procedure was the same as the baseline, when the experimenter made no response to the vocalization. The results indicated that the two days of social stimulation significantly increased the rate of vocalizations to nearly double the baseline rate; the two days of extinction reduced the vocalization rate almost to baseline level.

The authors pointed out that to conclude that the vocalizations were response dependent required further research in which social stimuli are given with the same frequency but are not contingent upon vocalization.

Incorporating these stipulations and a method similar to Rheingold's et al., Weisberg (1963) carried out a study with 3-month old infants, using a procedure in which random, noncontingent social stimuli were given. The results clearly indicated that vocalizations were relatively more affected by contingent conditions than by random noncontingencies.

Weisberg's findings were accepted as definitive until Bloom and Esposito (1975) reported on their research, also with 3-month-old infants. In one experiment with two groups of infants, they used a "yoke-control" procedure, rather than the random procedure, for distributing stimulation in order to make certain that the noncontingent,or response-independent treatment condition, would be identical to the contingent, or response-dependent treatment condition. They found that in both groups, vocalization rates increased from baseline to stimualtion periods and decreased from stimulation periods to extinction periods.

Bloom and Esposito found in their second experiment that vocalization rates were similar under conditions of continuous social stimulation and under conditions of omission training in which there was no social stimulation for a 5-second period following each vocalization. They also found that both rates decreased when social stimulation was replaced with exposure to a mobile.Findings from these two experiments seem to demonstrate that social stimulation facilitated vocalization, that facilitation was independent of the amount of stimulation and the contingency applied, and that omission training did not suppress response rate.

In a follow-up study consisting of two experiments, Bloom (1975) first confirmed the findings of Bloom and Esposito (1975) that social stimuli in the operant conditioning paradigm also **elicit** vocalizations, and then demonstrated that both response- independent and response-dependent social stimulation increased the rate of vocalization only when the infants could see the eyes of the adult delivering the stimulus.

The conclusions that antecedent auditory social stimulation increases vocalizations during the first year of life (Chang and Trehub, 1977; Dodd, 1972) and that consequent auditory social stimulation increases both vocalizations and non-nutritive sucking behavior (Trehub and Chang, 1977; Williams and Golenski, 1978) have been borne out by the cited investigators and others as well.

**Social conditions affecting vocalizations.** The social conditions influencing the transition of vocalizations to conventional speech, and the characteristics of the final speech products are studied as both group and individual phenomena. Data from both types of research are acceptable in an interbehavioral analysis provided they are actual organism-environment interactions.

For analytical purposes, the social conditions that modify infant vocalizations are divided into two categories: Specific stimulus events and setting factors (Bijou and Baer, 1978; Kantor and Smith, 1975). A mother's verbalizations together with her intonation, inflection, timing,

220

substances, etcs., are examples of specific stimulus events. In general, when mothers talk to their babies they tend to use limited vocabularies, simpler grammatical structures, fewer pronouns, frequent repetitions, and lower speech rates. A specific finding on differential verbalizations of middle socioeconomic class mothers to infants in the 4, 6, and 8-month-age range, is provided by Sherrod, Friedman, Crawley, Drake, and Deview (1977) who found that mothers made shorter utterances when talking to their 8-month-old infants than did mothers of 4 and 6-month-olds, and that they used more complex verbal structures when talking to their 4-month-old infants than mothers to their 6 and 8-month-old infants.

One characteristic of the verbalizations of middle socioeconomic class mothers is its reciprocal relationship to the infant's vocalizations. Andersons, Veitz and Dikecki (1977) found that in the natural environment both mothers and their 3-month-old infants were more likely to vocalize in the presence of a vocalizing partner and that mothers tended to terminate their vocalizations when the infants were quiet. These results are compatible with findings that babies with meager vocabularies and limited verbal fluency are often reared by mothers who speak sparsely and without much affect and enthusiasm, and interpersonal characteristic frequently encountered in mothers in the lower socioeconomic brackets (e.g., Kilbride, Johnson and Streissguth, 1977).

Setting factors, or the context of linguistic interchanges, the second category of the social conditions mentioned, may take organismic, physical, and social forms (Bijou, 1980; Kantor and Smith, 1975). As Bloom (1975) noted, eye contact was a necessary social setting factor for both the antecedent and consequent stimulus condition to be effective, a finding consistent with Todd and Palmer's conclusion (1968) that consequent social stimulation is more powerful when the person providing the stimulation is present.

Largely through the auditory and virbratory stimulus consequences of vocalization (ecological reinforcers) and the social reinforcement of imitative responses, random babbling moves toward those sounds that are more universal in the language, and drifts in intonation, inflection,etc., toward the language system to which the baby is exposed. One bit of evidence for this transformation is the finding by Condon and Sander (1974) that infants' micromomentary movements synchronized with adult utterances whether or not the adult was present or whether the speech was on an audiotape with American or Chinese voice sounds. Drifts toward the mother tongue are followed by (a) the formation of expressions, or idiosyncratic nonconventional utterances witha mixture of functions, such as demanding, indicating, and expressing (Cruttenden, 1979), and then by (b) first approximation words and phrases, used as word-sentences (holophrastically) with functions similar to those for expressive utterances.

## Development of Comprehension Repertoires

An infant responds non-verbally to words and short phrases at about 9 months of age, several months before he or she communicates verbovocally (Goldin-Meadow, Seligman and Gelman, 1976; Huttenlocker, 1974). Beyond this statement very little else can be said at present about comprehension prior to verbovocal language. Cruttenden (1979) tells why:

> It is difficult to present anything as a hard fact in
> the development of comprehension. Not only has
> individual variation in children to be taken into account
> but methods of gathering information about compre-
> hension vary enormously from recordings of natural
> conversation,through tests of productive capacity
> giving proof of understanding, to matching a sentence
> produced by an experimenter with one of a number of
> pictures (p. 70).

The relationships between the receptive repertoires and the productive repertoires that follow shortly are neither simple nor direct. Comparisons of first words comprehended, and first words produced reveal low correspondence between the lexical items in the two systems (Benedict, 1976; Goldin-Meadow et al., 1976).

## Development of Gestures

Hard facts on the onset of gestures as referential linguistic behavior are also limited, primarily because of equivocal criteria. For example, Brazelton (1974) claims that mothers communicate with infants through gestures soon after birth, and Trevarthen (1974) maintains that 2-month-old infants hold conversations with rudimentary sounds and also imitate segments of conversations. The indications are that gestures probably begin later than two months and at a time when an infant has attained the biological equipment to perceive (discriminate) and to explore the immediate physical enviornment. The latter is essential for the development of the primitive motor skills required for this mode of communication (Bijou, 1980). One might speculate that the repertoires acquired through exploratory behavior carry over to those interactions (Kinklestein and Ramey, 1977), including those with social properties, and serve as a basis for the evolution of gestures.

The origin of specific gestures may be an infant's partial or complete response to objects or events that are interpreted as communicating "inner needs." Allowing food to dribble out of the

222

mouth with the tongue, or turning the head away from the nipple are forms of behavior that amy be taken as the infant's satiation for food (Hurlock, 1977).

An analysis of gestures as referential linguistic behavior involves three components: (a) The infant, as gesturer, or referor, (b) the person interacted with, as referee or auxilliary stimulus, and (c) the object or activity, designated as referent. Kantor (1977) refers to the relationships among these components as bistimulational. Consider, for instance, two situations. In the first one an infant in interacting with his or her mother with gestures about an object or activity as referent. In the second situation a mother is responding to her infant about the referent with speech, gestures, actions, and facial expressions. The context or setting of both interactions is the setting factors (SF) . The behavior of an infant is a function of his o her history and the current situation, consisting of the mother, the referent, and the setting factors; the behavior of a mother is a function of her history and the current situation, consisting of her infant, the referent, and the setting factors.

## Stage Two: Simple Referential Utterances

In Stage Two of initial linguistic development, which begins 9 and 15 months and ends between 22 and 24 months, simple referential utterances develop into more precise and more complex referential utterances (two-and three-word approximations). During this stage, gestural repertoires increase and integrate with the verbovocal system (but also continue to function independently) and comprehension repertoires become part of verbovocal referential behavior.

### Simple Utterances as Referential Behavior

First-approximation verbovocal utterances are analyzed functionally as behaviors just as gestures are analyzed: A baby as speaker, a mother as listener, and an object or activity as referent. The relationships among speaker, listener, and referent are essentially the same as those in the analysis of gestures described above, the only difference being that the speaker's behavior here is not limited to gestures; it is combination of verbovocal utterances, gestures, actions, tactile contacts, and facial expressions.

The functions of initial referential utterances are classified in different ways depending on the theoretical orientation of the writer. In general, a distinction is made on the basis of whom the baby is talking to. When talking to him or herself the behavior is described as ideational (also egocentric and expressive); when talking to a person the behavior is designated as (a) demanding, pragmatic, and mediation-

223

al), or (b) attributive (also mathetic, tacting, and narrative). In most interpersonal situations, a baby's utterances have more than one function.

According to Kantor (1977) verbovocal repertoires expand primarily through the interactions between a baby and his or her natural environment. That is, "...linguistic development of children does not take place as a matter of learning and teaching. Language as adjustment implies that the development is mainly casual and greatly dependent upon the exigencies of the moment" (p. 191).

Yet during child-rearing activities, mothers, particularly middle socio-economic class mothers, continuously provide their babies with carefully graded langauge lessons: Their speech contains much repetition, simple grammatical structures, and fewer pronouns, and they talk slowly, using smaller vocabularies. They tend to respond to the baby's speech by expanding on utterances, asking questions and providing answers, and demonstrating meanings by gestures and actions (Cruttenden, 1979). And mothers (reference here again is primarily to middle class mothers) also tend to devote themselves to teaching their babies the names of objects and actvities . The procedure usually followed fits the operant conditioning paradigm in which a mother points out an object, for example, a pet kitten or a stuffed toy kitten, and at the same time says "Kitty, kitty." Responding at first to the sound of the word, the baby imitates perhaps with "kid-dee, kid-dee," a response the mother usually follows with attention, approval, or affection. If these contingencies are repeated often enough, "kid-dee" becomes a discriminated stimulus not only to the mother's saying "Kitty"--which initially prompted the response--but also to the sight of the kitten. It is less likely that the baby would be reinforced if he or she were to say "Kid-dee" when the kitten was not in view.

## Expansion and Coordination of Gestural Repertoires

A baby's gestural repertoire expands rapidly during the second year and becomes a part of his or her preconventional utterances--("idiosyncratic expressions"). since many of the gestures in these early interactions are not specific to the referent, the listener has to rely heavily on the context of an interaction to understand a baby's communicative behaviors.

In the transition from "expressions" to first approximations of conventional utterances, gestures change in topography, and because of the greater specificity of even first-approximation conventional utterances, they serve to increase the precision of verbovocal referential behavior.

224

A person's gestural repertoire continues to be modified as changes in cultural practices take place and are retained as a viable separate communication system. One is never more aware and appreciative of his or her gestural repertoire until stranded in a foreign country whose language he or she neither understands nor speaks.

## Integration of the Receptive Repertoire with Referential Verbovocal Behavior

That a baby's language comprehension increases steadily is evident: he or she learns to comply with simple requests, answer simple questions, and indicate or call attention to a specific change or changes in the immediate environment. Oviatt (1980) found, for example, that three groups of babies--10 between the ages of 9 and 17 months, 10 between 12 and 14 months, and 10 between 15 and 17 months--all showed a steady increase in "recognizatory" language comprehension.

As a baby begins to use first-approximation conventional utterances together with gestures and other actions, his or her comprehension repertoire combines with utterances to form full-fledged referential language in which the baby serves as both speaker and listener in relation to a referent.

## Stage Three: Complex Referential Utterances

During Stage Three of initial linguistic development, which begins 21 and 24 months and ends between 28 and 32 months of age, one and two word-sentence utterances expand into larger and more complex units approximating four or more words. At the terminus of this stage, the vowel system of verbovocal referential behavior is complete, and utterances contain most of the conventional grammatical forms. The child's verbovocal referential behavior repertoire continues to expand throughout the later stages and gradually takes on all the grammatical forms of his or her culture.

## Functions of Referential Linguistic Behavior

Earlier in Stage Two, we labeled the function of pre-holophrastic and holophrastic utterances with terms suggested by several writers. Now, to make our analysis with the interbehavioral approach, we classify the functions of referential linguistic behavior into narrative and mediational language. Narrative language operates as specific autonomous adjustments; in other words, it is not related to non-referential activity. In contrast, mediational language has a close connection with non-referential performance, as the following subcategories indicate (Kantor, 1977): (1) **Preceding language** mediates

225

a nonlinguistic activity. Example: "Pass me the juice, please." (2) **Accompanying language** serves to bring about, further, or aid a final adjustment. Example: A teacher seeing a child write his name correctly says, "You did that well, Bobby" in the hope that he will do it again. (3) **Following language** verbalizes a close relationship between linguistic and nonlinguistic behavior. Example: A child puts the last block on the castle she has been building and says, "Well, that's done." (4) **Substitutive language** substitutes language behavior for a nonlinguistic final adjustment. Example: A child who allows the string of his balloon to slip through his fingers, cries out, "My balloon, my balloon" as his precious balloon floats away.

Referential behavior may also be distinguished as communicative or expressive on the basis of whether a person, as an auxiliary stimulus, is involved (Kantor, 1977). In communicative language, what the speaker says is not only an adjustment but is also a stimulus for the listener, as in a lively conversation. Expressive language, on the other hand, constitutes only the speaker's own immediate adjustment, as when a child talks to him or herself, whether or not another person, as an auxiliary stimulus, is present.

## Summary and Conclusions

The initial development of linguistic behavior presented here is based on the assumption that language is psychological behavior and as such it develops in the same way as other categories of behavior. The theoretical frame of reference for our analysis is the interbehavioral, which posits that psychological linguistics are the adjustments that human organisms make as they adapt to circumstances, either directly, by verbovocal language and gestures, or indirectly, by means of symbols and writing.

The initial development of linguistic behavior spans the first two-and-a-half to three years, the time it takes a normal child to acquire the quasi-adult skills necessary to interact linguistically with members of the family and others. Since the circumstances of development and coordinated linguistic behavior change rapidly during the formative years, the analysis is divided into three stages which are distinguished by landmarks in the transition from random babbling to first-approximation conventional utterances.

From the literature on infancy we learn that even though a neonate's voluntary response equipment is in the performed stage (random activity), he or she can react differentially to sensory stimuli, can utter potentially all the speech sounds of the culture, and can be operantly and respondently conditioned.

In Stage One, approximately the first year, there is a close relationship between changes in biological maturation and changes in vocalization, similar to the close relationship between biological maturation and the early development of prehension and locomotion. Social interactions enhance the rate of vocalizations and influence their forms, much as exploratory interactions do in the development of prehension and locomotion. Babbling drifts toward the topography of the family's language patterns, evolves into idiosyncratic expressions, and then into holophrastic utterances with mediating and narrative functions. Comprehension and gestural repertoires also take shape in Stage One.

During Stage Two, which coincides with about the second year, biological maturation continues its important role, although in a somewhat diminished form, and social conditions (both general and family tutorials) move verbovocal behavior toward conventional language practice. Comprehension repertoires expand and become more refined. In Stage Three, which extends well into the third year, biological maturation plays a relatively small role; social stimulation assumes greater importance; and verbovocal behavior changes form holophrastic utterances to longer and more precise units.

The analysis of the initial development of linguistic behavior has implications for theory, research, and practical application. Theoretically, it calls for a theory of initial linguistic development that (1) focuses on progressive interactions between the functions of linguistic referential behavior and successive changes in the circumstances that constitute the environment, and (2) distinguishes between actual interactions and their products, such as words and sentences. We have attempted to do this in the light of some of the relevant research findings. There is need for a more elaborate theory, one which would refine the analysis of initial development and extend into later childhood, adolescence, and adulthood. Because the relationship involved in such an analysis are complex and because the conceptions of the theoretical system are incompatible with the Zeitgeist, this undertaking will, predictably, not be achieved readily.

The research implications are both methodological and substantive. Much needed investigation should focus on events in natural settings in order to obtain descriptive and field experimental data on linguistic interactions, first, to verify findings from studies with other theoretical orientations, and second, to contribute new information on linguistic development. The latter boils down to studying the functional relationships among speaker, listener, and referent under various biological maturational conditions, setting factors, and social stimulating conditions. It also includes studying situations in which the child is speaking to him or herself, and which a referent is absent. Since the methodology for field studies of this sort is well advanced (e.g., Bakeman and Brown, 1977), technological considerations should not be a deterrent to progress in this direction.

The practical implication of this analysis, although considered a first-approximation effort, is that communication problems of retarded, emotionally disturbed, and particularly autistic children should be based on the assumption that language is adjustive behavior that develops through interactions with objects and events, primarily social. According to this view, those children who need help in developing linguistic behavior should be treated by the systematic modification of social conditions and setting factors; whereas children who have difficulty in learning symbols, words, phrases, and sentences and their meanings should be taught through procedures based on learning principles.

## References

Anderson, B.J., Vietze, P. and Dokecki, P.R. 1977. Reciprocity in vocal interactions of mothers and infants. **Child Development,** 48, 1676-1681.

Bakeman, R. and Brown, J.V. 1977. Behavioral dialogues: An approach to the assessment of mother-infant interaction. **Child Development,** 48, 195-203.

Benedict, H. 1976. Language comprehension in 10-to-16-month old infants. **Unpublished Doctoral Dissertation,** Yale University.

Bijou, S.W. 1980. Exploratory behavior in humans and animals: A behavioral analysis. **Psychological Record,** 30, 483-495.

Bijou, S.W. and Baer,D.M. 1978. **Behavior Analysis of Child Development** (Revised edition). Englewood Cliffs, New Jersey: Prentice-Hall.

Bloom, K. 1975. Social elicitation of infant vocal behavior. **Journal of Experimental Child Psychology** , 20, 51-58.

Bloom, K. and Exposito, A. 1975. Social conditioning and the proper control procedure. **Journal of Experimental Child Psychology,** 19, 209-222.

Brazelton, T.B. 1974. The origins of reciprocity. In M. Lewis (Ed.) **The Effects of Infant on its Care Giver.** New York: Wiley.

Chang, H.W. and Trehub, S.E. 1977. Infants' perception of temperal grouping in auditory patterns. **Child Development, 48,** 1666-1670.

Condon, W.S. and Sander, L.W. 1974. Neonate movement is syncronized with adult speech: Interactional participation and language acquisition. **Science,** 183, 99-101.

Cruttenden, A. 1979. **Language in Infancy and Childhood.** New York: St. Martin's Press.

Dodd, B.J. 1972. Effects of social and vocal stimulation on infant babbling. **Developmental Psychology,** 7, 80-83.

Finkelstein, N.W. and Ramey, C.T. 1977. Learning to control the environment in infancy. **Child Development, 48,** 806-819.

Goldin-Meadow, S., Seligman, M. and Gelman, R. 1976. Language in the two-year old. **Cognition,** 4, 189-202.

Hurlock, E.B. 1977. **Child Development** (6th edition). New York: McGraw-Hill.

Huttenlocker, J. 1974. The origins of language comprehension. In R.L. Solso (Ed.) **Theories in Cognitive Psychology.** Hillsdale, New Jersey: Lawrence Erlbaum Associates.

Kantor, J.R. 1970. An analysis of the experimental analysis of behavior (TEAB). **Journal of the Experimental Analysis of Behavior,** 13, 101-108.

Kantor, J.R. 1977. **Psychological Linguistics.** Chicago, Ill.: Principia Press.

Kantor, J.R. and Smith, N.W. 1975. **The Science of Psychology: An Interbehavioral Survey.** Chicago: Principia Press.

Kazdin, A.E. 1979. Fictions, factions, and functions of behavior therapy. **Behavior Therapy,** 10, 629-654.

Kilbride, H.W., Johnson, D.L. and Streissguth, A.P. 1977. Social class, birth order, and newborn experience. **Child Development,** 48, 1686-1688.

Lewis, M.M. 1959. **How Children Learn to Speak.** New York: Basic Books.

Lipsitt, L.P. and Kaye, H. 1964. Conditioned sucking in the human new-born. **Psychonomic Science,** 1, 29-30.

Mowrer, O.H. 1954. The psychologist looks at language. **American Psychologist,** 9, 660-694.

Osgood, C.E. 1953. **Methods and Theory in Experimental Psychology.** New York: Oxford.

Oviatt, S.L. 1980. The emerging ability to comprehend language: A experimental approach. **Child Development,** 51, 97-106.

Papousek, H. 1961. Conditioned head rotation reflexes in infants in the first months of life. **Acta Paediatrica,** 50, 565-576.

Rheingold, H.L., Gewirtz, J.L. and Ross, H.W. 1959. Social conditioning of vocalizations in the infant. **Journal of Comparative and Physiological Psychology,** 52, 68-73.

Ribes, E. 1977. Relationship among behavior theory , experimental research, and behavior modification techniques. **Psychological Record,** 27, 417-424.

Risely, T.R. 1977. The development and maintenance of language: An operant model. In B.C. Etzel, J.M. LeBlanc and D.M. Baer (Eds.) **New Developments in Behavioral Research: Theory, Method and Application.** Hillsdale, New Jersey: Lawrence Erblaum Associates.

Siqueland, E.R. 1968. Reinforcement and extinction in human newborns. **Journal of Experimental Child Psychology,** 6, 431-442.

Siqueland, E.R. and Lipsitt, L.P. 1966. Conditioned headturning in newborns. **Journal of Experimental Child Psychology,** 3, 356-376.

Skinner, B.F. 1957. **Verbal Behavior.** Englewood Cliffs, New Jersey: Prentice-Hall.

Sherrod, K.B., Friedman, S., Crawley, S. Drake, D. and Deview, J. 1977. Maternal language to prelinguistic infants: Synatic aspects. **Child Development,** 48, 1662-1665.

Todd, G.A. and Palmer, B. 1968. Social reinforcement of infant babbling. **Child Development,** 39, 591-596.

Trehub, S.E. and Chang, H.W. 1977. Speech as reinforcing stimulation for infants. **Developmental Psychology,** 13, 170-171.

Trevarthen, C. 1974. Conversation with a two-month-old. **New Scientist,** 62, 230-235.

Weisberge, P. 1963. Social and nonsocial conditioning of infant vocalizations. **Child Development,** 34, 377-388.

Williams, L. and Golenski, J. 1978. Infant speech sound discrimination: The effects of contingent versus non-contingent stimulus presentation. **Child Development,** 49, 213-217.

# HAS BEHAVIOR ANALYSIS ACTUALLY
# DEALT WITH LANGUAGE?

Emilio Ribes

> Without the word there would be no history nor love;
> we would be as the rest of animals, mere perpetuation
> and mere sexuality. Speaking ties us as couples, as
> societies, as countries. We speak because we are,
> but we are because we speak[1].

Language has always been an omnipresent subject for discussion in psychological theory, mainly because its analysis seems to be crucial for testing the power and soundness of the various methodological approaches to behavior. Questions regarding language do not seem to be indigenous to psychology , itself, but rather derive from disciplines foreign to the study of behavior: Phonology, linguistics, grammar, neurology, anthropology, semantics, and even philosophy. Therefore, an essential first step is to relate psychology to the study of language, and to point out the theoretical and empirical relevance that language may have to a behavior theory in general. However, before examining this problem, it may be well to discuss some other topics relevant to language in a behavioral analysis and the kind of empirical relations that are involved.

Language in psychology has been related to many different topics such as thinking, communication, concept formation, meaning, and problem solving. However, all are central to a theoretical question: Is there a basic difference between animal and human behavior? Many criticisms of a behavioral analysis of language stem from the assumption that language is something more than behavior, and that to understand language, we need concepts and principles that are different from those used to explain "behavior" properly stated. Let us concentrate on the two fundamental issues that underlie this position. First, is animal behavior different as a subject matter from human behavior? Second, if it is different, is it nevertheless possible to analyze human behavior on the basis of the same assumptions used for animal behavior; or if it is not the same, do we need to appeal to concepts that refer to a different set of events?

## Animal and Human Behavior

Let us begin by stating that, in fact, human behavior is both similar to and different from animal behavior. They are similar in the evolutionary sense that complex phenomena or events include as part of their organization or structure the properties and determinants of simpler events. Human behavior is affected by the same variables and laws that determine animal behavior, but not by those alone. Social influences render human behavior highly specific in relation to the various classes of non-human behavior defined by non-social environments. What is the specificity of human societies in relation to animal "social"environments? Group life and social interaction, in terms of the mutual influences of organisms, are not peculiar to human individuals. Nevertheless, human society differs in a fundamental way from any other kind of inter- or intra-specific interaction group environment. Human society organizes interactions among individuals in terms of conventions that are set up by agreement, at least for some of the members of the group, and these conventions overcome the concrete relations and interactions that may be established by particular individuals on given occasions. These conventions allow for the detachment from concrete situations in terms of the functional properties of the behavioral interactions involved in the establishment of the conventions themselves. From a behavioral point of view, the detachment is the functional consequence of the arbitrariness of the conventions involved. Behaviorally speaking, what is the nature of these conventions? Conventions are nothing more than linguistic interactions , and linguistic interactions consist of complex mediations between individuals in terms of reactional systems, socially established independently of the nature of the objects, events, or individuals to which they might be related. This functional independence, which biologically bound behaviors lack, allows linguistic interactions to set up the boundaries between animal and human behavior. Animals are unable to set up conventions that can be separated from the concrete situations in which interactions occur. Communication in animals is, in this sense, non-linguistic, since the reactional system consist of the same set of responses biologically bound to concrete situations. Human conventions are independent of concrete situations, both in space and time, and this is determined by the arbitrary nature of the linguistic interaction defining the conventions **as** behavior.

Having decided that human behavior is different from animal behavior in the sense previously described, let us move to the second question. Is it possible to analyze human behavior in the same terms as animal behavior? Or do we have to have an additional level of concepts not referrable to direct behavioral terms? This question has been answered in two different ways, both, in my opinion, misleading.

One way assumes a dualistic position, either in terms of the stuff of which events are made, or in terms of the possibility of knowing the events. In any case, behavior is restricted to: (a) an index of different type of phenomenon or event, or (b) the public epiphenomenon of the crucial process, which is unobservable. Behavior is cancelled out as the basic datum and its relevance is only methodological in relation to the inference of inner entities or processes. These may be behaviorally phrased events, e.g., meaning responses (Osgood, 1958; Mowrer, 1960), or definitely mentalistic cognitive terms, e.g., deep structures (McNeil, 1971). But, independently of the particular conceptual form that they adopt, their formation signifies setting up an insurmountable boundary between behavior and these different phenomena. Dualism is thus formalized.

The alternative and misleading answer to this question has been to affirm that concepts derived from the analysis of animal behavior are sufficient to describe and explain human behavior. This position has taken two modalities. One, illustrated by Watson (1924), reduces interactions organic actions, and therefore to movements, e.g., the analysis of thinking as subvocal language. The other one recognizes that human behavior is different in quality, but at the same time, assumes that analytic concepts formulated in simpler situations are amenable to extrapolation to more complex phenomena. Skinner (1957) represents this position. Although he says in relation verbal behavior that "behavior which is effective only though the mediation of other persons has so many distinguishing dynamic topographical properties that a special treatment is justified and, indeed, demanded" (p. 2), his analysis of verbal behavior falls short of conceptually identifying these properties because of the three-term contingency paradigm used: Ribes (1979) and Whitehurst (1979) have pointed out some of the shortcomings of Skinner's analysis of verbal behavior both on theoretical and empirical grounds.

Although terms employed to explain animal behavior are inadequate to describe the complexity of human behavior, we do not believe this fact justifies the use of dualistic concepts. In other words, the recognition of qualitative differences in an empirical domain does not necessarily justify the existence of two different domains. Human behavior is different from animal behavior not only in terms of its appearance or morphology, but because of its functional organization, since language and society define and allow for different dimensions of interaction between individuals and objects. These dimensions involve complex processes of mediation of the interactions, external mediations which constitute , in terms of a field organization, qualitatively distinctive behaviors. Quality difference does not refer to the hypothetical stuff of which behavior or "mind" is made, but to the field structure of objects, events, and individuals interacting, which defines the functional organization of behavior. Language and social environment define a distinctive quality of human behavior, but this distinction simply means that new elements and relationships encountered in human interactions are not possible in animals. Nevertheless, the laws and processes governing animal interactions are necessary conditions to understand and explain human behavior in such a way that concepts describing human interactions do not exclude concepts related to animal behavior, but on the contrary, include them as a necessary subset of the field of interactive events under study. Let us summarize by saying that, although human behavior requires a new set of concepts adequate to the properties of the complex field of interactions involved, these new concepts are based on and include the constructs employed to analyze animal behavior.

It is our intention to sketch some of the necessary distinctions between language, as a conventional structure and social product, and behavior, as the interaction of individual organism with other individuals and objects in the environment. This strategy will enable us to show that "language" in humans serves different behavioral functions, and that these functions must be described and explained according to different dimensions of interactive organization. To do so, we shall begin by discussing how these various functions have been confounded in behavior theory (theories?) in order to proceed to a more thorough analysis of the issues involved in the relation between language and human behavior.

The confounding of language is a formal product of social interaction between individuals with the linguistic interaction itself, resulting in, to a great extent, the failure to produce a behavioral account of language as human behavior. We shall illustrate this failure by concentrating on Skinner's (1957) analysis of verbal behavior.

### The Operant Analysis of Language Behavior

The purpose of Skinner's analysis is to study language from a functional viewpoint, but since "...it has come to refer to the practices of a linguistic community rather than the behavior of any one member...the term 'verbal behavior' has much to recommend it...it emphasizes the individual speaker shaped and maintained by mediated consequences" (1957, p. 2). He adds that the behaviors of speaker and listener taken together compose what may be called a total verbal episode. There is nothing in such an episode which is more than the combined behavior of two or more individuals. Although we shall try to show some inconsistency between these statements and other assertions, our intention is to emphasize the conception of language as the behaviors of speaker and listener in a **total** episode. Behavior should be understood as the complete segments involving the speaker and the listener. Even when isolated "the speaker can be studied while assuming a listener, and the listener while assuming a speaker" (p. 2). However, there seem to be theoretical and empirical restrictions to this separate account of each of the members of the episode if the episode is to be preserved as a unified interaction.

The separate analyses of the speaker and the listener have, in fact, missed the fundamental issue: The particular behavioral interaction taking place when a speaker mediates the interaction of the listener with other indviduals or events is a bi-directional and reciprocal process. The isolation of the controlling relation in terms of the speaker alone takes out of context the speaking behavior itself, resulting in a twofold negative problem. First, there is the problem of reference (i.e., when talking about objects and events) abstracted from the relation determining who is being spoken to. This restores the whole problem of meaning and expression of ideas characteristic of cognitive and methodological behavioristic approaches. Although Skinner says that "in very general terms we may say that behavior in the form of the tact works for the benefit of the listener by extending his contact with the environment," he considers that " a tact may be defined as a verbal operant in which a response of given form is evoked or at least strengthened by a particular object or event" (pp.81-85), stressing thus the relation between the stimulus boejct and the response of the speaker. Second, the fragmentation of the verbal episode conflicts with the whole notion of **communication**, or referring function of the speaker (Kantor, 1977). If language is to some degree of interest to psychology it is because language, as the behavior of speaking, writing, and reading affects the behavior of a reader or listener, not as a single effect, but also in his relation with other individuals and events, including the speaker himself. Catania (in press) singles out this issue when he states that "verbal behavior derives its power from this relation (the tact), because without it there would be nothing of which we could speak."

The isolation of the verbal episode as the separate behaviors of the speaker and the listener (with a very light dedication to the latter) not only neglects the mediation function of the speaker in relation to the contact of the listener with other individuals and events, but inverts the issue in stating that the speaker is the medited component of the interaction. The speaker is said to be mediated in the reinforcement of his behavior by the listener. The listener is just a formal surrogative of the reinforcing stimulus in the operant relation. This logical substitution is questionable for several reasons. First, it reduces an interaction which involves mediated relationships to a non-mediated interaction. Linguistic interbehavior is a complex sequence of actions of objects, events, and individuals with a speaker who mediates those actions by a linguistic act to another individual (the listener) who in turn reacts both to the speaker and the the objects, events, and individuals. The complex sequence is therefore reduced to a single component: The speaker tacts an object or event and is reinforced by the listener's behavior. Second, the concept of reinforcement becomes so loose that it turns out to be not only circular, but also meaningless and unnecessary. Reinforcement is equated with any consequence of the speaker's behavior, but this equivolence violates four assumptions originally defining the concept of reinforcement. First, the verbal unit is not a punctate repetitive response. Second, there are no independent conditions, previous to the "effect," that allow for establishing, with an actuarial criterion, that a particular event is going to be reinforcing, e.g., deprivation, etc. In fact, it seems that in a verbal episode there is always a consequent event, including the speaker's behavior itself, so that reinforcement always occurs as a universal predication of the speaking action, without being any longer an empirical issue. Third, there is no classical effect of reinforcement in terms of the increase or maintenance of the frequency of a response relative to a particular time period. Verbal behavior always fills up the whole episode, without leaving any empirical gap to be completed by a reinforcement effect. Fourth, except for the mand relation, reinforcement plays a secondary role as a generalized stimulus that frees the controlling relation from specific motivational determinants, moving the control to the antecedent or "discriminative" stimulus, which paradoxically becomes a strong functional event in spite of being associated with weak reinforcers. To summarize, reinforcement in the analysis of verbal or linguistic behavior plays a role very similar to some monarchs in modern countries: Pure adornment!

We shall end our discussion of Skinner's **Verbal Behavior** (1957) by raising one additional issue: Is it possible to carry out a genuine functional analysis of verbal behavior when the episode that defines the event being studied is divided into separate components? We believe that the answer is negative, and that , in fact, the analysis drifts toward a formal description in behavioral terms.

Three problems arise in the treatment of language in terms of the displacement of a functional analysis towards a formal description of the speaker's behavior. First, the classification of verbal behavior, as an alternative to descriptions akin to a structural view, is presented as an (incomplete) taxonomy of the controlling relations between formal dimensions of stimuli and formal dimensions of responses. Second, although phonetic and linguistic units such as phonemes and words, are set aside as irrelevant to the analysis of the verbal episode, most of the relations described involve single stimulus objects or events and words or short phrases, as a consequence of an explicit interest in the acquisition and maintenance of responses instead of functional interactions. Third, formal structural problems remain as shown in the postulation of autoclitic functions. Syntax and grammar become behavioral problems and specific concepts are coined to deal with them, despite the initial aim of the analysis to formulate language in terms of legitimate behavioral concepts.

238

**Verbal Behavior** (1957) is in some sense a classificatory effort. This is emphasized by Skinner in saying that "our first responsibility is simple **description:** What is the topography of this subdivision of human behavior?" (p. 10). A substantial part of the theoretical exercise is to identify relevent controlling relationships between vocal or written responses--since gesturing is merely mentioned--and different types of antecedent stimuli and reinforcers (although as previously pointed out reinforcement is never central to the theoretical analysis). Catania (in press) summarizes the treatment of reinforcers in **Verbal Behavior:**

> To show that (such) consequences can affect the frequency of verbal classes make it appropriate to call such consequences reinforcers. But to fail to do so does not bear on whether it is appropriate to deal with verbal behavior in terms of reinforcing consequences. The concept of reinforcement is simply a name that tacts a particular behavioral relation...: if a response is maintained because the response has had a particular consequence is called a reinforcer. Failure to demonstrate that a particular event serves as a reinforcer in a particular situation simpy means that the term reinforcer is inappropriate in that instance" (p. 38).

The theoretical problem, however, is concerned with the meaning of "maintained" or "acquired," and that "inappropriateness of the term," since, as we mentioned above the use of the concept of reinforcement in the description of a verbal episode is highly questionable in terms of the logical and empirical boundaries of the construct. In recognition of this fact the classification of verbal behavior rests upon the antecedent stimulus condition, even in the mand, which evokes the tacting response to an object or event.

Although formal classes of verbal behavior point to relations between mophological properties of stimuli and responses, they do not discriminate adequately among the functional properties that a single class may have. In some sense this is a consequence of the choice of words as the criterion for defining responses. Catania states (in press) that "formal verbal relations are defined in terms of the correspondence between verbal stimuli and verbal responses (in the colloquial vocabularly, we would say that the stimuli and the responses use the same words)" (p. 7). And although the placement of the same "word" in a different formal medium or dimension of relation overcomes some of the problems intrinsic to the conception of words as units themselves (e.g., the difference between saying **fire** when the word is read or when we are looking at a house burning) it is not sufficient to prevent neglect of the functional processes mediating the verbal episode. Thus, the word **fire** is different when it is read from when it is emitted to a physical phenomenon, such as combustion. However, this does not mean that the functional property of the speaking response is different. In fact, saying **fire** when a text is presented and when a house is seen burning may even have no verbal property at all, except for the morphology of the relationship. I see no difference between the fact of speaking, that is, vocalizing a response with a particular topography when a stimulus is presented (it does not matter if it is a text or an object), and the behavior of pecking a disc by a pigion when the disc is associated with a physical property such as temperature, or when the disc is illuminated in such a way that a geometrical figure (a text) is discriminable from the "ground." The distinction between a tact and text, using the terms employed in **Verbal Behavior,** does not permit differentiating the verbal functions of speaking.

Let us take, for instance, the textual response **fire.** The controlling relation of the response by a printed stimulus may have different functions in the sense of describing different types of interactions. Thus, we may read **fire** in order to avoid entering an area where something is burning and we would be in danger. The stimulus **fire** is the written behavior of a "speaker" which is mediating our behavioral contact with physical event. This relation is different from the simple textual response of **fire** when as Spanish-speaking persons we learn to "read" English. It is also different when the stimulus **fire** is being read as the equivalent to a physical formula describing the fact of combustion. It seems obvious, then, that a formal classification of verbal behavior in terms of the correspondence between types of stimuli and responses falls short of a truly functional account of the behaivor of speaking as part of an interactive episode.

A second problem is the ubiquitous role of the word as a unit in the analysis of controlling relationships of verbal behavior. Although it is discarded as a basic unit of analysis--as is the case with other formal linguistic units--the word underlies most of the particular topics and issues discussed in **Verbal Behavior**
(1957). An example of this attitude is in Catania's review when he states that "particular words are uttered or written under particular circumstances. The different cirumstances that set the occasion for different words provide the basis for a behavioral classification of words" (in press, p. 1). Although beginning with the assumption that words are not the relevant issue in language as behavior, words again become the subject matter but are embedded in a formal definition of the written or spoken response relative to a particular stimulus condition.

In order to show the importance given to words (and to other linguistic or grammatic units such as phrases and sentences) we shall

240

briefly examine their treatment as tacts and intraverbal responses. In discussing the problme of an ideal language, Skinner (1957) states that "the most familiar examples of functional units are traditionally called words. In learning to speak the child acquires tacts of various sizes: words..., phrases..., and sentences" (p. 119), stressing the formal features of the response in terms foreign to a behavioral account. Or does this mean that structural units correspond to behavioral functional units? If this is so, what is the need for a functional behavioral analysis of language? Additional evidence is found with intraverbal responses in which a reasonable space is devoted to the discussion of chaining and word association. Even when the intraverbal unit is larger than the word (as happens with other verbal operants), chaining is raised as the theoretical mechanism responsible for the functional relation established among arbitrary responses and stimuli; that is, formal units correspond to words most of the time.

Finally, as a third related problem, we have the notion of autoclitic processes as behavioral equivalents of grammatic structures. We shall not enter into detail regarding the logical need to postulate such processes in a truly behavioral analysis of language (see, for instance, Kantor, 1936), but we shall stress the formalistic approach underlying Skinner's notion of autoclitic operants. He says: "The verbal operants we have examined may be said to be the raw material out of which sustained verbal behavior is manufactured. But who is the manufacturer?...The important properties of verbal behavior which remain to be studied concern special arrangements of responses" (1957, pp. 312-313).

Independently of the logical success with which autoclitic processes are postulated to deal with a problem set up by grammer and linguistics, it is evident that grammar or syntax should not be taken as a given issue for a psychological theory of language. Behavioral interactions involving language do not have grammar or syntax. Grammar and syntax are disciplines which deal with language product as things. As Kantor correctly points out, "grammarians, in other words, have not studied the actual speech of persons but rather have analyzed and described **things** word-forms, and even literary products-materials...far removed from speech" (1936, pp. 7-8). One of the shortcomings the operant analysis of language as behavior is that although it formally rejects a structural study of language (seen as complementary to a functional approach) it has imported from disciplines foreign to psychology a set of problems bound to the concept of structure itself. An additional issue is to clarify whether this misconception has been or has not been fostered by the atomistic nature of the concepts defined by the conditioning paradigm. However, this is not the place to examine that problem.

## Behavioral Dimensions of Language Interactions

We shall propose an alternative way of dealing with the problem of language as behavior, based upon conceptions advanced by Vigotsky (1934; Spanish translation, 1977) and Kantor (1936, 1977).

Our basic argument will be that certain functional properties of linguistic morphology are essential for the development of specifically human interactions, and that nevertheless, linguistic morphological behaviors may involve infra-human processes in human beings. In addition, linguistic interactions may play distinctive functional roles that a single concept such as verbal behavior would not differentiate. We shall point to five distinctive behavioral interactions involving linguistic morphology, three of them pre- or proto-linguistic and two actually linguistic.

**(1).** Linguistic actions require that a specific repertoire, although dictated by the biological endowment characteristic of human species, be shaped into different phonetic morphologies through the influences of social factors and rules. The modulating influence of society is so determinant that the final outcome in the form of a standard set of sounds and patterns of speech are relatively specific to every linguistic community and quite apart from the extensive biological repertoire. The acquisition of this phonetic-linguistic repertoire as a social reactional system is confounded frequently with the acquisition of the linguistic functions defining specific human interactions. Although phonetic repertoires, depending on social standards, reflect conventional properties, the fact of behaving in terms of the morphology typical of these conventions does not mean that an actual linguistic interaction is taking place. So, on the first level of the organization of language, we find the acquisition and establishment of the social reaction system defines the possibility of truly linguistic interactions. This process has to deal with the so-called "acquisition" of language, some of the problems related to "grammatical" language, and the expanding of vocabulary and syntatic forms. The process has been artificially separated into the learning of "words" and the "expression" of phrases or sentences, that is, meaningful syntatic units. On the one side, words seem to be related to the problem of "meaning" of language, and on the other side, phrases and sentences to the structure that allow conveying and creating "meaning." We shall not go into the details about "words" and "sentences." Kantor's (1936) discussion of the issue is still valid.

We shall limit ourselves to pointing out that the problem of the meaning of langue (either words or sentences) is not a problem of looking for univocal referents or rules to generate new descriptions, but is the problem of identifying the functional conditions that define a linguistic interaction as a substitutional process not restricted to the physical, existing **now-here** properties of objects and behavioral events. The acquisition of words and phrases are both, (as part of the establishment of a conventional reactional system) a matter of the acquisition of the style of speech, that is, the development of the patterning of phonetic (and gestural) responding specifically, to a particular linguistic community. Skinner's (1957) analyses of the textual, tact, intraverbal and echoic responses are relevant to different moments of this stage, since the patterning of the style of speech is not just a process restricted to the "association" of words and objects but also refers to the relations between words as stimulus objects, as in reading, imitation, and standard conversation.

To complete this behavioral interactive level involving language, we shall discuss an additional feature of this stage of linguistic aptitude development. The establishment of a reactional system that is not given as a biological, relatively invariant, repertoire involves the necessary interactions between the individual and contextual properties of stimulus objects and events. In this sense, speech responses become functional to the contextual properties of things, relations, and printed stimuli. The whole process of nomination and relations between word responses is based on this interaction between properties of stimulus objects contextualizing in time-and-space, phonetic and printed stimuli and corresponding morphological responding. This may be one reason for historically recurrent explanations of "meaning" in terms of classical conditioning or discriminated operants.

**(2).** Linguistic actions, although initially restricted to responding to functional proerties of contextual relations in the environment, become behaviors that may not only react to, but also produce, those functional properties. The individual, through speaking, affects the ways in which the environment is functional to him. Speaking is not only a way of making other individuals change in relation to objects which affect him or to their mutual interactions. When the individual speaks consequences in the environment are different than when he acts completely in non-verbal terms. Speech becomes a functional repertoire in producing specific effects in the environment, mainly through the mediation of other individuals. Speech allows the individual to be mediated in his interaction by other individuals, and in this respect becomes an essential factor in the socialization process. Mand responses, as described by Skinner (1957), are characteristic of this second stage of development. Nevertheless, it is important to stress that this stage of linguistic aptitude does not represent a truly substitutional linguistic interaction. The individual is mediated by the behavior of other individuals, but this mediation is still functional only in reference to concrete **here** and **now** interactions with objects and other individuals. The physical properties on which conventions are defined are not yet the functional properties of the interactions. The

243

individual is responding with the morphology of conventions but strictly on the basis of concrete properties of the situation. It is the situation understood as the behavior of others toward him that is beginning to put the behavior of the apparent speaker under the control of the mediation of conventional factors.

(3). The two previous levels of linguistic actions are in fact no different than the types of responding conceived by traditional theories based on classical and operant conditioning. It is important to stress, however, that some of the particular actions pointed out would transcend the restricted boundaries of this conceptual framework. In the third developmental or complexity stage of linguistic activities, interactions based on the physical properties of responding and the environment become mediated and conditional to their relation with conventional properties of linguistic stimuli and responses. The individual still interacts with the concrete events in a **here** and **now** fashion but the interaction itself becomes conditional to the linguistic stimuli and responses of other individuals who determine the specific relationship that takes place. Many of the problems traditionally encompassed under the label of concept formation and problem solving are relevant to this stage of linguistic aptitude. The individual may respond with a linguistic or non-linguistic morphology to a set of events with similar or dissimilar physical properties. Nevertheless, the factor or variable determining the interaction with the events is always related to verbal instructions, conventional cues, or conventional relationships between the events as defined by a third event. Obviously, this stage of interaction is not limited to protolinguistic conceptual behaviors; it also includes some forms of mediated imitational phenomena as well as some complex processes shared with higher vertebrates, as for example, non-linguistic communication and basic social non-linguistic interactions.

(4). The fourth stage of linguistic actions is properly related to langue as a genuine behavior event. Two factors influence this functional progress. On the one hand, true linguistic behavior is independent of concrete situational properties with which it is interactive. That is, conventional behaving, and in this sense, phonetic morphology--as the most prominent of linguistic actions--allows for detaching responses as such from any particular physical properties of indviduals and object events. The response "The house is green" as a truly linguistic behavior is independent of any particular concrete house, text stimulus, or any other present event in time and space. The detaching of responses from concrete situational conditions allows linguistic interactions which are independent on **here** and **now** contingencies. The fact of referring to past and future events, or to non-apparent observable but present events, is one of the defining properties of language as behavior. This referential function is different from traditional

244

concepts of meaning which are classifiable in the first two stages described earlier. It involves responding to present, past, or future events, not in terms of uniquivocal relations to their physical properties, but in terms of conventional properties that allow the individual to detach himself from the momentary circumstances limiting the concrete interaction. This is so because the linguistic interaction, as a socially imposed quality of contact to the individual, does not depend on the properties of physical events, per se, but on the conventional attributes that society defines as relevant ways to respond to what are considered pertinent properties. Thus, when we refer to a chair hidden under the table the response of speaking about the relation between chair and table without entering into direct physical contact would not be possible if linguistic topographies depended on the physical properties, per se, of a chair, the table, and their location in space. In fact, the independence of linguistic responses from the stimulus conditions interacting with them allows for interactions not apparent in the mere presence of events, that is, as if the responses were to the relations of events or to properties not directly observable in the concrete situation.

On the other hand, this detachment of linguistic responding from the concrete events to which an individual is referring makes possible the fulfilling of a second feature, which, integrated to the former, allows for genuine linguistic behavior. This second factor is that referring is not an isolated action to a referent object or event; it is only the first step in a non-divisible process of referrring to a referee. That is to say, linguistic interaction at this stage is bistimulational, since the linguistic response of the referee is controlled by both the referent and the referee, by the object or event one is speaking of, and the individual to whom one is speaking. In this sense, this first stage of genuine linguistic behavior depicts to a great extent the facts of communication through language.

The question thus arises: Is it necessary that a referee be present in order to have an actual linguistic interaction? We believe the answer is yes because the fact of speaking to somebody about something depicts a distinctive behavior in relation to language. The speaker or referor is substituting a contact of the referee (or listener or reader) with the object or event that is a referent stimulus. Not only does the speaker allow for an indirect contact between the listener and the stimulus object or event, but he or she also determines the nature of the concrete contact and the subsequent relationship between the listener, the stimulus event, and himself or herself. No real reference exists when there is no referee at all, and reference cannot be fully appreciated as a mediating interaction if the behavior of the listener is not taken as the relevant outcome of the speaker. It might be observed that, whereas in operant conditioning as a case of the second stage of linguistic aptitude the speaker shares consequences mediated by the listener, in a genuine substitutional linguistic episode it is the listener who is being meidated in his contact by the speaker, without conceiving the possibility of analyzing the speaker's behavior independently of the listener's behavior, since the behavior of the latter is relevant not only to the speaker but also to the stimulus event itself.

(5). Finally, a different level of linguistic aptitude is achieved when the mediating process of substituting through language behavior is not related to a referee. This is what Kantor (1977) calls non-referential language, and Vigotsky (1977) calls internalized speech. It deals with a vast number of complex human behaviors labeled symbolic and thinking interactions. In this substitutional class of interactions the individual reacts not to the events themselves but to the substitutional contacts to those events, a process that allows him not only to detach himself from time and space in which events occur but also from the concrete events themselves. The individual reacts to events not directly, but mediated by his linguistic interactions. He or she interacts conventionally with conventional responses to physical events and to individuals. Although in this type of linguistic interaction the individual may be in contact with another individual, he is responding to the conventional properties of the behavior and not to the concrete physical dimensions of events and individuals.

Concept formation and thinking interactions, in this stage , are different from those depicted in stage three. In the protolinguistic stage, individuals classify, for instance, responding directly to the physical properties or relations between events. In the substitutional stage that we are describing, individuals interact with their own linguistic interactions and those physical events and relationships. The substitutional behavior mediates contacts between linguistic events and interactions, and not between physical events. However, to become functional, this linguistic aptitude must be preceded in development by referential substitution. Otherwise, individuals would interact and live within a world of conventions without the possibility of contact with events and other individuals. Logic, mathematics, and musical literary compositions illustrate complex interactions at a non-referential substitutional level. Written language seems to be essential to this process.

## Some Final Remarks

Behavior analysis has been dealing, mainly, with linguistic morphologies that do not fulfill the substitutional functions of actual language behavior. Our emphasis has been on the first three pre- and protolinguistic behavioral stages of development. These functional stages are basic to a comprehensive knowledge of linguistic interactions only if their distinctive functional properties are not

246

confused with their similarity in topography.

Some concluding comments are relevant to this general issue. The first is related to the initially examined differences between animal and human behavior. After the review of the various stages in which linguistic action may be involved, it is apparent that although not every behavior sharing the morphology of linguistic behavior is truly language as interaction, these morphological properties (including their property of enduring as behavioral products, e.g., writing) are not irrelevant to the development of substitutional functions. The first three stages of interaction are found not only in man but also in animals, and the comparison of how they develop in both is not just a matter of drawing analogies, but is central to both a comparative and developmental theory of behavior. It is our assumption that equivalent stages of behavioral development are not the same in animals and man because of the conventional nature of the behavior topography in man and the historical nature of social variables affecting its functions. When man and animals are studied under similar conditions, man will show more complex and faster performance functions.

The second comment deals with the general research strategy for studying human linguistic processes. Traditional strategies, looking for associative processes or for reinforcement effects in language, have concentrated basically on the acquisition of the reactional systems and some elementary interactions involving the linguistic morphology. But they have not led to a break with their initial purpose of showing associations or increases and decreases in behavior, nor have they served as guides in producing data relevant to the actual processes underlying linguistic interactions. Furthermore, in spite of their claims, these approaches have legitimized problems and issues foreign to a behavioral view.

New research is needed to take into account: (a) The transitions between functional stages; (b) the fluctuation of levels of interactions in complex situations; (c) the role of linguistic morphology, especially of written langue, in the development of the detachment process essential to substitutional interactions; (d) the parameters involved in the complex external mediational processes between two individuals and the environment; (e) the process of responding to conventional properties of events in addition to their physical characteristics; (f) how referential and nonreferential langauge allow for an expansion of contacts between the individual and the environment, and also how the properties of the environment are changed due to the linguistic function.

To conclude, I would like to emphasize that if behavior analysis is to become a comprehensive behavior theory, standing as the body of psychological science, we must grasp the distinctive qualities of behavioral interactions without fear of questions relating to the extreme simplicity and linearity of present theoretical approaches. Our best recognition of past theoretical efforts may be to examine what they have correctly pointed out, instead of restricting the meaningful problems related to human behavior to the boundaries of their conceptual limitations.

## Acknowledgments

This paper was read as an invited address at the Seventh Annual Convention of Association for Behavior Analysis, Milwaukee, May , 1981. The author is grateful to J.R. Kantor and S.W. Bijou for their suggestions in improving the manuscript.

## Footnotes

1. Speech read in the Argentina Center in Defense of Human Rights, Madrid, March 23, 1981. Reproduced in **Uno Mas Uno,** May 2, 1981, Mexico City.

## References

Cantania, A.C. (in press). Language: A behavioral analysis. (English Translation) to appear in H. Zeier (Ed.) **Pawlow und die Folgen.** Zurich: Kindler Verlag.

Kantor, J.R. 1936. **An Objective Psychology of Grammar.** Bloomington, Indiana: University Publications, Science Series.

Kantor, J.R. 1977. **Psychological Linguistics.** Chicago: Principia Press.

McNeill, D. 1971. The capacity for the ontogenesis of grammar. In D. Slobin (Ed.) **The Ontogenesis of Grammar.** New York: Academic Press.

Mowrer, O.H. 1960. **Learning Theory and the Symbolic Processes.** New York: Wiley.

Osgood, C.E. 1953. **Method and Theory in Experimental Psychology.** New York: Oxford University Press.

Ribes, E. 1979. El desarrollo del legnuaje grammatical en niños: Un analisis teorico y experimental. **Mexican Journal of Behavior Analysis,** 5, 83-112.

Skinner, B.F. 1957. **Verbal Behavior.** New York: Appleton-Century-Crofts.

Vigotsky, L.S. 1977. **Pensamiento y Lenguaje.** Buenos Aires: La Pleyade.

Watson, J.B. 1924. **Behaviorism.** New York: Norton.

Whitehurst, G.H. 1979. Meaning and semantics. In G.J. Whitehurst and B.J. Zimmerman (Eds.) **The Functions of Language and Cognition.** New York: Academic Press.

250

# SYSTEMATIC FOUNDATIONS FOR THE CONCEPT OF "PRIVATE EVENTS": A CRITIQUE

Linda J. Parrott

The place of Behaviorism in psychology is being usurped by what has been called the "New Cognitivism." This movement must be viewed with alarm by psychologists whose aim has been to earn the status of a natural science for their discipline. After all, the "New Cognitivism" is, essentially, the same old mentalism that has always obstructed the scientific development of psychology (Observer, 1971, 1979; Kantor, 1979). The only novelty in the current formulation is the terminology with which mythical processes, held to underly complex psychological events, are described--a circumstance owing largely to recent developments in computer technology.

While many circumstances may have contributed to a cognitive revival at the present time, among them is the absence of a satisfactory behavioral account of complex human phenomena such as thinking, imaging, dreaming, and the like. The absence of such an account may be traced to the fact that the science of behavior has not progressed to any significant extent beyond a collection of principles and investigative procedures. The basic assumptions and presuppositions upon which the science rests are yet to be articulated.

While it is true that a science may not reach the postulational stage of systematic development for some time, the uneveness with which the science of behavior has developed suggests that reaching this stage may not even be a goal for behavioral scientists. Certainly such elaborate systemization as is here recommended may have seemed unnecessary for an understanding of the relatively simple animal activities that have occupied behavioral scientists for several decades. However, this situation changes when more complex human acts begin to be addressed. Particularly is this the case when the acts in question are not readily apparent to external observers.

When these more complex activities are addressed, the behavioristic position becomes especially vulnerable to corruption by the menace of mentalistic philosophies. This is the case both because traditional dualisms were originally invented to account for these com-

251

plex human events and also because the analysis of complex behavior entails a considerable measure of theoretical and methodological extension. In other words, a natural science account of complex activities is not only unfamiliar to the behaviorist, but it is also difficult to achieve.

The task of formulating an account of complex human activity is therefore not an easy one and the behaviorist is well advised to proceed with caution and restraint. It is at this point, however, that a problem arises: By what rules or guidelines are the behaviorists' speculations and extensions to be constrained? The answer, of course, is that in the absence of a satisfactory postulational system there are no rules. There is only the guidance provided by conventional philosophy.

Moreover, it is not a guidance that can be refused. Scientists always operate on the basis of presuppositions, whether or not they are aware of this fact or of the specific presuppositions adopted (Kantor, 1953). This being the case, failure to develop a new set of postulates may be taken as evidence for the adoption of more traditional views. Unfortunately, it has always been the argument of behaviorists that progress will be registered in psychology only when a natural science approach to psychological events is taken, which in turn, will be accomplished only if traditional assumptions about such events are abandoned (Skinner, 1953).

Needless to say, the behavioral account of complex human activity is influenced by conventional philosophy, and for this reason does not constitute a viable alternative to the interpretation advanced by the "New Cognitivist." Moreover, a careful analysis of the inadequacies of the behavioral account of complex activity reveals weaknesses in the approach to even the simplist of acts. These inadequacies should not be taken to imply that a satisfactory account of complex or even simple human behaviors cannot be accomplished within the boundaries set by a natural science. Instead, it must be realized that the adequacy of an analysis of complex behavior depends on the adequacy of the underlying **philosophy.** As Kantor (1969b) has argued: "a bad philosophy invariably comports with a bad psychology and vice-versa," (p. 617).

The purpose of this paper is to reveal the adverse influence of traditional philosophy on the behavioral account of complex acts and to prevent further adherence to a fruitless position. In so doing, more appropriate postulates and their implications for the analysis of complex as well as simple acts will be presented and discussed.

In preparing this paper I have selected B.F. Skinner as a spokesman for the mainstream behavioral position in psychology. While many who would identify themselves as behaviorists--even Skinnerians--would not find themselves in total agreement with Skinner, all appear to have adopted similar, if not identical philosophical assumptions. Since it is with respect to these foundations that the behavioral position is contested, I feel that Skinner's views may be regarded as representative.

## Complex Activities

Before embarking on a critical examination of the behavioral interpretation of complex activity, we must specify the activities included in this category and it is not without some difficulty that we do so. The difficulties arise from the fact that there are not fundamental differences between simple and more complex activities, hence all systems of classification are arbitrarily produced. Nonetheless, a relatively standard set of categories have been adopted by psychologists, and it is on the basis of these conventions that we may distinguish the simple from the complex.

Simple psychological phenomena are those in which a readily apparent response is coordinated with a readily apparent stimulus. Complex activities, on the other hand, are those in which one or the other of the coordinated factors is inapparent to an observer. For example, when presented with an arithmetic problem (stimulus) a solution is eventually achieved, as signified by the production of an answer (response). However, because the production of the answer does not occur immediately upon presentation of the problem, and some form of interaction between the problem solver and the problem appears to be taking place during this delay, there is reason to believe that the overt production of an answer constitutes an incomplete description of the response factor. The activities occurring during the delay constitute an example of complex behavior in which the response factor is inapparent.

The inapparent stimulus factor case is illustrated by instances of remembering. In such cases a response occurs which appears to be coordinated with stimulus events that are no longer present, and are hence inapparent to a present observer. Complexities are multiplied when both stimulus and response factors are inapparent. Such is the case with imaging and daydreaming activities.

From a behavioral standpoint, activities of the first type, and those in which both response and stimulus factors are inapparent to external observers, are discussed collectively under the heading "Private Events." The analysis which follows will address these events in particular.

## Private Events Distinguished From Public Events

Skinner (1953) argues that a psychological event is classified as private on the basis of its limited accessibility to an observer, not because it has any special structure or nature. The observer in this context includes both the person in whom the event is occurring as well as an external observer. With regard to the latter, limited accessibility is not intended to include circumstances under which an event is not observed simply because an observer is not present when it occurs. Rather, it refers to an impossibility of unaided observation resulting from the fact that the events to be observed re taking place inside the skin of another person (Skinner, 1953; 1974). The impossibility of observing such events must also be qualified as a temporary state of affairs. Eventually, Skinner (1974) argues, a complete, account o private events will be provided by anatomists and physiologists.

With regard to the former observer, that is, the person within whom the private events are occurring, limited accessibility to these events is a consequence of two circumstances. The first of these has to do with the physical structure of the human organism and its evolutionary history. Skinner (1974) claims that observation of events taking place inside one's own body is limited by the fact that certain areas of the body are not innervated to allow reactions to events taking place in those areas. One may react to conditions of the body produced by some malfunction or injury to the spleen, for example, but the spl een itself is not innervated sufficiently to allow the organism to identify the location of these conditions. This situation is owing to the fact that the conditions under which the species evolved biologically did not afford greater chances of survival to members capable of observing events taking place within their own skins.

The second set of circumstances which limit the accessibility persons have to events within their own skins is the social origin of self-knowledge. Skinner (1974) explains:

> We might expect that because a person is in such intimate
> contact with his own body he should be able to describe
> its conditions and processes particularly well, but the
> very privacy which seems to confer a special privilege
> on the individual makes it difficult for the community
> to teach him to make distinctions. The community
> can teach a child to name colors in various ways. For
> example, it can show him colored objects, ask him to
> respond with color words, and commend or correct him
> when his responses correspond or fail to correspond with
> the colors of the objects. If the child has normal color
> vision, we expect him to learn to identify colors accurate-
> ly. The community cannot, however, follow the same

254

practice in teaching him to describe the states of his
own body because it lacks the information it needs
to commend or correct him (pp. 22-23).

Despite these difficulties, the community can and does teach its
members to identify or otherwise react to events within their own
skins, primarily on the basis of correlated public events.   The fact
remains, however, that self-knowledge of this sort is limited even for
events taking place in appropriately innervated areas, and is lacking
altogether with respect to areas inadequately innervated.   For these
reasons, private events must be characterized as having limited
accessibility even to the person in whom the event is taking place.

## Varieties of Private Events

Private events may constitute stimuli or responses but are not
restricted to either, since events taking place at a neurological level
or which exist in unclear dimensions may also be included in this
category.

**Private stimuli.**   Private stimuli are distinguished from public
stimuli in two ways.   The first concerns their place of origin. The
second concerns the nature of the relations with response events.

With regard to the first criterion, stimulation arising from the
surrounding environment are regarded as public, while private
stimulation are:   The digestive, respiratory, and circulatory systems;
and "the position and movement of the body in space and...the position
and movement of parts of the body with respect to other parts ,"
(Skinner, 1953, p. 258).   Other internal sources of stimulation
mentioned by Skinner include conditions associated with behavior but
not necessarily produced by it (1967); and irritation or inflammation of
tissues, as in the cases of an itch and pain arising from a decayed
tooth, respectively.

Classification of events as stimuli, and further as private stimuli
on the basis of their place of origin is not accomplished without some
difficulty.   Particularly is this the case when proprioceptive sources
are at issue.   Inasmuch as "the position and movement of the body or
of its parts" constitutes a definition of behavior (Skinner, 1938, p. 6),
we may assume that this source of private stimulation is one's own
behavior, be it public or private. Consequently, from the standpoint of
the person being stimulated from this source, private behavior, as well
as at least some aspects of public behavior and private stimuli, amount
to the same thing. This deduction finds support in the following
passage:

255

The covert behavior evokes the same response as the overt behavior because it is essentially the same stimulus except for magnitude (Skinner, 1957, p. 142)1.

Feelings and emotions are analyzed in a similar manner. Skinner (1966) points out: "In a sense a feeling is both the thing felt and the act of feeling it" (p. 255), and our own behaviors are among the things felt.

Private stimuli are also distinguished from public stimuli on the basis of the kinds of relations they may have with response events. They may enter into controlling relations, particularly in a discriminative or elicitive capacity (Skinner, 1953, p. 275), although also in the capacity of reinforcers of an automatic sort (Skinner, 1953, 1957, 1974). But they are not regarded as having any "causal" status (Skinner, 1957, p. 437; 1969. p. 257). Causal properties are ascribed to stimuli arising from the surrounding environment only.

**Private responses.** Private responses are distinguished from public responses primarily on the basis of their magnitude (Skinner, 1953, p. 282; 1957, p. 141; 1969, p. 242; 1974, p. 27). As such, the public-private dichotomy is essentially a continuum: Private responses are executed with the same musculature as public responses but on such a small scale as to be invisible to an external observer-- or even to the person in whom the event is occurring.

Not all private responses are of this sort, however. In some cases the private response is assumed to constitute only a fractional component of its overt couterpart, not a miniature version of it (Skinner, 1974, p. 82). When a person sees or hears something in its absence, for example, the person is said to be doing in the absence of the thing some part of what he does in its presence.

Whatever is the precise nature of private responses, all are held to operate in the same manner as public responses, and are subject to the same laws. In fact, there are no important distinctions made between the two levels or forms of activity (Skinner, 1957, p. 437).

**Unclassified private events.** Private events which are not readily classified as responses or stimuli include those which apparently are not executed by the muscular apparatus and which exist in unclear dimensions. Fedings, as acts of feelings, must be included in this category. In an emotional or feeling episode one may react to various conditions of the body and its movement, however, the nature of such a reaction is not specified (Skinner, 1969). Presumably these reactions do not involve muscular action.

For the most part, events of unclear dimensions are regarded as response events as the following passage indicates:

> The range of verbal behavior is roughly suggested, in descending order of energy, by shouting, loud talking, quiet talking, whispering, muttering 'under one's breath,' subaudible speech with detectable muscular action, subaudible speech of unclear dimensions, and perhaps even the 'unconscious thinking' sometimes inferred in instances of problem solving (Skinner, 1957, p. 438)[2].

Although Skinner argues that "[t]here is no point at which it is profitable to draw a line distinguishing thinking from acting on this continuum," the point at which it would seem reasonable to do so is the point where muscular action is no longer involved. By his own declaration (1938, p. 6), events which do not involve movements of the body or its parts are not properly regarded as response events.

Events of unclear dimensions are also discussed in the context of rapid self-editing of ongoing speech. In such instances, "changes are made on the spur of the moment and so rapidly that we cannot reasonably attribute them to an actual review of covert forms" (Skinner, 1957, p. 371). It appears, instead, that we are able to react to and reject responses before they have occurred (1957, p. 435) or before they have reached their final form (1957, p. 371).

Unless one assumes that a response which has not yet occurred is intended to imply a "response which has not yet occurred on a muscular level," this interpretation is absurd. A nonexisting event cannot be reacted to. While Skinner is reluctant to specify the dimensions of these events, the only plausible naturalistic dimensions of a premuscular response are neurological. Hence, from Skinner's perspective, neural activity corresponding to a particular muscular event is believed to precede this event in time, and is further regarded as itself a response event.

**Summary of private events.** The behavioral position with respect to complex inapparent activity may be summarized as follows: Some of an organism's behavior, as well as the stimulus conditions responsible for the occurrence of behavior, take place within the organism's own skin. Events occurring within the skin are not distinguished by any special physical status, in fact, a more complete understanding of their nature is anticipated with advances in the biological sciences[3].

With respect to their operation, private responses are not held to differ in any fundamental way from their public counterparts. Private stimuli, on the other hand, do not appear to have all of the properties of public stimuli. Specifically, private stimuli lack causal properties.

## A Critique of the Private Event Analysis

Because events of the present sort have been traditionally assumed to exist in other than spatio-temporal dimensions, Skinner's contention that such events are not distinguished by any special physical status is widely held to mark a break with tradition. And, of course, to some extent it does. However, the emancipation from transcendental institutions is incomplete, resulting in numerous inconsistencies in the behavioral position. In fact, Skinner's analysis of complex activity reveals the influence of traditional philosophy at every turn, namely, in the conceptualization of stimuli, responses, and the relations between them.

Further, it is not only with respect to complex phenomena that these influences may be detected. Quite the contrary, since it is founded on such traditions, Behaviorism is rife with difficulties on even the most fundamental of issues. Among these must be included the essential character of the psychological datum. So critical in fact is this issue to the unfolding of the behavioral argument that it constitutes a perfect starting place for the critique that follows.

**Functional relations versus causal relations.** Skinner (1953, 1969, 1974) argues repeatedly that functional relations between stimulus and response events constitute the subject matter of behavioral psychology. Readers of this argument might assume that functions would constitute units of analysis in Skinner's system. This does not appear to be the case, however. Functions are not regarded as crude data for which explanations are to be found in the context of their occurrence. That is, behavioral events and their occurrence with respect to stimulus events are regarded as effects of prior[4] stimulus causes. This perversion of the concept of function is owing to the fact that functional and causal relations are totally confused in Skinner's system as the following passage indicates:

> The external variables of which behavior is a function provide for what may be called a causal or functional analysis. We undertake to predict and control the behavior of the individual organism. This is our "dependent variable" the effect for which we are to find the cause. Our "independent variable"--the causes of behavior--are the external conditions of which behavior is a function. Relations between the two--the "cause-and-effect relationships" in behavior--are the laws of of a science. A synthesis of these laws expressed in quantitative terms yield a comprehensive picture of the organism as a behaving system (1953, p. 35).

Skinner does not acknowledge a confusion in his thinking on this point. He frankly asserts that functional and causal relations amount to the same thing (Skinner, 1953, p. 23):

> The terms 'cause' and 'effect' are no longer widely used in science. They have been associated with so many theories of the structure and operation of the universe that they mean more than scientists want to say. The terms which replace them, however, refer to the same factual core. A 'cause' becomes a 'change in an independent variable' and an 'effect' a 'change in a dependent variable.' The old 'cause-and-effect connection' becomes a 'functional relation.'

According to Skinner, the scientific community adopted the newer terms simply to avoid the suggestion carried by the older terms as to how a "cause" causes its effects (1953, p. 23). According to other members of that same community (Kantor, 1970; Zimmerman, 1979), however, the adoption of the newer terms represents a revolution in scientific thinking. As Kantor (1970) has pointed out, the newer functional vocabulary originated in other sciences--specifically mathematics--and when mathematicians spoke of functional relations there was no implication whatsoever that traditional causal philosophy was reflected in their usage. "Mathematical functions simply imply absolute equivalence of variants and no existential or causal dependence or independence" (Kantor, 1970, pp. 106-107).

Moreover, given Skinner's understanding of the differences implied by the two sets of terms, it is not clear why he should prefer the functional vocabulary since he himself addresses the issue of how a "cause" causes its effect. In Skinner's system stimuli cause behaviors to occur with greater frequency and they do so by virtue of the fact that behaving organisms have inherited the capacity to be affected by the consequences of their actions (Skinner, 1969, 1971, p. 114). Obviously, then, the additional meaning carried by the older terms--to which contemporary scientists have taken issue--is precisely the meaning Skinner has improperly attached to the newer terms.

From these arguments, we may summarize the behavioral position with respect to the character of psychological data as follows: Psychological events are relations between stimuli and responses which require for their understanding some form of causative determination. Accordingly, stimulus changes--conceived as independent entities taking place at a particular point in time--are assumed to bring about behavioral effects at some later point. Furthermore, the causal power of stimuli to bring about such effects may be attributed to the biological structure of behaving organisms.

Needless to say, This aspect of Skinner's system must be regarded as deviant from the standpoint of the larger scientific community. Physicists have long abandoned simple causal doctrines of this sort. The same may be said of interbehavioral psychologists (Kantor, 1950). Moreover, equating functionality with causality is the source of numerous inadequacies in the Skinnerian account of complex activities. Because causes are concpetualized in autonomous entities, stimulus and response events may be described and discussed independently of one another. The outcome of this procedure is to regard stimulus events as physical objects and response events as organismic phenomena (Skinner, 1957, pp. 14-15). It is to these problems that we may now turn.

**Stimulus objects versus stimulus functions.** Difficulties arise when objects or situations are regarded as stimuli. Because any number of responses may occur with respect to the same object, it is difficult, if not impossible, to determine which stimulus is coordinated to which response for a particular organism. This problem then becomes which stimulus functionreside in a specific object for a particular organism (Kantor, 1933).

The power of the stimulus-as-function formulation is illustrated by Skinner's solution to the problem of identifying the physical dimensions of private stimulus objects. The stimulus-as-object conception appears to create no particular problems when these objects are observable events, although even here some difficulties are encountered (Skinner, 1969, p. 79). When stimuli are private, however, the problem of identifying their properties, and thereby distinguishing one from another, appears to be insurmountable. Consequently, a classification in terms of sources of stimulation is adopted (Skinner, 1953). The irony of this situation is that while Skinner regards this solution as less than satisfactory, a functional interpretation of stimulus events calls for just such an analysis. The point is that adequate descriptions emerge from actual confrontations with the events described, despite postulational improperieties. In the case of feelings, for example, the thing felt and the act of feeling seem to constitute a unity. Similarly, proprioceptive stimuli and reactions to them appear to be one and the same thing. These mergers present problems when stimulus events are regarded as prior and independent causes of response effects. However, from a functional standpoint, no problem exists. In each case what is observed is an interaction of the organism with conditions of his or her own body--a functional relation in which stimulus and response events constitute simultaneous phases of a single event.

Were Skinner's conception of stimui derived from actual observations of events, observations would not draw it into question. The fact that they do argues for reconsideration. However, no such action is taken.    Instead, the causal interpretation is vigorously defended, although not without an additional problem.  The problem concerns the causal status of private stimuli.

**The causal status of private stimuli.**  Despite the fact that private stimuli may have elicitive, discriminative, and reinforcing effectiveness, they are not regarded as having any causal status. Only public stimili may serve in this capacity.  By this restriction we must assume that causality refers to something other than elicitation, discrimination, and reinforcement operations.   However, in all other contexts, the stimuli invovled in these operations are regarded as the causes of behavior.    That is, these operations and their derivatives are taken to be    synonymous with the concept of causality.    Why this situation should change when stimuli become inapparent to an external observer is unclear.

It might    be argued that the restriction of causality to public stimuli is imposed on practical grounds. Events inside the skin of another organism are not only inapparent to an external observer, but they are also no directly manipulable. Because causality is believed to be demonstrated when events are manipulated and effects reliably produced,    the    causal    properties    of    private    stimuli    are    not demonstrable.    Hence, while private stimuli may have causal properties, it serves no useful purpose to make this inference since (whatever may be their nature) no practical action may be taken with respect to them.   In actual fact Skinner makes this  argument only with respect to private events of alleged nonphysical dimensions (1974, p. 210).  By contrast, the noncausal status of private stimuli is simply asserted.

It would be reassuring to think that the restriction of causality to public stimuli were made on the basis of observation.  This argument cannot be made however as causality is not among the events observed, be they public or private. From this standpoint, it is not the noncausal status of private stimuli that must be questioned but rather the causal status of their public counterparts. Skinner is totally unenlightened on this issue, however, and does not even question the causal role of public stimuli.  In fact, the attribution of causality to public stimuli is fundamental to the behavioral position:    Apart from an  explicit  denial  of  the  psychic  nature  of  private  events,  the principal   difference   between   Behaviorism   and   Mentalism   is   the **location of the alleged causes of behavior.**

**Organismic responses or behavioral fields.**   The causal inter-pretation  of  functional  relations  also  results  in  an  inadequate conception of response events.  When stimuli are regarded as causes of behavioral effects, behaviors come to be understood as exclusively organismic performance or movements (Kantor, 1970, p. 105).  This, in turn, leads to attempts to localize response events in particular muscle groups or other biological structures. Skinner's own position on response events varies with the occasion, since most often biological phenomena are described as psychological events. The outcome of this confusion is to assume, as Skinner does, that the observational problems posed by private events of psychological significance will eventually be solved by technologies designed to amplify biological occurrences (Skinner, 1953, p. 282). However, when psychological events are properly conceived as interactions between behaving organisms and stimulating environments, it becomes obvious that the problem of privacy will never be resolved in the manner anticipated by Skinner.

The assumption that a more complete description of psychological occurrences eventually will emerge from microscopic examinations of organismic structures is not the most serious consequence of failing to properly differentiate the psychological from the biologcial domain. A more serious problem is that when attempts are made to distinguish one type of event from another, improper relations between these events are constructed. In essence, psychological events are explained by way of biological phenomena. It is in keeping with such reasoning that Skinner (1974) makes the following statement:

> The physiologist of the future will tell us all that can be known about what is happening inside the behaving organism. This account will be an important advance over a behavioral analysis, because the latter is necess-arily 'historical'--that is to say, it is confined to fun-ctional relations showing temporal gaps. Something is done today which affects the behavior of an organism tomorrow. No matter how clearly that fact can be established, a step is missing, and we must wait for the physiologist to supply it (p. 215).

The point is that the manner in which response events are conceptualized determines how biological factors enter in their analysis. For example, when responses are conceived as organismic performances, they appear to demand a biological substratum or basis. Accordingly, changes in organismic performance--normally described as "learning"--appear to demand changes in an underlying biological structure. Hence the latter are simply asserted, despite the absence of any concrete evidence. Moreover, the two sets of changes are not regarded as simultaneous occurrences: The psychological changes are regarded as results of prior biological changes.

Alternatively, when responses are conceived as phases of functional relations, they exist as events without any substantive structure themselves and, consequently, are not dependent upon such a

262

structure at any other level of analysis. Given this view of response events, "learning" is something that happens to functional relations, not to organisms.

This is not to say that biological factors are not involved in psychological events, only that their involvement is not profitably described as causal. Kantor (1982) explains:

> When we think in terms of biological functions as comprised in psychological behavior situations, we are on our way to an accurate description of events, while in considering the two as separable and causally related, valid analysis of what happens in human behavior is completely forestalled. In other words, when we regard the organism's anatomical features (which have a part in every action) as parts (actually indivisible of course and therefore only logical parts) of an act going on, then we can account for the specific variations of action because of the size, weight, and other biological factors of a person. On the other hand, when we regard such anatomical features, whether definite organs, structures, or hypothetical biological factors, as determiners or foundations of conduct, then our psychological data are inevitably misinterpreted. By all means must we avoid here the logical error of confusing a necessary conditions with a cause (p. 72).

In summary, because the revolutionary concept of functionality is confused with traditional causality in behavior theory, psychological stimuli and responses are regarded as both separate and independent entities. Consequently, each is assumed to have, or to have a basis in, substantive structure. That is, stimulus-causes are regarded as physical objects, not phases of functional relations. Likewise, response-effects are conceptualized as strictly organismic phenomena. In other words, psychological events are reduced to the things and events of the physical and biological sciences.

Despite the fact that psychology--as conceived by behaviorists-- is the study of such causes and their effects, the causes appear to have less intellectual appeal than their effects. Psychology is rarely reduced to physics, in whole or even in part. On the other hand, the biological basis of psychological phenomena is heralded as revealed truth. This emphasis on response-effects and their biological bases may also be attributed to the influence of conventional doctrine concerning the causes of behavior, to which we may now turn.

**Internal causes.** A review of psychological history reveals that for the largest portion of that history, responses were believed to be caused from within. Originally, internal causes were of a spiritual sort; they were the directives of the transcendental soul. In more modern times, the mind has occupied this portion; and still more recently, the brain has emerged as the source and origin of an organism's activity (Kantor, 1963, 1969a). Needless to say, when the causes of behavior as well as the behavior itself are localized in the organism, interest in the stimulating environment wanes[5].

That behavioral psychologists have adopted the doctrine of internal causes is indicated in Skinner's (1957) discussions of self-editing. As previously mentioned, Skinner's contention that a person can react to and reject responses before they have actually occurred, or before they have reached their **final** form, must be taken to mean that respones occurring on a muscular level have their origin in the brain. However, there is no reason to assume that neural events at one point in time become muscular events at a later point (but by adherence to the doctrine of internal causes).

To deny neural events a causal role in the occurrence of psychological events is not to deny their involvement altogether. On the contrary, they may be assumed to participate in the psychological event. However, the neural activities pertinent to and participating in the occurrence of a particular response are those occurring at the same time as that response, not prior to it.

The doctrine of internal causes is also responsible for two other aspects of the behavioral interpretation of complex events: The public-private dichotomy; and the inadequate differentiation of classes of so-called private events.

**Public-private dichotomy.** Conventional doctrine holds that the brain, as well as its terminological predecessors, is not only the source and origin of behavior, but also the behaving entity. That is, throughout psychological history, complex acts have been held to be enacted by particular parts of the organism, namely the soul, mind, or brain (Kantor, 1963, 1969a). Hence thinking, reasoning, and the like were conceptualized as activities occurring inside the organism. The behaviorist, in keeping with this tradition, takes the position that some events occur within the skin. By this position the public-private dichotomy is established: Events occurring "within the skin" are private, while events occurring at the "surface of the skin" are public.

In what sense, however, does behavior occur at the "surface of the skin?" Furthermore, it is obvious that the whole organism--skin and all--is involved in every instance of psychological activity. Clearly it is only the behaviorists' unwitting commitment to conventional philosophy that leads them to regard obvious or apparent events as activities of a whole organism, and subtle or inapparent events as activities of its parts.

264

The behaviorists' dichotomization of psychological events into public and private classes is not of theoretical significance only. More important are the consequences of this analysis for the identification, differentiation, and investigation of events in the private class. Essentially, by classifying events as private on the basis of their inaccessibility ot external observers, these events are rendered inscrutable--at least for the present time. Moreover, by reducing psychological functions to biological occurrences, the responsibility for the analysis of private events is transferred to the biological scientist. Consequently, private events are not adequately differentiated because they are not currently possible to identify. Further, in the event that private events do become possible to identify (by means of technological innovations designed to amplify biological activities), and are thereby able to be differentiated one from the other, it will be the job of the biological scientist--not the psychologist--to investigate their nature and operation.

In short, some behaviorists are willing to consider the issue of private events, in large part to avoid being accused of neglecting them (Skinner, 1974). But, to avoid being identified as cognitivists, they are unwilling to elaborate upon the nature and operation of such events. As a result, the behavioral position with respect to complex human activity is fundamentally identical to that of the contemporary cognitivist, minus the detail of the latter's position. Little wonder it is, then, that Behaviorism has not been successful in preventing a cognitive revival in psychology.

## Summary and Conclusion

The behavioral position with respect to complex human activity is clearly influenced by conventional causal philosophy. This influence may be observed in the confusion of functional relations with causal relations, resulting in a causal interpretation of stimuli so conceptualized. That is, stimuli and responses may be regarded as separate and independent entities, localized in physical objects and biological organisms, respectively.

At this point in the analysis we see the influence of additional philosophical assumptions concerning the relationship between biological and psychological events. Under this influence, psychological events lose their distinctive character altogether. They are interpreted as organismic happenings, explained in terms of their underlying biological structure.

In accordance with these assumptions is the public-private dichotomy asserted: Public events are interpreted as activities of the whole organism, occurring at the surface of the skin; while private events are seen as activities of parts of the organism, occurring within the skin.

Events within the skin are not readily investigated, however. Moreover, should such investigation be undertaken it will not be undertaken by psychological workers, since the events of interest are biological rather than psychological in nature. Hence, the behavioral position with respect to complex human behavior both lacks detail and offers no promise of elaboration. As such, the behavioral position does not provide a viable alternative to traditional interpretations of this subject matter. It is, in fact, just an impoverished version of the traditional viewpoint.

No doubt, behaviorists would object to this characterization of their position, arguing that Behaviorism stands alone in its rejection of mind-body dualism. It is true that behaviorists have made a serious attempt to exorcise the spooks from their system. The problem is that a fully articulated system has failed to materialize. Consequently, behaviorists are at a loss to deterimine whether or not a particular theoretical argument is in keeping with their underlying postulates. With no guidelines by which to regulated specualtive analyses, as is required for an understanding of complex behavior, analyses fall prey to traditional philosophy. As a result the behavioral position lacks consistency and rigor.

What is needed is an acknowledgment of the logical character of science, and a commitment on the part of behaviorists to construct a satisfactory scientific system, for it is only with the development of such a system that a coherent analysis of complex human behavior may be formulated and a cognitive revival in psychology forestalled.

The selection and derivation of suitable postulates and assumptions implies a considerable familiarity with the origins and implications of these presuppositions--a prerequisite knowledge that may not be possessed by many behaviorists given their previous lack of concern for such issues. Fortunately, a system of science in keeping with the naturalistic aspects of Behaviorism has already been articulated by 1R. Kantor and it is in consultation with his works that Behaviorists are advised to undertake their task.

### Footnotes

1. Unclear by this exposition is the status of auditory stimuli arising from movements of the vocal apparatus. While these stimuli do not technically arise from the surrounding environment--the criterion by which public stimuli are distinguished--it cannot be argued that such events are impossible of observation by an external observer--the criterion by which private events are distinguished.

2. Nonverbal behaviors of unclear dimensions are also discussed (Skinner, 1953, p. 273).

3. Skinner is not entirely conistent on this issue. For example in 1969 (p. 226) he argues that the psychological problems of private events will never be resolved on physiological terms. However, the position most often taken is the reverse.

4. Behavioral effects are produced by prior stimulus causes even when the stimulus in question follows the response since consequences are not said to have an effect on the response they follow but on future responses of the same class.

5. It is in accordance with such understanding that behavioral psychologists describe their discipline as the science of behavior as opposed to behavior-stimulus relations.

### References

Kantor, J.R. 1933. In defense of stimulus-response psychology. **Psychological Review,** 40, 324-336.

Kantor, J.R. 1950. **Psychology and Logic** (Vol. 2). Chicago: Principia Press.

Kantor, J.R. 1963. **The Scientific Evaluation of Psychology** (Vol. 1). Chicago: Principia Press.

Kantor, J.R. 1969a. **The Scientific Evaluation of Psychology** (Vol. 2). Chicago: Principia Press.

Kantor, J.R. 1969b. Scientific psychology and specious philosophy. **Psychological Record,** 19, 15-27.

Kantor, J.R. 1970. An analysis of the experimental analysis of behavior (TEAB). **Journal of the Experimental Analysis of Behavior,** 13, 101-108.

Kantor, J.R. 1979. Psychology: Science or nonscience? **Psychological Record,** 29, 155-163.

Kantor, J.R. 1982. **Cultural Psychology.** Chicago: Principia Press.

Observer, 1971. Comments and queries: Revivalism in psychology. **Psychological Record,** 21, 131-134.

Observer. 1979. Comments and queries: What future for psychology. **Psychological Record,** 29, 297-300.

Skinner, B.F. 1938. **The Behavior of Organisms.** New York: Appleton-Century-Crofts.

Skinner, B.F. 1953. **Science and Human Behavior.** New York: The Free Press.

Skinner, B.F. 1957. **Verbal Behavior.** New York: Appleton-Century-Crofts.

Skinner, B.F. 1967. **Contingencies of Reinforcement: A Theoretical Analysis.** New York: Appleton-Century-Crofts.

Skinner, B.F. 1971. **Beyond Freedom and Dignity.** New York: Alfred A. Knopf, Inc.

Skinner, B.F. 1974. **About Behaviorism.** New York: Alfred A Knopf, Inc.

Zimmerman, D.W. 1979. Quantum theory and interbehavioral psychology. **Psychological Record,** 29, 473-485.

# THE ROAD TO SCIENTIFIC AGEISM

J.W. Herrick

Scientific ageism is the name I have given to the practice of conducting geropsychological research designed to discover the degree to which individuals become behaviorally incompetent in later life (Herrick, 1981). Unlike scientific racism, a la Jensen (1969), scientific ageism has as yet few critics. However, like scientific racism, its goal is to understand complex human behaviors in terms of simplistic biological explanations.

The road to scientific ageism is not a particularly long or hard one. In fact, it is easy to travel on and offers its adherents many attractive accommodations along the way. A much more difficult route to understanding the behavior of anyone at any age is found in interbehaviorism. This chapter will attempt to take the reader on this uphill journey.

After a brief comment on what it is like to be an interbehaviorist (The Interbehaviorist: Wrong Way on a One-Way Street), basic interbehavioral principles relevant to understanding geropsychological research topics (viz., declining intelligence, reaction times, motivational levels, perceptual abilities, memory, etc.) will be discussed (The Interbehavioral Detour),as will emotional or feeling and motivational behaviors that have survival value for us as a species (Evolution: A Public Thoroughfare). This is followed by discussions of how racist and sexist explanations for behavior are no longer in vogue among academicians and behavioral scientists (Racism and Sexism: Academic Dead Ends), while biological explanations for individual behavior and the behavior of elderly persons as a group are still tolerated (Green Lights for Elitism and Ageism). The cultural-historical bases to reductionistic explanations for individual behavior are reviewed (Biological Explanations for Behavior: Construction of the "Inner State" System), followed by a discussion of how certain unwarranted assumptions have combined with certain observations to create scientific ageism (Following the Yellow Brick Road). The role of hypothetical, brain-localized cognitive structures that, because of the normal aging process, are believed to deteriorate and generate declining "cognitive processes" is discussed in relation to reaction times and performance on intelligence tests and problem times and performance on intelligence tests and problem solving tasks

(Speed Limits), misconceptions regarding "senility" (Taking the Senile Route), and performance on memorization or learning tasks (Memory Lane). Finally, it is recommended that the road to scientific ageism be closed, and that future public monies be spent on repairing the economic and social positions of the elderly (Road Closed for Repairs).

## The Interbehaviorist:
## Wrong Way on A One-Way Street

It is not easy being an interbehaviorist. It is not easy because understanding, then accepting, the interbehavioral approach to behavior is tantamount to becoming a member of an alien culture. Being an anthropologist, I liken it to rejecting the world view of a modern-day member of Western culture and adopting that of the Hopi, Navajo, Iroquois or some other people with a radically different cosmological scheme. In fact, if one follows Maruyama's (1973) discussion of three of the many ways that various groups of humans may go about "reasoning" (what he calls the "unidirectional causal," or the "random process," and the "mutual causal" paradigms), it will be discovered that interbehaviorism fits best into the third category--one that is decidedly non-Western in nature.

After one has become an interbehaviorist there is the tendency to become a bit smug and self-righteous. You may, as Gibson (1970) has described its adherents, begin to see yourself as being a child of light fighting against the children of darkness. There may be some truth to this. There is definitely a feeling of brother-sisterhood that binds us together, and I sense that we do believe that it is "us against (in interaction with) the world." We have our prophet, and we do our share of proselytizing. So maybe Gibson is right. After all, interbehaviorism does qualify as a belief system. For some of us, it is our only belief system, with no truer true-believers to be found anywhere.

Our belief system, however, goes beyond simply ordering our world, lessening our anxiety behaviors, and providing us with something to believe in. It has given those of us who are genuinely interested in understanding human behavior the feeling that we have gotten pretty close to our goal. And even though we have become a bit "jargonized," it is a jargon that does not leave us with the sense that we are merely speaking one dialect of the usual social-behavioral scientific gibberish. On the personal level, it has allowed me to maintain a certain degree of idealism and optimism, and has indirectly made me an advocate of the down trodden--those with "less intelligence," the poor and disadvantaged, minorities, peasants, the humble and the aged. I am convinced that these people have much more to offer the world than our traditional scientists of behavior have wanted us to believe.

# The Interbehavioral Detour

The principles of interbehaviorism are neither easy to grasp nor to adopt. Nor on the surface does it appear as though they could possibly account for the complexities and, as we have come to expect, the mysteries of human behavior. Everything, including phantom limb phenomena, imaging, dreaming, nightmares, multiple personalities, hyponosis and hallucinations is explained in naturalistic terms. Interbehaviorism, then, is not very romantic or glamorous. However, it is a good approach if one's goals as a behavioral scientists are understanding, predicting and controlling behavior. It is not so good if one's goals include the appearance of profundity and erudition. This might account for why interbehaviorism has been so long in being accepted among those in society whose main job it is to be (or appear to be )profound and erudite.

With interbehaviorism we are always dealing with the event of a behaving organism as it interacts with various stimulating things and events, or substitutes for various things and events (e.g., stimuli that resemble or "remind" one of some nonpresent thing or event), within a context of setting factors. Any present stimulus is capable of serving as both a direct stimulus and a substitute stimulus. For example, interacting directly with a person who comes to "remind" you of your dead grandfather is a case where a direct stimulus may act as a substitute stimulus for another stimulus. This behavioral situation may result in that implicit behavior called "reminiscing." Responding to things and events when they are not present (i.e., responding to "substitute stimuli") constitutes what is called "implicit behavior." Both implicit behaviors and substitute stimuli have their origins in direct contact with things and events. "Pure" thoughts or ideas (uncontaminated by experience) do not exist for interbehaviorists. The "meaning," or, in the language of interbehaviorism, "stimulus function" of any stimulus (or substitute stimulus) is derived from one's past interbehavioral experiences with that stimulus. Implicit behaviors may act as precursors to overt behavior, or may remain strictly implicit. And because it is quite possible to be aware of the implicit behavior of a person one knows intimately, "privacy" is not necessarily a distinguishing feature of implicit behaviors. Of course overt behaviors are capable of being carried out in solitude, and may be quite private (cf. Mahan, 1968, p. 82). Finally, implicit behaviors are on a continuum with overt behaviors, and are regarded as being made up of interactional events just as any overt behaviors are (i.e., they are interbehaviors).

Included among implicit behaviors are (1) knowing behaviors (involving orientation to stimuli) that include conceiving, cognizing, recognizing, appreciating, and understanding interbehaviors; (2) intellectual behaviors, including opinions, attitudes, assumptions, expecting responses, guessing, conjecturing, convincing, postulating, hypothesizing, supposing, believing, disbelieving, and doubting interbehaviors; (3) thinking behaviors that include planning, problem solving, reasoning, abstracting, inferring, predicting, judging, speculating, reflecting, evaluating, explaining, estimating, deciding, choosing and criticizing interbehaviors; (4) memorial behaviors (e.g., Kantor and Smith, 1975) that include remembering and forgetting interbehaviors; (5) imagination behaviors, such as creativity and inventive interbehaviors; (6) imagery behaviors (e.g., eidetic imagery); (7) reminiscing, reverie, daydreaming, and fantasizing interbehaviors; and (8) dreaming interbehaviors. There are also broad classes of implicit behaviors termed "revived"(reliving an experience implicitly, such as during reminiscing), "continuative" (continuing to respond to a stimulus after the stimulus has gone), "incipient" (such as the implicit behaviors that may be involved in repeatedly trying, but failing, to remember someone's name), and "anticipation" interactions.

To appreciate the often times subtle distinctions between the implicit behaviors of "conceiving" versus "planning" or "cognizing" versus "recognizing," one must consult Kantor's (1924, 1926) classification, description and examples of them. Mahan (1968), Kantor and Smith (1975) and Pronko (1980) also provide examples that illustratemany of Kantor's typology of implicit behaviors. As in the case of any classification system, however, it should be realized that there will be some behavioral acts that do not fit neatly into any one category. Kantor (1924, 1926) is very aware of this. The blending of various types of implicit behavior is to be expected, as is the blending of implicit and overt behaviors (such as in a case in which implicit problem solving or imagining responses alternate with overt manipulative acts). In focusing on interactional processes, the interbehavioral perspective on behavior could almost be considered antithetic to the use of discrete categories. In fact, one should (after having understood the reasons behind this first goal or task of any scientific endeavor, namely, classification) pay less attention to categories and more attention to the continuum of interbehavioral events that constitute the authentic data of the science of psychology.

A type of behavior that well illustrates the interrelatedness of implicit and overt behaviors is seen in what has come to be called "perception." Perceiving, as Pronko (1980) has put it, "is a halfway house to implicit behavior" (p. 382). It is an interactional event that involves the preparatory act of attending to a particular stimulus or characteristics of a particular stimulus (an overt behavior), followed by recognition, identification, or discrimination behaviors. Attention may refocus on the stimulus and its characteristics of the original stimulus. This process of attending-discriminating, recognizing-attending-discriminating, recognizing-attending, and so on, is the basis of perceiving interbehaviors. It is, of course, an act that all humans (as well as rats and pigeons) can perform. It may involve any one or, more likely, any combination of the five senses. Individual differences in perceptual behaviors are, when there is nothing organically pathological with the behaving organism, due to contextual factors and the personal behavioral history of the organism.

The interbehavioral position on "intelligence" is simple: There is no such entity. Rather, "it is never anything but a name for the particular way the individual adapts himself to his surroundings" (Kantor, 1924, p. 128). It is an event, and the way any person adapts himself to surrounding circumstances will be a function of that person's behavioral history (cf. Baer, 1970; Bijou, 1968, 1971).

Just as there is no brain-localized structure that generates "powers of intelligence," so, too, is there no brain-localized structure that generates problem solving "abilities." To the interbehaviorist, problem solving is "concerned with the disentanglement of the person from some unsatisfactory situation, the resolution of some perplexity, or the overcoming of a difficulty (Kantor, 1926, p. 173). What type of problem solving strategy is employed, what techniques or methods are used, or whether or not a person even recognizes the presence of a problem, will depend on what stimuli are presented by the problem, the immediate context of the problem solving behavior, and, most importantly, the behavioral history of the individual. Problem solving is usually seen to involve alternating between implicit and overt interbehaviors.

Memorial interbehavior consists of remembering and forgetting behaviors. The former involve nonrepetitive, singular adjustments that are to be carried out at some future point in time. The concept of "forgetting" is used only in reference to remembering behaviors. Since remembering involves performing some behavior in the future, forgetting to perform that act is understood in terms of the organism not interacting with sufficiently meaningful or numerous substitute stimuli that serve as "reminders." Failing to learn nonsense syllables or anything else in experiments involving memorization tasks does not qualify as "forgetting." Instead, it would simply be considered a failure to learn under extremely unusual and contrived circumstances (cf. Kantor, 1926, p. 355), and would examplify "memorization" behaviors, involving the acquisition of behavior for the purpose of repetitively performing certain kinds of actions. Reminiscing is a type of implicit behavior involving responding to past events and is not to be confused with remembering behaviors.

Feeling behaviors derive or are abstracted from an organism interacting with stimuli (direct or substitute) within a specific context. They are not "states" generated by physiological structures, but they do (as do all behaviors) involve the participation of physiologic

273

structures and processes. In fact, very widespread physiological processes are seen to be involved in feeling behaviors (e.g., the interconnected involvement of the autonomic nervous system, glandular systems, and smooth muscles). The distinguishing characteristic of these behaviors is that they are not in themselves overt or "effective": But rather, an "affective." That is, they do not necessarily involve the organism having an effect on the stimulating thing or event with which it is interacting. When the organism experiences a general physiological arousal, but does not have any effect on the stimulating object or event it is interacting with, it may be said to be experiencing rage, guilt, anxiety, aggravation, jealousy, affection, hate, fear, anger, joy, sorrow, embarrassment, indignation, surprise, disappointment, repulsion, and so on (depending on the nature of the stimulus, contextual factors, and the history of the organism). These affective behaviors may, in some cases, be followed by effective (overt) behavior. In such cases , the feeling behaviors would simply precede the effective behaviors. Also, feeling behaviors may follow various types of implicit behaviors. Like implicit behaviors, feeling interbehaviors do not necessarily lead to overt behaviors. Nor do feeling behaviors inevitably lead to implicit behaviors. Contextual factors enter heavily here, especially as regards effective behaviors that follow feeling behaviors (e.g., whether the person you want to punch is alone or with friends, or whether the person hearing your confession is alone or with friends).

Why do individual differences in feeling interbehaviors exist? Again, the interbehavioral history of the individual and setting factors or context are the key variables. Because feeling interbehaviors are easily conditioned and because the range of possible stimulating things and events and contexts in one's behavioral history is so wide, there is necessarily a wide range of individual differences to be found in the area of feeling behaviors (e.g., the intensity of one's feelings, or the things, events or circumstances that make one happy, angry, etc.). At the same time, each individual shares with other members of one's culture, socioeconomic class or sex certain standardized feeling behaviors. Understanding the interrelatedness of these individual and shared factors as they enter into feeling behaviors is necessary for any attempt at understanding what are considered "psychosomatic" and "psychogenic illnesses" (cf. Herrick, 1976).

An equally important, frequently overlooked consideration, is the idea that feeling behaviors are expressed in culturally stylized ways. Some examples are giggling, instead of blushing, when embarrassed; wailing uncontrollably, instead of keeping a stiff upper lip, when grieving; and crying, instead of grinding one's teeth and starting unflinchingly, when enraged These exemplify the varying outward expressions of feeling behaviors. The function of such standardized ways of expressing (or not expressing) feelings is that of communication. The wailing, staring, giggling, or stoic person is trying to convey a culturally appropriate message to another or others. Szasz's (1974) discussion of "hysteria as communication" is especially relevant in this regard. And, although expressions of feelings undoubtedly have bioecological origins, they have long since been shaped, then reshaped, by what has come to be humankind's most important means of adaptation and survival, namely, culture (cf. Andrew, 1963; Kantor , 1959, pp. 49, 85, 86). So overwhelming are factors of culture, immediate context, and the behavioral history of the individual in understanding the development, experiencing and expression of feeling behaviors that it would seem to make any discussions of the organic make-up of individuals superfluous (cf. Kantor and Smith, 1975, p. 230).

When the comedian responds "We all have to be somewhere!" to the question "What are you doing here?" it is not unlike the kind of responses that might be given to the question, "What are the origins of motives?" The answer: "We all have to be doing something!"

During our waking and dreaming hours we are constantly interacting with stimuli and substitute stimuli. Some of these interactions involve our choosing to behave in one way over another or others. For the interbehaviorist, the choices that we make will be a function of contextual factors and our behavioral histories. Why any person is "motivated" to hoard his earnings may be due to a variety of past experiences and present circumstances: Having been broke, wanting to die rich, saving for a prestigious home or car, having no immediate needs for certain material goods, and so on. Why one hungry person resorts to stealing, while another starves himself for a political principle; or why one person embraces interbehaviorism while another totally rejects it can also be understood in terms of personal historical and contextual factors.

The interbehaviorist does not look inside the organism for "energizers," "drives," "motivational , drive or arousal states." Hunger, in the example just given, is but one element (an endogenuous stimulus) in a complex chain of interbehaviors. Nor does the interbeahviorist consider external stimuli to be "determiners" of motivations. Motives are always abstracted from the continuum of interbehaviors carried out by individuals or collections of persons.

### Evolution:  A Public Thoroughfare

What is the point of this discussion of how the interbehaviorist conceives of behavior? It is this: Implicit, perceptual, feeling and motivational behaviors are no more mysterious or arcane than are any overt behavioral acts. Furthermore, these "abilities" do not exist apart

275

from the organism as it engages in interactional behavior. These behaviors (events) do not exist as entitites, and, as such, cannot be possessed by individuals or groups in varying degrees. Understanding these points is one of the most difficult problems for non-interbehaviorists to overcome.

Implicit behaviors, for example, just happen to be among the many behaviors performed well by human beings. And it should be remembered that these behavioral capabilities differ from those of many nonhuman creatures in degree, not kind (cf. Schrier and Stollnitz, 1971). We are, so to speak, "stuck with them" just as we are stuck with bipedal locomotion or nails instead of claws, and just as **electrophorous electricus** is stuck with the equipment to generate an electrical charge. The facility with which we carry out these behaviors has unquestionably been of selective advantage through the ages for a not too strong, fast or ferocious species of primate. Planning ahead, drawing on the past (both of which involve response to stimuli not present), and creating order out of an unorganized universe have, with the help of conceptual and symbolic "tools," been made easier by our being able to behave implicitly. **Sapience,** not truculence, has accounted for our survival into the present. It would be a mistake, however, to think that it was our brains or our nervous systems that caused us to be so clever. Only a bioecological, evolutionary approach to human development will help us understand our behavioral equipment as a species (cf. Kantor, 1947, p. 100).

Our perceptual skills as a species have also contributed to our survival. The emphasis that is placed on visual perceptual processes by researchers is not without significance. A general primate characteristic or tendency is the development of visual equipment (viz., binocular, color, and steroscopic vision) over those of taste, touch, audition and olfaction (Cartmill, 1972). Those implicit behaviors called recognizing, identifying, and discriminating, and the development of the physiologcial equipment required for other types of implicit behaviors no doubt paralleled developments in our organs of vision.

Our species-wide abilities to reason, recognize, discriminate, solve problems, plan ahead, imagine, remember, use concepts and so forth have similarly allowed us to make choices that have contributed to both individual and group survival. Since both individual and group survival are necessary for the continuance of **Homo sapiens,** those behaviors that have permitted the dove-tailing of individually--and socially-oriented "motives" would be seen to be selected for culturally--at least in the cultural past.

Feeling behaviors and the stylized outward expression of them have likewise been of adaptive value to humans. The fact that all cultures have a multitude of concepts designed to describe how we feel under various circumstances is testimony to the value we and our cultural ancestors have placed on being aware of the subtleties of feeling behaviors. Without these concepts, empathy would not be possible. Such behavior has clearly had survival value for the vulnerable social creatures that we are. At the same time, it is this practice of emphathizing through the uses of concepts that is responsible for our having the distinction of being the only creature that may behave inhumanely.

### Racism and Sexism: Academic Dead Ends

Behaving implicitly, our perceptual abilities in the area of vision, making choices, and feeling behaviors have all played a role in our survival as a species. Similarities and differences in how we carry out each of these behaviors is, from the interbehavioral perspective, due to three interrelated factors. The cultural and social matrix within which individuals develop is one of these factors. How problems are solved or plans are made, what one dreams about, what one knows about, what things are recognized, what beliefs are held, the intensity of one's feelings, the stimuli that make one happy, the choices one makes when faced with alternatives, and how one interprets and responds to various things and events that are perceived will all be the product of shared cultural and social learning experiences (Herrick, 1974; Kantor, 1925). Often overlooked contextual factors or the immediate surroundings of the interbehaving organism also influence how these behaviors are carried out. Finally, the personal behavioral history of the organism enters into how that organism interbehaves with stimuli.

It is interesting that only the most unenlightened of the unenlightened in academic or scientific circles would ever seriously entertain the notion that the Australian Aborigines and New Yorkers solve problems, "perceive," or have the feelings they have about various things because of biological factors. Such racist ideas have long since been debunked and would surely be considered signs of ignorance. Similarly, biological or sexist explanations for the behaviors of men and women (e.g., women in our culture are generally aware of more colors than men, while men are generally aware of more automobile makes) would be frowned upon, although I suspect with less vehemence. But in the area of understanding differences and similarities in individual behavior, biological explanations are tolerated, and much more. The rule seems to be as follows: Where groups (e.g., races, ethnic groups, cultures, men and women) of people are concerned, biological explanations for behavior are perfectly respectable    There is one notable exception to this rule: The aged.

277

It is still acceptable to understand complex behaviors in later life both in terms of individual biologically-based explanations as well as group biologically-based explanations.

## Green Lights for Elitism and Ageism

In the real world, racist, sexist, and other group superiority-inferiority themes, as well as biological explanations for individual differences and similarities, reign supreme. Hsu (1972) explains this by pointing to the fact that we are a people who militantly defend our self-reliance, want to succeed on an individual basis in a highly competitive stratefied society, but are forced into conforming to the bigoted attitude held by those above us who have already eliminated economic competition on arbitrary bases (such as on the basis of skin color, sex, or some other biological trait). Our quest for status and our desire to elimiante competition, therefore, make us willing subscribers to group superiority themes. These same factors make biological explanations for human behavior on the individual level sound reasonable--especially when one is competing with someone of one's own race, sex, age, etc. But what about those academicians and social-behavioral scientists who steadfastly cling to the idea that there are biological causes for intelligence, perception, problem solving, emotions or feelings, reasoning, and so forth on the individual level and, in the case of the elderly, on the group level? Is it simply due to their being members of a Western, industrial-capitalist society? If what Hsu (1972) is saying is correct, this could be part of the answer, although such beliefs are equally popular among our comrades in socialist states. Were I not an interbehaviorist, I might credit such elitist attitudes to "basic human nature." Because I am an interbehaviorist, I suggest that such beliefs are held by the majority of academicians and scientists in societies of all economic and political bents because they areself-serving. That is, these beliefs serve to justify their exhalted positions in the social hierarchy and are, in short, merely further examples of arbitrary and contrived ways of preserving or enhancing social status. Clearly, personal and social "motives" have not yet blended in this area. And whenever personal motives take precedence over social motives, society as a whole becomes a little less efficient as a mechanism of survival. In the case of elitism, we all lose as a result of the waste of human resources.

Harris (1968) has used the term "scientific racism" to describe early attempts by certain social theorists (e.g., Spencer) to appear scientific through the use of biological and evolutionary explanations for complex human behaviors, as well as to justify and rationalize the social position of the bourgeoisie. As mentioned in the introduction of this chapter, I have suggested use of the expression "scientific ageism" to describe the assumptions held by geropsychologists that behavioral

278

incompetence necessarily accompanies biological changes in later life. Here, too, we find an appeal to biology for the sake of gaining scientific respectability. In the case of scientific ageism, however, it is the superior position of the "young" (along with the tacit superiority of those conducting the research) that is being rationalized and justified.

Serving as a backdrop to scientific ageism is what might be called "folk ageism." Folk ageist beliefs receive much support from (1) the relativistic nature of the terms "young" and "old"; (2) the familiar device of attending to only those characteristics that verify the inferiority or incompetence of the aged--a common practice accompanying stereotyping and prejudice; (3) adherence of the elderly themselves to negative images regarding the aged (cf. Harris and Associates, 1975); (4) an economic system that requires constant expansion and breeds a "throw away" mentality; (5) the myth that older workers are less productive (cf. McFarland, 1943); (6) the post-World War II practice of dumping elderly psyciatric patients in nursing homes, which bolstered the incompetent image of the institutionalized elderly (cf. Kahn, 1975); and (7) the role playing and self-fulfilling prophecy aspects of behavioral incompetence among the elderly (e.g., Kuypers and Bengtson, 1973).

### Biological Explanations for Behavior: Construction of the "Inner State" System

Understanding the cultural-historical roots and development of the idea that individual differences and similarities in behavior are the direct or indirect products of biological structures is made easy thanks to the work of Kantor (1947, 1963, 1969; cf. Mountjoy, 1966, 1970). From 5th century Augustine to the present, the history of psychology has been tainted with theories and constructs derived from what had been a strictly theological approach to understanding human behavior. The unknowable (except through introspection) soul principle of Augustine was, over a period of 800 years, gradually allowed to be joined with the body by St. Thomas Acquinas. As social and economic conditions slowly improved in Europe, Descartes made bolder connections between the spirit or mind and the body or brain. The Renaissance found Leibniz and Spinoza arguing that is was possible for a non-spatial, nontemporal soul or mind to interact with the material body through their doctrines of "parallelism" and the "double aspect theory. As the 17th, 18th, and 19th centuries further molded internal determiners of behavior, the institution of science continued to rise, and these internal determiners of behavior were ultimately reduced to hypothetical biological structures located in the new seat of the soul:The brain.

Most of today's psychologists persist in searching for ways of indirectly knowing about these various internal determiners of behavior (e.g., "associated machinery," "mental, cognitive, or central structures") that are housed in our brains and which manifest themselves through our "mental-cognitive," "process-states" and ultimately through our behaviors. It is believed that differences in these brain-localized, biological structures lead to differences in brain-generated "processes" or "states" that in turn lead to differences in performances on intelligence tests, in problem solving, in reaction times, in perception, in the rates at which individuals learn, in how well one remembers or forgets, in the feelings and the intensity of the feelings one experiences and expresses, in how creative or talented one is, or why a person has the personality he or she has. And because traditional psychologists continue to approach behavior from the standpoint of it being the product of experience as mediated or determined by brain-localized structures (things), it is not surprising to find them conceiving of various implicit and overt behaviors (events) as also being "things." For example, "cognitive structures" are believed to house "memories," "personality," "consciousness," "intelligence," "learning abilities," "creativity," "emotional states," "drives," and other constructs that have been contrived and reified through the ages. Since these entities are contained in biological structures, it is perfectly logical to expect them to decline as the biological structures within which they reside begin to deteriorate It is precisely upon this unwarrented assumption that the foundation for scientific ageism is built. It will be seen that this underlying assumption has further spawned a strange blending of observations and equally ill-founded assumptions that have become the stuff of which geropsychological research is made.

## Following the Yellow Brick Road

Much of the confusion that many of us have come to associate with the "minds" of the aged is, from the interbehavioral viewpoint, better placed within the minds of those who study them. For example, consider the following combinations of fact and fancy.

(A). Assumption: Biological , brain-localized structures mediate or determine "cognitive-processes" and, ultimately, overt behavior.

(B). Observation: Biological changes (particularly declines in functioning) occur in later life as a result of the normal aging process or senescence (such as the heart, lungs, kidneys).

(C). Assumption: Biological structures of the brain undergo declines in functioning just as other organs do during senescence, with this resulting in declines in "cognitive processes" mediated or determined by these structures.

(D). Observation: Senility or senile dementia occurs among some elderly persons.

(E). Assumption: Senility is but one end of a continuum of behavioral incompetence that begins in later life and increases insidiously · during the normal aging process.

(F). Observation: Psychogerontological research indicates that there are decreases in learning ability, perceptual ability, memory, hunger and sex drives, motivational levels, emotions, creativity, and intelligence among elderly subjects.

## Speed Limits

As discussed above, Assumption (A) is the product of transforming animistic, internal determiners of behavior into more scientific-sounding brain-localized structures that serve the same purpose. Both look for explanations for complex behaviors that come from within the organism, while little or no consideration is given to factors of context and the behavioral history of the behaving organism as it interacts with stimuli--the only factors that are of interest to the interbehaviorist.

Observation (B) is largely the product of Shock (1961, 1962, 1970; cf. Kantor, 1947, pp. 282-288), Birren , Butler, Greenhouse, Sokoloff and Yarrow (1963) and Palmore's (1970) research.     Age-related decreases incardiac output, vascular system funcitoning, maximal lung ventilation, aerobic capacity, muscular strength and fatigue, immune and endocrine system functioning, glucose tolerance, digestive system functioning, and nervous system functioning are well-documented. However, de Vries (1975) contends that dysfunctionings are declines in these areas may be due to factors other than age.    Inactivity or "hypokinetic disease" and unrecognized, incipient disease may also account for much of the observed declines.    Still, decreases in physiological funcitoning apart from disease, unrecognized disease, and inactivity seem inevitable during the middle and later years of one's life.  Stressful circumstances only make these declines in functioning more marked.

Assumption (C) is helped along by Assumption (A) and that part of Observation (B) dealing with declines in  nervous system functioning as it relates to reaction time.   Decreases in nervous system functioning is, in turn, believed to be related to cardiovascular impairments. Declines in cardiovascular, then,  are thought to account not only for the slowing of reaction time or "sensorimotor" performance, but also for declines in perceptual, problem solving, intellectual and memory functionings (cf. Birren and Spieth, 1962; Botwinick, Robbin and Brinley, 1959; Gerard, 1959; Simonson and Anderson, 1966; Walsh, 1976;

Welford, 1958, 1959).

There are attempts at accounting for these slowed responses or "cautiousness" behaviors observed during tests of reaction time through discussions of "arousal levels"--i.e., the supposed physiological correlates of "motivation" and "anxiety" which act to disrupt "cognitive processes." Heart rate changes as levels of attention change (Morris and Thompson, 1969), levels of free fatty acid mobilization into the blood plasma (Troyer, Eisdorfer, Wilkie and Bogdonoff, 1966), slowed alpha wave frequency (Busse and Obrist, 1965; Wang and Busse, 1969), and reticular system responding as it affects cortical activity and arousal ("motivational") levels (Obrist, 1965) are among such attempts. All of these reductionistic approaches designed to explain reaction times, decreased sensorimotor performance and, ultimately, cognitive or intellectual impairment among the aged imply the involvement of as yet unknown and undemonstrated structures of the central nervous system.

Interbehaviorism does not reduce complex behaviors to discussions of the nervous system, the brain, or the supposed physiological correlates of motivational or arousal "states." These physiological structures and processes, as do other interrelated physiological systems (e.g., the vascular or endocrine systems), merely participate in the whole of the psychological event. They do not cause or mediate behavior. Attempts at correlating "sensorimotor" measurements with "cognitive/central processes" may be seen as being more scientific-sounding ways of saying that there are internal structures or entities which largely or wholly determine human behavior.

From the interbehavioral perspective, factors other than deterioration or interference with cognitive structures would account for the slowed "sensorimotor," "intellectual," or "cognitive" performances observed among elderly subjects. Since biological structures do participate in all behavioral events, the role of hearing (presbyacusis) and visual (presbyopia and incipient cataracts) losses among elderly experimental subjects might well be significant factors in explaining slowed responses. Decreases in muscle size and strength (both the inevitable result of senescence, as well as forced or voluntary inactivity) would certainly affect muscular coordination. Muscle deterioration also affects retinal adjustments. Any so-called "noncognitive" factors of over-or under-arousal would be functions of (1) past behavioral experiences of the subject and (2) present contextual factors. It is these two factors--not hypothetical brain- or gland-generated arousal or motivational "states"-- that influence how an elderly person or any person performs on tests of reaction time. As for the more marked increases in reaction time when "cognitive organizing or reorganizing" is supposedly required by the task, there are a host of contextual, behavioral-historical, and generational variables that could be used to explain these poorer performances. Geropsychologists ignore, or assign only supplemental roles to these "noncognitive" variables (cf.Eisdorfer, 1968), and persist in talking about the supposed malfunctionings of hypothetical cognitive structures existing inside the heads of their elderly subjects. Even de Vries, who has made such a significant contribution by dispelling the myth that large declines in physiological functionings among the elderly are due to the aging process alone, succumbs to the myth of deteriorating cognitive structures in the heads of the elderly. For him, improvements in intellectual performance among elderly subjects that exercised was due to "central stimulation" (de Vries, 1970).

Geropsychological researchers also persist in designing newer and better strategies that will conclusively support the long held contention that intellectual "abilities" decline among the elderly. Most damaging in this area is their blind acceptance of Horn and Cattell's (1967) pronouncement that there exist two distinct kinds of intelligence. One, called "crystallized intelligence," is the product of learning. The other, called "fluid intelligence" is rooted in physiological structures, involves the ability to "reorganize perceptions," and may or may not be contaminated by experience--a watery theory, indeed. Even the most outspoken critics of theories of intellectual decline in later life are seen to apologize for not adequately dealing with fluid intelligence in their studies (cf. Nesselroade, Schaie and Baltes, 1972).

And what to do about the observation that scores on intelligence tests measuring verbal "mental abilities" remain the same or increase in later life (Bayley, 1968; Owens, 1963), while those measuring performance (e.g., visual-motor performance) show declines? Could it be that the same auditory, visual and muscular coordination problems resulting from senescence, inactivity or unrecognized disease might account for poorer performance by elderly subjects on intelligence tests where speed of responses, perceptual behaviors, and manipulative skills are required to obtain a good score? The answer is an emphatic "yes," but because it is believed that sensorimotor (e.g., visual-motor) behaviors are merely correlates or reflections of what is going on inside elderly subjects' heads. Again, factors such as sensory impairment, atrophying musculature, intimidating experimental conditions, and generational differences are viewed as constituting "noncognitive" variables that affect genuine declines in cognitive functionings. For the interbehaviorist, such noncognitive factors suffice in explaining both good and poor performances on so-called tests of intelligence.

# Taking the Senile Route

It would seem that in the area of senility, Observation (D), we would be dealing with an irrefutable case of dysfunctioning, brain-localized structures giving rise to disorganized cognitive processes or mental processes. So strong, in fact, is the cultural association between brain deterioration and the behavioral characteristics of senile psychosis (e.g., memory loss, disorganization, impairment of intellectual functions, depression, emotional lability, hallucinations, paranoid tendencies, incoherent speech, etc.) that to suggest that biological factors merely participate in these behaviors may sound like some sort of interbehavioral quixotism. Nevertheless, brain degeneration would merely participate in senile psychosis. And it should be realized that there are those who contend that much of what has been credited to arteriosclerosis of the brain is, in reality, a functional disorder resulting from what is commonly (though incorrectly) called an "emotional breakdown" (Oberleder, 1969). Of course the "functional" versus "organic" distinction has less significance for the interbehaviorist since there are biological (healthy or pathologic) participants in all behaviors. However, the spirit of Oberleder's (1969) point is supported by the often ignored fact that there are studies which demonstrate no strong relationships between visible brain changes and behavioral functioning in the aged (Blessed, Tomlinson and Martin, 1968; Busse and Wang, 1974; Kieve, Chapman, Gutherie and Wolff, 1962; Zarit and Kahn, 1975). Of much more importance to the interbehaviorist than the amount of brain tissue lost or the rapidity of brain cell loss would be the individual's behavioral history and contextual factors (the complexity and friendliness of the environment) as they influence how the elderly, potentially brain damaged, person behaves.

Among the complications are the fine and sometimes contrived distinctions that are made between "acute" organic brain sydromes (said to be reversible and resulting from stressful circumstances, strokes, medications, malnutrition and congestive heart failure) and "chronic organic brain syndromes (said to be irreversible and resulting from arteriosclerosis in later life), and the mistaking of the former for the latter among elderly persons. The labeling of the elderly person suffering from acute brain syndrome "senile" would undoubtedly have disastrous consequences in regards to any therapeutic measures taken or not taken. The notion that chronic brain syndrome exists only when therapeutic measures are forsaken is an intriguing one. Kahn's (1965) observation that institutionalized elderly persons behave at a level considerably below that which they are capable, as well as Kuyper and Bengtson's (1973) contention that much behavioral incompetence among the elderly is due to their succumbing to negative labeling by others, only adds to the multiplicity of contextual factors that may contribute to many of those disorganized behaviors

284

exhibited by the aged that have been traditionally credited to brain damage or deterioration.

Depression is the functional illness that is both most prevalent and most likely to occur in later life (Butler and Lewis, 1973). For the interbehaviorist, depressive behaviors constitute "moods." Moods are characterized as being unorganized affective or feeling responses that are not directed toward any specific stimuli (Kantor and Smith, 1975). Like all other behaviors, they are to be understood as resulting from interactions with stimuli (vaguely defined in this case) within particular contexts). The behavioral history of the individual is critical to understanding what mood is being experienced and why it is being experienced. For many of the elderly (86% of 65+ persons have at least one chronic condition), constant interaction with endogenous stimuli accompanying various chronic illnesses might well serve as reminders (i.e., substitute stimuli) of one's declining health (and the independence that good health connotes) or impending death. Feelings of despair, hopelessness or anger might then carry over into every aspect of one's life, and the result is chronic depression. Others, who have developed adaptive strategies throughout their lives for dealing with the problems of living, might not be depressed at all. Or perhaps every stimulating thing and event in an elderly person's social environment reminds him or her that the days of independence, self-worth adn social worth have left forever (cf. Clark and Anderson, 1967). Of course such depressive moods may occur at any age. Their prevalence among the elderly says much more about their place in society than it does about their brains or glands. The prevalence of hypochondriasis, anxiety neurosis, and suicide (especially among white, elderly males) in later life does likewise (cf. Busse and Pfeiffer, 1977; Butler, 1975).

Declinirg or disorganized emotional responses are among the behaviors incorrectly linked with both chronic brain syndrome and old age in general. Descriptions of the senile personality often include stubborness, irritability, as well as depression and emotional withdrawal. "Childish" is the most frequently used folk expression. It is, of course, as patently absurd to say that stubborness or irritability are caused by brain or gland deterioration or the aging process as it is to say that such behaviors are caused by the brains or glands of anyone at any age. Only recently have the myths regarding both the emotional physical symptoms of menopause been debunked (Boston's Women's Health Book Collective, 1976). It was concluded that the important variables in understanding what a women experiences during menopause were current circumstances (context) and the behavioral history of the individual.

The interbehaviorist would say that irritability and stubborness behaviors derive form contextual factors and one's behavioral history. A stubborn or irritable child may be reacting to his present circumstances(another person making demands) in relation to his past behaviors (rarely having to comply with others' demands). Stubborness and irritability among aged persons should also be understood in terms of contextual and behavioral historical factors. Stubborness, for example, might well be a reasonable behavioral response in certain contexts, such as when an adult child assumes the role of parent to his aged parent . In fact, these contextual and behavioral historical circumstances are quite common to the elderly. And if the overt expression of feeling behaviors has the function of communication, perhaps the irritability exhibited by elderly (or any) persons is an exaggerated attempt to convey a message to someone not in the habit of listening to less dramatic forms of communication. On the other hand, Dean's (1962) conclusion that elderly people show declines in their ability to exhibit such emotional responses as irritation and anger supports the idea tht all sorts of communication demand a listener. No listener, no attempt to communciate via stylized expressions of feelings. No communication, no empathy. No empathy, no humanity.

Since biological aging is a gradual process, and since senility is thought to be "caused" by the deterioration of structures inside the brains of elderly persons, it is not unreasonable to assume that one gradually eases into senility. If the cardiovascular system declines in functioning at approximately one percent per year after the age of 20, and if the cardiovascular system is directly responsible for deterioration of the brain (which then generates impaired "cognitive processes"), then perhaps one becomes increasingly senile at the rate of one percent per year after the age of 20. It might be thought that such reasoning (Assumption E) would more likely be found at the level of folk ageism, **vis a vis** scientific ageism. But if one looks closely at other assumptions, derived from Observation F, it will be discovered that many of our psychogerontologists are, in essence, searching for support or proof for a similar conclusion. Their application of a medical model to phenomena requiring a behavioral model is certainly responsible for this (cf. Szasz, 1974), but such a model seems perfectly appropriate to them in light of their accepting Assumptions A and C.

The traditional approach to "memory," especially as "it" relates to the behavior of elderly persons, will serve as a final example of how these erroneous assumptions and conclusions have operated.

## Memory Lane

Geropsychological research in the area of "memory" and aging is so laden with unfounded assumptions that one would do well to forget it.

286

There is talk of "information-processing" as it is involved in "primary" (when the retained material is still in mind and has undergone phonemic encoding only) and "secondary" (the organized and structured storage of semantically encoded material) memory--with the elderly having greater difficulty retrieving information in the latter (Botwinick and Storandt, 1974; Schoenfield and Robertson,1966; Waugh and Norman, 1965). Some (Atkinson and Shiffrin, 1971) believe that it is the "executive function" of the brain that moves information between one type of memory to the other and is responsible for these difficulties in secondary memory. Others speak of "perceptually processed" memory "traces" that are not processed at sufficient depths--with this resulting in secondary memory deficits among the elderly (Craik and Lockhardt, 1972). In paired-associate and serial learning tasks--tasks involving memorization or learning behaviors--deficits among elderly subjects were initially viewed as being the result of defective "associative machinery" (Gilbert, 1941). Many are now willing to accept the idea that certain "noncognitive" factors may account for or, more commonly, contribute to poor performances on these tasks by elderly subjects (Arenberg, 1965; Botwinick, 1973). Pacing variables (Canestrari, 1963), arousal levels (Eisdorfer, 1968; Powell, Eisdorfer and Bogdonoff, 1964) , the effects of using mediators (Canestrari, 1968) and "meaningfulness" of the information to be learned or memorized (Shmavonian and Busse, 1963) are included among these so-called noncognitive variables.

It will be remembered that for the interbehaviorist memorial behaviors involve carrying out or not carrying out behavior at some future point in time. Remebering is facilitated by the presence of substitute stimuli (stimuli not present that serve as "reminders"), while forgetting is understood in terms of having inadequate substitute stimuli in one's surroundings. And although there is most certainly physiological participation in memorial behaviors, "memories" are not viewed as being **things** that may be stored or processed anywhere. If anything, they are abstracted from interactional behavioral processes. Memories, in short, are **events.**

Experiments designed to test the "memories" of elderly subjects mainly involve memorization (which, unlike remembering and forgetting behaviors, involves behavior acquisition or learning behaviors) of words or nonsense syllables. In the case of nonsense syllables, it is worth noting that many elderly subjects have voiced the opinion that learning nonsense syllables is so much nonsense (Hulicka, 1967).

Performance on memorization tasks improves for elderly subjects when meaningfulness of stimuli increases; but, overall, they perform at a level below that of younger subjects. In addition, performance deficits may be accounted for by factors of context (e.g., intimidating experimenal conditions, or a very young experimenter) and behavioral history (e.g., having read that one's memory fails in later life and then becoming so preoccupied with wondering how much loss will show up on the test that one is uanble to concentrate on the stimuli being presented). The fact that the "younger" subjects used for comparison in such tests are nearly always college students is also significant. Perhaps their many recent experiences with having to memorize, or their recent experiences with having to compete with others for test scores contribute to the students' superior performances. The elderly, therefore, may simply be poor learners under contrived experimental conditions.

Not helping matters for the elderly are the "memory" problems encountered by the very few (5%) of those who are correctly or incorrectly diagnosed as being senile. It appears that geropsychologists are unwilling to separate pathological physiological structures that participate in the pathological behaviors sometimes exhibited by "senile" elderly persons from the memorial behaviors carried out by the very many elderly persons who are not considered to be senile. Again, this is a reflection of the widely held belief that "cognitive" incompetence is an inevitable and insidious process resulting from normal biological aging.

Contributions to both folk and scientific ageist attitudes toward the elderly is the fact that the elderly have a much better chance of living either highly structured or highly unstructured lives . The former case makes "reminders" or attending to reminders obsolete, while the latter produces few reminders or substitute stimuli (e.g., not having constantly to be looking at clocks or calenders). Fewer reminders leads to more forgetting, with more forgetting being used to support the folk and scientific beliefs that one's memory gradually fails in later life.

### Road Closed for Repairs

Since this is a radical reassessment in psychology, my radical reassessment is this: Because there is so much confusion and contradictory evidence resulting from geropsychological research, perhaps the fundamental assumptions from which researchers in this field proceed have been incorrect all along. That is, perhaps behavioral or "cognitive" incompetence (however one wishes to measure these nonexistent "abilities") has nothing whatsoever to do with the age of an individual's brain. If this is so, and I believe it is, it could be considered both unethical and immoral to continue conducting research in this area. Continued support of such research through public or private funds should be recognized as being no less a case of institutional ageism than is mandatory retirement. Unlike institutional racism, institutional ageism is made only that much more pervasive by the fact that our cherished institution of science is lending its considerable authority and prestige to what amounts to the sanctioning of negative stereotypes toward the aged.

The road to scientific ageism must be closed. Instead of giving monies to researchers intent on discovering the degree to which "mental" incompetence increases in later life, we would do well to channel these funds, however small, to the large percentage of elderly persons hovering near the poverty level--especially unmarried men and women. If social-behavioral scientific research must be carried out, let it be directed at repairing the damage done to the economic and social positions of the elderly by both folk and scientific ageist beliefs.

## References

Andrew, R.J. 1963. Evolution of facial expression. **Science**, 142, 1034-1041.

Arenberg, D. 1965. Anticipation interval and age differences in verbal learning. **Journal of Abnormal Psychology**, 70, 419-425.

Atkinson, R.C. and Shiffrin, R.M. 1968. Human memory: A proposed system and its control processes. In K.W.Spence and J.T. Spence (Eds.) **Advances in the Psychology of Learning and Motivation Research and Theory** (Vol. 2). New Jersey: Prentice-Hall.

Baer, D.M. 1970. An age-irrelevant concept of development. **Merrill-Palmer Quarterly of Behavior and Development**, 16, 238-245.

Bayley, N. 1968. Cognition and aging. In K.W. Schaie (Ed.) **Theory and Methods of Research on Aging**, Morgantown, West Virginia: West Virginia University Press.

Bijou, S.W. 1971. Environment and intelligence: A behavioral analysis. In R. Cancro (Ed.) **Intelligence: Genetic and Environmental Influences.** New York: Grune and Stratton.

Birren, J.E., Butler, R.N., Greenhouse, S.W. Sokoloff, L. and Yarrow, M.R. 1963. **Human Aging: A Biological and Behavioral Study.** Washington, D.C.: Government Printing Office.

Birren, J.E. and Spieth, W. 1962. Age, response speed, and cardiovascular functions. **Journal of Gerontology**, 17, 390-391.

289

Bleesed, G., Tomlinson, B.E. and Ruth, M. 1968. The association between quantitative measures of dementia and senile change in the cerebral grey matter of elderly subjects. **British Journal of Psychology,** 114, 797-811.

Boston Women's Health Book Collective. 1976. **Our Bodies, Ourselves.** New York: Simon and Schuster.

Botwinick,J. 1973. **Aging and Behavior.** New York: Springer.

Botwinick, J. , Robbin, J.S. and Brinely, J.F. 1959. Reorganization of perception with age. **Journal of Gerontology,** 14, 85-88.

Botwinick, J. and Storandt, M. 1974. Cardiovascular status, depressive affect, and other factors in reaction time. **Journal of Gerontology,** 29, 543-548.

Busse, E.W. and Obrist, W.D. 1965. Pre-senescent electro-encephalographic changes in normal subjects. **Journal of Gerontology,** 20, 315-320.

Busse, E.W. and Pfeiffer, E. 1977. Functional psychiatric disorders in old age. In E.W. Busse and E. Pfeiffer (Eds.) **Behavior and Adaptation in Late Life** (2nd edition). Boston: Little, Brown and Co.

Busse, E.W. and Wang, H. 1974. The multiple factors contributing to dementia in old age. In E. Palmore (Ed.) **Normal Aging II: Reports from the Duke Longitudinal Study,** 1955-1969. Durham, N.C.: Duke University Press.

Butler, R.N. 1975. **Why Survive? Being Old in America.** New York: Harper and Row.

Butler, R.N. and Lewis, M.I. 1973. **Aging and Mental Health.** Saint Louis, Missouri: C.V. Mosby.

Canestrari, R.E. 1963. Paced and self-paced learning in young and elderly adults. **Journal of Gerontology,** 18, 165-168.

Canestrari, R.E. 1968. Age changes in acquisition. In G.A. Talland (Ed.) **Human Aging and Behavior.** New York: Academic Press.

Carmill, M. 1972. Arboreal adaptations and the origins of the order primates. In R.H. Tuttle (Ed.) **The Functional and Evolutionary Biology of Primates.** Chicago: Aldine-Atherton.

Clark, M. and Anderson, B. 1967. **Culture and Aging.** Springfield, Illinois: Charles C. Thomas.

Craik, F.I. and Lockhart. T.S. 1972. Level of processing: A framework for memory research. **Journal of Verbal Learning and Verbal Behavior**, 11, 671-684.

Dean, L.R. 1962. Aging and decline in affect. **Journal of Gerontology**, 25, 325-336.

de Vries, H.A. 1975. Physiology of exercise and aging. In D.S. Woodruff and J.E. Birren (Eds.) Aging: **Scientific Perspectives and Social Issues.** New York: D.Van Nostrand.

Eisdorfer, C. 1968. Arousal and performance: Experiments in verbal learning and a tentative theory. In G.A. Talland (Ed.) **Human Aging and Behavior.** New York: Academic Press.

Gerard, R.W. 1959. Aging and organization. In J.E. Birren (Ed). **Handbook of Aging and the Individual.** Chicago: University of Chicago Press.

Gibson, K.R. 1970. Review of **The Scientific Evolution of Psychology (Vol. 2),** Granville, Ohio: Principia, 1969. In **Journal of the History of the Behavioral Sciences,** 6, 201-203.

Gilbert, J.G. 1941. Memory loss in senescence **Journal of Abnormal and Social Psychology,** 36, 73-86.

Harris, L. and Associates. 1975. **The Myth and Reality of Aging in America.** Washington, D.C.: National Council on Aging.

Harris, M. 1968. **The Rise of Anthropological Theory.** New York: Thomas Y. Crowell.

Herrick, J.W. 1974. Kantor's anticipations of current approaches to anthropology. **Psychological Record,** 24, 253-257.

Herrick, J.W. 1976. Placebos, psychosomatic and psychogenic illnesses and psychotherapy: Their theorized cross-cultural development. **Psychological Record,** 26, 327-342.

Herrick, J.W. 1981. Interbehavioral perspectives on aging. **International Journal of Aging and Human Development,** in press.

Horn, J.L. and Cattell, R.B. 1967. Age differences in fluid and crystallized intelligence. **Acta Psychologica,** 26, 107-129.

Hsu, F.L. 1972. American core value and national character. In F.L. Hsu (Ed.) **Psychological Anthropology.** Cambridge, Mass.: Schenkman.

Hulicka, I.M. 1967. Age differences in retention as a function of interference. Journal of Gerontology, 22, 180-184.

Jensen, A.R. 1969. How much can we boost I.Q. and scholastic achievement? Harvard Educational Review, 39, 180-184.

Kahn, R.L. 1965. Mental Impairment in the Aged. Philadelphia: Philadelphia Geriatric Center.

Kahn, R.L. 1975. The mental health system and the future aged. The Gerontologist, 15, 24-31.

Kantor, J.R. 1924. Principles of Psychology (Vol. 1). New York: Knopf.

Kantor, J.R. 1925. Anthropology, race, psychology, and culture. American Anthropologist, 27, 267-283.

Kantor, J.R. 1926. Principles of Psychology (Vol. 2). New York: Knopf.

Kantor, J.R. 1947. Problems of Physiological Psychology. Bloomington, Indiana: Principia Press.

Kantor, J.R. 1959. Interbehavioral Psychology. Bloomington, Indiana: Principia Press.

Kantor, J.R. 1963. The Scientific Evolution of Psychology (Vol. 1). Chicago: Principia Press.

Kantor, J. R. 1969. The Scientific Evolution of Psychology (Vol. 2). Chicago: Principia Press.

Kantor, J.R. and Smith, N.W. 1975. The Science of Psychology: An Interbehavioral Survey. Chicago: Principia Press.

Kiev, A., Champman, L.F., Gutherie, T.C. and Wolff, H.G. 1962. The highest integrative functions and diffuse cerebral atrophy. Neurology, 12, 384-393.

Kuypers, J.A. and Bengston, V.L. 1973. Social breakdown and competence: A model of normal aging. Human Development, 16, 181-201.

Mahan, H.C. 1968. The Interactional Psychology of J.R. Kantor: An Introduction. San Marcos, California: Project Socrates Press, Palomar College.

Maruyama, M. 1974. Paradigmatology and its application to cross-disciplinary, cross-professional and cross-cultural communication. **Cybernetica**, 17, 136, 205.

McFarland, R.A. 1943. The older worker in industry. **Harvard Business Review**, Summer, 505-510.

Morris, J.D. and Thompson, L.W. 1969. Heart rate changes in a reaction time experiment with young and aged subjects. **Journal of Gerontology**, 24, 269-275.

Mountjoy, P.T. 1966. New dimensions in the history of psychology. **Journal of the Scientific Laboratories, Dension University,** 47, 5-12.

Mountjoy, P.T. 1970. New dimensions in the history of psychology II: A review. **Journal of the Scientific Laboratories, Dension University,** 51, 1-8.

Nesselroade, J.R., Schaie, K.W. and Baltes, P.B. 1972. Ontogenetic and genetic and generational components of structural and quantitative change in adult cognitive behavior. **Journal of Gerontology**, 27, 222-228.

Oberleder, M. 1969. Emotional breakdowns in elderly people. **Hospital and Community Psyciatry**, 20, 21-26.

Obrist, W.D. 1965. Electroencephalographic approach to age changes in response speed. In A.T. Welford and J.E. Birren (Eds.) **Behavior, Aging, and the Nervous System.** Springfield, Illinois: Charles C. Thomas.

Owens, W.A. 1963. Age and mental abilities: A longitudinal study. **Genetic Psychology Monographs,** 48, 3-54.

Palmore, E. 1970. **Normal Aging: Report from the Duke Longitudinal Study, 1955-1969.** Durhma, N.C.: Duke University Press.

Powell, A.H., Eisdorfer, C. and Bogdonoff, M.D. 1964. Physiologic response patterns observed in a learnign task. **Archives of General Psyciatry**, 10, 192-195.

Pronko, N.H. 1980. **Psychology from the Standpoint of an Interbehaviorist.** Monterey, California: Brooks/Cole.

Schoenfield, D. and Robertson, E.H. 1966. Memory storage and aging. **Canadian Journal of Psychology**, 20, 228-236.

Schrier, A. and Stollnitz, F. 1971. **Behavior in Nonhuman Primates.** New York: Academic Press.

Shmavonian, B.M. and Busse, E.W. 1963. The utilization of psycho-physiological techniques in the study of the aged. In R.H. Williams, C. Tibbits and W. Donahue (Eds.) **Process of Aging: Social and Psychological Perspectives.** New York: Atherton.

Shock, N.W. 1961. Physiological aspects of aging. **Annual Review of Physiology,** 23, 97-122.

Shock, N.W. 1962. The physiology of aging. **Scientific American,** 206, 100.

Shock, N.W. 1970. Physiologic aspects of aging. **Journal of the American Diet Association** , 56, 491-496.

Simonson, E. and Anderson, D. A. 1966. Effect of age and coronary heart disease on performance and physiological response in mental work. **Proceedings of the Seventh International Congress on Gerontology,** Vienna, Paper no. 279.

Szasz, T.S. 1974. **The Myth of Mental Illness: Foundations of a Theory of Personal Conduct** (revised edition). New York: Harper and Row.

Troyer, W.G., Eisdorfer, C., Wilkie, F. and Bogdonoff, M.D. 1966. Free fatty acid responses in the aged individual during performance on learning tasks. **Journal of Gerontology,** 21, 415-419.

Walsh, D.A. 1976. Age differences in central perceptual processing: A dichoptic backward masking investigation. **Journal of Gerontology,** 31, 175-185.

Wang, H.S. and Busse,E.W. 1969. EEG of healthy old persons--A longitudinal study: I. Dominant background activity and occipital rhythm. **Journal of Gerontology,** 24, 419-426 .

Waugh, N.C. and Norman, D.A. 1965. Primary memory. **Psychological Review,** 72, 89-104.

Welford, A.T. 1958. **Ageing and Human Skill.** London: Oxford University Press.

Welford, A.T. 1959. Psychomotor performance. In J.E. Birren (Ed.) **Handbook of Aging and the Individual.** Chicago: University of Chicago Press.

Zarit, S.H. and Kahn, R.L. 1975. Aging and adaptation to illness. *Journal of Gerontology*, 30, 67-72.

# Part 3

# INTERBEHAVIORAL IMPLICATIONS FOR
OTHER DISCIPLINES

# AN INTERBEHAVIORAL AND HISTORICO-CRITICAL EXAMINATION OF ANTHROPOLOGY, ETHOLOGY, AND SOCIOLOGY

Michael H. MacRoberts

Barbara R. MacRoberts

Kantor's theme is that science has to be built upon naturalistic principles. This means that scientific work must begin with objects and events and in building constructions must not add to, change, abandon, or deviated from them. Unfortunately scientists do not always do this. Kantor's interest in the disjunction between objects and events and constructions purportedly built for their description has led to his interest in scientific and cultural history, for it is in the cultural past that Kantor has discovered the source of these divagations.

From a recognition of a hiatus between constructions and events and of the fact that much of prevailing wisdom consists primarily of traditional pronouncements, Kantor has not only developed a scientific psychology but a philosophy of science as well. Interbehaviorism is the result for psychology but the ramifications of interbehaviorism, as Kantor has shown (1953, 1959, 1981) are much wider. Interbehaviorism is what many philosophers of science and scientists-turned-philosopher might have articulated long ago had they not been prevented from doing so by their acceptance of culturally-derived ideas about sensation, knowing, being, mind, logic, and so on. It happens, then, that the stumbling blocks to the development of a scientific psychology are also the stumbling blocks to the development of a scientific philosophy.

It is not difficult, therefore, to see that Kantor's work would be of interest to non-psychologists. In this paper we look at psychology's sister sciences: Anthropology, ethology, and sociology. In the four essays that follow we show that scientists in these fields, just as in psychology, quickly abandon objects and events in favor of specious philosophy and cultural assumptions. While we have not attempted to integrate these essays, the overriding theme is Kantor's historico-critical method.

The first essay deals with palaeoanthropology. The history of human palaentology reveals the distance venerable tradition can spread from its origin. In such a field one might expect that objects and events (fossils and artifacts in a spatio-temporal sequence) would determine conclusions reached. Not so. Paleoanthropologists are as much victims of brain dogma as are psychologists.

The second essay deals with ethology. Its purpose is to show that the ethological paradigm is basically identical to that of mentalistic psychology. This is because both take root in precisely the same philosophical soil. The only difference between them is that psychology emphasizes one side of the traditional man-animal dichotomy and ethology emphasizes the other.

The third essay deals with holism in sociology and social anthropology. Here we find venerable tradition again at work, this time in a form that does not generally plague psychology. Anthropologists and sociologists, having steered clear of reductionism, have wrecked themselves in holism. They have reified society into a "superorganism." A precedent for doing so is to be found in two millenia of Christian theology.

A fitting closing essay deals with a new subdomain of sociology, the sociology of scientific knowledge, a discipline that takes as its subject matter the cultural aspect of science. Here the student of science would expect to find enlightenment. But no sooner found than straight away rejected, for the sociologist instead of rising above the murky waters of tradition finds himself at home in this medium. While this subdomain is to be commended for its attempt to wrench the study of science away from philosophers and bring it into the realm of science itself, it has achieved little of theoretical value. This is because its practitioners have chosen to join forces with the "New Philosophy of Science," which depicts science as little more than the subjective judgments of particular cultural groups. A knowledge of interbehavioral philosophy might have prevented the revival of the solipcism that this new "subjectivism" entails, but, as with the re-emphasis of cognitivism in psychology, we may attribute this reversion to the failure of philosophers and philosopher-scientists to recognize and avoid traditional pseudo-problems.

## The Brain and Palaeoanthropology

The nature of man has been a central concern of both philosophy and science. In philosophy, man has been defined as possessing a soul or mind, the operation of which sets him apart from other organisms. In science, the search for humanness has been characterized by an attempt to discover a biological basis for separating man from other species and the brain has become the focus of attention in this endeavor.

Thus, the purpose of this essay is to indicate the influence of brain tradition on palaeoanthropology and to indicate another anomaly in that tradition.

Since the time of Darwin, anatomists have found themselves in the ambiguous position of emphasizing the similarities between the brains of men and apes in order to establish evolutionary continuity while at the same time emphasizing the differences between the brains of men and apes in order to maintain the traditional man-animal behavioral dichotomy. While the former emphasis is a result of phylogenetic assumptions, the latter derives from traditional self-actional principles wherein the brain is regarded as the organ of behavior (Delprato, 1979; Kantor, 1947). In this view, it is assumed that because men and apes behave differently their brains must show a corresponding difference, the difference in brain explaining the difference in behavior. The origins of brain dogma will not concern us here as they have been discussed elsewhere (Kantor, 1963, 1969; Smith, 1974). Our only purpose is to examine its influence on palaeoanthropology.

At the time Darwin published **The Origin of Species** in 1859 the critical issue was man's uniqueness. The point of contention was whether man differed in kind or degree from other species and the neurological correlate of the difference. While brain size differences were recognized, size is not a matter of kind. What was needed to substantiate the dichotomy was some structure that man alone possessed and that accounted for man's uniqueness. Sir Richard Owen thought that he had found such a structure in the hippocampus minor,for, according to him, man alone possessed this neurological structure. The famous "hippopotamus" debate between Huxley and Owen is the classic wrange on this issue (Ayres, 1932).

The outcome of this search for unique structures was that there is nothing about man's brain that uniquely distinguishes it from the brains of his closest relatives. While there are differences, these are not of the type hoped for. Point by point, ape and human brains have the same structures, but they do not have the same proportions. The human brain is two to three times larger than the brains of apes and there are certain features of degree, not kind, that differ between them. Size and proportional difference, therefore, became the characteristics used to explain the man-ape behavioral dichotomy, with often some sort of "critical threshold" being posited above which the differences became one of kind.

Let us therefore briefly discuss these two aspects of neuroanatomy. We begin with size.

The reason that brain size has been emphasized as the major human hallmark is that man's brain is quite large, varying in volume from 1000 to 2000 cc in modern man. However, there are problems with the size theory. First, because there are no "mental" differences among individuals over this range, size alone cannot be all. Second, man does not have the largest brain in the animal kingdom, either in absolute size or in size relative to body weight. Third, it is becoming apparent that human brain size is more variable than is commonly recognized, often without correlated "mental" differences (Lewin, 1980). Finally, the fossil record shows that the human brain has not always been as large as it presently is yet without notable differences in behavior as far as can be inferred from archaeological associations.

Because the purpose of this essay is to empashize what the fossil record tells us about the brain and behavior, let us briefly review it (see Howells, 1966; Leakey, 1976; Trinkaus and Howells, 1979; Walker and Leakey, 1978).

Palaeoanthropology dates from the publication of **The Origin of Species** (1859). Although a few fossil hominids had been discovered prior to this, there was no framework for understanding their significance. However, with Darwin's publication this changed as evidenced by Huxley's quick off the mark, **Man's Place in Nature and Other Anthropological Essays** (1896). Since then the hominid fossil record has grown rapidly.

Briefly, this record shows that the "body" evolved prior to the "brain." By three to four million years ago hominids existed who were dentally and post-cranially "human" but who had brains no larger than those of apes (Johanson and White, 1979). Subsequent evolution has resulted in little post-cranial change whiel the brain has doubled or tripled in size.

The aphorism, "behavior does not fossilize," is, like most aphorisms, only partly true. Footprints, tools, hearths, food remains, and so on are preserved and give an excellent indication of behavior. Unfortunately the search has been primarily for the fossil hominids themselves and not for their "fossilized behavior." More to the point, there has been a separation of palaeoanthropology from archaeology to the extent that archaeological discoveries have not sufficiently influenced palaeoanthropological interpretations (Isaac, 1978). This however is changing, but it is only recently that very ancient hominid sites have been discovered and carefully excavated by archaeologists (Howell, 1972; Isaac, 1978; Leakey, 1966). What is being found was not expected: Approximately two to three million years ago small-brained hominids were fashioning stone tools (Anonymous, 1981)[1]. Table 1 is a simplified outline of the current state of the palaeoanthropological record.

| AGE (million years ago) | TYPE | BRAIN SIZE cc | CULTURAL ARTIFACTS |
|---|---|---|---|
| Present to .4 | Modern Cro-Magnon Neanderthal | 1000-2000 | Stone tools, fire,burial |
| .4 to 1.0 | Homo Erectus | 800-1200 | Stone tools, fire |
| 1.0 to 4.0 | Australopith-ecus,"Homo Habilis" | 400-800 | Stone tools, shelters, Carrying objects |
| 4.0+ | Unknown | Unknown | Unknown |

**Table 1**

While Table 1 gives an idea of the current state of knowledge, it does not give any idea of the actual history of palaeoanthropology, which is of interest to us because it can only be described as one long series of surprises. While evolutionists early on agreed that man and modern apes evolved from a common ancestor and thus as one went back in time these forms should converge, the exact path followed has been diametrically opposite to expectation. Nothing seems to have fit into the initial--and it might be added, continuing--preconception of how human evolution occurred, nothing, that is, except "Piltdown."

Whoever perpetrated the Piltdown fraud knew precisely what the palaeoanthropologists were looking for and created just that "fossil" by combining the cranium of a modern man (big brain) with the jaw of an ape and depositing them in a Pliocene bed with bone and stone tools. No"fossil" in the history of palaeoanthropology has been so gleefully and quickly embraced by the scientific community, for the Piltdown was precisely what the early evolutionists predicted: A large-brained ape, not a small-brained man. As one authority at the time put it, Piltdown was "a combination which had indeed been previously anticipated as an almost necessary stage in the course of human development" (see Weiner, 1955).

By the time Piltdown was exposed as a hoax it had become the anomaly in an otherwise relatively simple phylogenetic series. But

301

even its removal did not appreciably affect traditional assumptions, and most palaeoanthropologists have continued hypothesizing "big-brained" capacities of small-brained hominids. Consequently, when tools are found in association with small-brained forms they are attributed to some undiscovered but contemporary "advanced" species. But as the fossils come in, the hope for "cerebral" ancestor has not materialized, which does not prevent palaeoanthropologists from making heavy weather of a few cubic centimeters of brain in otherwise identical fossil forms.

However, if brain size does not account for man's behavioral differences, brain dogma may be salvaged by advertising to brain organization. Let us, therefore, turn to this facet of the problem.

Palaeoneurology (sometimes derogatorily referred to as palaeophrenology) is the study of the endocranial casts of fossil forms. Its purpose is to glean information about potential behavior by assuming that the surface features of the cortex can tell us something about behavior (see Holloway, 1974; Keith, 1931).

Setting aside the problem of what actually can be inferred regarding behavior from an examination of the brains of extant forms, palaeoneurology encounters two additional problems. First, it deals only with surface features, and second, the skull does not receive anything but the poorest impression of the brain housed within it. For example, as early as 1916, Symington, in response to claims then being made by palaeoneurologists, compared endocranial casts with actual brains examined in the postmortem room. "The results of these comparisons were disconcerting; they showed that, in fact, very little of the convolutional pattern of the human brain can be defined with any accuracy on an endocranial cast" (Le Gros Clark, 1967, p. 18). Of course, Symington's results were contested, in particular by an anatomist who had declared that the Piltdown "intercranial cast revealed the most simian brain so far known in the human family" (Boule and Vallois, 1957, p. 155).

These early criticisms, however, have not put an end to palaeoneurology. Although modern palaeneurologists do admit that "precise impressions" of the brain are not left on the skull, that the skull bears "only a minimal impression of the brain surface," and that, in fact, "the only detailed features that can be traced on the endocranial cast...are the paths of the meningeal blood vessels" (Holloway, 1974, p. 108). It is still generally accepted that "even a relatively featureless cast will reveal at least the general proportions and shape of the brain" (Holloway, 1974, p. 108). And what can be gleaned from the featureless endocasts of early hominids? According to Holloway (1974), "the **Australopithecus** brains were essentially human in neurological organization (p. 112).

302

In conclusion let us reiterate the aim of this essay. In the behavioral sciences, the brain has been made to do heavy duty as an explanatory principle and palaeoanthropology is no exception. But here, just as elsewhere, there is a lack of fit between theory and ata, and the palaeoanthropologists' predictions have clearly not been substantiated by the fossil record. In fact, having neither brain size differences nor substantial evidence of brain organizational differences, palaeoanthropologists have arrived at an impasse. As Isaac (see Anonymous, 1981, p. 84) describes the situation, two possibilities exist: Either the human way of life preceded the development of a significantly enlarged brain, or the trend toward brain enlargement began earlier than the oldest fossils we yet have. Consequently, while palaeoanthropologists still hope for a "cerebral" ancestor, from the evidence now available it looks as if bipedalism, tool manufacture and use, and other behaviors that are typically human (insofar as these can be inferred from the archaeological record)preceded the expansion of the brain (cf. Isaac, 1978; Lovejoy, 1981).

## Ethology and the Evolution of the
## Man-Animal Dichotomy

Kantor's historico-critical approach to psychology as represented by **The Scientific Evolution of Psychology** ( 1963, 1969) is a unique undertaking in the history of the behavioral sciences. The reason it is unique is that Kantor has traced from inception to present the evolution of traditional ideas in psychology. Ethology has had no such historian. However, **The Scientific Evolution of Psychology** can also be used as a history of ethology.

Specifically, as the soul construction evolved during the post-Hellenic period, so did the man-animal dichotomy. This dichotomy emphasized the difference between man and other animals in the sense that, while both men and animals have bodies, only man has a soul, or paraphrasing the words of medieval theologians, irrational creatures preceded the creation of rational man. This dichotomy remained throughout the Middle Ages and only started to be modified in the sixteenth and seventeenth centuries when Descartes and others began reflecting on the relation of the soul to the body. The period following Descartes, but especially after Darwin, saw the convergence of the souled-man and the soulless-animal views to such an extent that today both ethology and psychology stand on similar ground: Both prescribe to essentially the same type of mentalism.

Because we have only begun our study of the origin and evolution of the man-animal dichotomy, and thus cannot pretend to have traced ethology's exact course, let us describe the terminus of this evolution. Knowing the terminus, we are at least in a desirable position from which to begin a reconstruction of the origins of ethological ideas.

Briefly, ethology, like mentalistic psychology, begins with the assumption that organisms consit of two parts: The visible body and the invisible mind, and that the two interact (or more correctly), the mind directs the body[2]. Like mentalistic psychology, ethology links behavioral events to physiological and neurological occurrences wherein the brain is considered to be the master organ. Reductionism therefore is routine, and neurophysiology, especially conceptual neurophysiology, monopolizes the explanation of behavior. If the ethologist recognizes the hiatus between behavioral event and physiological information, then models to "help bridge the gap" are suggested. As with mentalistic psychology, the aim is to explain behavior by revealing the "ghost in the machine," the ghost being the brain, hormones,or various hypothetical powers and forces such as motivations, drives, tendencies, instincts, and acquired "mental templates." Hence the behavioral event is reduced to the organism itself seen as an entity self-activated by internal or internalized powers.

Because the behavioral event is equated with or reduced to various psychical or physiological factors, ethologists, like mentalistic psychologists, fail to understand the various roles of stimuli, setting factors, media of contact, and biological structures in behavioral responses and continue to overemphasize the importance of the latter. This is clearly indicated by brain extirpation experiments where the logic runs precisely as it does in physiological psychology:
Because the absence of a structure results in a deficiency in behavior, **ipso ffacto,** its presence causes the behavior.

The pattern that ethological causation studies follow is essentially the same as that in mentalistic psychology, because all self-reports are not available and the organism's behavior becomes the sole source of data. That is, because animal "minds" cannot be known through verbal reports, they can only be known indirectly through the study of "overt reactions. " The formula is: What an organism does reflects what is on his mind. If he flees, he is afraid or has actualized "fear" or a tendency to flee.

In all essentials, then, the ethological paradigm is identical to the mentalistic psychological paradigm, except for one thing, namely, man is said to possess a "cognitive" mind,wher eas other animals are said to possess "non-cognitive" minds. Although man is said to possess thought, reason, and consciousness, animals are said to lack these qualities. But both men and animals possess motivations, drives, emotions, and so forth, and it is these that run animals. The brain (or only a part of the brain) is considered to be the organ of thought, and that part is unique to man. Other animals lack these structures and for that reason cannot perform human actions.

Ethology, therefore, supports a body with a non-cognitive mind theory, which, except for the few missing powers denied non-human animals, is identical to psychology's body with a cognitive mind theory. In both paradigms the organism is considered to be run by its neurological wetware, which is taken to be the "real" or "ultimate" cause of behavior. Even in the most interactionalistic ethology, mentalism eventually bobs to the surface. **Cause,** in the final analysis, ultimately resides inside the organism whether it entered by way of "experience" and is stored as a "mental template" or whether it was there all along, having arrived somehow in the genes.

Historically, then, we are dealing with the terminus to two traditions. The first is the mind-body dualism and the second is the man-animal dichotomy. One is as old as the other, for they are simply two aspects of the same tradition. One reverses the world and the other orders nature. Both views fit the culture that developed them but neither fits well today. Nonetheless, we remain heir to these views attributing minds to man and other animals, and to man alone special mental powers and forces.

At this point we will give an example in order to illustrate what we have said. The example comes from linguistics (semiotics) and animal communicaiton (zoosemiotics). We simplify for the sake of brevity.

The referent of communication events has always puzzled semioticians and zoosemioticians. The reason for this lies in the fact that communication events are reduced to mentalistic occurrences. One need look no further than Locke, Berkeley, and Hume for the basis of this view. Thus, it is obvious when someone says "There is a cat" that the speaker is responding to an object, and that this statement adjusts the auditor to the same object. This common sense or realistic view has been so undermined by Western tradition that in semiotics the cat becomes, literally, a part of the responding organism (see Kantor, 1936, 1977; Pronko, 1946). Hayakawa (1949) expresses this clearly when he says:

> Now, human beings have agreed, in the course of cen-
> turies of mutual dependency, to let the various noises
> that they can produce...systematically stand for specified
> happenings in their nervous systems. For example, we
> who speak English have been so trained that, when our
> nervous systems register the presence of a certain kind
> of animal, we may make the following noise: 'There's
> a cat.' Anyone hearing us expects to find that, by
> looking in the same direction, he will experience a

similar event in his nervous system (p. 27).

Zoosemioticians also being heir to this tradition have the same problem. Because the referent of communication events is removed from its spatio-temporal location and is smuggled inside the organism, its "materialization" becomes decidedly difficult. For example, when a sparrow or other small bird gives an alarm call in response to a hawk, it is said to respond, not to the hawk, but to something inside itself (fear, a tendency to flee, etc.), and the auditor is referred to something occurring inside the communicator, not to the hawk.

We see in this example both the mind-body dualism and the man-animal dichotomy in action. In both semiotics and zoosemiotics communicators are seen as responding to and referring to events inside themselves and auditors are referred to those events occurring in the communicator. But only in man can the referent be an idea; animals are limited to emotional communication. As might be expected, these studies quickly degenerate into self-actional analyses in which any semblance of a field vanishes and the conceptual nervous system takes over (MacRoberts and MacRoberts, 1979, 1980a, 1980b).

In order to show the difference between this traditional approach and a naturalistic one, let us give the summary of a recent paper entitled, "Monkey Responses to Three Different Alarm Calls: Evidence of Predator Classification and Semantic Communication" (Seyfarth, Cheney and Marler, 1980).

> Vervet monkeys give different alarm calls to different
> predators. Recordings of the alarm played back when
> predators were absent caused the monkeys to run into
> trees for leopard alarms, look up for eagle alarms, and
> look down for snake alarms. Adults call primarily to
> leopards, martial eagles, and pythons, but infants give
> leopard alarms to various mammals, eagle alarms to
> many birds, and snake alarms to various snakelike objects.
> Predator classification improves with age and experience
> (p. 801).

Here, then, is a naturalistic approach to animal communication. Our reason for mentioning it is to contrast it with the traditional model of animal communication, which is still so much in evidence. That such naturalistic studies are the exception rather than the rule indicates the current state of ethology.

In conclusion, while ethology is obviously evolving toward an objective or naturalistic position, it, like mentalistic psychology, has yet to attain that status. Ethology is, therefore, in as much need of understanding its roots as is psychology. This task will require the scientific historian to span three millenia of Western tradition, paying particular attention to the first four centuries of the Christian era. While we have only begun to examine this history, some interesting points have definitely emerged. One is that the man-animal dichotomy was established very early on. It had already developed by the time of the early Patristics, and the only thing left was to decide on the fine points of the human soul, a topic that occupied most attention thereafter. At this early period also we see the consequences of considering man the microcosm of the macrocosm, for as his "nature" is distorted, so, too, is all nature distorted. The process, of course, is evident in Plotinus and Augustine, but by the time of John Scotus Erigena it had been carried to such an extreme that the only reality was transcendental, making confrontable things and events less substantial than the "reasoning processes" that supposedly maintained their existence. In this manner, reality moved "inside" man, and as a result, inside everything else as well. It was only when the soul or mind began to be identified with the brain that the issue of differences was forced to the front. Then, animals began to ascend to **scala naturae,** or more to the point, that man began to descend and today man and animals are essentially conjoined in one paradigm, the only differences between them being the particular powers attributed to the brains of each--all remnants of soul doctrine.

### Theodicy and Sociological and Anthropological Holism

Kantor is a scientific historian but not in the traditional mold. For him, history is as much a tool of the scientists as is the apparatus and data with which he works (Kantor, 1976; Observer, 1975, 1979). Kantor, in his concern to explain current psychological thinking, recognized that its source was not to be found in the "laboratory" but in pre-scientific tradition, which is why he is able to say that "probably the most important value of scientific history is the opportunity it offers for an evaluation of the preconceptions which lie at the basis of individual and institutional scientific practices and theories" (Kantor, 1971, p. 599). What Kantor has done, then, is to recognize " that the conceptions of psychology were not formulated by scientists" (Observer, 1980a, p. 584) and to proceed beyond traditional history to discover the actual assumptional origins of psychology (Observer, 1980b).

In this essay we examine holism in sociology and anthropology[3]. Our purpose will be to show no more than that before anthropology and sociology became sciences and "developed" their holistic paradigms there existed a precise duplicate of that paradigm in the culture at large.

As with the previous essay, what follows should be considered preliminary. Our research has not progressed to the stage where we actually trace the exact lineage of current theory; it is even possible that curent theory evolved independently of the tradition we shall discuss. But it is worthwhile to realize that pre-scientific tradition may have contributed more to current theory than has the confrontation of anthropologist or sociologist with his subject matter.

In their efforts to steer clear of biological and psychological reductionism, sociologists and anthropologists have landed themselves on the rocks of holism and as a result have reified society. This can be seen in almost any anthropological or sociological work dealing with theory (see, for example, Abrahamson, 1978; Cohen, 1968, Davis, 1958; Dray, 1967; Emmet, 1967). Briefly, holists construe societies or institutions as highly integrated, organized, purposive systems, much in the manner of an organism (see Gouldner, 1970; Jarvie, 1965; Munch, 1976; Spencer, 1965).

Merton (1957) clarified the sociological concept of function when he made his classic and very influential distinction between manifest and latent functions; in so doing, he provided the basis for alter usages. Merton defines "functions: as those observed consequences which make for the adaptation or adjustment of a given system and "dysfunctions" as those observed consequences which lessen the adaptation or adjustment of the system. He then divides the category function into two types: Manifest and latent. The former he defines as those objective consequences contributing to the adjustment or adaptation of the system which are intended and recognized by the participants of the system and the latter as those which are neither intended nor recognized. Thus, manifest functions are "conscious motivations for social behavior," or put another way, "those objective consequences for a specified unit (e.g., person, subgroup, social or cultural system) which contribute to its adjustment or adaptation and were so intended" (Merton, 1957, p. 63). In this category, the "end-in-view" is emphasized. Latent functions, on the other hand, are "unintended or unrecognized consequences" of the actions of individuals or group but consequences that nonetheless are beneficial (see Malefijt, 1974, for further examples).

In short, what we have in sociological-anthropological holism is a unit--society or culture--above the individual interbehavioral level, which, like a medieval "Real," is more substantial than the individuals themselves.

If we look at traditional sociological and anthropological history, we find that although these histories discuss the superorganic or holistic view--Spencer, Durkheim, Comte, Radcliffe-Brown, Kroeber, Malinowski, and scores of others ascribed to it--the historians fail to tell us not only where theses ideas come from, but insist that they have been abandoned. This is, of course, about what we find regarding the mind-body dualism when we turn to histories of psychology. Not only are modern histories of psychology devoid of the actual origins of mind-body dogma, but they also suggest that this view died fifty years ago because at that time the word "mind" fell into disgrace. Because holism, like mentalism, neither arose with the fathers of the social sciences nor was subsequently abandoned, it is obvious that we are simply dealing with traditional history and that we must go further afield: In fact, we must reexamine history[5].

Theodicy, for example, is the study of evil from the assumptional basis of Christian theology. It could be called theological functionalism. The problem of theodicy is this: How is the existence of evil to be reconciled with the theological account of holistic universe created by an omnipotent, omniscient, good, and creative being? Put differently, if God shows the qualities listed above, what is the source of war, plague, murder, disease, suffering, intolerance, **ad infinitum**? Note first the assumption of a unitary (monostic) and perfect universe. Note second the facts of pain and suffering. It would be a most obtuse individual who could deny these anomalies, and the Christian apologist do not deny them. But not denying them does not mean that they allow the facts to tamper with the assumptions. They neither admit a dualistic universe (e.g., good and evil coexisting) nor do they deny a purposive universe. What they do is to attempt to alter the interpretation of the facts.

We are interested in this process of fact reinterpretations for a number of reasons, the main one being that the line of argumentation used by theodicists is very similar--if not identical--to that used by holistic sociologists and anthropologists. It consists of shifting the angle of theoretical vision from consequences for individuals to those for social or universal systems.

Theologians have devised many arguments to reconcile the seeming paradox of a unitary-whole and perfect universe with the presence of evil, but only one will concern us here. This is the "aesthetic" argument. It has a long history but a simple one because its basic points have not changed much over time. It was used by Plotinus, Augustine, Aquinas, Spinoza, Leibniz, King, Kant and Hegel, to name only a few key figures[6].

We begin our very brief examination with Augustine, not because he expressed the aesthetic argument first[7] but because he was the pacesetter for Western theodicy until the eighteenth century.

Augustine presents a clear shift in theoretical vision--from an infinite point of view, each event or thing in the world is necessary to the whole and therefore in its own way good. Each event contributes to the completion of the whole and thus to perfection. To remove or eliminate anything would be to "destroy the order." A finite Being perceiving events from a very limited perspective is unable to see the whole and thus the good that would be evident from an infinitely wider perspective. As Hick (1966, p. 82) puts it: "seen in its totality...the universe is wholly good; for even the evil in it is made to contribute to the complex perfection of the whole." Thus, evil cannot be looked upon as dysfunctional or destructive but when viewed from the proper perspective must be seen as a necessary element, a part of the "wonderful harmony which is not only good but very good" (Hick, 1966, p. 38).

Thomas Aquinas, who symbolizes the transition from medieval to modern, adds little to Augustine. Moving forward quickly to the eighteenth century, we reach what has been called the "golden age of theodicy," for it is here, in the work of Spinoza and Leibniz, that the final form of the aesthetic argument crystallized.

Spinoza was not only a monist and holist but a determinist. All was created in a perfect holistic form and all that occurs is a part of that form. Spinoza, unlike his predecessors, abandoned free will. In many ways he championed the idea of the limited awareness of the whole as did all his predecessors, but by eliminating free will[8]. This concludes tht all things are determined from divine necessity to exist and to act in this manner. "Since everything is determined by a perfect Determiner, everything must be perfect" (Hick, 1966, p. 18); consequently, this world in every respect is perfect. Organisms are set on predetermined courses by a guiding hand and are unable to alter that course.

Leibniz, Spinoza's contemporary, but intellectual descendant, is perhaps the greatest of all theodicists. Spinoza allowed the assumptional basis of theology (monism-holism) to carry him to the conclusion that the world was perfect. Leibniz saw it differently. For Leibniz, the world was not perfect, it was only the best of all possible worlds. Leibniz's reasoning is simple. God, being absolute and perfect, could have created any world or, for that matter, no world at all. But God is not unlimited, he is bounded by logical necessity. He, for example, cannot create a triangular square. Now, God, finding that something is better than nothing and that much is better than little, surveyed all conceivable worlds, weighing this one in its totality against that one in its totality until he decided that this world (i.e., the one in which we find ourselves) was the best of all possible total creations. This was not the most perfect he could have created, but if he had created that more perfect world, that is, for example, one without death, famine, or war, it would have been, on the whole, not as good as this because death, famine, and war make for a more perfect whole than a world without them.  Accordingly: "so-called evil is bad when we judge it by itself, but once the universe as a whole is viewed, it ceases to be evil..." (Alpern, 1933, p. 156).

This brings us to an important part of Leibniz's system, his celebrated principle of sufficient reason.   While there is no general agreement among philosophers upon what this principle states, its general outline for our purposes is clear (see Leibniz, 1934; Lovejoy, 1936).   Holists are concerned with the interrelation of parts to wholes, and in particular with the underlying purposes.

Recall that Leibniz was a contemporary of Newton and lived at the time when the physical sciences were in their glory.  Recall, therefore, that scientific explanations were beginning to win ground at an ever increasing rate.  Scientific explanations are contingent, that is billiard ball A moving at velocity B colliding with billiard ball C causes C to behave in X manner.  Going back in time, billiard ball A was set in motion by pool cue P because it was moving in Q manner, and so on.  Such explanations are explanations for Leibniz in only a limited sense.  The real problem was not that all of this occurred in a regular manner, but that events occurred this way and not another way.  There were thousands of conceivable ways that billiard balls could behave, but they follow only one pattern.  Thus, there had   to be another explanation, and it is this explanation that Leibniz describes in the principle of sufficient reason.  It is the initial concept of the whole, and the whole as working in harmony, that requires it. While Leibniz would completely endorse the view that each thing is caused by its predecessor in a mechanical manner, he goes further and develops the view that each event is planned, guided, and structured relative to the whole by some force or power that he labels God. Sufficient reason, therefore, is final causation, theological necessity, or, in the terms of our present discussion, functionalism in its most blatent form.  Things are as they are and happen as they do because of the value they have in relation to the whole.  The notion, as Lovejoy (1936, p. 146) puts it, of good must be employed in order to understand Leibniz: "All events have **some** [non-contingent] reason;" they are "grounded in something else which is logically ultimate."

The form in which Leibniz cast the aesthetic argument, including his concept of sufficient reason, has determined the course of theodicy ever since.  It is repeated by Kant, "The whole is best and everything is good for the sake of the whole," by Hegel, "ultimate harmony of all contradictions," and by other philosophers and theologians.

Let us conclude this historical outline by briefly summarizing. The necessity to explain away evil rests with the intial assumption: In the Christian holism, "evil" cannot exist.  Evil, therefore, is an illusion, not a reality, and is also the mistaken impression of finite minds viewing only part of a whole. Evil would be recognized as good if it could be seen in its fullest context. Evil, therefore, is explained away. The basic assumptions are maintained or even strengthened.

By way of discussion and conclusion, little need be said because the reader cannot miss the similarities between sociological and anthropological holism and theodicy. They are, in fact, essentially identical and for the same reasons. Both are based on holistic assumptions, which in turn incline each to find purpose ("harmony of society") in all events. Berlin (1954), speaking of holists in general, captured the essence of the matter: Holists believe in invisible powers and dominions, conceived as impersonal entities at once patterns and realities, in terms of which men and institutions must behave the way they do. Something, therefore, beyond contingencies, causes them to behave the way they do, or put in other terms, something causes the contingencies to be in a certain way to produce the "best" results.

Envisioning society as an integrated whole leads to an attempt to explain anomalies by seeing them as somehow contributing to the whole. This can be done most effectively by shifting the focus of attention from the individual to the group and by shifting from manifest to latent functions. The sociologist steps back from the individual, as does the theodicist, to see the whole. If this does not produce the desired result, like the theodicist, the social scientists declares that because of a limited perspective, the observer (or native) may not be able to see the function of a particular activity, but if the whole were viewable in its entirety, the activity would be seen as functional for the whole. Like Augustine, the sociologist believes that if something "is," then, it must be "good" even though it does not appear to be so: That is, its very existence is proof that it is a part that functions for the whole. Anyone familiar with "role theory" in sociology and anthropology realizes that there is always something more than the interbehavior of organisms in "fields" involved in these explanations, and that this something is essentially what Leibniz was trying to express under the label "sufficient reason." Always, in sociology and anthropology, behind contingencies, there lies another "force" or structuring principle: Society.

## The Sociology of Scientific Knowledge

Any discipline that takes as it subject matter cultural influences on science would be of interest to interbehaviorism. Consequently, we take this opportunity to briefly discuss the newly emerged sociology of scientific knowledge. Here, one would think, is a discipline that might "help scientists to orient themselves with respect to the origin of doctrines and theories (Kantor, 1971, p. 599). But this is not what has

312

happened. Instead, sociologists in their efforts to stake out a subject matter spent their time discrediting science. This is because they felt they had to choose between one of two alternative characterizations of science: Either science is an objective and rational enterprise or it is a subjective and cultural one. No other possibility has suggested itself, and by opting for the subjective-cultural interpretation (the side they would have to take if they were to have a subject matter), sociologists of scientific knowledge have not only made a caricature of science, but have become the target of sharp criticism as a result.

Until recently sociologists of knowledge have excluded science from their purview. This was because they deemed science to be culture free. In this view, scientific facts, theories and laws are considered to be derived from observation and experimentation and are thus uninfluenced by the factors that mold other aspects of culture. As Mulkay (1979a) puts it:

> Because scientific knowledge is seen as an objective
> account of the real world, it is assumed that socio-
> logical analysis must stop when it has shown how
> the social organization of science enables scientists
> to observe and report the world objectively, with little
> sign of the bias and distortion which are thought to
> arise in other areas of cultural production through
> the impact of social and personal factors (p. 64).

This view contains within it a dichotomy between two fundamentally different types of "beliefs"[9]. On the one hand, there are scientific beliefs, which are called "rational." The study of rational beliefs, according to traditional sociologists, is best left to the philosopher and historian, while the irrational cues are proper sociological subjects.

It was not until the sixties when Feyeraband, Hanson, Kuhn, and others began to dispute the time-honored positivist position that sociologists found an opening into science as a subject matter. By this time, positivist philosophers had all but thrown up their hands regarding science's special epistemological status: Popper's "falsification" hypothesis, logical positivism's "neutral observation language," along with many other philosophical attempts had all been shown to be deficient. For their part, historians had made clear that science never seems to reach its final goal of "truth." In time even the most firmly established theory is overthrown. Finally, Kuhn's (1962) very influential **The Structure of Scientific Revolutions** with its thesis of paradigm replacement and theory-ladenness of observation cleared the ground for viewing science as a primarily cultural phenomenon. In short, these developments led to the conclusion that the general criteria by which scientific knowledge-claims are assessed (such as consonance with the evidence, replicability, etc.) have no meaning until they are interpreted in terms of scientists' particular intellectual commitments and in relation to specific interpretative and social contexts (see Mulkay, 1979a, p. 65). This "new" sociology of knowledge, therefore, argues that the conclusions of science are the outcome of the scientist's interactions, including his particular expertise and general cultural milieu (if this is influential).

This conclusion would not excite criticism if this were what the sociologist meant. But it is not. Instead of simply recognizing or understanding that scientists are not **tabula rasa** individuals registering and recording pure "sense impressions" about the "real" world and constructing theories directly from these pristine "sense impressions" but are people with special training engaged in a particular type of work, sociologists have proceeded to produce a caricature of science by selectively choosing examples and by emphasizing certain aspects of those examples. On the basis of this caricature, they have produced a skeptical and solipcistic philosphy, which meshes perfectly with the "new philosophy of science," as Mulkay (1979b) calls it.

We will very briefly illustrate the way sociologists have proceeded by examining some of their work. Because these few examples do not do justice to the effort, we invite those interested to examine this work in detail (see especially Barnes, 1974; Bloor, 1976; Mulkay, 1979b).

Barnes (1976), in a paper entitled "Natural Rationality: A Neglected Concept in the Social Sciences," attacks the traditional rational-irrational dichotomy between "belief" systems. His reason for doing this is clear: "Natural science, it is said, is an exceptionally rational activity; hence its beliefs are not amenable to study from the standpoint of the sociology of knowledge" (p. 124). Thus, if there is to be a sociology of scientific knowledge, the dichotomy must be discredited.

Barnes attempts to acheive this by way of cognitivism and enthnographical accounts of primitive belief systems[10]. By assuming that all people are alike and that the brain is the organ of thought, Barnes concludes that all thinking in all men must be the same, which he calls "natural rationality." His evidence for this is that all belief systems are intelligible; they do not possess disjunctions or elements that do not fit with the whole, and they are this way because of "cognitive propensities" inherent in the organism[11]. Put another way, man's innate cognitive capacities are not overridden by culture, but culture makes for different belief systems. Barnes (1976, pp. 123-124) concludes: "The general implication here is that there is, so far as we can tell, no institutionalized irrationality to be explained...,All institutionalized systems of belief and action appear to embody natural rationality alike--science no more or less than any other institution."

Barnes' procedure may strike some as unusual until it is understood that what Barnes has done is little more than to rely on traditional beliefs to argue for the "psychic unity" of mankind. Having done so, he simply declares that all men think alike, **ergo,** all men are rational and thus all belief systems are rational.

Concerning ethnographical evidence, let us only point out that Barnes attempts to make "primitive" beliefs look more scientific than they actually are (Barnes, 1974, Chapter 2).

Be all this as it may, Barnes' entire argument is best comprehended by realizing in exactly what sense he is using the term "rational," that is, as a synonym for "reason," meaning: The employment of the thinking faculty or power of the human mind. Thus, Barnes is apparently under the impression that when it has been claimed that science is extremely rational, what is meant is that somehow scientists are more "logical," "systematic" or "consistent" than are non-scientists. What, in fact we (and we believe most others who have mentioned this problem) have always assumed is meant by rational in this context is a second definition of "reason," that is, that sensible or observable things have to do with tangibles.

What we are left with, then, after dismissing the invocation of unviersal psychic powers as an illegitimate method of unifying mankind, is the fact that belief systems are **coherent** and **consistent.** However, from this "fact" it hardly follows that "no distinctiveness can be attributed to our existing natural science" or "that science should be treated as a part of culture like any other, to be studied by the same methods, explored by the same techniques" (Barnes, 1976, p. 124). It only means that systems, being systems, are systematic, and that in this regard science does not differ from other "belief" systems.

Consequently, because Barnes has tangled himself in both psychic and semantic problems, little or no gain has been made--certainly his point has not, for he has overlooked the essential feature of science that distinguishes it from other activities: Its adherence to objects and events in building constructions.

The second paper we will discuss is Mulkay's (1979a) "Knowledge and Utility: Implications for the Sociology of Knowledge." Mulkay abstracts his own thesis:

> It is suggested that in identifying scientific knowledge
> as epistemologically special, and as exempt from
> sociological analysis, sociologists have tended to make
> two basic assumptions; namely, that scientific theories

can be clearly validated by successful practical application
and that the general theoretical formulations of science
do regularly  generate such practical applications.  These
assumptions, as customarily interpreted, pose a major
challenge for any sociological analysis which views scientific knowledge as the contingent outcome of interpretative
and context-dependent social acts.  It is argued, however,
...that the validity of these assumptions is doubtful....(p. 63).

What Mulkay is saying is that if scientific knowledge leads to or is
validated by practical application (not just by laboratory
confirmation), this would provide independent or special evidence for
its epistemological distinction ("objective truth") and thus be a reasons
for excluding it from sociological analysis  because "it is particularly
difficult to accept that an idea can be socially determined and yet
valid" (Mulkay, 1979a, p. 66).  Because Mulkay is committed to the
view that the study of science falls within sociology, his aim is to
show that effective practical techniques are not a "fairly direct
porduct of scientific knowledge."  The "pragmatic" test of validity is
therefore applied to science on a practical level.

Before  continuing  our  discussion,  however,  let  us  agree  with
Mulkay on one point at least.  This is that when we talk of scientific
knowledge demonstrating its objectivity through successful application,
we are at most referring to a minority of scientific knowledge claims
within a limited number of research areas because most of science
does not lead to practical application in the sense being used by
Mulkay.

Within  this  qualification,  let  us  continue.   Mulkay  makes  a
distinction between pure science and applied science or technology.
We see why he does this: He is attempting to diminish the part the
pure scientists plays in producing "effective practical effects" but
cannot dismiss the technologist.  This uneasy dichotomy however is
not useful or justifiable because most scientists are, to a certain
extent, simultaneously technicians and vice versa.  It would be a peculiar  scientist, technician, engineer, doctor, architect, etc. who in their
daily practice did not rely on embodied scientific knowledge.  Kantor
(1953), discussing science and technology, sums  it up pretty well:

> But it would be unreasonable to assume that the tech-
> nologist cannot profit by his fellow worker who special-
> izes in the development of **principles.** Technological
> practice at certain points really depends upon pure
> science. 'What builder of steam boilers,' demands Le
> Chatelier, 'could do without the laws of water tension
> vapor investigated by Regnault?' (p. 323).

316

Indeed, looked at in this manner, what engineer, technician or physician is not dependent upon pure science?

Let us briefly consider two final and very typical examples of the way sociologists proceed in their efforts to cast doubt on the positivist account of science.

As part of Mulkay's (1979b) rejection of science's special epistemological status, he resorts to **both** the traditional model of seeing (Object-light-eye-brain-eidola, etc.) and an interactionist model (a la N.R. Hanson) to prove , first, that we cannot make direct contact with any object but only indirect contact, and second, that because seeing is a developed interaction ("theory-laden"), that is, the observer imposes "meanings" on the observed things, we cannot actually see the thing-in-itself but only what our culture has taught us to see. In this instance, Mulkay reaches into the grab-bag of philosophy, comes out with two essentially incompatible views of perception, and uses **both** of them as if this somehow strengthens his position: That seeing is a mysterious endeavor to be avoided at all cost.

The second example comes from Barnes (1974, pp. 9, 10, 12) whose thesis is that scientific theories are imposed on data (cf. Kuhn, 1962). But nowhere in his book does he allude to the other fact that such theories are also derived from the interaction of the observer with objects and events. While we do not doubt Barnes' statement, such one-sidedness of presentation does not give an accurate picture of the nature of scientific work and, in fact, displays the obvious bias underlying the sociologists' efforts.

The main result of this one-sidedness of presentation has been the rejuvination of solipcism. While the sociologist of knowledge quite justifiably takes exception to the absolutist position maintained by many positivists, he argues himself into the **cul-de-sac** of "relativism" or better put, "cultural solipcism." Briefly, this reduces science (and therefore sociology itself) to just another belief system with no special criterion of justification. Yet cultural solipcism could have been avoided if these workers had understood at the outset what science is, which it is obvious they do not. The sociologist have neither begun their studies of science by carefully preparing their own assumptional basis nor by detailing science's special features, including its metasystematic assumptions (see Lichtenstein, 1967; Kantor, 1953, 1959, 1973, 1978, 1981). Instead they have begun by hitting all the low dives of philosophy and have been so influenced by the "new philosophy of science" that it might be said that they are sociologists who speak with a philosophical tongue. As Mynell (1977, p. 490), criticizing relativism[12], put it, "'proof,' 'justification,' and 'validation, boil down to modes of behavior and ways of speaking which are characteristic of the ways of life of particular social groups, and which cannot be further justified..." But what the sociologist of knowledge have overlooked "is whether some philosophic or cultural attitudes are more conducive to the attainment of correct results ...than others" (Kantor, 1971, p. 176).

As might be expected, the sociology of scientific knowledge has become the target of a great deal of sharp criticism. This criticism has occurred not because, as Bloor (1976) suggests, scientists are afraid of being scrutinized and the "truth" told about them, but because scientists, like all other people, object to being misinterpreted.

But when all is said and done, what does the sociologist actually offer us? If we examine sociological case studies of science, do we find anything new and startling? Not at all. In fact, these studies are all very much in the manner that historians and philosophers of science have been writing for years (see Barnes and Shapin, 1979). The only disjunction is between what Barnes and Shapin (1979, p. 11) call "abstract arguments" (theory) and practice, for as they point out: The best way to establish the possibility of doing something is to do it," and this they have done.

We, therefore, do not believe that any scientists would object to a **scientific** sociology of scientific knowledge, recognizing as most scientists do (1) the history of scientific change, (2) the cultural and institutionalized nature of the enterprise, (3) the metasystemic underpinnings of science, (4) science's corrigibility, and (5) the inter-institutional (favorable and unfavorable) influences that occur between science and culture at large. In fact, Kantor (1963, 1969) has produced for psychology what the sociologists would label a sociology of scientific knowledge.

In conclusion, let us say that in the case of the sociology of knowledge, good intentions have spawned bad arguments. While the idea of a sociology of scientific knowledge is exemplary, those sociologists who have undertaken this task have themselves an insufficiently evolved scientific "culture" by which to promote their effort (this being indicated by their heavy reliance on modern philosophy), and they have chosen a most unfortunate method of getting their foot in the door. While there is no doubt that science can and should be treated as a cultural system, in the present sociological program its distinctive aspects, that is, its naturalistic orientation to objects and events and the derivation of constructs from them, have not been appreciated; indeed, they have barely been recognized. No other intellectual enterprise resembles science in this regard. As Mountjoy (1980) puts it:

Science is, of course, concerned with the development
of propositions that cannot be adequately evaluated
except by the criterion of science itself. That criterion
is the events which the propositions purport to describe.
I submit that this criterion is involved in all human intellectual enterprises, but the scientist is set apart from
other scholars by an exceptional faithfulness to the use
of events as the ultimate criterion fo the validity of
his constructs. In fact, in no other field of scholarship
has there been developed such a complex set of rules
and procedures to insure that a description of events
is accurate rather than misleading (p. 8).

That science regularly "fails" is nothing surprising, for scientific
work seldom if ever proceeds undisturbed by specious philosophy,
difficulties of contacting subject matter, inadequate data, over-influen-
tial theoretical assumption, personal bias, and so on. The task of
sociology with regard to scientific knowledge should be to show,
among other things, how traditional assumptions disturb the working of
the scientific system rather than to build a skeptical relativism
whereby the sociologist does nothing but undermine his own credibility
at being able to scientifically study science.

## Concluding Remarks

The common theme of the preceding essays is the hiatus so often
found in science between assertion, on the one hand, and objects and
events, on the other, and also the fact that much prevailing wisdom
consists of traditional pronouncements. Kantor's historico-critical
method offers a solution to this problem. That is, we must understand
clearly the cultural milieu out of which the sciences have developed
in order to separate scientific work from traditional philosophies, that
is, to allow objects and events their proper role in directing
conclusions, even if this should mean abandoning cherished
preconceptions.

## Footnotes

1. There is no reason to expect that more ancient sites will not    be
found once they are carefully looked for. Thus, a date of two to
three million years ago marks only the oldest known tools.

2. For reviews of mentalistic psychology see most of the references
to Kantor  as well as Lichtenstein (1980) and Smith (1973), among
other interbehavioral writings. For   examples   of   mentalistic
ethology, see any number of recent texts, but historically important
are Tinbergen (1951), Hinde (1966) and articles in  Schiller (1957).

3. The paradigm is the same in both. The reader is asked to note that holism as we use it in this essay applies to the practice of creating wholes where there are none, i.e., reification. A social scientist has three options: (1) Reduce "society" to atoms; (2) use "society" as a word denoting interebehaviors with cultural stimuli or denoting some type of mass action to cultural stimuli (Kantor, 1929); or (3) reify "society" into a superorganism with a group mind. In this essay, we are concerned with the latter position. Sociologists and anthropologists seldom opt for the former but move back and forth between the second and third positions depending on purpose and school affiliation.

4. The reader will note that functionalism of the type encountered in anthropology and sociology is often of a type referred to as "final cause," as developed during the predominance of religious traditions, and is not in any way comparable to Aristotelian functionalism (see Randall, 1960).

5. Kantor's (1929) critique of social psychology deals in part with this.

6. In this essay we rely mainly on Hick (1966) since his book deals specifically with theodicy. Lovejoy's (1936) **The Great Chain of Being** is also an excellent survey of holism and theodicy.

7. See for example Plotinus, **The Enneads**, II, 3, 18, translated by S. MacKenna, 1930, London: Faber and Faber: "the poisonous snake has its use--though in most cases their function is unknown. Vice itself has many useful sides: it brings about much that is beautiful, in artistic creations for example, and it stirs us to thoughtful living, not allowing us to drowse in security" (p. 104).

8. This elimination of free will logically follows from the initial assumptions of the argument but is ignored by Augustine and Aquinas for other theological reasons.

9. The reader should note that we often use the sociologist's terminology in this essay. Thus, the word "belief" as used in the sociology of science literature means something very different from what it means to interbehaviorists (see Observer, 1970).

10. Barnes actually never uses the word "brain." Instead he speaks of "natural rational processes; cognitive propensities," etc., which amount to the same thing.

11. Barnes errs badly here when he suggests that "belief systems" are rational, meaning logical or consistent. Most are badly self-contradicting, as Gruenberg (1978) has pointed out. For further examination see Kantor, 1945, pp. 187-188 and 170.

12. "Relativism" and "relative" have become very overworked words. In sociology and anthropology they usually mean no more than that different cultures are equally "good." Their use developed around the turn of the century in an effort to get away from ethnocentrism.

## References

Abrahamson, M. 1978. **Functionalism.** Englewood Cliffs, New Jersey: Prentice-Hall.

Alpern, H. 1933. **The March of Philosophy.** New York: Kennikat Press.

Anonymous. 1981. Oldest tool kit yet. **Science News,** 119, 83-84.

Ayres, C. 1932. **Huxley.** New York: W.W. Norton.

Barnes, B. 1974. **Scientific Knowledge and Sociological Theory.** London: Routledge and Kegan Paul.

Barnes, B. 1976. Natural rationality: A neglected concept in the social sciences. **Philosophy of the Social Sciences,** 6, 115-126.

Barnes, B. and Shapin, S. (Eds.) 1979. **Natural Order: Historical Studies of Scientific Culture.** London: Sage.

Berlin, I. 1954. **Historical Inevitability.** Oxford: Oxford University Press.

Bloor, D. 1976. **Knowledge and Social Imagery.** London: Routledge and Kegan Paul.

Boule, M. and Vallois, H.V. 1957. **Fossil Men.** New York: Dryden.

Cohen, P.S. 1968. **Modern Social Theory.** New York: Basic Books.

Davis, K. 1959. The myth of functional analysis as a special method in sociology and anthropology. **American Sociological Review,** 24, 757-772.

Delprato, D.J. 1979. The interbehavioral alternative to brain-dogma. **Psychological Record,** 29, 409-418.

Dray, W.H. 1967. Holism and individualism in history and social science. In P. Edwards (Ed.) **The Encyclopedia of Philosophy** (vol. 4). New York: MacMillan, pp. 53-58.

321

Emmet, D.M. 1967. Functionalism in sociology. In P. Edwards
(Ed.) **The Encyclopedia of Philosophy** (vol. 3). New York:
MacMillan, pp. 256-259.

Gouldner, A. W. 1970. **The Coming Crisis of Western Sociology.**
New York: Basic Books.

Gruenberg, B. 1978. The problem of reflexivity in the sociology
of science. **Philosophy of the Social Sciences,** 8, 321-343.

Hayakawa, S.I. 1949. **Language in thought and action.** New York:
Harcourt, Brace.

Hick, J. 1966. **Evil and the God of Love.** New York: Harper
and Row.

Hinde, R.A. 1966. **Animal Behaviour.** New York: McGraw-Hill.

Holloway, R.L. 1974. The casts of fossil hominid brains. **Scientific
American,** 231, 106-115.

Howell, F.C. 1974. Recent advances in human evolutionary studies.
In S.L. Washburn and P. Dolhinow (Eds.) **Perspectives in Human
Evolution.** New York: Holt, Rinehart and Winston.

Howells, W.W. 1966. Homo erectus. **Scientific American,** 215,
46-53.

Isaac, G. 1978. The food-sharing behavior of protohuman hominids.
**Scientific American,** 238, 90-108.

Jarvie, I.C. 1965. Limits to functionalism and alternatives to
it in anthropology. In D. Martindale (Ed.) **Functionalism in
the Social Sciences.** Philadelphia: The American Academy
of Political and Social Sciences, Monograph 5.

Johanson, D.C. and White, T.D. 1979. A systematic assessment
of early african hominids. **Science,** 203, 321-330.

Kantor, J.R. 1929. **An Outline of Social Psychology.** Chicago:
Follett.

Kantor, J.R. 1936. **An Objective Psychology of Grammar.** Chicago:
Principia.

Kantor, J.R. 1945. **Psychology and Logic** (vol. 1). Chicago:
Principia

Kantor, J.R. 1947. **Problems of Physiological Psychology.** Chicago: Principia.

Kantor, J.R. 1953. **The Logic of Modern Science.** Chicago: Principia.

Kantor, J.R. 1959. **Interbehavioral Psychology.** Chicago: Principia.

Kantor, J.R. 1963. **The Scientific Evolution of Psychology** (vol.1) Chicago: Principia.

Kantor, J.R. 1969. **The Scientific Evolution of Psychology** (vol. 2) Chicago: Principia.

Kantor, J.R. 1971. **The Aim and Progress of Psychology and Other Sciences.** Chicago: Principia.

Kantor, J.R. 1973. System structure and scientific psychology. **Psychological Record,** 23, 451-458.

Kantor, J.r. 1976. The origin and evolution of interbehavioral psychology. **Revista Mexicana de Analisis de la Conducta,** 2, 120-136.

Kantor, J.R. 1977. **Psychological Linguistics.** Chicago: Principia

Kantor, J.R. 1978. Cognition as events and as psychic constructions. **Psychological Record,** 28, 329-342.

Kantor, J.R. 1981. **Interbehavioral Philosphy.** Chicago: Principia.

Keith, A. 1931. **New Discoveries Relating to the Antiquity of Man.** New York: W.W. Norton.

Kuhn, T.S. 1962. **The Structure of Scientific Revolutions.** Chicago: University of Chicago Press.

Leakey, M. 1966. A review of the oldowan culture from olduvai gorge, Tanzania. **Nature,** 210, 462-466.

Leakey, R. 1976. Hominids in Africa. **American Scientist,** 64, 174-178.

Le Gros Clark, W.E. 1967. **Man-Apes or Ape-Men?** New York: Holt.

Leibniz, G.W. 1934. **Philosophical Writings.** London: J.M. Dent.

Lichtenstein, P.E. 1967. Psychological systems: Their nature and function. **Psychological Record,** 17, 321-340.

Lichtenstein, P.E. 1980. Theoretical psychology: Where is it headed? **Psychological Record,** 30, 447-458.

Lovejoy, A.O. 1936. **The Great Chain of Being.** New York: Harper and Row.

Lovejoy, A.O. 1981. The origin of man. **Science,** 211, 341-350.

MacRoberts, M.H. and MacRoberts, B.R. 1979. The referent in animal communication. **Bird Behaviour,** 1, 83-92.

MacRoberts, M.H.and MacRoberts, B.R. 1980a. Toward a minimal definition of animal communication. **Psychological Record,** 30, 387-396.

MacRoberts, M.H. and MacRoberts, B.R. 1980b. Animal communication theory: Mentalism versus naturalism. **Bird Behaviour,** 2, 57-86.

Malefijt, A. 1974. **Images of Man: A History of Anthropological Thought.** New York: Knopf.

Merton, R.K. 1957. **Social Theory and Social Structure.** New York: Free Press.

Mynell, H. 1977. On the limits of the sociology of knowledge. **Social Studies of Science,** 7, 489-500.

Mountjoy, P.T. 1980. Review of Daniel N. Robinson, An **Intellectual History of Psychology, The Interbehaviorist,** 10, 4-10.

Mulkay, M. 1979a. Knowledge and utility: Implications for the sociology of knowledge. **Social Studies of Science,** 9, 63-80.

Mulkay, M. 1979b. **Science and the Sociology of Knowledge.** London: Allan and Unwin.

Munch, P. 1976. The concept of function and functional analysis in sociology. **Philosophy of the Social Sciences,** 6, 193-213.

Observer. 1970. Belief and faith in science. **Psychological Record,** 20, 545-552.

Observer. 1975. History of psychology: What scientific benefits. **Psychological Record,** 25, 567-571.

Observer. 1979. Observations on the history of psychology. **Psychological Record, 29,** 567-571.

Observer. 1980a. Progress in general science and psychology. **Psychological Record, 30,** 581-586.

Observer. 1980b. Mythopsychology and its history. **Psychological Record, 30,** 429-432.

Pronko, N.H. 1946. Language and psycholinguistics: A review. **Psychological Bulletin, 43,** 189-236.

Randall, J.H. 1960. **Aristotle.** New York: Columbia University Press.

Schiller, C.H. (Ed.) 1957. **Instinctive Behavior.** New York: International Universities Press.

Seyfarth, R.M., Cheney, D.L. and Marler, P. 1980. Monkey responses to three different alarm calls: Evidence of predator classification and semantic communication. **Science, 210,** 801-803.

Smith, N.W. 1973. Interbehavioral psychology: Roots and branches. **Psychological Record, 23,** 153-167.

Smith, N.W. 1975. The ancient background to Greek psychology and some implications for today. **Psychological Record, 24,** 309-324.

Spencer, R.F. 1965. The natureand value of functionalism in anthropology. In D. Martindale (Ed.) **Functionalism in the Social Sciences.** Philadelphia: The American Academy of Political and Social Science, Monograph 5, pp. 1-17.

Tinbergen, N. 1951. **The Study of Instinct.** Oxford: Clarendon Press.

Trinkaus, E. and Howells, W.W. 1979. the neanderthals. **Scientific American, 241,** 118-133.

Twain, M. 1903. **Roughing It** (vol. 2). Hartford, Conn.: American Publishing Company.

Walker, A. and Leakey, R. 1978. The hominids of East Turkana. **Scientific American, 239,** 54-66.

Weiner, J.s. 1955. **The Piltdown Forgery.** London: Oxford University Press.

# PSYCHOLOGICAL INTERBEHAVIOR AS A FACTOR IN BIOLOGICAL EVOLUTION

Larry Shaffer

In the past decade students of animal behavior have increasingly conducted studies of behavior ecology (Alcock, 1975; Barnett, 1981; Krebs and Davies, 1978; Morse, 1980; Wittenberger, 1981). Behavior ecology, by the nature of the enterprise, should be more likely to take an approach consistent with the interbehavioral psychology of J.R. Kantor because Kantor has persistently stressed the role of behavior as a part of an interaction of the organism with environing circumstances (Kantor, 1924, 1926, 1959a).

Kantor (1959b) noted that Darwinian ideas about evolution have done much to free psychology from varieties of the immortal soul doctrine. Specifically, psychologists are more likely to view man as a part of nature as a result of Darwin's postulation of common ancestry. Unfortunately, the positive influence appears to be largely in one direction. Biologists have been only little influenced by scientific psychology and have yet to adopt a naturalistic, interactive view of behavior.

It is the purpose of this paper to discuss several of the stances taken by Kantor's scientific approach to psychology and to demonstrate how each of these presents a useful alternative to the student of evolutionary behavior ecology. In this process, the role typically assigned to behavior in biological evolution will be evaluated from an interbehavioral standpoint.

## Distinction Between Data and Interpretations

Kantor (1959a) has stressed that in science it is necessary to be very clear about the distinction between data and the interpretation of those data. The data are objects and events whereas the interpretations are constructs. Kantor (1959a) clearly distinguished among evolutionary concepts as first causes and suggested that evolutionary interpretations should be fashioned with close reference to concrete events.

In biological writing natural selection, in particular, is often cited as the cause of behaviors and structures. Natural selection may be best viewed as an interpretation that is placed on the non-random mortality which occurs among individuals in populations of animals and plants. In order to be used as a cause of behavior, natural selection must be reified and treated as if it were a force of some kind, a clear confusion of data and interpretation. This type of usage began with Darwin (1859):

> It may be said that natural selection is daily and hourly
> scrutinizing, throughout the world, every variation,
> even the slightest; rejecting that which is bad, preser-
> ving and adding up all that is good; silently and insen-
> sibly working wherever and whenever opportunity offers
> at the improvement of each organic being in relation
> to its organic and inorganic conditions (p. 133).

Darwin spoke in these metaphorical terms to help the general reader understand a new and difficult concept, but this non-scientific imprecision and confusion of data and interpretation has continued over the years in the writing of evolutionary scientists (e.g., Young, 1971).

In the introduction to the second edition of one of the cornerstone works in modern evolutionary thought Sir Julian Huxley (1963) quotes Dobzhansky (1955) as having said that "natural selection means differential reproduction" (p. xviii). Huxley footnotes the word "means" and says in the footnote that it would be mroe logical to say "operates by means of" differential reproduction. In this case, Dobzhansky avoided the confusion of data and interpretation only to have it reintroduced by Huxley.

A clear distinction between data and interpretations can offer solutions to some of the philosophic problems in evolutionary thinking. For example, allegations of tautology have often been made concerning the phrase "survival of the fittest" which Darwin borrowed from Herbert Spencer. Although this would seem to be a semantic and trivial problem, it has been the source of considerable discussion and confusion among evolutionary thinkers (e.g., Bethell, 1976; Plew, 1966; Hull, 1974; Manswer, 1965; Scriven, 1959).

Survival of the fittest becomes a tautology when fitness is treated as a general state of superiority which is reified and used as a cause of survival, but not defined independently of survival. The phrase then comes to mean "the survival of those who survive." Being aware of the distinction between data and interpretations, there are two ways to avoid this tautology and to clear the confusion.

The first approach is to define fitness as a particular object or event. For example, Garnett (1981) has found that the largest titmice in a population have a better chance of surviving the immediate post-fledging period. In this instance fitness could be said to be equivalent to size and survival of the fittest becomes survival of the large. This can be easily reformulated as a testable proposition wherein cause is left as an interpretation and is not confused with the data.

Another way to treat fitness is to use it as a label for those who survive. Survival of the fittest then becomes a definition, rather than a causal principle. Scriven (1959) has objected to this approach saying that it would be "fatal to all the scientific claims of the theory of evolution" (p. 478). Popper (1972) contended that evolution by natural selection is not a scientific theory in any event because all imaginable objects and events are consistent with it and therefore it cannot be tested. Olding (1978) objects to this Popperian approach as does Flew (1966) who said "We must on no account overlook that a theory may be in practice unclassifiable because it happens in fact to be true" (p. 75).

These authors seem to be missing the point that a scientific theory should be testable through observation of concrete objects and events if it is going to be of use.

Evolution and natural selection are not being        tested        in ethological studies. In practice studies of eco-ethology in natural settings examine ecological behavior to determine the degree to which it corresponds to ecological behavior in other situations or for other types of animals. These are the data in such studies and if a theory is being tested it is that behavior observed would or would not correspond to that observed on another occasion. Evolution by natural selection is brought in as an interpretation regardless of the outcome of the data.

## Distinction Between Psychological Events and Biological Events

Kantor (1959) has urged behavioral scientists to consider carefully the distinction between psychological and biological events. Biological events are seen as being the actions of cells, tissues and organ systems and are necessary but not sufficient for behavior. Psychological events, on the other hand, are interactions of the whole organism with objects, events and other organisms. Psychological events are not reducible to biological events . Biological events are an essential part of psychological events and can be studied as such, but mere biological events are no more basic to behavior than are other factors such as the characteristics of a stimulus object or the organism's past interactions with a stimulus object.

Interpretations involving Darwinian natural selection should be intimately involved with the interactions of organisms and environing circumstances. Neverthelss, many Darwinians make the reductionistic assumption that the interaction is based on or can be reduced to biological events. This assumption has denied the real importance of behavior in evolution because the behavior is seen as being a result of biological factors alone. Typically in this view, evolution by natural selection is seen to cause physiology and physiology is viewed as the immediate cause of behavior. For example Dawkins (1970) asserted that genes controlled the behavior of survival machines--his term for individuals--by controlling the brain and other neural physiology. The brain was thought to cause behavior by controlling and coordinating actions of muscles (for other examples, see Dewsbury, 1978; Marler and Hamilton, 1966; Sagan, 1977; Wilson, 1975).

Psychological events are derived from bioecological events in which the individual is engaged in finding food, shelter, or situations resulting in reproduction. The whole individual participates in these bioecological interactions (Kantor, 1959a).

Kantor (1959a) characterized biological events as resulting from events that occurred in the phylogenetic history of the individual. He asserted that species evolution involved changes resulting from specific interactions of the organism with the environment. Behavior is, in this way, given a role in evolution by natural selection. The structure forged in this way limits the functioning of the organism because the organism's shape, size and symmetry have definite influences upon the kind of psychological interactions that can be developed (Kantor, 1959). These structure-function influences can be seen either as limits or as predispositions. For example, ground squirrels have limited mobility in the air because of the absence of the loose skin attached between front and hind legs that predisposes gliding in flying squirrels. This flap of skin is only one factor in the bioecological events involving flying squirrels. It is not a cause of flying squirrel behavior, but rather a participating structural factor in those events.

### Continuity Between Man and Other Animals

Classic attempts of comparative psychologists to compare the behaviors of non-human animals were often based on a naive and probably mistaken view of biological evolution (Hodos and Campbell, 1969). In this view, existing species were arranged from the "oldest" to the "most recently evolved." Some existing animals were treated as if they were equivalent to the ancestors of other animals. The behaviors of these so-called ancestral species were examined in order to draw conclusions about the evolution of behavior (Bitterman, 1960).

330

An alternative approach, more consistent with current biological evolutionary thinking views existing species as contemporaries which are constantly involved in interaction with the environment. The ecological behaviors of various animals in various situations can then be compared because these behaviors are all seen as solutions to the ecological problems facing all organisms: Food, shelter, and reproduction. Recently this latter approach has encouraged comparative studies of the ecological behaviors of a large variety of animals (for examples see Krebs and Davies, 1978; Morse, 1980). In this view humans are not considered as discontinuous with other animals to any greater extent than is the case between other species. On the contrary, it is believed that through the study of other animals, solutions may be suggested to the problems that humans are experiencing in ecological matters (Kantor, 1969, p. 312; Tinbergen, 1972).

This denial of an absolute difference between organisms would be more likely to bear fruit in comparative studies if biologists were willing to abandon causal notions of automaticity. A consideration of the psychological behaviors of all animals can lead to an understanding of behavior that can not be achieved through simply viewing non-human animals as machines. As an example , we can speak of the ground squirrel being involved in psychological events because we can see the development of new functions for a given stimulus occurring during the ontogeny of the individual. A ground squirrel which discovers the unguarded burrow of another ground squirrel may explore it and steal stored food. After the first such raid the thief will quickly return at short intervals and will carry away food. At this point the burrow as a stimulus object has a new function. It is no longer just an unguarded burrow, but additionally it is a rich source of food. The stimulus function changes again when the thief is discovered by the burrow owner and is chased and bitten (Shaffer, 1980). The behavior of the ground squirrels can be understood as part of an interaction between the ground squirrel and its environing circumstances including as necessary factors the structural constraints that predispose the animal for feeding on the ground as well as the changing stimulus functions resulting from the animal's past interactions with the stimulus. Based on this understanding, predictions can be made, if so desired, of the outcomes of future interactions between the squirrel and the burrow.

Other examples of psychological responses are common in the literature of comparative psychology, although they are not usually interpreted as such. Studies of operant learning constitute the formation of new stimulus functions (for example see Barnett, 1981; Dewsbury, 1978; Hinde, 1970).

Psychological events are clearly a part of the daily lives of non-human animals beyond the context of the laboratory as well. Imitation, especially in feeding behavior seems to be a common type of psychological event (see Davis, 1973 for a review). One of the classic studies of this is the investigation of the opening of milk bottles by birds (Fisher and Hinde, 1949; Hinde and Fisher, 1951). The data presented indicated that this feeding habit was transmitted locally through observational learning, although it had a number of independent occurrences. It is interesting to note that the authors originally described the feeding behavior as instinctive and the imitation was thought to be the result of inborn mechanisms. Observational learning of feeding behavior in birds has recently been the subject of a careful experimental analysis and the importance of stimulus characteristics and the individual's past experience in the development of this behavior have been demonstrated (Krebs, MacRoberts and Cullen, 1972; Partridge, 1976; Smith and Sweatman, 1974).

## Behavior and Evolutionary Approaches

The three stances described above are all of importance to behavioral biologists who use evolutionary interpretations in their work. A failure to separate data and interpretations has resulted in misleading statements about the cause of behavior. Cause is always an interpretation. Constructs such as innate mechanisms, tendencies and drives are, unfortunately, still sometimes confused with objects and events.

A failure to appreciate the difference between biological and psychological events and their proper relations has resulted in frequent biological reductionism in evolutionary accounts of behavior. Probably the majority of behavioral scientists using evolutionary interpretations on behavior were trained in biological, rather than psychological disciplines. This may set the stage for reductionistic interpretations of behavior and its causation.

A failure to stress the continuity between man and other animals has resulted in behavioral biologists being likely to consider biological rather than psychological factors in the event field through a failure to appreciate that psychological factors exist for non-human animals.

A very serious shortcoming of most evolutionary thinking has been the failure to accord a meaningful role to behavior, that is, a role that takes account of its interactive nature. Rather than dealing with behavior in the manner suggested by Kantor and described briefly above, biologists have sought single causes of behavior.

Typically behavior has been treated in one of three ways. First, behavior has been viewed as instinctive, that is, as simply caused by genes and inherited (Lorenz, 1965). A second approach can be seen in evolutionary writings where the organism's inherited "traits" or "characters" are discussed (e.g., Hardin, 1959, p. 61; Huxley, 1942, p. 63; Mayr, 1965, p. 148; Simpson, 1949, p. 220). It is often clear from the context that the trait or character is a behavior although it is not specifically so defined. In this way the discussant manages to avoid actually saying that a behavior is inherited but also manages to avoid confronting any other role of behavior in evolution. In a third approach, behavior itself is not thought to be inherited, but the ability to perform the behavior is seen as inherited. Generally when biologists are speaking with what they consider to be great precision they will adopt this latter approach and will speak of genetically controlled phenotypes (Mayr, 1965, p. 138). This permits behavior to be part of an interactions with the environment but it does not abandon the notion of underlying genetic control and inheritance.

In the rest of this paper I shall examine neo-Darwinian evolution and three other approaches that can be seen as additions or contributions to neo-Darwinism. Neo-Darwinism and modern Lamarckism both are typically associated with traditional reductionistic assumptions about behavior. A third approach, organic selection, allows an interactive nature of behavior in some circumstances but it retains traditional assumptions as well. The fourth approach, evolution by behavioral initiative, can be viewed as being consistent with the interbehavioral stances described above. Further, this last approach offers solutions to some of the classical problems of biological evolution.

## Neo-Darwinian Approach

The term Neo-Darwinian will be used here to refer to the approach involving a synthesis of Darwinism and genetics as described by Huxley (1942, 1963) and others. This notion is based on the observation that individuals have enormous reproductive potential but that populations usually remain stable. The presumption is that those individuals which have more offspring have superior genotypes which are passed on to those offspring. Genotypes vary and some will be better adapted to the environment and preserved while others will be selected out through mortality or low reproductive rates. Variation among individuals is thought to be based on genetic variation resulting from new combinations of genes formed during sexual reproduction and from mutations. Traditionally mututations are said to be random, but as Barker (1969) has pointed out, they are not random physiological events rather they are random with respect to future benefit.

Darwin (1859) believed that instinct was an important cause of behavior. He stated that instincts were inherited and were slightly variable. This variability was thought to be subject to differential morality, or selection, just as with structural variation. Darwin (1871) did allow some classes of behavior that were not thought to be inherited, these being habit and reason. These were mentioned but they were not integrated into Darwin's evolutionary scheme. Later evolutionists preserved these notions and added Mendelian genetics. Usually, for neo-Darwinists, behavior is thought to be a product of the nervous system and the nervous system is thought to be a result of genetic instructions. Thus Barnett (1981) stated that "cognitive abilities represent one of the major unsolved problems of biology: how do nervous systems generate such elaborate behavior?" (p. 122).

Recently Wilson (1975) and Dawkins (1976) among others have suggested in a very overt manner that genes cause behavior. This doctrine had been called sociobiology. Wilson (1975) wrote:

> As more complex social behavior is added to the genes' techniques for replicating themselves , altruism becomes increasingly prevalent and eventually appears in exaggerated forms. This brings us to the central theoretical problem of sociobiology: how can altruism, which by definition reduces personal fitness, possibly evolve by natural selection? The answer is kinship: if the genes causing the altruism are shared by two organisms because of common descent, and if the altruistic act by one organism increases the joint contribution of these genes to the next generation, the propensity to altruism will spread through the gene pool (p. 3).

A more tangled web of reductionism and data-interpretation confusion is difficult to imagine. In this account genes and natural selection both cause altruism. We do not know what the behavior in question is because the interpretation "altruism" is used in place of a behavioral description. This type of genetic determinism as an extension of neo-Darwinism concludes that at the very least the genotype must determine the reproductive ouput of the individual. If this were correct, then both individuals within a pair of monozygotic twins would have the same number of children (Hull, 1974).

Dawkins (1976) allowed non-genetic influences, exhorting us to teach our children to be altruistic. He forgot that within the rest of his schema of genetic determinism those who did so would be selected out. As in the work of Darwin (1871) there is no attempt to integrate this non-genetic influence on behavior into the evolutionary system. One of Dawkins' primary evidences that genes cause behavior is the work of Rothenbuhler (1964) on cell-cleaning bees. Here Dawkins ignores the interactive nature of the bee's activities with diseased cells and concludes that a single gene can cause a behavior. He makes much of this example even though, earlier in this book, he states that "chosen examples are never serious evidence for any worthwhile generalization" (p. 7). Sociobiology has often been criticized (for examples see Montagu, 1980; Sahlins, 1977) for its reductionistic assumptions.

### Inheritance of Acquired Characteristics

Although the ideas of the inheritance of acquired characteristics are probably ancient, the name of the 18th century naturalist Lamarck is most often associated with such notions. In the simplest form of this view, structural variations of offspring are caused by parental development of structures. Perhaps the most common example involves the son of the blacksmith being supposed to inherit genetically the muscles that his father developed in the course of smithing. Cannon (1959) pointed out that Lamarck has been treated unfairly by historians and biologists. Lamarck was a highly competent naturalist and he recognized that some sort of evolution was a reasonable interpretation of the sorts of variety with which he was confronted. Suggestions that he made about the inheritance of acquired characters were merely the naive suggestions of a man working in the late 18th century. Lamarck's work was summarized and reinterpreted by anti-evolutionists after his death in an attempt to make his ideas appear less tenable.

Darwin (1859) renounced inheritance of acquired characteristics but had reintroduced it by the time the 6th edition of the same book appeared in 1872. He did not see how variations could be preserved without this type of explanation (Hardin, 1959).

Probably the most vocal proponent of this view at the present time is Arthur Koestler (1967, 1971, 1978). As Toulmin (1979) has pointed out, Koestler seems to be primarily objecting to the neo-Darwinian notion that behavior and structure come about as a result of mutations which are random. Koestler (1978) wrote:

> The purposiveness of all vital processes, the strategy of genes and the power of the exploratory drive in animal and man all seem to indicate that the pull of the future is as real as the pressure of the past. Causality and finality are complementary principles in the sciences of life; ....if you take out finality and purpose, you have taken the life out of biology as well as psychology (p. 226).

335

Koestler (1978) believed that events in the life of the organism must, in some orderly way, be the determiners of the genetic mutations that take place. He attacks the Weissman-Crick dogma which he describes as the unalterable germ track. In Koestler's view, genetic mutations are seen as basic to and causal of behavior and these mutations are determined, at least in part, by psychological events acting through biochemical channels. Strangely, Koestler considers himself to be a crusader against reductionism(Koestler and Smythies, 1972; Koestler, 1978).

Although this modern Lamarckism continues to be advocated in the professional literature (Ho and Saunders, 1979) many professional biologists and philosophers of science continue to oppose it. "Experiments in heredity in the present century not only have failed to corroborate that there is such a process but have also shown that it is highly improbable, if not impossible" (Simpson, 1944, p. 133). "With few and quite unimportant qualifications, **there's nothing in Lamarckism**" (Hardin, 1959, p. 110. "Lamarckism is conclusively discredited" (Ruse, 1969, p. 345).

## Organic Selection or the Baldwin Effect

As with the inheritance of acquired characteristics, this proposal can be seen as supplementary to neo-Darwinian natural selection rather than as opposition to it. It is important because it admits a role for behavior as an interactive process. The concept of organic selection appears in the work of James Mark Baldwin (1895) and is given formal statement in the next year (Baldwin, 1896a; Morgan, 1896; Osborn, 1896). Baldwin (1895) recognized that behavior was variable or plastic and that wihtin a group the individuals with certain types of behavior were more likely to be the survivors because they could adapt to new circumstances that might appear. This conflicted with the traditional view of behavior as rigidly controlled by instinct. Baldwin (1896a) certainly believed that behavior was caused by physiology but he was able to look beyond that level of analysis to see the organism interacting with its environment in its ecological behavior. "We find a superb series of adaptations by lower as well as higher animals during the course of ontogenetic development...The progress of the child in all the learning processes which lead him on to be a man just illustrates this higher form of adaptation" (Baldwin, 1896a, p. 445).

In his proposal of organic selection, Baldwin allowed the individual modification of behavio to keep the individual alive until such time as
the right chance variations in heredity occurred to preserve these modifications in the future. Organic selection raised little comment for almost half a century. Sir Julian Huxley (1942) included mention of it in his classic summary of evolutionary thinking. While Baldwin (1896a,

1896b, 1896c) thought that organic selection would act as a bridge between Darwinian and Lamarckian thoughts, Simpson (1953) rejected this idea. Simpson did not deny the possibility of organic selection but he said that there was no evidence for it and that the examples often used to illustrate it were trivial. He further stated that "the ability to 'acquire' a character has, in itself, a genetical basis" (Simpson, 1953, p, 116). In so doing he negated any small gains that might have been made in the recognition of the role of behavior in evolution through organic selection.

### Evolution by Behavioral Initiative

The inheritance of acquired characteristics was only part of the evolutionary mechanism proposed by Lamarck. Another of Lamarck's proposals suggests something completely different. Lamarck said "The production of a new organ in an animal body results from a new need (**besoin**) which continues to make itself felt, and from a new movement that this need brings about and maintains" (translated by Cannon, 1959, p. 51). there has been confusion over the translation of this passage and **besoin** has been variously translated as **need** or **want** (Cannon, 1959). When the meaning is "want," the suggestion is that the animal can create new structures in some way through desiring them. When, however, the meaning is "need," as Cannon (1959) and Hardy (1965) suggest, then the behavior of the individual is given a role in subsequent evolution.

Hardy calls this evolution by behavioral initiative. Although Hardy gives credit to many others for first having these ideas (Lamarck, 1816; Baldwin, 1896a; Morgan, 1896; Osborn, 1896; Ewer, 1960) he has nevertheless given the most complete presentation of the proposal. Evolution by behavior initiative is also implied by Jepsen (1949) and McAtee (1936) as well as being clearly stated by Stern (1959) who called it the bonus principle.

In this approach, the structure of the animal is not merely the result of the ancestral biological events of gene mutation and recombination as is stressed by the neo-Darwinians. Rather the interbehavior[1] of the ancestral individual plays a large role in the eventual structure of the species. A documented example from Ewer (1960) concerns bushpigs. The bushpig is a fairly unspecialized feeder, eating all sorts of things. The related warthog is a specialized feeder, eating mainly grass from among the weeds. The bushpig has short, unspecialized teeth, rather like those of a domestic pig whereas the warthog has teeth specialized for grass feeding. The warthog chews with a sideways grinding movement which grinds the grass seeds. This behavior can be directly observed or inferred from the architecture of the skull and the polish that the teeth attain in so doing. A number of fossil South African pigs show different stages in the development of the structural adaptations that accompany the grinding of specialized feeders. If behavior initiates structure, then we would expect to find the characteristic tooth wear of the specialized feeder earlier in the fossil record than we find the changes in skull structure that accompany specialized feeding. That is, we should expect to find that the animal was involved in new interactions with the food in the environment first and that these new psychological events made certain biological events (the mutations and recombinations predisposing skull changes) worthwhile. According to Ewer (1960) this is found in the case of the fossil pig.

Ewer(1960) stressed that within animal populations there is always variability among individuals with respect to biological structures. If this variation is, for example, normally distributed, then perhaps a new interbehavior would be most useful to those individuals within a species with structural variation occurring on one or the other tail of the distribution. Imagine a new interbehavior which may involve feeding and which may be most successfully accomplished by individual birds within a species which have the longest bills. If these individuals can feed themselves more successfully because of the coincidence of bill length and psychological interbehavior the result will follow one of two possible scenarios. The long-billed individuals might rapidly increase in frequency in successive generations at the expenseof their short-billed conspecifics. This will happen if, even with the new food supply, long-billed birds and shorter-billed birds are still competing for food, space, or mates. The other possible outcome would be a divergence of the long-billed birds from the rest of the population without extinction of the shorter-billed birds. This would occur in situations in which the long-billed birds invaded a new ecological niche to the extent that they were no longer in direct competition with the shorter-billed animals.

As a contribution to evolution, behaviorally initiated evolution solves some of the problems of classical neo-Darwinism. Ho and Saunders (1979) noted the problem that rigorous natural selection, which would occur in conditions of high intraspecific competition, has not been associated with major evolutionary advance. They report, however, that when selection is relaxed and a species invades a new ecological niche or is isolated geographically in a new habitat, rapid evolution does occur. The new circumstances occasioned by a niche invasion or isolation are just those in which we would expect animals to interact with the environment in new ways resulting in differential survival for structural variations in the longrun.

Two problems confront the stance of the neo-Darwinians that the only source of variation for evolution by natural selection is recombination and mutation of genes. First, as Ho and Saunders (1979)

338

have summarized, the evidence suggests that most genetic changes are irrelevant to evolution. This is not surprising, nor is it a problem in the light of behaviorally initiated evolution. Second, mutation and recombination are slow, steady processes yet it is clear from the palentological record that evolutionary changes have not happened at a steady rate, but, at times, surged ahead (Grould, 1980; Jepsen, 1949). This is what would be expected if some of these changes were behaviorally initiated. A new behavior could sweep through a population by imitation, as with the milk bottle opening in birds mentioned above. Suddenly birds with certain structural variations, for example long bills, would be feeding mroe efficiently than the rest of their conspeicifics and as a result they would raise more offspring. Rapidly the population would move toward being long-billed through the differential mortality that is called natural selection. Evolutionary changes would be very rapid for a number of generations while the average bill length of the population increased.

An additional problem, mentioned by Huxley (1953) was that because of the steady and slow mutation rates the operation of neo-Darwinian evolution might be viewed as too slow to account for the rich variety of organisms in the time available. Behaviorally initiated evolution, as an interpretation, leads to acceptance of faster rates of evolution that appear to happen at times. Baldwin (1896) recognized that it was possible for successive generations of parents to pass a behavior along by teaching it to their offspring. He called this social heredity and he suggested that it was really just another means of transmitting variation from one generation to the next. If the behavior resulted in increased reproductive output, it would increase in frequency within the population. Huxley (1953) has called this cultural evolution but dicusses it only in the context of human populations. Problems may arise for the neo-Darwinian when animals learn new and useful behaviors from unrelated individuals as certainly happens frequently (Barnett, 1981). Neo-Darwinian evolution depends on benefits being passed on to related individuals because each individual is seen to be in competition with unrelated conspecifics for resources. Benefits passed on to unrelated others would only interfere with and further slow the rate of neo-Darwinian evolution.

A number of authors have commented that much mortality will be simply accidental, having nothing to do with the superiority or inferiority of the organism (Dewar, 1926; McAtee, 1937; Scriven, 1959). This type of mortality has been called the survival of the lucky, survival of the ordinary or survival of the fortunate. It would only further slow neo-Darwinian evolution making behaviorally initiated evolution even more essential as an interpretation.

Behavior varies from individual to individual as a result of a number of factors including the individual's past interactions and it is

339

only common sense that this variation must be allowed a large role in the reproductive success of the individual. There is a considerable confusion on this point among the evolutionists which could be cleared up by the acceptance of an interbehavioral view of behavior. Most neo-Darwinians allow that selection acts on variations occurring in the phenotype. They further assert that the phenotype is not identical with the genotype. They are aware that the behavior and structure of animals are phenotypic. Having acknowledged all this they tend, nevertheless, to discuss behaviors and structures as if they were simply caused by an identifiable portion of genetic material. Further, they suggest that the variation important for evolution must be genetic variation (Huxley, 1942, p. 115; Mayr, 1965, p. 148; Simpson, 1949, p. 213; Dawkins, 1976, p. 18; Wilson, 1975, p. 14). This is clearly false as it is the phenotypic variations that result in mortality and reproductive success.

If the biological establishment is to accept evolution by behavioral initiative as part of its evolutionary doctrine, it must be prepared to accept that the events interpreted as natural selection act on all variation in a population, not just variation in genetic structure and events. This has been recommended by Hardin (1959) and by Stern (1970) in other contexts. If variation is the raw material of natural selection then the inclusion of interbehavior as part of this variation would tend to accelerate rates of evolution because behavior differences between individuals of the same species are probably greater than structural differences. More variability means a greater range of adaptation. These behavior differences must be closely linked to mortality. Manser (1965) has pointed out that neo-Darwinians lack a complete theory of variation although it is critical to an understanding of natural selection.

It is, of course, essential that the variation in question be transmitted from one generation to the next but the means of transmission does not matter. Indeed, to try to say that the means is genetic or non-genetic is to fall into the old and useless nature-nurture dichotomy. As has bene clearly pointed out by Murphey and many others, behavior and structure cannot be dichotomized on a nature-nurture dimension (Murphey, 1973). If we accept the arguments against this dichotomy, then we are forced into admitting that differential mortality results from all variation and that selection of variation, regardless of the source of means of transmission, results in evolution.

In spite of the age of the behaviorally initiated evolution notion, it continues to be largely ignored by the biological establishment and, more strangely, by behavioral biologists. Recent thinking about the evolution of hominoids is consistent with evolution by behavioral initiative but this idea is not specifically mentioned (Lovejoy, 1981).

340

It seems reasonable that behaviorally initiated evolution has been largely ignored because it steps away from the view of behavior as having biological causes. Acceptance of behavioral initiative requires behavior to be viewed as an interaction between the individual and the environment. The acceptance of this interbehavioral view by evolutionary biology would not be the mere acknowledgment of an alternative explanation. It is essential to a complete understanding of biological evolution that all variation be understood. The interbehavioral perspective encourages the understanding of behavior as part of a organism-environment interaction and in concert with behaviorally initiated evolution it can offer resolution of a number of classical neo-Darwinian problems.

## Footnote

1. I consider that for the purpose of this paper, interbehavior is equivalent to behavior. In places I shall use the term interbehavior to additionally stress the interactive nature of the behavior in question.

## References

Alcock, j. 1975. **Animal Behavior. An Evolutionary Approach.** Sunderland, Mass.: Sinaver Associates.

Baldwin, J. 1895. Consciousness and evolution. **Science, 2,** 219-223.

Baldwin, J. 1896a. A new factor in evolution. **American Naturalist,** 30, 441-451, 536-553.

Baldwin, J. 1896b. Heredity and instinct. **Science, 3,** 438-441.

Baldwin, J. 1896c. Heredity and instinct II. **Science, 3,** 558-561.

Barker, A. 1969. An approach to the theory of natural selection. **Philosophy, 44,** 271-290.

Barnett, S. 1981. **Modern Ethology. The Science of Animal Behavior.** New york: Oxford University Press.

Bethell, T. 1976. Darwin's mistake. **Harpers,** 252, 70-75.

Bitterman, M. 1965. The evolution of intelligence. **Scientific American ,** 212, 92-100.

Cannon, H. 1959. **Lamarck and Modern Genetics.** Springfield, Ill.: Charles C. Thomas.

Darwin, C. 1859. **The Origin of Species By Means of Natural Selection or the Preservation of Favored Races in the Struggle for Life.** London: Murray.

Darwin, C. 1871. **The Descent of Man and Selection in Relation to Sex.** London: Murray.

Davis, J. 1973. Imitation: A review and critique. In P. Bateson and P. Klopfer (Eds.) **Perspectives in Ethology.** New York: Plenum.

Dawkins, R. 1976. **The Selfish Gene.** London: Oxford University Press.

Dewar, D. 1926. **Indian Bird Life or the Struggle for Existence of Birds in India.** London: John Lane.

Dewsbury, D. 1978. **Comparative Animal Behavior.** New York: McGraw Hill.

Dobzhansky, T. 1955. A review of some fundamental concepts and problems of population genetics. Cold Spring Harbor **Symposium on Quantitative Biology, 20, 1-15.**

Ewer, R. 1960. Natural selection and neoteny. **Acta Biotheoretica, 13, 161-184.**

Fisher, J. and Hinde, R. 1949. The opening of milk bottles by birds. **British Birds, 42, 347-357.**

Flew, A. 1966. The concept of evolution: A comment. **Philosophy, 41, 70-75.**

Garnett, M. 1981. Body size, its heritability and influence on juvenile survival among great tits **Parus Major. Ibis, 123, 32-41.**

Gould, S. 1980. **The Panda's Thumb.** New York: Mentor.

Hardin, G. 1959. **Nature and Man's Fate.** New York: Mentor.

Hardy, A. 1965. **The Living Stream.** New York: Harper and Row.

Hinde, R. 1970. **Animal Behavior: A Synthesis of Ethology and Comparative Psychology** (2nd edition). London: McGraw Hill.

Hinde, R. and Fisher, J. 1951. Further observations on the opening of milk bottles by birds. **British Birds, 44**, 392-396.

Ho, M. and Saunders, P. 1979. Beyond neo-Darwinism. An epigenetic approach to evolution. **Journal of Theoretical Biology, 78**, 573-591.

Hodos, W. and Campbell, C. 1969. Scala naturae: Why there is no theory in comparative psychology. **Psychological Review, 76**, 337-350.

Hull, D. 1974. **Philosophy of Biological Science.** Englewood Cliffs, NJ.: Prentice-Hall.

Huxley, J. 1942. **Evolution , the Modern Synthesis.** London: Allen and Unwin .

Huxley, J. 1953. **Evolution in Action.** New York : Harper.

Huxley, J. 1963. **Evolution , t he Modern Synthesis** (2nd edition). London: Allen and Unwin.

Jepsen, G. 1949. Selection "o rthogenesis" and the fossil record. **Proceedings of the American Philosophical Society, 93**, 479-500.

Kantor, J.R. 1924. **Principles of Psychology** (Vol. 1). New York: Knopf.

Kantor, j.R. 1926. **Principles of Psychology** (vol. 2). New York: Knopf.

Kantor, J.R. 1959a. **Interbehavioral Psychology.** Granville, Ohio: Principia Press.

Kantor, J.R. 1959b. Evolution and the science of psychology. **Psychological Record, 9**, 131-142.

Kantor, J.R. 1969. **The Scientific Evolution of Psychology** (Vol. 2). Chicago: Principia Press.

Koestler, A. 1967. **The ghost in the Machine.** New York: MacMillan.

Koestler, A. 1971. **The Case of the Midwife Toad.** New York: Random House.

Koestler, A. 1978. **Janus: A Summing Up.** New York: Random House.

Krebs, J., MacRoberts, M. and Cullen, J. 1972. Flocking and feeding in the great tit **Parus major**--an experimental study. **Ibis,** 114, 507-530.

Lamarck, J. 1816. **Histoire Naturelle des Animaux Sans Vertebres.** Paris: Verdiere.

Lorenz, K. 1965. **Evolution and Modification of Behavior.** Chicago: University of Chicago Press.

Lovejoy, K. 1965. The origin of man. **Science,** 221, 341-350.

Manser, A. 1965. The concept of evolution. **Philosophy,** 40, 18-34.

Marler, D. and Hamilton, W. 1966. **Mechanisms of Animal Behavior.** New York: Wiley.

Mayr, E. 1965. **Animal Species and Evolution.** Cambridge, Mass.: Belknap.

McAtee, W. 1936. The role fitness in evolution. **Ohio Journal of Science,** 36, 237-241.

McAtee, W. 1937. Survival of the ordinary. **Quarterly Review of Biology,** 12, 47-65.

Montagu, A. (Ed.) 1980. **Sociobiology Examined.** London : Oxford University Press.

Morgan, C. 1876. On modification and variation. **Science,** 4, 733-740.

Morse, D. 1980. **Behavioral Mechanisms in Ecology.** Cambridge, Mass.: Harvard University Press.

Murphey, R. 1973. Genetic correlates of behavior. In G. Bermant (Ed.) **Perspectives on Animal Behavior.** Glenview,Ill.: Scott Foresman.

Olding, A. 1978. A defense of evolutionary laws. **British Journal of Philosophy and Science,** 29, 131-143.

Osborn, H. 1896. Ontogenic and phylogenic variation. **Science,** 4, 786-789.

Partridge, L. 1976. Individual differences in feeding efficiencies and feeding preferences of captive great tits. **Animal Behavior,** 24, 230-240.

Popper, K. 1972. **Objective Knowledge.** London: Oxford University Press.

Rothenbuhler, W. 1964 Behavior genetics of nest cleaning in honey bees. IV. Responses of F, and black cross generations to disease-killed brood. **American Zoologist,** 4, 111-123.

Ruse, H. 1969. Confirmation and falsification of theories of evolution. **Scientia,** 104, 329-357.

Sagan, C. 1977. **The Dragons of Eden.** New York: Random House.

Sahlins, M. 1977. **The Use and Abuse of Biology.** London: Tavistock.

Scriven, M. 1959. Explanations and prediction in evolutionary theory. **Science,** 130, 477-482.

Shaffer, L. 1980. Use of scatterhoards by eastern chipmunks to replace stolen food. **Journal of Mannalogy,** 61, 733-734.

Simpson, G. 1944. **The Major Features of Evolution.** New York: Simon and Schuster.

Simpson, G. 1949. **The Meaning of Evolution.** New Haven: Yale University Press.

Simpson, G. 1953. The Baldwin effect. **Evolution,** 7, 110-117.

Smith, J. and Swatmen, H. 1974. Food searching behavior of titmice in patchy environments. **Ecology,** 55, 1216-1232.

Stern, C. 1959. Variation and hereditary transmission. **Proceedings of the American Philosophical Society,** 103, 183-189.

Stern, J. 1970. The meaning of "adaptation" and its relation to the phenomenon of natural selection. **Evolutionary Biology,** 4, 39-66.

Tinbergen, N. 1978. Ethology and the human sciences. In N. Tinbergen (Ed.) **The Animal in its World.** Cambridge, Mass.: Harvard University Press.

Toulmin, S. 1979. Arthur Koestler's theodicy. On sin, science and politics. **Encounter,** 52, 46-57.

Wilson, E. 1975. **Sociobiology.** Cambridge, Mass.: Belknap Press.

Wittenberger, J. 1981. **Animal Social Behavior.** Boston: Duxbury Press.

Young, R. 1971. Darwin's metaphor: Does nature select? **The Monist,** 55, 442-503.

# AN OBJECTIVE ANALYSIS OF
## SPECIES-TYPICAL AND OTHER BEHAVIORS

Donna M. Cone

During recent decades, ethological studies have yielded data which appear incompatible with the extremely environmentalistic bias of American psychology. Certain behaviors seem to be unacquired and display little or no improvement with either maturation or practice. These behaviors characterizes given sex or species, are closely related to certain physiological states of the organism, and are primarily involved in adaptive biological functions such as ingestion, metabolism and growth, symbiosis, and reproduction. In attempting to interpret these data, certain psychologists (e.g., Herrnestein, 1972) posit a sort of equivalence between 'drive" and "instinct" and contend that a primary task of behavioral psychology is to specify the number of innate drives and how they interact with each other. This analysis overlooks the fact that both "drive" and "instinct" are mentalistic concepts which evolved in response to cultural influences rather than the observation of psychological events. The present paper proposes that species-typical behaviors can be more completely and objectively assessed by an analysis of the confrontable events. Several examples of such an analysis will be detailed to support this contention.

## Scientific Field Analysis in Psychology

A scientific analysis of confrontable events presupposes an appreciation of their complexity. Psychological events occur only as intricate interactions in spatio-temporal fields. While traditional theorists have focused on the responding organism, it is only one participant in the field event. This approach fails to take into account the other critical factors in the psychological event. A more complete analysis is offered by Kantor (1959, p. 16) who views the psychological event (PE) as centering around a response function (rf), which consists of an action of a living organism, and a stimulus function (sf), which consists of a reciprocal action of a stimulus object. The historical interbehavioral process (hi) in which these functions are generated in an important factor, since most psychological interbehaviors have evolved through a series of contacts between organism and objects. In addition, there are setting factors (st), or immediate circumstances, influencing which sf-rf will occur.

Finally, there is a medium of contact (md), e.g., light, by which organisms and objects are able to contact each other. The roles played by these factors can be represented in this formula for the psychological event: PE=C(k, sf, rf, hi, st, md), in which k symbolizes the uniqueness of each interbehavioral field and C indicates that the field consists for an entire system of factors in interaction.

## Problem of Species-Typical Behaviors

Species-typical behaviors constitute a special class of interbehaviors in which the **individual** historical interbehavior process is minimal while the critical setting factors largely comprise physiological states of the organism. The stimulus function (i.e., what traditional ethology calls the "releasing properties of the sign stimulus") in species-typical behaviors is the outcome of long periods of interbehavior in biological evolution.

## A Comparison of Species-Typical and Psychological Behaviors

Such biological interbehaviors contrast with psychological interbehaviors along several dimensions. Biological interbehaviors consist of the functioning of cellular structures either in isolation, as in nerve-muscle preparations, or in integral systemization, as in species-typical behavior of entire organisms. Psychological interbehaviors are relatively independent of localized structures or systems, always consisting of the acts of organisms evolved in relatively short-term intervals of individual interbehavioral history. Where biological interbehaviors are concerned, stimulation is based exclusively upon the intrinsic properties of objects (e.g., the red breast of a male robin) and the immediate contingencies of events (e.g., the securing of a territory). In psychological interbehaviors, stimulus functions are not limited to physiochemical properties of objects, but may be built up under social, or cultural auspices. The development and alter performance of psychological interbehaviors occur in complex fields comprised of either idiosyncratic or cultural components, or both.

## Nonreductionistic Relationship Between Biological and Psychological Interbehaviors

Psychological interbehaviors are not related to biological interbehaviors in a reductionistic fashion. Rather, each is independently definable according to objective criteria. Psychological interbehaviors that are very similar to biological inerbehaviors may occur if conditioning procedures are instigated. For instance, in the Pavlovian paradigm, the UR of salivation is a psychological inter-behavior. Recently, species-typical behaviors, or biological interbehav-

348

iors, involving the entire organism have been classically conditioned. For example, Farris (1967) conditioned male Japanese quail to display courting behavior at the sound of a buzzer (a previously neutral stimulus) by pairing buzzer presentation with the presentation of a female quail for several trials. Here the UR of courting to the female quail is a biological interbehavior, while the CR of courting to the buzzer is a psychological interbehavior. Both unconditioned salivation and unconditioned courting characterize the species, while conditioned salivation and conditioned courting merely characterize the individual. In most situations occurring in a natural environment, biological interbehaviors of a species-typical type occur only to the so-called "sign stimuli."

### An Interbehavioral Analysis of Fish Behaviors

In order to demonstrate the interbehavioral analysis of species-typical behaviors, the reproductive behavior of the bitterling (**Rhodeus Amarus Bloch**) will be considered. The following description is taken from Wiepkema (1961) who observed this fish in tanks, using fresh-water mussels of the genera **Unio**:

> The bitterlings swim around these mussels and perform reactions to them which are typical of the reproductive period. After some time the males start defending an area around a mussel. Other males or females are chased away, but ripe females are permitted to enter this area. These females are led by the males towards the mussel. During leading the male swims in front of the female and quivers with its entire body. The female deposits its eggs within the gills of the mussel by means of the long ovipositor. There usually are a number of spawning acts a day. Both before and after egg laying the male makes swimming movements over the siphons of the mussel. Simultaneously with swimming the male may eject sperm, which may be drawn into the inhalent siphon of the mussel and thereby reach any eggs lying within the gills. After a development of about 4 weeks the young fish leave the mussel through the exhalent siphon. There is no parental behaviour in the bitterling (p. 105).

A careful analysis of Weipkema's (1961) data reveals the presence of a number of significant stimulus objects and several relevant setting factors. The primary setting factor for the female is that she be in the physiological state of oestrus. This state will not develop except in water of a certain temperature (normally this occurs from April to June in the ponds of Holland) and can be postponed even then if mussels are not available in her immediate environment. Under optimal conditions, once every 6 to 12 days the ovipositor of the female becomes very long and the female deposits 1 to 4 eggs during each of 10 to 15 spawning acts. While a female which is prevented from spawning for many hours by keeping her separated from males and mussels may deposit her eggs in a mussel in the absence of a male, the mussel and the male generally act as stimulus objects for spawning. Initially, the female follows the males to the mussel, a behavior which constrasts markedly with her typical non-estrous behavior of schooling or fleeing and remaining in the pond's vegetation. The relevant stimuli presented by the male just prior to spawning by the female appear to be his head-down positioning over the mussel, his skimming and sperm ejection, and his remaining nearby while performing a quivering movement.

There are physiological setting factors for the male bitterling, as well as for the female, The first observable sign of the coming reproductive period in the male is a brightening of the red eyepatch and the blue tail line and a reddening of the anal fin. Two white wartlike structures develop just above the mouth, the so-called pearl organs, and contrast sharply with the dark head colors. Only males which will defend an area around a mussel perform courtship movements in the presence of a female. Thus, the mussel is, for the male as well as the female, an essential part of the reproductive field. If only males are present in the defended area, various predictable agonistic movements are made by the defending male. When a female first enters the defended area, she is rushed at by the male. However, if the female possesses a long ovipositor, his initial head-butting agonistic movement is quickly replaced by quivering and leading movements. Since the female's coloration remains constant throughout her reproductive period, the presence of the long ovipositor appears to be the only relevant stimulus she presents for the male.

The entire reproductive sequence in the bitterling thus results from the complex interplay of physiological setting factors, with structural and movement stimuli within a field that has a certain temperature and a particular organism of another species. The modification of any one of these factors can drastically alter this biological interbehavior. For example, eggs deposited beside the mussel rather than in it are usually devoured immediately by both male and female.

### Inheritance vs. Evolution of
### Biological Interbehaviors

The above characterization of the stimulus functions in biological interbehaviors as "the outcome of long periods of biological evolution" must not be viewed as saying that biological behaviors per se are inherited.  As Klopfer (1969, p. 559) points out, modern theories of gene action do not conceptualize the gene as a "repository of data or a blueprint from which the organism can be constructed," but rather as "an information-generating device which exploits the predictable and ordered nature of its environment." As shown above with the example of bitterling reproductive behavior, biological interbehaviors do not occur unless the predictable and ordered nature of the environmental field is present.  Biological interbehaviors, then, are not stored up in the organism as "instincts," or "tendencies" to be exhibited when certain "sign stimuli" appear.  The predictability of a given biological interbehavior is a function of the ability to predict the entire field, including setting factors and contact media, as well as stimuli.

### The Traditional Approach of Biologists to the Evolution of Functions

Since before Darwin's time, biologists have approached the problem of the evolution of structures and functions by comparing them across species.  As Sir Richard Owen indicated in 1843 (Gray, 1973), the basic principles of similarity and dissimilarity in structure and function can be specified by a factorial design. Comparing the structures of two species will show them to be similar (homlogous) or dissimilar (nonhomologous), while the functions of these structures are similar (analogous) or dissimilar (nonanalogous).  If the structures are similar in both structure and function, a homologue is present. If they are similar in function but not in structure, an analogue is present.  If they are dissimilar in both structure and function, there is no basis for comparison.   If they are similar in structure but not in function, a spurious comparison has been made.   Atz (1970),for instance, has discussed at length the special problems involved in attempting to trace the evolutionary history of functions. Recently Klopfer (1973a) has pointed out that the distinction between analogues and homologues is largely dependent on the observer's prior knowledge of the phyletic relationship and physiology of the animals being compared.  He gives as an example the status of wings in bats and insects:   If one already knows that bats are mammals and flies are insects, then their wings are classified as analogous structures, a convergent response to a common problem.  If such taxonomic data are absent, the observer cannot deny that the wings may be homolgues.

### Traditioinal Approach to the Evolution of Display Behavior

Display behavior has been extensively studied by ethologists interested in the evolutionary origins of biological behaviors.  Daanje (1950) first argued that intention movements, the initial parts of an action performed without leading to completion of the action, are a major evolutionary source of displays. Comparisons across closely related species reveal the states through which intention movements passed and evolved into a display. For example, Lorenz (1958) compared "inciting" movements in several species of ducks. The shellduck displays a primitive, unritualized set of movements, while the mallar merely points its bill over the shoulder in a hihgly stereotyped fashion.

Displacement behaviors comprise a second evolutionary source of displays. For example, a comparison of the form of the threat display of the Manchurian crane with threat displays of other species of cranes allows one to trace it through a series of variations, which began as unritualized displacement preening (Dewsbury and Rethlingshafer, 1973).

A third evolutionary source of display components is found in peripheral manifestations of autonomic change. Morris (1959) showed that feather posture such as crest-raising and sleeking of feathers in birds is affected by temperature in ways which suggest its evolutionary basis.

The evidence cited above to support an evolutionary origin of displays belongs to what Klopfer (1973b) calls "comparative studies." He distinguishes between "strong" comparative studies, in which an array of species exists providing a spectrum of behavioral types, and "weak" comparative studies, in which an array of species has a variety of traits,some elements of which are held in common. Klopfer (1973) discusses four other sources of evidence to support the evolution of biological interbehavioral response functions. One is a type of "behavioral fossil," as when footprints preserved in mud reveal data about the gait of the animals which made them. A second is when one can directly observe natural selection at work, as in the correlative changes of moth and butterfly coloration with changes in industrial soot deposits in England over the past century. Third, one can infer certain things about the evolution of behavior by knowing the character of the organism's environment (e.g., one can estimate the degree of dispersal of ungulates if one can reconstruct the vegetation and climate of an area). The fourth type of evidence relates to the variability in populations now alive. While in some cases variability indicates evolutionary pressures at work, in other cases, variability itself may be adaptive, for example, when the environment shifts drastically.

## Coexistence of Biological and Psychological
## Interbehaviors in Complex Psychological Events

Simply knowing what class of behavior is involved does not always allow one to identify a behavior accurately as either biological or psychological. This has already been noted by comparing the biological URs of salivation and courting with psychological CRs of salivation and courting. Another example comes from the ethological studies of bird song (for a review of the literature, see Thorpe, 1961; for a synthesis of the research, see Marler, 1963). Singing in a manner characteristic of their species appears to be a biological interbehavior in domestic fowl (Konishi, 1963) and European black birds (Messmer and Messmer, 1950) since adults of these species sing normally even if deafened shortly after hatching. Parasitic African finches, however, appear to learn the song patterns of their hosts through an imprinting-like process (Nicholai, 1964); and several species, including the white-crowned sparrow (Marler and Tamura, 1964), either fail to develop full song patterns or develop abnormal ones if deafened or isolated soon after hatching. The chaffinch presents an intermediate case in that some aspects of its complex song appear to represent biological interbehaviors, while others represent psychological interbehaviors (Thorpe, 1961). The general structure of the repetitive notes of the song develop normally regardless of rearing experiences. However, the perfection of these notes and the division of the song into its characteristic three parts depends upon the bird's hearing the song from adult males during the first few weeks after hatching. The terminal flourish and other details of the song develop during the bird's first spring, after it has occupied its territory, and seem to result from imitation of the songs of neighboring males.

### Problems Inherent in the Deprivation Experiment

This discussion of the classification of bird songs call attention to the deprivation experiment, a procedure which has characterized the work of behaviorists who seek to counter claims that certain behaviors are innate or instinctive. Despite the repeated observation that total deprivation of contact with stimuli critical to the behavior under study is rarely possible without damage to the structure of the organism, this approach remains widely used. By adopting the presently proposed taxonomy of biological vs. psychological interbehaviors, one can properly analyze the results of deprivation experiments. As noted earlier, a biological interbehavior is closely associated with a given structural system, and its response function has evolved gradually over many generations. Using these criteria one would readily predict that the immobilized salamanders in Charmichael's classic studies (1926, 1927, 1928) would swim normally when released from the drug's effects. After all, the salamander is a swimming organism! Contrast these results to what would likely happen if a young ape were kept anesthetized in water for the first few months of its postnatal life. Here one would be testing an organism whose biological evolution has resulted in a terrestrial existence. Some deficits in walking and tree-climbing would likely follow such deprivation, as well as deficits in swimming. In these cases, it is an oversimplification to say that swimming is innate in salamanders and learned in apes. The deprivation experiment may aid in classifying interbehaviors as either biological or psychological, but such results should not be the only criterion used.

## Proper Use of the Deprivation Experiment
## In Analyzing Species-Typical Bird Behavior

While many researchers have relied solely on the deprivation experiment to indicate how great a role environmental factors play in the development of a particular behavior, other workers have correctly seen the procedure as one of several to be used when classifying behaviors. Hailman's classic work (1967) on the development of bill-pecking in the laughing gull (larus atricilla) and related species demonstrates a desirable interplay between the descriptive field study and analytic laboratory work. Field observations from a blind indicated that parents regurgitate semi-digested good onto the ground in response to pecking by the chick, and leave the food there as long as the chick pecks. If the chick does not peck, the parent takes the food into its mandibles. If the chick still does not peck, the parent reswallows the food. Recently fed chicks peck only if the food is taken into the parent's mandibles. As the chick grows older, more pecks are directed at the parent's bill and the coordination and aim of the pecking response improves. Analysis of the motion pictures of chicks pecking reveals considerable inter- and intra-individual variation in the performance of four motor components of the pecking response. Rotation of the head, which allows the chick to grasp the vertically positioned bill of the parent, is not performed by newly-hatched chicks but becomes increasingly frequent during development in the nest. Two types of deprivation experiments, force-feeding chicks raised in the dark and raising chicks in the laboratory for several days without feeding, reveal that the anticipatory head rotation movements do not develop when normal early environmental contacts are prevented.

Using Kantor's formula for the psychological event, one can summarize the complex interactions which comprise bill-pecking in the laughing gull. In the newly-hatched chick, the primary stimulus for pecking is the parents' head and its spotted, vertically-positioned, horizontally-swinging bill. The stimulus function of the parents' bill is refined during the first week of pecking so that the bill's form becomes more important than its speed of movement. If siblings are present, their bill tips also serve as stimuli for bill pecking. Through contacting food while pecking at the bill, food itself develops a stimulus function for pecking. While the general pecking response is present soon after hatching, one component (rotation of the head) develops during the first few days of life if the gull is allowed to remain in the nest. Accuracy of the pecking response is improved somewhat through simple motor maturation but reaches its normal accuracy only through repeated interbehavioral contacts. The chick's responses serve as stimuli for the parents, in that food is not picked up and reswallowed as long as the chick pecks. Several setting factors are indicated. The presence of other chicks leads to a more rapid finding of the food, but exactly how this social setting factor operates depends on whether the companion chicks are naive or experienced (here the interbehavioral history of a setting factor is important). The degree to which a chick has been deprived of food is also an important setting factor, in that deprived chicks display a higher overall pecking rate than do satiated chicks. In addition, recently-fed chicks peck only after the parent takes the regurgitated food back into its mandibles. Time of day is a relevant setting factor in that the laughing gull feeds in the daytime, while its close relative, the Galapagos swallow-tailed gull (larus furcatus) feeds at night. The relevance of the interbehavioral history of a given chick is seen in the change in bill-pecking accuracy from 50 % to 85% during the first two days of life, that is, the development in a few days of visual recognition of the food and the development within a week of a marked preference for a life-like model of the parent's head, regardless of its rate of movement. These changes indicate the development of stimulus and response functions within a specific environmental setting. Such normal development does not occur in a deprived setting. The relevance of light as a contact medium in bill-pecking behavior is indicated by the results of its removal during the deprivation experiments. By carefully combining field observations, deprivation experiments, and contrived laboratory tests, Hailman has described the post-hatching development of a behavior once labelled as "instinctive." By classifying his findings according to the interbehavioral model, we have summarized in a straightforward manner the complexities of a behavior pattern which contains both biological and psychological interbehavioral components.

## Problem of the Evolution of Human Behavior

In the preceding paragraphs we have presented an objective analysis of species-typical behaviors in birds and fish, the two groups of animals most frequently studied by ethologists. The present approach applies equally well to the behavior of mammals, including man. Behavioristic psychologists challenged McDougall's characterization of man as the possessor of varied instincts and concludes instead that all man's behavior is learned. It should be obvious that adequately describing behavior requires more than making a simple binary choice. Expect for Eibl-Eibesfeldt's (1970, p. 398) study of human expressions and gestures, little ethological work has been done using man as a subject. In Eibl-Eibesfeldt's organocentric approach, man is a repository of pre-determined responses, yet he possess free will! If one looks at events instead of manipulating traditional terms, one can objectively describe human behavior, giving man his proper place in the animal kingdom.

## Evolution of Adult Human Interbehaviors

Adult human interbehavior, like that of all other organisms, results from four types of evolutionary development (Kantor, 1959, p 44): Planetary, phylogenetic, ontogenetic, and interbehavioral history. The study of naturl history focuses on planetary evolution, during which the habitat of living organisms developed . The study of phylogenetic evolution points to man's behavior as a member of the species **Homo sapiens.** The process of species or variety development constitutes phylogenetic evolution. For man, we can point at the possibilities for the development of psychological interbehaviors which result from the evolution of the hand, an erect posture, and a general agility.

The third evolution, the ontogenetic biological evolution, begins with the union of the gametes. At this point, a complex set of interactions of the new individual with intrauterine environmental conditions is begun. Since the present zygote is a link in the reproductive cycle which continues the life of the species, early ontogenetic interactions are influenced by the prior phylogenetic developments of the species. During the embryonic and fetal periods, numerous physical, chemical, and biological interactions occur. If abnormal conditions exist during this time, a malformed organism may be produced instead of the average biological product. Any psychological interbehavior which depends upon specific biological characteristics cannot occur if they are absent, e.g., a person born without legs cannot walk though he may transport himself by other means. When ontogenetic evolution reaches a certain point, psychological development begins. At first, psychological interactions are scarcely differentiable from biological interactions. They consist of fetal adjustments to such factors as varying pressure and temperature. When the organism is born, and thus comes into direct contact with a complex world of stimulus objects , psychological development proceeds rapidly. Early post-natal psychological development continues to parallel biological development; e.g., before an infant can turn his head toward his mother in response to her call, he must develop the necessary neuromuscular coordination. As the infant grows older, psychological activities become relatively more independent of biological development, being composed of interactions with stimulus objects . At this point, we can properly speak of the importance of an individual's interbehavioral history. This fourth evolution continues throughout the life of the individual. Man's psychological interbehaviors are involved with what are called social factors, The essential human features of one's surroundings; consequently, individuals build up specific ways of speaking and feeling and of appreciating the nature and uses of objects. A characteristic human development involves learning to name things in the environment. A given object sitmulates different people in different ways, e.g., a statue is reacted to as a fertility god by one person and as an art object by another. Thus psychological activities are not merely the coordinated action of muscles, nerves, and glands, but a specific form of activity interrelated with a stimulus function of an object. Crosscultural comparisons of social behaviors, such as are being done by Eibl-Eibesfeldt, will reveal similarities and differences in sociological evolution. Phylogenetic influence must necessarily be indirect; that is, man's evolutionary history affects his gestures and expressions by limiting the anatomical structures which participate in these social interbehaviors.

An appreciation of the natural development of the human organism through four evolutions renders unnecessary any appeal to traditional mentalistic concepts of innate determiners and internal motivators. By the same token, it is no longer possible to view man as some half-free, half-chained animal struggling to use his mental powers to lift himself about his predetermined role as a brute.

### Concluding Remarks

Since Verplanck's (1955) paper, a growing number of psychologists have realized that species-typical behaviors play a participative role in many of the contrived behavioral studies conducted by psychologists. Breland and Breland (1961) viewed this role as one of "misbehavior" since species-typical factors seem to place limits on what behaviors are operantly conditionable. In recent research on auto-shaping (e.g., Jenkins and Moore, 1973), the form of the response directed toward a stimulus is viewed as resulting from an interaction of species-typical consummatory movements and the physical properties of the stimulus object. Observations like those of the Brelands and Jenkins and Moore have stimulated a growing research interest in what is called "biological constraints on behavior" (for an introduction to this area, see Hinde and Stevenson-Hinde, 1973). The present paper has demonstrated that the interbehavioral approach to the activities of living organisms provides a means by which species-typical behaviors can be systematically incorporated into the body of psychology.

By distinguishing between biological interbehaviors and psychological interbehaviors and by indicating that both of these classes of activities result from intricate interactions in spatio-temporal fields, the need for any unobservable, mentalistic constructs have been eliminated. At the same time it has been shown that the behavior of all mature organisms develops through four evolutions, each containing many interacting factors. Such an evolutional approach stands in sharp contrast to the traditional binary explanations of behavior as either instinctive or learned.

Such a sophisticated field approach to animal behavior is not without historical antecedents (e.g., Kantor, 1971; Klopfer, 1969, Kuo, 1967; Schneirla, 1966). However, the interbehavioral approach goes beyond the approach advocated by these antecedents, not only in dividing the continuum into two classes of behavior, but also in pointing to specific types of participating factors, such as physiological setting factors and media of contact. Moreover, both participating factors may be isolated and experimentally manipulated. While the interbehavioral model provides an analysis of behavior somewhat more complex than that of earlier writers, it remains easy to understand and amenable to empirical verification.

## References

Atz, J.W. 1970. The application of the idea of homology to behavior. In L.R. Aronson, E. Tobach, D.S. Lehrman and J.S. Rosenblatt (Eds.) **Development and Evolution of Behavior.** San Francisco: W.H. Freeman.

Breland, K. and Breland, M. 1961. The misbehavior of organisms. **American Psychologist,** 16, 681-684.

Carmichael, L. 1926. The development of behaviors in vertebrates experimentally removed from external stimulation. **Psychological Review,** 33, 51-58.

Carmichael, L. 1927. A further study of the development of behavior in vertebrates experimentally removed from the influence of external stimulation. **Psychological Review,** 34, 34-47.

Carmichael, L. 1928. A further experimental study of the development of behavior. **Psychological Review,** 35, 253-260.

Daanje, A. 1951. On locomotory movements in birds and intention movements derived from them. **Behaviour,** 3, 49-98.

Desbury, D.A. and Rethlingshafer, D.A. 1973. **Comparative Psychology: A Modern Survey.** New York: McGraw-Hill.

Eibl-Eibesfeldt, I. 1970. **Ethology and Biology of Behavior.** New York: Holt, Rinehart and Winston.

Farris, H.E. 1967. Classical conditioning of courting behavior in the Japanese quail, Coturnix coturnix japonica. **Journal of the Experimental Analysis of Behavior,** 10, 213-217.

Gray, P.H. 1973. Comparative psychology and ethology: A sign of twins reared apart. **Annals of the New York Academy of Science,** 223, 49-53.

Hailman, J.P. 1967. **The Onttogeny of an Insttinct.** Leiden: E.J. Brill.

Hinde, R.A. and Stevenson-Hinde, J. 1973. **Consttraints on Learning.** New York: Academic Press.

Jenkins, H.M. and Moore, B.R. 1973. The form of the auto-shaped response with food or water reinforcers. **Journal of the Experimental Analysis of Behavior,** 20, 163-181.

Kantor, J.R. 1959. **Interbehavioral Psychology.** Granville, Ohio: Principia Press.

Kantor, J.R. 1971. In memoriam: Zing-Yang Kuo 1898-1970. **Psychological Record,** 21, 381-383.

Klopfer, P.H. 1969. Instincts and chromosomes: What is an "innate" act? **The American Naturalist,** 103, 556-560.

Klopfer, P.H. 1973a. Does behavior evolve? **Annals of the New York Academy of Science,** 223, 113-119.

Klopfer, P.H. 1973b. Evolution and behavior. In G. Bermant (Ed.) **Perspectives on Animal Behavior.** Glenville, Ill.: Scott, Foresman.

Konishi, M. 1963. The role of auditory feedback in the vocal behavior of the domestic fowl. **Zeitschrift fur Tierpsychologie,** 20, 349-367.

Kuo, Z.Y. 1928. The fundamental error of the concept of purpose and trial and error fallacy. **Psychological Review,** 35, 414-433.

Kuo, Z.Y. 1967. **The Dynamics of Behavior Development:** An **Epigenetic View.** New York: Random House.

Lazar, J.W. 1974. A comparison of some theoretical proposals of J.R. Kantor and T.C. Schneirla. **Psychological Record,** 24, 177-190.

Lehrman, D.S. 1970. Semantic and conceptual issues in the nature-nurture problem. In L.R. Aronson, E. Tobach, D.S. Lehrman and J.S. Rosenblatt (Eds.) **Development and Evolution of Behavior.** San Francisco: W.H. Freeman.

Lorenz, K. 1958. The evolution of behavior. **Scientific American,** 199, 67-78.

Marler, P. 1963. Inheritance and learning in the development of animal vocalizations. In R. Busnel (Ed.) **Acoustic Behaviour of Animals.** New York: Elsewiere.

Marler , P. and Tamura, M. 1964. Culturally transmitted patterns of vocal behavior in sparrows. **Science,** 146, 1483-1486.

Messmer, E. and Messmer, I. 1956. Die entewicklung der lautausserungen und einiger verhaltensweisen der amsel. **Zeitschrift fur Tierpsychologie,** 13, 341-441.

Morris, D. 1956. The feather postures of birds and the problems of origin of social signals. **Behaviour,** 9, 75-113.

Nicholai, J. 1964. Der bruntparasitismus der viduinae als ethologisches problem. **Zeitschrift fur Tierpsychologie,** 21, 129-204.

Schnierla, T.C. 1966. Behavioral development and comparative psychology. **Quarterly Review of Biology,** 41, 283-303.

Thorpe, W.H. 1961. **Bird Song.** New York: Cambridge University Press.

Verplanck, W.S. 1955. Since learned behavior is innate, and vice versa, what now? **Psychological Review,** 62, 139-144.

Wiepkema, P.R. 1961. An ethological analysis of the reproductive behavior of the bitterling (Rhodeus amarus Bloch). **Archives Neerlandaises de Zoologie,** 16, 103-199.

# INTERBEHAVIORAL SYSTEMS, TEMPORAL
# SETTINGS AND ORGANISMIC HEALTH

Roger D. Ray


This chapter has its origins in a decade of research that probes contextual setting influences on organismic-environmental interactions. The program began with a doctoral dissertation (Ray, 1970) investigating curare-form drugs and other contextual "setting operations" using Pavlovian heart rate conditioning (Ray and Brener, 1973). Kantor (1959), Lewin (1951) and several other authors have detailed the importance of interaction settings. But, with the possible exception of Barkerand his colleagues (cf., Barker, 1968), empirical research on this topic has been slow to develop. One of the limiting factors to progress has been the lack of suitable methodologies for discerning the impact of historical field factors, immediate contextual settings, and momentary interactions. Thus development of methodological technologies suitable for pursuit of the "setting" phenomenon has beena·primary focus of our research program.

While progress has been slow, we believe some important issues are beginning to develop. This chapter speculates on the character of one of these issues: Temporal settings and systemic synchronization. We are especially interested in pursuing the suggestion that temporal setting factors influence psychosomatic health and pathology. As such, we will be reviewing work which focuses upon overt behavioral actions and cover psychophysiological activities.

Until recently, our research has attended to behavioral, as opposed to physiological, processes and capitalized upon methodological progress extant in the fields of ethology and operant psychology. Our "interbehavioral systems approach" to behavioral and setting analssis has been outlined via a series of professional papers and publications (cf., Ray and Brown, 1975, 1976; Ray and Ray, 1976; Ray, 1977b; Ray, Upson and Henderson, 1977. 1978; Ray, Carlson, Carlson, and Upson, 1982; Upson, Carlson and Ray, 1981). Pilot probes of our systems approach to psychophysiological processes have also been reported (cf., Ray, Brown and Greenspan, 1975, Ray and Upson, 1975; Ray, Hobbs and Upson, 1976; Ray, et al., 1977; Ray et al., 1982), and are quite compatible with the "systems" methodologies being explored by other psychophysiological researchers (cf., Clynes, 1960, 1970; Sayers. 1973, 1975; and Porges, 1979).

Our methodological model closely corresponds to Kantor's (1959) conception of the research mission in Psychology, which includes the naturalistic description of reciprocating stimulus and response functions occurring within field or setting conditions. As does Kantor, we stress (1) the temporal continuity of behavior-environment reciprocity, (2) the functional correspondence of multiple behavioral modes (i.e., skeletal, tendonal, muscular, glandular, peripheral, nervous, autonomic nervous, central nervous, etc.), and (3) the importance of both organismic and environmental contextual setting condtions. As noted, our methods share conceptual elements with Kantor's "Interbehavioral Psychology" and paradigmatic elements with Operant Psychology, European Ethology, and modern Cybernetic Control Systems Analysis. We refer to the approach as "Interbehavioral Systems Analysis."

Our research model stresses the functional nature of stimulus antecedents- instrumental actions, and eventul consequences defined both by ethologists and by operant psychologists (cf. Skinner, 1969, 1972). Ethology has its origins in naturalistic descriptive investigations and field research, and the operant paradigm underlies many applied behavioral analysis programs (cf., Thompson and Dockens, 1975; Tharp and Wetzel, 1969; Ulrich, Stachnik and Mabry, 1970), as well as laboratory-based efforts. As such, each lends itself to naturalistic human behavioral analysis involving even the most sophsiticated questions (cf., Ray and Ray, 1976 for cross-cultural applications and Brady and Emurian's 1979 extension to human motivational and emotional research). However, unlike others using the operant paradigm, we stress temporal, sequential- organizational , and setting dimension as important additions to the antecedent-behavior-consequences model. Further, insteand of emphasizing singular categories of operant behavior we incorporate an ethological emphasis on continuous behavioral-behavioral , as well as behavioral-environmental , interactions (Ray and Brown, 1975).

Two vital components make up the interactional process. An organism behaves (B1, B2,...., Bn) and the environment reciprocates with stimulational change (s1, s2,...., sn). This all takes place within the context of relatively stable environmental (Es) and organismic (Os) settings, as well as historical fields (implied by the time element) which contextually influence the present interaction via the character of former interactions.

The organism's behavior can be described in categorical terms. This is a common methodological practice in ethology (cf. Hinde, 1970), where both global (Macro) and fine-grained (micro) movement patterns are catalogued for analysis. Such behavioral catalogues are called "ethograms" (cf. Cofer and Appley, 1964) and they closely parallel the Kantorian concept of "reactional biography" (cf., Kantor

362

and Smith, 1975). Environmental elements are also catalogued according to physical-chemical attributes. This follows the common editorial practice of professional journals for defining independent variables. Such initial catalogues are considered to be the "structural" definitions of systemic components. Functional, as opposed to structural, depictions of behavioral and environmental contributions emerge when specific sequences of environmental antecedent behavioral, and consequential events are described, as in the case of taxes, tropisms, reflexes, discriminative operants, etc. Such terms as these refer not to behaviors or stimuli per se, but rather to the relatively predictable relations which can be defined between stimuli and behaviors. Thus, for example, a reflex is not a behavioral act, but rather is a relationship with particular lawful properties extant between certain classes of eliciting stimuli and certain classes of elicited behavior. Such transactional elements eventually string together to constitute a temporally coherent "stream" of functional interactions involving an organism and specific extra-organismic (i.e., environmental and social) events.

Surrounding these successions of interactions are more stable contextual events, or "settings." Contextual settings are relatively stable processes which serve as background for each specific organismic-environmental transaction. Settings can be considered as only relativley stable in that they change at somewhat slower rates than do momentary transactions.

This schema is somewhat simplistic at first. The structure of macroscopic transactions depicted in our analysis should also include micro-level dynamic patterns within each macro-depicted state. As such, practical analyses rely upon inclusive taxonomic lists of macro behavioral states (all Bl's) but must further allow for any singular categorical state (i.e., any specific Bl) to include many, more elemental, behavioral components which are probabilistically organized as to sequential pattern. These micro-defined components may also include physiological modes of behavior.

In such a conceptual magnification, the smallest micro unit of importance may be argued as paralleling the synergisms of kinesiological movement (cf. Bernstein, 1967; Gelfand, Gurfinkel, Fomin and Tsetlin, 1971; Holst, 1973) or, phenomenologically, the "perceptual moment" of time perception research (cf. Efron, 1972). To help clarify the idea that probabilistic sequences of micro units make kup larger, macro-behavioral units, we can refer to this phenomenon in psycholinguistic studies where phonemes, the most elemental units of sound, eventuate in words and phrases (the macro organizations of phonemic sequences, cf., Bennett, 1977).

Interbehavioral relations suggested by this model determine a continuum of behavioral probabilities which are measurable and affected by stimulus schedules, setting factors, place of interface in the flow of behavioral sequencing, rate of event flow, etc. Empirical assessments of event changes (i.e., interbehavioral kinetics) allow for: (a) An analysis of the sequential integration of interbehavioral events by assessing particular probabilities of behavioral component change patterns (behavioral kinetic syntax); (b) the relative measurement of rates of change from behavioral category to behavioral category (behavioral kinetic velocity); and (c) the measurement of variability in the particular types of behavioral sequences which occur (syntax pattern variability).

Our research on such variables has suggested a unique interpretation of a persistent otpic of interest to both theoretical an applied psychophysiologists: The relation between somatic and autonomic activities. Such relational questions have been the foundation for severl learning theory issues (cf. Smith, 1954, 1964a, 1964b; Black, 1965; Black and Lang, 1964; Miller, 1969), motivational issues (cf., Elliott, 1974, 1975), and psychosomatic theory (cf., Gantt, 1953, 1957, 1964; Miller, 1969).

The views on psychosomatics we are about to detail evolved from a hypothesis first elaborated by the popular journalist Alvin Toffler in **Future Shock** (1970). This hypothesis holds that the rate-of-change in informationally laden or adaptationally relevant settings serves as a vital source of psychophysiological stress. Our form of the hypothesis holds that such settings have a temporal rhythm to them which has to successfully synchronize with biological rhythms intrinsic to an organism. Rhythmic perturbations and desynchronizations can occur within the biological rhythms of the organism. Such desynchronizations of ten are manifest between the somatic activity rhythms and ryhthmns in autonomic functions, and are thus open for diagnostic assessment.

In the present discussion we will thus be drawing upon the increasing interests of chronobiologists (cf., Luce, 1971; Scheving, Halberg, and Pauly, 1974; Wever, 1979) as they relate to psychosomatic dysfunctions. Such researchers have clearly demonstrated that autonomic functions involve periodic fluctuations which are both relativley slow (e.g., cycle approxcimatley once in 24 hours--the "circadian" rythms) and relatively fast (i.e., cycles every few seconds or minutes--the "ultradian" rhythms). There is literature that details rhythmic fluctuations in very gross somatic-motor activity, such as spatial movements (cf., Cofer and Appley, 1964; Kavanau and Peters, 1976), but we have recently extended this literature via demonstrations of clear ultradian and circadian rhythms in specific somatic functions (cf., Ray et al., 1977; Ray et al., 1982).

We intend to build upon the premise that one of the more diagnostically useful asepcts of such rhythms is the varying degree of temporal synchrony, or "coherence," extant among various systemic components. This coherence occurs as a result of natural "dynamic couplings" which exist between multiple subsystems in the autonomic and somatic nervous functions under healthy setting circumstances. We believe a substantive case exists for the view that such dynamic couplings may undergo significant alterations under psychologically stressful setting conditions, and that such alterations manifest themselves via a desynchronization in subsystem oscillations. We further believe that dominant contributions to psychological stress involve not only the physical characteristics of psychological setting (including setting syntax and variability), but also the temporal pace of setting-to-setting change (i.e., setting veleocity). Thus setting kinetics are an important contributors to the dynamics of organismic kinetics.

Because both the conceptual problem and the methodological approach we are positing are radical departures from much available research in psychsomatic psychophysiology, some outline of the more salient issues to be discussed is in order. Thus, prior to a more detailed literature discussion, we presently emphasize that four important assertions are explicit in our thesis:

1. The rate of change experienced when transiting from one psychological setting to another is an important, but highly ignored, stress agent which carries psychosomatic implications.

2. Modern systems control theory can be a valuable source of methodological and theoretical guidance when dealing with behavioral and psycophysiological phenomena involving time-series qualities.

3. Additional methodological and theoretical contributions of importance can be realized from behavioral biology (ethology). The kinetic techniques developed for ethological investigations and analysis, especially as they can be adapted for physiological investigations, have been largely ignored by psychosomatic investigators.

4. Chronobiological research on circadian and ultradian rhythms is highly relevan to consider for a more substantive conceptual foundation in the emergent field of behavioral medicine--especially when dealing with cardiovascular psychosomatics.

Finally, there is an additional point which is implicit in these four points when considered as a collective. The traditional use of static

365

statistical methods for the description and analysis of even the most typical data bases in modern psychophysiology are far from adequate techniques. The existence of hierarchically nested, sequentially organized, and temporally periodic data bases call for radically different mathematical techniques . Some of these techniques such as power-spectral analysis (cf., Sayers, 1973, 1975; Chatfield, 1975), cross-spectral coherence and weighted cross-spectral coherence analysis (cf., Bohrer and Porges, 1981; Porges, Bohrer, Cheung, Drasgow, McCabe and Keren, 1980), and kinetic path analysis (cf., Ray, 1980) are promising supplements to those already in use by chronobiological researchers (cf., Halberg, Tong and Johnson, 1967). In addition, there is a small, but growing, literature showing promise for a control systems modeling procedure applied both to physiological (cf., Clynes, 1960) and to behavioral (cf., Ray et al., 1977, 1978) phenomena. We shall thus begin the more formal arguments for our thesis by considering some details of various control systems.

## The Influence of Setting Operations
## On Behavioral Kinetics

We have mentioned that an ethological perspective on behavior concentrates on the kinetic sequencing of behavior. Ethologists have focused their analyses almost exclusively on categorical behavioral sequence probabilities as a function of preceding behavioral category (i.e., the syntax fo behavioral kinetics). With few exceptions (e.g., Fentress, 1976; Siegman and Feldstein, 1979), researchers applying this technique to analyze behavioral kinetics have not been interested in the timing of categorical behavio change. As such, multi-behavior analyses have failed to provide a complete description of kinetic processes by ignoring two crucial dimensions of behavior, viz., temporal locus and temporal extent. We shall argue that we have improved upon this analytic approach by measuring temporal parameters which ultimately yield measures of: (1) Specific behavioral durations; (2) temporal locus of specific behaviors; (3) rate of general behavioral change (or kinetic velocity); and (4) correspondent physiological velocities. In addition, we feel that the moment-to-moment changes in the complexity of behavioral patterning (i.e., syntactic variability) is an important measure. An analogy might help to clarify these behavioral processes and their potential relations.

Suppose a driver is considering an automobile trip. He might decide to be expeditious and thus choose to drive tenaciously a very direct route offering few, if any, avenues of choice (i.e., limited opportunity for variability in route patterns). This fixed route could then be driven at different speeds depending upon a number of factors, such as the driver's time table for arrival at the desired destination. On the other hand, the driver may plan his trip to include highly circuitous and alternative routes which offer a great

366

variety of route patterns. But, again, the speed at which this chosen route is traveled will vary depending upon other factors. Conceptually at least, the driver might drive fast enough to traverse the more variable route even faster than the less variable route.

Similarly, an exerimental subject may have the alternative of many or few combinations (or patterns) of behavioral sequence, but also have the alternative of various velocities of sequencing through these patterns. Each measure is theoretically independent of the other, and each tells us something different about behavioral kinetics.

Results from our earliest studies (Ray and Brown, 1975, 1976) found that the sequential pattern variability in behavioral change (i.e., the Kinetic Syntax Variability) was increased relative to Baseline by injections of sodium pentobarbital (an organismic setting condition), by pre-session satiation (another organismic setting), and by manipulations of increased and decreased ambient temperatures (environmental setting conditions). This implies a less coherent organization in behavioral change under these various setting circumstances. Such increases in kinetic syntax variability occurred, however, only during the discriminative setting signalling the opportunity for responses to be reinforced . During those setting periods when reinforcement contingencies were not in effect, kinetic syntax variability remained consistent with Baseline levels.

On the other hand, the kinetic velociity of behavioral change slowed considerably under all impositions and in both the contingency and noncontingency periods. In essence, subjects became more lethargic whether the general setting involved organismic setting perturbations such as drug injections and satiation, or external perturbations, such as ambient temperature changes.

### The Influence of Setting Velocity On Behavioral Kinetics

It was during this experimental series that we first explored the sensitivity of kinetic velociity and syntactic pattern variability to changes in the temporal parameters of ambient settings (i.e., setting duration and rate of change). Generally, research which focuses on such temporal setting factors does so within the context of temporally organized biological factors. This interface between environmental and organismic temporality is typically the purview of the field of chronobiology (cf., Scheving, Halberg and Pauly, 1974; Wever, 1979). Circadian variations in rest and gross motor activity in behavioral susceptibility to drugs and ambient stress agents, and in almost every known physiological measure are now well documented (cf., Luce, 1971).

367

Typically, circadian rhythms are the result of interactions between externally paced environmental events ("zeitgebers") and endogenously determined oscillators, or "biological clocks." If these endogenous oscillators are allowed to control behavioral or physiological responses independently of environmental influence (e.g., under experimental isolation conditions which screen off environmental changes, such as experiments inducing "free running" procedures), the periodic fluctuation in these measures are somewhat different form the 24 hour circadian period (cf., Wever, 1979). In some subjects response systems cycle faster, while in others, they cycle more slowly than the usual 24 hours . When placed back into the normal environment, subjects' response system return to a nearly perfect 24 hour cyclicity. Thus the pace of change in the external environment serves to capture, or "entrain," the endogenous rhythms and makes them synchronous with the cyclic temporal fluctuations of the environmental zeitgebers. The determinants of these external zeitgebers are usually temporally regulated events such as the rising of the sun or the passing of the moon (cf., Kavanau and Peters, 1976).

The existence of another class of biological rhythms oscillating with frequencies considerably shorter than the 24 circadian cycle is also well known. These "ultradian" rhythmic fluctuations are most typcially seen in physiological systems, such as the cardiac arrhythmia cycle (cf., Clynes, 1960; Luce, 1971; Sayers, 1975). Other ultradian rhythms include the respiratory inhalation-exhalation cycles, and the highly dominant 90 minute cycle of general central nervous system arousal which often manifest itself in "sleep stage" EEG patterns (cf., Dement and Kleitman, 1957), oral activity (cf., Friedman and Fisher, 1967), daydreaming (Othmer, Hayden and Segelbaum, 1969), work performance (Globus, Drury, Phoebus and Boyd, 1971), and physiological activities of the cardiac and gastric systems (Hiatt and Kripke, 1975; Orr and Hoffman, 1974).

### Circadian Periodicities in Behavioral Kinetics and Their Implications for Physiological Rhythms

Subsequent to our investigations of ultradian rhythms in settings and behavior, we conducted a series of investigations on circadian rhythms in kinetic velocity and respiration. To summarize our results, we found that Killer Whales have very prominent and independent circadian rhythms in (1) respiratory rate, (2) the initiation frequency of each macro behavioral state, (3) the temporal duration of each macro behavioral state, (4) the percent of total time they spend in each macro behavioral state, (5) the kinetic syntactic variability of macro behaviors, and (6) the kinetic velocity of macro behaviors. Further , we found that mathematical models of micro-behavioral kinetic velocity during the macro behavioral category of "free swimming activity" suggest the presence of an ultradian rhythm which is variably damped as a function of preceding behavioral conditions. In fact, these are the same mathematical equations which successfully modeled the behavioral kinetic velocity of the rats in the contingency and noncontingency pace study.

We also found that the circadian rhythm in respiratory rate disappeared when we analyzed respiration by each specific macro-behavioral category. Respiratory rates were very different for each category when compared to the other categories, but the variability within each category across the circadian period remained apparently random. Implications of this are that behavioral variations (i.e., changes in the initaition frequency of one behavioral state vs. another, plus changes in behavioral durations, etc.) across the circadian period are sufficient to account for rhythmic variations in respiration across the circadian period. This relationship suggests that physiological processes, such as somatic-cardiac activity couplings, deserve further exploration by our particular interbehavioral systems analysis methodology. To that end we now turn to issues related to cardiovascular psychophysiology.

## The Interjection of Systems Theory into Cardiovascular Psychophysiology

It was partly in an attempt to refocus the basic researchers back to more fundamental and theoretical kinds of questions that Brener (1974) offered his conceptual model outlining the dynamics of voluntary control over cardiovascular activity via internal information (i.e., interoceptive) feedback-control systems. While most would probably credit Brener's as among the first recognizable attempts at modeling cardiovascular control via control-systems theory, the model fails substantially when one looks for concrete variables or parametrics suitable for empirical evaluation. As such, the model qualifies more as a descriptive analogy, rather than a serious modeling effort. Thus one must search elsewhere for serious systems theory applications in cardiovascular psychophysiology.

One example of this systemic approach is Sayers' (1975) investigation of informational loads and their influence on cardiac activity. A major distinguishing characteristic of Sayers' work is its reliance on power spectral analysis techniques for data treatment. Sayers' use of time series methods more fully recognizes and accounts for the dynamic control properties inherent within the cardiovascular system. These control properties result in cardiac rates being highly rhythmic or oscillatory. As such, the mathematical treatment of choice must be sensitive to each of the fundamental frequency components, for each component contributing to cardiovascular dynamics has a unique oscillation frequency (e.g., Sayers, 1973). Sayers argues that such differing oscillation frequency signatures can be determined for respiratory compensation mechanisms, for blood pressure compensation mechanism, and for temperature compensation. Power spectral analysis allows one to track varaitions in each contributor and to study their sensitivity to perturbation by such psychological factors as informational load.

It is a relatively small conceptual step from Sayers' interests in informational load and our conception of environment velocity, especially when viewed within the context of Khananashvili's informational neurosis paradigm. One may thus susupect that contextual complexity and velocity might well create stress loads sufficient to induce pathology if such conditions were sustained for long periods. To successfully asses such a condition, it would be most beneficial to assess multiple systemic components simultaneously with time-series techniques. Fortunately, some data already exist which address this situation.

## Multi-System Component Analysis:
### Cross Spectral Coherence

The technology for comparing multiple components of a system, or even multiple subsystems has been developed recently. This technology results in two or more dynamic oscillation spectra and their respective power function (as in comparing the ultradian variations in cardiac velocity with ultradian variations in behavioral velocity). Porges and his colleagues (1980a) have pioneered a cross spectral technique for analyzing the weighted coherence between two independent but synchronized systems. These workers have documented the spectral coherence between respirations and cardiac sinus arrhythmia, and a significant diagnostic potential for this measure is subjects and situations as diverse as hyperactive children (a cardiac-somatic comparison . mortality risk in newborn infants (multi-physiological comparisons), and animal intervention studies involving manipulations of vagal tonus (Porges, et al., 1980b).

### Timing Influences on Health and Pathology

Investigations of oscillation frequencies and the degree to which they are coherently integrated, or synchronized, is a potentialy powerful methodology. That this concept is health and stress related is further bolstered by the work of Stroebel (1969) and Wever (1979). Basing his work on previous contributions from such chronobiologists as Gjessing, Richter, and Halberg, Stroebel pursued the idea that even if biological rhythms do not cause mental illness, the failure to assess them might well result in an early diagnostic error. In an experiment designed to develop behavioral stress in primates, Stroebel found two very important and distinct reactions to that stress. In one group of subjects he discovered a tendency to desynchronize temperature rhythms away from the circadian cycle, even though a dominant synchronizer in the form of 12 hours light on and 12 hours light off was constantly present in the subject's environment.

This desynchronization accompanied behavioral symptoms which are pathological in nature. Stroebel's subjects developed asthmatic breathing patterns, duodinal ulcers, gastrointestinal disturbances, eruptive skin lesions, and excessive water consumption--all symptoms typically found in dogs in the informational neurosis paradigm.

A second group of animals adopted a predominant 48 hour cycle of brain temperature with a progressive suppression in the usual 24 hour peak in the second day. This longer rhythm developed as a gradual lengthening of the dominant peak, and was associated with behavior that was highly maladaptive . This included animals spending many hours trying to catch imaginary flying insects, excessive masturbation, compulsive hair pulling, stereotyped movements, and alternations of movements with severe lack of interest in the surrounding environment.

Another of Stroebel's primary contributions to his concept of synchronization-desynchronization in psychosomatics is his use of long running data reporting procedures and a reliance upon a large range of variable measures. Here Streobel relies on spectral analysis as the preferred data analysis technique.

To complement Stroebel's argument that disrupted timing in biological systems is health related, we also point out that there is evidence that disturbances in the timing of psychologically relevant external events might also be involved in health and disease. The importance of this observation is easily overlooked. Both Selve (1976) and the legions of researchers following his lead in stress research have not, to our knowledge, demonstrated that time parameters are important stress factors. Certainly the literature relating time and health (e.g., Cohen, 1967) recognizes that disease has the potential for altering psychological perceptions of the passage of time (e.g., Frazer, 1966), but this literature includes little suggestion that effects may work the other way around--i.e., that time or time perceptions affect health.

Such a suggestion, of course, would have to take into account that **time** is not a stimulus per se, at least in the traditional sense of that term. Rather, it is the temporal characteristic of psychologically relevant stimuli or settings, including their temporal duration and their relative temporal distribution (i.e., their kinetic velocity and syntax), that defines variables of interest and relevance.

371

Traditionally the most interested researchers in this phenomenon have been those studying both the entrainment of, and the potential alteration of, biological rhythms (e.g., Sheving, Halberg and Pauly, 1974). But researchers in other areas have also directed their attention at related issues, including the ergonomic study of work-rest schedules (e.g., Luce, 1970), the Soviet research on informational neurosis in animals (e.g., Khananashvili, 1976), and the operant literature on stimulus schedules and their implications for the temporal organization of behavior (e.g., Schoenfeld and Cole, 1972; Killeen, 1975).

In our view, it is unfortunate that none of the systemically oriented investigations to date have incorporated a measure more suitable for assessing behavioral timing, or rhythmicity. Our own research in this area strongly suggests that such measures are among the most sensitive somatic measures which could be included. If this is so, they should also have significant early diagnostic implications. In fact, on the level of common observation, every mother will tell you when her child is "coming down ill," first by the child's behavioral velocity changes, and only subsequently by such "medical diagnostics" as temperature and other physiological symptoms.

The potential in analyzing for spectral changes and for the cross-spectral coherence between behavioral oscillations and their related, or integrated, autonomic oscillations, be they circadian, as in Stroebel's work, or ultradian, as in Porges' and Sayers' research, seem sespecially promising. The evidence available comes from a series of observations on a pair of Killer Whales and the serendipitous occurrence of illness and the subsequent death of one of our subjects.

In these observations we were interested in the analysis of social synchrony and dominance in two Killer Whales who had been housed together for several years. The observations were conducted across a continuous 96 hour period to allow for the determination of circadian periodicities in social organization parameters. We found the pair to be highly synchronized in making behavioral changes during the night, but hardly synchronized at all during the daytime . In addition, we found the female of the male-female pair to be most likely to initiate paired-behavior changes, and the male likely to lag by a few seconds in imitating the change.

Thus, along with individual behavior dynamics, social organization and dominance seem to be highly influenced by temporal-environmental setting parameters. But more important to the topic of illness and spectral dynamics, we also found spectral changes in the records of the male during the last day of our observations, which was the first day he demonstrated any signs of illness. These early signs included marked behavioral changes, such as balking at show performance cues ( quantifiable element we have studied in the laboratory under the guise of "interbehavioral sensitivity," cf., Ray and Brown, 1975), a hightened aggressiveness toward trainers, and a failure to eat.

More importantly, our formal data indicated temporal shifts in the data of the dying animal which suggest diagnostic criteria for future assessment. The first of these data was a decline in circadian peak levels in respiration rate. The second, and more unique finding, was a prominant departure from the singular circadian fluctuation that is normal for the behavioral velocity of these animals. The normal pattern, as determined by Ray et al. (1977) and the data from our female subject which was healthy, is a singular circadian variation in behavioral rates of change. Such a rhythm results in mid-day peaks and mid-night lows, which is also the normal periodic fluctuation for respiration rates.

However, the male in this study demonstrated both a mid-morning peak and a mid-afternoon peak which were separated by a mid-day velocity low equivalent in level to his night-time low. A spectral analysis supported our interpretation of the appearance of this bi-modal, or ultradian, oscillation in behavioral velocity, as well as the normalcy of the male's unimodal, or circadian, respiratory oscillation. Thus, a desynchronization in the normal rhythms is suggested.

We were also able to record the female a couple of weeks subsequent to the death of the male. During this latter analysis period, the female's circadian peak levels for respiration were quite elevated above previous levels. Further, during this period of adjustment to the absence of her long-term social companion she had a behavioral velocity which was markedly elevated and which contained a 2 hour spectral periodicity. This ultradian rhythm appeared without any concomitant change in syntactic variability, but with some specific behavioral probability or frequency changes. In fact, the behavioral velocity considered against other behavioral occurrences suggested an animal oscillating between hyper-kinetic and hypo-kinetic behavioral patterns on an ultradian basis.

### Some Final Considerations

The research we have accomplished thus far is clearly only a small beginning. Our systems approach has, to date, rested largely upon animal research in laboratory or other confined environments. We have not ignored the human dimension (cf., Ray and Ray, 1976), but the complexity and ethics of such research is highly limiting. As a conclusion to the current review of temporal settings and the quality of organismic functioning, the results of our most recent efforts in applying our methods to human subjects should be highlighted (Upson, Carlson and Ray, 1981).

This descriptive study utilized continuous self-report logs which included records of internal states, behavioral activities, and both physical and social settings. Eight human subjects maintained these logs by recording the most prevalent data available in these categories every 5 minutes for all waking hours over 17 days of experimental conditions. These experimental conditions were created within the context of a course on the psychology of consciousness which was offered during a Winter interim-term period at Rollins College. For the first 7 days, subjects attended a 2-hour class session during which they were instructed to place themselves in one specific type of setting during the remainder of the day (i.e., normal stimulus environment with "other-induced" time schedules). These settings were chosen to present various types of environmental stimuli, such as music, dancing, sitting in chapel, etc. During the subsequent 6 days, subjects were free to choose their own settings as long as they remained in the vicinity of the College campus (normal stimulus environment with self-induced time schedule). The final 4 days were spent in a remote out-island Bahamian village where subjects were given a free choice schedule (i.e., limited stimulus environment with self-induced schedule).

Since over 275,000 observations are involved in this study, it is clearly beyond our current purpose to review it in detail here. However, one highlight will serve to illustrate the effort. We found that, as a subject moves from an other-paced to a self-paced environmental schedule, there is an increase in the rate at which the subject changes settings during the evening hours. When in the limited stimulus environment of the Bahamas, subjects reduced their early morning setting velocities and, compared to other experimental conditions, maintained a flattened, or more consistent, setting velocity throughout the rest of the day.

In the other-paced setting, power-spectral analysis revealed a highly prominent 24 hour oscillation in setting velocity. Next in relative power inder these conditions was a 12 hour ultradian periodic fluctuation followed by a 6 hour fluctuation in the self-paced settings, setting velocity followed the prominent 24 circadian cycle, with the less dominant 6 and 12 hour ultradian periodicities still the strongest secondary rhythms. However, in the Bahamian environment, ultradian oscillations in setting velocity shifted in periodicity. Instead of the previous 6 and 12 hour rhythms, 7 and 4.5 hour periodicities were observed. The more dominant 24 hour rhythm remained unaltered.

Another finding of significant interest was the comparison between the total number of different settings experienced and the velocity of moving through these various settings. Not surprisingly, the imposed setting conditions of the first few days resulted in the greatest variety of different kinds of settings experienced. Next highest in variety of settings experienced was the self-scheduled college environment. Finally, the fewest different kinds of settings existed in the out-island Bahamian environment. However, when setting velocities were measured, we found that only the other-imposed environment was different. When setting velocities were other-imposed, the velocity was approximately 50% greater on the average than when self-selected. And self-selected velocities were equivalent in both the college and the Bahamian environments. Thus, even when variety of settings increases, subjects maintain a consistent level of changing from one to the other. However, they do shift the ultradian periodicities of these setting changes.

Thus our preliminary findings suggest that human studies using our systems model for the investigation of temporal setting parameters are quite feasible and may result in highly unique data bases. We believe, along with Toffler, that research on the pace of environmental settings and their implications for the quality of human life should be given a significant priority.

Thanks to the conceptual efforts of theoreticians such as Kantor (1959) and Lewin (1951), as well as the pioneering efforts of ecological researchers interested both in humans (e.g., Barker, 1968) and in lower animals (e.g., Hinde, 1970), settings are found to be easily defined and measured. Only the temporal dimensions seem to have eluded most theoreticians. Yet the temporality factors made explicit by chronobiological researchers offers a clear call for such theoretical efforts. And we believe that sufficient data already exist to suggest that these issues are of more than theoretical interest. We believe these factors may eventually play a very fundamental role in organismic health and systemic maintenance.

### References

Barker, R. G. 1968. **Ecological Psychology.** Standord: Stanford University Press.

Bennett, W.R. 1977. How artificial is intelligence? **American Scientist,** 65, 694-702.

Bernstein, N. 1967. **The Coordination and Regulations of Movement.** New York: Pergamon Press.

Black, A.H. 1965. Caridac conditioning in curarized dogs: The relationship between heart rate and skeletal behavior. In W.F. Proasy (Ed.) **Classical Conditioning: A Symposium.** New York: Appleton-Century-Crofts.

Black, A.H. and Lang, W.M. 1964. Cardiac conditioning and skeletal responding in cruarized dogs. **Psychological Review,** 71, 80-85.

Bohrer, R. and Porges, S.W. 1981. The application of time-series statistics to psychologial research: An introduction. In G. Keren (Ed.) **Statistical and Methodological Issues in Psychology and Social Science Research.** Hillsdale, N.J.: Lawrence Erlbaum and Associates.

Brady, J.V. and Emurian, H.H. 1979. Behavior analysis of motivational and emotional interactions in a programmed environment. In H. E. Howe and R.A. Dienstbier (Eds.) **1978 Nebraska Symposium on Motivation.** Lincoln: University of Nebraska Press.

Chatfield, C. 1975. **The Cerebral Cortex and the Internal Organs.** London: Champman and Hall.

Clynes, M. 1960. Respiratory sinus arrhythmia: Laws derived from computer simulation. **Journal of Applied Physiology,** 15, 863-874.

Cylnes, M. 1970. Biocyvernetics of the dynamic communication of emotions and qualities. **Science,** 170, 764-765.

Cohen, J, 1967. **Psychological Time in Health and Disease.** Springfield, Illinois: Charles C. Thomas.

Cofer, C.W. and Appley, M.H. 1964. **Motivation: Theory and Research.** New York: John Wiley and Sons.

Dement, W.C. and Kleitman, N. 1957. Cyclic variations in EEG during sleep and their relation to eye movements, body motility, and dreaming. **Electrencephalography and Clinical Neuro-physiology,** 9, 673-690.

Efron, R. 1972. The measurement of perceptual duarations. In J.T. Faser, F. C. Haber, and G.H, Muller (Eds.) **The Study of Time.** New York: Springer-Verlag.

Elliott, R. 1974. The motivational significance of heart rate. In P.A. Obrist, A.H. Black, J. Brener, and L.V. DiCara (Eds.) **Cardiovascular Psychophysiology.** Chicago: Aldine Publishing.

Elliott, R. 1975. Heart rate, activity, and activation in rats. **Psychophysiology,** 12, 298-305.

Fentress, J.C. (Ed.) 1976. **Simpler Networks and Behavior.** Sunderland, Mass.: Sinauer Associates.

Fraser, J.T. (Ed.) 1966. **The Voices of Time.** New York: George Braziller.

Friedman, S. and Fisher, C. 1967. On the presence of a rhythmic, diurnal oral instinctual drive cycle in man. **Journal of the American Psychoanalytic Association,** 15, 317-343.

Gantt, W.H. 1953. Principles of nervous breakdown: Schizokinesis and autokinesis. **Annals of New York Academy of Sciences,** 56, 143-164.

Gantt, W.H. 1957. Normal and abnormal adaptations--homeostasis, schizokiness, and autokinesis. **Disorders of the Nervous System,** 18, 30-33.

Gantt, W.H. 1964. Autonomic conditioning. In J. Wolpe, A. Salter and L.J. Reyna (Eds.) **The Conditioning Therapies.** New York: Holt, Rinehart and Winston.

Gelfand, M., Gurfinkel, V.S., Fomin, S.V. and Tsetlin, M.L. 1971. **Models of the Structural-Functional Organization of Certain Biological Systems.** Cambridge, Mass.: The MIT Press.

Globus, G.G., Drury, R., Phoebus, E. and Boyd, R. 1971. Ultradian rhythms in performance. **Psychphysiology,** 9, 132.

Halberg, F., Tong, Y.G. and Johnson, E.A. 1967. Circadian system phase--an aspect of temporal morphology: Procedures and illustrative examples. In H. von Mayersbach (Ed.) **The Cellular Aspects of Biorhythms.** Berlin: Springer-Verlag.

Hiatt, J. R. and Kripke, D.F. 1961. Ultradian rhythms in waking gastric activity. **Psychosomatic Medicine,** 37, 320-325.

Hinde, R.A. 1970. **Animal Behavior: A Synthesis of Ethology and Comparative Psychology.** New York: McGraw-Hill.

Holst, E. 1973. **The Behavioral Physiology of Animals and Man.** R. Martin (Trans.) Coral Gables, Fl.: University of Miami Press.

Kantor, J.R. 1959. **Interbehavioral Psychology.** Bloomington, In.: Principia Press.

Kantor, J.R. and Smith, N.W. 1975. **The Science of Psychology: An Interbehavioral Survey.** Chicago: Principia Press.

Kavanau, J.L. and Peters, C.R. 1976. Activity of nocturnal primates: Influences of twilight zeitgebers and weather. **Science, 191,** 83-85.

Khananashvili, M.M. 1976. Experimental neurosis in unrestrained animals. **Pavlovian Journal off Biological Review,** 85, 571-581.

Killeen,P.R. 1975. On the temporal control of behavior. **Psychological Review,** 82, 98-115.

Lewin, K. 1957. **Field Theory in Social Sciences: Selected Theoretical Papers.** In D. Cartwright (Ed.) New York: Harper and Row.

Luce, G.G. 1971. **Biological Rhythms in Human and Animal Physiology.** New York: Dover Publications.

Miller, N.E. 1969. Learning of visceral and glandular responses. **Science,** 163, 434-445.

Othmer, E., Hayden, M.P. and Segelbaum, R. 1969. Encephalic cycles during sleep and wakefulness in humans: A 24-hour pattern. **Science,** 164, 447-449.

Orr, W.C. and hoffman, H.J. 1974. A 90-minute cadian biorhythm: Methodology and data analysis using modified periodograms and complex demodulation. **IEEE Transactions on Audio and Electroacoustics,** BME-21, 130-143.

Porges, S.W. 1979. Innovations in fetal heart rate monitoring: The applications of spectral analysis for the detection of fetal distress. In T.M. Fields, A.M. Sostek, S. Goldberg, and H.H. Shuman (Eds.) **Infants Born at Risk.** New York: Spectrum.

Porges, S.W., Bohrer, R.E., Cheung, M.N. Drasgow, F., McCabe, P., and Keren, G. 1980. New time-series statistics for detecting rhythmic co-occurrence in the frequency domain: The weighted coherence and its application to psychophysiological research. **Psychological Bulletin,** 88, 580-587.

Ray, R.D. 1970. Classical conditioning of hear rate in restrained and curarized rats. **Dissertation Abstracts International,** 31, 2324- B.

Ray, R.D. 1977. Physiological-behavioral coupling research in the Soviet science of higher nervous activity: A visitation report. **Pavlovian Journal off Biological Sciences,** 12, 41-50.

Ray, R.D. and Brener, J. 1973. Classical heart-rate conditioning in the rat: The influence of curare and various setting operations. **Conditional Reflex,** 8, 224-235.

Ray, R. D. and Brown, D.A. 1975. A systems approach to behavior. **Psychological Record,** 25, 459-478.

Ray, R.D. and Brown, D.A. 1976. The behavioral specificity of stimulation: A systems approach to procedural distinctions of classical and instrumental conditioning. **Pavlovian Journal of Biological Sciences,** 11, 3-23.

Ray, R.D., Brown, D.A. and Greenspan, J.D. 1975. Cardiovascular-behavioral relationship changes in rapidly paced environments . Paper presented at Pavlovian Society Meetings, Little Rock, Arkansas.

Ray, R.D., Hobbs, F. and Upson, J.D. 1976. Sport psychophysiology and kinesiology: Somatic-autonomic coupling from qualitative empirical behavioral perspective. Paper presented at Pavlovian Society Meetings, Louisville, Kentucky.

Ray, R.D. and Ray, M.R. 1976. A systems approach to behavior II: The ecological description and analysis of human behavior dynamics. **Psychological Record,** 26, 147-180.

Ray,R.D., Upson, J.d. and Henderson, B.J. 1977. A systems approach to behavior III: Organismic pace and complexity in time-space fields. **Psychological Record,** 27, 649-682.

Ray, R.D. , Upson, J.D. and Henderson, B.J. 1978. The structural-functional analysis of interbehavioral systems. In G.J. Klir (Ed.) **Applied General Systems Reserch.** New York: Plenum Press.

Ray, R.D. and Upson, J.D. 1975. A behavioral systems analysis of oscillatory heart rate arrhythmias. Paper presented at Animal Behavior Society , Wilmington, North Carolina.

Ray, R.L. 1980. Path analysis of psychphysiological data. **Psychophysiology,** 17, 401-417.

Sayers, B. 1973. Analysis of heart rate variability. **Ergonomics,** 16, 17-32.

Sayers, B. 1975. Physiological consequences of informational load and overload. In P.H. Venables and M.J. Christie (Eds.) **Research in Psychophysiology.** London: John Wiley and Sons.

Scheving, L.E. , Halberg, F. and Pauly, J.E. 1974. **Chronobiology.** Tokyo: Igaku Shoin Ltd.

Schoenfeld, W.N. 1976. The "response" in behavior theory. **Pavlovian Journal of Biological Science,** 11, 129-149.

Siegman, A.W. and Feldstein, S. 1979. **Of Speech and Time: Temporal Speech Patterns in Interpersonal Contexts.** Hillsdale, N.J.: Lawrence Erlbaum Associates.

Skinner, B.F. 1969. **Contingencies of Reinforcement: A Theoretical Analysis.** New York: Appleton-Century-Crofts.

Smith, K. 1954. Conditioning as an artifact. **Psychological Review,** 61, 217-225.

Smith, K. 1964a. Curare drugs and total paralysis. **Psychological Review,** 71, 77-79.

Smith, K. 1964b. Comment on the paper by Black and Lang. **Psychological Review,** 71, 86.

Stroebel, C.F. 1969. Biological rhythm correlates of disturbed behavior inthe Rhesus monkey. In F.H. Rohles (Ed.) **Circadian Rhythms in Nonhuman Primates.** Basel: S. Karger.

Tharp, R.G. and Wetzel, R.J. 1969. **Behavior Modification in the Natural Environment.** New York : Academic Press.

Thompson, T. and Dockens, W.S. 1975. **Applications of Behavior Modification.** New York: Academic Press.

Toffler, A. 1970. **Future Shock.** New York : Bantam.

Ulrich, R., Stachnik, T. and Mabry, J. 1970. **Control of Human Behavior** (Vol. 2): **From Cure to Prevention .** Glenview, Ill.: Scott, Foresman and Company.

Upson, J.D., Carlson, M.L. and Ray, R.D. 1981. Setting changes and the quality of human life. In G.E. Lasker (Ed.) **Applied Systems and Cybernetics.** New York: Pergamon Press.

Wever, R. A. 1979. **The Circadian System of Man.** New York: Springer-Verlag.

# THE COMPUTER ANALOGY IN PSYCHOLOGY: MEMORY AS INTERBEHAVIOUR OR INFORMATION-PROCESSING?

Edward Blewitt

Psychology is in a state of crisis. Since the beginning of this century the behaviourists and the mentalists have fought a ferocious battle over what psychology is. The behaviourists have adopted an atheist position with regard to the phenomena of "mind." They have claimed the brain as the locus of psychological events. But in attempting to naturalize "mind" the behaviourists have denied to people their most intimate characteristics. These have been appropriated by the mentalists who appeal to a quasi-religious transcendental Mind. A newcomer to psychology is presented with these two approaches as the only alternatives. Each camp proclaims "If you are not for us, you are against us." Anyone wishing to challenge this carve-up of psychology faces a daunting task: Neither camp is prepared to give them a fair hearing. The interbehvioural psychology developed by J.R. Kantor is such a challenger. Fortunately the contradictions of the behaviourist and mentalist positions are beginning to become apparent: Neither camp offers an answer. These contradictions cannot be resolved by the joining together of behaviourism and mentalism. Such eclecticism merely multiplies the contradictions and leads to confusion. the contradictions have to be transcended. Both behaviourism and mentalism deal with legitimate psychological phenomena, but because their postulate systems are inadequate to deal with the whole range of psychological activities they need to be replaced by a system which can (see Schoenfeld, 1969).

The aim of this paper is to examine the ways in which the activities of memory have been dealt with. It begins by looking at how the ancient Greeks, with their naive naturalism, handled these activities. With the degeneration of classical Greek society naturalism was replaced by supernaturalism. The transcendental soul displaced the activities of biological organisms as the subject matter of psychology. This tradition is still with us. In its modern form it is expressed in the information-processing approach. It is this which is dealt with in the second section. In the third section we discuss some of the criticisms levelled at this approach. Finally, we outline the interbehavioural approach to memorial activitivities.

381

# The Classical Approach to Memory

In a society without the sophisticated printing techniques available today which allow the fossilization of verbal behaviour, the ability to remember is greatly prized. Because of the wide range of activities whch remembering makes possible, it is very likely that the poets and priests as the guardians of the tribes' history and complex rituals devised techniques to enable them to pass these to the next generation.

The only complete source of the art of memory in antiquity is the text known as the **Ad Herennium** (circa 86-82 B.C.) (Yates, 1966). This distinguished between natural and artificial memory. Natural memory is that with which the person is born, whereas artificial memory is a memory improved by training. As with so many other things, the art of memory can be traced back to the Greeks. It is unlikely that the Greeks invented the various aids to memory, but they were the first to codify and elaborate the rules. Why this was so is unclear, but may have been due to the changes which Greek society was going through at the time. Yates (1966) suggests that an important reason for the condification at this time was that the poets were given a definite economic position in society. Whatever the reasons for this condification, teaching the art of memory was a significant part of education, especially that provided by the Sophists. Seneca, the father of the philosopher, claimed that he was able to repeat two thousand names after a single hearing, or repeat in any order two hundred disconnected lines of verse shouted out by members of an audience (Yates, 1966). The art of memory was usually taught as one part of five parts of rhetoric, as a technique by which the orator could improve his memory, though Aristotle believe it was useful as a part of dialectic.

Although the origins of the art of memory are lost in antiquity, the Parian Chronicle, a marble tablet from about 264 B.C. attributed its invention to Simonides of Ceos (circa 556-468 B.C.), one of the most admired lyric poets of Greece, and called the "honey-tongued." Simonides was said to excel in the use of visual imagery, and was the first to equate the methods of poetry with those of painting. The recognition of the power of visual imagery in poetry and painting was paralleled in the use of visual images in the art of memory. Cicero, the Roman orator (106-43 B.C.) vividly described the invention of this art in his text **De Oratore** (55 B.C.):

> ...He inferred that persons desiring to train this faculty
> (of memory) must select places and form mental images
> of the things they wish to remember and store those
> images in the places, so that the order of the places

will preserve the order of the things, and the images of things will denote the things themselves, and we shall employ the places and images respectively as a wax writing-tablet and the letters written on it.

Thus, the general principles of the mnemonic are very simple. The first step is to memorize a series of loci or places. The commonest type of mnemonic place system used by the Greeks and Romans was the architectural type. Quintilian (circa 35-100 A.D.), the first Professor of Rhetoric in Rome, described the process in his **Institutio Oratoria** (circa 100 A.D.) . In order to form a series of places it is necessary to remember a spacious and varied building, with its forecourt, living room, bedrooms and parlours, and the statues or adornments which decorate the rooms. The images by which the speech is to be remembered are then placed in imagination on the places which have been memorized in the building. Once this is done, as soon as the memorized facts have to be remembered, all the places are visited in turn and the various "deposits demanded of their custodians" (Yates, 1966, p. 18). Whilst making his speech, the orator imagines himself moving through the building. The principle of loci is common to all the varied memory systems .

In addition to the principle of loci, there were also rules for the kinds of images to be used. The anonymous author of the earliest complete source of the art of memory discusses why some images are suitable for memorizing whilst others are not (see Yates, 1966, pp. 25-26).

The principles of loci and images are the most important rules concerning the art of memory. These rules could then be applied to the "memory for words," where there is an image for every word that is to be memorized, or to the "memory for things," where there is an image for every notion or argument used. It was considered that "memory for things" was usually adequate for most cases. Concrete applications of these basic rules are given only occasionally in the texts as the instructors considered it preferable for the students to devise their own method for formulating suitable mnemonic images. One example is provided by the author of the **Ad Herennium.** The author asks us to suppose that we are the counsel for the defence in a law suit. A man has been charged with killing another by poisoning. The prosecutor has stated that the crime was committed to gain an inheritance, and declared that there are many witnesses and accessories to the crime. Adding certain symbolic devices for a point of reference, a cup would remind the prosecutor of the poison, tablets of the inheritance, and the testicles of the ram through verbal similarity with "testes," of the witnesses. While, no doubt, such images may aid the person in remembering, sometimes the images are more complex and varied than the things to be remembered.

383

From the brief extracts presented one cannot but be impressed with simplicity and clarity with which some of the classical writers dealt with the topic of memory. An outstanding feature of the approach is that it is done without reference to any form of reductionism, that is, without any attempt at reducing the memory events to the constructs of physiology and physics. Neither is memory considered as a hidden process underlying the specific acts; rather, the acts are the memory. Perhaps one reason for such clarity is that the writers were concerned with the practical problems of improving the ability to remember and memorize things.

## Aristotle on Remembering and Recollecting

The most detailed discussion of remembering and recollecting in Aristotle is his **De Memoria et Reminiscienta** ( On Memory and Reminiscence). This group of lecture notes is the second in a group of treatises known as the **Parva Naturalia.**

Aristotle regarded remembering and reminiscence as classes of sense perception. The topic of the first part of the text is to discuss memory and remembering, what their object is, and what part of the "soul" they belong to. In referring to memory Aristotle does not mean a structure or a faculty. Rather, it is used to refer to the ability (tendency or disposition) to perform specific remembering acts. In other words, memory does not refer to the present performance of an act, but to the potentiality of performing. Aristotle uses the term "remembering" to refer to the specific act of remembering.

Although remembering is continuous with perceiving, it is distinguished from it in that remembering involves the elapse of a time interval. Whereas perception involves interaction with present events, memory involves past events (judgment and prediction involve future events). That is, the organism is not interacting with present events but to past ones; it is reacting to absent events. Thus, in the act of remembering a person "always says in his soul (to himself) in this way that he heard, or perceived, or thought this before" (Sorabji, 1972, p. 48). This entails that remembering is an ability only of those animals which are aware of the passage of time between the past event and the present (Aristotle held that animals other than man had memory). In remembering a past event what a person is engaged in is imagining the past event. For Aristotle, the image has to be a likeness or copy to the event or thing remembered. If the image is not a copy, then the person is not remembering; although one might be said to be "trying to remember" in trying to imagine what the thing was--but this trying may either be successful or not. If it is the former, the person is said to have remembered. Taking into account these two characteristics of remembering (perception of time, and seeing an image) it is clear why Aristotle considered memory to belong to the primary activities of sense-perception.

In explaining how it is possible to react to a thing which is absent, Aristotle argued that memory involves an imprint derived from past perceptions:

> For it is clear that one must think of the affection,
> which is produced by means of perception in the soul
> and in that part of the body which contains the soul.
> as being like a sort of picture, the having of which
> we say is memory. For the change (i.e., the perceptual
> process) that occurs marks in a sort of imprint, as it
> were, of the sense-image, as people who seal things
> with signet rings (Sorabji, 1972, p. 50).

A couple of points can be made about this statement. If one adheres to a dualistic interpretation of Aristotle, it would appear that the terms "soul" and "body" refer to two different substances, and that Aristotle is talking about two effects: An image in the soul and a physical change in the body. But this is not a correct interpretation. Rather, what Aristotle is saying is that there is one effect, namely , the image. Aristotle refers to the body for he simple reason tht the soul is a function of the body: When a person has an image it necessarily involves a physiological occurrence. But this is not to say that an image can be reduced to a physiological occurrence. The image is part of an interactional event involving the organism and the environing conditions. This leads on to a second point. When Aristotle says that the perceptual process "marks in a sort of imprint," it appears to imply that the having of an image is a physiological process involving the retrieval of a physical trace.

It certainly is true that Aristotle does not keep the concepts of image in the soul and physiological change clearly distinct. However, what is imagined is not the physical trace, but simply that the image requires a physiological component. So, even though the person is changed physically in its continuous interaction with the world, it does not follow that what is remembered is a physical copy. The confusion is not in Aristotle. It is in the reader. Contemporary thought is almost wholly impregnated with dualistic assumptions, and has been for the past 2000 years. In looking at the past we too easily assume that it shared in our dualism: We tend to appropriate the past as if it were continuous with us . However, the past had its own assumptions, problems and solutions. If we are to understand the past, instead of extracting from it only that which is relevant to us, we need to know the context in which it existed: What did people in the past see as their problems, what were the implicit assumptions which were so widely accepted that they did not need to be made explicit?

Considering these points, Aristotle did not share in our dualism. Neither did he share our problems. Therefore, we should not expect him to have an explanation for problems derived from dualistic postulates.

The main topic of the second part of **De Memoria** is recollection. For Aristotle, recollection is the active search to recover some knowledge or sensation one had in the past. Recollection involves the presentation of a succession of images which terminate in the recovery of the object or event sought, that is, the person remembers. In the recollection the earlier images in the series put one in mind of the succeeding ones. In this sense, recollection is similar to the process of reasoning. Hence, Aristotle confines recollection to those animals which are able to deliberate. For Aristotle, only human beings have this ability.

Recollection may result in successful remembering of a past event or not. It is in discussing recollection that Aristotle refers to the use of mnemonic techniques as aides to successful recollection. The use of mnemonic techniques illustrates the serial nature of recollection. Aristotle refers to mnemonic methods to demonstrate that links in the series can be connected by artificial means. There is no natural relationship between the links except those given to them by the person. The mnemonic techniques imposes order on the things to be imagined which otherwise would not have it. Although mnemonics relate objects and events artificially, there are natural relations between them: Those of similarity, dissimilarity, contiguity (temporal and spatial), and habit. These natural relations are not between the images but between the things imagined. Aristotle is not referring to the association of ideas but to the association of events.

From this discussion of **De Memoria et Reminiscentia** it is clear that Aristotle did not refer to any hidden processes which were the real processes of memory. All the phenomena of memory were described at their own level; they were not reduced to physiological events, although physiological events are involved in remembering (and any other interaction of the organism with its environing conditions). There is no reference to non-naturalistic events. However, the naturalistic orientation of the early Greeks was soon to be replaced by supernatural ones. Instead of viewing psychological events as the functioning of a biological organism, of persons interacting with their surroundings, human beings were split into a naturalistic "body," which occupied time and space, and a transcendental soul, which occupied time but not space. Although the soul has been naturalised in the form of the Brain, the supernaturalism still remains. An example of this in contemporary psychology can be seen in the view of persons as "information-processing systems."

386

## Man as an Information-Processor

The view that man is an information-processing system has its origins in Wiener (1948) and Shannon and Weaver (1949). The significance of Wiener's book was that it provided a model which described the structure of information flow within and between systems. Furthermore, Wiener conceptualised neuronal synapses as analougous to the switching gates of computers, in that both operate on an "all-or-none" principle.

While Wiener was more concerned with the biological applications, Shannon was more interested in the application to engineering communication. The importance of Shannon's work was to conceptualise information as a measurement of organisation, and to devise a mathematical measure of the amount of information. In their more popular presenation of information theory, Shannon and Weaver defined communication as "all of the procedures by which one mind may affect another" (Shannon and Weaver, 1949, p. 95) and that:

> In oral speech, the information source is the brain,
> the transmitter is the voice mechanism producing the
> varying sound pressure (the signal) which is transmitted
> through the air (the channel)...and your ear and associated
> eighth nerve is the receiver(Shannon and Weaver, 1949,
> pp. 98-99).

This view is not a new one. In fact, it goes back at least to de Saussure's representation of what is supposed to occur when persons speak. According to de Saussure, the ideas in A's mind are translated into words that are transmitted by sound waves to B's mirdwhere they are translated back into "ideas" (Kantor, 1977). Shannon's introduction of quantification into this process gave it a scientific respectability, and no doubt contributed to the initial widespread acceptance of the information-processing model in the 1950's.

Messages are complexes of data transmitted from one physical system to another, and they convey "information" only if they are not predictable from the data previously received. Thus, incomplete knowledge of the future, and also of the past of the transmitter from which the future might be constructed, is at the heart of the concept of information. On the other hand, complete ignorance also precludes information; a common language is required, that is, an agreement between the transmitter and the receiver concerning the elements used in the communication process.

The symbols used in the messages can be anything: Words, letters, digits, etc. The communication process is conceived as an act of selection out of these. A series of selections of symbols constitutes the message, which is itself a selection from all possible messages.

A selection form **n** symbols can be broken up into a sequence of selections from a smaller number of possibilities. This is usually achieved in terms of binary digits or "bits." For instance, any number up to 32 can be defined by 5 binary choices or bits. This, the information of a message can be defined as the minimum number of binary decisions which enables the receiver to reconstruct the message on the basis of the data already available to the receiver. It was Shannon's achievement that he was able to provide a mathematical measure of the amount of information carried. The number of bits is simply the logarithm (to the base two) of the number of possible choices: That is, $\log_2 n$, where "n" is the number of choices. Thus each letter of the alphabet carries $\log_2 26 = 4.70$ bits of information.

In communication theory, information refers to what a person **could** say rather than to what a person **does** say. That is, it is a measure of the freedom of choice when selecting a message. It does not apply to individual messages, but to total number of messages which could be transmitted. The unit of information indicates the amount of freedom of choice a person has in selecting a message. In dealing with the problem of how precisely the transmitted symbols convey the desired meaning, Weaver stated that the basic model would have to be altered only by the addition of a Semantic Receiver between the engineering receiver (which changes signals into messages) and the destination. This Semantic Receiver would decode the message for a second time, matching the statistical semantic characteristic of the message to the statistical semantic capacities of the totality of receiver. Similarly, there would be a box for Semantic Noise.

Given this approach, different questions concerning the process of communication arise, These questions are concerned with: Amount of information; channel capacity in terms of bits; the nature of coding and decoding processes and their degree of efficiency; the effects of noise and their reduction; and, the differences between a continuous and a discrete signal. Researchers into the problem of memory who have adopted the information-processing model have been interested mainly in the study of memory structure, the number of memory stores, and the storage and retrieval of information.

In order to better evaluate the value of this approach to the events of memory in human beings, two models of memory will be presented. Following this presentation, the problems arising from this approach will be discussed.

## Information-Processing Models of Memory:
## Broadbent, and Atkinson and Shiffffrin

One of the earliest attempts at constructing a model of memory based on information-processing was Broadbent's filter theory (1958). Broadbent's conception of what occurs in the nervous system (1958, p. 27) follows. Stimuli that impinge on the sense organs go into a temporary buffer or short-term store. The process of attention is conceptualised as a selective filter that allows only part of the information through.

Physical properties of those events which increase the probability of information being passed through the limited capacity channel include: Physical intensity, time since the last information from that class of event entered the limited capacity channel, and high frequency of sounds as opposed to low frequency. States of the organism which increase the probability of selection are those sometimes classed as "drives," such as degree of food deprivation. The limited capacity channel is where the "bottleneck" in the processing of information occurs.

Broadbent also proposed that there is a short-term store at a stage prior to the limited capacity channel, so that when two messages arrive simultaneously one of them is transmitted instantly, whereas the other is held in store until the line is free. During its time in store, the representation of the message fades due to autonomous decay, so that by the time the message is transmitted it will be degraded.

The long-term or secondary memory consists of, among other things, a store of conditional probabilities. These are associations between events, but they form associative networks in which some associations are more probable than others. Matching of spoken words to stored representations in this "neural dictionary" is what taxes the system.

One of the problems raised by the filter model is what happens to the information not selected. One view, and the one originally held by Broadbent, is that the filter actually blocks all unattended messages so that nothing gets through. However, on the basis of experiments conducted by Moray (1959) and Treisman (1960), this "blocking" by the filter was found not to be a valid description of the process. It is now generally held that the filter "attenuates" signals rather than eliminates them, and that the weakened signal can still be picked up by specially attuned cognitive systems (see Moray, 1966 and Neisser, 1967).

Broadbent's model was very influential on the thinking of later theorists. Newer models have been developed not so much because Broadbent's model is wrong, but because it is incomplete. It describes the overall operation of the system, not the detailed functioning. One of the most successful modifications of Broadbent's general structural model was the buffer model of Atkinson and Shiffrin (1968). The buffer model was first proposed in 1965, and has been undergoing elaboration and refinement since then.

According to Atkinson and Shiffrin (1968), memory consists of two major dimensions: (1) Structural features; and (2) control processes. The structure of memory consists of three stores: (1) The sensory register; (2) the short-term store; and (3) the long-term store. So far, this system resembles that of Broadbent. An important aspect of this model is that the character of the information in the short-term does not depend upon the form of the sensory input. Thus, a visually presented item may be encoded as an auditory item in the short-term store.

The second dimension of memory is the control process. Control processes refer to those processes that are not permanent features of memory, but are instead transient phenomena under the control of the subject; their appearance depends on such factors as instructional set , the experimental task, and the past history of the subject (1968, p. 106).

For example, in a paired-associate learning task involving a list of stimuli each paired with either an A or a B response, the subject may try to learn each stimulus-response pair as a separate integral unit, or may, more efficiently, answer B to any item not remembered, attempting to remember only the stimulus paired with the A response. These two methods will yield sugnificantly different results, indicating the importance of the control processes. Although the variety of controlling processes is virtually infinite, and are under the control of the subject,  they are, nevertheless, dependent upon the permanent memory structures.

Perhaps the most important aspect of the Atkinson and Shiffrin model is the significance of the rehersal buffer in maintaining an item in the short-term store. Although rehearsal also formed a part of Broadbent's filter model, it did not receive the detailed discussion afforded to it by Atkinson and Shiffrin. In order to explain the rehearsal buffer, Atkinson and Shiffrin use the analogy of a bin always containing N items, with each new item entering the bin knocking out an item already there. The content of the buffer is constructed from items that have entered the short-term store, either from the sensory register or long-term store. A long-term trace is built up during an item's stay in a buffer. Afterwards, the input of a new item into the buffer causes an item currently there to be bumped out; this item then decays from the short-term store and is lost (except for any long-term trace built up while in the buffer). An item dropped from the buffer is likely to decay more quickly in the short-term store than a newly presented item which has just entered the short-term store. This is because it is already in a state of decay when dropped, and the information making up the item in the buffer is likely to be only a partial copy of the ensemble present immediately following input.

Two other processes are involved. First, the subject may decide not to enter every item into the buffer store, for example, because the rate of presentation of items is too fast, or because the subject does not want to break up an easily rehearsed combination of items. Secondly, there is nothing indicating the choice of items to be eliminated from the buffer store. The elimination of items may be randomly determined, depend on the state of decay of items in the buffer, depend on the ease of rehearsing certain items, or depend on the length of time items have been in the buffer.

Finally, it is useful to distinguish between the different experimental procedures typically used in the study of short-term and long-term memory, and the separate memory systems assumed to underlie the distinction. Thus, the short-term memory procedure refers to recall of material after a few seconds, or a minute at most, whereas the long-term memory procedure refers to recall after minutes, hours, days, and years. It is on the basis of difference in results due to the use of different procedures that theorists have postulated separate short-term and long-term memory systems underlying and accounting for these different results. However, the correspondence between short-term and long-term experimental procedures and system is not perfect, as the long-term system may contribute to performance using short-term procedures.

### Some Criticisms of the Information-Processing Model

The information-processing approach is the dominant paradigm within memory research (and is at the stage of imperialist aggrandisement, challenging the ruling paradigms in other areas). Controversy is conducted within this model rather than directed against it. However, not all is well within this camp. As the edifice of information-processing gets bigger cracks are beginning to appear: It is no longer able to support the weight of experimental evidence. Recently, Neisser (1976), one of the chief architects of this paradigm, has retracted somewhat from his earlier position (Neisser, 1967) as a result of his encounter with the work of J.J. Gibson (e.g., 1966, 1976).

Now, Neisser is not so enamoured with the information-processing approach.

Nevertheless, Neisser still cannot tear himself away from the edifice he did so much to construct.   But there are fundamental reasons for abandoning the paradigm.  In this section, we will attempt to weaken the information-processing edifice at its most vulnerable point--its foundations.  Rather than trying to dismantle the paradigm brick by brick starting from the top (that is, by questioning the mass of experimental findings), we will start from the bottom.   By questioning the assumptions of the paradigm, it is hoped that the whole edifice will come tumbling down.

Bridgman (1927) stated that any concept is nothing but the set of operations used.   In psychology, the most influential exponent of operationism was Stevens, who published a number of papers in the 1930's on this topic.   However, the conventional interpretation of operationism as expounded by Stevens and Boring, tended to confuse the operations, and the words used with the events themselves (see Moore, 1975).

This is certainly what has occurred in the domain of memory research.  Having clearly defined short-term and long-term memory as experimental operations, researchers take the unwarranted step of transforming these experimental operations into memory systems; they assume that there must be corresponding systems underlying these operations.   They are not concerned with showing that these underlying systems exist as neural structures, and are prepared to accept them as hypothetical constructs.

Cognitive psychology appears to be satisfied with this status of cognitive systems as hypothetical constructs.  It is claimed that other sciences, especially physics, have found the use of hypothetical constructs to be of great value.  But this is no justification for their adoption of psychology.  In the other sciences, the subject matter is often very difficult to observe, but this is not the case in interbehavioural psychology.  There is no warrant to fill an explanatory space by the use of unobservables.  This merely gives the illusion of knowledge.  Also, in those sciences where hypothetical constructs are resorted to they are usually defined in terms of space-time location, so that their relationships to observable events can      be tested experimentally(Ebel, 1974).  So, cognitive psychology has to define its hypothetical constructs so that they can be located.  If they are supposed to be neural events, what evidence is there?   The problem cannot be passed on to the physiological psychologists.   The buck stops with the cognitive psychologists.   If the hypothetical constructs are postulated merely to fill an explanatory gap, then it is better if they are rejected.

Cognitive psychologist are concerned solely with the hypotheses generated by their models and how well these fits the data. That is, they assume that because their model-generated data are a close fit to the experimental data that the actual functional relations are the same as the ones contained in their model. However, there is a danger that they are committing the logical fallacy of affirming the consequent. Thus, if it is true that "If A then B," it does not follow "If B then A" is true. That the computer analogy predicts certain experimental findings does not mean that the same processes are involved in the production of the prediction as in the original event. Just because a computer can engage in action which has a topographical similarity to that of human memorial behaviour does not mean that the controlling relations are the same in the computer as in the human. This problem can be solved only if the controlling relations in the human and computer are studied and compared.

In order to avoid the problem of existential reality, it is often claimed that the models used to explain the experimental resuts are only "as if" models or metaphors, and do not imply that the organism studied is functionally similar to the models. This is a strange form of defence. Assuming that researchers are intersted in understanding the process under investigation, it is surely impossible to achieve this goal if the events are conceptualised as something which they are not. Although most discussions of the computer model are prefaced by a statement that the metaphor is only a way of speaking about the events, this is soon forgotten (**sic!**). For example, Simon (1977), one of the leaders in the area of artificial intelligence, has written that "the elementary processes underlying human thinking are essentially the same as the computer's elementary information processes" (p. 422).

It seems clear that the achievement of the traditional interpretation of operationism has been to maintain the dualism which has dominated psychology for so long (Kantor, 1963, 1969). As Moore (1975) notes: "Operationism has been subverted to support the resulting mentalistic analyses of behavior" (p. 124). The existence of mentalistic entities are supposedly assured by performing a publically observable operation: "Intelligence is what intelligence tests measure" is the most well-known example. Thus, instead of exorcising the "spooks" of dualistic psychology, the traditional interpretation of operationism secured their legitimacy. However, there were others who did not adhere to the traditional interpretation.

Probably the two most prominent figures in the development of behaviourism as a philosophy of science were J.R. Kantor and B.F. Skinner. Unlike most psychologists, however, they did not adhere to Steven's interpretation of operationism. Kantor and Skinner clearly distinguished between events and constructs. For example, Kantor (1957) wrote:

> Events may simply be described as anything that happens
> which may or may not become known or studied....But
> unless our thinking is debauched by epistemological in-
> stitutions we will not think that when scientists discover-
> ed electric induction, radio waves..., or the psychological
> processes of color discrimination, learning and unlearning,
> they somehow created these events. Constructs may
> best be described as products derived from interbehaving
> with events (pp. 258-259).

Following the distinction between events and constructs, operationism for Kantor and Skinner is a matter of assessing the conditions which lead the scientist to use a term in a particular way.

The behaviouristic interpretation of operationism emphasises the conditions that control the verbal behaviour of the scientist. It is not always the case that the scientist is under the discriminative control of properties and elements of the investigative event. The scientist may be under the control of conventional linguistic practices. Indeed, this is to some extent an inevitable condition, as each scientist is a member of a specific verbal community which adheres to certain, often implicit, assumptions. Scientific work involves reducing the role of conventional linguistic practices. Although constructs (the scientist's verbal behaviour) and events must not be confused, there must be a continuity between them. It is always the case that genuine scientific constructs are derived from interbehaviour with events. When constructs are imposed on events, that is, are derived from interbehaviour with traditional linguistic practices and socio-cultural traditions, their functions are scientifically meaningless. This continuity between events and constructs is clearly stated by Kantor (1959, pp. 89-99).

It is clear that the analogical models used by Broadbent and Atkinson and Shiffrin are derived from contact with non-psychological events--telephone engineering and computer engineering and programming. It is also clear from what we have referred to as the behaviourist interpretation of operationism that such a procedure is of no scientific value. The study of human memorial behaviour must develop new terms and interpretations on the basis of interbehaviour with events, and must not borrow terms and hypotheses from investigative domains dealing with events bearing no resemblance to psychological events. Indeed, to what features of psychological events do such terms as "input," "output," "encoding," "decoding" refer? Observer (1968) remarks that they refer to none:

> Instead they suggest that the organism is simply an
> electronic contrivance, a servo-mechanism, or a computer
> that can achieve remarkable results when properly program-
> med. Moreover, the terms 'encoding' and 'decoding'

especially, imply psychic substances and mystical processes. In no sense does such terminology describe the complex origins, operation, and resultants of human behavior (p. 112).

It is not that models and analogies are necessarily worthless. On the contrary, they can perform valuable functions. What is important is the **choice** of the analogy: The analogy has to be appropriate to the subject matter. Moreover, the analogy has to be justified: What are the similarities between the analogy and the original event it represents? The danger with constructing analogies is that they are primarily subject to distortion, and hence adoption of them into the linguistic community transcends this distortion across different fields of study.

Do the concepts of information-processing provide any additional understanding to the concepts developed by behaviourists such as Kantor and Skinner? Although the cognitive psychologists claim to be using the same model as computer engineers, is this in fact so? They may well use the same terms, but that does not ensure that they refer to the same kind of events. Indeed, it seems clear that in psychology "information" terms do not refer to the same type of event. For example, when it was first introduced into psychology, the concept of "information" had a very precise mathematical definition, and was used to quantify the structural characteristics of a message. However, it soon became clear that this notion of information was not an especially useful one for psychology, and the term "information" gradually approached its everyday meaning. A reasonable conclusion is that the use of information-processing terms is merely a terminological change. These terms replace the old mentalistic ones. The information-processing model is simply the traditional dualistic psychology in a different guise. Information-processing tells us a great deal about how computers operate but nothing about how people remember. Human behaviour is not in any significant way similar to that of the computer.

People do "code" information, but it is an activity of the person and not of a cognitive structure. Coding is used to mediate between a stimulus and a response. For example, a beginner in Morse code first copies all the dots and dashes and then translates them into words. It is only after this activity that the person comes up with the content of the message. But as he gets better there is no need for this elaborate mediating activity (the translating). Instead, he is able to read the message straight off the wire. This is possible not because the translating or coding process has been speeded up to a very high speed and occurs unconsciously (by the cognitive system), but because the process has been dropped. The dots and dashes now perform the same stimulus function once performed by the mediating process. Thus, the dots and dashes have the same function as ordinary language does for the person who does not know Morse code.

Neither is there any need to reduce events to "information." Rather, events should be conceptualised at the same level at which we interbehave with them in our everyday lives. Furthermore, cognitive behaviour is performed by organisms as a whole and not by a person's brain. The absurdity of thinking that the brain performs cognitive functions is strikingly made by Malcolm (1977b).

A fundamental source of error in the information-processing model is its organocentric assumption that psychological events are located **inside** the organism. Thus, between the contact of people with their environment and their activity in that environment, there are intervening cognitive processes through which "the sensory input is transformed, reduced elaborated, stored, recovered and used" (Neisser, 1967, p. 4). Therefore, the aim of the cognitive approach is to "trace the fate of the input" (Neisser, 1967, p. 4), and to discover what happens to the stimulus once it impinges on the sensory systems. The "causes" of behaviour are placed inside the organism. The concept of causality in this approach is a linear one of S-->O-->R, in which behaviour is a manifestation of the underlying processes inside the organism. But the environment does not somehow enter the organism to be processed by the cognitive structures. The environment stays where it is. What goes on in the organism are physiological, neurological, and chemical processes, not psychological processes. Kantor (1978) has written:

> Perversely to make the brain into a computer that
> thinks, invents, and plays clearly wrenches a major
> organ from its proper place in the biological economy
> in which it forms one of many interacting functions.
> This violence done to the biological organ gives rise
> to all sorts of theoretical and factual absurdities, for
> example, making neurons into magnetic tapes for
> storing information or knowledge and neural synapses
> into electronic connections of wires in cables. Basical-
> ly the comparison of the brain with the operations of
> electronic machinery reduces to the coining or convert-
> ing of terms without regard to the things and events
> involved (p. 581).

Reference to events inside the organism does not account for psychological events, but merely provides a more detailed description of the resposne phase of the event. Viewed in isolation from the stimulus context, the responding of an organism is a purely biological event. Psychological events are not localised in biological structures; biological structures attain the status of psychological ones only when related to the stimulus context. Psychological processes are not organocentric, rather they involve the interaction of a biological organism with a physical and social environment. The organism does not consume the environment, process it, and regurgitate it as a response; there is no "input" or "output." Organism and environment come into contact with each other, and it is the various forms of contact that constitute the subject matter of psychological events. In terms of psychological events nothing goes on between "input"and "output" because nothing goes in or comes out. The subject matter of psychology is not the "stuffing" in between the stimulus and response. Rather, the interaction between the stimulus and response is the psychological event. Whereas in the cognitive approach stimulus and response are peripheral factors in the psychological event, in the interbehavioural one they are the central factors. Physiological research can search as much as it wants to discover the "causes" of human behaviour within the organism. Such a search will prove futile (see Bentley, 1940, pp. 238-239).

The locus of psychological events is not in the organism but in the spatio-temporal setting in which stimulus-response interactions occur. The organism is only one phase of a larger event. Any explanation of psychological happenings ought, therefore, to be focused on the current and historical setting, and not resort to filling the organism with pseudo-psychological functions.

One source of the cognitive appraoch's difficulties lies in its concept of "stimulus." Cognitive psychology distinguishes between a nominal and a functional stimulus. The nominal stimulus is the stimulus which is presented by the experiment to the subject. It is defined in physical terms. Now, since this physical "input" is equivalent, in physical terms, to the response or "output" of the subject, varies from subject to subject. and even varies with the same subjecy under different circumstances, it is assumed that the nominal stimulus must be processed by the subject's cognitive structure and transformed into the functional stimulus ( the stimulus for the subject). Thus, if one nominal stimulus is correlated with two different responses, this is because the functional stimulus is different in both cases. Similarly, if two different nominal stimuli are correlated with the same response,this is because the functional stimulus is the same in both cases.

The objection to this view is not that the distinction between nominal and functional stimuli is not a valid one. On the contrary, such a distinction is a necessary one if the apparent inconsistencies of (1) the same nominal stimulus being correlated with different responses and (2) different nominal stimuli being correlated with the same respone, are to be understood. Rather, the objection is to the postulation of an internal transforming mechanism. Instead of resorting to internal intervening variables: the interbehavioural approach is to examine the historical development of the organism and environment and the current setting conditions. Stimulus functions are not developed inside the organism but in the history of stimulus-response interactions. By adopting naturalistic postulates interbehaviourism has been able to avoid the problems which arise from the concept of internal transformation of stimuli. In place of the distinction between nominal and functional stimulus, interbehaviourism refers to stimulus object and stimulus function. Stimulus functions are located in stimulus objects, which are defined in physical terms. However, stimulus functions cannot be reduced to stimulus objects. In many cases, the stimulus function has very little connection with the physical properties of the object. Whether a particular function of a stimulus object is actualised depends on the current setting conditions. Whereas in the information-processing model the stimulus is conceived as an antecedent cause in a linear causal chain, in the interbehavioural scheme, the stimulus is conceived as a part of the psychological event, as one phase of a bi-phasic event occurring in a field of other events.

In the information-processing approach remembering is separated into an inner, hidden memory process, and an external manifestation of these processes. When I am asked "Where is the book?" and reply "on the table," it is assumed that there is a mental or brain process which occurs so that I am able to reply to the query. The reply itself is not regarded as the remembering, rather it is the result of an underlying memory process. It is this underlying process which is really what memory is. Often this process is not something people are aware of. When asked the question, "Where is the book?" I replied promptly and without effort. It is in such cases that it is assumed that the process is a hidden one. Although it is not a conscious process it is assumed that it **must** occur. This hidden process is regarded as being similar to that which occurs when someone is trying to remember where he left his keys. He is unable to provide a prompt answer, and goes through an elaborate process of imagining where he last had them: "I had them when I came home because I used them to open the door; I'm sure I the put them back into my pocket; Then I went into the kitchen and made a cup of tea..." This goes one until either (a) he gives up in exasperation, that is, he has failed to remember, or (b) he suddenly exclaims "They're still in the keyhole in the front door!" In this example, the remembering is the result of a long series of acts which preceded it. Supposedly, a similar series of activities is carried out by my "cognitive system" when I remember something without hesitation.

The philosopher Malcolm in a paper entitled "The Myth of Cognitive Processes and Structures" (1977a) has pointed out that the belief tht there are hidden cognitive processes is a piece of bad philosophy. Although he uses the example of recognition to illustrate his argument, it applies equally well to remembering.

What is so interesting from an interbehaviourist standpoint in this analysis is the emphasis on the context of behaviour as that which identifies it as a recognition interaction or not. The structure of the behaviour itself is of no value whatsoever in determining "Hi, John" as a recognition. Only when it is put into the historical context of each of the individuals does this occur. We have to know that the two people met before to call it a recognition situation. Even a complete description of the situation at the time of meeting will not be adequate. To use a cinematic metaphor: An analysis of each frame independently of those which precede and follow it is of no value at all; we need to analyse the whole movie. Thus, in order to describe and understand any act of remembering, we need to know its history. Remembering is an extended temporal act.

The importance of the specific context on whether a response is a remembering or not is clearly indicated when we change the context. Consider the example of my going over to the drawer to take out a set of keys. If someone had said to me beforehand "Where are the keys?" this act of getting the keys would be an example of "remembering where the keys are." But suppose instead that someone had said "Go and fetch me the keys from the drawer." In this case, the act of getting the keys would be an example of "carrying out a request."

Going inside the organism is going in the wrong direction; it throws us off our track. It prevents us from "observing the situations and activities, the contexts, to which the words'remember,' 'think,' etc. belong and which give them all the significance they have" (Malcolm, 1977a, p. 142). Contrary to the view of the information-processors, their analogy is not a useful heuristic device. Insofar as it directs us inside the organism it is a harmful influence: "You become a fly in a fly-bottle" (see Malcolm, 1977b).

Remembering can take a variety of forms. There is no hidden essence common to them all. This is one of the errors of the information-processing approach. It recognizes that the act of remembering takes many forms, but holds that these are mere manifestations of a hidden common process. There **must** be more to remembering than the observable acts themselves. But the philosopher Wittgenstein argued that there is no must about it: "I have been trying in all this to remove the temptation to think that there must be what is called a mental process of thinking, hoping, wishing, believing, etc. independent of the process of expressing a thought, a hope, a wish, etc." (Wittgenstein, 1958, p. 41). Ryle (1948), too, has argued against the view that there are mental processes under-

399

lying the performance of particular acts. A person is not a "ghost in the machine." there is no mind and body.

In talking of "mental acts" there is no justification in holding that they occur behind the publically observable "bodily acts." Instead, when we refer to mental acts "we are referring to these overt acts and utterances themselves..." (Ryle, 1949, p. 26). For Ryle, the belief in a "ghost in the machine" is an example of a category mistake, of representing the facts of mental life as if they belonged to one logical type when they belong to another.

Apart from the criticisms of those working within the Anglo-American philosophical tradition, the information-processing approach has also been criticised from the "Continental" tradition. One example of this is what has come to be known as dialectical psychology. The general tenor of this approach to memorial behaviour is seen in a recent paper by Steinar Kvale (1976). Kvale's radical dialectical phenomenology rejects the separation of the world into an inner and an outer. Persons are conceived as being in direct contact with a socially constructed world, and not with inner representations of it. The concept of "being-in-the-world" emphasises the continuous interaction with the social world. Thus, memory is not a thing or a faculty, but an activity of a person in interaction with the past. A consequence of viewing memory as a thing is that it has diverted research into investigating the supposed structure and function of "metaphysical memory castles." However, an emphasis on memory as an activity in the world orients research to the observation of memory in its everyday contexts.

In this section we have examined a wide range of criticisms of the dominant information-processing model of memory which conceives of memory as a hidden process underlying the overt acts of memory. This approach merely perpetuates the dualism of the past 2000 years in a scientific guise by appropriating constructs from another subject matter which has a scientific respectability. The only way to resolve the probems is through the rejection of dualistic postulates. Within psychology Kantor's interbehaviourism is a non-dualistic alternative. In the following section we outline Kantor's approach to memorial activities.

## Kantor's Interbehavioural Analysis
## of Memorial Activities

The importance of memorial activities to human interbehaviour is clearly indicated by Kantor (1926). For Kantor, memory is neither a faculty of the mind or brain nor a hidden cognitive process, but a specific form of interaction between an organism and its surroundings. Memorial interactions can take many forms: Verbal, perceptual, motor, implicit, overt, partially implicit, etc. When one arranges to meet someone at the pub at eight o'clock, and meets them at the appointed time and place then one is performing a memorial activity. Failure to meet the appointment is an act of forgetting (Kantor and Smith, 1975). In a naturalistic account to memorial behaviour there is

> no room in our description for the sorcerous reinstatement of mental states in the remembering mind through a mysterious association of ideas, a process usually made still more mysterious by means of various forms of imaginary neurology. And in the second place, we abjure the notion that memory behavior consists merely of a reaction system acquired, functioning later whenever the adjustment stimulus is presented. The latter is merely a general property or condition of psychological organisms and is the basis for all psychological responses, not merely the memorial behavior (Kantor, 1926, p. 89).

In this quotation we see an opposition to mentalistic conceptions as well as to the universalisation of memory. When I stop typing this paper so that I can go and meet that person in the pub at eight o'clock....and resume typing the following morning, my ability to type is not a case of remembering how to type," or "remembering how to sit down in the chair." The use of the concept of "remembering" in these examples is meaningless. However, memorial activity did play a part in this example of "resuming to type." It was not an example of "remembering **how to** type" but an example of "remembering **to** complete the paper." This distinction points to the defining charactersitic of memorial activities: They are delayed activities in which the delayed response is correlated with a substitute stimulus. It is the delayed nature of memorial behaviour and the interaction with a substitute stimulus rather than original adjustmental stimulus that distinguishes it from, say, perceptual behaviour in which the organism is in immediate contact with the adjustment stimulus (Kantor, 1926; Kantor and Smith, 1975).

The delayed nature of memorial activities ensures that they are tri-phasic: (1) the initiation or projective phase; (2) the delay phase; and (3) the consummatory recollective phase. These three phases are temporally continuous. The three phases are not independent, discontinuous activities, but a part of one activity. The memorial activity is occurring throughout all the phases, even though it does not appear so in the second phase (in fact, this phase can be a very active one, such as when the person implicitly performs the behaviour to be carried out in the consummatory phase). While in many projective examples the time of the completion of the response in the third phase is clearly specified (e.g., A agrees to meet B at 2:30 p.m. next Thursday), this is not always the case (e.g., A says that he must tell B about the lecture he heard at the conference whenever he sees him).

Kantor distinguishes between two types of memorial behaviour: (1) Remembering, and (2) reminiscing or recollecting. Remembering is characterised by being projective. That is, the response to be remembered is projected to a future time (specified or indefinite), and performance is delayed until that time. Recollecting, unlike remembering, does not involve the postponing of a response to be performed at a later time, but is backward looking, and involves implicit responding to past events--a "re-living" of an event no longer present. Although remembering and reminiscing are opposite in terms of their time reference, they are still types of memorial activity; they are both tri-phasic. The difference lies in the phase which is dominant. In remembering, the projective phase is emphasised, whereas in reminiscing, the third phase is emphasised.

How the projection of a response to a future time is possible is shown by briefly discussing the three phases of the remembering act. As an extended temporal act, remembering must have a beginning time. This is the projective phase. During this period there is a co-ordination of sitmulus and response factors. If two people arrange to meet at a later time, this agreement cannot function as the stimulus at the later time as it is no longer a part of the immediate environment. Therefore, it is necessary for a substituute stimulus to be presented. It is during the projection phases that associations between the act, the adjustment stimulus, and the substitute stimulus are arranged. These are achieved in a variety of ways: Writing down the time of the meeting in a diary or appointment book, marking the date on a calender, asking someone to remind you, using a mnemonic, and so on. However, it is not always the case that the association is so deliberately arranged. Sometimes it involves just stating the time when action is to occur: "I'll see you on Friday," or "I must send that letter off tomorrow." If the projection is over a fairly brief period, the person may continually repeat to himself the relevant stimulus throughout the delay phase: "05948648" or "Second left at the traffic lights, third right after the shoe shop, the fifth house on the left," or "Mr. Alexander." The role of repetition or rehearsal indicates that the delay period can be an active one and not necessarily passive. In most acts of remembering, however, it is a passive phase. The consummatory phase of remembering involves the performance of the projected act when the substitute stimulus is presented. Depending on the associations arranged in the projective phase, contact with the substitute stimulus may be either deliberate (looking in the diary, referring to the shopping list, repeating the mnemonic, etc.) or casual (noticing the time on your watch, seeing the person you arranged to meet, etc.).

Reminiscing compared with remembering has many different characteristics. Reminiscing is distinguished from remembering in that it involves a reference to past events, rather than the projection of an act into the future. In reminiscing or recollecting the final phase is more prominent than the first one. It is still a delayed activity as the person is responding to original events in their absence through interaction with substitute stimuli. Reminiscing need not involve imagery, but may take the form of verbal descriptions of the past events. Kantor distinguishes between three types of reminiscing. First, **casual reminiscence** is engaged in for no particular purpose other than to review past events themselves. There is no change in the surrounding environmental conditions. Such behaviour is usually initiated by an unimportant or obscure stimulus. Typically, the person is passive, and, once initiated, the responses themselves function as stimuli for further reminiscing. An example of such behaviour would be reminiscing about that second shot on the tricky left-hand dogleg. You struck that four-iron with such ease. You didn't see the ball finish, and when you got to the green the ball was nowhere in sight. It was in the hole! Fabulous! Or, perhaps, you're worrying whether you sent off that letter in time. Secondly, in **direct** or **determined recollection,** the activity is carried out for a specific purpose. As an example, Kantor gives that of a witness in a trial being asked to recall a specific event. In such a context, the witness is not free to recall the event in all its detail, but only those details which are relevant to the question. If the same event was recalled in casual reminiscence, the person would not be so constrained. Another example would be hunting for the set of keys you thought you left in the doorknob. You try to retrace your past actions from the time you came into the house. Lastly, in **memorial recovery,** the activity is engaged in not to alter the surrounding conditions, as in determined recollection, but because of the effect of the act on the person. A case in point is the religious confession.

Memorizing as a type of learning and not memorial interbehaviour is a special case. Memorizing for Kantor is not a kind of memorial activity, but a type of learning. This is in complete contrast to the contemporary view in which memorial activity has been reduced to memorizing. The probable reason for the confusion between the two types of interbehaviour is that both are tri-phasic. Memorizing is usually conceived as involving the stages of acquisition, retention, and recall. However, this similarity is a superficial one only. Kantor goes so far as to say that "greater differences can hardly exist between remembering and memorizing" (Kantor and Smith, 1975, p. 258). The most important difference is that memorial performances are activities that occur only once in the lifetime of a

403

person. "Never again will 'A' remember to meet 'X' at the club at eight o'clock p.m. August 15, 1973" (Kantor and Smith, 1975. p. 258). The nonrepeatability of remembering in comparison with memorization ensures that there are differences between the two types of activity in all three stages.

In memorization, the first stage involves the acquisition of a response, whereas in remembering it involves the projection to a future time the performance of a response which is already a part of the person's repertoire. The second, non-performative stages differ in that in memorization it is only a period in which the adjustmental stimulus is absent. That is, if the stimulus was present the memorised stimulus is absent. That is, if the stimulus was present the memorised response would occur. However, in remembering, the second stage can only be a period when the projected response must not occur (although the response can be rehearsed). Thus, if A agrees to meet X at eight o'clock August 15, 1973, the response cannot occur until that time. It cannot occur at nine o'clock on August 14, 1973. In remembering, the third stage is the performance of the delayed response. This stage is continuous with the other two stages, in that it is the completion of a response initiated during the first stage. Furthermore, the performance of the response requires the presentation of a substitute stimulus. In memorizing, however, the third stage is merely a period for the re-performance of a response in the presence of the direct or original adjustmental stimulus. It is another response, and not the completion of a response. These differences between memorizing and remembering do not imply that the two activities cannot be involved in the same behaviour situation. Thus, it is possible for a person to memorize a response and project its performance to a future time, as, for example, in cramming for an examination on a particular day.

Kantor's approach to memorial behaviour draws upon the naturalistic analysis of Aristotle and completely rejects the dualistic conceptions of the dominant psychological theories. But Kantor does not simply repeat Aristotle's analysis. To ignore the discoveries of the last 2000 years would be foolish. Kantor has appropriated what is living in Aristotle's approach (especially his naturalism), insofar as memorial behaviour is responding to absent events through the mediation of a substitute stimulus. At the same time he rejects that which is dead, especially the naive physiology and the central role of the image. Memorial activities are recognized as taking a wide range of response forms, from the most subtle to the grossest. Most importantly, memorial activities are not considered to be solely backward-looking but also forward-looking.

## Conclusion

The introduction of psychology of the concepts developed by communication and computer engineers was seen by many as a revolution. It appeared as if the oppression of the dominant behaviourist "ruling class" had been lifted off the backs (or perhaps heads) of the subjects of psychology experiments. People were now free to talk of such things as "thinking," "internal processes," "cognitions," and "intervening variables" without having to look over their shoulders to see whether the behaviourist "thought police" were hovering about. The mentalists could now come out into the open; no longer were they forced to "translate" mentalistic phenomena into "Behaviourese." The **samizdat** publications now became the best-sellers. But the revolution wasn't really a revolution-- it was a **coup d'etat.** The new ruling class simply spoke in a different jargon. Underneath the argot there lay the traditional adherence to dualistic postulates of mind and body. Whereas the previous behaviourist ruling class has merely lopped off the "mental" side of the dichotomy (Off with her head!!" cried the Queen of Hearts), the cognitive ruling class wanted to rehabilitate the "mental" ("All the kings horses and all the kinds men tried to put Humpty together again").

For a revolution to occur in psychology dualistic assumptions themselves must be overthrown. It is these assumptions that are the basis of oppression of the psychological subject. Adhering to the dualistic assumptions only results in the cyclical repetition of history Behaviourism-mentalism-behaviourism-mentalism... To get out of this vicious circle requires a revolution which transcends the dichotomy. This does not mean giving equal emphasis to mind and behaviour: "Psychology is the study of mind and behaviour," as a kind of peaceful co-existence. It means to both negate and affirm behaviourism and mentalism in a comprehensive naturalism. "Psychologists of all countries.....UNITE!"

## References

Atkinson, R.C. and Shiffrin, R.M. 1968. Human memory. In K.W. Spence and J.T. Spence (Eds.) **The Psychology of Learning and Motivation** ( vol. 2). New York: Academic Press.

Bentley, A.F. 1940. Observable behaviors. **Psychological Reviews,** 47, 230-253.

Broadbent, D.E. 1958. **Perception and Communication.** Oxford: Pergamon Press.

Cicero, 1942. **De Oratore** (Book 2). E.W. Hutton and H. Rackham. London : Heinemann.

Ebel, R.L. 1974. And still the dryads linger. **American Psychologist,** 29, 485-492.

Gibson, J.J. 1966. **The Senses Considered As Perceptual Systems.** Boston: Houghton Mifflin.

Gibson, J.J. 1976. An **Ecological Approach to Visual Perception.** Ithica: Cornell University Press.

Kantor, J.R. 1926. **Principles of Psychology** (vol. 2). Granville, Ohio: Principia Press.

Kantor, J.R. 1957. Events and constructs in psychology. **Psychological Record,** 7, 55-60.

Kantor, J.R. 1959. **Interbehavioral Psychology.** Granville, Ohio: Principia Press.

Kantor, J.R. 1963. **The Scientific Evolution of Psychology** (vol. 1). Granville, Ohio: Principia Press.

Kantor, J.R. 1969. **The Scientific Evolution of Psychology** (vol. 2). Granville, Ohio: Principia Press.

Kantor, J.R. 1977. **Psychological Linguistics.** Chicago, Illinois: Principia Press.

Kantor, J.R. 1978. Man and machine in psychology. **Psychological Record,** 28, 575-583.

Kantor, J.R. and Smith, N.W. 1975. **The Science of Psychology: An Interbehavioral Survey.** Chicago, Illinois: Principia Press.

Kvale, S. 1976. Dialectics and research in remembering. Paper presented at the fifth Life-Span Developmental Psychology Conference, Morgantown , West Virginia.

Malcolm, N. 1977a. **Thought and Language.** Ithica: Cornell University Press.

Malcolm, N. 1977b. **Memory and Mind.** Ithica: Cornell University Press.

Moore, J. 1975. On the principle of operationism in a science of behavior. **Behaviorism,** 3, 120-138.

Moray, N. 1959. Attention in dichotic listening. **Quarterly Journal of Experimental Psychology,** 11, 56-60.

Moray, N. 1966. **Listening and Attention.** Harmondsworth: Penguin Books.

Neisser, U. 1967. **Cognitive Psychology** New York: Appleton-Century-Crofts.

Neisser, U. 1976. **Cognition and Reality.** San Francisco: W.H. Reeman.

Observer. 1968. Descriptive relevance of psychological language. **Psychological Record,** 18, 111-113.

Ryle, G. 1949. **The Concept of Mind.** Harmondsworth: Penguin Books.

Shannon, C. and Weaver, W. 1949. **The Mathematical Theory of Communication.** Urbana, Illinois: University of Illinois Press.

Simon, H. 1977. What computers mean for man and society . **Science,** 195, 187-1094.

Sorabji, R. 1972. **Aristotle on Memory.** London: Duckworth.

Treisman, A.M. 1960. Contextual cues in selected learning. **Quarterly Journal of Experimental Psychology,** 12, 242-248.

Wiener, N. 1949. **Cybernetics.** New York: Wiley.

Wittgenstein, L. 1958. **Blue and Brown Books.** Oxford: Blackwell.

Yates, F.A. 1966. **The Art of Memory.** Harmondsworth: Penguin Books.

# A HISTORY OF PSYCHOLOGICAL TECHNOLOGY

Paul T. Mountjoy

The evolution of scientific psychology from its inception in ancient civilizations up to the present has been described comprehensively , and appropriately evaluated, in two volumes by Kantor (1963, 1969). In these works he followed closely his suggestion (long familiar to his students) that the study of the history of science, and especially of the history of psychology, was a valid scientific enterprise which could significantly contribute to the current evolution of a science (Kantor, 1960). Specifically, the proper pursuit of historical research in psychology provided further validation of conclusion which has become more firmly grounded in recent years--there have never been any psychic data. Thus, the traditional approach to psychological history as the ever increasing accumulation of knowledge concerning the psychic attributes of mankind (e.g., Brett, 1912-1921) must be abandoned. Instead, the notion of a partially psychic and partially physical universe stands revealed as an intellectual construct which evolved under quite social and political conditions in a definite place and time (Kantor, 1963).

Although many modern psychologists claim that they have discarded psychic factors in their constructs, that claim alone does not guarantee the development of an adequate psychological science. Indeed, Kantor (1969) has exhaustively documented the manner in which attempts to base a scientific psychology upon biology, quantization, experimentation, and evolution have merely served to obfuscate the nature of an authentic natural science of psychology. Furthermore, historians of psychology have erred by failure to apprehend this pervasive continuation of psychic doctrines in their disguised forms (Kantor, 1964) and consequently continued to interpret the career of psychology as having been furthered by the utilization of these trappings of science (e.g., Herrnstein and Boring, 1965).

Interbehavioral psychology offers a viable alternative which promises to result in more satisfactory solutions to psychological and historical problems than do the conventional approaches. The proper study of scientific history does not disclose that the brain is the organ of mind, or of behavior, or even of adjustment. Instead, it is seen that all psychological fields are a function of prior psychological fields and of present circumstances. An interbehavioral analysis of the hisotry of psychology, then, is freed from the conventional shackles of the presupposition that only eminent historical personages may ahve contributed to the evolution of psychology. The interbehavioral position that psychological fields are continuations of past fields, as modified by current circumstances, may be verified both by investigation of contemporary events in the field and laboratory, as well as by historical investigations into earlier approaches to psychological events.

Clearly, then, the interbehavioral psychologist uses historical research as a tool to sharpen his constructs rather than as a justification for the continuation of venerable and out-moded conceptions of the nature of psychological events . In actuality, the most important result of proper historical research is the severe pruning of a no longer viable psychic underbrush which serves only to hinder scientific achievement by concealing the vigorous new growth of adequate interbehavioral constructs and consequently impedes their growth and development. The discarding of those metaphysical constructs which were never of service in the evolution of scientific psychology can serve as a potent stimulus for that energetic cultivation of new constructs, without which all sciences are foredoomed to become intellectual fossils.

An investigation of psychological technology may appear to be a sterile enterprise **a priori** to one who assumes, that until the flowering of experimental science in the Renaissance, mankind was basically superstitious and unable to cope effectively with events. However, the history of technology indicates that human beings adjusted adequately to a wide variety of events long before any scientific understanding of those events had begun to emerge. Examples are numerous, but only selected instances are presented here as illustrations. Historical studies of alchemy have indicated that a number of the operations of modern chemistry (e.g., sublimation, fermentation, distillation, etc.) were developed by alchemists and incorporated into chemistry when it evolved into a science. Similarly, certain of the basic operations of modern medical science (e.g., administration of iodine for thryoid hypofunction and variolation for the prevention of small pox were practiced by the ancient chinese ) had been in widespread use for centuries prior to any approximation of a rational account of their effectiveness. Studies of psychological technology may reasonably be expected to disclose the existence and use of psychological operations before their investigation in the psychological laboratory.

Historical research into mankind's technological control of physico-chemical events (e.g., pottery and metalurgy) and biological events (e.g., domestication of plants and animals) has long been a subject of scholarly activity (Singer, Holmyard, Hall, and Williams, 1954, 1956, 1957, 1958a, 1958b; Zeuner, 1963). Psychological technology has, however, largely been ignored. Kantor (1963, 1969) has argued that the physico-chemical, biological, and psychological sciences have evolved in parallel with each other. That is, all three are at roughly the same level of development at approximately the same historical period. A basic assumption which guided the present research was that a similar relationship would be found between physico-chemical, biological, and psychological technologies (for an outline of the evolution of physico-chemical and biological technologies see Cipolla and Birdsall, 1980).

The present paper reports the results of preliminary explorations into this complementary aspect of the history of scientific psychology—the technology of behavior as it existed before the scientific advances which occurred in psychology in the twentieth century. Investigation of behavioral technology was stimulated by Kantor's discussion of prescientific and protoscientific stages in the evolution of psychology (and it should be noted that his discussion of these stages is suggestive of their potential for research as the preponderance of the two volumes is devoted to the third and final authentic scientific stage).

What advantages may we expect to accrue from an investigation into technological aspects of psychology as opposed to the purely scientific developments? The demonstration that human beings predicted and controlled behavior long before the occurrence of the "behavioral revolution" in the twentieth century appears to bear the seeds of increasing our contemporary understanding of behavioral events—when behavioral events are taken to include the behaviors of investigative scientists—since at least three major and four minor benefits flow from this demonstration. These advantages are here stated in the form of hypotheses to be investigated, although their direct derivation from the system of interbehavioral psychology (Kantor, 1959) is obvious.

## Hypotheses

### Major Hypotheses

1. We expected verification of the assumption that psychological events have always been open to inspection and have never been manifestations of postulated and in principle unobservable, inner essences. As a corollary, we anticipated the discovery of historical evidence that psychological events are functions of organismic and environing variables in the sense that the operation or environmental manipulations were tailored to suit the species whose behavior was of interest. Parenthetically, evidence for the field nature of

411

psychological events may well be found in technological descriptions of operations designed to produce some desired behavioral outcome as well as in experiments designed to test a scientific hypothesis.

2.    Verification of the assumption that the behavior of both scientists and non-scientists lies upon a single continuum was foreseen. Evidence was sought in the form of an identity between the operations of the psychological technician and the behavioral scientist.

3.    The complexity of the event continuum studied by psychologists led to the prediction that behavior technologists of the past had described behavioral events which have not been and are not currently under investigation by scientific workers. Descriptions of "unknown" behaviors were foreseen because of the necessity for scientists to select events for study and a consequent inability to be completely inclusive in the range of events to be studied. It was hoped that these events would not represent trivia, but would be important contributions along the trail to a comprehensive scientific psychology.

## Minor Hypotheses

1.    It was presumed that an investigation of the history of behavioral technology would amount to a desirable elucidation of an aspect of our cultural heritage about which little was known, and which actually is being ignored by historians.

2.    The prediction made was that once the elucidation of psychological technology was underway, there would result discoveries of relationships between science and technology in the manner that such relationships have already been discovered between alchemy technology and scientific chemistry, and between folk medicine and modern medical science.

3.    It was contemplated that vigorous pursuit of historical records would lead to formulations concerning the existence of general relationships between animal behavior technology and human behavior technology.

4.    Finally, and not necessarily of the least importance was the prospect of broadening our general appreciation of the historical continuum.

## Behavioral Technologies

The data of this investigation consist primarily of historical documentation, and an enormous number of relevant documents have been discovered. For purposes of the present report selected examples

412

are cited and arranged primarily in a chronological schema.[1]

**Prehistory**

## Hunting Technology

Archeological evidence abounds concerning the ability of preliterate peoples to predict and control the responses of the prey species upon which they were predatory. Cornwall (1968) has organized this evidence into a compelling summary of the ancient kill sites which have been excavated. The oldest layers of Olduvai Gorge (Bed I, which dates to at least one and one-half million years ago) record that our earliest known humanoid ancestors were somewhat inefficient carnivores, evidently subsisting primarily upon small organisms (e.g., lizards, snakes, and rodents) and juvenile or aged members of larger species. It appears that the evolution of both more effective weapons and behavioral knowledge concerning prey species were necessary in order for more efficient predation by human beings to occur. Evidence for these parallel evolutions became striking during the upper Palaiolithic when cave paintings and engravings representing traps, enclosures, fences, nets and nooses were created. At Solutre (ca. 15,000-20,000 B.C.) a site has been excavated at which wild horses were driven over a cliff. The numerous remains indicate that this site was exploited over a period of many years and it must be assumed that exploitations of such a nature required a high degree of behavioral knowledge concerning the horse.

We should be careful neither to overestimate nor underestimate the efficiency as predators of our distant ancestors, however. Martin and Wright (1967) have suggested that the five mammoth kill sites excavated in North America (and other considerations) are compatible with the hypothesis that the late Pleistocene extinctions of more than 24 genera were the direct consequence of paleoindian hunting pressure. In addition, Moisimann and Martin (1975) have demonstrated by means of computer simulation that the extinction of mammoth, mastadon, camels, horses, ground sloths, etc., in North America by human predation is at least within the realm of possibility.

## Domestication Technology

About 11,000 years ago man and dog entered into a symbiotic relationship which culminated not merely in the domestication of the dog, but of various other species as well. Zeuner (1963) has summarized the evidence regarding the process of domestication, and it shall not be repeated here. Nevertheless, it is clear that domestication required a high degree of sophistication regarding the behavior of the species undergoing domestication. Among the behavioral skills which must be possessed in order for domestication

413

to occur we mention only the following. What environmental stimuli provoke attack responses directed toward the human captor? Obviously such stimuli must be withheld. What are the conditions necessary for members of a species to copulate and successfully rear offspring in captivity? These stimuli must be provided if the process of domestication is to occur.

## Primitive Societies

In our modern age of literacy there still exist preliterate social groups whose way of life has not appreciably changed in certain respects for centuries, or even millenia, until quite recently. We are indebted to numerous explorers and missionaries who painstakingly recorded detailed observations of the hunting technology of those societies which they encountered. Among the prominent examples available we list only the polar Eskimo and the Maori of New Zealand.

The polar Eskimo's astuteness regarding the behavioral propensities of prey species has been exquisitively documented by Nelson (1969) who traveled with hunters of acknowledged ability and observed their highly skilled performances. Not only did the Eskimo know the preferred pathways and flyways of migrating animals and birds (and concentrated their hunting efforts along these favored areas) but they also presented stimuli which attracted their prey. For example, they were skilled at mimicry of bird calls, and could lure seals within range by scratching upon the surface of the sea ice.

Best (1856-1930) devoted his life to the study of the Maori of New Zealand and the fruits of that work were reported in a posthumous volume (Best, 1942). From this lengthy report emerges a picture of behavioral sophistication that is astounding. Lack of projectile weapons dictated that the various species of birds (the dominent phylum in Polynesian New Zealand) be lured within range of nooses, thrusting spears, etc. This end was achieved by imitations of calls, artificial or captive speciments. In all cases, hunting behaviors were directed toward a specific species at any one time, and the simulations presented were appropriate to that particular species.

Psychological technologies are not limited to animal behavior technologies but include as well technologies designed to control the behaviors of the human animal. Mankind's cultural organizations may all be so regarded. The complex interplay among physico-chemical and behavioral technologies is illustrated by the navigational systems of teh aborigines of the Pacific islands, including as they do meteorology, geography, astronomy, etc., and even a system of education. Lewis (1978) has documented the incredible complexity of the navigational technology practiced by these illiterate people who are customarily regarded as "ignorant and superstitious savages." The oral traditions which preserve nagivational skills extend at least back to the second millenium B.C., and have been transmitted from generation to generation in organized schools which continued to exist into the twentieth century. Tyro navigators are taught the names of some 178 stars and constellations and their positions at different times of the night for all seasons of the year and varying latitudes and longitudes. At one point in their training the scholars are seated in a "stone canoe" on shore and both instructed and interrogated about the changes in appearance of the heavenly bodies during a simulated voyage.

## The Ancient Near East

With the advent of writing our data base begins to expand enormously. The first documents devoted exclusively to the behavioral management of animals are cuneiform tablets which date to the 14th century B.C. The most famous of these are the five tablets which describe in detail the training regimen of the horses which pulled the war chariots of the ancient Hittites. These were among the approximately 10,000 tablets excavated by Winckler in 1906-1907 and 1911-1912 when he discovered the royal archive at Boghazkoey. Decipherment of the cuneiform inscriptions was begun by Hronzy who published a French translation of the first tablet (Hronzy, 1931) and it has been vigorously pursued by other scholars since that time. Shortly afterwards Potratz (1938) issued a German translation of all five tablets, and later Kammenhuber (1961) rendered into german the five tablets as well as other tablets which had been discovered more recently. The first tablet begins: "The following are the words of Kikkuli, horesman, from the land of Mittani..." (our translation). Consequently, we ascribe to Kikkuli the position of being the first animal behavior technologist identifiable by name and nationality.

The five tablets of Kikkuli (composed in the fourteenth century B.C.) were completely rational descriptions of the day by day procedures to be followed in order to produce teams of horses capable of the sustained effort necessary to pull war chariots at high speeds over long distances as well as being responsive to the commands of the charioteers. The procedures advocated were directly comparable to those described by later writers who were concerned with training trotters and pacers for drawing sulkies in harness races (e.g., Woodruff, 1869; Harrison, 1968).

Salonen (1955) has presented a catalog of the Mesopotamian terminology related to the management of asses, horses, mules, hinnies, oxen, camels, and elephants. His lexiographic efforts have revealed the high state of development of equipment for behavioral control of animals at that time. Among the items he enumerated we mention only yokes, bits, reins, whips, spurs and devices to protect the hooves of the animals. Modern animal behavior technologists display great interest in the continual refinement of these items of equipment (Harrison, 1968) and thus provide testimony concerning the necessity and utility of such devices.

Even as the Hittites and Mesopotamian peoples founded a behavioral technology which was destined to evolve continuously during succeeding centuries and millenia, records of a similar (but different) technology appeared in ancient Egypt. This is the technology of the sorcerer or magician, and this, too, has undergone a continual evolution since its earliest beginnings. A tomb painting of circa 2500 B.C. at Beni Hasan depicts the cups and ball trick, which not only remained popular during the Roman and Medieval periods (Christopher, 1973), but continues to exist in modified form in the 20th century. We submit that a sequence of stimulations which result in desired behavioral outcomes (e.g., purchase of tickets to a performance) represents a human behavior technology. In later sections of this essay more recent occurrences of magical technology shall be discussed.

The earliest magical performance designed purely for entertainment of which a record exists is described in the Westcar papyrus (ca. 1700 B.C.), but the command performance was given for the Pharaoh Cheops whose reign is dated at about 3000 B.C. Among the feats presented by the magician Didi were the decapitation illusion (which survives today in the form of "sawing a woman in half") and a tame , well-trained lion which followed Didi without a leash (an early example of "off-lead heeling"). To be sure, priests had undoubtedly performed magical feats in connection with religious rituals before this, but Didi may be regarded as the earliest professional magician on whom we have any record (Erman, 1894; Christopher, 1973).

### The Far East

The Chinese are well known for their ability in various branches of animal behavior technology, e.g., falconry (Mountjoy, Bos, Duncan and Verplank, 1969). This essay shall confine itself to the manipulation of human behavior; two examples of the use of aversive control are instructive. During the Period of the Warring States (the battle of Ching-Hsing in 205 B.C.), a military leader showed great acumen by placing his green troops with their backs to a river which effectively prevented their retreat and forced them to fight to a victory (Kierman, 1974). The tale is told that a prince of Wu (6th century B.C.) asked a military aspirant to demonstrate his ability to command by drilling the prince's concubines. The aspirant divided the concubines into two groups and placed each under command of a favorite concubine of the prince. When the "troops" failed to obey, the aspirant ordered the two "commanders" beheaded on the spot. The tale indicates that from that time forward, the surviving concubines displayed the most exemplary obedience toward the orders of their new "commanders." The prince's behavior which followed the executions convinced him of the necessity for strict discipline in military affairs (Gulick,1961).

The ancient Chinese should not be regarded as having been obsessed with sexuality. However, the prevailing cultural conditions (polygamy, among others) resulted in the development of manuals of sexual technology which have often been imitated (though probably not surpassed). These manuals were serious attempts at instruction rather than pornographic works (Gulick, 1951, 1961) because sexual activity had important religious connotations. Much of the content centered on techniques by which the male could arouse the female to orgasm while himself refraining from ejaculation. These techniques were practiced for over 2000 years, but were abandoned in the seventeenth century.

The first table recording a human behavior as a function of a physically definable independent variable was presented in these ancient sex manuals; it consists of a plot of the number of allowable ejaculations for the male as a function of age. Comparison to the observed frequency of orgasm as a function of age reported by Kinsey, Pomeroy and Martin (1948) leaves little doubt that the Chinese table was obtained by empirical observation since the correspondence between the two is so striking. The table may be found in the **Yu-fang-pi-Chuck** which dates from the Sui Dynasty of 590-618 A.D. (Gulick, 1961).

### Classical Antiquity

The late fifth and early fourth centuries B.C. were a time of intense intellectual activity in Athens; we need cite only Socrates, Plato, and Aristotle as indicative of the importance of that time for later developments. Xenophon (ca. 430-355 B.C.), contemporary of Socrates, produced three important works of behavior technology. They contained many practical procedures for the training of horses and men.

The translation of Xenophon's **Hippike** by Hull (Xenophon, 1956) is of exceptional interest because of Hulls' expertise in horsemanship; indeed, he comments that modern riders will find material of great utility in this ancient treatise. It should be noted that Xenophon refers in laudatory fashion to a now lost prior work by Simon. Both of these classical authors deplored the use of severe punishment for attaining desired behaviors, and advocated instead techniques which modern behaviorists refer to as stimulus fading (small increments or decrements in stimulation), and shaping (constantly changing behavioral requirements). Xenophon indicates the high level of expertise among ancient Greek horsemen when he remarks that there were specialists who broke colts for riding. The esteem in which skilled horsemen were held is illustrated by the well known story of Bucephalus and his taming by Alexander the Great. Briefly, Bucephalus had unseated everyone who attempted to ride him. Alexander succeeded where all others has failed since he noted that Bucephalus bucked when he saw his own shadow, and positioned him so that stimulus was not observed. Clearly the tale functioned to elicit admiration for Alexander's unique acumen , and may be apocryphal rather than veridical.

Xenophon contains detailed descriptions of the manner in which pairing of stimuli with responses of the horse will result in those stimuli acquiring a functional relationship to the response. These descriptions should be of especial interest to the modern psychologist since Xenophon clearly indicates that the nature of the stimuli may be irrelevant ("neutral" in modern terminology), and that the important variable is the pairing of a specific stimulus with a specific response. Although it is the case that controversy now exists as to whether classical conditioning and operant conditioning are distinct processes, it is evident that in the fourth century B.C. Xenophon presented the first accurate description of the conditioning process.

Xenophon must also be credited with having founded the literature of hunting technology with **Cynegeticus,** the first book devoted to explication of the procedures to be followed in the successful pursuit of game. The work abounds with accurate descriptions of behavioral propensities of various species of prey and accounts of the reaction to be expected of a specific species to specific stimuli. Furthermore, Xenophon described behavioral indices whch indicated the initiation of a behavioral sequence. For example, the hunter was told how to anticipate the actions of a wild boar by watching its eye movements (a matter of great concern when the hunter was expected to kill boars with a spear while dismounted--prediction of the charge was an absolute necessity).

Xenophon's treatise was followed shortly by the **Cynegeticus** of Flavius Arrianus (ca. 96-180 A.D.), and translations of these two works have been rendered by Hull (1964). Hull also included an excerpt from Julius Pollux's **Onomasticon,** a late second century A.D. ten volume dictionary which listed terms and definitions by topics (rather than alphabetically). The topic presented by Hull is hunting. The last great work concenring hunting from the Roman era is another **Cynegetica** by Oppianus (ca. 163-ca. 217 ), who also wrote a work on fishing (**Halietica**) (Oppianus, 1928).

## The Middle Ages

Medieval documentation is difficult to access since most works exist as unique documents in various libraries throughout the world and many are not generally available in modern editions. This gap is partially filled by secondary sources, but remains a serious problem whihc must be solved in the future. We have elsewhere (Mountjoy, 1980, p. 136) published a tabular list of the most important medieval manuscripts devoted to hunting and falconry, with commentary concerning relationships to later works on these topics.

A useful secondary source is Strutt's (1876 edition) **The Sports and Pastimes of the People of England.** Strutt (1749-1802) perused the manuscript collections of the Bodleian, Cottonian, Harleian, Royal and Ben'et College Libraries, as well as private collections, and summarized the activities indicated by his title. Book I contains two chapters on hunting, hawking, and fishing while Book III has a chapter largely devoted to trained animals exhibited for amusement. This latter chapter is illustrated with 13 drawings of trained bears, dogs, monkeys, horses, rabbits, and cocks which Strutt has redrawn from various manuscript sources. Other renditions of trained animals, and discussion of the manuscripts in which they are found, are scattered throughout the work. No techniques of training are presented by Strutt; the burden of the discussion is that trained animals were commonly exhibited for amusement in England during the Middle Ages. We infer, from the terminal behaviors described, that there were sophisticated practitioners of animal behavior technology in this historical period.

Frederick II, Holy Emperor, King of Sicily and Jerusalem (1194-1250) stands out from among his contemporaries as a harbinger of many modern developments in the art of establishing social institutions. For example: In 1224 he founded the first charted university in Europe at Naples. He devoted a significant portion of his later years to a masterpiece of animal behavior technology, **De Arte Venandi cum Avibus** (Frederick II, Holy Roman Emperor, 1943 Edition). This work was only partially completed at the time of the Emperor's death and portions were added by his favorite son and successor, Manfred, King of Sicily (ca. 1232-1266). Manfred's unique personal copy is preserved in the Vatican Library as Ms. Pal. Lat. 1071, and a modern facsimile edition has been issued (Fredericus II, Holy Roman Emperor, 1969 Edition; Mountjoy, 1976). In literal translation the title (**The Art of Hunting with Birds**) fails to indicate the wealth of behavioral observations contained therein. We have already made a behavioral analysis of portions of this work available in the literature (Mountjoy, et al., 1969) and hence merely state that the Emperor's treatise serves as a standard of excellence against which modern books on falconry may be measured. The descriptions of the procedures of the falconer are readily analyzable into many of the operations of the modern experimental and applied analyses of behavior (e.g., deprivation, satiation, fading, and shaping).

Gaston De Foix (also known as Gaston Phoebus) produced the most famous and detailed work on hunting **La Livre de Chasse** between May 1, 1387 and August of 1391 (Grohman, 1919). It abounds with detailed descriptions of the behavioral tendencies of various species of game and how the hunter could best utilize knowledge of these tendencies to successfully (yet chivalrously) bag his prey. A readily available version of **La Livre** with color reproductions of the exquisite illuminations, verifies the behavioral sophistication of medieval hunters (Phoebus, 1978 Edition). The illustrations are from Ms. Francais 616, Bibliotheque National, Paris (but, this is not a facsimile edition).About 1406 Edward, second Duke of York, translated **La Livre** into early English with additions reflecting the differences between the continental and insular conditions and entitled it **The Master of Game** . The Baillie-Grohmans (York, Edward of Norwich, 2nd Duke of 1909 Edition) have translated the **Master of Game** into modern English and have provided scholarly commentary concerning the significance of this work in the early literature of hunting.

The most useful secondary source which is concerned with the literary and artistic tradition of hunting during the Middle Ages and up through the nineteenth century is **Sport in Art** (Grohman, 1919 Edition). Baillie-Grohman had amassed a personal collection of more than 4,000 prints and drawings, of which nearly 250 were reproduced and dicsussed in this work (still unsurpassed in scholarl and artistic merit more than 60 years after its publication). He described the contents of many Medieval manuscripts which were devoted to hunting technology, and thus provided indirect access to documents which would otherwise be difficult to examine. An aspect of this hunting technology is of interest today because of its similarity to modern reinforcement operations. **La Livre** contained a written description and an illustration of the Curee (ceremonial meal) given to the hound after a successful chase and kill. The pack had been food deprived prior to the hunt, and the blood and minced internal organs of the game were mixed with bread and flour upon the flayed hide of the trophy from which the dogs were allowed to consume the reinforcer. Incidently, modern veterinarians recommend that cereal grain products be mixed with meat before it is fed to dogs; indeed a diet consisting solely of meat is eventually lethal to dogs.

# The Scientific Renaissance

It is no idle jest to regard the advent of the printing press in about 1450 as one of the important criterion of the Scientific Renaissance. All who conduct historical research are struck by the increased dissemination of the accumulated books from past centuries and the acceleration of the production of new books. That is, not only were the authors of classical antiquity made available in relatively inexpensive editions (e.g., Xenophon) but numerous works by contemporary writers appeared, among which were many devoted to animal behavior technology. We list illustrative examples: Turbervile's (1575b) **The Noble Arte of Venerie or Hunting**, (1575a) **The Booke of Falconrie**, and Blundevill's (1580) **Fouer Chiefyst Offices Belonging to Horsemanshippe.** No longer is the problem one of locating works concerning psychological technology--from this time onward the problem is the selection of the most significant works.

Frequently we find assistance in secondary sources, the authors of whch are experts in some field. An example is the analysis of the evolution of the art of riding from 1500-1670 given in **Bridleways Through History** (Apsley, Lady Viola, (Meeking) Bathurst, baroness, 1936). The baroness was a skilled horsewoman who had a wide acquaintance with the relevant literature. Her explanation of the manner in which a well-trained team of horse and rider were a potent unit in the type of warfare prevalent during this period is most enlightening. She explained, e.g., that the horse was trained to respond to leg signals in order to free the hands of the horseman to manipulate his sword and shied.

Other works cannot be ignored primarily because of their aesthetic appeal. Such a publication is offered by Suleiman (1970) who reproduced the miniatures of the incomparable British Museum manuscript of the **Babur-Nama.** Babur (1483-1530) founded the Moghul Empire in 1526 and was one of the first rulers to record his memoires. This manuscript version of his memoires (although it is dated to the end of the 16th century) was lavishly illustrated with minatures of high artistic merit. In addition, the illustrations indicate how falcons were carried at that time and place, many details of other aspects of hunting technology, etc.

Works which are the first to discuss a specific topic are always of interest, and the first book concerned with the dogs of England (Caius, 1945, p. 32) contains the following timeless piece of wisdom.

> For there be some....Which barcke only with free and
> open....throate but will not bite,....Which doe both barcke
> and byte,....Which bite bitterly before they barcke

The first publication in English to present a naturalistic explanation of conjuring or sleight-of-hand was that of Scot (1584). Not only did he attack the then almost obsessive craze of witchhunting but he also devoted some 30 pages and four plates to descriptions of the cups and ball, various coin, card, handkerchief, and paper tricks as well as the decapitation illusion. In the description of the decapitation illusion Scot gave painstakingly detailed directions for the arrangements of candles and drapes (thus controlling visual stimuli) and provision of distracting auditory and olfactory stimuli to the audience in order to produce a compelling illusion.

Accounts of displays of trained animals are common at this time, and we have selected a description which is more detailed than most. In the early sixteenth century, a Moor, John Leo, traveled widely in Northern Africa and about 1526 wrote an account of his travels and adventures in Arabic and Italian. This was later translated into English by John Pory and published in 1600 under the title A **Geographical History of Africa** (Leo Africanus, 1600). Its original author, now known as John Leo Africanus, recounts that in a suburb of Cairo there were numerous animal trainers. One had trained an ass to play dead when verbally threatened with imminent hard labor, and to persist in this perverse immobility even when beaten. However, when the trainer began to speak of special meals of oats"...the ass suddenly starteth from the ground, prancing and leaping for joy..." (p. 942). Amusing as this anecdote is (and clearly the trainer was an excellent showman) it resembles many accounts of trained animals--no specifics of the training nor of the signals given to the ass were reported. We assume that the signals to which the ass responded were not discriminable to the audience.

Later, however, Leo Africanus did describe the training of a camel to "dance" by pairing a heated floor with a drum beat. He reported that after 10 months to a year of training, the camel would "dance" on an unheated floor when a drum was beaten. In our opinion this was a tale told by a trainer wishing to preserve the secrecy of his methodology since the procedure of elicitation and pairing as described is far too demanding of equipment and of time as compared to other available techniques. However, it does raise a question which could be answered by appropriate historical research, the question of the relative importance of elicitation and of reinforcement in the history of behavioral technology.

### The Seventeenth Century

The first book in English devoted entirely to conjuring appears to have been **The Art of Jugling** by "Sa: Rid" (1612). (It is unknown whether this represents an abbreviation of the author's name or was a

422

pseudonym.) **The Art** discussed the famous horse Morocco exhibited by an equally mysterious personage named Banks. Morocco could count the number of dots exposed by the roll of a pair of dice, and even "read the minds" of members of the audience in the sense of pawing the proper number of times if a member of the audience first whispered the number of shillings in his pocket into Banks' ear. Sa: Rid was apparently an eyewitness to one of these performances as he reported the behavioral cue Banks presented to enable Morocco to perform these feats in the following words.

> ...and marke the eye of the horse is alwaies upon his
> master, and as his master moves so goes he or stands
> still...then the horse paws with his foote whiles the
> master stands stone still; then when his master sees
> hee hath pawed so many as the first dice showes itselfe,
> then he lifts up his shoulders and stirres a little...and
> note that the horse will pawe an hundred times together,
> untill he sees his master stirre: and note also that
> nothing can be done, but his master must first know,
> and then his master knowing, the horse is ruled by him
> by signes (no pagination).

The similarity between Banks' Morocco of the seventeenth century and von Osten's **Kluge Hans** of the twentieth century is obvious (and indeed there were many educated animals which could count, read, etc., in the seventeenth, eighteenth, nineteenth and twentieth centuries). A behavioral analysis of an eighteenth century educated pig will be presented in the section of this essay devoted to the eighteenth century.

Although Sa: Rid did not speculate concerning the training procedures utilized by Banks, five years earlier Gervaise Markham in his **Calvelarice, or The English Horseman** (1607) had described in detail exactly how to train a horse in order to produce such apparently marvelous behaviors. The operations are presented in sufficient detail to allow us to state that Markham used the operations of deprivation, primary and secondary reinforcement, successive approximations, backward chaining, and fading. Markham specified the length of time the horse was to be food deprived, the use of food as a consequence for a desired response (primary reinforcement), the requirement that only the trainer present food and water (thus, many responses of the trainer--e.g., caresses--would become secondary reinforcers), the respone criteria to be followed in shaping (successive approximations) the horse to pick up a glove with its mouth (utilizing backward chaining) and present it to the trainer, and the attenuation (fading) of a cue--i.e., the trainer was to gradually decrease the magnitude of an arm movement at the point at which an audience could no longer discriminate the motion, but the horse's behavior remained under the control of the cue.

It is desirable to mention at least one other of Markham's numerous publications, **Hungers Prevention: Or the Whole Arte of Fowling by Water and Land** (1621) because of th detailed accounts of various methods by which one could take advantage of behavioral propensities of diverse species of fowl in order to effect their capture. One especially interesting device is the lark mirror. This is of unknown origin and great antiquity; it was well known prior to Markham's description. Briefly, it consisted of an upright cylinder with small bits of mirror fastened to its exterior so that when rotated upon its axis the mirrors would reflect light in all directions. The cylinder was mounted upon a vertical axle inserted into the ground, and in Markham's time rotated by a string extending to the blind in which the hunter was concealed. More recent versions had spring powered motors to provide rotation (Brusewitz, 1969). The use of the lark mirror illustrates that knowledge of behavioral principles necessary in order to be an effective hunter since the lark mirror attracts larks only at sunrise during the fall migration. A search of the modern ethological literature has failed to reveal any discussion of the specific response of larks approaching flashes of light in the manner reported by Markham and others, even though the lark mirror continued to be used into the nineteenth century after shotguns had replaced the nets of the seventeenth century.

William Cavendish (1593-1676) the lear, marquis and duke of Newcastle published in 1658 **La Methode Nouvelle et Invention Extraordinaire de Dresser Les Chevaux,** which was shortly followed (1667) by a modified English version **A New Method and Extraordinary Invention to Dress Horses** (Newcastle, Duke of, 1970). The **Methode** of 1658 was so important a contribution to the development of dressage riding that it was reissued in 1737, and finally produced in an English translation entitled **A General System of Horsemanship** in 1743, which was reissued in 1748. This work is of interest not only for its great influence upon horse training, but also because of its utter rejection of the savage use of aversive techniques which evidently were pervasive at that time. In addition, in his introduction, Cavendish expounded upon the generality ot training and psychological principles for both horse and human (as well as denying the validity of Descartes' dictum that only human beings think).

We cannot leave the seventeenth century without indicating that the tradition of literary and artistic works depicting the technology of hunting continued to be vigorous not only in England (Grohman, 1919, Markham, 1612) but also upon the Continent. For example, by 1614 Wolfgang Birkner (1582-1651) was court painter to John Casimer (b. 1654, reigned 1586-1633). Birkner's "Old Hunting Book" is apparently lost as it has not been reported since 1910. However, the "Younger Hunting Book" (which was begun early in 1639 and probably finished circa 1649) has been reissued in facsimile with commentary by Lindner (1969). The work consists of 39 exquisite paintings in India ink, watercolor, and tempura, which depict in detail the hunting technology of Duke Casimir of Saxony. It is remarkable to note the manner in which Medieval traditions of the hunt have persisted into the seventeenth century. We merely note that plates 12 and 13 record the ritualistic gralloching (dressing) of the game and plates 14, 15, and 16 show various aspects of the ceremonial "partnership feast" of the hounds (or **Curee** as it was called in France and England). These ritualistic aspects of hunting technology were already highly developed during the Medieval period (Grohman , 1919) and we reiterate that the **Curee** involved the operations of both deprivation and primary reinforcement as we indicated in our discussion of the Middle Ages.

## The Eighteenth Century

The origins of the pursuit and capture of the largest animals ever to live upon this earth are lost in the mists of antiquity since scavenging of stranded whales was practiced by preliterate peoples who lacked the technical expertise necessary to pursue free swimming cetacians. However, these technical abilities were observed among many preliterates when they were first observed by Europeans during the age of exploration. Whaling is recorded as a behavior technology of the Basques by the end of the first millenium of our era, but reached its full flowering in the eighteenth century (**Enclyclopedia Britannica**, 1910-11; Goode, 1887; Jenkins, 1971). The pursuit of the sperm whale led American seamen to be among the       first       to explore the far reaches of the Pacific Ocean, although British whalers were in the vanguard. In addition to the geographical knowledge accumulated (which contributed to the opening of trade routes among other things) an enormous amount of expertise concerning cetacian behavior was gathered. Descriptions of breeding grounds, maternal behavior, and migration routes were quite detailed (Beale, 1839; Bennett, 1840; Davis, 1926). Practitioners of whaling were sophisticated in terms of the sensory capacities of, and probable reactions to specific stimulus situations by the various species. Indeed, great expertise was essential when mammals over 50 feet in length were attacked and killed by means of hand held harpoons and lances from fragile rowboats only half the length of the prey (Cheever, 1850; Scoresby, 1823). The hardships and dangers faced by whalers before the advent of steam powered ships and explosive harpoons in the nineteenth century cannot fail to excite our admiration for the courage and skill with which they confronted an extremely hostile environment. Accounts of damaged or destroyed boats and dead, maimed and injured seamen are common in the literature of whaling.

Examples of human behavior technology are not far to seek. For example, de Latude (1725-1805) attempted to manipulate the behaviors of Madame de Pompadour (mistress of King Louis XV) and a consequence of his bungling he become famous as "the prisoner of the Bastille." His two successful escapes from the prison at Vincennes, and an additional one from the Bastille (1756) testify to his success as an amateur behavior modifier (Mountjoy, 1972). Benjamin Franklin (1706-1790) recounted in his memoires a system of behavioral self-management which contained many modern components (Mountjoy and Sundberg, 1981).

Displays of trained animals continued to be popular in this century and Strutt (1876 Edition) has described a complex performance he observed in 1789. Some 12 or 14 "little birds" (species not identified further) wearing paper caps and carrying miniature wooden muskets marched a "deserter" in front of a very small cannon. An "executioner" applied a lighted match to the touchhole, and at the report the condemned bird fell and lay motionless while the "soldiers" marched away. Strutt also described a pig which responded to oral questions by selecting pieces of paper on which were written the appropriate answers. Somewhat earlier a popular article (Anonymous, 1753) summarized the performance of "Mrs. Midnight's Animal Comedians." They consisted of a troupe of monkeys and dogs who enacted a drama which (among other things) the dogs besieged a castle defended by the monkeys. Neither Strutt nor the anonymous reporter described training procedures, but confined themselves solely to the terminal performances; it is obvious, however, that complex shaping procedures could have produced these terminal behaviors.

The actual complexity of the shaping procedures used by seventeenth and eighteenth century horsemen may be gleaned from reading Newcastle (1970) and examination of the many engravings which illustrate the techniques verbally described in the text. A modern edition of d'Eisenberg's 1747 **Description du Menege Moderne** displays exquisite color reproductions of the 55 goach paintings which served as the basis for the engravings which illustrated **du Menege.** Illustrations such as these indicate the behavioral sophistication and attention to small detail which is the hallmark of the competent behavior technologist.

Much scholarly interest has been directed toward the impact of the horse upon the culture of the American Indian. Prior to the arrival of the Europeans upon the North American continent the sole domesticated animal of the Inidan tribes was the dog. There is little evidence that the Indians adopted the horse in the seventeenth century, but there is considerable evidence that the process of adoption commenced in the eighteenth century. Both Wilson (1924) and Roe (1939) have summarized the historical documentation and described the manner in which the insertion of the new domesticated animal changed the Indian culture in numerous ways. Although the Indians had trained dogs to carry packs, and to pull the travois, the introduction of a new species required the development of a new animal behavior technology and many cultural traits as well.

Wilson (1924) reported how Indians broke two year old colts for riding and further training for war ponies. Prospective war ponies were trained to turn toward the side on which the rider's weight was placed by pairing the shift of seat with reining. The reining was then gradually attenuated and the weight shift was similarly faded until the pony would respond to very subtle leg pressure of the rider. It must be noted that similar procedures are followed by modern horse trainers, although the actual training procedure today is much more complex than this brief account is able to indicate. It is assumed that the eighteenth century Indians were quite sophisticated concerning horse behavior since they were among the great horsemen of world history. To illustrate: "Reining" was actually a pull upon a rope secured about the Indian pony's lower jaw, and hence technically an aversive stimulus which elicited escape by turning. The turning did remove the aversive pull (achieved escape) since the rider would then slacken the rope. Thus, the turning was maintained by negative reinforcement. The shift in seat reliably preceeded the pull, and responses to that shift were in essence avoidance--and the well trained pony could be guided solely by slight leg pressure which left the rider's arms free to manipulate weapons.

An extreme example of the manipulation of stimuli to predict and control the behavior of an untrained animal is to be seen in the bullfight. Since its origins in Minoan Crete, long before the Christian era, the skill and courage of those confronted the charge of a bull have elicited admiration among spectators. The modern bullfight evolved on the Iberian peninsula from the hunting of wild bulls on horseback, and assumed its modern form in the eighteenth century (Fulton, 1971) when the techniques of eliciting charges were expanded to include control over the charge by manipulation of the cape so that the bull could be killed by a man on foot armed only with a sword. Joaquin Rodriguiz Costillares (1729-1800) is widely regarded as the innovator who is responsible for the essentials of the modern bullfight (Alvarex, no date; Conrad, 1961; Fulton, 1971). The skilled **torero** evaluates the propensity of each bull to establish its own "territory" within the bullring, and proceeds according to that and other individual behavioral tendencies. Once a charge has been elicited the cape is moved at a velocity which corresponds to the speed of the charge in order to control the bull's behavior. All of this must be done in the manner prescribed by rules which insure that the bull has a "fair" opportunity to gore the bullfighter. The list of bullfighters who have been killed and injured in the bullring testifies to widespread adherence to those rules. Breeders of bulls have for centuries been skilled in the administration of behavioral tests for "bravery" (and other behaviors) and have demonstrated their expertise in selective breeding by producing strains of fighting bulls whose behavior are remarkably predictable (Macnab, 1959) and always dangerous to the **torero**.

## The Nineteenth Century

An English magician, William Frederick Pinchbeck was the author of the first two books on conjuring to be written and published in the United States (Beck, 1975). One of these "throwaways" (the little books sold at the performance) was entitled: **The Expositor: Or Many Mysteries Unravelled**[2] (Pinchbeck, 1805). This work is of especial interest to the historian of behavior technology as it described in detail how to train a pig to not only answer questions put to it in ordinary speech, but even to "read the mind" of a member of the audience. The day by day minutia of the training regimen was so detailed that one may discern the use of the operations of reinforcement, backward chaining, discrimination training, successive approximations, and stimulus fading.

Pinchbeck surpassed Marham's (1607) description of how to fade stimulus cues until they were no longer discriminable by the audience and clearly anticipated Pfungst's (1911) research upon **Der Kluge Hans** a century later. The important contribution of Pfungst was the experimental documentation that the trainer, or indeed any member of the audience, could give cues to the animal while being unable to report that he was doing so. Pinchbeck stated that after the fading process had been completed the trainer would find that he could dispense with the cue altogether and still the pig would continue to respond correctly. Pinchbeck lacked the technical terminology necessary to describe such a complex interbehavior, but it is evident from his repeated attempts to describe the interaction that he possessed an adequate technological understanding of this complex event in the sense that he spoke of a postural cue which he could not further identify. The early nineteenth century report of the manner in which a trained animal (and an audience?) would shape an "unobserved" response in the trainer is relevant to recent research on learning without awareness (Hefferline, Keenan and Harford, 1959; Hefferline and Keenan, 1961; Hefferline and Keenan, 1963; Hefferline and Bruno, 1971; Sasmor, 1966). The burden of this recent research is the demonstration that a response may be shaped by contingencies even though that response is so minute that sophisticated electronic equipment is necessary for detection and recording. In the case of Pinchbeck and his pig it may be argued that the pig "taught" the trainer in the same sense that the trainer "taught" the pig--and this

428

is clearly an example of **interbehavior.**

We have briefly traced chronological examples of the tradition of animals which have been educated to read, count, etc., from the seventeenth century accounts of Sa: Rid (1612) and Markham (1607), through Strutt's (1876) eighteenth century descriptions, and into the nineteenth century exposition of training procedures by Pinchbeck. This historical series is incomplete as we have other examples which have not been mentioned. However, the vitality of the tradition is testified to by the twentieth century claim of Borgese (1966), that she has taught her dog to typewrite meaningful prose.

Numerous individuals shaped exceptionally complex behaviors in a wide variety of species. An example may be found in the following quotation which was attributed to Audobon (Browne, 1850). Speaking of the American Goldfinch he states:

> One of them...would draw water for its drink from
> a glass, it having a little chain attached to a narrow
> belt of soft leather fastened round its body, and ano-
> ther equally light chain fastened to a little bucket,
> kept by its weight in the water, until the little fellow
> raised it up with its bill, placed a foot upon it, and
> pulled again at the chain until it reached the desired
> fluid and drank, when, on letting go, the bucket immed-
> iately fell into the glass below. In the same manner,
> it was obliged to draw towards its bill a little chariot
> filled with seeds...(p. 52).

Almost in the exact center of the nineteenth century the Reverend Lorenzo L. Langstroth revolutionized the technology of apiculture or beekeeping. The honey produced by various species of the genus **Apis** provides a convenient source of nourishment for many animals, including mankind. It is likely that our protohumanoid ancestors robbed the nests of wild bees, and that apiculture had developed at least by neolithic times. Indeed, it has been argued that **Apis mellifera** is the first domesticated animal (Zeuner, 1963). Apiculture, in its early form, was inefficient as the entire comb was destroyed in order to extract the honey. In fact, the entire populations of hives were killed in order that the comb might be harvested without the keeper being stung (Butler, 1609; Hill, 1568; Remnant, 1637; Southerne, 1593). This necessitated that new colonies be obtained and developed--or at the very least that the bee colony expend considerable time and energy in reconstructing combs before they could begin to replenish the supply of honey. Many persons attempted to develop hive from which combs could be removed easily,emptied, and replaced intact to be refilled by the busy workers. All these

429

attempts failed until Langstroth discovered the behavioral principle known to modern apiculturists as "the bee space" during an ingenious investigation. In the summer of 1851 he demonstrated that bees would not fill in a one-quarter inch space (the bee space) but would instead crawl through it (Langstroth, 1862). If the gap exceeded one-quarter of an inch the bees built combs in it; a lesser space will filled with propolis (which resembles the resinous pitch of conifers). In either case the frame containing the comb had to be cut out--which enraged the bees and resulted in a stung beekeeper. The beespace (which was ensured by Langstroth's movable frame hive) enabled the comb to be removed and emptied by the centrifugal force produced by rapid spinning--a procedure developed by Hruschka in 1865. The replacement of the frame containing the new empty comb stimulated the bees to begin gathering nectar rather than to sting the beekeeper. Langstroth obtained U.S. Patent number 9,3000 on October 5, 1852. In the book which described his observations Langstroth (1862) concluded that slight distrubances of the inhabitants of a hive resulted in them filling their stomachs with honey, and that the probability of a satiated bee stinging the keeper was for all practical purposes "zero." He, therefore, suggested small stimulations prior to removing frames in order to avoid stings. Because of his astute observations, and ability to turn these observations to practical application, we regard the Reverend Langstroth to have been one of the most competent animal behavior technologists known from the historical record.

An example of an historical document which reports another behavior that has essentially been forgotten by scientists is to be found in Sir Ralph Payne-Gallwey's **The Book of the Duck Decoy** (Gallwey, 1886). This neglected behavior is the mobbing of predators by flocks of avian prey species. The few modern reports of mobbing are confined to the passerine birds and they have been summarized by Hinde (1970) and Thorpe (1956). However, Sir Ralph reported many instances of **waterfowl** mobbing predators, and a search of the modern ornithological literature has failed to uncover any discussions of this behavior. Payne-Gallwey (1886) described the historical evolution of a system of ponds, canals, and nets into which waterfowl (especially ducks, but also geese and swans) could be enticed and captured because of the tendency for flocks to approach a predator and to follow it if it fled (mobbing). Sir Ralph also presented detailed instructions concerning how to construct and operate a duck decoy (Gallwey, 1882. 1886). The English word "decoy" is stated by Sir Ralph to be a corruption of the Dutch term "en die kooi" which literally means the "duck cage," and the term is descriptive of the system of netting which secures the waterfowl.

The operation of a duck decoy was so complex that it was entrusted to a specialist in behavior technology, the "decoy-man." He not only oversaw the physical maintenance of the decoy, but also trained the "decoy-ducks" (which attracted wild ducks to the pond in the first place) to approach the canal upon cue--thus enticing the wild ducks into position from which they could observe the "decoy-dog." This dog was a specialized breed, which resembled a fox in appearance, and was trained by the decoy-man to be responsive to commands. A series of opaque fences concealed the decoy-man from the wild ducks while he signaled the decoy-dog to retreat in front of the advancing ducks. They mobbed the predator by following the fleeing dog. At the appropriate time the decoy-man revealed himself in order to flush the ducks into a restraining net at the far end of the canal, from which they were readily removed and killed. All of this may sound rather simple and straightforward-- but the successful execution of the procedure involved a high degree of behavioral acumen.

The utilization of mobbing to capture birds is an extremely ancient tradition. As early as the thirteenth century, the Emperor Frederick II (1943) commented that bird catchers took advantage of this behavioral tendency by using owls to attract other birds into nets, and Baillie-Grohman (1919) reproduced a rendition of a duck decoy by Hans Boll (1534-1539). Markham (1621) discussed the fact that a model of an owl would entice birds into traps, while Blaine (1856) wrote of the duck decoy as if it were a well-known phenomenon, and Cox (1874) briefly described the operation of a decoy. This traditional use of mobbing behavior has not only persisted into the twentieth century (Gibson, 1905), but is still used at this date by modern hunters who use either live predators or models of them to lure flocks of passerines within shotgun range.

In this last quarter of the twentieth century Americans have become so dependent upon mechanized transportation that they tend to forget that most human beings still live as they did in prior centuries, at least in the sense of relying completely upon animals for transport. In an attempt to illustrate this continued dependency upon animal behavior technology we cite examples drawn from nineteenth century American circumstances.

Horses were the primary method of transport in these United States, and as a consequence there arose an almost overwhelming concern with the methodology of horse training. One reason for this excessive interest probably was the result of the well-known tendency for Americans to rely over much upon punishment as a training technique with the consequent development of "vices" (handbooks on the management of horses almost universally contained a section on the curing of vices, and the development of vices were frequently attributed to improper punishment procedures). A seminal figure in the shift to more rational training techniques was Rarey (1857). Although we cite only one of his many publications, he was continually cited in later works (e.g., Stewart, 1869), and frequently his techniques were dipicted **without** citation of their source (e.g., Magner, 1980). Indeed, Rarey was so famous that he toured Europe, where among other feats, he tamed a man-killing horse owned by Prince Albert. This so impressed the royal family that Rarey was invited to attend the wedding of one of Victoria's daughters. One of the most eminent nineteenth century British horsemen (Hayes, 1894, pp. 98-110) has testified to the importance of visiting American "Professors" as influences in the evolution of European horsemanship techniques.

Rarey's techniques for extinguishing excessively fearful responses in the horse appears to resemble implosion in the sense that the horse was essentially immobilized by a set of special straps, thrown, and then stimulated repeatedly with the feared object. For example, an umbrella would be forcefully opened repeatedly and directly in front of the horse's head.

Itinerant trainers, who traveled on as soon as the behavioral problems in the immediate area were solved, were common in the later portion of the nineteenth century. The self-styled "Professor" Oscar R. Gleason (1892) represents an example of these itinerant individuals, and an interesting contrast to Rarey since Gleason advocated beginning with less intense stimulation and fading in more intense stimulation over an extended period of time for the treatment of phobic horses.

The extent of interest in horses and their training may be judged by the existance of another self-styled "Professor" Oliver W. Gleason (1900). Part II of this work is a reissue of his 1889 **System** and contains a brief description of how to train a carriage horse to be guided without reins. To be sure, teaching a carriage horse to be guided purely by the visual cue of the motion of the whip was not new, as Jennings (ca. 1866) had given a detailed discussion of the procedures some years earlier. Nevertheless, the continued interest in such a feat testifies to the pride taken in a well-trained horse during the nineteenth century. The behavioral sophistication necessary to successfully train and manage horses is apparent in the complex behavioral descriptions and prescriptions presented in a late nineteenth century classic now readily available in a modern facsimile (Magner, 1980).

Additional evidence of the behavioral sophistication of horsemen is found in the treatment of punishment given by Fillis:

432

...if punishment is not administered at the precise moment the fault is committed, it will lose all its good effect...For instance if a horse which kicks receives punishment when his hind legs are off the ground, he will remember that he got hurt for kicking. If, on the contrary, the punishment is received after his hind legs have come down, he will be unable to connect in his mind the ideas of these two acts; in fact, the pro- bability is that he will try, by a fresh kick, to get rid of the person who is hitting him.

I have said that every deliberate act of disobedience committed by a horse should be punished; but I do not hesitate to add that it is better not to punish him than to do it too late. Both are bad, but it is better to choose the lesser of the two evils (1889, p. 17; 1902, pp. 9-10).

Clearly, Fillis viewed punishment as a procedure which interfered with the completion of a response sequence rather than as a weakener of behavior a la Thorndike (1911 and later).

The importance of animals for transportation may be judged by the attempt (now almost forgotten) to introduce the camel for use in the arid southwestern portion of the United States prior to the completion of the transcontinental railroad. Congressional documents (Executive Document No. 62, 1856-7) have preserved the correspondence between the then Secretary of War Jefferson Davis and other government officials which recorded the details of this effort. The procedures for training camels were described in other documents (Micellaneous Document No. 271, 1858). Among the factors which doomed this enterprise to failure were the advent of the Civil War (with consequent diversion of resources to other affairs) and the subsequent meeting of the east and west bound railroad tracks in the Golden Spike ceremony at Promontory Point, Utah. Half a world away, in Australia, where there was neither a war nor a successful railroad, camels were imported by the thousands in the nineteenth century and they continued to be of great importance almost until World War II (McKnight, 1969).

One last example must suffice to round out this survey of psychological technology. Since we (Mountjoy, 1974) have reported in detail upon the matter, we briefly sumamrize it here. Between 1856 and 1919 the United States Patent Office granted Letters of Patent for a total of at least 49 devices which were designed to prevent masturbation. Although 35 were intended to be applied to stallions and jacks, 14 were designed to be used by human beings. A number of these artifacts are instructive concerning the level of behavioral sophistication reached at that time because they were essentially designed to automatically respond to penile tumescence by providing feedback which would reflexly produce detumescence. The similarity of the stimulation provided by certain of the devices to the squeeze technique of Masters and Johnson (1970) is striking. To illustrate: Most of the devices were designed to apply pressure at the juncture of the penile head with the shaft--and this is precisely the technique advocated by Masters and Johnson.

## Evaluation of Hypotheses

We have surveyed a portion of the available historical data which indicate that viable behavioral technologies have existed since an extremely early period in the evolution of the human species; it is now appropriate to evaluate to what extent these data support or fail to support the hypotheses enumerated at the beginning of this essay.

### Major Hypotheses

1. Have psychological events always been open to inspection rather than being manifestations of postulated and in principle unobservable inner essences? The evidence is compatible with such an hypothesis in the sense that until the advent of psychological dualism in the Christian era the behavior of organisms was predicted in the field (and controlled in specific circumstances ) solely by consideration of the behavioral propensities of the species and the nature of environing circumstances. Following the advent of dualism some behavior technologists discussed psychic components--while others did not. Further research and analysis is necessary to determine the extent to which adherence to psychic explanations hindered or was irrelevant to the evolution of a behavioral technology. It appears to be the case that psychic constructs distracted the technologist from actual variables and contributed to the development of irrelevant (largely verbal) rituals.

**Corollary.** Are psychological events functions of organismic and environing variables in the sense that operations were tailored to suit the species under consideration? The evidence supports this generalization (e.g., Frederick II warned against the use of punishment with falcons, but advocated it in the case of dogs).

Is there evidence for the field interpretation of psychological events? There is in the sense that whenever events were described in any detail, it is obvious that ancient authors knew full well that very minor changes in environing conditions produced marked changes in the events under consideration. The most important single document discovered has been Pinchbeck's (1805) description of the interbehavior

434

of the learned pig and its trainer. While he lacked the technical vocabulary which facilitates our contemporary discussion of psychological interbehavior, i.e., those dynamic changes in stimulus and response functions which occurred during a sequence of behavior segments. The description of those dynamic changes which constitute an interbehavioral field remains the fundamental task of the objective psychologist today. We submit that given the limitations inherent at his place on the historical continuum, Pinchbeck produced a remarkably accurate description of a psychological field when he described the manner in which the trainer taught the animal to respond in a specific fashion and at the same time the animal was also teaching the trainer to respond in another manner. This mutual interdependence of stimulus and response functions is of central concern to interbehavioral psychologists, and Pinchbeck's nineteenth century description of this interdependence supports the interbehavioral approach to the subect matter of psychology.

2. Does the behavior of scientists and non-scientists lie upon a single continuum? They appear to do so since there is essentially an identity between certain operations performed by behavior technologists of the past and behavior scientist of the present. Among those we have identified are deprivation, positive and negative reinforcement, successive approximations, stimulus fading, backward chaining, and punishment. The point on the continuum which separates scientists from non-scientists is, of course, the concern of the scientist to develop explanatory constructs. However, in at least some instances the technologist has evaluated the effects of behavioral operations more adequately than the scientist. An example is Fillis' treatment of punishment as contrasted to that of Thorndike.

3. Did behavior technologists describe events not currently under investigation by scientific workers? They did, and two striking examples are the utilization of mobbing behavior to entrap waterfowl (the duck decoy) and the lark mirror. A search of the contemporary ornithological literature has revealed current disinterest in the mobbing behavior of waterfowl--and only a slight interest in the mobbing behavior of passerine birds. The obvious survival value of mobbing indicates that this is not a trivial behavior in the species under consideration. A similar search has failed to uncover any descriptions of the behavior elicited by the lark mirror.

## Minor Hypotheses

1. We have been able to begin an elucidation of an aspect of our cultural heritage which actually is ignored by historians. As this line of investigation is prosecuted in the future it is hoped that behavioral technologies will be placed in appropriate historical perspective.

2. At the present time little evidence concerning relationships between behavioral technology and behavioral science has been discovered. It appears that as a group modern behavioral scientists (because of the tendency of many to be ahistorical) have been forced to rediscover the techniques of past behavior technologists. The modern scientist has far surpassed the behavior technologist of the past in the development of an adequate technical vocabulary and appropriate explanatory constructs.

3. Some evidence exists that historical figures discussed the application of identical behavioral principles to both human and nonhuman organisms (e.g., Xenophon cites Simon as having discussed the different procedures to be used in training horses and slaves). The fact that eminent animal behavior technologists were also able politicians in at least some instances (e.g., Frederick II and Babur) points the way for future research efforts.

4. Has our appreciation of the general historical continuum been broadened? We must answer in the affirmative so far as we ourselves are concerned. It has become more apparent that whenever a complete discontinuity has been proposed careful investigation discloses the intermediate points on a continuum which unites the supposed independent entities.

### Conclusion

The thrust of this essay should not be misunderstood as containing an implication that pre-twentieth century behavior technologists were actually interbehaviorists since that viewpoint is a unique twentieth century development. However, pre-twentieth century peoples did adjust effectively to their behavioral environment. That is, they were able to isolate and to some extent to manipulate those aspects of that environment which we now speak of as setting factors, interbehavioral history, and stimulus objects, etc., in order to develop coordinated stimulus and response functions. Although it is the case that all of the evidence has not been isolated and evaluated to date, that evidence which we have discovered (and examined in this essay) is compatible with the general assumptions that all human technologies (behavioral as well as physio-chemical and biological) evolved in a parallel fashion which is analogous to the parallel evolution of the various sciences.

### Footnotes

1. No attempt is made to provide complete publishing histories of the historical works cited. However, when modern editions are known to be available these are also cited--and in those cases in which only the modern versions have been consulted they are listed first in the citations.

2. I wish to thank Mr. Leonard N. Beck, Curator, Special Collections in the Rare Book Division of the Library of Congress and his staff for allowing and assisting me in the examination of the **Expositor** and other rare volumes.

## References

Alvares, R.V. (no date). **El Toro (The Art of Bullfighting).** (Translated by Enrique Inigo y Samaniego). Lago Alberto, Mexico: Editorial Eduardo Cabal.

Anonymous. 1753. The explanation of Mrs. Midnight's animal comedians. **The Universal Magazine**, February, 90-91.

Apsely, Lady Viola, (Meeking) Bathurst, baroness. 1936. **Bridleways Through History.** London: Hutchinson.

Beale, T. 1839. **The Natural History of the Sperm Whale, to which is Added a Sketch of a South-Sea Whaling Voyage.** London: John Van Voorst.

Beck, L.N. 1974. Things magical in the collections of the rare book division. **Th Quarterly Journal of the Library of Congress,** 31, 208-234.

Bennett, F.D. 1840. **Narrative of a Whaling Voyage Round the Globe from the Year 1833 to 1836.** London: Richard Bentley.

Best, E. 1942. **Forest Lore of the Maori.** Wellington, New Zealond: The Polynesian Society.

Blaine, D.P. 1856. **An Encyclopedia of Rural Sports.** London: Longman, Brown, Green , Longmans, and Roberts.

Blundevill, T. 1580. **The Fouer Chiefyst Offices Belonging to Horsemanshippe.** London: Wyllyam Seres.

Borges, E.M. 1966. **The White Snake.** London: MacGibbon and Kee.

Brett, G.S. 1912-1921. A **History of Psychology** (3 vols.) London: Allen.

Browne, D.J. 1850. **The American Bird Fancier.** New York: C.M. Saxton.

Brusewitz, T. 1969. **Hunting.** New York: Stein and Day.

Butler, C. 1609. **The Feminine Monarchie: Or a Treatise Concerning Bees: And the Ordering of Them.** Oxford: Joseph Barnes.

Caius, J. 1945 (edition). **Of Englishe Dogges.** (Translated from the Latin by Abrahm Fleming). Washington, D.C.: Milo G. Denliger. Latin edition, London: 1570; English translation, London: Rydhard Johnes, 1596; reprinted, London: A. Bradley, 1880.

Cheever, H.T. 1850. **The Whale and His Captors.** New York: Harper and Brothers.

Christopher, M. 1973. **The Illustrated History of Magic.** New York: Crowell.

Cipolla, C.M. and Birdsall, D. 1980. **The Technology of Man.** New York: Holt, Rinehart and Winston.

Conrad, B. 1961. **Encyclopedia of Bullfighting.** Cambridge, Mass.: The Riverside Press.

Cornwall, I.W. 1968. **Prehistoric Animals and Their Hunters.** New York: Frederick A. Praeger.

Cox, I.E.B. 1874 . **Facts and Useful Hints Relating to Fishing and Shooting** (3rd edition). London: Horace Cox.

Davis, W. M. 1926 (edition) **Nimrod of the Sea.** Boston: Charles E. Lauriat Co. (1st edition, 1874)/

Eisenberg, Baron Reis d'. 1979 (edition) **The Classical Riding School.** New York: Vendome Press . **Description du Menege Moderne** (1st edition, 1747).

**Encyclopedia Britannica,** 1910-1911. (11th edition). Whale-fishery. 28, 570-573.

Erman, A. 1894. **Life in Ancient Egypt.** (Translated by H.M. Tirard). Bronx, New York: Benjamin Blom. (Reissued, 1969).

Executive Document No. 62, 1856-57. Report of the Secretary of War, etc. **The Executive Documens of the Senate of the United States 3rd Session,** 34th Congress, Vol. 8.

Fillis, J. 1899. **Principles de Dressage et D'equitation.** Paris.

Fillis, J. 1902. **breaking and Riding: With Military Commentaries.** (Translated by M. H. Hayes.) London: Hurst and Blackett.

438

Frederick II, Holy Roman Emperor. 1943 (edition). **De Arte Venandi Cum Avibus, The Art of Falconry.** (Translated by C.A. Wood and F. Marjorie Fyfe.) Stanford: Stanford University Press.

Fredericus II, Holy Roman Emperor. 1969 (edition). **De Arte Venandi Cum Avibus, Facsimile at Commentarium.** Graz, Austria: Akademische Druk-u. Verlaganstalt.

Fulton, J. 1971. **Bullfighting.** New York: Dial Press.

Gallwey, Sir R. P. 1882. **The Fowler in Ireland.** London: John Van Voorst.

Gallwey, Sir R.P. 1886. **The Book of Duck Decoys.** London: John Van Voorst.

Gibson, W.H. 1905. **Camp Life in the Woods and the Tricks of Trapping and Trap Making.** New York: Harper and Brothers.

Gleason, O.R. 1892. **Gleason's Horse Book and Veterinary Advisor.** Chicago: M.A. Donohue and Company.

Gleason, O.R. 1900. **Gleason's Veterinary Handbook and System of Horse Taming.** Chicago: Thompson and Thompson.

Goode, G. B. 1887. U.S. Commision of Fish and Fisheries. **The Fisheries and Fishery Industries of the United Stated.** Section V, History and methods of the fisheries. Volume II, Part XV, The Whale Fishery, pp. 3-293. Washington, D.C.: U.S. Government Printing Office.

Grohman, W.A. Baillie. 1919 (2nd edition). **Sport in At.** London: Simpkin, Marshall, Hamilton, Kent and Company.

Gulick, R.H. Van. 1951. **Erotic Colour Prints of the Ming Period, with an Essay on Chinese Sex Life from the Han to the Ch'ing Dynasty, B.C. 206 A.D. –1644** (3 vols.). Tokyo: Author.

Gulick, R.H. Van. 1961. **Sexual Life in Ancient Chinese.** Leiden: E. J. Brill.

Harrison, J.C. (Ed.). 1968. **Care and Training of the Trotter and Pacer.** Columbus, Ohio: The United States Trotting Association.

Hayes, M.H. 1894. **Among Men and Horses.** London: T. Fisher Unwin.

Hefferline, R.F., Keenan, B. 1961. Amplitude-induction gradient of a small human operant in an escape-avoidance situation. **Journal of the Experimental Analysis of Behavior**, 6, 307-316.

Hefferline, R. F. and Bruno, L.J. 1971. The psychophysiology of private events. In A. Jcabos and L.B. Sachs (Eds.) **The Psychology of Private Events**. New York: Academic Press.

Hill, T. 1568. **the Profitable Arte of Gardening**. London: Thomas Marsne.

Hinde, R. A. 1970. **Animal Behavior** (2nd edition). New York: McGraw-Hill.

Herrnstein, R.J. and Boring , E.G. 1965. **A Source Book in the History of Psychology**. Cambridge: Harvard University Press.

Hronzy, B. 1931. L'entrainment des chevaux chez les anciens Indo-Europeans, d'apre un texte Mittannien-Hittite provenant du 14e Siecle Av. J.-C. **Archiv Orientalni**, 3, 431-461.

Hull, D.B. 1964. **Hounds and Hunting in Ancient Greece**. Chicago: University of Chicago Press.

Jenkins, J.T. 1971 (edition). **A History of the Whale Fisheries**. Port Washington, New York: Kennikat Press (1st edition, 1921).

Jennings, R. ca. 1866. **Horse Training Made Easy**. Published by author.

Kammenhuber, Annelies. 1961. **Hippologia Hethitica**. Wiesbaden: Otto Harrassowitz.

Kantor, J.R. 1959. **Interbehavioral Psychology** (revised edition). Bloomington, Indiana: Principia.

Kantor, J.R. 1960. Perspectives in psychology: XV. History of science as scientific method. **Psychological Record**, 10, 187-189.

Kantor, J.R. 1963. **The Scientific Evolution of Psychology** (vol. 1). Chicago: Principia.

Kantor, J.R. 1964. History of psychology: What benefits? **Psychological Record**, 14, 433-443.

Kantor, J.R. 1969. **The Scientific Evolution of Psychology** (vol. 2). Chicago: Principia Press.

Kinsey, A.C., Pomeroy, W.B. and Martin, C.E. 1948. **Sexual Behavior in the Human Male.** Philadelphia: W.B. Saunders Company.

Kierman, F.A. (Ed.). 1974. **Chinese Ways in Warfare.** Cambridge: Harvard University Press.

Langstroth, L.L. 1862. **A Practical Treatise on the Hive and Honey-Bee** (3rd edition). New York: Saxton.

Leo Africanus, J. 1600. **A Geographical Historie of Africa.** (Translated by John Pory.) London: Impensis George Bishop. (Reissued , 1896, Hakluyt Society.)

Lewis, D. 1978. **the Voyaging Stars.** New York: W.W. Norton and Company.

Lindner, K. 1969. **The Hunting Book of Wolfgang Birkner.** (Translated by A. Havlu.) New York: Winchester Press.

McKnight, T. L. 1969. **The Camel in Australia.** Carlton, Victoria: Melbourne University Press.

Macnab, A. 1959. **Fighting Bulls.** New York: Harcourt, Brace and Company.

Magner, D. 1980 (edition). **The Classic Encyclopedia of the Horse.** New York: Crown Publishers, Inc. (First edition, 1887.)

Markham, G. 1607. **Cavelarice: Or the English Horseman.** London: E. White.

Markham, G. 1621. **Hungers Prevention: Or the Whole Arte of Fowling by Water and Land.** London .

Martin, P.S. and Wright, H. E. 1967. **Pleistocene Extinctions.** New Haven: Yale University Press.

Masters, W.H. and Johnson, V.E. 1970. **Human Sexual Inadequacy.** Boston: Little, Brown, and Company.

Miscellaneous Document No. 271, 1858. Letter from W. Re Kyan Bey to Edwin DeLeon, Esq. Dated November 17, 1857. **The Miscellaneous Documents of the Senate of the United States for the First Session of the Thirty-Five Congress,** Vol. 4.

Moisimann, J.E. and Martin, P.S. 1975. Simulating overkill by Paleoindians. **American Scientist**, 63, 304-313.

Mountjoy, P.T. 1972. Jean Henri Masers de Latude (1725-1805): An unappreciated practical psychologist. **Psychological Record**, 22, 145-149.

Mountjoy, P.T. 1974. Some early attempts to modify penile erection in horse and human: An historical analysis. **Psychological Record**, 24, 291-308.

Mountjoy, P.T. 1976. The **De Arte Venandi Cum Avibus** of Frederick II: A precursor of twentieth century behavioral psychology. **Stuides of Medieval Culture**, VI and VIII, 107-115.

Mountjoy, P.T. 1980. An historical approach to comparative psychology. In M.R. Denny (Ed.) **Comparative Psychology: An Evolutionary Analysis of Animal behavior**. New York: Wiley.

Mountjoy, P.T., Bos, J.H., Duncan, M.O. and Verplank, R.B. 1969. Falconry: Neglected aspect of the history of psychology. **Journal of the History of the Behavioral Sciences**, 5, 59-67.

Mountjoy, P.T. and Sundberg, M.L. 1981. Ben Franklin the proto-behaviorist I: Self-management of behavior. **Psychological Record**, 31, 13-24.

Nelson, R.K. 1969. **Hunters of the Northern Ice**. Chicago: University of Chicago Press.

Newcastle, Duke of (William Cavendish). 1970 (edition). (Facsimile Edition, New York: Winchester Press). **A General System of Horsemanship**. London: J. Brindley, 1743. (Translation of **La Methode Nouvelle et Invention Extraordinaire de dresser les Chevaux**, Antwerp, 1658.)

Oppianus. **Colluthus Tryphiodonis** (1928 edition). (Includes both **Cynegetica** and **Halietica**.) (Translated by A.W. Mair.) Cambridge: Harvard University Press.

Phoebus, G. 1978 (edition). **The Book of Hunting**. (Text by G. Bise; Translated by J.P. Tallon.) Fribourg-Geneve: Productions Liber SA.

Pinchbeck, W.F. 1805. **The Expositor: Or Many Mysteries Unravelled**. Boston: Author.

442

Pfungst, O. 1911. **Clever Hans.** (Translated by C.L. Rahn.) New York: Henry Holt and Company. (Reissued, 1965, New York: Holt, Reinhart and Winston.)

Potratz, H.A. 1938. **Das Pferd in Der Fruehzeit.** Rostock: Carl Hinstorffs Verlag.

Rarey, J.S. 1857. **The Modern Art of Taming Wild Horses.** Cincinnati: Henry Watkin.

Remnant, R. 1637. **A Discourse or Historie of Bees.** London: Thomas Slater.

Rose, F.G. 1939. From dogs to horses among the western Indian tribes. **Transactions of the Royal Society of Canada, 33,** Section 2, 209-271.

Salonen, A. 1955. **Hippologica Accadica.** Helsinki: Suomalainen Tiedeakatemia.

Sa: Rid. 1612. **The Art of Jugling or Legerdemine.** London.

Scoresby, W. 1823. **Journal of a Voyage to the Northern Whale-Fishery.** Edinburgh: Archibald Constable and Company.

Sasmor, R.M. 1966. Operant conditioning a small scale muscle response. **Journal of the Experimental Analysis of Behavior, 9,** 69-85.

Scot, R. 1584. **The Discoverie of Witchcraft.** London: William Brome. (Reissued, 1964, Carbondale, Illinois: Southern Illinois University Press.)

Singer, C., Holmyard, E.J., Hall, A.R. and Williams, T.I. (Eds.) 1954, 1956, 1957, 1958a, 1958b. **A History of Technology** (5 vols.). New York: Oxford.

Stewart, R. 1869. **The American Farmer's Horse Book.** Cincinnati: C.F. Vent and Company.

Strutt, J. 1876 (edition). **The Sports and Pastimes of the People of England.** (Edited by W. Hone.) London: Chatto and Windus. (1st edition, 1801.)

Southerne, D. 1593. **A Treatise Concerning the Right Use and Ordering of Bees.** London: Thomas Woodcocke.

443

Suleiman, H. 1970. **Miniatures of Babur-Nama.** Tashkent: Fan.

Thorndike, E.L. 1911. **Animal Intelligence.** New York: Macmillan.

Thorpe, W.H. 1956. **Learning and Instinct in Animals.** London: Methuen.

Turbervile, G. 1575a. **the Booke of Faulconrie or Hauking.** London: Christopher Barker.

Tubervile, G. 1575b. **The Noble Arte of Venerie or Hunting.** London.

Wilson, G.L. 1924. The horse and dog in Hidatsa culture. **Anthropological Papers of the American Museum of Natural History,** 15, (Part II), 127-311.

Woodruff, H. 1869. **The Trotting Horse of America.** New York: J.B. Ford and Company.

Xenophon. 1956 (edition). **About Horsemanship.** (Translated by D.B. Hull.) Published privately.

York, Edward of Norwich 2nd Duke of. 1909 (2nd edition). **The Master of Game.** (Translated and edited by W.A. Baillie-Grohman.) London: Ballentine, Hanson and Company.

Zeuner, F.E. 1963. **A History of Domesticated Animals.** New York: Harper and Row.

# INTERBEHAVIORAL IMPLICATIONS FOR BEHAVIOR THERAPY: CLINICAL PERSPECTIVES

Douglas H. Ruben

Up to this point, examinations of interbehavioral psychology in preceding chapters have been largely concerned with the solution to one major problem in Kantor's entire system--namely, does it possess heuristic validity? Heuristic validity is imperative only so that every discipline into which interbehaviorism has probed can profit from the interpretation. In contrast to the Skinnerian revolution, interbehavioral psychology has struggled around the barriers of philosophical and nonexperimental hypotheses. Propositions, postulates, protopostulates, and metapostulates, among many others, all inherently constitute a new scientific foundation but there is little demonstrable research in interbehavioral **methods** or **technology** to verify these tenets on human and infrahuman subjects (see Ray and Brown, 1975). However promising this scientific foundation appears, it finds itself an unwelcome guest against the orthodoxy of traditional operant or instrumental psychology, the psychology whose roots have actually been planted by Kantor himself.

In this final chapter responding to a reassessment in psychology we shift gears to a vastly different perspective, that of examining interbehavioral psychology as it may apply to clinical situations or be interpreted for **psychopathological analysis.** Psychopathology, in synonymous relation to terms such as pathology, psychopathy, sociopathy or even neurosis or psychosis, means a **behavioral disorder,** nothing more. We define disorderly behaviors by the impact they produce upon environing conditions in any set of circumstances in which there are organisms that interact with stimuli. Psychopathology is not always entirely traceable to disorderly behaviors or even to a field of situational events. Complex behaviors, or those behaviors most clinicians attend to in diagnosis, result from three major influences upon the organism. They are the typical (a) genetics, (b) socio-environmental agents or "institutions," and (c) behavioral history of conditioning or "reactional biography."

Through variations of these three influences, new disciplines in medicine, psychology, and sociology have emerged seeking rapprochemment with behavioral psychology in regard to its ideologies and methodologies. Evolving from this cabaret of integrations have been such creations as mathetics, behavioral pediatrics, behavioral neurology, behavioral geriatrics,behavioral engineering, behavioral sociology, industrial behaviorism, multi-modal behaviorism, eclectic behaviorism, behavioral ecology, cognitive behaviorism, and, adding the hybrids from philosophy, social behaviorism, analytical behaviorism, radical behaviorism, methodological behaviorism, epistemological behaviorism, and metabehaviorism. All of these neonate combinations seek professional recognition in their own unique styles. So, too, as these new "disciplines" literally "invade" the territory of behavioral sciences they seize upon whatever principle or dogmatism is practical for immediate application in their own domain. Pirating of this sort is perforce not new, nor is the plagiarism that results from the gradual convergence of two fields. Descartes swiped early Aristotelian notions about anatomy; Galton filched the notion of intelligence from his cousin Darwin's evolutionary theory; and Pinel's humanism during his campaign to convert mental asylums from warehouses to homes of rehabilitation was an almost perfect replica of Plato's prescription for human betterment in **The Republic.** In short, combinations between and within disciplines are one among many predictable consequences when genes, environment, and behavior are allowed to define the constituency of psychopathology.

Formation of these integrative disciplines was for another reason as well. In order to jump on the behavioral bandwagon, evidence from the experimental analysis of behavior had to be **valid.** Validity, in other words, played a key role. Evidence that did not receive support from valid experimentation was inadequate for pursuasion since nonpsychological disciplines only wanted a system of procedures for achieving their own goals. Hence, this explains the unsuccessful marriage Miller and Dollard attempted in 1950 between psychoanalysis and early Hullian Behaviorism (1941; 1948; 1951) and again, with similar fervor, by Watchel in the early 1970's (1973). Inadequate empirical validity becomes even a more serious drawback when a psychological theory resists or slowly approaches experimentation and coasts along on primarily hypothetical topics. Skinner's early introductions of operant theory, for instance, in his book **The Behavior of Organisms** (1938) , consisted largely of speculative hypotheses derived from the lab oratory but which were lacking extensive verification. By the late 1950's, with the advent of the **Journal of the Experimental Analysis of Behavior** (1958), and Skinner's two publications of **Science and Human Behavior** (1953) and **Verbal Behavior** (1957), experimental replications of human and infrahuman laboratory research had made a definite name not only for B.F. Skinner, but largely for the "revolutionary" operant position. Such a revolutionary profile for interbehaviorism is less visible primarily as the result of Kantor's early publications (e.g., 1924, 1926) and later "refinements" (e.g., 1982) being concerned with theoretical clarity. While much of Kantor's writings did describe intricate details of psychological processes (e.g., for perception, imagination, memory, etc.), organismic development (e.g., reactional biography), and stimulus effects (medium of contact), very little, if any of these details culminated in the erection of **experimental interbehavioral paradigms.**

It is the purpose here, then, in introducing new concepts relative to Kantor's interbehaviorism, to show there are methods derivable from his paradigm for clinical application. However, in constructing any methodology there are, initially, many interpretations of behavior that are understandable in theory but which make no sense at all for practical application. Alterations we explore in this chapter focus on the reactional biography in relation to the Skinnerian concept of "repertoire." These revisions then assist us in developing a methodological model for clinical diagnosis and treatment.

### Reactional Biography

Reactional biography is the total summation of experiences by an organism during its lifetime, evolving through germinal, embryonic, and fetal periods. Conceptually this construct is a replacement for "interactional" or "interbehavioral" history (Kantor, 1933)--two terms Kantor used, initially, to stress the reciprocal interchange stimulus events have with organismic behavior. During a single behavioral segment the setting factors with which behavior and stimuli interact are said to "possess" all the "controlling functions" rather than the controlling functions being inside the organism itself. This position abounds in later arguments concerning where the behavior is located. By contrast, behavior is traditionally assumed to lie in internal processes, encoded and decoded for storage. Language research with apes, for example, has had the misfortune to receive much scientific approval for this practice; mentalistic or "cognitive inventions" that explain "referential " and "emotional" factors make it more of a **dressage** than **apprentissage** form of science. Attributional personality theories akin to this practice also treat the "repertoire" as a construct existing inside the organism's skin, or something that collects and cumulates behaviors from birth until death.

However, because behavior is developmental, that is, it proceeds through gradual biological and psychological changes for adaptive reasons, some amount of **cumulation** does in fact occur. Kantor's incremental ladder from integration, modifiability, and variability to differentiation and so on (1924, pp. 162-3) illustrates this hierarchical schema, similar in many respects to Skinner's concept of learning history. The learning history (cf. Ferster and Skinner, 1957; Skinner, 1959) is also a production of historical interactions between stimuli and organisms and allows for the relocation of controlling variables from inside the organism to outside in the environment. From this conditioning history the organism develops a composite of response types or "classes," translated into the convenient term "repertoire." A repertoire by most definitions is a facsimile of some combinatory process of storage into which learned responses enter and multiply through interaction with the environment. Because the multiplicative effect is cumulatory, rather than accumulatory--that is, each new response builds upon a previously learned response--acquisitional training must take into consideration both the **prior** and **current** response class. Alphabet-letter discrimination tasks, for instance, employ a procedure known as "match-to-sampling" that involves trial and error responding to different alphabet stimuli. Before an accurate discrimination is performed, it would seem reasonable to first teach the child how to point his finger (i.e., for identifying alphabet cards). Accordingly, by teaching the motor coordination for fine digital movement the child then has prerequisites to perform letter discriminations.

Cumulatory responses are not to be confused with consummatory responses. Kantor's sequential structure from precurrent to consummatory action is but one way to distinguish the execution or consummation of some act from the anticipation or inception of it. Assuming, for the moment, that if anticipatory reactions belonged to a separate class of responses, then consummatory responses would be the **production** of responses in any given behavioral segment. Cumulatory responses, by comparison, are not an act of production but rather the **process** going on between learned responses and different spatio-temporal behavioral segments. Put differently, the cumulatory process is a developmental process, not in a psychosexual sense but in the way changes in response topography multiply when combined with the topography of new responses.

At the same time, to make cumulatory responses a "process" may be tantamount to making it a separate "inter-active" entity. Skinnerianism or radical behaviorism, we already said, has conventionally delegated this change in response topography to the environment. But where in the environment is it? Does it belong to some structural or stimulus dimension such that the organism's interaction with it yields new responses? Kantor, too, in exorcising homonculi spooks from the organism (i.e., expunging dualism) puts this active cumulatory process in the stimulus field. It is here where the organism can create new topographies. But, again, the question behaviorists and interbehaviorists must be brought to ask is upon us: Where in the environment does this active process, this cumulatory repertoire reside?

One solution Kantor offers is through an examination of memory (1926, pp. 92-94). Memorial behavior occurs in projective or recollective acts. Projective acts are intentional or unintentional

448

"retrievals" of pertinent information from the setting events that make it possible for past behavior to recur. More than their counterpart, they are dependent upon the personal disposition (i.e., wants, needs, desires, etc.) of the organism who in turn seeks from the stimulus setting those properties relevant for satisfaction. Recollective memorial acts rely less upon dispositional features and more upon stimulating conditions prevalent in a given behavioral segment as they relate spatio-temporally to preceding and succeeding segments. Memorial acts, like cumulatory responses, are not the act of production; as precurrents or, in Skinner's language, "antecedents," they set an occasion for past response topographies not demonstrated over a period of time to "re-assemble" and recur. This is why, for example, "forgetting" happens when a stimulus is no longer present during a response. "Remembering," the solutional step, is thus achievable when a stimulus object (adjustment, substitute, etc.) that for some reason was unavailable returns to the sensory field.

Memory or memorial behavior may explain an organism's ability to reproduce past behaviors a la some setting events, but only if we presume the repertoire lies outside in the stimulus field. Here, again, our frustration swells on how to account for the locus of a repertoire.

There is little risk to interbehavioral integrity in describing repertoire functions as cumulatory. Whether we use Kantor's terms, "reactional biography," or Skinner's terms, "learning history," the same repertoire action boils down to one thing: Does the cumulatory effect and hence the repertoire itself occur inside or outside the organism? The answer, we propose, is **both**. It takes an organism's morphological maturation (from neural, skeletal, muscular and glandular to internal kinesthesia) in a sequential progression in order for other changes to occur. Morphology represents half the total constituency of a repertoire, because in producing behavior the organism's amenability or response tendency is subject to fluctuations with structural formity or malformity.

A second feature in defining repertoires lies in the environment. Disciples of Kohler's Gestalt Psychology concerned with perceptual manipulations or those occurring in a psychological field (e.g., Tolman, Lewin, Brunswick, Barker, Lashley, etc.) made some useful distinctions in how the organism moves through space dimensions. Hodology and topology, for instance, were two nonmetric scales of geometry upon which theorists could base a conceptual representation of psychological interactions. Hodological space had its vectors or "connections" that gave some perspective on directionality in one's life dimensions and interpersonal relationships. Later replaced by two-dimensional linear graphs (see Cartwright, 1959), this tool permitted at least some estimation of symmetrical and asymmetrical human movement or "locomotion" in synchronicity with physical barriers through the space of one's entire experiences. Diagrams used in formulating these predictions were to later give impetus to laboratory investigations of trial and error learning with rodents (e.g., Tolman and Hoznik, 1930). But for now, hodological and topological assumptions are important because they help organize the matrix of stimulus events into scientifically meaningful data.

Stimuli generated from two different sources are the ones discussed here. One sort of stimulus event evolves through conditioned or discriminative learning, as it becomes identified with circumstances either appropriate or inappropriate for producing behavior. Discriminatively trained stimulus events are ones that most Skinnerian psychologists or "behavior modifiers" work with in skill acquisition tasks (e.g., match-to-sampling, etc.). Secondly, stimulus events may evolve from the production of responses in an existing behavioral segment that affect response topography in successive segments. Here is how the response and stimulus event would interact. Take a single behavioral segment involving a response, some medium of contact, and a stimulus object, the total of which we now call $B_{s1}$. Where there to be three rapidly occurring segments in consecutive succession (e.g., $B_{s1}$, $B_{s2}$, and $B_{s3}$), the responses produced in each segment may or may not have similar topographies, but they will still all "interrelate" as long as the response repertoire is cumulatory. In other words, vocal pronunciations made in $B_{s1}$, gestural commands in $B_{s2}$, and swimming in $B_{s3}$, while composed of different musculature, are all integrative by being a member of the same cumulatory response repertoire. Stimulus changes in $B_{s1}$ produced by vocal pronunciations are in turn the stimuli affecting gestural commands in $B_{s2}$, and so on into $B_{s3}$. Moreover, Kantor's requirement that before an individual can perform an act he must first attend to it would make another feature of the transition from $B_{s1}$ to $B_{s3}$ become important. This feature deals with "contingencies." Just as the organism in the precurrency or attending stage identifies stimulus features such as movement, intensity, repetition, size, novelty, color, and cessation of energy, so it would also identify external "contingency relations."

**Contingency relations** is a derivative from the Skinnerian concept of operant contingencies. A contingency is any demonstrated relationship in which behavior is under the control of setting events. Contingencies also assume a reciprocal interaction with surrounding and biological stimuli in that behaviors can produce a consequence as negative or positive, while those consequences will reciprocally determine the future strength or weakness of behaviors. Operant psychology puts contingencies on a pedestal tantamount to Kantor's conception of setting factors, since for every behavioral segment,

450

single or multiple contingencies comprise an organism's hodology. Responses we observe in $B_{S1}$, $B_{S2}$, and $B_{S3}$ all must revolve around not only stimulus objects, but also the contingencies by which they are inclined to occur. Vocal pronunciation made through a loud speaker (object) are thus contingent on additional features related to many media such as, say, an audience hearing the transmission (sound waves or phonoreception) of the pronunciation, or another audience watching the visual display (light waves or photoreception) of the topography.

We now have two features about setting events from which a repertoire develops. One is the **change** in stimulus events produced by behavior. Stimulus changes made in one's behavioral segment prepare conditions for behavior in successive segments so that, at all times, there is continuity along every behavioral segment during an organism's lifetime. To explain fluctuation in the repertoire **we** had to include contingencies in Kantor's system. And second, behaviors observed in one behavioral segment are logically interrelatable to behaviors in successive segments because a repertoire is cumulatory.

By way of summary we can conclude that a location for the behavior repertoire is neither entirely inside nor outside the organism itself. There is no storage tank filled with individual response topographies, all very distinctive and noncombinatory. Rather, physiology--the malleable quality of somatic responses--depends on skeletal and muscular growth as much as it does upon contingency relations within the behavioral segment in order for changes in physical topography to multiply as the organism passes through different cumulative stages of adaptation. At any given time the behavior we observe consists of **one** topography, a topography instrumentally and morphologically erected so that every new response assimilates in succession.

## Clinical Application

Clinical diagnosis is still greatly embedded in subjectivism. Judgments about human nature tend to rely on inferences or assumptions drawn from observed contingencies dealing with one person (idiographic) or with many people (nomothetic) (cf. Ruben and Ruben, 1982). Behavioral clinical psychology tries to resist subjectivism by emphasizing aspects or "variables" relevant to a person's reactional biography that are observable or "confrontable" or have potential for observability (e.g., Erwin, 1978; Yates, 1975). For instance, subvocal statements or "thoughts" only become clinically relevant when amplified in magnitude to observable levels. And even then, once behavior occurs through a medium perceivable by an observer it may still lack stimulus or topographical features that are necessary for accurate clinical judgments (Ruben, 1982a).

451

Kantor has provided some direction for clinical judgments with his classifications of behavior. Four major classification by which all response patterns are described include suprabasic behaviors, contingential behaviors, idiosyncratic behaviors and cultural behaviors (1924, pp. 188-213). Suprabasic behaviors are those actions typically responsible for the expansion of simpler responses, such as when infants learn to walk and then run. Contingential behaviors are ones that are occasional or incidental as governed by specific stimulus events. We only wear tuxedos, for instance, to attend formal engagements rather than to the beach. Idiosyncratic behavior includes the "Socratic introspectionism" we use to evaluate our own behavior, independent of stimulus demands. Contemplation, retrospection, and anticipation fit into this category. Cultural behavior is a learned reaction to "fixed" or discriminative situations for which only one behavior is appropriate. This differs from contingential behavior by its more frequent occurrence.

Unfortunately, in a very short time the clinician using Kantor's taxonomy confronts a problem. Much overlap exists among the categories in terms of both verbal and nonverbal behavior insofar as topography and even setting events are concerned. Distinct acts consisting of morphology, the cumulatory repertoire, and setting factors are all collapsed in accord with the laws of behavior into "behavioral" types that attempt to qualify within a nonmetric system the distribution of external changes upon an organism. But the classification system **qua** system is incomplete.

Toward a solution, Kantor offers a further division of 10 categories. This list includes reactions that are compensatory, productive, manipulative, approbative, recessive, accommodative, acquisitive, expressive, exhibitive, and defensive (1924, p. 173). While, by current standards, this typological list reminds the naive clinician of a family of psychiatric nosology described in the **Diagnostic and Statistical Manual of Mental Disorders** (DSM-III, 1980), this is not to assert that "behavioral" descriptors are entirely worthless. In many ways they represent a precursory effort toward a new kind of **clinical reductionism.**

### Clinical Reductionism

The reductionistic notion persists despite the fact that the era of conditioning and learning has demonstrated that experimental and quantitative descriptions and laws are readily available when concrete interbehaviors are studied without any attempt to reduce them to something else (Kantor, 1966, p. 382).

This familiar advice is against an overzealous approach to reductionism in analyzing salient or confrontable behaviors that are already quantifiable. Behavioral diagnostic practices, on the other hand, consider this overzealous reductionism a norm in understanding external dynamics of causality. Typically an assessment of behaviors during an intake interview or initial session involves a twofold decision. One decision is to determine, by observation alone, whether physical symptomatology in general appearance indicates the presence or absence of some disease or illness requiring a medical emergency alert. Physical symptoms of heroin addicts in withdrawal, for example, serve as stimulus cues to which counselors have reacted in the past by calling for immediate ambulance transportation. While there are clearly confrontable stimuli, withdrawal symptoms may also stimulate formulations of a diagnosis unrelated to its confrontability and which instead rely upon intangible or capricious processes. A case in point was when a recognized clinician from the local university, in examining the author's reaction to a potentially hostile client interaction, commented that there must have been some "unconscious statement" underlying the client's actions, that hostility alone was not explanatory for repressive or otherwise pathologic reactions in the client's childhood." Of course, in hearing this explanation the author had a few explanatory words of his own.

Jungian, Freudian, humanistic, or any theoretical paradigm to which clinicians subscribe is actually harmless unless, as in the above case, it distorts the heuristic value of confrontable events. A psychological diagnosis which ruins the **purity** of scientific events is one that attributes fictitious myths to causal explanations of behavior and therefore preserves the status of reification in clinical subjectivity. That is, as clinicians diagnose patterns of behavior they are determining a point at which **physical symptoms** , such as heroin withdrawal, diverge from **psychological symptoms,** such as the "underlying unconscious statements." Because of this twofold explanatory process, clinical reductionism is always subject to abuse.

Behavioral and interbehavioral reformulations of this twofold process would put "physical" and "psychological" explanations together under a single umbrella and dismiss implications of dualism. Inasmuch as this combination would seem to solve diagnostic dualism, what in fact results is a collapse in the logical construction of reasons for behavior occurrence. Suppose that we put an elderly institutionalized patient who is "shy" under surveillance to determine deficits in her interpersonal social skills during different interactions. Observed passivity, motoric inhibition to enter the social hall, or even escape responses such as urinating in her outfit would all confirm, to a large extent, the incidence of social skill deficits. But a behavioral deficit is not a deficit by how imperfectly or unsuccessfully behaviors achieve a desirable consequence. In solving a problem, for example, Skinner disagrees with this assertion ; he instead contends that

> A person has a problem when some condition will be reinforcing but he lacks a response that will produce it. He will solve the problem when he emits such a response....Solving a problem is, however, more than emitting the response which is the solution; it is a matter of taking steps to make that response more probable, usually by changing the environment (1974, p. 123).

Problem solving demonstrates a glaring example of the behavior therapist's misinterpretation of a deficit. Just how necessary is it to **emit** a response for completely eliminating some problem? **Emission** is a process that describes an executory function and stimulus function working in some degree of causal harmony with each other to produce a response topography. A response topography, on the other hand, is not definable by a **process** but by that which the process leaves imprinted upon the organism in successive behavioral segments. Usually this imprint is either momentary or protracted. Momentary is when topographical deficits that interact with setting events have ephemeral or short-term locomotion and impact within a stimulus field, and reduced potential for producing successive responses. Protracted means the topographical deficiency has lasting or immutable dimensions that come more rapidly to observable attention within the stimulus field. Deficits, therefore, refer to a **set** or **class** of responses features all of which lack some critical feature leading to either momentary or protracted production of **one** topography. This definition does differ from saying, as Skinner does, that improvements in behavioral deficits lead to desirable consequences. Attainment of desirable consequences, by our reformulation, is a secondary and more remote goal. Again consider Skinner's strategy for the elimination of problems:

> There are many ways of changing a situation so that we are more likely to respond to it effectively. We can clarify stimuli,change them, convert them into different modalities, isolate them, rearrange them to facilitate comparison, group and regroup them, "organize" them, or add other stimuli (1968, p. 132).

When Skinner speaks of "changing a situation," the manipulation he describes is actually between stimulus objects and response topographies , nothing more. For example, suppose the elderly woman who had a language impediment and poor interpersonal skills also had weak visual coordination, no finger-pointing skills, and no ambulatory potential without physical assistance. Does this mean her only deficit was still "improper social skills?" Or, was it that **combinations** of deficient responses in mutual interrelationship prevented the production of one topography in one behavioral segment from enabling attainment of desirable consequences?

There is a shift in paradigm implied here. A shift from a repertoire consisting of responses learned as a function of only consequences to responses learned as a function of the cumulatory process. Since any learned behavior is interbehavioral, it must proceed through two stages of development beginning with a morphological change and ending with however the setting events shape it to occur. Even the most simple responses--that of raising one's index finger--is at first a physiological act, constriction of muscles, which involves smaller or molecular response interactions of ligaments, tendons, nerves, arteries, and muscles all occurring beneath the skin. That this interaction is private does not disqualify its existence nor potential to enable, or, as the case may be, disenable changes in digital coordination that allow extension toward an upright finger position. Once an upright finger position is achieved and changes thereby become visually observable, the behavior of "pointing" can itself be said to produce external ("social") consequences.

Insistence that a diagnosed deficit or, for that matter, excess is really a function of the response itself has the surface appearance of sounding ignorant of subtler consequential effects. Skinner's analysis of superstitious behavior (1948, 1957; also see Staddon and Simnelhag, 1971), for instance, clearly documents an illustration of how anecdotal or irrelevant adaptations in response topography can come under the control of discrete properties of the organism itself. That is, the organism can provide its own antecedents and consequences in much the same way as humans self-talk or find "games" self-reinforcable (Ruben, 1979). Subtle, almost indistinguishable manipulations resulting in self-reinforcement are said to occur when, for example, untying one's shoelaces is reinforced by easy removal of the foot from the shoe. So, too, we would assume that those responses actively involved in the "untying response" (e.g., finger dexterity, vestibular coordination, etc.) might also receive reinforcement by the foot's removal. To speak of reinforcement in this way, however, means there is a chain of multiple response topographies linked in some relatively complex sequence that becomes stronger in occurrence. Linkage of responses in, say, an Ebbinghaus sense of connectionism, would take unusual exception to interbehavioral as well as to behavioral principles because there is no **lawful** way to explain operant "pairing" between respones. Finger dexterity and vestibular coordination, in other words, do not pair in order to acquire mutual strength. Operant theory suggests that the presentation of some reinforcable event is responsible for increasing this pairing strength, while an interbehavioral explanation is that both responses bilaterally develop with whatever stimuli confront them. According to our cumulatory notion, it is more the case that one response produces the successive occurrence of another response through nothing more than topographical interactions with setting events. As one raises his index finger, the flexion extension can only persist when mechanoreceptors remain uninhibited by environmental barriers. If pressure stimulation, on the other hand, is felt when raising the index finger it inhibits digital abduction below .5 millimeters. Resistance against moving the finger, in other words, prevents digital extension. Removal of this resistance from mechanoreceptors allows further digital abduction to occur until the index finger reaches a desirable vertical position. After reaching this position, it becomes possible for the index finger to function as a nonverbal (gestural) or verbal request (mand) for reinforcable events, the attainment of which would strengthen future occurrences of "finger-raising" topography.

## Clinical Application

On a theoretical basis, redefining the concept of "repertoire" so that it clearly distinguishes response interrelationships from interactions with setting events helps to avoid the Skinnerian trap of having only consequences exert control over behavior. When we apply this reductionistic analysis to psychopathology, it greatly expedites our understanding of large response topographies faced in clinical practice. Topography, by itself, is often mistaken for being the sole explanatory cause of pathology, that nothing around it had more influence than the behavior or behaver himself. His "existential" or "phenomenological" disposition becomes a thing around which symptoms manifested as behavior revolve and lead to treatment intervention. But false predictions of this sort do more than simply distort pure empirical facts regarding what is under control. The lucunae in these diagnoses lay in distortions of response relationships. While nobody denies the role consequences play in development of behavior repertoires, consequential influences are only secondary in determining behavior outcomes. Primary influences, we said, happen on a morphologic level and involve inter-topographical relationships prior to the production of responses controlled by "consequences." A good example is with amaurosis. Amaurotic reaction is when there is a decay in vision occurring without perceptible external changes. Alterations in physical topography occur on a morphologic or biological level and are precipitory to the actual vision loss during interrelations with physical stimulus objects. In other words, retinal deterioration that occurs beneath the skin is a physical topographical interaction not producing environmental consequences until it interferes with visuality--until our visual perceptions are obscured.

Let us consider the following case study of obesity with respect to this interbehavioral approach. A single woman around 25 years old with severe thyroid problems came to a behavior therapy clinic seeking an effective and harmless weight loss program. During her initial intake we learned of her past heterosexual failures, her discontinuation of school after her mother died, and many drug-related "cures" for obesity taken over the past 5 years. Initially the assessment revolved around places, persons, events, behaviors, and either punishment or reinforcement in those situations. When the session ended, she wanted a prognostic statement predicting her ability to lose weight through the clinic's help.

Most behavior therapists at this point, presuming they agree to risk a prognosis, would identify the source of weight accumulation in interpersonal deficits, poor knowledge of caloric or nutritional diets, poor food consumption control, or possibly even because the thyroid imbalance was a medical contraindication to behavioral solutions. All four diagnoses relate to some identified deficit, not from direct observation in her natural environment, but rather from observing **potential causes** of actual behavior. Diagnosticians can only exercise speculation at this point until they perform more assessments which invoke real-to-life situations (cf. Ruben, 1982b).

Behaviors which we can describe in terms of repertoire effects of by topography, however, only include interpersonal deficits and poor food consumption control. To interpret "poor knowledge" of nutritional and caloric diets would engender an epistemological assumption that distinctions in expressive and receptive language are relative to some internal mechanism's capability--an assumption heavily couched in mentalism. A physical thyroid dysfunction, on the other hand, is improperly diagnosable using our own technology and should instead be determined by a medical consultant. This leaves the first two behaviors for investigation. In order to perform any further scientific analysis free of subjective distortion, some system of clinical reductionism must be constructed that organizes response interrelationships in a logical format and reveals weak and inappropriate topographies. Because a response topography is cumulatory and definable by its preceding and current behavioral segments, our analysis must also supply a way to "predict" potential interactions, or factors likely to influence this interaction. This second feature in our evaluation is called **interbehavioral potential.** An interbehavioral potential, said differently, is a nonmetric predictive measure of probability regarding the chance that some behavior will bring about changes in the environment. Because it is only a probabilistic "guess," more data has to be accrued before it genuinely contributes evidence to a diagnosis. Interbehavioral potentials are usually confrontable responses or events (also historical) but may also bear relation to "covert" or "hidden" activities such as in the case of deprivation.

A clinical tool that records interbehavioral events must further contain categories arranged in a lawful schematic order for every topographical or environmental change occuring in mutual contact. From this evaluatory system we can draw simpler and more accurate conclusions about skill deficits. We do so by adding to the list of diagnostic categories the following information: (A) Media of contacts; (B) the behavioral segment in question; (C) those stimulus objects with which behavior interacts; (D) responses (only one execution of action is analyzable in any single behavioral segment)-(1) responses are reducible to (a) magnitude (how big, small, loud, quiet, etc.), (b) duration (how long), (c) latency (elapse of time between first stimulus contact and response), (d) rate (how fast), and (e) frequency (how many); and (E) time constraints, which consist of (1) contingencies and (2) parameters of stimulus function (frequency, magnitude/intensity, operation, duration, and rate/latency).

Let us now apply these descriptions in the diagnosis of obesity. Specifically, we wish further clarification on where the deficits lie for poor food consumption control, as shown in Table 1 on the next page.

This diagnostic chart lists a series of interactive elements during one behavioral segment $(B_{S1})$. This diagnostic chart is capable by itself of a diagnosis regarding behavior deficits or pathology, although there are no categories into which "cognitions" or "emotions" are placed, since they constitute variables at an inferential level of analysis and are frequently inaccessible and meaningless for **initial** clinical judgments. With the exception of interbehavior potentials, all the categories directly reflect expressive descriptors by the client of inappropriate or "maladjusted" areas relevant to weight gain. Like any diagnostic instrument, however, the Interbehavioral Chart for Clinical Diagnosis is subject to potential flaws in its structural design in that it may not provide interpretable information for the construction of remedial or "treatment" plans. Treatment plans that clinicians establish from many assessment forms (e.g., Cautela, 1977,1981a, 1981b) will often times be based on other supplementary materials in order to develop ideas for homework assignments, ethical issues, or procedural techniques. Resorting to his compendia of psychological information assures the therapist that, from his assessment data, "brilliant" interventions can be discovered which perfectly satisfy all the client's needs. But when treatment decisions shift from scientific deductions to a ritual of consulting "cook-book" recipe procedures, all of which provide temporary solutions, then treatment efficacy is obviously going to suffer. This is what cynical critics and infrequent users of behavior modification programs have

# INTERBEHAVIORAL CHART FOR CLINICAL DIAGNOSIS

**General Behavior:** Food consumption
**Behavior Segment:** $B_{s1}$ (Behavior Segment-1 in Kitchen)
**Stimulus Objects:** Refrigerator handle
**Media of Contact:** Light waves (visual stimuli); air waves (tactile stimuli)

**Response:**
Magnitude-Below 10 decibels (acoustic range from 1 to 130)
Duration- 3 seconds
Latency- 4 seconds (from "seeing" to "touching" refrigerator)
Rate- 1 squeeze per 3 seconds
Frequency-1 time

**Time Constraints:**
Contingencies: Opening refrigerator door--> (yields) light on and food presented.

Parameters of Stimulus Function:

Frequency- Opens 1 time
Magnitude/
Intensity- Low-pitch squeak when opens
Operation- Squeeze down on handle, pull forward
Duration- Door remains open indefinitely until person shuts it
Rate/
Latency- Door opens within 3 seconds per response

**Interbehavioral Potentials:** Deprivation (hunger, thirst); clock shows time when usually eat

Table 1

referred to as the "band-aid" effect; the effect of unresolved maladaptive behavior disorders after a superficial modification technique was implemented and failied. Of course, what both critics and "cook-book" users fail to recognize through ignorance of science and human behavior is that, it is not that **behavior modification** fails, but that **behavior modifiers** fail to use it correctly.

Creation of this interbehavioral chart is a viable step toward attenauting these type of artifact errors in clinical designs and subsequent treatment planning. Omitted from the schematic list, we said, are also references to "cognitions" or affective processes. Although, currently, the zeitgeist in behavior therapy is for a marriage between learning theory and mentalism to advance toward the forefront of psychology (e.g., Beck, 1970; Bergin, 1970; Foreyt and Rathjen, 1978; Goldfried, 1982; Mischel, 1973; Mahoney, 1977; Meichenbaum, 1979), the resistance against this crusade continues strong because of operant psychology's rejection of dualism and potential to provide solutions to more pragmatic problems (Locke, 1971. 1979; Nawas, 1970; Skinner, 1977; Ulmann, 1970). Pragmatism has been an historical advantage of behavioral applications unshared by competitive psychologies (see Baken, 1966), much as interbehaviorism's continual emphasis upon confrontable events. The opposite is true for cognitivism. Cognitivism is an example of how events become abused because there is no traceable explanation for confrontable phenomena. When, for example, clinicians hypothesize that the locus of behavioral control resides in hopelessness, helplessness, powerlessness, resigned and inhibitory affectations, as in the cognitive reformulation of learned helplessness syndrome (e.g., Abramson, Seligman and Teasdale, 1978), all they really mean is that response or stimulus functions are inescapable, unavoidable, indiscriminable, or unpredictable and that resulting response topographies are fragmented. Confrontable events, in other words,undergo a transmutation at a level where pure scientific facts are distorted and acquire descriptory power over causal explanations. Here we agree when Skinner says,

> The simplest and most satisfactory view is that thought is simply **behavior**--verbal or nonverbal, covert or overt. It is not some mysterious process responsible for behavior but the very behavior itself in all the complexity of its controlling relations, with respect to both man the behaver and the environment in which he lives (1957, p. 449).

We therefore conclude there is little value in entering cognitive or affective descriptors in the interbehavioral chart.

Pressing onward, clinical diagnosis is only a facilitator if it accomplishes another goal. This goal, in essence, is to provide a clear indication about the treatment direction using as few subjective interpretations as possible. In the interbehavioral chart shown in Table 1, for instance, each category that we completed earlier is revised with changes in "refrigerator-opening" behavior that we determine, clinically, to be appropriate for a weight loss program (see Table 2 on next page).

Since a behavioral segment $(B_{S1})$ contains only one stimulus-response interaction, changes in setting factors will result in revisions of the media of contact, response, time constraints, and interbehavioral potentials. We add the medium of **sound waves** because in the Parameters of Stimulus Function there is a new mechanical change described that sounds an alarm as the refrigerator is touched. By the contingency, "touch refrigerator--> alarm on/door remains shut," it means the same magnitude, latency, and frequency of responding occurs prior to the alarm being triggered, but that duration and rate vary in relation to the unsuccessful attempts to open the door. Holding the refrigerator handle now lasts 20 seconds at a constant rate of 2 muscular "squeezes" (on the handle) per 3 seconds, thus amounting in total to approximately 6, as opposed to 1, attempts to open the regrigerator door. Also, by the new stimulus operation we know that it takes a thermal skin response (i.e., heat generated from the hands and fingers when clasping the refrigerator door) in order to evoke both the alarm and closed door, i.e., the door handle functions as a thermocupler registering electrical currents transduced from the heat. Further parameters of the stimulus function include: (a) The alarm and closed door last for 30 seconds; (b) there is a loud intensity by a siren tone that repeats itself every 3 seconds for a total of 10 revolutions; and (c) there is no centrifugal resistance from the tight door.

Quantitatively, these revisions in the Interbehavioral Chart for Clinical Treatment represent a methodological procedure operant psychologists would refer to as **positive punishment**. Positive punishment has a "deceleration" effect upon behavior, much as "positive reinforcement" produces an "accelerational" effect. In other words, between the aversive sound of the siren alarm and intense expenditure of effort in trying to open the door, the behavior topography of going into the refrigerator for "food consumption" reduces in future occurrence. As reduction begins, behaviors consisting of new topographies may emerge in order to escape or avoid the aversive consequences. We call this newly formed topography an **incompatible** behavior, since it is a behavior that increases concurrent with the deceleration of inappropriate or "opening-the-refrigerator" response. Clinically, we say that the person

# INTERBEHAVIORAL CHART FOR CLINICAL TREATMENT

**General Behavior:**    Food consumption
**Behavior Segment:**    $B_{s1}$ (Behavior Segment-in Kitchen)
**Stimulus Objects:**    Refrigerator handle, noise alarm
**Media of Contact:**    Light waves, air waves, sound waves

**Response:**

Magnitude-Below 10 decibels
Duration- 20 seconds
Latency- 4 seconds (from seeing to touching refrigerator)
Rate- 2 squeezes per second
Frequency-1 time

**Time Constraints:**    Contingencies: Touch refrigerator-->alarm on/door remains shut.

Parameters of Stimulus Function:

| | |
|---|---|
| Frequency- | Rings 1 time |
| Magnitude/ | |
| Intensity- | loud noise, door tight |
| Operation- | Thermal skin response (heat converted into electricity) triggers alarm/ tight door |
| Duration- | 30 seconds |
| Rate/ | |
| Latency- | Siren alarm repeats every 3 seconds |

**Interbehavioral Potentials:**    Deprivation removed; interference from new setting events

Table 2

who used to desire food at improper time intervals during the day has now **learned** an alternative response topography to opening the refrigerator door. That new topography is a product of "punishing" or reducing inappropriate behavior.

This relatively harmless conclusion is, as we said, typically what clinical behavior therapists would assert. Implicit in this assertion, however, is that the heretofore "opening-the-refrigerator" response is now gone. But, alas, where did it go? Development of incompatible responses implies a process involving a bilateral or mutual exchange whereby one response--presumably the inappropriate one in question--is **replaced** by a topographically different structure which occurs in the identical or approximate spatio-temporal interval. This substitutional process further implies the existence of a repository of response classes located somewhere inside or outside the organism, in which the "new" topography now resides. Our argument regarding a cumulatory repertoire, however, firmly challenges this operant assertion and instead would describe the incompatibly developed (or appropriate) response as an outgrowth of new structural adjustments in topography, wherein the "opening-the-refrigerator" response **interacted** with new setting events (shown in Table 2) , this produced changes in the reponse topography, and eventually what resulted was a combination of the "old" topography and those biological and psychological changes incurred during the behavioral segment. In other words, we explain the surprising retention of those behaviors observed in the "opening-the-refrigerator" response (e.g., visual-motor coordination, tactile discriminations, etc.) and also observed in the "new" topography by the fact that all topography is a function of continuous convergence, not substitution.

At this point, loyal behavior modifiers versatile with many operant techniques may object to the originality of clinical reductionism as it is discussed here, or to displaying it on a chart. Were they to accuse clinical reductionism and interbehavioral charting of emulating existing operant logistics and claim that nothing new is gained by further investigations of response topography, might the rebuttal be simply that operant procedures omit recognition of the entire stimulus field in reciprocal interaction? Not really. This only glosses the real bedrock of problems. Solutions that behavior therapists have for dealing with all aspects of the environment lay in the invention of "comprehensive treatment packages." Comprehensive treatment packages are programs which provide several techniques in tandem for bringing about multiple changes in the person. Toilet-training programs, for example, tend to go beyond **prima facie** goals around excretory control and will provide additional goals on assertiveness control for parents or children who are reclusive from social interactions for fear of enuretic or encopretic accidents.

From this expansive system for treatment coverage has come one serious error that reduces clinical efficacy. This error lies in assuming that **causal connections** exist between (a) variables in the environment indirectly responsible for the behavior and (b) those variables of which the behavior is definitely a function. Causation presents a problem for the same reason that the clay statue of Zeus is not identical to the clay statue of Apollo, even though both statues are made of clay and represent mythical gods. That is, in any constellation of setting events there are stimuli that bear physical resemblance, functions that bear operational resemblance, and interbehaviors in between these things and the organism that resemble similar interbehaviors. Similarities, however, are inconclusive variables for a causal analysis if further attempts to confirm or disconfirm their **controllability** never occur. As the statue of Zeus is distinct from that of Apollo, so the relationship of stimuli and responses presumed to be causal is distinct from authentic causal relationships. Interbehaviorism, by contrast, makes no assumption about causality. Kantor warns us in regards to his causal postulate that

> Both the causalists and acausalists indulge in metaphysical
> thinking. Moreover, they hardly ascend above the level
> of traditional common sense. They do not therefore
> keep within the range of physical research as a con-
> crete enterprise (1959, p. 213).

The expense of "causal analyses" and its siblings "prediction and determinism" upon scientific psychology is that it diminuates veridical explanations of phenomena. This is not to say causality and predictability are worthless concepts in scientific investigation. Quite the contrary, they represent the foundation of all science. Interbehaviorism, however, treats the concepts of causality and predictability by emphasizing relations between properties of an event system. In this system all variables that are **mutually corresponsive** rather than emissive (Kantor, 1970, p. 106) act in a potentially predictive motion so that the propagation of change results from complex interactions, not from isolated causal relations.

The interbehavioral charts attend to this pitfall in their composit-ion. Stimuli, responses, and those variables through which inter-behaviors pass are identifiable by their **topographical** features, rather than by their relational or causal features. While in any clinical diagnosis some degree of causal latitude is necessary for treatment planning purposes, interbehavioral assessments limit the intrusion of causality to only interbehavioral potentials and, in doing so, lift any restrictions on the propriety of other stimulus-response combinations. Different, then, is the way the chart identifies large or molar assemblage of responses, segregates their functional and topographical features using a metric and nonmetric classificatory scheme, and, finally, can introduce corrections in behavior by a single adjustment of quantifiable properties.

Intentional or not, Interbehavioral Charts for Clinical Diagnosis and Treatment offer still a further advantage. Efficiency is difficult for clinicians to acheive during these days of economic stagnation. Efficiency in a procedure means that two goals are achievable prior to intervention. First, whatever behavior a client brings forth as troublesome must undergo a scientific "dissection" so that the topography is clear. Secondly, reductionism of any sort must take into account a client's entire social system (cf. Wahler and Fox, 1981). For busy, underpaid or poorly managed clinicians faced with these two "goals," interbehavioral charting is a nice safeguard against the risk of making quick decisions about causality. With the chart, moreover, even pressures to run through a diagnosis quickly will not sacrifice specificity as long as all the categories are completed. And, considering that in most clinical facilities the administration places a high premium on finishing "paper work," diagnosticians would be encouraged to comply with standards and hence finish the entire chart.

## Summary

This chapter dips a bit farther into the boiling cauldron of non-traditional psychological topics, that of human psychopathology. We entertain the notion that a repertoire is a **cumlatory** process, not just a functional one. It is a process which consists of one response topography assimilating in part with newly acquired topographies as they both develop in coordination with morphological maturity and concrete changes in setting events. To say a repertoire "resides" in the organism or stands aloof somewhere in oblivion as a reified storage tank for "a history of conditioning" puts it on an invisible pedestal unreachable by behavioral scientists. Cumulatory repertoires are repertoires the organism strengthens or weakens through a procession of interbehaviors, interbehaviors that possess as much importance in their own topographical composition as they do in the composition of their relationships with objects, events, and other setting factors. Once grounds for understanding topography are satisfied, relationships with other factors in the behavioral segment can be analyzed.

Toward this end, a clinical diagnostic and treatment chart was introduced. It showed how to catalog all important interbehavioral phenomena by virtue of its reductionistic ("or more organized") orientation. Were the job of diagnostician that of labelling maladaptive behavior, volumes of nosological syndromes would already be available for practical use. But in behavior therapy a psychometric role is a self-denial of empirical competency. While for many behaviorists intelligence tests are still acceptable in assessment (e.g., Nelson, 1980), these devices are not replacements for scientific and naturalistic observations. So, too, psychiatric terminology and personality inventories may refine the labyrinth of "physical and mental" symptoms, but they certainly lack rigorous explanatory power for nearly all interbehavioral predictions. This is simply because cognitive science and behavioral science are irreconcilable as far as being monomorphic disciplines. Alternatively, clinicians with an operant or scientific background for whom a broader or more conclusive analysis is attractive should employ strategies unlimited by traditional behavioral assessment. Applying the interbehavioral chart system is one approach to this strategy by the fact that it can initiate progress toward a more prudential goal--that of conferring heuristic validity upon interbehavioral psychology.

## Acknowledgments

Completion of this manuscript was with the warm, empathic support and editorial assistance of my wife, Marilyn J. Ruben, and also professional encouragement from my colleague, friend, and mentor--Paul T. Mountjoy.

## References

Abramson, L., Seligman, M. and Teasdale, J. 1978. Learned helplessness in humans : Critique and reformulation. **Journal of Abnormal Psychology,** 87, 49-74.

Bakan, D. 1966. Behaviorism and american urbanization. **Journal of the History of the Behavioral Sciences,** 1, 5-28.

Beck, A. 1970. Cognitive therapy: Nature and relation to behavior therapy. **Behavior Therapy,** 1, 184-200.

Bergin, A. 1970. Cognitive therapy and behavior therapy: For a multidimensional approach to treatment. **Behavior Therapy,** 1, 205-212.

Cautela, J. 1977. **Behavior Analysis Forms for Clinical Intervention.** Chicago, Illinois: Research Press.

Cautela, J. 1981a. **Behavior Analysis Forms for Clinical Intervention** (vol. 2). Chicago, Illinois: Research Press.

Cautela, J. 1981b. **Organic Dysfunction Survey Schedules.** Chicago: Illinois: Research Press.

Cartwright, D. 1959. Lewinian theory as a contemporary systematic framework. In S. Koch (Ed.) **Psychology: A Study of a Science** (vol. 2) **General Systematic Formulations, Learning and Special Processes.** New York: Mcgraw-Hill.

**Diagnostic and Statistical Manual of Mental Disorders.** 1980. Washington, D.C.: American Psychiatric Association.

Erwin, E. 1978. **Behavior Therapy: Scientific, Philosophical and Moral Foundations.** New York: Cambridge University Press.

Ferster, C.B. and Skinner, B.F. 1957. **Cumulative Record.** New York: Appleton-Century-Crofts.

Foreyt, J. and Rathjen, D. (Eds.). 1978. **Cognitive Behavior Therapy: Research and Application.** New York: Plenum Press.

Goldfried, M.R. (Ed.). 1982. **Converging Themes in Psychotherapy.** New York: Springer Publishing Company.

Kantor, J.R. 1924. **Principles of Psycology** (vol. 1). New York: Knopf.

Kantor, J.R. 1926. **Principles of Psychology** (vol. 2). New York: Knopf.

Kantor, J.R. 1933. **A Survey of the Science of Psychology.** Chicago: Principia Press.

Kantor, J.R. 1959. **Interbehavioral Psychology.** Granville, Ohio: Principia Press.

Kantor, J.R. 1966. Feelings and emotion as scientific events. **Psychological Record,** 16, 377-404.

Kantor, J.R. 1970. An analysis of the experimental analysis of behavior (TEAB). **Journal of the Experimental Analysis of Behavior,** 13, 101-108.

Locke, E. 1971. Is "behavior therapy" behavioristic? (An analysis of Wolpe's psychotherapeutic methods). **Psychological Bulletin,** 76, 318-327.

Locke, E. 1979. Behavior modification is not cognitive--and other myths: A reply to Ledwidge. **Behaviour Therapy and Research,** 3, 119-125.

Mahoney, M. 1977. Reflections on the cognitive-learning trend in psychotherapy. **American Psychologist,** 32, 5-13.

Meichenbaum, D. 1979. Cognitive behavior modification: The need for a fairer assessment. **Behaviour Therapy and Research,** 3, 127-132.

Miller, N.E. and Dollard, J. 1941. **Social Learning and Imitation.** New Haven: Yale University Press.

Miller, N.E. 1948. Theory and experiment relating psychoanalytic displacement to stimulus-response generalization. **Journal of Abnormal Psychology,** 43, 155-178.

Mischel, W. 1973. Toward a cognitive social learning reconceptualization of personality. **Psychological Review,** 80, 252-283.

Morse, W.H. and Skinner, B.F. 1957. A second type of superstition in the pigeon. **American Journal of Psychology,** 70, 308-311.

Nawas, M.M. 1970. Wherefore cognitive therapy? A critical scrutiny of three papers by Beck, Bergin and Ullmann. **Behavior Therapy,** 1k 359-370.

Nelson, R. 1980. The use of intelligence tests within behavioral assessment. **Behavioral Assessment,** 2, 417-423.

Ray, R. and Brown, D. 1975. A systems approach to behavior. **Psychological Record,** 25, 459-478.

Ruben, D.H. 1979. Are game behaviors self-rewarding: A behavioral analysis. **Proceedings of the Heraclitean Society,** 4, 78-93.

Ruben, D.H. 1982a. Philosophical and methodological adaptations in assertiveness training programs designed for the blind. Presented at the meeting of the Association for Behavior Analysis, Milwaukee, May.

Ruben, 1982b. Analogue assessments in the behavioral treatment of drug addictions. **The Catalyst,** in press.

Ruben, D.H. and Ruben, M.J. 1982. Applying behavioral principles to interpersonal employee relations: Control or manipulation? Unpublished manuscript under review.

Skinner, B.F. 1938. **The Behavior of Organisms.** New York: Appleton-Century-Crofts.

Skinner, B.F. 1948. Superstition in the pigeon. **Journal of Experimental Psychology,** 38, 168-172.

Skinner, B.F. 1953. **Science and Human Behavior.** New York: Macmillan.

Skinner, B.F. 1957. **Verbal Behavior.** New York: Appleton-Century-Crofts.

Skinner, B.F. 1959. **Cumulative Record.** New York: Appleton-Century-Crofts.

Skinner, B.F. 1968. **Technology of Teaching.** New York: Appleton-Century-Crofts.

Skinner, B.F. 1974. **About Behaviorism.** New York: Knopf.

Skinner, B.F. 1977. Why I am not a cognitive psychologist. **Behaviorism,** 5, 1-10.

Staddon, J.E. and Simmelhag, V.L. 1971. The "superstition" experiment: A reexamination of its implications for the principles of adaptive behavior. **Psychological Review,** 78, 4-43.

Tolman, E.C. and Hoznik, C.H. 1930. "Insight" in rats. **University of California Publications in Psychology,** 4, 215-232.

Ullmann, L. 1970. On cognitions and behavior therapy. **Behavior Therapy,** 1, 201-204.

Watchel, P.L. 1973. **Psychoanalysis and Behavior Therapy.** New York: Basic Books, Inc.

Wahler, R. and Fox, J. 1981. Setting events in applied behavior analysis: Toward a conceptual and methodological expansion. **Journal of Applied Behavior Analysis,** 14, 327-338.

Yates, A. 1975. **Theory and Practice in Behavior Therapy.** New York: John Wiley and Sons.